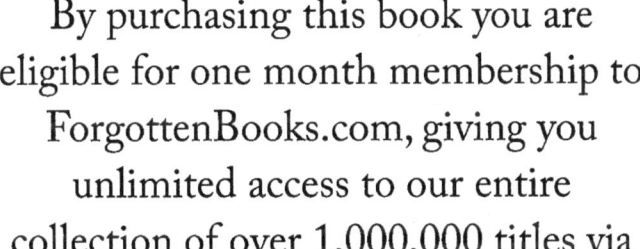

ISBN 978-0-484-16826-7
PIBN 10803876

This book is a reproduction of an important historical work. Forgotten Books uses
state-of-the-art technology to digitally reconstruct the work, preserving the original format
whilst repairing imperfections present in the aged copy. In rare cases, an imperfection in
the original, such as a blemish or missing page, may be replicated in our edition. We do,
however, repair the vast majority of imperfections successfully; any imperfections that
remain are intentionally left to preserve the state of such historical works.

PERSONNEL
Journal

Index to Volume 23

May 1944–April 1945

Managing Editor—CHARLES S. SLOCOMBE
Business Manager—HAZEL HIMSWORTH

Published by
PERSONNEL RESEARCH FEDERATION
60 East 42nd St., New York 17, N. Y.

INDEX

ARTICLES

CONTRIBUTORS

BOOKS REVIEWED

Book Review Editor—EVERETT VAN EVERY

PERSONNEL

Journal

The Magazine of

LABOR RELATIONS AND PERSONNEL PRACTICES

Published by PERSONNEL RESEARCH FEDERATION

Lincoln Building, 60 East 42nd Street, New York City

Volume 23   *Number 1*

Contents for May 1944

EDITORIAL BOARD

Industrial Companies Are More and More Adopting Personnel Counseling to Aid Employees in Their Adjustment to Factory Conditions Under War Stress. It Is Very Advisable that These Counselors Should Know as Much Psychology as Possible.

What Is *a* Normal Mind?

By Nathaniel Cantor
University of Buffalo,
Buffalo, N. Y.

THE simple question, "What is a normal mind?" covers many difficult problems. If we could all agree on what is meant by "normal" and by "mind" the answer would be as simple as the question. The likelihood is that few of us would agree on the definition of these terms. The problems involved in answering the question will be more clearly seen by raising the question, "What is a normal, healthy body?" The first answer which occurs is the negative one, "A body which is not diseased." Obviously, we can exclude all those who are physically disabled or suffering some definite chronic illness. Does this mean that the rest of us are physically well?

A Healthy Body

CAN a person still be considered well if he has fallen arches, an occasional cold, a headache or hangover, artificial teeth or a bald head? What, indeed, is normal health? Many of us feel well. Some of us go about our daily affairs more or less dyspeptic, anemic, diabetic, with high or low blood pressure, and raised eyebrows. We fill our lungs with smoke and our stomachs with alcohol. Are we enjoying normal health? It would seem so. Yet each of us has his particular complaints which differ from the particular aches and pains of others.

The situation is no different with regard to mental health. It is easy to exclude the definitely insane and the pathological personalities. Those of us who are not in institutions or under the care of psychiatrists feel that we possess normal minds. Nevertheless we each have peculiarities. Many of us go about our daily affairs more or less afraid of the boss, our mother-in-law, the loss of our job, communists, or landlords. We fear the impressions we make on others and underestimate or exaggerate the achievements of those whom we dislike or like. Wives henpeck their husbands, husbands the children, and the children each other or the dog.

Some of us suffer from timidity, others want always to be heard. Some feel they must fail in everything they do; others that they can succeed in anything they undertake. Few of us take kindly to criticism but most of us are ready to give advice to others. How many and what kind of individual peculiarities may we possess and yet remain mentally normal? Apparently most of us are abnormal in certain respects.

Our problem, however, is not to find out how we each differ from the others, but to discover in what respects, if any, we are all alike. If we could discover such common traits we could define the average normal mind.

Happiness and Adjustment

IF WE examine the many popular definitions of a normal mind, i.e., the attempt to classify mental traits common to most people, we find that they fall into two principal groups: those using happiness as a standard, and those depending upon the criterion of adjustment to reality. A moment's reflection shows, however, that both standards, that of happiness and adaptation to one's surroundings, do not help much. A normal personality may be a "happy" or a "well-adjusted" one but unless we define what is meant by "happy" and by "well-adjusted" we are no wiser as to what characterizes a normal mind. We shall return to the matter of happiness and adjustment later.

Is there any one general standard upon which we can all agree that will indicate normality of mind? It seems we are on safe ground in believing that any standard used to define a normal mind will be concerned with the *feeling attitudes* that an individual experiences in his relations to other persons. The central factor in any criterion of normality will deal with the fundamental psychological needs of every person. What are these needs?

Basic Psychological Needs

TO FIND out something about the character of the basic psychological needs of human beings we must turn to those who are professionally interested in such matters—the psychiatrists and psychoanalysts. A word of caution is necessary. Students criticize, and rightly so, the speculative and sometimes even fantastic ideas in the fields of psychoanalysis and psychiatry. There is a great deal of disagreement on the part of psychiatrists as to fundamental theory and specific processes. On the other hand, there is almost complete agreement as to the significance of the attitudes we are to deal with. One can accept the general point of view made possible through the work of psychoanalysts and the mental hygiene movement without subscribing to any particular schools or theories.

Outward Appearances Deceptive

IT IS safe for all of us to agree that we are deceived by outward appearances in our behavior and that the face value of ourselves and others with regard to behavior is extremely untrustworthy. All behavior is symptomatic of the needs of individuals. Every individual possesses dynamic drives which must be expressed in one form or another. The pressure of one's surroundings—the family, school, neighborhood, friends, and so forth—largely determines the expression taken by the drives. In the process of adjusting to these pressures one's needs conflict with the needs of others (the surroundings). Adjustments, inhibitions, balances, repressions, sublimations, identifications, displacements, and projections are required.

Many of us manage to strike working balances between what we want and what others demand. The demands or wishes of others become incorporated in one's own personality and subsequently become part of one's own desires. The most thorough assimilation of the wills of others takes place during infancy, childhood, and adolescence. Very few people are aware even part of the time, and no one is aware all of the time of this process of assimilation.

The incorporation of other selves into one's own personality brings exceedingly painful experiences. Individuals fight to be "themselves," that is, to express their unique differences, and resent being what others insist they shall become. On the other hand, these same individuals long to depend upon others and do not want to be different but desire to be like those around them. This conflict continues throughout life. If the conflict becomes too sharp, if working balances are not struck, if one does not yield often enough to others or surrenders too often, an unusual distortion of the personality arises; unusual behavior follows.

What is Abnormal Behavior?

ABNORMAL behavior, then, is in part symptomatic of the needs of individuals which have been frustrated by their culture, that is, the demands of others. Viewed from the other side, abnormal behavior is symptomatic of the demands of others (society) which have not been met by the individual. In order to make this clear it is necessary to explain what is meant by the "needs of individuals," the "demands of others," and what happens when no effective compromise is established between them.

It is significant for our theses that however wide the theoretical differences between the psychoanalytic "schools," there is universal acceptance of the ideas that all individuals want and need to express themselves, that they want and need to feel secure, and that they must face reality and adjust themselves to authority.

Dynamic Drives

EVERY individual comes into the world possessed of dynamic modifiable drives which demand expression from the moment of birth until death. The organism seeks to express itself and release its tension regardless of time, place, objects or people. Very soon the infant is made "aware" that such free expression or assertion of the self is unacceptable. Adjustments to the demands of persons and objects around him must be made. The need for protection and security is won at the cost of submitting to authority and curbing self-expression.

This may be stated in another way. Every individual seeks to assert himself, to be independent, to express himself in accordance with his own peculiar temperament. But the harsh world of reality, in the form of dangerous parental and social prohibitions, and the relentless right-of-way of objects, cannot be easily overcome. Problems and dangers which cannot be conquered oppose the individual. The unknown is feared. Security, warmth, protection, and dependence is longed for, sought for, and achieved—only to be repudiated by the incessant demand to express oneself, to dominate—and the pendulum starts its counterswing. One rebels at being dependent and secure, settled and safe. The urge to dominate, to express one's peculiar difference, to be an independent individual, reasserts itself. More prohibitions and other dangers are encountered giving rise to fear and the need for security and dependence. The pendulum repeats its arc although in a slightly different path directed by the ever new constellation of experience.

The Basic Conflict

Most individuals are neither anarchic in their claims for self nor beaten into dulled submission by the claims of others. Most people achieve a working balance between the claims of self and society or reality which is discovered and rediscovered in the light of their own dynamic experience. The achievement is neither static nor gained without ceaseless struggle. The balance is constantly being shifted, redefined, and paid for at the cost of emotional disturbance to the self and to others. An Emily Post balance will carry one along life without the risk of landing in a psychiatric clinic or the possibility of becoming an immortal creator. Most individuals are not handicapped by this bipolar conflict. They manage more or less "to get along" with themselves and with others, unmindful of what is taking place.

What happens, however, to those who succumb to the fear of a reality, that is, parents, schoolmates, business associates, and so forth—a reality which dominates them or which they insist upon dominating? They are trapped by society or by their own self. They live according to an all-or-none principle. They are consumed by fears or consume themselves and others by their hunger for power. Everything stands in the way of the one, and the other seeks to stand alone. Neither one can get along with reality. Both are neurotic, unhappy and abnormal.

Too Much or Too Little

Their surroundings, or reality, culture pressures, parents, friends and so forth, have provided them with too much or too little security, too much or too little authority. The over-protection of self-sacrificing mothers, who do everything *they* want for *their* children and make little effort *not* to do some things for their children, leads to timidity, dependence, fear, and lack of initiative. It weaves apron strings about the neck of the child choking the joy of life out of him. The rejected child, on the other hand, who never acquires the feeling of "belongingness" from his parents, friends or school is isolated, anxious, restless and ill at ease. Too much authority of parents and society breeds resentment, hostility, guilt, aggression, and too little authority nourishes overconfidence and disregard for others. Such personalities are out of balance with their environments and with themselves. Instead of recognizing and accepting this fact, they deny it and then either conceal, distort or create attitudes and engage in the appropriate behavior which justifies their attitudes

Culture Pressures

THE preceding discussion of personality needs is relevant to an understanding of the cultural pressures upon the individual. Security and affection having been denied him, the individual seeks reassurances against the dangers of reality in other ways. The ways which are open to him will depend upon the culture in which he lives and the kind of reassurance sought. It is necessary at this point to distinguish between the assurance of security and the reassurance of adequacy since it is chiefly the preservation of one's ego that is sought by those who are insecure.

The first deep contacts of an infant are with the mother. "Satisfactory breast-feeding or cuddling experiences do more than whole dictionaries of later words in the establishment of security in the family group." The infant rapidly acquires a sense of "belongingness." The emotional ties binding families together defy all logic. The enveloping affection is the result of the mother-child relationship and in no wise depends upon objective judgments of any kind. Whether the child is good or bad, ugly or handsome, healthy or sickly, a leader or a follower—all of this is irrelevant to parental love. A mother's arms is the child's harbor. In a slightly less but still intense degree the father, where the relationship to the wife is one of "belongingness," transmits this feeling of "at-homeless."

Adequacy Floats with Opinion

As THE child develops from infancy through childhood and into adolescence he is judged more and more by *what* he is and by *what* he can do. Comparisons with others are made, scolding and nagging, praises and compliments fill the days. These judgments determine the child's feeling of adequacy or inferiority. Children who are secure, who sense they are loved, pay little attention to what their parents *say* about their inadequacies. The pervasive awareness of security shields the child from the disquietude of not measuring up to brothers, sisters or schoolmates. Children who sense their rejection and feel insecure seek to acquire feelings of adequacy which, however, never quite give them a basic sense of security. If they fail in showing that they possess some outstanding trait, the inevitable feeling of inferiority in addition to the basic sense of insecurity leads them to become "problem children."

It is difficult for children and adolescents to obtain security or love through accomplishments since affection is built on the "psycho-motor tensions" of the first few years. Reassurance against anxiety and insecurity is sought in another direction, that of doing something better than others, of attracting attention by asserting themselves. Security is dominantly an *emotional relationship* while feelings of adequacy flow from what others *say* about one's abilities or achievements. Security is rooted in affection. Adequacy floats with opinion.

Economic Status Paramount

WE NOW come to the principal thesis. How can one acquire a normal mind? What are some of the ways which modern society offers to the protesting individual who seeks release of tension, fear, hostility, aggression? To answer this question one needs to examine our culture for the factors and attitudes which bring feelings of adequacy. In other words, what does being "successful" mean in our society? One can be successful in school, sports, art, learning, friendship or profession. Primarily, however, economic status sets the standards of success.

Competition is the life of our economic activity. The competitive spirit wells up from its economic center, spills over and floods all other activities. Success in school, sports, art, and so forth means that someone has competed with and prevailed over others. Competitive striving in itself is normal in our culture and indeed in all group life. It is the struggle for economic dominance which characterizes our particular society. Competitive striving in itself does not signify a distorted personality. Almost everyone is seeking advantage at the cost of disadvantage to others. We want to excel in what we are doing. We seek "power, prestige, and possession." This is quite normal activity in our economic society. We proceed to get ahead because *objective* realities compel us to match our strength against the strength (or weakness) of others. We face the hard *fact* of the struggle for economic security. (And many want to be economically secure not merely to obtain food, clothing and shelter, but to win approval by acquiring the power, prestige and possession which money commands.)

The Positive Drive

IT is important, however, to distinguish the strivings of those who are psychologically secure from those who are insecure. In the former case the struggle for approval, in addition to security, is a *positive* one, while in the latter the striving is for feelings of adequacy as a *substitute* for the lack of security and affection. Weakness, fear, and insecurity are denied and the quest for reassurance becomes the struggle for power, prestige and possession. The attitudes behind competition, the meaning of the struggle to the individual, will determine whether the activity is normal or neurotic. In the one case the quest rests upon "objective" fact and in the other upon "subjective" denial.

The distinction between normal competition to win approval, and competition as a substitute reassurance for the lack of affection, represents the two limits of a continuous series. Actually, all social relations reflect both the positive and negative attitudes of individuals, that is, the need to be independent, to assert one's differences and the need to depend upon others. When the balance between depending upon others and being oneself (which is different and changing for every individual) is seriously interfered with (too much or too little security or too much or too little fear and guilt in self-expression) the individual tends to behave abnormally from a social standpoint. The needs of the disturbed personality are oppressing and will find outlet (justification) in behavior which is psychologically normal for the particular individual, but socially unacceptable.

The overtones of success and competition reverberate through all the major institutions of our economic society. To be someone or something (to be successful, financially secure, admired for the values accompanying wealth) is harped upon in the family, school, radio, newspaper and movies. Individual needs are artificially stimulated by advertising. To acquire automobiles, clothes, schoolgirl complexions, white teeth, soft hands, Hollywood facials, furniture (the kind the "best," i.e. the wealthiest, people possess) and thousands of other things is to obtain status. The wherewithal to satisfy many of these artificial status-preserving needs is not present and their frustration makes for dissatisfaction and unhappiness.

Rugged Individualism

OUR early training leads us to believe that rugged individualism is the road to success. We need but to try hard enough and we will get what we seek. As a matter of fact, there is little equality of opportunity. Individual effort, no matter how sincere, is pitifully feeble compared to the dominating pressure of circumstances and the role of accident in one's life. Most people do not get very far in achieving wealth, fame or power. Instead a sense of helplessness and failure slowly corrodes one's self-esteem.

Emotional conflicts are generated by our competitive society from still another angle, that of the conflict between the formal ideals of, and actual practices in, society. Parents, teachers and religious leaders impress youth with ideals of cooperation and loving one another. The virtues of kindness, modesty, charity, tolerance and understanding are *talked* about. But, generally, in our society, if one is retiring, genuinely cooperative, unassuming and unaggressive, he does not get very far. He is a failure as judged by present standards. His self-esteem is crushed. He fears the adverse judgment of others. He feels inferior and inadequate. This, in turn, breeds hostility in him and fear of hostilities of the more successful. He is afraid to compete not only because *he* fears he will fail but also because he fears *others* will feel hostile to him if he succeeds.

Some Leaders

CONTRARIWISE, the aggressiveness of many basically insecure but successful people (leaders in industry, society, business, politics and law) serves to justify and release the hostility, guilt, and anxiety generated by the conflict between their aggressive behavior and their earlier emotional impressments about cooperation. This conflict is denied and in its place are substituted contributions to community funds, libraries, providing work for the unemployed, and "safeguarding the morals of the community" by carrying out the law. They display self-righteousness because of the desperate need to appear justified in their own eyes for their dimly felt unrighteousness. The "self-made" man in many cases, *must* be proud of the fact because he seeks to deny the guilt for shortcomings he senses but covers up.

In brief, in our culture, the contradictions of (1) stimulated needs and their frustration, (2) individual effort and institutional pressure, and (3) competition and cooperation affect all of us more or less. When emotional stresses become too intense some individuals are unable to make normal adjustments

Creators and Destroyers

THESE deviating types become either creators or destroyers. Social maladjustment, that is, behaving differently from accepted normal standards, can assume creative forms in art, science, business, politics, religion, industry, or personal relations. In these instances the individual dares to be himself, he is unafraid to express his differences. He stands out because of his strength, the positive organization of his personality-pattern, and he is ready to accept the consequences of daring to be different. Social maladjustment also takes the destructive form of abnormal behavior. In these cases the individual is afraid to express his differences. He cannot accept responsibility for positive behavior, is overcome by guilt and fear. He stands out because of his weakness, the negative expression of his creative ability. He is blocked because of an inability to accept himself as he is. There has been too much or not enough external interference in his life; he has become too dependent upon, or too independent of, others. He is afraid to live in terms of his own positive, creative needs. The emotional conflicts are disruptive.

The feelings of frustration, fear, guilt, inadequacy and restlessness cannot be admitted and recognized. They are denied or "repressed" and compensation, that is, substitution or justification, is set up not creatively but destructively.

Internal Freedom

WE ARE prepared to return to the main question, what is a normal mind? Anyone who has achieved a satisfactory dynamic balance between the need for self-expression and the needs for self-repression has a normal personality. Such person will possess *a sense of internal freedom, a feeling of inner confidence and a lack of disruptive fear*. These attitudes will prevent one from reacting too violently to the opposition or hostility of others. Those who lack an inner confidence show inordinate fear, resentment, hate and guilt. These unsocial attitudes are defenses of the personality reflecting an inner anxiety, an inner uneasiness which the individual is unable to control.

Normality of mind is characterized by a friendly relation to others, by a tolerance toward those who differ. The expression, "To live and to let live" best characterizes a normal mind. To be yourself, accept your own limitations, recognize the inconsistencies in your own behavior without feeling too guilty, and to recognize the inconsistencies in the actions of others without feeling too hostile, is to approach normality of mind. To accept fearlessly whatever life's circumstances bring, is a sign of an emotionally mature personality.

No One is Normal

WHO of us, then, is normal? None of us, is the answer. No one in our society has attained an ideally well rounded, nicely balanced personality. We dare not, most of the time, spontaneously express ourselves nor permit others the freedom to express themselves when our toes are being stepped on.

The kind of society in which we live does not help in the formation of well-rounded balanced personalities. Our social life is unbalanced. Modern civilization is "neurotic." To develop a normal mind we need economic security and opportunity for creative self-expression. We live in constant fear; fear of not obtaining work or losing our job, fear of sickness, dependency, of bills and landlords, fear of being ourselves. Desires are set up but the means for satisfying them are not at hand. Dissatisfaction and unhappiness result. We use most of our energy in seeking to get ahead financially and not in learning how to live satisfactorily. In short, the conditions under which most people live today breeds fears and insecurities of all sorts. Life becomes drab, uncertain, unsatisfying and disquieting. We feel isolated and frustrated. We fear to be unaffectedly kind and to cooperate in collective effort.

No Answer Known

THE conclusion is not to be drawn that a collectivist society will guarantee the development of normal personality. Abnormal behavior follows from the inadequacy of social institutions in meeting the basic needs of human drives. In every society there will be gaps between individual drives and the social means of satisfying them. It is the *tragic* inadequacy of our *present* institutions to meet the needs of people that has been emphasized. Whether, and to what extent, we can build a society in which men and women can be provided with greater opportunities to develop balanced personalities, time and an active participation in the contemporary scene will tell.

Reprinted from The American Journal of Orthopsychiatry, Vol. XI, No 4, October, 1941.

The U. S. Steel Corporation Issues Annually an Excellent Report Which Shows Not Only Its Financial Operations But Also Gives Much Information about Its Actual Working Operations. Here is Shown How a Personnel Department Attempts to Do the Same Thing.

Annual Report of Personnel Department

By Edward N. Hay

Pennsylvania Company,
Philadelphia, Pa.

A LTHOUGH the past year brought still further contractions in the supply of suitable persons seeking employment, we have succeeded in meeting the demands for replacements. Officers and employees helped us considerably by referring their friends and acquaintances. While the figures which follow will reveal that we had a considerable number of applicants for positions, they will not reveal the large percentage who were utterly unsuitable for employment due to age, health, physical disabilities, and other reasons. Nor will they reveal the large number of persons who are termed 'floaters'" due to their continual search for positions which pay a little more than their present position. We have considered it unwise to employ this type of person.

Employment, Resignations and Separations

OUR turnover was higher than ever (28.8%), but compares favorably with other companies. The siphoning-off of men for Military Service contributed to this, of course, although the major portion of our turnover has been due to employee leaving for higher-paying positions.

Despite these difficulties, the qualifications of those we have employed have not been appreciably lowered and the toral number of employees was reduced during the year by 43 persons. As of the end of the year we had 1097 employees (including permanent and temporary), as compared to 1140 on 12–31–42 and 1245 on 12–31–41, a two-year reduction of 148 persons.

The following tables will show the activities in these matters as compared to recent years:

VISITORS RECEIVED IN PERSONNEL OFFICE

	New applicants	Applicants calling back	Total calls
1943	2298	554	5648
1942	3346	1045	6529
1941	2756	1107	5909
1940	2673	931	5168
1939	2454	1098	4237

SOURCES OF APPLICANTS

Sent by	1941	1942	1943
Officers of the bank....................	195	193	147
Other employees...........................	216	256	279
Customers............................	3	4	18
Schools, agencies, etc......	575	408	100
Walked in and miscellaneous..............	1622	1736	878
Newspaper advertisements	145	749	876
Total.................................	2756	3346	2298

	1941	1942	1943
Applicants referred elsewhere.	155	75	92
Applicants placed elsewhere................	22	15	24
Credit inquiries answered..	669	418	231

SOURCES OF EMPLOYEES HIRED

	1941 No.	%	1942 No.	%	1943 No.	%
Bank customers	29		23		22	
Officers..	24 } 81	28	20 } 90	31	19 } 121	37
Other employees........	28		47		80	
Applied on own initiative.........................	60	21	81	28	67	21
Fee-charging agencies..........................	32	11	30	11	3	1
Schools and non-fee agencies....................	83	28	23	8	6	2
Advertisements................................	7	2	45	16	84	26
Former employees rehired.. :	27	10	11	3	42	13
Penna. Co. Pensioners...			11			
Total..	290		291		323	

The Labor Turnover

THE labor turnover has continued to rise, although compared to most firms we had a very favorable turnover rate. The following table shows the rise in turnover for the past five years:

Year	Turnover
1943	28.8%
1942	23.9%
1941	13.6%
1940	8.5%
1939	7%

RESIGNATIONS

	1941	1942	1943	%—1943
Marriage	37	72	52	19%
Another job	53	130	114	41.5%
Dissatisfied	3	9	18	6.5%
Military service	31	110	61	22.2%
To attend school	—	18	10	3.6%
Health reasons	3	15	20	7.2%
	127	354	275	

SEPARATIONS

	1941	1942	1943
Dismissed, under 3 yrs. service	13	10	26
Dismissed, over 3 yrs. service	15	10	9
Resigned	127	354	275
Pensioned	7	5	3
Died	2	9	10 (incl. 4 pensioners)
Total	164	388	323

SEPARATION ALLOWANCES

1943	$6602.05
1942	5957.50
1941	5680.23

Religion of Persons Employed

EVERY effort has been made to keep our hirings in balance with the religious proportions for this locality, although this has become increasingly difficult in recent years.

	Protestant	Percentage Catholic	Jewish
Population average	62%	25%	13%
Hired in 1943:			
Men (no. hired—47)	83%	17%	—
Women (no. hired—276)	63.4%	35.9%	.7%
Total (no. hired—323)	66.2%	33.2%	.6%
Proportion, all departments, Jan. 1, 1944, (Not including officers, pensioners, and cafeteria employees)			
Men	65.4%	30.2%	4.4%
Women	60.3%	36.2%	3.5%
Total	62.3%	33.8%	3.9%

Testing

THE number of persons who were tested was smaller than for any recent year, which is a further indication of difficulty in obtaining suitable applicants for replacements.

Persons Tested

	1941	1942	1943
Applicants:			
Men..	371	303	61
Women...	802	775	640
Total...	1173	1078	701
Employees and others.................................	531	355	220
Total	1704	1433	921

Summary

REFERENCE to the various tables above shows that for each employee placed on the payroll there were on the average:

	1941	1942	1943
New applicants.......................................	9	11	7
Applicants calling back................................	4	3	1.7
Interviews of applicants by personnel officer...............	1	.5	.034
Applicants tested.....................................	4	4	2
Persons employed.....................................	1	1	

Pensions

DURING 1943 three persons were pensioned, and four pensioners died, making a net decrease of one.

Pension payroll	No. on pension	Amount per annum
12-31-43	67	$147,469.44
12-31-42	68	148,202.72
12-31-41	70	138,668.80
11-30-40	73	133,208.16
11-30-39	55	117,656.40

Employee Loans

THERE has been a noticeable decrease in loans to employees in the past year:

Employees' Social Service Fund

Date	No. of loans	Amount outstanding
12-31-43	39	$2647.00
11-30-42	92	4698.75
12-31-41	60	4230.50

Time Sales Loans to Employees

Date	No. of loans	Amount outstanding
12-31-43	71	$ 8,419.12
12-31-42	161	16,522.16
12-31-41	250	36,807.80

OVERTIME PAYMENTS

	1942	1943
Average number of persons receiving overtime pay in each pay period..............	227	232
Average amount each pay period...	$1460.90	$1851.29
Total amount during calendar year...	$35,061.66	$44,431.00

Hospitalization

DURING the year the Associated Hospital Service paid for 565 days' hospitalization of our employees.

	1941	1942	1943
No. of members as of end of year......................................	732	674	626
No. of claims...	95	136	59
Amount of benefits paid employees.....................................	$5987.76	$7666.53	$4973

REPORT ON LENGTH OF SERVICE

(Excluding Cafeteria and Pensioners)

Length of service	Officers 5-1-42	Officers 12-31-43	Other employees Male 5-1-42	Other employees Male 12-31-43	Female 5-1-42	Female 12-31-43	Totals 5-1-42	Totals 12-31-43
Under 5 yrs.............	4	3	160	75	284	323	448	401
5-9 yrs.............	8	6	106	61	48	72	162	139
10-14 yrs.............	16	9	117	84	58	30	191	123
15-19 yrs.............	22	23	87	81	73	72	182	176
20-24 yrs.............	16	20	51	46	54	43	121	109
25-29 yrs.............	15	18	11	25	3	22	29	65
30-34 yrs.............	7	10	9	9	1		16	19
35-39 yrs.............	7	9	8	4		1	15	13
40-44 yrs.............		2	2	6	1	1	3	9
45-49 yrs.............	1	1					1	1
50 and over............	1	1					1	1
Totals................	97	102	551	390	521	564	1169	1056

SUMMARY OF NURSE'S ACTIVITIES

	1941	1942	1943
Minor illnesses, treated on premises......................................	2052	2047	1792
Minor illnesses, treated at main off.....................................	2	7	12
Minor surgical cases treated on prem...................................	771	694	474
Visits to hospitals and employees' homes..............................	238	268	362
	3063	3016	2640
First aid to outsiders on business in bank................................		3	12
Visits by Dr. Macfarlan to infirmary......................................	31	17	7
Employees sent to Dr. Macfarlan..	64	44	27
Employees' eyes examined by Dr. Gifford................................	6	22	15
Employees vaccinated by Dr. Macfarlan.................................	156		485
	257	86	546

	Male	Female
Employees absent due to illness and accidents.............................	326	591
Days lost due to illness and accidents.....................................	2964½	4076

COMPARISON

AVERAGE SALARY BY AGE GROUPS

(Does not include Cafeteria or Pensioners)

Age group	Males				Females				Officers			
	No. as of 5-1-42	Ave. Salary	No. as of 1-1-44	Ave. Salary	No. as of 5-1-42	Ave. Salary	No. as of 1-1-44	Ave. Salary	No. as of 5-1-42	Ave. Salary	No. as of 1-1-44	Ave. Salary
Under 20	37	73.89	1	85	96	73.72	103	84.28				
20–24	33	101.15	1	125	143	88.98	135	98.08				
25–29	54	137.17	11	154.99	61	101.79	72	108..10				
30–34	112	163.61	27	171.30	67	120.42	48	120.44	7	433.33	4	310.41
35–39	84	178.88	62	186.39	76	132.31	81	128.25	11	391.84	13	415.38
40–44	78	179.22	72	188.26	52	142.36	54	141.81	21	481.69	15	451.94
45–49	46	174.62	50	166.10	38	138.39	36	143.90	18	582.92	24	566.49
50–54	35	177.74	49	191.55	15	148.31	24	151.02	19	882.12	21	649.27
55–59	21	197.76	28	153.73	6	124.26	7	138.19	13	982.69	12	1456.94
60–64	22	147.20	17	196.17	1	116.66	4	133.12	3	484.72	6	469.45
65–69	21	151.67	22	139.27	3	158.54	1	165.00	2	833.34	3	662.50
70 and over	9	175.65	16	156.14	1	135.00	2	167.50	3	620.13	4	690.10
Total.....	552	158.01	356	175.45	550	108.32	567	114.14	97	644.00	101	644.11

Job Analysis

DURING 1943 the Job Analysts presented 140 job descriptions and ratings to the Job Valuation Committee with the following result:

> 81 raised in grade
> 4 decreased in grade
> 22 unchanged
> 7 returned for further study
> ___
> 114
> 26 new positions
> ___
> 140

We have continued to make surveys of other banks and companies, for comparison purposes, as to salaries paid for particular positions. Also, we again participated in the Chamber of Commerce Salary Survey. Comparison of our rates with those reported in the survey indicates that our salaries compare favorably with the average rates paid in this area.

Central Stenographic Unit

DURING the calendar year an average of fifteen girls worked 27,876 hours, of which 5,567 hours (an average of three girls for the year) were expended in assisting or substituting in other departments.

A considerable amount of work which was in previous years handled in various other departments was absorbed this year, including the following:

Tax Department: In all, 16,110 pieces, including addressing envelopes, were typed by the Central Stenographic Unit. This total included also:

5688 Information Letters
2429 Fiduciary Returns
1995 Capital Gains and Losses Statements
388 Individual Returns

Court Accounting Division: Absorbed all the typing which in previous years was performed in the Division. This included 650 Schedules and Court Accounts, varying in size from 8 to 353 pages and averaged 45 pages for each account.

Trust Investment Department: Took over the work of four of the six girls who formerly performed the typing work in the Department.

In addition to the above, the following were also typed in this Unit during the year:

60,629 Letters
1,291 Trust Dockets
90,013 Miscellaneous Pieces of Copy Work
12,474 Cylinders transcribed

This volume of work was produced despite the fact that during the year nineteen new girls were trained in the Unit. Seven girls were promoted to other positions, two were separated, three resigned and one joined the WAVES.

Payroll Division

THE increased volume of work made necessary the addition of a third clerk in the payroll division. By adding an additional clerk excessive overtime was practically eliminated and the work was handled with a maximum of efficiency and a minimum of error. Since it may be of interest the duties of the payroll division during the past year are listed below in some detail as an illustration of how involved payroll work has become.

1. Four times during the year complete new figures had to be set up. This involved changing all the payroll cards in three places for some changes and in four places for others. They were as follows:

January 15th   Philadelphia Wage Tax 1½ to 1% Victory Tax adtion

March 8th (S. C.) Income Tax and Victory Tax—Change in rate of bonus (changed all figures on payroll cards)

July 15th   Change from Victory Tax to Income Withholding Tax

Sept. 8th (S. C.) (Change from Victory Tax to Income Withholding Tax

2. In addition to the four complete changes two additional payrolls were run: February 2, 1943 Adjustment of increase in Special Compensation

paid December 8, 1942, and increased as of September 1, 1942. (Had some help from Audit Department.)

December 29, 1943 Officer increase adjustments effective 12-1-43.

3. Two big War Loan Drives—average 350 pay changes per Drive, plus 120 charged against the Special Compensation checks of December 8, 1943.

4. In order to set up the Withholding Tax of July 1, 1943, it was necessary to secure from every person on the payroll (including pensioners) a regulation Government statement stating marital and dependency status for the purpose of computing tax exemptions. These statement files had to be maintained and kept up to date throughout the year.

5. Late in 1943 work was begun on monthly listings from the Salary Review cards for the purpose of computing comporatio figures. Special reports based on Salary Review files were prepared when requested throughout the year. These included special listings for various officers and supervisors.

Payroll Deductions

1. Maintained and made the required reports on the following payroll deductions:

 a. City Tax
 b. Victory and Income Withholding Tax
 c. Social Security
 d. Bonds
 e. Loans—both Personal and Social Service
 f. United War Chest
 g. Hospitalization

2. Because of the large turnover a definite routine had to be worked up for quick handling of separations from the payroll. Roughly, this routine was as follows:

a. Receive verification of employee's leaving, checking on dates, extra pay and reason for leaving.

b. List employee's deductions to be adjusted:

 Hospitalization
 Bonds
 Loans
 United War Chest

c. Get in touch with employee to determine how far he wished to pay hospitalization in advance; whether he wished a bond refund; how he was going to complete his payments on any loans; what he intended to do about completing his United War Chest subscription.

d. Have proper forms signed for hospitalization transfers and advance payments; notify Audit Department about bonds; make arrangements with Time

Sales about loans (verification of arrangements mostly); notify United War Chest of pledge to be removed from payroll deduction plan.

e. Draw advance checks for pay due employee.

f. Accumulate earnings and tax withheld figures for current year to date of leaving and prepare W-2 statement in duplicate to be issued to employee at time of departure. Duplicate filed until end of year.

g. Accumulate wages paid for past nine quarters for reporting to Pennsylvania Unemployment Compensation Bureau.

This routine is given in detail so that it can be seen how much time is involved. With 323 separations in 1943 and an allover average of 1 hour's work per separation, it is not difficult to see where a great many work hours are spent merely to remove a person from the payroll.

3. Insurance records were maintained as in previous years.

4. With the introduction of the policy of paying time and a half for holiday and extra work throughout the year, computation of overtime became more complicated and increased in volume.

5. Our most successful innovation in the year was the issuing of checks on bright green paper printed in purple ink. This completely eliminated past complaints on the part of tellers and transit clerks about difficulty in reading our checks.

6. A new system for keeping records of insurance refunds to men in military service was devised. A card file is now maintained for each man in the service and details all information pertaining to the issuance of insurance checks. It also serves as a tickler file to determine when the year has expired and another check is due. During the year one hundred and fifty checks were sent to men in service, each accompanied by a letter of explanation and tidbits of news.

Women on Night Forces

DUE to difficulties in securing suitable male replacements for our evening and night forces, we have been using women on those shifts since January, 1943. We were the first bank in the city to adopt this course and it has proven to be successful in borh the Transit and Tabulating Departments.

Training Stenographers

THE innovation of sponsoring five girls, who were graduating from High School, for an intensive secretarial course at Temple University has proven to be successful. One girl has resigned, refunding over half of the cost of the course to the Company; two are proving to be capable clerk-typists; and two are rated as exceptionally good prospects for secretarial positions. At a time when stenographers are difficult to find at reasonable salaries, the small cost of the course at Temple University ($80. for each girl) is proving to be a good investment.

Requests for Military Deferments

UNTIL December 1943 it was not the policy of the Company to request employees' deferment from military service for occupational reasons. However, due to the imminent loss of a number of trained men in the Company—men whom it would be difficult to replace—it was finally decided to request some deferments on the requests of Senior Officers in charge of Departments.

At the time of writing this report, 21 requests for occupational deferments had been filed, with the following results:

> 6 Deferments granted (from 3 to 6 mos.)
> 5 Rejections
> 10 Have received no answer
> ——
> 21

EMPLOYEES IN MILITARY SERVICE

	12-31-42	12-31-4
No. of men in military service.....	140	180
No. of women in military service	2	13
Total in military service................	142	193
Deaths of employees in the service.......	0	

Total Annual Salaries of Employees in the Armed Services as of January 1, 1944

	Male	Female	Total
Employed *before* December 8, 1941....................	$315,558	$9,888	$325,446
Employed *after* December 8, 1941...	14,844	4,140	18,984
	330,402	14,028	344,430
Less: annual salaries of those who died and of those who have returned to their jobs...	17,148		17,148
	313,254	14,028	327,282
Less: allowance now being paid to those in military service (6)	7,756		7,756
	305,498	14,028	319,526

Conclusion

THE Department has continued to function smoothly despite additional burdens caused by withholding taxes on salaries; rationing of food in the dining rooms; increasing requests for new job descriptions and ratings caused by changes in jobs in all departments; additional record-keeping as a result of increased hirings, transfers, promotions and resignations.

In the past year there has been a noticeable increase in the tendency of supervisors and division heads to seek test results and recommendations in matters of making promotions and transfers within the departments. This growing awareness of the value of tests has been mentioned by several supervisors, which is a healthy sign. At the very least, this would indicate that more careful consideration is being given to promotions and that the old rule of length of service as the deciding factor no longer prevails.

On a number of occasions in the past two years we have offered suggestions as to methods of reducing the number of employees, many of which were accepted and proved to be satisfactory. The same result was obtained in a number of instances merely by urging division heads to try to manage without a replacement. During the present year we shall continue to seek means of further reducing the number of employees wherever possible.

How Many Returning Service Men Will be
Satisfied with the Sedentary and Unspectacular
Life of an Office Worker after Experiencing the
Thrills of Combat? It will be Quite a Come-
down for a Bomber Pilot to Go Back to Posting
Ledgers and Reviewing Files.

The Future
Office

By Ross Stagner

Koppers Co.,
Pittsburgh, Pa.

THE functions of an office in a business organization include the maintenance of
records, communications between various operating units, preparation of
reports, supplying necessary data to management.

When the war is over, and perhaps governmental controls somewhat relaxed,
I do not think it safe to assume that this will necessarily lead to a reduction in office
staff or office functions.

Assumptions

You may find, upon assaying the work in your office, that some functions are
not being handled efficiently and you may, as soon as the emergency is over,
desire to add to the types of record-keeping and communication devices employed.
The volume of office work you will anticipate must, of course, be related to anticipated sale and production of your product. This phase of postwar planning, of
course, is outside your province, but you need some such estimates before starting
on your own work.

In planning, you are therefore going to start with certain notions of the kind
of office functions to be carried out, and the volume of paper work you will be given.
To proceed intelligently from this point, you will have to make certain assumptions
about the postwar world. Here are the assumptions I would make:

I venture the assumption that paper work will not decrease very much for a
year or two after victory, if then. And this statement holds regardless of the November election. Some types of records which have been established pursuant to

governmental requirements may even find their way into permanent office practice—
e.g., salary controls.

Two Basic Choices

I SUGGEST that office equipment is not going to change very much. The marvelous
gadgets which the "imagineers" are picturing may, or may not, appear in the
average home. In the office, there will not be many such. I anticipate a general
increase in the use of punched card and automatic equipment, for example, taking
over functions like checking purchase orders against invoices; probably more records
will be filed and located by automatic devices. But we shall still have only two
basic choices with regard to the organization of office routines:

(A) one person handles all aspects of a single function;
(B) several people handle selective details of a function

Type B corresponds to mass production; it is unquestionably adapted to handling a greater volume of work, and you have probably installed such procedures
under the stress of war conditions. Workers of limited intelligence and experience,
for example, can be trained fairly quickly to check one specific detail on a series of
forms, even if they do not understand where the forms came from, where they go or
what they accomplish. (Not necessarily good management to leave them in this
state of ignorance.)

Type A, in which a single person handles an entire function in all aspects, is
more flexible, more interesting, and trains a rounded employee who is a better prospect
for advancement in the company. However, it takes a better quality of raw material
than has always been available in the last year or so.

Happy Little Morons

WHEN you have decided which of these two types of job organization your
postwar office will utilize, you can start realistically on the problem of job
specifications. Obviously, if you adopt the production line type of office structure,
you will want a considerable number of girls of fairly low intelligence. Not too
low, or they will be incapable of even automatic work accurately; not too high, or
they'll get bored, make errors and quit soon. They will not need much work experience, and you will not have to worry about traits of judgment, initiative and
speed of decision. However, if you get an office full of these happy little morons,
you may have to worry about where your future supervisors and trouble shooters
are coming from.

The alternative type of job organization that I suggest (and of course varying
combinations of these two types can be set up) is to have one person, exercising
judgment and responsibility, handle a larger work cycle without a breakdown of the
job into simple successive steps. This has the advantage of imparting—and requiring—wider knowledge of the work and its significance in company affairs. It trains

new supervisors and future executives. It runs the danger that there will still be a substantial residue of routine work which will bore your competent employee, causing him to make errors or to quit.

Superior Intellects

JOB specifications in this type of job are different. You would want people of considerably above average intelligence; older employees, more settled, and with wider business experience or technical education; people with decisive, aggressive personalties, but not carrying such traits to the extreme of being impulsive or bull-headed.

Naturally, each of you already has job specifications in your mind. You interview and employ people, or reject them, according to certain standards. However, in most cases those standards are purely mental and subjective—they are in your head, not in the records. This in itself is a violation of good office practice, because in a properly organized office, all essential records are reduced to writing to prevent the loss of valuable information.

Fuzzy Job Specifications

FURTHER—and I say this with no intent to be critical—many of your job specifications are fuzzy, unscientific and perhaps actually misleading. Many executives still cling to notions—established from hearsay or from chance acquaintance with a single man—about whom they should hire and whom they should reject. People are selected according to race and religion, instead of on ability to deliver the goods, in some cases. The realistic, practical, business like kind of job specification is the one that emphasizes a man's ability to carry the duties of his job. Scientific personnel research can give the answers more accurately than gossip or hunches.

In preparing job specifications, you will find it best to start with detailed *job descriptions*. That is, have every employee now at work write down a fairly detailed statement of his daily duties. (You may be surprised at some of the answers you get.) Classify together those doing similar work, and check on their backgrounds. You may find, e.g., that a girl with two years of college does no better than those with only a high school education, on a certain job. In this case you can set up high school as the minimum education for this position, instead of hunting for college students who will render no better service, and may very likely leave in a short time. If you have given standard tests for intelligence, stenographic skill or clerical ability to all applicants for employment, you can state your specification in terms of minimum score for each grade of clerical work performed.

Scientific Psychological Methods

IN ADDITION to intelligence and education, job specifications commonly include a statement as to previous work experience; physical or mechanical skills, such as blueprinting, comptometer, etc.; physical effort and physical discomfort associated with the job, such as excessive standing and walking; eyestrain, special visual acuity needed, etc.; and less tangible personal qualities such as initiative, good supervisory personality, cautiousness, persuasiveness; and ability to take responsibility for cash, valuables, etc., if those are handled in the course of the job.

While most of these personality traits are still in the stage of judgment by interviews, scientific psychological methods particularly in the field of temperament are bringing advances all the time in accuracy of measurement of these traits. Some of the wartime work in classifying and adjusting soldiers will prove of considerable value to business in the postwar world. Even if you can find no way of measuring such characteristics, it is better to list those which you deem essential in a given job and make a deliberate effort to decide whether an applicant for a job possesses the kind you need.

Reemployment of Veterans

HERE is one concrete example of how adequate job specifications may be of value to you in the near future. Your company is obligated, under the Selective Service Act, to re-employ returning veterans. Morally, if not legally, you are required to take in disabled men and give them the nearest thing to their old jobs, in status and pay.

You may very well have a considerable number of skilled production employees coming back—disabled as far as heavy work goes, but physically and mentally capable of office work. Can you place them? To do this, on other than a trial-and-error basis, calls for good job specifications and measures of the soldier's ability. He may never have had an office job before—but may turn out to be a valuable employee—if you fit him into the right slot without too much fumbling. Putting him into an unsuitable job on which he will fail, is going to be bad for his morale and bad for your office efficiency.

Develop Special Skills

TRAINING programs to fit old and new employees into their jobs can obviously be prepared more accurately if you have good job specifications. Instead of giving training for many office duties, only a few of which will be exercised on the job, you can concentrate on those special skills which are most needed and least developed in this employee.

When you have obtained and analyzed your job descriptions, you may find it desirable to subject each job to the following four questions:

Can it be eliminated? This will obviously be true of certain jobs which have developed because of regulations during the war; it may even apply to traditional jobs which no longer serve any valuable function.

Can it be merged with others? By having the same person handle two operations, you sometimes telescope procedures—e.g., pulling correspondence from file once instead of twice. Sometimes two forms are doing the work that could be done by one. Sometimes an extra copy of a form would replace a letter or another form.

Can it be done by machine? Punched card and similar equipment is going to be cheaper and more versatile after the war. There will be a considerable number of skilled operators available, as compared with their relative scarcity in prewar days. Many records may be printed on tabulating cards which can be punched for sorting and filing, thus decreasing the amount of routing work in the office.

Correct Faulty Records

Is IT set up so as best to serve its function? A job may conceivably be made more complex, rather than simplified, if that will give the results needed. I have in mind, for example, labor turnover records, which are almost universally unsatisfactory. War Manpower Commission people have found that almost anything can be proved from turnover statistics, like absenteeism statistics, including the fact that "there ain't no such thing." Turnover records, to be of use, must have far more detailed breakdowns than are customary at present. And, I should add, good turnover records are a cornerstone for many personnel and industrial relations policies.

Sometimes merely re-arranging the sequence of steps in an operation will result in greater efficiency. As a very small example, we found that the girls in our Personnel Dept. were checking personal histories and rather often had to go to the payroll and other departments to get missing information. Now it was found that, at one step in the cycle, that all of these forms were pinned to the personal history record. By simply switching the point at which the check was made, much waste time was eliminated. In this particular case, since some confidential information was also attached, it was necessary to have a more responsible employee do the checking; but you are just as likely to turn up cases where a junior clerk can do a job and still eliminate waste motion.

Summary

In summary, let me state the following points which seem to me to be the irreducible minimum on postwar planning for the office.

(1) Set up a clear statement of functions to be accomplished by the office force;
(2) Obtain clear descriptions of every job in the office.
(3) Plan your postwar organization around either present jobs or a definite, written revision of these jobs.
(4) Set up job specifications which will be:
(a) neither too high nor too low, in terms of job duties;

(b) definite so that some one else can take over if needed;

(c) realistic—including factors related to efficiency, excluding factors having nothing to do with efficiency;

(d) scientific—as far as possible, can be measured by objective, tests, not relying on recommendations or guesses.

The establishment of such a system of job specifications will not issue in a period of heaven on earth. It will not solve all your office management problems. But it will assure you of getting the human material most suited to your needs, and from that point onward, the job is up to you to make it work.

From a paper presented before the Pittsburgh Chapter, NOMA.

An Historical Survey of the Development and Underlying Philosophy of Supervisory Training in One Company.

Servel Trains Supervisors

By Gerald E. Stedman

FOREMANSHIP development is a critical productive consideration at anytime—particularly during war time. As contact between management and labor, foremen are non-coms of our war shops. They catch all the grief, often win too little credit, wield indispensable influences upon production. The show couldn't go on without them. It sometimes is badly acred because of them. And it is always difficult to give singular credit to such a plural group.

Tact Talent and Training

FOREMANSHIP development is often the most mishandled, poorly handled, or simply "unhandled" of all production essentials. That conclusion is based on widespread observations as a technical writer that have taken me into many plants of all sizes and descriptions throughout .the country. Along with being technically superior at the jobs concerned under his supervision, a foreman must be an economist, psychologist (often, now a psychiatrist), humanitarian disciplinarian and statesman with judicial wisdom, unusual poise and much forbearance. He has many unconscious opportunities to create individual grievances, which in an atmosphere of collective bargaining, can spin themselves into united distortions of complicated effects. It takes much talent, tact, and training to become a good foreman. All over the country men are being upgraded from machine hands to group leaders, to assistant foremen, to general foremen, in huge batches; sometimes selected helter-skelter and with but a few hours' training. This is necessary because of the urgency of war. Nothing so proves the inherent might of the United States as that so many workers have so quickly been promoted into supervision and have done such a good job at it with as little labor trouble and lost time.

Slow-paced Schedule

HOWEVER, I have been in large plants that give foremanship development no particular attention; in others where they are being trained on a slow-paced schedule that would require seven training years; in others where managements actually refuse to permit general foremanship meetings for fear such will provide the opportunity to organize in some manner.

From my contacts, I am delighted to record that Servel, Inc., Evansville, Indiana, is doing one of the most difficult, thorough and able jobs of foremanship development in the United States. It is difficult, because Servel has engaged in a more completely varied war production than any other plant of my knowledge. It is thorough because Louis Ruthenburg, Servel president, pioneered foremanship development, being widely known as the primary organizing influence of the National Association of Foremen.

The Great Kettering

A FLASHBACK into the history of foremanship development has value here. In 1912, Charles F. Kettering was in charge of the Dayton Engineering Laboratory Company. It is interesting to realize how many exceptional industrial leaders grew from these old Delco days. Louis Ruthenburg joined him as assistant chief engineer, having concluded a rounded journeymanship in numerous small shops.

From the start, Ruthenburg had been a student of human relations. In 1913, a crisis developed from an altercation between the Delco chief inspector, a typical academician with technical ability but lacking knowledge of how to get along with people and his departmental workers. This resulted in a round robin letter threatening a strike unless he was fired. "You know what's going to happen," Ruthenburg parried Kettering's query as they talked after quitting time. Kettering wondered where another man could be found to take the job. Ruthenburg assured him that it was no job, rather a whipping post, and that no one could survive it. So Kettering gave Ruthenburg the job—he will declare to this day though he tried to refuse it, the job started the most valuable three years' experience of his career. It gave him first contact with requirements for handling successfully the human factor.

Racehorse Stopwatches

AN INTERESTING aside is that Ruthenburg dug deeply into the fundamentals of quality control, established intimate customer contact, set up acceptance standards reflected in final tests of materials, tools, sub-assemblies and complete inspection control. This reduced return of goods to suppliers from nine per cent to .003 per cent during the three year period. During this time Delco was growing too fast to grow soundly. There had been no attempt at scientific setting of work standards. An impulsive superintendent, using racehorse stop watches with secret timers spying from behind posts, ordered a speed-up that had cataclysmic results. Men stalled machines, injured tools, and walked out. Ruthenburg learned his second lesson—that labor trouble doesn't start the day before . . . it has its roots in the years. He couldn't blame these men. During the cussing matches between management and labor, they asked: "Can we join a union?". That was the start of the Screw Makers Union.

Three years went by and Ruthenburg had risen to assistant superintendent. In the A. F. of L. revival, a general Dayton strike was ordered in which Ruthenburg's shop was most seriously affected. Though there was no grievance and the plant had played no part in the altercation, production was held up and employees walked out. Seeing the sheer waste to all concerned, Ruthenburg settled his strike by methods then in vogue, and without concessions in two weeks' time. But he was so mightily impressed with the waste to all that he decided to assay all relationships between supervisors and workmen. It was obvious that sound relations would forever be impossible unless supervisors could be trained properly to handle their men as human beings.

Questionnaire Used

ONLY one text on the subject had been written by an able shop man, issued by the Business Training Corporation. Recognizing that technical text material needed supplementation, Ruthenburg searched for the first essential: "What are the ideal qualifications of a good foreman?" With that answered, he could get somewhere, and so, as he does everything, Ruthenburg approached his answer in an engineering manner—sent a request to a tremendous list of shop superintendents, manufacturers, psychologists, educators, including his own foremen. This was a basic questionnaire concerning qualifications, asking each to add, strike out, or list others—all weighted in their relative importance.

At that time Walter Dill Scott was applying lessons learned from his War I experience in army personnel administration to the industrial picture, and Ruthenburg arranged with Professor Hayes of the University of Chicago, a Scott associate with a statistical flair, to reduce this tremendous questionnairing by some proper rating scale. This was the first basic development in foremanship training.

Foreman Score Low

ONE of the results of the Hayes analysis was to prove that the average foreman possessed only about 15 per cent of the knowledge he should have. It was also indicated that shop training should be supplemented with outside technical, trade, and related foremanship training. Weaknesses had been previously concealed because there had maintained a common level of mediocrity with no critical rating to follow in classification. Then, too, no careful appreciation could be developed in an atmosphere of semi-compulsion. A true reading is possible only when one is led, not forced.

Mr. Ruthenburg proceeded to develop a training procedure that would correct conditions. He keenly felt that industrial education was a *leading out* rather than a *driving in* process. He decided to encourage the voluntary interest of his foremen in establishing a system of industrial education. Avoiding hackneyed and generalized material, making no promises, he invited foremen participation in an experiment in which each section of study would develop in an interval of two meetings, each participant to plan his part in development by contributing his wisdom through questionnaire methods.

Conviction of Sin

As FOREMEN studied these subjects," Mr. Ruthenburg is quoted, "it brought about a 'conviction of sin'. They realized they needed to be converted but had difficulty telling how or in what way. They were thrown into a receptive atmosphere where, although entirely voluntarily, the first year's attendance was perfect, appreciation was great and even outsiders began to attend these foremanship development classes. Of course, the fair test was 'would they ask for more'; their second year desire was unanimous. Because of 1920 business conditions, it was decided that foremen produce their own classes, each acting as chairman to cover the subject he knew most about. This method proved very successful. It convinced foremen that there was a great deal to learn—even about that which they were supposed to know. It helped others to lose their inferiority feeling, never before having been called upon to present a subject to a critical audience. Management helped edit the papers which brought greater concord. The papers were surprisingly creditable. This procedure continued year after year—the studies having become fundamental in economics and psychology. From it, many of our fine industrial leaders have developed."

The technique permitted foremen to think concretely, rather than abstractly. The aim was to illustrate the principle by some familiar practice rather than the reverse, which is the stumbling block in too many training programs. At this time, a foremanship group meeting at the Dayton Y.M.C.A. used canned material, teaching by the reverse method. Mr. Ruthenburg was invited to become its conference leader. Anxious to test his principles, he accepted. The Dayton Foremen's Club was formed and a class of 50 foremen, widely varied from wood shoe lasts to foundry practise, started training. This became the nucleus of other clubs in neighboring cities, and finally evolved into the National Association of Foremen. It is significant to realize that industry had one of its greatest preparedness measures in that movement. It was too little conscious of it then, and for that matter, is today.

Idea Spreads

To conclude this historical flashback, Mr. Ruthenburg later delivered a "Foremanship Development" paper before an annual convention of the National Metal Trades Association. This aroused request for him to reorganize its industrial education program. Ruthenburg accepted the assignment as Chairman of the Industrial Education Committee of that association, and developed a technique and materials for members that have stood the test of time—20 years with but little modernization. Several units of General Motors Corporation, among these members, became enthused about the course. That corporation asked Ruthenburg to discuss the matter with its Works Managers Committee, and thus General Motors Institute was born.

"It was interesting," Mr. Ruthenburg reminisced to me, "to find many of my 1919–20 friends on the Works Managers Committee of General Motors, who at that time had criticized my foremanship development effort as too theoretical, had so changed heart in the few intervening years as to heartily favor General Motors Institute."

The difficult Servel problem of war conversion and the ease with which talent within his factory organization has been so swiftly upgraded to entirely new skills under violently different conditions is testimony of the importance of adequate foremanship development practises. Without that, no firm can expect to do its complete part in war production.

Skills Completely Changed

With proper foremanship development, a plant can do most anything. Servel proves that. Its former production was largely in sheet metal and steel tube bending, assembly and welding. Now it is producing complete wings for the Republic P47 in a huge new plant; breech blocks for anti-aircraft guns, requiring 174 operations of the most precise nature, cartridge cases, aluminum castings for the Jacobs aircraft engine; wooden cargo bodies for military trucks; range burners for the quartermaster corps. These skills are so varied and different that it would be difficult to find anyone among Servel's thousands of employees who is now doing anything of any kind similar to what he had formerly been skilled in.

Servel Foremanship Development considers the supervisor as a critical management link. Throughout each year a chart is used constantly to emphasize the interdependence of stockholder, employee, customer, government, with the management always in the middle. It can be applied to any enterprise. It provides an excellent worksheet to isolate the relation and function of any detail. It is based upon the necessity of balance and the requirement of give and take. There is not a human, technical, or economic consideration but what can be fitted into this diagram. The chart is constantly before foremen with space for notes and remarks. Thus, every subject discussed finds itself being analyzed from the standpoint of this interdependability.

Human Technical and Economic Triangle

SERVEL makes much use of the triad of human, technical and economic considerations as the triangle by which the successful Servel supervisor can measure his education in relation to his job. This diagram is based upon Mr. Ruthenburg's analysis of industrial problems and the duties of supervision. It is important to note that the base of the triangle is " human relations". Note again how this simple treatment reduces all complexities to a few general heads, providing an easy symbol around which the foreman groups his detailed understandings.

Servel constantly emphasizes the three functions of the foreman: (1) As supervisor, (2) As manager, (3) As instructor. Foremanship Training Meetings are ever at work training foremen to be more artful at these three functions.

Advance Knowledge

LAST of the Servel techniques I shall mention is a method to assure maximum delivery of any impression from executive through foreman into employee mind, with least chance of being misunderstood, distorted, or forgotten. Each month, Servel holds an evening Foreman-Executive Conference at which time, talking directly to the foremen, Servel executives take up policies, plans, considerations to be passed along to employees. Foremen are given advance knowledge and training on every policy and practice. Later, in the Foreman-Employee Meetings, using identical charts and procedure, each foreman passes on the information with minimum distortion. Employees know the foreman is talking directly from management. They have respect for this unwasteful method of receiving full import of executive plans, policies and suggestions. No other method is encouraged. Good educational control with minimum confusion and interference is thereby established.

Foremanship development is so critical to war production that it is wise to re-examine training methods to assure that all concerned are gaining maximum application of industrial education. Grievances, lost time, wild cat strikes, and very much of all that frustration and waste which can be considered as direct or unconscious sabotage, can be prevented by the fine relationships and the mutual understandings that are produced by such a simple program of foremanship development as that of Servel, Inc.

News Notes

Wellesley School of Community Affairs

T HE Board of Trustees and Academic Council of Wellesley College have approved the inauguration of the Wellesley School of Community Affairs, which will be opened this summer on the Wellesley Campus. The program of the School for the summer of 1944 will be built about the theme, "Cultural Differences within the American Community." The purpose of this study is to bring to citizens of a democratic world a new awareness of the problems which lie within their own towns and communities, and to develop in them skills with which these problems may be met. It has seemed to the College that the responsibilities which citizenship entails have grown to a new magnitude because of the war and the period which will follow. As a result, the College felt that responsible Americans should have an opportunity to learn to meet these responsibilities through courses of study not unusually given in undergraduate or professional institutions of learning. The present time seemed appropriate to try out a new kind of adult education, one which would be given at a college level, but which would be more concrete and direct than the ordinary summer conference or institute. Wellesley College has, therefore, opened its resources of buildings, library, and campus facilities to those who will attend the school.

Dr. Margaret Mead, well-known anthropologist and author of "Coming of Age in Samoa," "Growing Up in New Guinea," "And Keep Your Powder Dry," and other books and articles, will be the Director. While the study will be focused on the various ethnic groups in New England, it is applicable to situations in any American community. Greater Boston presents an unusually interesting field of study.

The School will run for six weeks, in three separate but related two-week periods. Lectures, discussions, and project groups will be directed by a staff largely from outside the College. While membership will, in the main, be open to those whose vocations are concerned with the problems of the School, a limited number of those whose interest is general rather than specific will be admitted.

The first fortnight, June 29–July 13, will be designed for teachers, for youth leaders, and for others who encounter intercultural situations in dealing with young people. The second unit, July 13–July 27, for personnel officers, trades-union educational secretaries and vocational guidance counselors, will deal with the problem of group relationship in industry. The third fortnight, July 27–August 10, will be planned for community and social workers, local governmental agents, group leaders both lay and clerical, including voluntary board members of civic associations, and members of interracial committees.

Further details will be announced on the prospectus for which those interested may apply to Miss Edith R. West, Executive Secretary, Wellesley School of Community Affairs, Wellesley College, Wellesley, Mass.

Typing Tests

THE *following information supplied to Mr. Willard E. Parker, the State Director of Personnel, Baton Rouge, Louisiana by Mr. Edward N. Hay, Pennsylvania Company, Philadelphia, Pa. may interest those concerned with these matters.*

In answer to your query, I am enclosing a copy of a very satisfactory typing test, the Thurstone. We have used this here for nearly ten years with entire satisfaction. We do not, however, score it exactly as described in the manual of instructions. One reason for this is that they recommend adding errors for typing and spelling to produce a single score, and we think this is illogical.

Another very satisfactory typing test developed in industry by a competent psychologist is that sold by Science Research Associates, 1700 South Prairie Avenue, Chicago. This is a test devised by Jurgensen. It is rather like Thurstone.

We do not use a stenographic test of the ordinary kind. We and some other companies I know of read a letter to the applicant and then she reads back from her notes. We do not have it typed.

There are very few good stenographic tests, and I cannot at the moment recommend any. You might ask Science Research Associates whether they have one and also the World Book Company whose address is on the bottom of the Thurstone Test. I suggest that you also write to the Psychological Corporation, 522 Fifth Avenue, New York.

Probably you are familiar with the United States Civil Service Commission Stenographic and Typing Tests. They are elaborate and require a long time, but they are very good. You might be able to obtain information about them by writing to Dr. L. J. O'Rourke, U. S. Civil Service Commission, Washington, D. C.

Study-Employment Scholarships

THE University of Chicago and Marshall Field & Company have had three very highly satisfactory years of experience with a Study-Employment Plan for students. This plan enables self-supporting students to synchronize their class and work schedules. Students have an exceptional opportunity by this arrangement to acquire an excellent education, earn money and get valuable work experience. It regularizes employment and provides work experience of a much higher order than the typical part-time jobs obtained by students who work their way through college. It is not, however, a cooperative plan in the usual sense of that term because class instruction is not formally coordinated with work experiences. The program is open to both men and women. Students engaged in this plan are usually registered for courses four quarters per year instead of the typical three quarters per year program. The Study-Employment Plan has been extended to other Chicago corporations.

The plan as it operates at Marshall Field & Company received a most stimulating kind of incentive last autumn. The decided interest which this corporation has always shown in this plan was further made known at that time by an announcement of 25 full scholarships. These scholarships pay tuition to the extent of three hundred dollars per year and are in addition to the amount earned by the student for the part-time work. Individuals assigned these scholarships must be on the Study-Employment Plan or applicants for it and must be approved by the Scholarship Committee of the University and by the Director of Personnel of Marshall Field & Company. Those interested in the Study-Employment Plan should write to the Board of Vocational Guidance and Placement, University of Chicago, and applicants for the Marshall Field & Company Scholarships address the Scholarship Committee, Room 203 Cobb Hall, University of Chicago. Chicago, 37, Ill.

Book Reviews

Book Review Editor, Mr. Everett Van Every

California Personnel Management Association, Berkeley, Cal.

GOVERNMENTAL ADJUSTMENT OF LABOR DISPUTES

By Howard S. Kaltenborn. Chicago. The Foundation Press, 1943. Price $3.50

Much is said today about the rule of government in the adjustment of labor disputes and there is much speculation about how far Federal and State intervention will go in attempting to regulate unlimited economic sway in the field of labor differences.

Studies such as this one will have a sobering effect upon rash and ill-planned acts of mass defiance and work stoppage. Both management and labor can derive much benefit from this sane reflection on labor disputes and what governmental machinery has sprung up to handle them. To some this governmental influence is a growing monster that may take sides or destroy what we now call a democratic era. Others prefer to look upon federal and state roles as a natural development to be expected, and anticipate for greater control over labor-management quarrels in the near future.

Howard Kaltenborn, not to be confused with the radio and news reel commentator, is connected with the University of Nebraska and chief wage analyst for the Regional War Labor Board in Detroit.

He has given us a thorough description of Federal and State agencies and their legislative powers in controlling labor disputes. The many tables and statistics are valuable and well chosen in showing the role of the government in attempting to bring peace and orderly bargaining between management and labor. The study, too, is a good contribution in labor history and labor economics—two fields in which many personnel men are not sufficiently well-informed.

One statement that annoyed me, and marred the entire book, was the author's assumption that strikes "in the net balance usually benefit no one." How else could labor have made its gains? Certainly there is no doubt that strikes have benefitted labor. The strike and the threat of strike has been the main weapon of organized labor since its conception. If he means that the greatest good has not been shared by the greatest number—or that in the last analysis there is much injury done—that is another question. But it cannot be denied that labor unions have not benefitted by strikes, net or gross.

Edwin E. White, Chairman of the XI Region War Labor Board, writing in the forward part of the book, says he has become convinced that there is no way compatible with democracy in which strikes can be eliminated. He is equally convinced, however, that government would be derelict in its duty if it did not make available the most effective possible machinery for an amicable and fair adjustment of labor disputes.

The reader may readily conclude that government's part (both Federal and State) in industrial relations differences is here to stay, and that personnel executives have a rapidly growing responsibility in this direction.

INDUSTRIAL SAFETY

Edited by Roland P. Blake. New York. Prentice Hall Inc. 1943. 435 pp. $5.00

Industrial safety has taken on a new meaning in war industries. More and more engineers, plant executives and top management, as well as the workers themselves are realizing that the practice of the fundamentals of industrial safety reduces accidents, saves lives and represents a huge economic gain. More than fifty thousand key men from industry have enrolled in safety courses in our engineering colleges and schools during the past two years. This wide spreading of safety training is having a definite effect in better utilization of material and manpower and is rapidly being recognized as a prime factor in efficient operation of war plants.

But not all safety men have access to war training classes. Not all safety departments have good reference material or a suitable library of stimulating reading that will serve to aid the beginners and a review for veterans. And too many times the responsibility for safety is suddenly thrust upon an inexperienced supervisor or foreman. In these situations there is no better text and reference material than Blake's volume on Industrial Safety.

The last two years has found several safety engineering books on the market, but none is more complete than this one. This is the best business book on safety management we have seen. It is prepared by leading men with long experience as active workers in industrial safety and presents an excellent analysis of the principles which must be practiced by every industrial plant today.

In addition to the conventional headings to be found in most studies of this kind, are several excellent chapters on the Safety Organization, the New Employee, Methods of Promoting Safety Practice and other similar chapters.

In addition to serving as an authentic handbook on Industrial safety this work should prove particularly useful as a textbook for safety engineering classes. It is a complete course in industrial safety and safety engineering and is a valuable contribution to the field of new business books. Recommended for every organization where safety is a factor in the personnel program—and to all persons interested in industrial health and safety.

HANDBOOK OF LABOR UNIONS

By FLORENCE PETERSON. Washington, D. C. American Council on Public Affairs. 1944. 415 pp.

A handbook is usually thought of as a complete and exhaustive reference guide to the field covered. In this respect the study is not a handbook at all, but rather a very valuable roster of 183 of our principal unions with a complete full-page description of the organization of the unions, their trade jurisdictions, membership qualifications, dues and finances, agreements, strikes and walkouts, etc.

No one who deals with organized labor should be without this valuable work. It gives in handy reference form a complete candid picture of the principal labor unions and should be available to all persons engaged in labor relations work. The author is in charge of the Industrial Relations Division of the Bureau of Labor Statistics, U. S. Department of Labor.

ORGANIZED LABOR AND THE NEGRO

By Herbert R. Northrup. New York. Harper & Bros. 1944. 312 pp. Price $3.50

Sumner Slichter calls this book a searching and comprehensive analysis of the influence of unions upon economic opportunity for Negroes.

It is not only an examination of the nation's most important racial minority, but it raises certain fundamental questions about unions. Northrup's book also digs up some deeply rooted problems in our whole social structure. Have the white workers, through their unions, excluded the Negro only where the Negro was pretty much excluded to begin with, and have they accepted him only where he already had a pretty good foothold? What are the differences in policies between the industrial and craft unions? Are the policies of unions the same in depression as in prosperous times?

Throughout the book we notice that the industry studies are for the most part those in which the Negro factor is significant and in which labor unions are an important part in determining personnel policies.

The author devotes a chapter to policies and experiences of unions in each of eleven American industries. Most of the exclusionist unions are found in the railroads, where most of the unions came into being as paternal and beneficial societies. To admit Negroes to their ranks on an equal footing would be in the minds of many white members tantamount to admitting that the colored man was a social equal, and this the majority of railroad white workers has always refused to countenance.

It is extremely important to note that nearly all unions practicing discrimination are organizations of skilled craft workers. The author believes that the well-known work-scarcity consciousness of most craft unionists is a major factor—a desire to restrict competition so as to safeguard job monopoly.

The book constantly points out the fundamental inconsistencies between the racial policies of most organizations and the oft-repeated principles of the National unions. The author says they never tire of "reiterating, re-endorsing, and reaffirming" the fact that they have no color line, and of proclaiming that the "workers must organize and unite under its banner without regard to race, color, creed, or national origin".

The study brings out a variety of methods by which unions handle racial differences in the labor market. The first section of the book deals with the fundamental reasons for the variations in union policies. The second section is devoted to questions of public policy raised by the union policies. The third section looks toward government possibilities for relief and equality, or at least for a curbing of discrimination. The fourth section surveys in general terms the future hope of Negro labor.

The author builds a pretty damaging case against the shipbuilding industry in respect to discriminatory unions. The prevalence of the closed shop and incidents such as those of the Tampa and Kaiser Yards show quite conclusively that these unions must bear the primary responsibility. Even when the metal trades unions relaxed their exclusionist rules, their uses of such devices as working permits and auxiliaries assumes that the jobs which remain in shipyards after the war will go to white workers exclusively.

Personnel executives will be interested in this study because it brings out a fundamental trend in labor relations that is even wider than Mr. Northrup's premise concerning discrimination and the attitude of unions toward the influence of racial minorities. As Sumner Slichter so ably points out in the introduction, the very fact that labor unions are collecting dues from Negroes means that sooner or later they must give them full voting rights. It appears to be making less difference whether unions are set up as private clubs or quasi public institutions. The way in which organized labor exercises discipline over its members and deprives men of membership is increasingly becoming a matter of public concern.

PERSONNEL
Journal

The Magazine of

LABOR RELATIONS AND PERSONNEL PRACTICES

Published by PERSONNEL RESEARCH FEDERATION

Lincoln Building, 60 East 42nd Street, New York City

Volume 23   *Number 2*

Contents for June 1944

Let Us Put First Things First. Improve Methods, Standardize Designs and Equipment, Train Employees, Develop Supervision, and Master Techniques of Control. The Possibility of Increasing Production in These Ways is Enormous.

Wage Incentives
and War Production

By Victor V. Veysey

California Institute of Technology,
Pasadena, Cal.

An INCENTIVE is a carrot held before the donkey's nose." So runs the definition in Mark Spade's humorous description of modern business methods, "How to Run a Bassoon Factory." Unflattering though the analogy is to business management and to the working man, there is much to be learned from the comparison of this age-old application of the incentive principle with its modern counterpart, wage incentives in industry.

Difference Between Peace and War

So far as is known, the use of carrots as bait for the donkey has neither universally nor permanently solved all of the knotty problems in the relationship between the driver and the cart's prime mover, although the device may have served usefully on many occasions. Likewise, wage incentives have been used with success under proper circumstances, but they have not proved to be a panacea for industrial ills. There is little reason to believe that the widespread and immediate application of wage incentives to the complex problems of production and industrial relations in wartime will increase factory output by 30 per cent to 100 per cent as certain spokesmen of management, labor, and government have claimed. No one would deny that the need for rapid production is pressing, and that the possibilities for improvement exist. The question is: Will wage incentives as they are likely to be applied today, increase war production?

The widespread use of wage incentives is being advocated by management representatives, seeking the same low costs and high rates of output in war plants that have been achieved through the judicious use of incentives in stable, peacetime industries. Unions see in incentive-wage plans a chance to increase employee earnings in spite of "wage freeze" restrictions. Government production men join in on the chorus by advocating a modified, innocuous type of incentive plan for which there is yet little proof of effectiveness. All groups are currently emphasizing the "win the war" possibilities of incentives.

Engineers Developed Plans

STUDENTS of management in America have been tinkering with wage-incentive plans since 1880 when the American Society of Mechanical Engineers devoted considerable attention to the effects of wages on the output of machine operators. Although a group of engineers pioneered in the development of wage-incentive plans, the subsequent application of the plans has proved to be a problem involving many intangible elements of industrial relations. The idea of buying extra work through a wage incentive appears to be disarmingly simple; the application of the incentive in a practical industrial situation has proved to be full of pitfalls. As we shall see in the following discussion, the use of incentives in war plants will require much preparation before success can be attained.

Neatly Packaged Plans

THE action desired from a wage incentive in industry is increased effort by the workman resulting in a high rate of production. There are innumerable neatly packaged plans or formulas through which the compensation of the individual is adjusted according to his production, in order to encourage and reward his effort and ability. These plans range from the simple, direct proposition of piece work, whereby the worker is paid so many cents for each unit completed, to the highly complex empirical plans which rely on intricate tables and charts for the determination of the compensation for a given rate of work. All of these plans are incentives designed to induce the worker to produce more in a given length of time; in certain applications, however, many of these plans have had exactly the opposite effect, have deterred men from working rapidly, have produced endless grievances, and have resulted in work stoppages until the "incentive" was removed.

The application of the incentive principle in industry is much broader than the adoption of a plan; it involves consideration of the immediate and the long-run effects on the employer-employee relations of installing an incentive plan under given conditions in the shop, or of following the alternative, payment on a straight hourly rate.

Time Rate or Incentive

THERE are at least four important reasons why an incentive-wage plan may produce disappointing results as compared with an hourly-rate wage plan:

1. The desire of a man to work rapidly is heavily influenced by his feelings toward his job, his supervisor, and his company. Morale is not necessarily purchased with an incentive plan.

2. The incentive effect of extra compensation for extra work is small at the present time because money cannot be translated into an electric refrigerator, a new car, or a new home.

3. A well-designed and properly-administered program based on hourly- or day-rate wages contains many elements of incentive.

4. An incentive-wage plan, applied without knowledge of what is a fair rate of production, will result in inequalities in wage rates which may disrupt production.

Let us examine each of these considerations:

First, is extra money the most important incentive? There are many incentives which may affect the activities of any working man. Certain incentives center in the wage structure; others have little relationship to compensation. One man works hard because he likes his work; another because hard work is an escape from a distressing home problem. One man wants the security of cold coin in his pocket; another wants the power of advancement and authority. At the initial meeting of a class in wage incentives conducted recently for a group of union officials, one of the members introduced his wife and baby boy, explaining, "This is my incentive plan." Certainly a strong incentive is the offer of secure employment with fair treatment both now and after the war.

The Hawthorne Experiments

THE Western Electric Company in its celebrated "Hawthorne Experiments" discovered that a man's feelings toward his work, his supervisor, and his fellow employees have a great effect on his production. It was discovered that if a man felt that his job was "right," that supervision was fair, and that his ability and achievement were recognized, he would automatically work rapidly without being aware at any time of the fast pace. This effect was so strong that it outran the influence of an incentive plan of long standing. Men and women will work rapidly if their adjustment to their job is right, but the money of an incentive plan will not buy extra effort unless their basic job relations are acceptable.

Money Incentive Today?

SECOND, how strong is the incentive of money today? In normal times there is, for the working man, a real problem in making his wages stretch to cover some of the luxuries which he and his family desire. In wartime, most employable men and women have jobs paying good wages, with ample overtime. The problem is: What, beside war bonds and essentials, can they buy with their earnings? One of the principles of a sound incentive plan is that the reward should be closely associated with good performance. Today, the real reward must be postponed until after the war when consumers' goods are again available in quantity. This delay

negates the incentive effect of added compensation. Most people enjoy the possession of goods much more than they do the accumulation of money which cannot be
spent for 10 years.

Promotion Incentive

THIRD, what financial incentive can be offered without an incentive-wage plan?
We must not believe that because a certain group of plans for increasing production and lowering costs have been labeled "incentive-wage plans," the more standard hourly wage system does not offer incentive. Any properly-administered wage
program offers certain and substantial financial reward for well-rounded achievement
on the job. This is accomplished by providing a range of rates for each job so that
the competent operator can be paid 20, 30, 50, or even 100 per cent more than the
novice on the same job. The individual's hourly rate within this range is established by an appraisal of the employee's worth at regular intervals by his supervisors.
Additional financial incentive for good work is provided through transfer of capable
employees to more difficult and more important work which, in a well-administered
wage system, carries increased compensation. Proper administration will assure
that superior performance on the job is rewarded by regular merit increases and by
advancement to better jobs for qualified men. This can readily be accomplished in
wartime when the pressure of work and the shortage of men cause the employer to
greet with shouts of joy and offers of more money any demonstration of ability on the
part of an employee.

A sound wage policy calls for financial incentive for all-round performance
above standard. This is in contrast to the wage-incentive plans which hang their
offer of more money on a single phase of the work, speed of production, with the
consequent tendency to neglect quality, careful use of material, proper maintenance
and utilization of tools, safety, flow of work, and other essential factors of the job.
In most jobs well-rounded attention to all phases of the work is necessary to achieve
maximum production. If the operator is coaxed, for example, to neglect quality
by placing a money reward on quantity, supervision must be prepared to balance
the scale on that job by controlling more carefully than ever the quality of output,
and the other de-emphasized phases. Today, supervision is poorly prepared to assume added functions. Wage incentives will mean that management's job is made
more, rather than less, complex. Wage incentives can never serve as a substitute
for good management, and they can seldom succeed in the absence of good
management.

Test of Wage Structure

FOURTH, will wage incentives disrupt the wage structure? This consideration is
particularly significant in plants producing war materials. A consideration of
some of the major tests of a justifiable wage structure will reveal that the unsound

application of a wage-incentive plan may do violence to the principle of fair wages, a prime essential of good industrial relations. What are the tests by which management and employees, organized or unorganized, may judge the fairness of a wage structure? The following are suggested as a partial list of comparisons:

1. How do the rates paid for various jobs within a company compare with the skill, responsibility, physical and mental application, and working conditions of the job? Are rates internally consistent with the requirements of the job?

2. How do rates paid by the company compare with those paid for the same work by other companies in the industry or area?

3. How do earnings compare with the social needs of the employee to maintain or attain a desirable standard of living?

4. How do wages compare with the ability of the company to pay, in view of its competitive position?

How Workers Judge Fairness

NOT all of these comparisons are of equal importance. At one time the discussion over wages may center in the study of prevailing rates in the area; at another time the emphasis may be on the standard of living. But the first comparison, the internal consistency of the wage structure, is the test which is of great and continuous importance. Every employee easily judges the fairness of his treatment by comparing his rate with that of others doing similar work for the same company. The bulk of grievances in wage matters arises out of this comparison. There is no argument which will adequately defend the payment of widely differing amounts for similar work.

A wage structure is composed of many complex job-to-job differentials which arise out of long usage as a reflection of the relative contributions of the jobs to production. Furthermore, these wage differentials carry with them the mark of social status. A man's worth is, rightly or wrongly, commonly measured in terms of his earnings, and his self-esteem tends to follow this measure. These long-established differentials between jobs cannot be torn up by management without major repercussions in the relationship between management and labor, yet that is exactly what an incentive plan will produce if it is installed without a careful determination of a fair rate of production.

Standards Are Important

WHY is this standard or fair rate of production so important? Every wage-incentive plan must be based on some concept of a fair day's work. This means a normal rate of output which is fair to the employer and employee alike. Additional production over this level will be compensated for according to the particular incentive plan which is used. The heart of the incentive plan, then, is the standard. If the standard is set too high, even extreme effort and great skill will not enable a man to achieve standard performance; if the standard is set too low, incompetent men may receive incentive payments, and a capable man using real effort will send his earnings soaring to high levels. There is nothing inherently objectionable about uniform high-incentive earnings, indeed high earnings indicate the power to stimulate production which incentives possess.

Workmen certainly do not object to high earnings, and management should not, for high-incentive earnings mean lower total unit costs because output is increased and overhead is consequently spread more thinly. Employees, however, do object, and rightly so, to the disruption of established and tested wage differentials through the operation of an incentive plan based on standards of uneven difficulty on the various jobs.

An Example

SUPPOSE that we consider two jobs:

Job	Rate
1. Drill-press operator	$0.80 per hour
2. Lathe operator	1.20 per hour

The rates given are accepted by management and by employees as representing the proper relationship between the rates of pay, considering the work performed. If, on this structure, we install an incentive plan based on loose standards for drill-press work, and tight ones on the lathe work, we create a serious problem. The drill-press operator may increase his earnings so that he receives $1.60 per hour, whereas the lathe operator may be unable to earn more than $1.20. This situation, it will be agreed by unions, individual employees, and management, "just doesn't make sense." Yet that is exactly what happens to wages if standards are not accurately set and maintained.

Possible Troubles

THE situation mentioned above is unstable; one of three things is likely to happen:

1. The lathe operators, individually or collectively, will bring pressure to have their standard rate of production relaxed so they can make good earnings to restore the original wage differentials. The drill-press operator's earnings will be used as a lever to pry the whole wage structure upwards.

2. Management may "cut the rate" on drill-press work to restore the traditional differential. This is always morale shattering, and if it happens to many employees the incentive plan will be branded a "speed-up system" under which a man works harder and gets nothing for it.

3. The drill-press operators, fearing management's action, may deliberately

work slowly, thereby reducing their earnings and protecting their easy job standard by preserving the original wage differentials.

If these results take place, the incentive plan has brought new troubles to the shop—troubles of a type that causes bitter feelings, work stoppages, and a determination to discredit and eliminate the incentive plan. Production may well be reduced rather than increased.

The real trouble is not in the incentive plan, but in the unfair standards of production. Throughout the history of wage-incentive installations, those which have succeeded have been based on sound and fair standards, and failure has inevitably attended those with haphazard standards.

Setting Standards

TIME- and motion-study men, since the time of Frederick W. Taylor, have worked with the problem of production standards with various degrees of success. Through the stop-watch and the motion-picture camera they have developed techniques, which permit the setting of accurate standards, provided:

1. All conditions under which the work is performed are well planned and controlled. This means that supervision must have mastered the problems of training men in a uniform method of doing the work, supplying uniform materials at a constant pace so that the work is not interrupted, providing standard and uniform maintenance on machines and equipment, holding conditions of light, temperature and other environmental factors at a constant level.

2. Designs and methods of performing the work do not change so rapidly that the investment in careful setting of standards is too great to be economically justifiable.

3. Adequate time can be devoted to methods for improvement in advance of installing the incentive.

4. A thorough, competent, and fair job of standards setting is done by an impartial time-study man, uninfluenced by pressure to find a predetermined answer.

5. A well-selected work force is employed so that the range of skill and ability is not too wide on any job.

Frequent and Drastic Revisions

THE conditions called for above do not just happen; they are brought about by long and careful work on the part of management. These conditions obviously are most likely to exist in an industry where product design, equipment, methods, and volume of output are stable. But what are the conditions which exist today in war production? Our worst problems of production exist where companies are producing items of different design from their peacetime line, and where the contingencies of combat require frequent and drastic revisions of design. There is not time to standardize on methods, equipment, or work place layout. The flow of materials is uncertain, and substitutes must often be used. The work force consists of anyone who can be induced to work, ranging from highly skilled and experienced hands to complete newcomers and to incompetents. Supervision is inexperienced and badly overloaded. Under these circumstances, can any fair standard of output be set? The average war-production job simply will not hold still long enough to be carefully studied.

Industry has used two compromises to avoid the difficulty of inaccurate standards:

1. A very mild incentive prevents earnings from getting far out of line, even with defective standards. This is generally unsatisfactory because the incentive exerts little beneficial effect.

2. Individual standards are avoided by hanging the incentive on total output of the plant rather than on individual achievement. The incentive effect is doubtful because reward does not necessarily follow effort; the lazy workman is rewarded equally with the energetic and capable man.

Labor Board Attitude

THE National War Labor Board, in a recent decision, granted the Grumman Aircraft Engineering Corporation permission to use a plant-wide incentive plan, but included reservations as to the general adoption of such a plan. The Board recognized the underlying principles as untested but stated, "This is no reason for denying a trial of the plan. There is a possibility that in certain situations it may, without an increase in costs, result in an expanded production of urgently needed war materials from present facilities and presently employed manpower. It seems clear, however, that only under an unusual set of circumstances do the plant-wide or company-wide wage-incentive plans offer sufficient promise to invite experimentation with them. The Grumman plan cannot be used as a readymade model for extensive application. On the contrary, it has a highly limited application."

Move with Caution

PERTINENT to the issue are the 800 applications for approval of various types of wage-incentive plans received by the National War Labor Board and the Regional Boards since the issuance of Executive Order No. 9328 on April 8, 1943. Many of these applications have been only a means to provide "hidden wage increases" contrary to the national wage stabilization program; many of them have been based on a desire to attract additional manpower rather than to stabilize the existing facilities and manpower; and others have been honest attempts prescribed without fundamental knowledge of wage-incentive plans or have been haphazardly constructed. The Board, which must approve each new wage-incentive installation, is moving with caution in granting permission because it fears that great damage can be done with poorly conceived incentive plans.

Wage-incentive measures, in the contention of the Board, will not automatically result in a startling increase in production. The Board strongly urges management and unions not to approach the incentive wage question as a cure-all for the solution of production problems. The Grumman decision states, "Actually, the fashioning of a wage-incentive plan adapted to the particular needs of any company is a major and a complex problem which requires the combined best efforts of specialists and of top executives. Its adoption is a major policy decision. It is not a casual undertaking. Even a properly designed plan may be likened to a highly specialized tool with a sharp cutting edge. Wielded by experts, it can be highly productive. On the other hand, it can cut off the fingers of the inexpert who attempts to use it. There is also a question of adapting any program to significant changes in operating conditions if the plan is to have a continuing influence on production. This must be anticipated at the time a plan is being developed. The determination to install an incentive wage-payment plan is not a light matter; it is a policy decision of the first magnitude."

War Production

WHAT, then, is the place of wage incentives in the war production picture? There is real need for development of the incentive principle in industry, but not at the cost of disrupting the wage structure and jeopardizing good industrial relations. Incentives can be developed through a well-administered hourly wage structure, or through the proper use of non-financial incentives. Wage incentive plans are only to be used safely under conditions of careful standardization of the work, and when proper and fair standards of performance have been set. Installation of wage incentives in the absence of these conditions is likely to bring about serious trouble, interfere with production, and result in ultimate abandonment of the plan.

The use of wage incentives in many war plants will only increase the burden on supervision already overtaxed to the breaking point. The manager who adopts wage incentives in the hope that they will substitute for good supervision is likely to find that he has started more than he has finished. Wage incentives cannot succeed unless management has mastered its job.

Let us, then, put first things first. Improve methods, standardize designs and equipment, train employees, develop supervision, and master techniques of control. The possibilities for increasing production in these ways are enormous. After that, incentives can be profitably employed. The wise driver of the donkey mends the broken wheel of his cart before he uses the carrot incentive to produce action.

Reproduced by permission from the January, 1944 issue of Engineering and Science Monthly, published by the Alumni Association, California Institute of Technology.

The Ideal Combination of Experience and Train-
ing for Orientation Instructors is Public School
Teaching with Considerable Training in Social
Psychology or Experience in Dealing with Public
Opinion.

Orientation
Training Today

By Earl Planty

Johnson & Johnson,
New Brunswick, N. J.

B EFORE the war, new industrial workers usually became oriented to company
policies, to their jobs, to their supervisors, and to fellow workers in either of
two ways. Some few companies maintained organized, orientation training
programs for getting new workers adjusted. Where these were lacking, the new
employee painfully, and with needless expense to the company, learned his way
about through trial and error or by "asking someone else". If learning by experience was costly in normal times, how much more so is this true in times when the
average length of service in some industries is less than a year, and where a worker
may ask information from half a dozen persons, each as new and ignorant of the
rules and regulations as himself.

Objectives

T ODAY most successful industries are recognizing the advantages of offering organized programs of orientation training. However, the objectives in these
activities vary widely. Many training programs have limited their objectives to
imparting knowledge of company rules and policies; a few others, more alert to the
psychology of public opinion, of propaganda, and of attitude building, have gone
further and made an open attempt to influence favorably the attitudes of their employees.

One of the major functions of any personnel department is to build job satisfaction, and its emphasis should be placed upon direct improvement of working
conditions. However, this alone in these unusual times will not suffice. Many

workers who have every reason to be satisfied with their conditions of employment are not so. There are too many outside distracting psychological tensions and hysterias which must be met and reduced if progressive industry is to receive full benefit from whatever actual improvements it makes in working conditions.

Credit Legitimately Due Employer

WORKERS become dissatisfied with their jobs through many abnormal, wartime factors, including imminence of induction, worry over relatives already in service, increasing cost of living, juvenile delinquency, rationing, crowded living conditions, stories of high wages elsewhere, migration mania, post-war uncertainty, political confusion, changing values, and through contacts with the neurotic, abnormal individuals whom industry has found it necessary to employ. All or any of these anxieties for which the employer is not in the least responsible may be projected into dissatisfaction with working conditions, which, considered objectively, may be wholly satisfactory. *It is not enough to improve working conditions; workers must be constantly kept aware of what has been done. They must be "sold".*

When an employer is doing all in his power to add to the comfort of his workers, it should not be considered immoral for him to attempt to stabilize and improve his workers' attitudes toward his efforts, especially where he is competing for attention among so many social and psychological distractions peculiar to the times.

Worker Attitudes Are Controllable

MANAGEMENT must recognize that attitudes are controllable, a fact that allows the political propagandist to function. Once an American newsman talked with Goebbels. It was at the time when Germany had just signed a pact with Russia, and Goebbels was busy building among the Germans a love of the "great Russian people". The American asked Goebbels this question, "Suppose you Germans found it necessary in a year or two to fight Russia, then wouldn't the respect which you had built among your people for Communism be dangerous?" Goebbels replied, "In six months my propaganda can make them hate the Russians as they now love them". In short, public opinion is controllable, and our best industries are engaging psychologists to measure and build industrial opinion (morale) just as carefully as they measure and increase production, for the latter depends upon the former.

Two generalizations, discussed above, underlie any attempt at orientation training. They may be restated briefly as follows: First, workers' attitudes toward their jobs do not always bear a close relation to actual working conditions. Even good conditions may result in poor employee attitudes or morale. Secondly, job attitudes can be controlled. Management which spends so much to improve working conditions is shortsighted indeed if it does not take the added steps necessary to see that these improvements do result in better morale. An orientation training program is the follow-up step necessary in guaranteeing to management that the expenditure of time and money on improved working conditions does result in favorable attitudes.

New Goals in Orientation Training

ORIENTATION programs that are alert to wartime pressures, serve their sponsors through an attempt to build and maintain satisfactory job attitudes by the following specific activities.

Traditional

Traditional Orientation Programs Inform Workers about Rules, Regulations, and Policies, and Thereby:

A. Reduce ill will, disciplinary action, and dismissals caused where employee did not know rules or consequences of violating them. Reduce "take a chance" attitude by showing even before the violation occurs the certainty and fairness of the penalty.

B. Reduce waste time on employee's part—he will know what to do or where to go with problems—he will ask fewer questions. He will be more secure, satisfied, less frustrated with unrecognized anxieties.

C. Reduce foreman's burdens in teaching and explaining company rules and policies.

D. Reduce fear of the unknown. New workers are timid, sometimes afraid. Oftentimes this fear, which may be sub-conscious, acts as a block or barrier so that the new worker never realizes his top production level until his fears are removed by slowly accumulated knowledge and understanding of the (unknown) new job. Unless assistance is given, this accumulation of knowledge and elimination of fear may take many months. Orientation helps remove the barrier at the outset.

More Advanced

MORE *Advanced Orientation Programs Instruct about Company History, Personalities, Products. They Show the Stability of the Company, its Reputation, its Post-War Possibilities. They Explain the Services Rendered the Employees: Explaining What the Company Has Done for Workers and Getting the Employees to Use Some of These Services. This Will:*

A. Build up an original reserve of high morale to a point where a new worker has some resistance power to rebuffs or disappointments which he must inevitably meet on his job. Help keep workers from quitting before they can give the job an honest try out.

B. Show that as good or better opportunities exist with the present company and reduce the part of labor turnover produced by indiscriminate job shopping.

—53—

C. Give management a chance to explain its position before the worker is misinformed by others. *Since first impressions are lasting ones*, this is an advantage which should be realized. This explanation, given directly by an orientation training specialist who uses all the devices of persuasion and conviction known to psychology, salesmanship, and education, can usually be more effective than distant or less well organized competitive attractions or distractions.

D. Build wholesome attitudes toward the job and the employer. Many American workers who have every reason to be satisfied with their jobs are not so. This is because disgruntled persons "work on" them or outside tensions provoke worries which are carried to and inseparably attached to the job. Opinion can be built as well as destroyed. Orientation will build an advance job satisfaction which helps counteract the activities of those present, even in the best of industries, who complain, criticize, and destroy good will.

Exceptional

A FEW *Exceptional Programs Show How the Company Depends upon the Workers, How the Workers Are the Company. They Show the Importance of the Product and Explain and Illustrate Each Worker's Contribution to the Finished Article. They Build up the Self Respect of the Worker and the Importance of his Job. This Will:*

A. Make workers feel they belong, that management needs them, respects them. Build the workers' confidence in the employer and in themselves. Reduce shopping for a job where the work might be more "important" or the worker "treated better."

B. Keep old and new workers satisfied by giving them an opportunity to have questions answered and their opinions considered, since it is informal and conversational.

C. Provide management with a planned opportunity to discover workers' attitudes and to isolate sore spots for treatment. It lets management get "inside" the workers' thinking, and thereby spot incipient trouble.

Most Farsighted

THE *Most Far-Sighted Administrators Use Orientation Training to Provide a Permanent Channel for Presenting Information to Employees and Influencing their Reaction to It.*

A. Orientation provides the workers with common knowledge and attitudes. People who think alike on some things have a basis for continued understanding. Orientation training is management's great opportunity to get workers integrated along constructive lines.

B. It provides a contact, a channel whereby management can, whenever a special occasion arises, get into contact with workers without disturbing foremen and without taking the risk that a few foremen might misinterpret whatever they are conveying to workers, or do a poor selling job of it. If emergency changes in policy arise needing explanation or "selling," an orientation training unit provides direct contact between workers and employer. Workers are not suspicious, since they usually regard orientation favorably.

Experience Necessary

Any training program which sets out to attain one or more of the above mentioned major objectives can go far toward arresting labor turnover, absenteeism, worker indifference or dissatisfaction with management. Such a program, however, can easily become a boomerang unless taught with extreme care. Ordinary production specialists or even shop teachers are usually incompetent to handle these activities.

The ideal combination of experience and training for orientation instructors is public school teaching with considerable training in social psychology or experience in dealing with public opinion. Above all the instructor must be enthusiastic, personally attractive, pleasant, and be able to interest groups. A high degree of social intelligence is required plus ability and willingness to keep abreast of changes in company policy and practice. Failing to obtain the services of experienced classroom teachers or psychologists, a few industrial concerns have tried salesmen and newspaper men with some success. Many women are proving highly capable at the work.

If Counseling is a Necessary Function—as Well
It May Be in the Face of New Conditions in
Industry—Care Should be Taken that the Work
is Organized on a Sound Personnel Basis.

Women's Personnel Division

By Hedwig H. Ellsley

Grumman Aircraft Engineering Corp.,
Bethpage, L. I.,
New York

To us, at the Grumman Aircraft Engineering Corporation, counseling is a unique function. It does not mean merely lending a sympathetic ear to the verbalized outpourings of the worker. Nor does it signify the "passive approach." It is, instead, a very active process. This means the consideration of our employees as mature adults, and the placement within their reach (to use or not, as they choose) such aids as will assist them in working out their own problems. The philosophy behind this theory is thus not a paternalistic one, but one that recognizes the right of the individual to the elements of a satisfying adjustment, and the right to make his own decisions toward achieving it. We recognize that there is nothing original in this theory. We have merely used an approach which is psychologically sound, and have found it to be very workable.

No Feminine Fripperies

Inasmuch as it has been axiomatic with us, ever since our inception a year ago, to consider the problems of women always as those of any *workers*, rather than from the much over-worked "woman's angle," our department functions not as an adjunct to the organization as a whole, but as an integrated part of it. The Women's Personnel Division at Grumman Aircraft is not a separate unit, operating with an eye to glamorizing industry for woman-appeal.

Among all our many services, there is not a single feminine frippery designed as bait for recruiting women workers. The specifics of our whole program have come out of an expression of need from women already employed, and facilities have been set up to meet that expressed need. Since such procedure is in line with good personnel practice, our department naturally functions as a part of the whole machinery of personnel administration under the supervision of Mr. Paul S. Gilbert, Personnel Director.

For "service" means to us providing avenues of assistance in areas where there is an indigenous need, rather than the artificial setting up of extraneous aids, and bidding women make use of them. When it became apparent that many of our women workers were in danger of being forced to leave their jobs because of the inadequacy of child care facilities, we established a series of three Child Care Centers in geographical areas where there was the greatest concentration of our women workers with children of pre-school age, and where there was not already community provision for their care. In cases where the children of our women employes are making use of the Lanham Fund Centers, our company makes a per capita financial contribution through the Nassau County War Council. Unlike many existing centers, ours were set up on a twelve hour basis to serve the needs of our mothers working for ten hours a day. The centers are staffed by well-trained specialists in nursery education, with whom the mother is certain her child is happy, safe and well.

Husband Called Up

WHEN we became aware of the fact that transportation difficulties obliged a worker who was not feeling well to stay at the plant until her driver finished work at the end of the shift, we were able to enlist the aid of the American Women's Hospital Reserve Corps to take her home. This unit has since extended its services to our workers, being on call through the Women's Personnel offices for any emergency not regularly covered by other divisions. For example:

Mrs. B——'s husband was unexpectedly called into service, and she was faced with the emergency of placing her children in a boarding home. She made an appeal to the counselor who suggested three possibilities selected from an extensive list of foster mothers compiled by our department [after having been cleared through the State Department of Social Welfare]. Mrs. B—— then requested a leave of absence for two days in order that she might have time to get about the area by public conveyance to visit the homes suggested, and to make arrangements for the care of her children if she found a home which was satisfactory. The counselor offered her the service of the A.W.H.R.C., and she was able to make her visits in the space of a single Saturday morning.

In the same way, our other services have developed. It is readily apparent that we cannot echo the cry of so many war industries which exclaim: "We're offering the women all these services, and they just don't use them!" *Services developed out of the expressed need of the worker do not lie fallowing.*

A Service Unit

ONLY in terms of this philosophy is the Women's Personnel Division of our company a service unit. Its ideal purpose is to serve the administration by interpreting to it the needs of its women, and to serve the women employees by helping them to meet the complexities which the war emergency has brought into their lives. It strives to help women workers to function as adequately as each is constitutionally able in an accustomed industrial situation, despite the exigencies entailed in maintaining the home; despite economic and personality barriers; and despite the very real obstacle of masculine prejudice engendered by the threat which women in industry inevitably bring to their security.

Although we can understand the basis of this prejudice and recognize it as a human one, it nevertheless continues to be one of the stumbling blocks for women in industry, just as it was from the beginning of the establishment of the Women's Personnel Division at Grumman Aircraft. The administration at the head of the organization saw the need for a service to women. However, it was readily apparent that such a service could not be imposed on the organization without nurturing the latent fear that we had come to usurp managerial functions. There was a manifest need for patient education toward an understanding of our place in the organization, and for painstaking cultivation of confidence in it.

First Woman Worker

THE story of our struggle for acceptance is in so many ways like that of any woman worker, that we know of no better way to demonstrate how this confidence has grown than to quote from a letter written by one of the first women to work in the shop:

". . . . Then came the red-letter day when we reported for work. . . .and pandemonium broke loose—whistlings, catcalls and wolf cries! You'd think that they had never before seen a woman, and they never had—not in this setting. An harassed lead-man received us and with a 'what-on-earth-am-I-going-to-do-with-them' look, put us to doing the simplest of chores. (Later we found that he had promised his men that we should do only the work they disliked.) . . . . We were the butt of a hundred jokes and became aware of the concealed hostility behind them. Lunch times were board of strategy meetings and one by one we all did the kind of work for which we had been trained. This I like to call woman's 'termite' approach and it worked! At the time, progress seemed maddeningly slow but over a span of one short year and a half, I can see that it was amazingly rapid— women doing everything but the extremely heavy work—even in sacred Tool and Die. And to think that now women are in Engineering and actually testing the Grumman Hellcats! . . . . Those old days are so close to me that even now I positively glow when you write me of a foreman's blocking a transfer of a woman, saying, 'She's a darn good worker and I need her,' when but yesterday he would have said, largely, 'Take 'em all—I don't want any part of 'em.' Shades of Sam Johnson—that we did it all—is remarkable!"

Remain Inconspicuous

AND so our growth, too, was a slow one, geared so precisely to the needs of the company, that we succeeded in remaining inconspicuous until we were able to prove our intentions. It was a gradual and unobtrusive sort of infusion. We came one at a time, setting up offices first in one plant and then rather diffidently but resolutely in another and another. In this fact, we feel, lies much of our strength. Not until our department had been functioning for nearly a year did we feel that we had been able to demonstrate to foremen and plant managers that we regarded ourselves always as a service, and never as a managerial unit. By now it is apparent that much of the doubt and even resentment which had smoldered perceptibly and threatened many times to break into open flares in the earlier days of our coming, has died. One counselor reports these as typical foreman requests today:

"I've got a girl here I don't know what to do with. I thought I knew about girls, but this one is too much for me. Do you mind if I send her over to see you?"

"We have a girl in our department who has been out for two weeks. Can you find out what's the trouble? She's a good worker and we don't want to lose her."

With certain inevitable reservations, we have been accepted.

Duties of Division

THE Women's Personnel Division, working under individual plant managers, is responsible to the Personnel Director. It consists of a Co-ordinator of Women's Personnel and fourteen staff members, three of whom serve the women on the night shift. One counselor represents Women's Personnel in the training schools. This same counselor is not confined by the nature of her work to any one plant, and so is free to circulate among them. This gives her the opportunity to undertake surveys and research projects objectively, for the purpose of inaugurating new services or modifying existing ones. This peripatetic member of the staff is also free to seek out community resources, and by personal contact to establish a reciprocal working relationship with them in order to interpret their functions to those in need of such services.

In order to carry out such a program as ours, the women chosen for the position of Personnel Counselor need to bring more to their jobs than that they are "motherly" or that they have had "experience in raising families." The Co-ordinator sought as members of her staff well-balanced individuals who could bring to their work the dignity of a professional attitude; a warmth of personality, and the responsiveness to make her interest felt by the woman worker; a sense of humor and the ability to see a problem in its proper perspective. Although she felt that the counselor should have a good measure of educational and cultural training, a glimpse of the backgrounds of the present staff members shows that the appraisal was hardly academic. They range all the way from one year in college to varying degrees of post-graduate study.

Professional Attitude

THE previous work experiences of the counselors include such fields as education, social work, music, psychology, and personnel, but in each case there has been experience in working with people in some capacity. Since we are still pioneering in the field of Women's Personnel, and since the stress of war time takes its toll of us as it does of other women workers, both flexibility and physical stamina were regarded as essential characteristics of the successful counselor. Lastly, but of highest importance, is the fact that each candidate was viewed not only in the light of her value as an individual, but also in the light of her possible contribution to Women's Personnel as a group, functioning with a scope so broad that the only limitations on it are the limitations imposed by intelligent and progressive management upon personnel workers anywhere.

In order to orient the counselor to her position, she is taken on the staff as a trainee and spends several weeks in one of the training schools learning shop techniques and the reactions of women, who in many cases are finding it necessary to adjust to a wholly unfamiliar situation. This training is supplemented by an apprenticeship under the guidance of one or more of the counselors in plants which already have an established counselor service. During this period, the counselor attends staff meetings and can begin to visualize the goals of the Women's Personnel program and at the same time formulate her own philosophy and techniques. Such a comprehensive orientation broadens the counselor's viewpoint and permits her to identify herself with the worker in establishing her own security on the job during the period of apprenticeship.

Regular Staff Meetings

THE Co-ordinator not only initiates some of the activities of the personnel counselors, but integrates them as well. The machinery behind this co-ordination program consists of regular weekly staff meetings in which problems concerning women as workers are discussed, and the solutions proposed scrutinized in terms of their practical application to real situations. The meetings are conducted by the Co-ordinator and attended by all the members of the Women's Personnel staff. In addition, the woman representative of the Employment Division attends the meetings, and serves by this expedient to aid in the business of correlating problems and policies of Women's Personnel with Employment, by interpreting each to the other. The Director of our Child Care Centers is usually also in attendance, inasmuch as the matters discussed have a bearing on the women workers whose children attend the nurseries.

From time to time representative members of other departments, such as, for instance, the health or the safety departments, are invited to participate in these meetings. In this way we provide an opportunity for exchange of advice and suggestions in matters of mutual concern, and attempt to foster a spirit of integrated action, which can only result from a reciprocal understanding of the points of view and the goals of these categorically separate units.

Decentralization

THIS function is especially important in an organization in which there are several plants each with its separate manager, and hence its specialized routines and its distinct problems. The very fact of this separateness, however, brings to our department the advantage of being forced to consider our common problems in the light of a more variegated experience, and to engage in a far more active exchange of ideas than if we were concentrated under one roof. This decentralization of our productive units also helps to provide for growth, inasmuch as we have upon occasion been able to put a new project across through all or several of the plants, by trying it out first in one of them. There can be no doubt that such an arrangement provides a constant challenge to all of us, and especially to the Co-ordinator whose task it is to present to the administration for approval the projects which from week to week present themselves to us as new ways to serve Grumman by serving the women who have so suddenly become a part of it.

Flexibility

THE functions of the counselors are characterized by complete flexibility. In each plant the counselor service differs from that in the other plants as the plant management differs, and as the personality and training of each counselor causes her to emphasize certain aspects of the implications in the term "counseling." Her tasks have no clearly defined lines except, of course, that *service* is the core of her operations. There is no kind of help which the counselor is not willing to offer, but each act of service carries with it the special sort of dignity implicit in her professional attitude. Although she has no disciplinary functions as such, there are occasions when she is called upon to give authoritative reprimands.

Since it has been one of our goals to encourage in the worker a feeling toward us of respect without awe, such reprimands administered by the counselor in the privacy of her office, usually foster better working attitudes than any punitive measures can ever hope to do. But no matter what sort of problem confronts the counselor, there is an ever present challenge to evolve techniques for bringing into living practice those sound psychological principles which are the essence of our philosophy.

In a culture such as ours, where work is a significant part of our mores, and where perhaps the greatest compliment one can pay another is to say he is a hard worker, we recognize that the person who is not a successful worker, especially when she has the added stimulant of war demands, has some very basic reason for failing. From her very first contact with her, the counselor, through a gracious, friendly, and non-judgmental approach, tries to *know* the worker; her home conditions and responsibilities; her motivation for work; her early background; her work experience; her health history; her personality characteristics; and the strengths and weaknesses which arise out of them. When she knows these things about the worker, she tries to help her to remove, or to view in appropriate perspective, those things which interfere with her functioning as well as she is able.

Counselor Aids Placement

Mℴℝᴇ concretely, this is how it works. When an applicant appears to present herself for a job, she is interviewed by a member of the employment division, who tries to learn pertinent facts about conditions in her home, the solution she has made for her child care and housekeeping responsibilities, and other information of a similar nature. Needless to say, no matter how skillful the interviewer's techniques may be, the agitated applicant, so unsure of her qualifications that she feels that any revelation may prove fatal, cautiously guards and frequently falsifies the facts.

However, the successful applicant is given a training period of about five or six weeks before she enters a plant. During the third or fourth week of this training period, when she feels quite at home in the training school atmosphere, and is anticipating the plant experience always with some apprehension and sometimes with genuine fear, she has an opportunity to make her first real contact with the company, by meeting one of the personnel counselors. The counselor meets with her in a group of her classmates at the training school and describes to her in concrete terms salient aspects of life at the plants. She is given a handbook which contains rules and regulations, policies and traditions of the company and many of these are interpreted and discussed.

The counselor strives to create an atmosphere conducive to a relaxed and free give-and-take. Since the women already feel a measure of security in having been on the company pay-roll for weeks, there are frank and eager questions from them. The close of the discussion always finds one or two women who linger to ask the counselor advice before she gets away, despite the fact that they have been told that the counselor will see each one individually before she completes her training period, to answer further questions and to get better acquainted personally. Hardly a meeting ends without some renewed evidence of the need of the worker for such a contact before she sets foot in a plant.

Orientation

THE group meeting is intended to aid in the process of orientation and to establish a working relationship between the women workers and the Women's Personnel Division, so that the worker will always feel free to talk over her difficulties with any member of the staff. The individual interview which follows the group discussion is intended to strengthen that feeling and to aid the worker in solving some of her difficulties *before* she actually enters the shop.

The counselor, by her permissive attitude, encourages the worker to talk freely. Often the talking itself may bring relaxation and relief of tension, and problems which seemed entangled in a devastating confusion in the mind of the worker, sometimes assume an ordered pattern as she verbalizes them. For instance, the girl who confides in the counselor to the extent of telling her of the unsanctified conditions attending her birth, or of the ruthlessness with which she has treated a non-conformist sister, feels that she has faced her problem by revealing herself honestly, and has been accepted by a person of integrity. The counselor, by her acceptance, takes an active part in increasing the feelings of self-esteem and security in a disturbed worker. It is a widely accepted fact that the greater the feeling of security and self-confidence, the greater the potentiality of the worker for success on the job.

Environmental Advice

IN OTHER instances, where the worker's problem may have an environmental solution, the counselor informs her regarding established services she is free to use. If her problem centers about child care, she is given information about child care centers, boarding homes, camps, play schools, or private schools according to her need. If her transportation will be difficult, train and bus services are examined, and the operation of our Transportation Division explained. If she knows she will be obliged to move a month after she starts work and has not been able to find a place to live, the counselor tells her about our Employees' Housing Service. If she is in need of domestic help, lists of high school girls who are willing to work after school and on Saturdays are made available to her along with the names of some adult domestic workers. These and other concrete aids are offered her.

The worker thus frequently is relieved of some of her major sources of concern before she starts work at the plant. At the same time, the pre-placement interview gives the counselor the opportunity, through informal conversation, to find out as much as she can about the worker as a human being and as a potential part of our particular industrial pattern. The counselor has an excellent opportunity here to get a more valid picture of the worker who by now feels an increased confidence and a fuller measure of security than she did in her pre-employment interview, and who therefore dares to be more truthful. The interview is recorded, and the counselor makes recommendations about the worker in her report.

Better Stay at Home

SURELY the employment interviewer would have rejected this woman if he had been able to ascertain these facts which the counselor gathered weeks later in the pre-placement interview at the training school:

Husband enlisted. Four children: boy, 14; girls 12 and 7; infant, 8 months. Twelve-year-old a retarded student because of consistent ill-health. She cannot read at all. Has had St. Vitus Dance. Is about to have a chest x-ray, because school nurse suspects tuberculosis. Mother plans to leave the entire responsibility of the home to her. She will care for the baby; clean the house; plan, shop for, and prepare the meals. Mother declares daughter is more capable at these tasks than she is.

Needless to say, the counselor recommended that the first duty of this mother, (who, incidentally, owned property from which there was an income) was obviously in her home.

The record of the pre-placement interview is highly confidential. Outside of our own department, only one person sees it. He is the member of the employment division who assigns women to their specific jobs after the training period is over. In as far as he is able, he attempts from the start to assign each one to the job which, in terms of the pre-placement interview, seems best to suit her capabilities and her needs. To those who have any part in allocating workers to jobs under the frustrating pressures of these times, we need not say that this seems to be a visionary goal, actually achieved in too small a percentage of cases.

Transfer Information

HOWEVER, even in cases in which the information in the pre-placement interview seems to have been overlooked at the employment office, if the worker fails at the task to which she has been assigned, or if she shows dissatisfaction with it, the interview record gives a clue to her failure or dissatisfaction, and it serves as a guide to the next step to be taken in her case. She may be transferred to a situation better for her, she may be encouraged to take a leave of absence until home affairs are settled, or she may simply be permitted to sever connections with the company if there are indications that she would never be able to adjust at all.

In a sense, the orientation program is a prophylactic measure. When the pre-placement interview record is sent from the employment office to the counselor in the plant to which the worker has been assigned, she has the opportunity to read it before the worker arrives and to anticipate what her difficulties may be, or what productive attributes she brings to the job. She knows which worker will need constant encouragement, which one may have difficulty in being accepted by her fellow workers, which one is inclined to tire easily, which one resents authority, and which one will be a first-rate morale builder. Equipped with this information she is frequently able to take steps to prevent incipient problems from materializing or at least to temper the effect they may have upon the worker and those who have contact with her.

A Seemingly Hopeless Case

FOR instance there was the case of K——. When recruiting for women workers seemed to have reached the saturation point, K—— was accepted for training in a moment of frenzied desperation well-known to any employment interviewer who is able to produce only one-tenth of the number of workers requisitioned. This is, in part, the description of K—— which the counselor who interviewed her at the training school sent first to the employment office, and then to the plant which was to receive K——:

Age: 42

Marital Status: Single

Education: 6th grade

Work Experience: None

Health: Had to wait a month to begin work because of a thyroid condition. Has gained a great deal of weight which she cannot lose. Has only one upper tooth.

Interviewer's Impression: Long history of maladjustment. Born on Long Island, reared in Brooklyn, but has never been in New York City. Has never had any interest in going. Quit school because teachers "weren't very nice." Declares she's very happy in her new-work. Even her brother notices a great change in her. Her brother helps her to read and study the work, and asks her questions about it afterwards. Explains the absence of teeth by the fact that years ago she bit on a hard nut shell. Posture poor. Expects to drive a car to work next week, though she's never tried to drive. Childish. Feels insecure. Eager to get to the plant to work. Should be carefully guided and checked for adjustment.

Becomes Good Worker

THE plant counselor, having read the report days before K—— presented herself at the plant, advised the foreman to whom she had been assigned, that K—— had never worked before, that her appearance was not attractive, and that she felt insecure and would probably need help in adjusting to the job. She suggested that K—— might present other difficulties, but that she was eager to try, and that perhaps with some special attention she might succeed in adjusting. When K—— arrived, the foreman tried her first at one job, and then with great patience at another. When she did not succeed, he hit upon the happy idea of putting her under the wing of an older woman who was one of his good workers, and who was kind and willing to help. The result has been that K—— is a valuable and loyal worker, who never fails to turn out her share of the work.

The Dead Donkey

THE pre-placement interview (not to be confused with the pre-employment interview) is the first step in executing our philosophy of promoting healthy and productive attitudes through a personal contact which, though relatively intimate, strives always to respect the integrity of each woman as an individual human being. The follow-up which the counselor makes more or less methodically after the worker is established at the plant is only one of the succeeding measures which carries out the principles of that philosophy. But it is the woman who came in disquieted haste to one of the counselors the other day, for advice about what to do with her donkey which had inopportunely fallen dead at her feet that morning, who bears witness to the fact that in some cases we have done our work too well.

At least there is evidence that, to offset the numbers of women who have not gained enough confidence in us as yet to consult us in matters in which we are prepared to give help, there are many women who have established the habit of seeking the advice of the counselor not only when the problems are co vergent upon job performance, but when they strike an impasse of almost any description.

The Women's Personnel Division at Grumman Aircraft does not limit its activity to conferring with women with "problems." Realizing that the worker who is to succeed first of all be in good health, much attention is given to this facet of her well-being. But to us, "health" is no circumscribed conception signifying absence of pain. It is rather a conception sensitized to the viewpoint that emotional and physical health are unitary and interactive. The happy, well-adjusted, productive worker is the healthy worker, and vice versa.

More Painful than Pain

OUR extensive recreation program operates as a palliative to the worker whose task has been so simplified that the monotony and boredom create in her tensions often more painful than "pain." In addition, we have been able to provide rest rooms for women which are not only utilitarian but attractive and relaxing in their decorative schemes as well. There can be no denying the fact that two minutes of rest in such an atmosphere is more re-vivifying than ten minutes under less favorable conditions. As a contribution to the mental health of the worker, we have striven to carry out the company tradition of allowing the worker to feel that production is a co-operative enterprise, and that the only coercion she feels is imposed by her co-workers who see the reasonableness of regulations, and so assist in their enforcement.

In almost all of our plants, for instance, we now have a House Committee composed of representative women from the shop who, under the leadership of the Personnel Counselor, and with the sanction of the Plant Manager and the Building Maintenance officer, formulate the policies which govern the rest rooms. Policies thus determined are inevitably enforced by public opinion, with little need for punitive measures. In another one of our plants, there are daily group meetings of a small number of women at a time, selected by the foremen at the counselor's request. These groups meet with the counselor, and sometimes also with one of the nurses, to discuss informally problems of health, and adjustment of attitudes on the job.

Here again, the lecture method is avoided, and active participation of workers in this small and intimate group is encouraged and achieved, and solutions arrived at not by the counselor, but by stimulating the worker to self-activity in thinking about the subjects discussed. The absence of any member of the supervisory staff at these meetings allows for open discussion of practices thought by the worker to be unsatisfactory; for suggestions for improvement of working conditions; and for the simple catharsis of just letting off steam.

Work with County Medical Society?

ALL these techniques are directed specifically toward the mental health of the worker. But we have not failed to be attentive also to her physical health. To supplement the activities of the Health and Safety Departments, we have initiated at least one large-scale project. Through work with the county medical society, we have secured the services of a panel of physicians which acts in an advisory capacity. This panel, known as the Industrial Hygiene Committee of the Nassau County Medical Society, consists of ten physicians, representing ten areas of medical specialty. It is this panel which has helped us to formulate a pregnancy policy, to disseminate among our worker information for cold prevention, and which is now revising our pre-employment medical examination form in terms of its value to the worker and to our organization, and at the same time in terms of its practicality from the point of view of local physicians already over-burdened on account of war procurements. The panel acts thus not only as a consultant body, but also as a medium of interpreting the special needs of the industrial worker, and the condition under which she works, to the physicians in the community.

It has doubtless been noted that throughout this description of our program there has been no mention of absenteeism. Publications are overflowing with accounts of the use of telegrams, charts, posters, interviews and contests to lure the worker to appear on the job each day, and the conscientious reader of them has his brain teeming with these schemes. Our philosophy of sound personnel practices permits us little confidence in such peripheral methods to combat a condition the cause of which so often lies deep. It is our conviction that the worker who has a need for work—be it a financial, an emotional, or a social need—will stay on the job if the conditions under which she works are attractive and practical for her; if she feels a reasonable degree of security; if she can have the satisfaction of accomplishment and recognition; and if in the maelstrom of production pressures, she can still feel the peculiar exhilaration and the precious dignity of being regarded as a human being.

It is toward this end that we have focused all our activity.

Dr. Lorraine Abel
    Co-ordinator of Women's Personnel
Hedwig H. Ellsley
    Women's Personnel Counselor
Ruth W. Johnson
    Women's Employment Representative
Elizabeth M. Junken
    Women's Personnel Counselor
Estelle N. Meeker
    Women's Personnel Counselor

Study Shows that Many Reasons Given by Workers for Their Absenteeism—and so Recorded—Are Either Incorrect or Superficial. Only by Getting at the True Facts Can It Be Properly Dealt With.

Motivation
and Absenteeism

By Karl R. Kunze and Randolph Branner,
Lockheed Aircraft Corp., Burbank, Cal.

A short time ago a committee representing certain West Coast industries met to study the problem of absenteeism. The principal product of these meetings was a list of some thirty so-called causes of absenteeism. It was a quite complete list of the reasons resorted to by employees in explaining absences. It offered a means for recording and reporting absentee data in a standardized form for the comparison of different companies.

Superficial Factors Misleading

However, as time went on it became evident that this list contained many superficial factors which were *vehicles of absenteeism*, facilitating an unrestrained action of deeper, prime causes. Oftentimes these superficial factors were misleading because they directed attention away from the underlying cause. These instances brought to mind the physician who interprets shooting pains in the hand as possible heart trouble, or the horticulturist who treats a tree with wilted leaves, by providing nourishment to the roots. A personnel man, as well as the physician, must realize that sometimes the manifest factor and the causal factor are quite apart from one another.

A consideration of the reasons for absence given by employees indicates that some reasons are related to factors *inherent in the job*, and others *external to the job*. That the factors inherent in the job, matters of plant or department, machines or materials, co-workers or supervision, are possible of control by management is readily acceptable. But to what extent are the factors external to the job, factors

—69—

outside the plant, possible of control by the individual where they are outside the control of management?

Many companies have attempted to redesign the community by bringing pressure to bear here and there in an effort to provide facilities, the lack of which keeps employees off the job. Some efforts in this direction have helped, but for the most part these changes have not affected community life sufficiently to cut down absenteeism.

Why have not these attempts of industry to better community facilities met with much success? One reason is that inadequate community facilities are secondary causes—factors that could be controlled by the employee if primary causes were non-existent or less intent.

A Few Examples

To FOLLOW this line of thinking, let us take a few alleged reasons (as given by employees) that occur frequently in most company records:

> Minor ailments suffered by the employee
> Personal business
> Transportation failures

It is not uncommon to consider such reasons as being beyond the control of the employee. And to an extent, that is correct. But beyond that, it is quite in order to consider how such reasons might be brought within the employee's control.

Minor ailments for instance, are merely circumstances beyond control until they are approached by the worker with a conviction that because they interfere with his desire to be on the job, something can and will be done by him to reduce or eliminate them.

Personal business, or some of it at least, can be regarded as an inevitable cause of periodical absence until it is approached by the employee as a source of undue interference with his desire to be on the job. As such, something can and will be done about it by the worker himself.

Transportation failures, despite all that most companies have done and are doing to eliminate them, are easily accepted as an unavoidable reason for absence until the employee comes to regard his transportation difficulties, or at least part of them, as interfering too seriously with his desire to be at work regularly. Approached in that manner, how long would transportation difficulties be permitted to become more than an infrequent impediment to regular attendance?

Attracting and Repelling Values

On THE surface it would seem that the employee's desire to be regularly on the job, is assumed. The truth is, however, that while that desire may actually exist, it is not powerful enough to overcome the worker's willingness to accept the cause of absence as inevitable.

Here we are dealing with the relative potency of numerous attracting and repelling values within a worker's environment. For example, upon awaking a worker might think of a new assignment he was given at the plant that particularly appealed to him. His meditations might then bring him to a realization that his supervisor will evince no great enthusiasm if the job, when completed, is well done. Pondering over the pleasures of a golf game the worker might rationalize that he could not get to work any way because his automobile battery is sluggish. Should this absence be considered due to a transportation difficulty? Obviously not, but chances are that it would go on record as such. In this instance repelling values outweighed attracting values, culminating in a lack of proper motivation.

The situation adds up to a conflict between the willingness and the unwillingness of a worker to tolerate any recurring hindrance to his being regularly at his work. This obviously implies the building up of his unwillingness so that it will be powerful enough to prevail in the conflict. In practical terms, that means making the job so attractive to the employee that his desire to be at it will be stronger than the hindrances that prevent his being at it. And this brings the problem into the range of things about which management can legitimately do something.

Whenever consideration is given to making the job attractive to the employee, the usual procedure is to turn to the things that surround the job: the plant or department, machines or material. These are important and weigh heavily in determining the employee's job-satisfaction.

People Contacted

But, just as important, and weighing at least as heavily in the employee's evaluation of his job, are the people he is called on to contact in the course of his work—especially those in supervision. In fact, relations with his supervision can be the determining factor in the worker's attitude toward his job and everything that springs from it.

In the final analysis, a worker's loyalty or enthusiasm can be best aroused by an individual and for an individual. A worker's overpowering determination to exceed what is expected of him can be engendered only by that worker's desire to "go to bat" for an individual. And the proposal here made is that this individual should be the worker's immediate supervisor.

The reasons why supervision at the lower levels does not generally command full support from workers is that supervisors come to their jobs by reason of their knowledge of machines, materials and methods involved in the work done in their respective sections—not their knowledge of people and how to get co-operation from them. The man-factor in the job is least understood by supervision at the lower levels.

Man-Factor in Job

It is only natural that a man who reaches the first or second rung in the ladder of supervisory responsibility should place emphasis on the impersonal aspects of his job. It is also natural that any man in any job places his emphasis on those phases of his job that he knows best. Both of these facts indicate the reasons why the man-factor in the job gets the least attention.

It is through human contact, particularly with supervision, that a worker experiences a sense of achievement or of frustration, a desire to be identified with or disassociated from his group, a feeling of enjoyment or distaste for his job. Employees often express their feelings in this fashion: "Even though my job is not so hot, I wouldn't leave it for anything. My supervisor is tops."

It is not our intention to discuss the philosophy of supervisory relations. There are excellent treatises on this subject. However, it can not be too strongly emphasized that in the case of absenteeism, we are not dealing with a simple cause and effect relationship, we are concerned with a concatenation or possibly a pattern of factors, many of which stem from a primary cause—defective supervisory relationships.

Spotting Poor Areas

Poor supervisory areas may be spotted by grouping on paper, sections of the plant engaged in comparable types of work. The absentee rates by department or section of a department should then be analyzed. If it can be assumed in your plant that (1) employees of different departments are faced with similar problems of housing, transportation, etc., (2) sex, race and seniority distribution are roughly comparable, (3) and the nature of the work is not significantly different, variations in the absentee rate can be attributed, at least in part, to differences in supervisory relationships.

If such a study is conducted in your plant, even if your overall plant rate is not excessive, you may find some department or section rates to be four or five times higher than others. In this method, you will be utilizing absenteeism to advantage, by converting it into an index of supervisory relationships.

In summary, much of absenteeism can be explained in terms of human motivations. Many causes for absences given by employees can be eliminated if basic and often non-manifest causes are treated successfully. The worker who has recurring minor ailments which he now accepts as inevitable, can be brought by the proper approach and an understanding supervisor to realize that while any one cold may not be prevented, recurring colds need not be tolerated. To make such thinking possible on the part of a worker, he must be provided with a better reason for wanting to come to work than he now has for staying away.

We May Think of an Industrial Organization as a Social Structure Through which Individuals are Moving in Time and Space. Their Interrelations are Not Altogether Determined by Management But Should be Studied by Management.

Interpersonal Relations

By Forrest H. Kirkpatrick,

Radio Corporation of America, Camden, N. J.

THE effective functioning of social groups, as well as the full realization of individual personality, depends upon the spontaneity with which individuals accept each other as co-workers and participants. Such a thesis seems to be the basic concept of the science of sociometry. It is well for personnel men to become aware of this vital new field of research for it may some day recast the study of interpersonal relations in the factory or business setting.

To Work, Play and Live With

SOCIOMETRY was devised by Dr. J. E. Moreno and Dr. Helen H. Jennings for the primary purpose of finding ways which would enable people in a community to live happily together. Attractions and repulsions were discovered. Charts were made after asking members of a group with what kind of people they preferred to work, play, and live. The questions were accompanied by promises that reforms would be undertaken. This procedure sets sociometrical investigations apart from the usual questionnaire, which promises nothing.

Dr. Moreno's book, "Who Shall Survive," appeared just ten years ago and in the years since its appearance, this "sociometric" approach has been effectively applied in urban and rural situations, in situations involving racial and religious tension, and in a variety of institutional situations in which the forced assignment of people to the same community made especially imperative their discovery of their own effective form and locus of participation. Sociometric assignment of the individual to the right group did much more than produce "efficient groups." It liberated the deeper forces of creativeness within the individual.

The primary method consists in asking each member of a closed group of 20 or 30 to choose the individual person he likes best, the person with whom he would prefer to work. In order to avoid extraneous restraints in such choices, Moreno has insisted that the choices insofar as possible, be functional in the sense that the chooser has an opportunity to live or work with his choices.

The Poor Isolates

IN VARIOUS groups the proportion of "isolates" (those not preferred by anyone) varied from 15% to 35%, even when each person was asked to name three choices. The percentage of mutual pairs (each member naming the other first) reached a maximum of 27% in the fifth grade of the school system, whereas more complex constellations such as triangles and chains are found among older children.

Among a group of girls in a home-cottage assembly, it was possible to determine and chart each person's "social atom", which is Dr. Moreno's term for a person's social attraction and repulsion. When individuals are allowed to choose those outside the group, Moreno considers that extensive preferences outside the group are indicative of extraversion in that group, and probably in the individuals so disposed.

The Leader Nucleus

THIS technique was used in New York's Training School for Girls—a social cosmos of 450—and it was found that a "leader nucleus" could be selected from the total group. Seven girls from one much larger group apparently cornered almost all the first and second choices. These girls were also strongly attached to one another. The actual "sociogram" could often be changed radically by altering the individuals in a group even a little, suggesting that popularity itself is not too stable.

The results of sociometry's most recent findings have just been presented in Dr. Jennings' new book, "Leadership and Isolation." Out of her pages emerges the encouraging possibility that, without assistance, ordinary people choose their leaders rather soundly and constructively in response to social needs. Exception might be taken to the use of the term "leaders" in this study because it refers only to persons with whom people like to live and work.

Three groups could be clearly defined by Dr. Jennings in this limited population. There were the "over-chosen", who were wanted as associates. Then there was a large group which stood for the average citizen and which was located in the middle of the range of psychological choice. Lastly, there were the "isolated" or "under-chosen."

Character of Leaders

THE "over-chosen" or leaders were described by the house-mothers as cooperative, requiring no special attention, making the most of opportunities, doing more than their share of work, and having greater insight into their own and others' behavior. They are not "glamour" personalities. They are chosen consciously or unconsciously because of unusual gifts or points of view which are essential in effective group organization. This small nucleus leavens the social structure and keeps it alive.

There was some similarity in the personality patterns of leaders. Thus leaders always see their own problems in the light of the group's problems. They show planfulness, initiative, and ingenuity. On the other hand, the rejected are more concerned with their own personal likes and dislikes, hopes and frustrations. "How does this affect us?" ask the leaders. "How does this affect me?" ask the isolates.

Leaders rebel against abuse of authority which affects the group as a whole. Unlike isolates, they are more reticent about their personal dilemmas and accept trouble as something that must be dealt with by themselves. The under-chosen show little of this group responsibility, and passively or actively frustrate the activities of the group.

Isolates want to be accepted. Hence, some make themselves Cinderellas of the group and others try to have themselves accepted through displays of temper or through self-assertion. Yet the self-assertive type and the willing drudges are equally shunned.

Up and Down Movement

IT ALSO appears from Dr. Jennings' study that, no matter how static or dead a community may appear, it is dynamic. Always there is a slow but measurable current that carries some members up and on. Lincoln is credited with the remark: "I have not made events; events have made me." But those who are carried on by the current of events do not always fulfill expectations. Whereupon they are rejected. When this happens, they must readjust themselves. Sometimes they do this so effectively that they may rise again. Members of the great middle group also move up and down.

Dr. Jennings' findings leave no doubt that groups will overlook objectionable qualities if the chosen leader has compensating virtues. It even seems safe to say that the maladjusted or self-centered isolate may perform a useful function. By hitting on a formula that expresses the will of the people, he may become the man of the hour whatever his shortcomings may be. Thus a Hitler becomes possible, a man who was for years a frustrated isolate.

Democracy rests on the assumption that the people know what they want and that, if they are free to express themselves and to act, they will choose wisely. In a measure Dr. Jennings' study supports this assumption. But it is also apparent from her work that if the choice is to be effective, it must be free and unlimited.

A Fresh Approach

SOCIOMETRY may seem distant and academic to the personnel man or production manager, but the findings of studies completed to date can not be tossed aside lightly. The terminology may seem grandiose and the Jennings study a bit overloaded with correlations that are not altogether convincing, but new doors are opened and we have a fresh approach to the study of compatibilities and antipathies. Such techniques may even suggest a new pattern for the selection of foremen and group leaders. Certainly few places offer a greater opportunity for better understanding of interpersonal relations than the factory or business enterprise.

References

(1) ALLPORT, FLOYD H. "The Group Fallacy in Relation to Social Science." *Journal of Abnormal and Social Psychology*, XIX: 60–73, April–June, 1924.
(2) JENNINGS, HELEN H. "Sociometric Studies," a supplement in J. L. Moreno, *Who Shall Survive?* Washington, D. C.: Nervous and Mental Disease Publishing Co., 1934.
(3) ——. "Structure of Leadership—Development and Sphere of Influence." *Sociometry*, I: 99–143, July–October, 1937.
(4) ——. "Individual Differences in the Social Atom." *Sociometry*, IV: 269–277, August, 1941.
(5) ——. "Sociometric Measurement of Personality." *Psychological Bulletin*, 39: 457–458, 1942.
(6) ——. *Leadership and Isolation.* New York: Longmans, Green, 1943. Pp. xv + 240.
(7) MORENO, J. L. *Who Shall Survive? A New Approach to the Problem of Human Interrelations.* Collaborator: H. H. Jennings. Washington, D. C.: Nervous and Mental Disease Publishing Co., 1934.
(8) ——. "Sociometry in Relation to Other Social Sciences." *Sociometry*, I: 206–219, July–October, 1937.
(9) ——. "Foundations of Sociometry." *Sociometry*, IV: 15–35, February, 1941.
(10) —— AND JENNINGS, H. H. "Advances in Sociometric Technique." *Sociometric Review*, 26–40, July, 1936.

What the Machine Age Has Done *For* the Worker
is Seldom Squared with What the Machine Age
Has Done *To* the Worker.

Psychological Aspects

By Carl W. Drepperd,

American Arbitration Association, New York, N. Y.

IN TERMS of their importance to the nation at large, perhaps the most underestimated group of men in America today are the Personnel Directors and Managers. The only reason "perhaps" is injected is because there is also an unknown and therefore underestimated group of some 9,000 men in a comparable position. They are the expert arbitrators on the panels of the American Arbitration Association.

Word "Management" Misused

THE first step in the direction of an analysis of the Personnel Managers' problems was made not last year, nor in 1930, nor in 1790 but was made in the 16th century by the Spaniard Huarte, whose work "Examen De Ingenios" was subtitled "The Examination of Men's Wits," which "by discovering the varietie of natures, is shewed for what profession each one is apt, and how far he shall profit therein." This work was published at London, in 1616. It is beyond question the work from which was borrowed the German psychologists' claim to the invention of aptitude testing. This bit of history is injected here to show that personnel problems are not primarily new problems but they are as old as commerce and industry itself.

Perhaps the most common error of locution of the American people occurs in respect of the word "management." Most people think of management as representing the directing heads of productive enterprise. They fail to realize that management is "direction" and that labor as well as industry has its duly elected or appointed management. To speak of controversy between management and labor is inaccurate. Most often it is controversy between owner-management and labor-management.

Yet it is management that must always rise to difference, to controversy or to dispute and be responsible for its resolution. The productive worker, putting his case in the hands of his chosen and elected management, is in the same position of the owner of a productive dollar invested in management that promises some security for the dollar plus continuous yield. The productive worker is doing identically the same thing with his capital—his ability to work at some particular trade or task and to earn money thereby. He wants the most security, the most safety, and the greatest assurance of continued maximum return.

Conscientiousness of Desires Varies

THE wants, desire, yearnings, and ambitions of people are common to all. The office boy, worker, straw boss, foreman, superintendent, personnel manager, treasurer, president, chairman of the board, as individuals, all seek the same objectives. These can be listed as follows: personal survival, money gain, overcoming of frustration, expansion of ego, development of pride and prestige, achievement of social significance, avoidance of unpleasantness, satisfying of hunger, improvement of health, increase in enjoyment, achievement of progress, and joy in work. The only difference between the man at the top of the ladder and the man at the bottom of the ladder is to be found in the degree of consciousness of desire for these things as conditions, and circumstances.

Viewed in this light, labor relations ceases to be a problem and becomes a privilege—a privilege in that the task becomes a matter of revealing to the worker, individually and collectively, his true aims and objectives, plus his opportunities of achieving them.

Worry and frustration are the major ills of the productive worker. All of his worries and all of his frustrations derive from the fact that he is consciously aware of his non-attainment of the things that make up his category of desires.

Upward or Downward?

IT HAS been revealed by able business psychologists that any effort made to enter the minds of the people must be made in a zone of initial impact within the realm of experience and natural capacity of the individuals involved. When made, this impact causes either (1) movement upward on an *intellectual* reaction ladder, or (2) downward on an *emotional* reaction ladder. When whatever is proposed, or offered, appeals to reason, wit, and judgment, then upward, intellectual movement is at once established. That generates self reliance which, in turn, makes for stabilization, understanding and convincement. When moving downward, however, there is first question, then misunderstanding, and finally doubt, which in turn generate confusion, anxiety, opposition, and hatred. The top of the scale represents wholehearted cooperation. The bottom of the scale represents disintegration.

There is one process for the settlement of disputes and controversies between the managerial group of labor and the managerial group of industry which appeals to the reason, wit, and judgment of both. That process is arbitration. In almost every case of settlement of disputes and controversies by arbitration there is certainty of upward direction; of the development of self-reliance, and a stabilization and consolidation of interest. Better understanding is developed and acceptance of the rightness of the general objectivity of both the management of labor and the management of industry obtains.

Arbitration

THE process of arbitration is so utterly democratic, and common-sense, that it has appeal to all people. The process of arbitration is self-regulatory. The decision to arbitrate is voluntary. The decision to provide for arbitration as a means for settling any dispute is voluntary. And the decision to abide by the award of the arbitrators is voluntarily made, although in many states the awards of the arbitrators are in fact legal and binding. It is perhaps significant that very few attempts to upset an arbitrator's award in court have been successful and that the judiciary seldom finds justification to confirm the allegation of bias which is the usual point of attack when trying to upset an arbitrator's award.

Generally speaking, any democratic method which gives the parties equal rights and power starts a proceeding on a constructive basis. Legal talent can be used by either or both parties at their discretion and yet, while the process of arbitration is democratic in all of its aspects, it has also the added value of resolving the dispute behind closed doors as all family squabbles should be resolved. The major portion of labor disputes involve a resolution of deep seated psychological ills which should be recognized as such in order that the cure may be administered. And the cure in almost every case is *not* to be found in nostrums or in sops to injured vanity, but in a common-sense removal of the actual causes, and of exposure of the imagined causes of resentment and frustration.

To and For

WHEN a hard-headed man of business takes time out to remark that in his opinion "Most of the differences between labor and employer are to be found in the lack of spiritual preparation for a mechanical age" those who read his words without understanding think the man is balmy. That's because almost invariably we give the word "spiritual" a religious or mystical connotation instead of its forthright definition of mental attitude. What the machine age has done *for* the worker is seldom squared with what the machine age has done *to* the worker. And the same is true in considering what the machine age has done *to* and *for* the employer of labor.

Let's take labor's relationship to the machine first. The machine age has not merely used machines to produce goods but has produced a multiplicity of other machines which are either sold, or rented, to the public at large. There is the telephone. The radio. The automobile. There are mechanical refrigerators, washing machines, vacuum cleaners, toasters, automatic stoves. There are mechanical gadgets of all kinds. Everybody who owns one gets a tremendous satisfaction out of the exercise of control over that machine. Among all productive workers this memory of control over personally owned or leased machines persists when using machines belonging to somebody else in the pursuit of earning the daily wage.

At that point a frustration is generated. Now frustrations in themselves are not evils. They give birth to ambitions—ambitions born of a desire to overcome the frustration. Therefore the apparent evil of frustration may, in the hands of a personnel director, be made a force for good. And in this case the job is not adjusting the man to the machine, but adjusting the machine to the man's concept of himself. This cannot be done to the machine. It can only be done in the man's mind.

The Death of Dinosaurs

To MANAGEMENT, the machine age of production has acted as a screen hiding the obvious fact that mechanical production must forever be directed and controlled by human beings. And personal relationships must inevitably, and eternally, be with people. Management no less than labor needs the advanced spiritual understanding required to keep in step with scientific mechanical progress. The body that progressed faster than the mind produced dinosaurs. Dinosaurs were never able to adapt themselves to environmental pressures. They died by the million, millions of years ago, because they had achieved twenty tons of body for every quarter-ounce of brain.

Man is a success because he realizes, either consciously or sub-consciously, that his brain is far more valuable than his body. Yet many of us have heard the phrase "survival of the fittest" with something of a shudder. We picture the superman who by sheer strength and power overcomes all others—a la Hitler's attempt. But survival of the fittest has nothing whatsoever to do with brawn as such. Man has survived not because he could hit faster and run faster but because he could think faster than any other form of life.

Therefore, personnel relations is a matter of dealing with man's greatest asset, his ability to think, to reason, and to decide. It is in this arena that every program of personnel relations either succeeds or fails. The personnel managers of America realize this, either as a well defined fact or suspect it as a possibility. Proof of the fact can be found in further use of arbitration wherever and whenever any kind of dispute or controversy arises. Arbitration has many facets all of which reflect the best attitudes, abilities, and possibilities of man. In an arbitration the rightness of the premise "all people are basically fair minded" is proved time after time. There is no greater basic hater of special privilege and biased justice than the working man of America.

PERSONNEL
Journal

The Magazine of

LABOR RELATIONS AND PERSONNEL PRACTICES

Published by PERSONNEL RESEARCH FEDERATION

Lincoln Building, 60 East 42nd Street, New York City

Volume 23   *Number 3*

Contents for September 1944

EDITORIAL BOARD

"Bodily Labor . . . Has Everywhere been Changed into an Instrument of Strange Perversion; for Dead Matter Leaves the Factory Ennobled and Transformed, Where Men are Corrupted and Degraded." (Pope Pius XI in Quadragesimo Anno.)

Democracy *and* Capitalism

Review and Interpretation
By Charles S. Slocombe
Personnel Research Federation
New York, N. Y.

ONLY about ten percent of the people on this earth live under a democratic form of government. Even these democracies are not as pure as Ivory soap is advertised to be, but are contaminated by undemocratic elements in greater or less degree.

A little over two hundred million people live in the democracies, United States, Great Britain, Canada, Australia, South Africa, New Zealand, Eire, Sweden and Switzerland. The remainder of the two billion people on the earth live under systems of dictatorship, communism, feudalism, imperialism, etc. In some there is a slight flavoring of democracy used to make the prevailing abuses more palatable.

For some years after the last war the number of people living under democracy was twice as great as now, if we consider Germany, Austria, France, Italy, Norway, Denmark and Czechoslovakia as democracies. Our avowed purpose in this war is to restore democracy in these countries, on the assumption that that is what the people in them will want.

More Modesty Required

WE SHOULD therefore be a little more modest in thinking of our democracy, and while thinking of it as the highest form of government yet realized by man, realize that it is really not more than 150 years old, that it has suffered a severe setback in the last 25 years, and that as yet the vast majority of the people in the world manage to live in greater or lesser degrees of comfort without it.

Democracy must therefore be regarded as still on the defensive, not only in regard to its foreign enemies, but also as against those internal elements which may tend to pervert it, or to destroy it.

It so happens that the countries listed above as democratic are all capitalistic. It does not necessarily follow that democracy cannot exist without capitalism or vice versa. For example, both socialism and communism can theoretically exist under a democratic form of government, and forms of capitalism exist, particularly in Asiatic countries, without the semblance of democracy.

The Condition of Man

However our thinking in America is that both democracy and capitalism are the systems which we most desire to live under, and have continued. What are the historical forces which have led us to this conclusion? What are the disrupting and perverting forces that we must constantly be on guard against? What are the positive thoughts and actions necessary for the preservation and improvement of our democracy and our capitalism?

In attempting an answer to these questions we shall use as a base the recent book by Lewis Mumford, titled *The Condition of Man*.

The first real democracy, or at least the one which opens Mumford's story, existed in Greece 2500 years ago. It lasted for about 200 years and was then wiped out owing to its own internal weaknesses, which were not remedied, and to the invasion of foreign foes. Well over 2000 years of world history then passed by without any democracy anywhere.

The success of the Greek democracy was due to the rise of law and reason as the basis of freedom, supplanting the rule of custom or strong rulers, leading to civil responsibility, and common sacrifice for the good of the whole. There was a wide participation in culture, an appreciation of learned men, and a unified view of man, in which a poet might also be a statesman, a stonecutter a philosophical teacher and a dramatist a great general.

Whole Personality

Mumford stresses much this idea of the development of the whole personality of man as a fundamental of democracy, says that it existed in Greece, but says that it has not yet come to fruition in our own democracy, and that this is a basic weakness in our democracy.

The causes of the final demise of Greek democracy he sees in the fact that it was based primarily upon law—that is reason—and that in its organization it neglected to take into account man's instincts and reflexes. To the Greeks, and to us, man's unconscious impulses, their obscure origins and their apparently uncontrollable character are little understood. That they upset the rule of law and reason is however recognized today. (We shall come across this conflict of reason and impulse repeatedly, and many attempts to explain it.)

Other causes of the downfall of this democracy, as listed, were the fact it contained the institution of slavery, (a canker we abolished 80 years ago); an unreadiness to control new processes of economic expansion; inability to deal with the new political problems arising out of commercial intercourse and rivalries, both domestic and foreign; the rising rule of the monied classes, with their increasing covetousness and insolent attitude toward the law, the state and the people. (We are all familiar with these potential dangers to democracy inherent in our own current situation.)

So after 200 years, behind a facade of continued prosperity and cultural vitality, this disintegrated democracy died under the heel of the Roman legions. Not until 150 years ago, with the American Constitution of 1787, the Constitutional Convention of the French Republic in 1792, and the English Reform Bill of 1832 was the world to see the democratic form of Government tried again. Can we make our modern attempt at democracy last longer than the Greeks managed to do?

Roman Empire

L ITTLE need be said about the Roman Empire, though it existed as an empire longer than any other western empire has done from that day to this. It was essentially utilitarian and materialistic, based upon a predatory economy parasitic upon exploited conquered peoples. Its free citizens lived a life of unemployed ease, with free bread, bestial and pornographic circuses, and its wealthy indulged in played out pleasures. Only its soldiers, military leaders and governors were men of action and ability.

Rome achieved its greatness because the surrounding countries which it overran were in a state of dissolution and decay. It conquered these peoples, exploited them, but gave them peace and orderly administration. The order achieved was real, but repressive.

Three forces led to the fall of the Roman empire. All have significance for democracy. These were the internal feeling among the people of devitalization, discouragement and bitter self-disgust at their modes of life; the growing opposition and strength of conquered peoples and barbarians surrounding the empire; and last, but most important for us, the rise of Christianity.

Democracy and Capitalism from Christianity

B OTH capitalism and democracy as we know them rose directly or indirectly from Christianity and the forms and institutions which it developed. An understanding of the historical development of Christianity is therefore necessary in order to see the pitfalls that surround the progress of democracy and the quicksand foundation upon which capitalism rests.

Neither, of course, came within the orbit of the preaching of Jesus Christ, though His basic concepts have been used to bolster the acceptance of both, sometimes with considerable distortion of His original meanings.

Christ came of a conquered people, and His own personal contacts were largely confined to such people. The revolutionary aspect of His preaching was yielding rather than opposing and dominating. He apparently saw the futility of the poor conquered people successfully entering into a frontal engagement with the Roman legions, and advised them to mitigate their tolerance of the harsh conditions imposed upon them by developing in their characters and in their own social milieu what we have come to know as the Christian virtues. Only by so doing, as He saw it, could they make life bearable on this earth, situated as they were. In fact, the practice of these virtues leading to simplicity, spontaneity, integrity and freedom, to His way of thinking, were the conditions for man's growth, and put man into the Kingdom of Heaven on this earth.

Release from Bondage

In this sense His doctrine was one of release from the irksomeness of bondage, because the inconveniences of life under tyrants were relegated to a status of relative unimportance. In addition there was of course the prospect of an everlasting life in heaven, after death.

One of the constant difficulties that Christianity has faced, and does even to this day, perhaps more today in a capitalistic democracy than ever, is the fact that Jesus was born and lived in a limited country environment, and taught people who were similarly limited. He had no knowledge of science or culture, or politics or government, and apparently did not know that the survival and promulgation of the gospel He preached depended upon the development of leaders, and the organization of an institution, which later became the Church.

Even if He, in view of a divine origin, might have been held to know of these matters He said nothing of them, or they were omitted in the record of His sayings left by His untutored followers.

Apparent Ambiguity

Hence there has been, throughout all Christian history the difficulty of applying the precepts of Jesus to the material, spiritual and cultural environments that have developed. The Church has taken upon itself this task, but has apparently had only a modicum of success in so doing, and hence in many cases the social message of Jesus has appeared ambiguous, and has been used by the unscrupulous to justify inhuman actions that must appear vile in the sight of God, as well as of man. Capitalism has perhaps been the chief offender in this respect.

We may now follow the history of Christianity as it developed into a Church with large temporal and material power, essentially undemocratic, and finally gave birth to capitalism.

The churchless stage of Christianity, after the death of Jesus, had only a short career. The essential ideas of Christianity had long been in existence in the Jewish faith, and indeed in some of the pagan religions.

Persecuted Become Persecutors

B UT Christianity revitalized these, and sloughed off much of the institutionalism that encrusted and deadened them. It became a mystery religion. Very soon however Christianity, through written communications between leaders in different places became doctrinized and developed into a dogma. These dogmatic beliefs acquired a rigidity, which appealed to the persecuted souls who sought something solid to cling to, and did not look too closely to see whether they originated in Christ, or came from more human sources.

Moreover persecutions led to the lopping off of the fainthearted, and the acceptance of dogmatic discipline by individuals in the interest of survival. Hence nonbelievers in the strict dogma became heretics, and the persecuted became persecutors. This pattern was followed in the New England states of America shortly after their settlement, and has occasioned much brutality in Russia since communism became the religion there.

Gradually the inevitable happened, and Christianity became institutionalized in the form of the Church. In so far as it did so the original simple ideas of Jesus began to alter and fade into the background. This change due to institutionalization was not due to any deliberate perversion on the part of early Church leaders, but is a universal pattern. (For example, the institution of democracy as it exists in America today is far far different from that anticipated by those who signed the Declaration of Independence. Even the Constitution is far different from what they apparently sought. Communism under Stalin is far different from what Marx or Lenin thought it would be.)

Henry Wallace

I N THE history of the Church therefore we constantly find people arising who think that it has drifted too far away from the original ideas of Jesus, and seek to lead or force it back to the original concept. In our democracy we constantly find it necessary to refer back to the original concepts of our constitution to offset our natural tendency to drift away from them. We even have men like Henry Wallace trying to halt the drift of democracy and capitalism into erring ways by referring back to early Christian concepts.

As the Roman empire rose to power through conquest of surrounding countries and cultures that were disintegrating and decaying, so the Church rose to power through the declining strength of Rome. The victory of the Christians in the 4th century after Christ was the capitulation of a confused, self-distrustful, greedy, superstitious, defeatist majority to an organized minority that knew what it wanted Upholders of the old culture fought only delaying actions, being incapable of inventing positive strategy for a new campaign.

(The establishment of communism in Russia, the rise of fascism in Italy, of nazism in Germany, the overrunning of France, Austria, and other European countries by Hitlerism, and of China by Japan, are all examples of the same phenomenon Let us take warning, and not carry out internal disagreements to the point of national weakness.)

As the great empire began to fall apart churchmen gradually managed to free themselves from the control of government. They then proceeded to assume themselves many of the duties of government.

Church Becomes Government

HERE was a monumental change in Christianity. The Church, under the bishop of Rome, or the papacy as it later became, developed into an agent of political organization, not as a repository of spiritual enlightenment. With the dissolution of the control of Rome the authority of barbarian kings was not sufficient to keep their countries in order. There were many wars, but little organization of government. The Church therefore extended its powers, not only over Rome, but over surrounding states. In fact it became in essence, the government of these states.

Its bishops thus were selected and appointed by the Church, not because of their excellence as promulgators of the Christian doctrine, but because of their abilities as efficient administrators and bureaucrats. Their democratic election locally gave way to nomination by the Pope. The finances of the Church were centrally controlled.

Gregory the Great gave the final blow to what little shreds of democratic thought remained by discarding the idea of tracing political authority back to the people. He placed sovereignty in the hand of God, thereby taking it out of the reach of the people. But as the Pope was God's representative on earth, he naturally assumed full sovereignty over both the religious and political matters in the world.

Continued Exploitation of Lowly

LITTLE need be said in detail of the next 700 years of Church domination. The lowly were exploited just as they had been in the time of Jesus. Only now they were kept in bondage by the Christian Church, and by the kings and nobles with the consent of the Church.

In so far as Jesus had not promised low born Christians an amelioration of their hardships under exploitation, on this earth, it is in a way not surprising to find them still in this condition 1200 years after His death. What is surprising is that the oppressors and exploiters now were not the barbarians and pagans of long ago, but professing Christians under the leadership of him called the Vicar of Christ. Truly the institutionalization of Christianity in the Church had led it far from the original tenets of the Christian faith.

As a result, in the period which is now some 700 years ago, according to Mumford, capitalism was born. The Church had acquired so much wealth that it had a surplus to invest. It therefore loaned money to the traders and business men of the time for profit, and to aid in the commercial expansion which had been prevented by the absence of surplus capital funds.

At this time, about the year 1200, arose the first two great protestors against the direction in which the Church had drifted, Francis of Italy and Dominic of Spain. They preached the doctrine that the function of the Christian Church was to minister to the spiritual wants of the poor. This they did with the approval of the Pope.

700 *Years of Capitalism*

THE history of capitalism, from the 13th to the 20th century, is one of vivid contrasts. As a method of business, and a way of life, it undermined the ethical standards of medieval life, and its notions of a holy and seemly life. The capitalist personality, directed to self-help and gain was the antithesis of the Christian, who sought to love his neighbor as himself.

The change in the moral climate may be summed up by saying that the seven deadly sins became the seven virtues. Avarice, the minute care of worldly goods, the hoarding of pennies, unwillingness to spend one's surplus on others, was a motive for capital saving. Greed, gluttony, envy and luxury were constant incentives to industry.

Human purposes, human needs and human limits no longer exercised a directive and restraining influence upon industry.

500 *Years Ago*

As MUMFORD says, all the articles of the capitalist faith today are implied in a classic statement made by a group of financiers in replying to an inquiry into monopolistic practices 500 years ago. "It is impossible to limit the size of companies, for that would limit business and hurt the common welfare; the bigger and more numerous they are, the better for everybody. . . . If a merchant cannot do business above a certain amount, what is he to do with his surplus money? Some people talk of limiting the earning capacity of investments. This would be unbearable and would work great injustice and harm by taking away the livelihood of widows, orphans, and other sufferers, noble and non-noble, who derive their income from investments in companies."

Yet in the early stages of capitalism, at least, we must give it credit for originating the release from the fixed usages of medieval society. Money provided an instrument for wide trade, as contrasted with local barter; it was a symbol of freedom from feudalism and a means of getting away from feudal compulsions. It was even used by cities as a means of purchasing their political freedom. In its early stages it was a healthy liberating influence—one very badly needed.

A Pious Formula

CAPITALISM took over for its own purposes some of the Christian doctrines and habits. For instance, the core of the doctrine of heavenly salvation was the concept of the postponement of present pleasures for the sake of much greater future reward. Capital saving was based on this pious formula. A well regulated sober life of work, with fairness and honest dealing with neighbors was part of the Christian ideology taken over by early capitalists.

But capitalism soon ran into the same conflict which we saw earlier leading to the demise of democracy in the Greek states—namely the conflict between the rule of reason in the guidance of conduct and the seemingly non-logical, biological and social needs of man. The Church had been, at all times, faced with this same problem.

Original Sin

THERE now appeared men who sought to explain this basic conflict. Machiavelli derided the Christian ethic. He justified the exploitation of the underdog by the despots and capitalists, with whom they were allied, on the grounds of the original dogma of the Christian religion—the original sin of man. According to him, men are inherently base and bad and will do no good unless they are made to. If they are such, then only despotism and oppression are possible forms of government.

This was a dastardly distortion of the Christian doctrine, which while admitting the original sin concept of man, yet held up the possibility of grace, redemption and perfection.

Working forward from the Machiavellian conception of man as essentially base, and therefore suitable only to be ruled by despots, Hobbes later brought forth the notion that man was nothing but an automaton obeying blind impulse. He should therefore be used by the despot simply as a mechanical tool. Thus we have the beginnings of the theory of man as a cog in a machine, trained to obey signals under a rigorous centralization of despotic power, and a ruthless dehumanization of the worker.

We shall come across these concepts of Machiavelli and Hobbes again in relation to our own contemporary situation.

Meantime the corruption of the Christian doctrine, the growing commercial spirit of the Church, and its open alliance with capitalism and despotism led to the rise of Protestanism. It came from those, within the church, who wished to do away with the venal elements that were making a mockery of its sacred professions. Protestanism was therefore not an ally, but an enemy of capitalism, as it then existed.

Essentially with the Waldensteins in France, the Wycliffes in England, and others, the revolt concerned itself with the advocacy of a return to Christian economics, and an attempt to bring Christianity back to poverty in which the mass of humanity lived, and to give Christianity its original foundation in daily life.

Luther's Reformation

LUTHER followed in Germany. Starting out by pitting himself against the materialist vices of the Church as had the first protestants his followers thought that he was interested in the lowly. His servile fear of external authority however led him, after his opposition to and clear break with the Church, to bolster the authority of the ruling secular princes. All he did for the lowly was to release them from exploitation by the church, and the ruling princes, and hand them over to the sole despotism of the princes.

Luther, in the eyes of Mumford, was responsible for a more serious ill that fell to the lot of man. Having weakened the foundations of the Church, he helped to lay the foundations of that arch enemy—nationalism, particularly German nationalism. Upon that sketchy foundation was built the rise of Bismarck, the Kaiser of the last war, and the Hitler of this one. His reformation brought no improvement.

So the shadow of Luther stretches across the pages of world history, and will make exceedingly difficult our attempt to set up a new democratic order in Germany after this war. For, from his time to the present day, with the exception of the brief period of the abortive Weimar republic after the last war, the German people have never experienced a democratic government.   .

Calvin, the First Christian Democrat

CALVIN, the founder of the Presbyterian Church, is the next of the great reformers. He, according to Mumford, is important for his influence upon American democracy and capitalism. He started from a protest against the prevailing abuses of the Catholic Church, and advocated a return to the Bible as a guide to conduct—regarding it as an infallible revelation of God, and thus unseating the Pope as the residual legatee of God's infallibility.

Thus he laid the foundation for civil liberty and self-government—the bases of democracy. For if an individual took to himself the teachings of the Bible as a guide to conduct, there was no need for him to have his conduct determined by a despot, as was thought to be necessary on the theory that man was innately bad. The individual who strictly adhered to the moral precepts as a guide to conduct was therefore qualified for civil liberty. In so far then as this was so, it was proper and correct that the sovereignty should pass to the people, with democratic self-government as the logical outcome.

This was the most revolutionary theory that had yet developed from protestantism, and that is why the followers of Calvinism were so hotly persecuted. Under the doctrine of the Catholic Church as expounded by Gregory the Great, 1000 years before, sovereignty rested in God, but was administered by God's representative on earth, namely the Pope, who had the sole and infallible right to interpret God's will. Hence the 1000 year grip that the Church held over the lives of people.

Hold of Church Broken

BUT Calvin's theory was that the written word—the Bible—was the revelation of God, and therefore infallible. With the invention of printing, the Bible, which was the first large book printed in 1456, became accessible to almost everyone, so that each man could go directly to it. God thereby retained His sovereignty, but man could now learn of and try to carry out the sovereign will, without the need of an intermediary such as the Pope. It is not difficult to see how this undercut the authority and hold of the Catholic Church.

But it is to be noted that only to the extent that the individual lived according to the rules laid down in the Living Word was he entitled to civil liberty and capable of self-government. Hence the function of the democratic governing authority was to see to it that men lived without sinning against the Holy Word. Theoretically then every man dedicated his life to the service of God. The job of the state and of the local congregations from which the state derived was to see that every man toed this line.

As the very strength and survival of the Church, so erected, and the democracy which accompanied it, depended upon strict adherence to the doctrine, there was more spying of neighbor on neighbor, more tittle tattle, and a harsh severity meted out to backsliders by congregations than it was humanly possible to endure. We know all this from the history of the Puritans in the early settlement of the New England states. Hence the rise of hypocrisy.

Calvinism and Capitalism

CALVINISM's main fields were preaching, moral admonition, law, administration government. Wordly vanities were dethroned and demolished. In place was enthroned the machine, the symbol of Calvin's unrelenting God and His predestined order. The factory, filled with material and human machines, was the place in which Calvinism and capitalism made use of each other. The driving discipline of the factory, with its discomforts, self-denials, deadly fatiguing routines and long hours gave no time for idleness and therefore no opportunity to sin, as well as being a punishment and penance for the odd sins that inevitably crept in.

And, of course it produced profits in sizable quantity, as the wealth of New

England testifies. Thus the exploiters found in Calvinism a new excuse for continuing the exploitation of the lowly. The change from the Catholic Church to the Calvinist Church, from despotism to democracy left the lowly still oppressed. Thus the Christian doctrine that the purpose of man's life on this earth was to develop a full balanced personality—to establish the kingdom of heaven on this earth—was again passed over.

Cursed Concept of Work

THE cursed Calvinistic conception of work as a soul stultifying moral discipline is still accepted as a sound tradition and continues to cast its blight over large areas of the American industrial picture. It undoubtedly has had its effect in determining the peculiar structure of American industry with its monotonous machine tending, and its sweating assembly lines.

Only in recent years has there come to be a recognition of the basically Christian concept of work as an activity that man indulges in as an expression of his own urge toward personal development, and in accordance with his own dignity as a human being, working in a social setting with others similarly motivated.

As the lash of threatened starvation is increasingly removed, through such measures as social security, industrial policies and practices will have to be modified in the light of this newer motivation to work. Opposition to social security has been based on the idea that if men are able to live without working they will not work. That is true—in part. They will not work under the conditions of present industrial organization, based on the traditional Calvinistic curse, unless driven to. Industrial management naturally hates the idea of having to make the necessary change.

The opening of the 17th century saw the beginning of scientific discoveries about the physical universe, and of new inventions based upon these discoveries. The use of these discoveries was of course profitable, as well as enhancing the physical pleasures of living.

No Humanistic Science

HOWEVER, there was no accompanying cultivation of humanistic knowledge. There was seen no economic motive for this being done. Thus there was, and continues almost to this day, a general indifference to the actual consequences of a new invention upon the lives of workers, or the social state of the whole community.

We do not know what would have been the results of a rigorous, extensive and energetic study of humanistic sciences, equal to that of the physical sciences, and how much it would have helped us in solving our social and political problems. We do know that without this knowledge we use the most primitive and brutal tools in meeting these problems today.

We could not deal with slavery without a bloody war; we cannot deal with national minorities without oppression, and the denial to them of the right to vore; we cannot deal with the growing protest against the Calvinistic concept of work except through an attempted suppression of the labor movement; Stalin could not deal with the peasants of Russia other than by mass murder and imprisonment; and the so-called civilized nations could not deal with the barbarities of German nationalism except through the means of a barbarous war.

So while the half-world of physical science uses the tools and instruments of precision, in the absence of any comparable humanistic science, we use the axe, the bludgeon and the bomb to deal with the problems of the other half-world, of human behavior.

But the humanities were not entirely neglected, even if the approach to them was not very scientific. The 18th century brought in a crop of social and moral philosophers, metaphysicians, economists, and utopians,—most of whom were not human.

But fortunately one was human—Jean Jacques Rousseau. According to Mumford, the ideas of Calvin and Rousseau largely determined the form of our American constitution, and our way of life. There is little evidence that the framers of our constitution, well read men as they were, had read either Calvin or Rousseau, but their ideas were currently abroad in the world.

Broad Humanism of Rousseau

IT is also fortunate for us that the broad humanism of Rousseau as represented in our constitutional convention of 1787 by the southern delegates, particularly those from Virginia, outvoted the narrow moralism of Calvin, represented by the northern delegates, chiefly from New England.

Rousseau started out with a bitter personal revolt against contemporary despotism, regimentation, exploitation, slavery, polite conformity, callous mechanization, stifling luxury and life-denying custom. He held then—in contradiction of current ideas—that man is naturally good, and that the evils he shows are due to the demoralizing influence of the arts, sciences and institutions. He therefore advocated the simple life, away from the temptations of civilization—the ever recurrent escapism.

The Social Contract

HE LATER came to realize "the other truth, no less certain, that men are bad." "Deceit and falsehood are born along with conventions and duties. As soon as we can do what we ought not to do, we try to hide what we ought not to have done. As soon as self-interest makes us give a promise, a greater interest may make us break it." Thus in living in civilized society he finds original sin coming up, fighting with the natural goodness of man.

What is to be done about it? Rousseau proposed the Social Contract, of which the American Constitution is now the only living written example.

If man recognizes his own limitations and tendencies to yield to the temptations of impulse, and similar characteristics in his fellow man, he enters into a contract with the state, by which the state is empowered to curb the evil impulses. Thus man creates a state to govern him in his anti-social weak moments. This it does largely by la v. "The mere impulse of appetite is slavery, while obedience to a law which we prescribe to ourselves is liberty."

Basis of American Constitution

THE central doctrine of the Social Contract, as later incorporated, particularly in the general welfare clause of the Constitution is that the well-being of all citizens is the prime object of civil government.

"By equality we should understand, not that the degree of power and riches are to be absolutely identical for everybody; but that power shall never be great enough for violence, and shall always be exercised by virtue of rank and law; and that in respect of riches, no citizen shall ever be wealthy enough to buy another, and none poor enough to be forced to sell himself; which implies, on the part of the great, moderation in goods and position, and on the side of the common sort moderation in avarice and covetousness. . . . It is precisely because the force of circumstances tends continually to destroy equality that the force of legislation should always tend to its maintenance."

Thus we see the foundation of our democracy. The implementation of this thesis resulted in the setting up of our three branches of government, the legislature, the executive branch and the courts—a system of checks and balances, providing the best representation possible, and a system of checks and balances to control all appetites for power, even those that might arise within the government itself.

Naturally the main onslaughts against this democratic government have come from those who are irked by the limitations it places upon their selfish appetites— deriving from the original sin component in their characters—for greater power, wealth, privilege and license.

New Century of Science

THE next century, the 19th, was one of territorial and colonial expansion, of scientific discoveries and inventions, of revolutions and wars. (According to our count there were some 35 wars of greater or less size, and over 45 revolutions.) Such was the result of a devout faith in the "New World" of science, capitalism, mechanization and colonial expansion.

Mumford sums up this threatened reversal of the course of Western civilization thus: "In the lions' den of Wagner's youthful disciple, Nietzsche, with his cult of superman, the stinking hyenas of Nazism already lurked. Nor was the Western hemisphere immune to these dark forces. In the United States, the South's attempt to revive and extend the long-moribund institution of slavery brought with it all the characteristic phenomena of fascism: racism, militarism, caste, theological perversions and scientific lies." Generally in the world, "The nihilism of brute impulse now became as it were the last refuge of vitality. To rape, to torture, to hate, to kill became a method of redemption: in fantasy if not in fact."

Empirical Humanistic Science

AT THE end of the 19th century, and in the beginning of our own present one, there came into being the first crude beginnings of a long overdue empirical humanistic science, which tried, on the basis of observation and experiment to understand the nature of man. One of the earliest of these human scientists was Sigmund Freud, though his methods were so crude, and his conclusions so startling, that he has been denied the status of a scientist, though all students of this science use his results today.

Working in the field of non-logical human behavior he naturally tackled the age old problem which others such as the Church, Machiavelli, Rousseau had described in terms of original sin or natural goodness in man. "By charting the dark repressed side of life, to which he first gave the label of the unconscious he made it possible to describe and evaluate the whole personality: to understand its drives, desires, wishes, lusts, both in their infantile nakedness and in the elaborate garb that maturity devises for society."

Without going into the details of his theory we may perhaps summarize it thus: man has certain biological impulses, largely according to Freud based upon sex and its various sublimations and symbolisms: these impulses he would not label as good or bad, labelling them as man's ego or id: there exists also a super-ego, which is in effect society acting as a checker, a curber and a censor of these impulses, forbidding, threatening and punishing.

This super-ego imposed by his contemporary environment upon the ego becomes in effect an equally strong component of a man's whole personality. So there is set up a perpetual internal conflict between deep non-logical subjective impulses and more realistic induced impulses to conform to the cultural pattern of society, and so avoid its punishments.

Freudian Conflicts

THUS Freud in a sense recreated man's original sin, without the hope of redemption, necessitating external control over his actions. Later psychoanalysts, such as Jung and Rank, modified this thesis, holding that the job of the super-ego was to nurture and liberate the positive expressions of life, that were potential in the id, as well as to curb those that could not be sublimated into constructive social drives.

The more the super-ego can liberate the creative elements in the original basic impulses, the less necessity will there be for the exercise of its repressive role.

Unfortunately many who have been affected by Freudian theory have thought that the needs of the impulses, the ego or id, are more important than the curbs of the super-ego. The fascists and nazis have thought so, and many of our own younger generation in America, as well as some of our business leaders, are impatient with the curbs on impulse and appetite contained in our Constitution.

Projected Across World Stage

THE great tragedy of our century so far, is that the Freudian conflicts within man's personality have been projected across the world stage, with the impulses from the blindest levels of the id, irrationalities, phobias, humorless limitations, colossal brutalities and a perverse animus against all life very strong.

For an explanation of how this came about Mumford goes to the writings of Oswald Spengler, whose main work "The Downfall of the Western World" was conceived before the first world war, and published in Vienna in 1918.

Spengler's thesis was that the promise of culture's springtime in Western Europe was about to end in a dormant frigid period of civilization's winter. The liberating function of the super-ego leading to the development of the positive expressions of life embodied in a civilized culture had not materialized. Instead the curbing function placed in the hands of technicians, engineers, business men who glorified the machine, as a machine, and devoid of any concern for life or the values of life, was leading to an empty civilization on an earth "plated with stone and steel and asphalt, in which men dreamed of growing crops in tanks, taking food in capsules, transplanting foetuses to protoplasmic incubators, conquering the air in stratoliners by means of oxygen tanks, and burrowing into underground cities to have security against the consequences of his conquest of the air."

So, in 20th century civilization, the individual man shrinks to a mechanical atom in a formless mass of humanity. He becomes merely an inane user and consumer of such mechanical gadgets and processed foods and drugs as the super-ego of the engineers and business men forces him to make, and foists upon him.

The Way of Escape

WAS there no way of excape from this living death to which a technological civilization had condemned man? Spengler said Yes. Let loose the id, the basic impulses: let us live again and live strenuously in a life of brutality, and brutal conquest. Let us overcome the technicians who would stifle our lives, and make *them* subservient to our brutal conquest of weak nations and cultures devitalized by subservience to the god of the machines; the finance machine, the industrial machine and the educational machine. So said Spengler.

The Allies are dedicated to the job of smashing the power of the brutalistic ids that have been let loose in Germany, Italy and Japan. In a sense then we have assumed the role of a cosmic super-ego. But in terms of the psychology we have been discussing, it is not sufficient for us to rely upon repression only when we have won the military victories. We must keep the more evil impulses of these countries under control, meantime attempting to liberate and nurture the rudiments of constructivism that surely must exist. This will be a long job, but is our only hope of avoiding another resurgence of brutality.

What of Ourselves?

WHAT of our own democracy and capitalism? Accepting, at least in part, the theories of Calvin and Rousseau upon which our Constitution was founded, and the subsequent elaborations by Freud, Jung and Rank, and heeding the warning of Spengler as to consequences of drifting into faulty policies, what are we to do?

In the field of labor relations the first thing to do, obviously, is to cast off the Calvinist doctrine of work as an imposed discipline to curb the evil components of man's character. In the light of Rousseau's theory of life as growth, (also contained in the Christian doctrine) and of the Jungian theory of the need for liberating and encouraging the positive elements in character, work of man should provide an opportunity for the growth and development of his character.

In other words, work should be so designed that man wants to work in a way that he enjoys and which provides him with an opportunity for making a meaningful contribution to the progress of his country.

Few men work in our industrial establishments today because they want to, or enjoy it. They work under the lash of threatened discharge and starvation, or because they have family responsibilities which motivate them, and cause them to endure soul destroying occupations in which they are entirely uninterested.

Modern Trend of Labor Relations

THE whole trend of our labor relations practices since the last war has been in the opposite direction: Jobs have been broken down into little bits requiring monotonous repetition: scientific management and work simplification have studied man as a machine which is to make a predetermined number of automatic movements: psychologists have developed aptitude and intelligence tests to help determine those who will fit the machines best, and to select happy little morons (many companies will not hire any but sub-normal people for their factory and some office jobs): job analysis and job evaluation are deliberately designed to disregard the personality of the worker: and so on.

Hence we have increasing labor turnover, absenteeism, tardiness and strikes— all indicating the worker's increasing hatred of increasingly soul stultifying jobs. The demand for more pay, shorter hours, vacations, etc. is all part of the same picture.

It is high time the trend was reversed, though actually the trend is continuing, with repressive measures advocated to put labor back in its place. Thus the long shadow of Calvin darkens our industrial scene. Unfortunately only the unsound part of Calvinism has been retained in industrial thinking. His concept of man as a responsible person capable of self-government is not allowed inside the factory gate and what is worse, is seldom allowed to enter the minds of industrial executives.

Brutality

THERE is another aspect of this work picture, and that is the case of types of work which by reason of their brutal inhumanity, breed brutality in the workers. There can be no question but that Hitler's brutalities could only have been carried out by men who had already been brutalized by their previous work experience. The necessity of reducing the number of occupations which brutalize workers, as a national safeguard is obvious.

The brutality exhibited in recent strikes in America is some indication of the industries in which this situation is worst. We may take the strikes in the automotive industry and the brutal race riots in Detroit as indicators that things are far from non-brutal in that industry, the steel strikes indicate a similar situation, as do the maritime and farm labor strikes of the Pacific Coast.

The mining situation is the worst. Its brutalities were graphically described by Mr. Justice Murphy in the Supreme Court decision, granting portal-to-portal pay. We quote.

Supreme Court Decision

"The miners," the Court says, "begin their day by arriving on the company property at a scheduled hour and going to the bath house, where they change into working clothes. They then walk to the tally house near the mine entrance or portal; there they check in and hang up individual brass checks, furnished by petitioners, on a tally or check-in board. This enables the foreman and other officials to tell at a glance those individuals who have reported for work and those production and service crews that are incomplete and in need of substitutes. Vacancies are filled and the head miners and crews receive any necessary instructions. In addition, each miner either rents a battery lamp for the day or buys a can of carbide each day or two for underground illumination purposes. And at some of the mines, many miners stop at a tool box or tool house on the surface to pick up other small supplies and tools necessary for their work. These activities consume but a few minutes.

"The miners thereupon are required to report at the loading platform at the mine portal and await their turn to ride down the inclined shafts of the mines. Originally the miners could reach the working faces entirely by foot, but as the shafts increased in length petitioners provided transportation down the main shafts. The miners accordingly ride part of the way to the working faces in ore skips or regular man trips, which operate on narrow gauge tracks by means of cables or hoisting ropes. The operation of the skips and man trips is under the strict control and supervision of the petitioners at all times and they refuse to permit the miners to walk rather than ride. Regular schedules are fixed; loading and unloading are supervised; the speed of the trips is regulated; and the conduct of the miners during the rides is prescribed.

Odors of Human Sewage

"About three to six trips are made, depending on the size of the mine and the number of miners. Ten men sit on each man trip car, while from 30 to 40 are crowded into an ore skip. They are forced to jump several feet into the skip from the loading platform, which not infrequently causes injuries to ankles, feet and hands. The skips are usually overcrowded and the men stand tightly pressed together. The heads of most of them are a foot or more above the top of the skips. But since the skips usually clear the low mine ceilings by only a few inches, the miners are compelled to bend over. They thus ride in a close 'spoon-fashion,' with bodies contorted and heads drawn below the level of the skip top. Broken ribs, injured arms and legs, and bloody heads often result; even fatalities are not unknown.

"The length of the rides in the dark, moist, malodorous shafts varies in the different mines from 3,000 feet to 12,000 feet. The miners then climb out of the skips and man trips at the underground man-loading platforms or 'hoodlums' and continue their journeys on foot for distances up to two miles. These subterranean walks are filled with discomforts and hidden perils. The surroundings are dark and dank. The air is increasingly warm and humid, the ventilation poor. Odors of human sewage, resulting from a complete absence of sanitary facilities, permeate the atmosphere. Rotting mine timbers add to the befouling of the air. Many of the passages are level, but others take the form of tunnels and steep grades. Water, muck and stray pieces of ore often make the footing uncertain. Low ceilings must be ducked and moving ore skips must be avoided. Overhead, a maze of water and air pipe lines, telephone wires, and exposed high voltage electric cables and wires present ever-dangerous obstacles, especially to those transporting tools. At all times the miners are subject to the hazards of falling rocks.

"Moreover, most of the working equipment, except drills and heavy supplies, is kept near the 'hoodlums.' This equipment is carried each day by foot by the crews through these perilous paths from the 'hoodlums' to the working faces. Included are such items as fifty-pound sacks of dynamite, dynamite caps, fuses, gallon cans of oil and servicemen's supplies. Actual drilling and loading of the ore begin on arrival at the working faces, interrupted only by a thirty minute lunch period spent at or near the faces."

Spengler and Calvin

SEVERAL things may be said about this case. In the first instance, it is a glaring example of what Spengler talked about, namely that the technician and engineer is either incapable of, or deliberately neglects, consideration of human values in his technology. This is an extreme example of this fact, but others are easy to find, and lead to the conclusion that engineers must be dethroned from their present too important place in our industrial picture, or humanized.

The second thing is that labor union philosophy still accepts the Calvinist conception of work, and in large part limits its function to getting increased pay for increasingly unpleasant work. Anathema was poured on the head of John L. Lewis because he demanded that the miners be paid for enduring these conditions. He should have been drowned in the flood of protests of those who should have demanded that he insist that these conditions be abolished entirely.

Apart from the brutalizing nature of some occupations, there is, for all work designed in accordance with the Calvinistic concept, another most serious argument for change. That is the reaction on democracy.

Effect on Democracy

CALVIN held that man was capable of self-government if he ordered his life according to Christian principles. Rousseau held that man is capable of self-government, because he is naturally good, presumably meaning that he has a natural inclination to live according to the Christian ethic. But Rousseau also held that the function of life is individual growth, and that growth makes possible man's overcoming of the dark temptations of social living.

The later psychoanalysts, such as Jung and Rank, held that the baser components of man's personality can be counterbalanced by the development of the more constructive components.

Adding the results of these theories, they amount to a recognition that democratic self-government requires men who have developed, and continue to grow in the understanding of the broad bases of true living, and the problems to be faced in so doing.

Eroticism Chief Amusement

UNDER the work conditions described above this is impossible. When a man spends the greater part of his waking day in brain-dulling monotonous attachment to a machine he is fit at the end of it only for passive amusement requiring no thinking. The amusement joints surrounding every shipyard, steel mill, automotive plant, etc. is evidence of this, as well as the incredible futility of most films and most radio programs. The prevailing motif in all these is a thinly disguised erotic symbolism and exhibitionism, as might be expected from Freud's writings.

Amusements such as these have, since the days of Greece and Rome, presaged the decline and fall of many empires. Certainly these conditions do not add to the possibility of our continuing a healthy democracy. In fact, as our problems, both domestic and foreign, increase in complexity, requiring greater and greater understanding on the part of the electorate, we are faced with industrial conditions which increasingly make any understanding impossible.

Regression of Capitalism

WHEN we come to capitalism we again find the writings of Rousseau and Freud helpful in interpretation.

When capitalism started some 700 years ago it freed the peoples of the then world from the limitations of trade by local barter, from the poverty of individual handcraft, and the use of surplus funds only in elaborate meaningless luxury and self-gratification. It gave promise of enriching the life of man by making available to him the products of other countries, and of increased quantities of the products of his own land, and freeing him from the dull grind of his slavish occupations and the boredom of unoccupied leisure. For lending the money to do this and managing the trade, industry and commerce thus made possible the capitalist was expected to obtain a reasonable compensation.

In essence then, its primary function was to improve the lot of man on this earth. It has done so in many parts of the earth, but its accomplishments have been accompanied by a mountainous and increasing toll of "blood, sweat and tears." Had the Church, which was the first great capitalist, foreseen the monumental debasement of Christianity that followed its new endeavour, it is unthinkable that it would have launched it upon the world.

For while there were great virtues in capitalism, there were also presented the greatest set of temptations that man has ever been faced with. As we now know from Freud, the base non-logical elements in human personality, greed for power, lust, envy, dishonesty, etc. all had to be kept under control if the primary purpose of capitalism was to survive. In his terms, this was a job for the personal super-ego of the capitalist. In Rousseau's terms it was the job of the state, and was so recognized in the first written Social Contract, the Constitution of the United States.

Too Big a Job for State

BUT it has been becoming increasingly evident, particularly since the turn of this century in America that the job has grown too big for the state. Except for a minority of business corporations, growth of size has led to an increasing insolence toward the state, and a growing attempt to pervert the basic instrument of our democracy—the Constitution.

If the present trend continues, it can lead in either of two directions: the industrial worker will be so brutalized, stupefied and impoverished by capitalist production that he will believe the promises of release from this condition made by ardent revolutionaries, who will promise, as in Russia, a dictatorship of the proletariat: or the capitalists will be so blown up by their empty success that they will take the state over and establish fascism. In either case, at least in the beginning, the Freudian non-logical id will be the ruler.

There is no reason why either eventuality should come to pass in America, but every reason to think that we are drifting in these directions.

What Capitalism Could Do

IF WE go back to the original concept of capitalism we see the opportunities it has in this country to fulfill its unfulfilled promises. If it could shake off its non-logical components and live according to the Constitution it would find such things to do as the following:

It could release its workers from the soggy-minded condition into which it has thrust them. The initiative and drive that would then be put into action would bring about an undreamed of demand, not only for more gadgets and automobiles, but for schools, parks, libraries, homes, theatres, and other facilities for cultural development.

It could work out some method of lifting the millions of poor whites (and negroes) in the South from the conditions of physical and mental poverty to which they have been condemned for the past 80 years. (At present the only way of dealing with these people is to keep them disenfranchised to prevent their active protest against their inhuman treatment.)

It could see to it that the educational opportunities and facilities particularly in the rural areas were adequate to develop a basis for a sound understanding of our national democratic problems. These last two items would release demands similar to those made possible if industrial workers ever became liberated.

It could see to it that the most intelligent liberal forms of social security were granted, freeing every American possible from the distresses of life arising out of natural causes, international conditions beyond our control, and the inevitable going awry of the best laid plans of man. Thus instead of a man or his wife having to worry over possible hazards and old age, or having to thrust their children into the maw of the industrial machine before adequate preparation, their mental energy could be devoted to the fulfillment of their proper life purpose, as portrayed by Christ and Rousseau.

What Will They Do?

IT COULD help to work out foreign policies, not based upon narrow selfish economic nationalism, but for the purpose of improving the lot of all humanity and protecting the world against the periodic resurgences of the blind id, with its recourse to war and revolution.

This list could be vastly extended, but basically the problem is not what can be done, but what the capitalist is willing to do.

Is the capitalist, the labor leader, the governmental administrator, the preacher, the citizen, ready to ask these questions constantly? "What is the nature of this or that industrial or social achievement—does it produce material goods alone or does it also produce human goods and good men? Do our individual life plans make for a universal society, in which art and science, truth and beauty, religion and sanctity, enrich mankind? Do our public plans make for the fulfillment and renewal of the human person, so that they will bear fruit in a life abundant: ever more valuable, ever more deeply experienced and more widely shared?"

If he is, well and good. If not, then we are about to enter Spengler's frigid winter of a dead civilization, in which only wolves survive.

Review and Interpretation

The above is a review, with interpretations relating to labor relations of the most recent book by Lewis Mumford. It is entitled, "The Condition of Man," published by Harcourt, Brace and Company, 383 Madison Ave., New York 17, N. Y. Pp. 467. Price $5.00.

To our mind it is the most important book that has appeared this year, or for many years. We are accustomed to going about our business, hiring and firing workers, training, collective bargaining, and electing or objecting to this or that president.

Too seldom do we take time off to wonder what we are all so busy about—where we are heading. Mumford gives us an opportunity of sitting back, and taking a look at ourselves. He does not provide a blueprint for the future, post this war or the next ones. He does suggest that if we wake up we will be able to do something with this world, out of our own wise thinking. He seems a little doubtful as to whether we will wake up.

Next time you go through your plant, and watch your employees, making toys or tanks or tires or typewriters, or silks and stockings—not to mention radio sets—think of what they and you are actually busy about in relation to matters that might be regarded as important in these terms: "Only after the human voice had been transmitted around the world with the speed of light did it become plain that the words so widely disseminated might still be the same words one could hear from the village gossip of the village idiot or the village clown or the village hoodlum."

There is Need to Divide Counseling into Two
Distinct Jobs, Done by Different People: One
to Deal with Administrative Problems; the Other
to Deal with the Psychological Problems of
Employees.

Functions *of* Personnel Counselors

By Nathaniel Cantor and John C. Bonning
University of Buffalo
Buffalo, N. Y.

Industry has had personnel departments for many years. During the past two years, however, these departments have made impressive advances in the breadth of the service they render. The experience of war industries, especially the airplane, shipbuilding, and ammunition plants revealed certain definite needs, both of supervision and employees, which require an entirely new type of personal service.

Reading in Too Many Directions

To meet those needs several hundred of America's leading corporations and approximately fifty shipyards have adopted some kind of personnel program embodying the use of personnel "counselors." There is little agreement on the part of these various corporations as to the qualifications, standards, or duties of the personnel counselors. In almost all of the plants, the personnel counselors are assigned a hundred or more different taks, chiefly of an administrative character.

Recent literature on the whole field of personnel counseling covers many aspects of the problem such as qualifications of staff; the organizational set-up of a program, its relation to supervision, management, and labor; selection of staff; in-plant training; etc. The careful reader of this literature is impressed, on the one hand, by the virility and rapid expansion of the movement and, on the other hand, by its loosely defined structure. Two of the most recent reports are striking illustrations of this two-fold character of the counseling movement.

We refer to a report to be sent out by the Community War Services of the Federal Security Agency, and a report of the Russell Sage Foundation of New York City.

The careful reader of these reports cannot fail to note that the counseling movement in industry is being firmly rooted while, at the same time, because of its rapid growth, it is trying to reach out in too many directions.

Perhaps the most important question to be raised is: "What is the function of the industrial counselor?" It is a most important inquiry because once there is agreement as to the function of the counselor many other questions can be more easily answered. For example, the problems of the qualifications, selection and training of the counselors, their duties, their place in the industrial organization, and their relations to management, labor, and community agencies can all be more clearly answered if the function of the counselor is understood.

The Personnel Counselor

THE uncertainty regarding the counselor's proper role in industry, we think, is due to the fact that very few of the plants have distinguished between the important administrative aspects of the personnel counselor's job, and the equally important function of dealing exclusively with employees who, for *psychological* reasons, are dissatisfied with or discontented on the job.

The counselor organization as conventionally set up today unquestionably renders a service of great value both to the company and its workers. It provides a fact-finding agency on any phase of employee activity. It communicates and clarifies company policies and procedures. It serves as an accessible information center on all subjects related to the employee's work. It acts in an advisory capacity to the employees on a wide variety of work problems. But the very extensiveness of its activities and the consequent limitations of time have prevented the counselor organizations from functioning effectively on problems arising out of workers' emotional maladjustments.

This latter phase of employee relations is too important to neglect and with the staggering problem of re-absorption and re-orientation of servicemen who will be returning, it will become increasingly important.

Employee Consultant

IT CAN readily be seen, therefore, that the activities of personnel counselors must be differentiated. This can be accomplished by dividing the counselor organization into two groups—one to handle the miscellaneous duties now associated with the counselor's function, the second to deal solely with the worker's psychological problems. In the interest of clear definition of function and proper identification, the latter group may be called "employee consultants." Actually this title better expresses the concepts underlying the consultant's field of service.

But regardless of what terminology is used to distinguish between the two groups, divorcing their activities is essential to effective results. Requiring a single group to perform duties which involve making recommendations or giving advice, and at the same time to handle interviews which to be successful must be permissive and free from any semblance of advice, is asking that group to be "fish and fowl" at the same time. It cannot help but dilute the sincerity and effectiveness of the relations with the employee.

The position of an interviewer is not that of a friend, although he must be genuinely friendly; his position is (or should be) that of a person engaged in the profession of interviewing. He cannot, on one occasion, in an administrative role, tell an employee what or what not to do, then on another occasion expect the employee to find his own way out of a dilemma. He cannot soundly undertake to perform an act of service for an employee today, and not expect the employee to make similar demands during an interview when the employee is trying to clear up some emotional difficulty.

Employee Confusion

IT is not surprising then to find the employee confused and disturbed by these inconsistencies. He rightfully could say, "I don't understand you. A few weeks ago you yourself advised me not to see so and so but to give you time to see what you could do. Now you tell me this is my own problem and I've got to decide for myself what I want to do about it. If you helped me then, why can't you help me now?"

Relations between individuals are never static. The feelings which arise during any contact are part of the succeeding contacts between the individuals involved. If A has been led to feel he can depend upon B for answers to his problem, he will expect B, subsequently to answer further problems which may arise.

In a word, the personnel representative cannot recommend at one time and refuse to find the answers for the employee at another time (the adjustment to an intra-personal difficulty) without adding to the confusion of the employee. It is wiser, it seems, to give one group of workers authority to recommend or to exercise discretion in granting or denying requests, and to place the responsibility of interviewing on another group of workers who have no power of authority or recommendation.

Furthermore, under such separation of function, the interviewer can live up to his understanding with the employee that all matters which arise will be held in the strictest confidence. Under the dual function of the personnel workers, this would become almost impossible.

Arguing Aloud with Himself

THE function of the employee consultant is, broadly speaking, to improve the effectiveness (the "morale") of the worker so that he can become more efficient. Hence almost any employee problem arising in or out of the plant can properly be presented to the consultant *insofar as* that problem interferes with the maximum effectiveness of the worker. Obviously, the consultant will have to be extraordinarily competent in his understanding of dynamic psychology and skilled in the techniques of conducting interviews.

Consulting consists of an ability to help people to define their problems, to come to grips with them, and to resolve them through their own efforts. The skilled consultant knows how to direct an interview so that the employee feels free to express just what he feels without fear of being blamed or disapproved of.

The employee consultant creates an atmosphere in which the employee really argues aloud with himself, being helped in this by the consultant who skillfully defines the problem rather than taking sides. The employee, in a word, is given a chance, in a free and friendly atmosphere, to discover just what it is he is after. Since he cannot fight against the consultant, who does not criticize him, he must fight with himself.

This art of interviewing is a well-established and well-recognized skill which is used in every reputable child guidance clinic in the country, as well as in the better social agencies.

Increased Self-Respect of Employee

IF PROPERLY conducted, the interview gives the employee a feeling of importance and an increased measure of self-respect. He gets a feeling that the corporation is sincerely and genuinely interested in him as a human being who is willing to cooperate with a large group and in a common interest. If management (and labor) feels this way, then the consultant in charge will inevitably transmit that feeling to the employee. This sort of atmosphere and relationship cannot be created without certain skills possessed by certain types of people who possess a genuine interest in and understanding of other people's problems.

It is not to be expected that anyone can undertake this work without the development of the required skills. To hire adults from such miscellaneous fields as advertising, sales, manufacturing, insurance, or what-not, and to expect professional consulting is as absurd as to call in former plumbers, pipefitters, or butchers to perform surgery. In the latter case, one would expect a frightful mortality rate and would be correct.

Consultant as Professional

EMPLOYEE consulting is a profession which has to be learned. It possesses its own peculiar content and techniques. Not all individuals are suited for this type of work. Growing older and "mixing" or "knocking around" do not necessarily qualify one for helping other people to help themselves.

The growing literature on the function of the individual who engages in this work reiterates that he must learn how to get people to talk about matters which are important to them and how to interpret what they say. He is told to listen rather than to talk. He is warned never to argue or to give advice. But such rules are as easy to state as they are difficult to follow. The consultant must have a framework of knowledge in which his thought is set, and a wealth of inner experience out of which his own sensitivity has developed, in order to know how to interpret and evaluate what the employee says in order to help him. In a word, it is the "how" of interviewing which cannot be so readily taught by rote but which must be achieved through the painful and laborious *professional* growth of the consultant.

We agree that at the present time the industrial counselor (as conventionally set up) performs a multitude of important administrative tasks. This is understandable in light of the accelerated growth of industry due to the war emergency. Such matters as transfers, gas and tire rationing, absentee control, induction of new employees, bond and insurance service, credit union, housing and transportation problems, care of children of women at work, and dozens of other matters are outgrowths of the emergency war situation in which industry finds itself. There has been insufficient time to centralize and clarify the functions of the various departments in industry. The "personnel counselor" group has become the available staff to act as a catch-all and to carry out the duties other departments could not or would not assume.

Unquestionably, they are doing an important job, but if the term "personnel counseling" has already become traditional for this kind of performance, then some other title such as "employee consultant" must be used to distinguish the counselors from the consultant staff which works with the employee on more intensive and deeper levels.

Cannot Remake Personalities

NAMES are less important than the functions they describe. It is arbitrary what we call whom. What is important is to recognize the distinctions. In the final analysis personnel management or industrial management is primarily a matter of human relations. Every large scale organization may be viewed as consisting of physical plant, equipment, and capital, formal organization, and people who do the work. It is a matter of common observation that happy people work more efficiently. The function of the employee consultant, then, is to make unhappy and psychologically ineffective people feel less unhappy and more content.

It should be emphasized that no one claims that the employee consultant is going to remake the personalities of employees. The function and effort of the consultant is definitely limited. He contributes to better productive effort by helping the employee get rid of disturbed feelings and, hence, making him more content on and with the job.

Limits

THE activities of the consultant, however, should not extend beyond the plant proper. In the exploration of the employee's problems instances inevitably will arise involving the need for environmental adjustment and contacts with persons other than the employee himself. For the consultant to invade this field of service would be prohibitive both from the standpoint of time, cost, and effort. To provide for adequate attention to such cases, the consultants should be fully informed on the various social agencies—public and private, within the community and their services. The consultants then will be qualified to make referrals to these agencies, either through the company's own welfare department or directly to the agencies.

Obviously, when the present emergency will have passed many of the now existing services of the personnel counselor no longer will be required. By and large there will be no labor shortage. The problem of transfers will have been stabilized. Housing shortages and transportation difficulties will have become things of the past. Procedures and policies with regard to labor codes and labor grievances will have become more settled. The worries over absenteeism will have largely disappeared. Other problems of like importance today will have ceased to exist or their handling will revert to Supervision. The reasonableness of this prediction will be apparent to anyone who makes a realistic examination of the subject.

Value Can Increase

RECOGNIZING this inevitable trend, however, does not imply the elimination of opportunity for today's personnel counselors. With their varied experience in industrial and employee relations and their understanding of supervision's problems, it takes but little imagination to conceive of assigning to them new responsibilities in personnel administration, coordination and guidance. Their value in their special field, rather than diminishing, can increase.

It goes without saying, too, that there are many men and women now serving in the role of personnel counselors, who by inclination, temperament and background, soundly qualify to enter the consulting field. Certainly the work of consulting should possess tremendous appeal for those counselors who have envisioned the post-war problems of human relations within industry. One of the most serious personnel problems which management will have to deal with after the war will be the conflicting *intra-personal* feelings of employees in relation to their fellow workers, supervision, and their jobs.

Troublesome as they are today, with thousands of discharged veterans being reabsorbed in industry, they will in all probability, be greatly intensified. We may expect that the impact of the war on the attitudes of the returning soldiers who re-enter industry and on the wives who are now in industry and who will return in large numbers to their household duties, will give rise to all sorts of disturbances which will be reflected in dissatisfactions on the job. Many different kinds of frustrations accumulated during and after the war, both on the part of wives and husbands, will find their outlet in disguised and distorted aggressions. The job will serve as a convenient target for the felt dissatisfaction.

Period of Human Readjustment

SERIOUS effort already is being made by various national agencies to anticipate and properly organize for this period of human readjustment. Industry inevitably will have to share the burden of restoring normalcy to human hearts and minds. And through this difficult period, the consultant can perform an invaluable service to industry. For through him, the employee is afforded a means of emotional release—a medium by which he can explore his problems in absolute confidence, with the assurance that whatever he says will be received with understanding.

The skilled consultant will communicate to the employee a feeling of sincere interest, which means that the employee, in turn, will feel that he counts as an individual, that *how* he feels and what happens to him *really* matters.

The soundness of that relationship will be apparent to those who recognize the definite bridge between an employee's emotional state, his effectiveness on the job, and his worth to himself as a human being. If then, we accept the validity of the consultant's place in industry; if we grant that this is a major work calling for deep reservoirs of sympathetic human understanding and psychiatric perceptions, we must likewise grant that it cannot soundly be merged with the functional heterogeneity of counseling as generally practiced today or as it will likely be in the future.

If Management's Interest Continues?

To BE effective and valuable, those who plan a career in what, by omnibus description, is now commonly defined as personnel counseling, had best decide whether it is counseling they wish to do—or consulting. They are distinctly different fields of service, calling for totally different interests, abilities and skills. And, if management's interest in the worker as a human being continues, there will be room for both in the post-war industrial world.

If We Isolate the Group or Groups of Employees
with the Highest Labor Turnover Rates We can
Analyze Their Causes of Termination and Plan
Appropriate Action to Keep More of Them on
our Rolls.

Why Workers Quit

By Dwight L. Palmer, Eugene R. Purpus and
LeBaron O. Stockford

Lockheed Aircraft Corporation
Burbank, Cal.

IN THE solution of the many problems in the field of Industrial Relations, too much
attention has been given to the symptoms of our "diseases." Too little attention has usually been paid to the more important underlying causes which lead
to these symptoms and to the "diseases" themselves.

The following study is one of several which have been carried on by the Industrial Relations Research department of Lockheed Aircraft Corporation in an
attempt to isolate and study these basic causal factors rather than to analyze further
the symptoms with which all of us are already familiar.

The Exit Interview

FOR example, most studies of the much discussed problem of voluntary turnover
have sought to analyze the frequency with which certain reasons for termination
are given. This approach, when used by itself, has two major limitations: (1) The
analysis is usually based upon reasons given during the exit interview; and it has been
found, beyond reason for doubt, that under such circumstances employees do not
give statements which are honest and reliable. (2) Major stress is laid upon an
analysis of the reasons themselves, whereas the really significant factor is an analysis
of the underlying causes which bring about termination within different groups and
under varying conditions.

The approach which we have taken to the problem of voluntary turnover (as
well as to other problems in Industrial Relations) may be explained by an analogy.
Suppose, for example, that eight people in a large family sit down to a dinner of liver

and onions, and six of them do not eat. If we examine only the *apparent* reasons for not eating—the reasons given at the table by each of the six—we may conclude that four of them were "not hungry" and that two of them "didn't feel well." Such information will be of little use to the cook; it will offer no practical basis upon which she can plan action to eliminate the resultant waste in time and material involved in producing the meal. If, however, a friend of the family has an individual talk with each of the members who did not eat the meal, he may be able to analyze the *real* reasons: two of the children had "dates" that evening and didn't want to eat onions before going out; the father knew that such a combination of food would upset his stomach; the youngest boy had been stuffing himself on ice cream all afternoon and wasn't hungry; one of the girls was mad at her mother and was on a "hunger strike"; one of the boys was coming down with chicken pox.

Real vs. Apparent Reasons

O N THE basis of this factual analysis of underlying causes the cook could effect an improvement of the problem, though she could not eliminate it entirely. For example, in the first three instances a separation of the two items of food would make it possible for half of those who did not eat to get at least a part of the dinner. In the fourth case, a little disciplinary action on between-meal snacks would eliminate the difficulty. The fifth case might be corrected through a counseling technique. Only in the sixth case was there a physical limitation which could not be overcome at the time.

If we merely summarized *apparent* reasons, we would have concluded that 50% of the people didn't eat because they weren't hungry, and 25% didn't eat because they didn't feel well. However, the real solution to the problem lay not in analyzing the *apparent* reason as given when the incident occurred, but in a later investigation of the individual persons involved and the basic forces operating upon their immediate needs.

The same methods of approach will yield similarly effective results when applied to the problem of voluntary turnover in industry. If we do no more than analyze the reasons given by employees during exit interviews and summarize the resultant answers, we shall achieve a result which is both unreliable and useless as far as industry is concerned. To obtain really useful results, we must make a different approach.

Study Ex-employees

W E MUST gather our data from ex-employees *after* they have left the company and are no longer influenced by the circumstances of employment or the confusion of termination.

We must pay less attention to the *overall frequency* with which reasons for termination are given, and shift our emphasis to (a) an analysis of the people who give these reasons, and (b) a consideration of how the real reasons for termination differ by groups in accordance with sex, marital status, age, shift, seniority, pay, etc.

If the employees who quit comprised one single, homogeneous group, it would be sufficient to know that 16% of them give "poor health" as the reason for termination. However, the working population in most industrial plants (particularly during war times) is made up of many different groups or types of people. The major reason for termination may vary considerably from group to group, and within each group it may differ markedly from the reason most frequently given during the exit interview. This latter information must be clearly delineated if management is to be able to approach and solve the real problem of voluntary turnover.

The following discussion outlines the way in which (on this basis) we approached the study of voluntary terminations at Lockheed Aircraft Corporation, and it presents the conclusions which were derived from this study.

Procedure

SELECTION *of Cases to be Interviewed:* This study is based upon the results of a series of interviews with 421 ex-employees of the Lockheed Aircraft Corporation. The people to be interviewed were selected at random from the lists of voluntary terminations for the months of August, September, and October, 1943. In all, 625 cases were selected, but 204 were not investigated because the ex-employees had left the Los Angeles metroplitan area or were part-time student workers who returned to school.

Of the 421 ex-employees studied, 174 (41.3%) were men and 247 (58.7%) were women. The age range of the men was from 16 to 77 years, with the average at 37 years 3 months. For the women, the age range was from 17 to 57 years, with the average at 29 years 7 months. The men had been employed at Lockheed from 1 to 78 months, with an average seniority of 10 months. The women had been at Lockheed from 1 to 19 months with an average service record of 5 months. The distribution of these people over the three shifts was approximately the same for both the men and the women: 45 per cent were on the day shift, 37 per cent were on the swing shift, and 18 per cent were on the graveyard shift.

The Interviews: Two to four weeks after leaving Lockheed, each of the 421 individuals was interviewed in his or her home by a trained investigator from an outside agency. In order to insure that complete information would be obtained, each investigator was given a list of 35 questions or topics to be discussed with the ex-employees. These items were used to broaden the coverage of the interview so that we could ascertain not only the reasons for termination but also some measure of each person's attitude toward his job, working conditions and supervisor.

Results

WHEN we analyze workers by groups, we find that the influence of different factors causes a difference in reasons for termination. For example, the kind and frequency of reasons for termination vary considerably among groups arranged according to sex, age, marital status, shift, seniority, and wages. Secondary factors (such as attendance records, merit reviews, type of work) which have no important influence upon causes of termination are not discussed in this study.

The reasons which ex-employees gave for voluntary termination were divided into two groups: (1) Occupational: In the order of importance, these reasons which relate to factors within the working situation are *placement, desire to take another job, general dissatisfaction, wages, shift, excessively heavy work, supervision,* and *working conditions.* These reasons accounted for 48 per cent of the terminations. (2) *Personal:* In the order of importance, these reasons which relate to factors beyond the scope of the working situation are *health, child care, transportation,* and *home responsibilities.* These reasons accounted for 52 per cent of the terminations.

The importance of each of these reasons varied in accordance with different groups, as is indicated in the following sections.

Summary of Results

Sex:	Three-quarters of the men quit for occupational reasons, whereas three-quarters of the women quit for personal reasons.
Age:	Most frequently, the younger men quit because of *placement* and and *job dissatisfaction;* men between 24 years and 37 years quit because of *wages;* and men over 37 quit because of *personal reasons* (largely *health*).
	Younger women quit because of *child care;* women in all age groups quit because of *health.*
Marital Status:	*Health, wages* and *personal problems* as reasons for termination are given more frequently by married men than by single men.
	Married women quit largely for reasons of *child care* and *health;* single women for reasons of *health, transportation* and *placement.*
Shift:	Among the men, *health* is the reason most frequently given for termination by those on the swing and graveyard shifts. The percentage of men on the swing shift who quit because of *wages* was twice as large as the percentage of those on both the day and graveyard shifts who quit for this reason. The percentage of women who quit the graveyard shift because of *child care* was twice as great as the percentage of women on either the day or swing shifts who quit for this reason.
Seniority:	As seniority increases, the frequency with which men quit because of *wages* decreases. Among women (especially those who are married) the percentage who quit because the *work is too heavy* increases with seniority.
Pay Status:	Men who received an increase in pay on coming to Lockheed stayed with the company twice as long as did those men who "took a cut in pay." The relationship of starting pay at Lockheed to previous earnings had no direct bearing on the reasons why women quit their jobs.

Influence of Sex

THERE are marked differences between the two sexes in the frequency with which certain reasons for termination are given. Whereas 48 per cent of the total group gave "occupational" reasons, 73 per cent of the men and only 31 per cent of the women gave such reasons.

The reasons most frequently given by the men were *health* (16%), *desire to take another job* (14%), *placement* (12%), *general dissatisfaction* (11%), *wages* (10%), and *transportation* (9%). These six reasons accounted for 72 per cent of all terminations among the men. The reasons most frequently given by the women were *health* (28%), *child care* (19%), *other domestic problems* (10%), *work too heavy* (6%), *placement* (6%), and *transportation* (6%). These six reasons accounted for 75 per cent of all terminations among the women

Three reasons, *health, job placement* and *transportation*, appear among the six most important reasons given by both the men (37%), and the women (40%). The remaining important reasons show the areas in which the most definite sex differences occur. About 35 per cent of the men quit to *take another job*, because they were *generally dissatisfied*, or because they disliked their *wage rates;* only 8 per cent of the women gave these reasons. On the other hand, 35 per cent of the women left their jobs so that they might *care for their children*, because they had *other domestic responsibilities*, or because they found factory *work to be too heavy*. Only 2 per cent of the men gave any of these reasons for termination.

Influence of Age

THE frequency with which certain reasons are given for termination varies with age. To approximate the relationship between age and reasons for quitting, the ex-employees were divided into five classes, each of which consisted of 20 per cent of the total group. The youngest 20 per cent of the men ranged in age from 18 to 24 years, the next 20 per cent from 25 to 29 years, the third from 30 to 38 years, the fourth from 39 to 49 years, and the oldest 20 per cent ranged from 50 to 77 years. For the women, the five age ranges were 17 to 21 years, 22 to 26 years, 27 to 32 years, 33 to 40 years, and 41 to 57 years of age.

Among the younger men (18 to 24 years), unsatisfactory *job placement* was the reason most frequently given for termination. As age increased, this reason was given less frequently. Only one man in the oldest group (50 to 77 years) quit because of faulty *job placement*. The converse is true of the frequency with which *health* was given as a reason for termination. Among the youngest 20 per cent of the men, only 6 per cent gave this reason, whereas 30 per cent of the oldest men quit because of poor *health*.

The reason for termination which was most closely related with the men in the middle age ranges was dissatisfaction with *wages*. Whereas only 6 per cent of the youngest men and 8 per cent of the oldest men gave this reason, 20 per cent of the men between 30 and 38 quit because of *wages*.

Among the women, health is a serious problem in all age groups. Because of the close relationship between the health of the worker and the strenuousness of the work, these factors should be considered together. These two reasons accounted for 21 per cent of all terminations (health 20%, and work too heavy 1%) among the youngest group of women (17 to 21 years). These reasons became increasingly important among the older women: of those over 40 years of age, 40 per cent gave *health* and 10 per cent gave *work too heavy* as reasons for termination. As might be readily assumed, *child care* was given as the reason for termination by more than 40 per cent of the women between the ages of 22 and 27. This cause was of little importance among women under 22 (14%), and of even less importance among women over 40 (2%).

Transportation

TRANSPORTATION is a relatively unimportant problem among both the men and the women who are between the ages of 25 and 40. Only 5 per cent of all people between these ages gave this reason for termination. Among men and women who were younger than 25 and older than 40, some 15% terminated because of transportation problems.

Influence of Marital Status

AMONG the married men, personal problems are far more important than they are among the single men. *Health* and the need for greater income (*desire to take another job* and *wages*) are the reasons most frequently given by the married men. These reasons accounted for more than half (57%) of the terminations within this group. These same reasons were given by only 33 per cent of the single men. The two reasons most frequently given by the single men were *placement* (23%) and *general dissatisfaction* (16%). These two reasons accounted for only 16 per cent of the terminations among the married men.

Again, among the married women the most important problems are personal, whereas among the single women occupational problems enter to a greater extent. Although an equal percentage of both married and single women gave *health* as a reason for termination, the percentage of married women who quit because of *too heavy work* (10%) is more than twice as great as that for the single women who gave this reason (4%). The percentage of single women who quit because of dissatisfaction with their *shift* (7%), faulty *job placement* (9%) and *desire to take another job* (9%) is almost four times as great as the percentage of married women who gave these same reasons for termination (7%).

Influence of Shift

AMONG the men, *health* was given as a reason for termination by 11 per cent of those on the day shift, 17 per cent of those on the swing shift, and 25 per cent of those on the graveyard shift. Among the women, *health* was equally important on all three shifts. To the women on the graveyard shift, *child care* was a particularly important problem. Thirty-three per cent of the women on this shift gave *child care* as a reason for termination, whereas only 16 per cent of the women on either the day or swing shifts gave this reason.

Among the men on swing shift, dissatisfaction with pay was indicated by the fact that 16 per cent of the men on this sift gave *wages* as a reason for quitting. In sharp contrast, only 5 per cent of the men on the day shift and 3 per cent of the men on the graveyard shift gave this reason for quitting. An equal proportion of men on all three shifts quit because they were dissatisfied with their *job placement* or to *take another job*.

Among both the men and the women, *shift* was given as a reason for termination by those on the swing shift only.

Influence of Seniority

FOR the purpose of determining the influence of seniority, both the men and the women in this study were separated into five equal groups according to length of service record with the company. For the men, the five groups were as follows: 1 to 3 months, 4 to 6 months, 7 to 10 months, 11 to 20 months, and 21 to 74 months. For the women, the five groups were 1 month or less, 2 to 3 months, 4 to 5 months, 6 to 9 months, and 10 to 19 months.

Irrespective of seniority, *health* was a serious problem among the men. The percentage of men who stayed with the company 3 months or less and who gave this reason for termination (19%) was the same as the percentage of men who quit because of poor *health* after they had been with the company 2 years or more. Pay was a very important problem among the newly hired men. One out of every seven men who quit within 3 months after employment gave dissatisfaction with *wages* as the reason for termination. However, the frequency with which this reason was given decreased with added seniority; only 1 out of every 25 men who had been with the company 21 months or more quit because of dissatisfaction with *wage rates*. This inverse relationship between seniority and dissatisfaction with wages undoubtedly has several causes: (1) as a group, the men who are recent hires are being employed at a pay rate which is considerably lower than that of their previous jobs; (2) the merit system permits a gradual adjustment in wage rates; (3) those who are dissatisfied with their wages tend to eliminate themselves during the first few months of employment.

Too Heavy Work

Among the newly-hired employees, *transportation* was a serious problem for both men and women. With the passing of time, this problem was adjusted and the number of people who gave this reason for termination gradually diminished. Among the women, *child care* was a constant problem; 19 per cent of those who quit in the first month and 19 per cent of those who quit after a year of employment gave this reason for leaving the company. However, the frequency with which women quit because of *poor health* increased with seniority. Whereas only 16 per cent of the women who quit in the first month gave this reason, 39 per cent of those who quit after 10 months left because of *poor health*.

It is interesting to note that *too heavy work* was not frequently given as a reason for termination by those women who quit after only 3 or 4 months of employment; but it was a very important reason among those women who remained with the company 7 months or more. An analysis of the data showed that all of the women who gave this reason for quitting were in direct manufacturing jobs, and that two-thirds of these women were married. It may be concluded that there is an accumulative effect of fatigue upon married women, who evidently find it too difficult to continue factory work and still keep up their household responsibilities.

Influence of Pay Status

Among the men there was an extremely strong relationship between the reasons for which they quit their jobs and their pay status at Lockheed. Absolute wages in themselves appear to have little or no bearing upon termination; however, the amount of money that a man earns on one job in relationship to his earnings on his previous job is an extremely important factor. The men were divided into thre groups: (1) those who received a definite increase in weekly earnings on coming to Lockheed; (2) those who received approximately the same wages as they did on their previous job; (3) those who took a definite reduction in earnings.

The percentage of men who received an increase in pay on coming to Lockheed and who quit their jobs because of dissatisfaction with *wage* rates (4%) was only one-fourth as large as the percentage of men who had taken a cut in pay and who quit because of unsatisfactory *wages* (17%). Although not to so great an extent, the same relationship is true among those men who quit because they were *generally dissatisfied*. *Health* was the reason most frequently given by those men who had received an increase in pay (24%). This reason for termination was given by only 6 per cent of those men who had taken a cut in pay on coming to Lockheed.

The best single indication of the effects of "relative pay" is to be seen in the relationship between starting pay and length of service. The men who received an increase in earnings when they started to work at Lockheed remained with the company for an average of 17 months; those whose starting pay was about the same as their previous earnings stayed with the company for an average of 9 months; and those who took a cut in pay remained with the company less than 7 months.

Among the women it was found that wages had little or no direct or indirect bearing upon termination.

Conclusion

V OLUNTARY termination is not, to the same degree, characteristic of all industrial workers. It is a changing and irregular phenomenon which varies in different groups and under different conditions. As a basis for control of excessive termination, we cannot rely upon analyses of the excuses and explanations which workers give, particularly during the exit interview. We must study the basic make-up of the total work force to see which sub-groups are under specific strains that might lead to termination at a rate higher than normal.

Instead of emphasizing the overall turnover rate and the reasons which employees give upon terminating, we must study the incidence of turnover within different groups which are separated on the basis of age, sex, shift, working conditions, etc. Having isolated the group or groups with the highest turnover rate, we can analyze their basic causes of termination and plan appropriate action within the limited area.

Book Reviews

Book Review Editor, Mr. Everett Van Every
California Personnel Management Association, Berkeley, Cal.

WARTIME LABOR RELATIONS

By John N. Mariano.   New York.   National Public and Labor Relations Service.
1944.   216 pp.   Price $2.75

This book throws the spotlight on labor and management and may cause both of them to squirm in discomfort.   Government, too, in wartime business, comes in for careful scrutiny.   The author believes that post wartime labor relations must distinguish itself by the manner in which it hands back the native peace-time skills and physical assets to our citizens.

We all realize that the end of the war will create acute problems in labor relations; many of us, too, realize that profitable operations of huge industries would prove unprofitable if older types of thinking in private management prevail.   And now a wartime labor relations econo ny calls for a fundamental modification of the private enterprise system which Mariano describes very well.

Probably a high light in the book is the careful analysis of the War Labor Disputes Act and the splendid section of case situations, including the U. S. Gypsum Company, Atlantic Base Iron Works, Brewster Aeronautical, Allis-Chalmers, Republic Steel, Illinois Coal Operators.

In the chapter in "A Labor Relations Decalogue" Mariano coasts along in his vigorous editorial style.   Wartime labor relations must not be deemed a terribly weighty subject fit only to be understood by top executives.   It is something everyone working in the plant should come to easily understand.   And the rank-and-file of labor must share the responsibility with its leaders for making the decisions which determine profitable or unprofitable employer-employee relations.

The author devotes one chapter to fifty wartime and post war labor relations changes which he says are reasonably safe and predictable.   Many employers will recognize definite trends in Mariano's quick summary of what he thinks are dominant changes to come.

Some of my fellow readers, who shared this book with me, contend there is little new in it, but all agreed that it is a forceful and challenging presentation of what management and unions are facing in this country.   We agreed, too, that tomorrow's labor relations no longer describes the free-enterprise system we once knew, but something resembling a permanently planned economy.   It is evident that the profit system of production will never again find itself standing alone and apart from a host of regulatory government agencies.

PERSONNEL
Journal

· *The Magazine of*

LABOR RELATIONS AND PERSONNEL PRACTICES

Published by PERSONNEL RESEARCH FEDERATION

Lincoln Building, 60 East 42nd Street, New York City

Volume 23   *Number 4*

Contents for October 1944

EDITORIAL BOARD

The Suggestion is Made that New or as Soon as Possible Each Company and/or Local Committee for Economic Development Should Establish a Vocational Information Shelf for Facilitating Transfer of Employees in Present War Industries.

Aid *for* Post-war Employment

By George F. Davenel

Flushing, New York

ANY organization engaged in post-war planning must include a program of vocational direction for personnel hired during the war emergency. It is imperative that this program be started at once because unemployment six months after the war may reach from 7 to 12 million (Bureau of Labor Statistics). To avoid such economic disruption, we must keep the national income at a level which will allow for a healthy consumption of goods and services. Legally, any man or woman returning from service has the right to his job if he files for it within 6 months after his discharge.

Are These Skills Just Waste?

WHAT then becomes of those who filled in during the emergency? These are the people who turned the wheels for you, the ones who kept your plant open, who earned your Army-Navy "E" rating, and who made your profits. What can these people do with their newly acquired skills learned at your expense? Are these skills just waste—something to be forgotten the day after the armistice? Suppose that it is possible for you to find openings for your veterans and to retain those now engaged who were working before the war. What shall we do with the men and women who are working for the first time—the housewives, the handicapped, the pensioner out of retirement? What will happen to women who have entered into jobs like bank teller, railroad and street car conductor, bus and taxi driver, engineering positions, supervisory jobs, and others that by precedent were formerly held only by men?

We cannot tell these various groups to go back where they came from and to fit themselves into a pre-war pattern of living. As a group they are different! They have tasted the satisfaction of a day's pay for a day's work. They know the financial and emotional independence that means! They have proved themselves to be occupationally necessary now.

Right to Jobs

MANY of them will want to be necessary later! If the criterion of life in a democracy is the right to self-determinism as long as it does not interfere with the good of the group, then these people have the right to further employment. Barring individual maladjustments and personality misfits, a high percentage of them must find it! After the last war, fascism, nazism, and communism became popular due to the highly regimented "efficiency" of their planned economies. Too often these economies offered popular sedatives to a problem such as this. In a democracy, however, we recognize the individual in each worker to allow for individual choices.

The rapid advance of the totalitarian states in the early days of World War II should serve as a reminder that people need at least the stimulation of well-rounded information to make wise choices. Selfishly, too, you must be interested in these new workers because this vast horde represents your actual buyers now, your potential buyers of the future, and your best piece of company advertising. Therefore, patriotically, socially, and economically, it is your duty to redirect their efforts and training to families of jobs—jobs related to those in which they are now engaged by common work or worker characteristics—where there will be opportunity for placement either in your own company or elsewhere. The medium for this direction is the establishment of a well-rounded program of vocational direction.

In such a program, vocational guidance plays the major part. Scientifically, vocational guidance is "the process of assisting the individual to choose an occupation, prepare for, enter upon and progress in it." It is not fortune telling, crystal gazing, phrenological reading or emotional diaper changing. It involves the distribution of occupational information, followed by interviewing, testing, counseling, placement, and follow-up. How much or how little your organization engages in will depend upon the extent of your resources. But anything you do will bear fruit in the good will and the economic betterment of your displaced workers. What then are the basic technics that any good personnel department could employ?

Vocational Information Shelf

THE first thing that the office should do is to establish a vocational information shelf. The material should be classified and indexed by title, author, and subject. A simple file of three by five cards with the typed notice is adequate as a catalogue. The material should be up-to-date and varied in scope. The basic aim is to widen the vocational horizon of the workers. Just telling a man that there are

30,000 different occupations helps to free him from the rich man, poor man, beggar man, thief, type of generalized reasoning. Some companies may wish to prepare a series of job charts showing the interrelated nature of the various positions and the opportunities for horizontal and vertical development within them. In this connection, THE JOB FAMILY SERIES, 1943, published by Superintendent of Documents, Washington, D. C. should prove helpful. This shows groups of related occupations, sources of upgrading, and inter-department transfer of personnel.

Additional information about specific occupations is obtainable from various sources. A few companies publish career monographs, which are booklets usually written by a worker in the field and therefore authenticated and well-rounded. Also, there are organizations which study labor trends and prepare monthly bulletins of these. The United States Department of Labor publishes a wealth of material. A handy reference is the OCCUPATIONAL INDEX, a quarterly bibliography of current publications, "which contains, or professes to contain, occupational information that will be helpful to an individual in choosing a field of work." The index lists material obtainable without charge, information that sells from 1¢ to 25¢, and over 25¢. A handy subject listing on the front cover shows the occupations referred to in the issue with the appropriate paragraph key number. In addition to this, Science Research Associates of Chicago publishes VOCATIONAL GUIDE, a monthly annotated bibliography of current articles on occupations.

Selected List Below

SINCE no one book could possibly answer all the questions your workers will have to ask, it is necessary to be familiar with a number of references. For your convenience, a list of books and magazines that should prove provocative to any one seeking vocational information is included at the end of this article.

A digest of this material prepared by your personnel department could serve as a handy reference sheet. Placing much of this literature on open shelves and turning your workers loose on it will produce results. If they can be directed by a member of the staff, the results should be just that much better. This is the simplest and easiest type of vocational guidance for groups. Certain readers may be interested in seeing the application of this technic on a college level described in the author's article VOCATIONAL INFORMATION FOR ALUMNI, IN OCCUPATIONS, THE VOCATIONAL GUIDANCE MAGAZINE, May, 1944.

Having motivated the workers to thinking about the occupational world in general, many companies will want to aid them further in the refinement of this thinking. Any attempt at measurement should be scientific. Conversely, the term scientific implies the most careful type of measurement. Therefore, if we are to evaluate and to direct the choices of these people, we need the support of a sound testing program.

Testing.

Howfrom, the whole field of testing is at present so indefinite that it is extremely difficult to segregate one type of test to be used for general guidance. A battery of tests will yield much more accurate results from which to predict. But it is only when we have used a number of tests, fused the results with the individual's education and work record, evaluated this information in terms of a health report and interviewed the worker to obtain information about his social life (the term social being used in its generic sense), that we get anything like the complex picture that is Mr. Jones.

When used this way, tests are helpful to estimate in a broad way, the probabilities of success in an occupation. Tests for *manual aptitude* like the Minnesota Manual Dexterity Test, Finger Dexterity Test of Johnson O'Connor, Tweezer Dexterity Test, Manual Versatility Test of L. R. Frazier, I.E.R. Assembly Test for girls; of *mechanical aptitude* like the Minnesota Mechanical Assembly Test, Minnesota Spatial Relations Test, the Wiggly Blocks, Minnesota Paper Form Board, T. W. MacQuarrie's Test for Mechanical Ability, L. J. O'Rourke's Mechanical Aptitude Test, J. L. Stenquist's Mechanical Aptitude Tests; of *clerical aptitude* like the Minnesota Vocational Test for Clerical Workers, Number Checking and Word Checking of Johnson O'Connor, General Test for Stenographers and Typists developed by the Research Division of the United States Civil Service Commission; of *scientific aptitude* like the Stanford Scientific Aptitude Test; of *art judgment* like Meier-Seashore Art Judgment Test and McAdory Art Test; of *vocational interest* like Strong's Interest Blanks and Manson's Occupational Interest Blank for Women and Garretson and Symonds' Interest Questionnaire for High School Students were all trail blazers and opened the door for experimentation and development of additional tests by commercial agencies.

Indirect Help

Even though many of our present aptitude tests do not show a sufficiently high enough validity and reliability (the measurement of an aptitude in the abstract may not be a true indication of the functional possibilities of that aptitude in a given occuparion), they are helpful in an indirect way in indicating latent potentialities in stimulating the person tested to think intelligently about his future and about possibilities that he might not have considered. They sometimes bring to light unsuspected talents or limitations which must be met in a practical way.

In addition to specific aptitude tests, general intelligence tests can be helpful, but here again caution in the use of them must prevail. There is a school of thought which has endeavored to classify positions according to intelligence levels. Accepting the value of critical scores (limits above and below which it might be unwise to hire people), in general it is not wise to restrict placement according to a score on an intelligence examination alone. The relation of the value of test scores to the balance of the material known about the individual will have to remain an indefinite quantity till the test scores themselves prove their worth.

Assistance Available for Publishers

WITH these reservations holding the interpretations of test results in check, it is safe to consider the actual selection of tests. What type of test for a specific job? The answer is the type of test that best measures the thing that the job requires of its workers. As we mentioned before a battery of tests and as much additional information that can be obtained about an individual are necessary for sound guidance. To determine whether the test in practice is worth the cost of administration, it is necessary to know the reliability (consistency of result) and the validity (does it measure what it purports to measure) of the test on a large number of cases (at least over one hundred). The reliability can be obtained by the use of the split-half (odd-even) method or by the test-retest method. The validity can be established by the method of correlation; per cent of agreement; critical scores. The reliability of the test must be at least .95; the validity at least .75. If the measures fall below, the use of the test should be seriously considered. To safeguard their professional use, organizations publishing tests usually restrict distribution to qualified users. Many of the tests are prepared in booklet form and can be reused by inserting a separate answer sheet for each applicant tested. Organizations publishing tests usually provide assistance in their selection and use.

Further Assistance

SO FAR we have assisted our workers to choose some phase of an occupation and we have explained to them how much preparation they will need. How far should we go to help them enter upon it? If we have surveyed our own possibilities by a thorough plant analysis and find that relocation within the organization is impossible, we might carry our program one step forward and prepare lists of possible lines of contact. It is probably not practical to think in terms of actual jobs, but if we supply the address of the local Committee for Economic Development, the War Manpower Commission office, the special branch of the United States Employment Service, dealing with the problems represented by our particular group (over-age, or handicapped, or junior groups, etc.), names and addresses of companies engaged in activities similar to our own, lists of good employment agencies from which we hire personnel, names and addresses of agencies offering free placement services, lists of civil service opportunities open, and suggest that those concerned register with the National Roster of Scientific and Specialized Personnel—the men and women themselves will get the jobs! Any follow-up work done will help to evaluate the worth of your project.

Pragmatism must get a word in and it will not be edgewise! Granted, that your personnel department is overworked and this plan entails expenditure of time and money, it is imperative that you help this group to the limit of your possibilities. Anything that you do along these lines will be individually important now and will cultivate the kind of "firm" reputation that reaps dividends later. The vocational information shelf will help you too after the war to say "no jobs today" gracefully to new applicants who do not meet your standards. While we are graceful, why not be practical? If a man has thought enough of your organization to single it out for application you ought to meet that trust with equal sincerity. A reference to your current vocational literature will at least put him a step in the right direction.

Selected List of Books

SOME general books that should prove helpful are the following:

Dictionary of Occupational Titles, United States Employment Service, Department of Labor, Washington, D. C. (For sale by the Superintendent of Documents, Washington, D. C.) The dictionary covered about 90% of the American workers employed in 1939. It is divided into four sections: Part I—Definitions of Titles contains job definitions of 17,452 separate jobs known by 29,744 job titles. Part II—Titles and Codes contains all the job titles listed in groups according to their occupational code number of which there are 7,000. Part III—Conversion Tables which facilitate the conversion of registration fields in public employment offices to the code structure in the dictionary. This is now obsolete. Part IV—Entry Occupational Classification Structure for those people who cannot be called experienced workers in terms of any one job. In addition, there is a supplement to parts I and II that contains an extra 4,201 job definitions known by 6,619 titles, thus making a total of 21,653 defined jobs known by 36,363 titles.

Occupations and Vocational Guidance, prepared by Wilma Bennett, New York, New York, H. W. Wilson Co. This is a source list of pamphlet material and contains statements from various sources.

Books about Jobs, Willard Parker, Chicago, Ill., American Library Association. A bibliography of occupational literature.

Index to Vocations, Willodeen Price and Zelma E. Ticen, New York, New York, H. W. Wilson. A subject index to 1,950 careers.

Find Your Own Frontier, Arthur C. Bartlett, Boston, W. A. Wilde Company.

I Find My Vocation, Harry Dexter Kitson, New York, McGraw-Hill Book Co.

Business Opportunities for Women, Catherine Oglesby, New York, Harper Brothers.

Careers for Women, Catherine Filene, New York, Houghton Miflin.

Careers for Men, Edward L. Bernays, New York, Garden City Publishing Company.

Choice of an Occupation, Edmund G. Williamson and Milton Hahn, The General College, University of Minnesota, Minneapolis.

You and Your Future Job, William G. Campbell and James H. Bedford, Los Angeles Society for Occupational Research. (This is especially good for young workers.)

How to Pass a Written Examination, Harry C. McKown, New York, McGraw-Hill Book Co.

Everyday Occupations, Mildred A. Davey, Elizabeth M. Smith and Theodore R. Myers, Boston, D. C. Heath and Co.

The Personnel Bibliographical Index, W. H. Cowley, Columbus, Ohio, Ohio State University. While this reference is designed mainly for work in the field of student personnel administration, there is much in its 2,000 references that can help anybody desiring information on occupations.

Economic and Business Opportunities, D. Clyde Beighey and Elmer E. Spanable, Chicago, Winston.

Exploring the World of Work: A Guide Book to Occupations, G. V. Bennett and Georgia M. Sachs, Los Angeles, California, Society for Occupational Research.

They also Serve, Merrill Bishop and Arda Talbot Allen, Austin, Texas, Steck Co. A group of stories about persons who are doing menial but necessary jobs such as garbage men, elevator operators, etc.

Careers, I. David Cohen and Mary K. Ganley, New York, Nelson and Sons, 1938. One of the Life Career Books, consisting of a collection of articles by various writers describing the nature and opportunities in different kinds of work.

Solving the Job Puzzle. A Guide Book in Vocations, Robert Gunning, Columbus, Ohio, American Education Press. This book is particularly helpful in outlining possibilities open to people without college training.

New Business Opportunities for Today: A Survey of Money Making Possibilities, H. S. Kahm, New York, Harper. This helpful book describes many ways to invest small amounts of capital. A handy book for your better-paid workers.

Start Your Own Business, H. S. Kahm, New York, Hillman-Curl. Another book by the same author about several kinds of retail shops.

Changes in the Occupational Pattern of New York State, Bradford F. Kimball, Albany, The University of the State of New York.

Getting and Holding a Magazine Job, Gertrude B. Lane, New York, Crowell Publishing Co.

Fashion Is Spinach, Elizabeth Hawes, New York, Random House. The author's experience in fashion work and her method in establishing an independent business.

Modeling for Money, Carol Lynn, New York, Greenberg.

Your Place in Life and How To Find It, John McDonnell, Champaign, Urbana, Ill., The Trailblazers.

The Road To Anywhere, Opportunities in Secretarial Work, Frances Maule, New York, Funk and Wagnalls.

This Business of Singing, P. V. Key, New York, Pierre Key, Publishing Corporation.

One Thousand Ways to Make $1,000, F. C. Minaker, editor, Chicago, Ill., The Dartnell Corporation.

A Preface to Advertising, Mark O'Dea, New York, Whittlesey House.

Front Page Story, Robert Van Gelder, New York, Dodd Mead.

Business Behavior, Ray Abrams, Cincinnati, Ohio, South-Western Publishing Co.

What's Holding You Back? Allan B. Chalfant, Whittlesey House.

The Romance of Candy, Alma H. Austin, New York, New York, Harper. Presents the field of candy making as an occupation.

SUGGESTED MAGAZINES

It would be wise to be familiar with a number of the following magazines in the field.

Ava Journal and News Bulletin, published quarterly by the American Vocational Association at 1010 Vermont Avenue, N. W. Washington, D. C. A good general reference.

Employment Security Review, published monthly by Social Security Board, Superintendent of Documents, Washington, D. C. Contains articles on population trends, job openings, unemployment and employment figures, etc.

Industrial Arts and Vocational Education, published monthly, except during July and August, by the Bruce Publishing Co., North Milwaukee Street, Milwaukee, Wisconsin. While this periodical is mainly of interest to workers in this field, there are general articles helpful in counseling.

Labor Information Bulletin, published monthly by U. S. Department of Labor, Superintendent of Documents, Washington, D. C. A very important reference.

Monthly Labor Review, published by Bureau of Labor Statistics, U. S. Department of Labor, Washington, D. C. Another important reference.

Monthly Vital Statistics Bulletin, Department of Commerce, Bureau of Census. Statistics relating to the industrial, commercial, and governmental life of the nation.

Occupations, the Vocational Guidance Magazine, published by the National Vocational Guidance Association, 525 West 120th Street, New York 27, New York. Articles on vocational guidance as a technic as well as on various vocational fields.

Survey of Current Business (weekly and annual supplements), U. S. Department of Commerce. Studies of business trends.

Vocational Guidance Digest, published monthly by Stanford University Press, Stanford University, California. A digest of material in periodicals and leaflets.

Vocational Trends, published monthly by Science Research Associates, Chicago, Illinois. A magazine covering employment possibilities and professional development.

Women's Work and Education, published four times a year—in February, April, October, and December, by the Institute of Women's Professional Relations, New London, Connecticut.

A Code System is Suggested by Which the Physical Classification of an Applicant and the Physical Requirements of the Job Are in Harmony with One Another.

Employing Physically Handicapped

By R. T. Mann

Consolidated Vultee Aircraft Corp.,
Vultee Field, Cal.

IF YOU are an employment man and you think you have reached the bottom of the barrel, it might pay you to take another look. This article does not pretend to be a panacea, but thoughtful consideration of its suggestions may help to supply you with additional man hours. The average employment man would surely agree that we are scarcely in a position to leave any stone unturned, no matter how small, in an effort to alleviate the manpower situation.

Need for Scientific Approach

THE acute shortage of labor that we have felt in the West Coast area for the past few months shows no signs whatever of improvement, and yet the manpower need continues to grow. It is only too apparent that we must not only take extra precautions to prevent or pass up any untapped or semitapped source of labor as well as to be absolutely certain that we are fully utilizing the manpower already acquired.

Consolidated Vultee has found that a scientific approach to the placement of physically handicapped workers is a very definite means toward this end. Many corporations have already employed a certain number of workers with major physical disabilities. While we can recognize and appreciate this more dramatic phase of the placement program, we are convinced that the so-called minor disabilities and limitations are a great deal more important. Principally because they concern a great many more people.

Employment men and department heads are prone to think of a physically handicapped individual as someone with a major or obvious physical defect. However, for practical purposes, in considering a program of this kind, we must recognize that the loss of the tip of a finger or slightly impaired vision or hearing actually constitute a physical handicap.

Wide Range Included

THINKING in such broad terms, our program becomes comprehensive enough to take in a wide range of so-called limitations or handicaps, and thus opens the way for greater flexibility in the actual placement of the workers on the job.

Before outlining the actual program itself, it would seem practical to clarify our objective. A preliminary survey would indicate that our object is three fold: To gain as many new workers as possible; to better utilize the abilities of present workers; and, to offer the most scientific and humane placement service possible to the men and women of our armed forces who are returning in increasingly large numbers with physical problems needing special consideration.

Our first problem, that of providing new workers, becomes not so much a matter of discovering an "Open Sesame" that would reveal hitherto untapped sources but rather that the small number of new workers that are available will be placed in the position which will completely and fully utilize their present and potential ability.

It is wise that the approach be made from the standpoint, not of making it easy for the physically handicapped, but rather to place them in a position on which, in spite of some minor or even major physical limitation, they will be able to produce on a competitive basis with the physically normal. It has been said that the handicapped person is like his fellows in far more ways than he is different. His physical disability may seem to be permanent but it is entirely possible to completely remove his vocational handicap.

The Get By Theory

THE customary reaction of the employment interviewer in many plants, when confronted with the physically handicapped individual, is to mentally go over the available jobs, in a not too scientific manner, in an effort to determine whether the person could "get by" on one of the jobs. Any success resulting from hiring methods of this kind is apt to be a matter of coincidence. There is too much chance in this situation that the individual will be placed on a job on which it is true he can "get by" but on which he can scarcely produce a really satisfactory amount of work. In addition, there is a possibility of endangering the safety record of a department by introducing workers in this manner.

It would seem necessary to have at the disposal of the hiring interviewer an entire, complete set of supplemental information to the job descriptions normally available. Information which will quickly and easily indicate to the interviewer the physical requirements of the job under consideration as applied to the physical classification of the worker. A very exact determination of each of these factors is necessary for a successful program.

Use of Present Workers

IN CONSIDERING the second phase of our program, how better to utilize present workers, it falls as a natural course of events that to ensure a completely effective plan a thorough survey should be made of physically handicapped workers who are already on the job to determine whether they might not become more productive if they were to be reassigned to jobs more compatible to their physical requirements.

This information, once obtained, will accomplish more than the obvious immediate purpose. It will prove to be a very helpful tool at such time that group transfers should be necessary. The plan being used here, of course, in the same manner as it applies to assigning workers to their original jobs.

Low Absentee Rate

THE importance of such procedures becomes more clear in the light of recent surveys on absenteeism and turnover. Our San Diego plant reports that preliminary attendance studies, made on the over one thousand men and women at that plant having physical limitations, have shown that the absentee rate among these people is less than one half of the average rate for the plant.

From a moral standpoint, tying in with reducing turnover, the resultant benefits of the program are obvious. The individual feels that a conscientious attempt has been made to place him on a job which he can properly handle. As a result, he will make a stronger attempt to stay with his job assignment.

We have had many expressions of gratitude, here at the Vultee Field plant, from those who were appreciative of the manner in which their particular physical condition was handled. Along this line, it has been found wise to be particularly careful in our attitude in dealing with these individuals. Any trace of false sympathy or pity must be thrust out and replaced with a feeling of sincerity and a conscientious desire to benefit both the individual and the company by intelligent placement.

The third item, that of guaranteeing a scientific, accurate and humane placement service for those returning from the armed forces might easily be considered our most important point. It will become obviously more important in the coming months as the number returning to this area becomes increasingly large. It is at this point that our moral responsibility for getting the ex-serviceman or woman on the right job surpasses even the more practical implications of the program itself.

The beauty of the program is that it constantly serves an imminently practical purpose while at the same time, in this particular respect, provides a full moral satisfaction. The same factors apply here as in the other two points we have considered. Their importance is simply crystallized and colored because of our obvious debt to this group. This one point alone would seem to completely justify the plan.

The Actual Plan

Now let us consider the actual plan. There are two prime factors involved in the placement program itself. The first concerns the physical classification of the worker. The second concerns the physical requirements of his new job. It will be seen that the same code numbers can be used for both purposes. The plan becomes only as complex as the number of jobs under consideration.

The plan in use at our Vultee Field plant was originally developed by Dr. Alfred C. Dick, Medical Director, and his staff, of the medical division of the Industrial Relations Department of the San Diego plant.

The letters A, B, C and D were used to indicate the general classifications of Heavy Sustained Labor, Moderately Heavy Labor, Light Labor and Very Light Labor, respectively. It is possible that a worker might be capable of doing heavy labor and still have other defects and limitations that would affect his work. These defects or limitations might include defective vision, defective hearing, skin sensitiveness, nervous instability and many others. Therefore, in addition to the A, B, C and D code classifications a series of numbers as a modification of this general code were set up.

Modification

1. Worker with monocular vision or severe visual defect.
2. Worker with severe defect of hearing.
3. Worker who should have partial sitting.
4. Worker capable of sitting job only.
5. Worker with poor coördination.
6. Worker with nervous instability.
7. Worker with sensitive skin.
8. Worker with one arm. (amputation)
9. Worker with hernia.
10. Worker with tendency toward developing hernia. (Relaxed rings, large abdominal scars.)
11. Worker with history of back strain or injury.
12. Worker with chronic illness. (cardiac lesions, nephritis)
13. Worker with aphrasic characteristics. (Senile)
14. Worker with arrested T.B.C., asthma, chronic bronchitis.
15. Worker unsuitable for climbing, working around dangerous machinery. (By reason of age, weight, or other factors—diabetes, epilepsy, hypertension, leg defects.)
16. Worker with partial limitation of one hand.

For example, a worker with defective vision and otherwise able to do heavy work would be coded "A-1." A worker capable of doing moderately heavy work but who is underweight would be coded "B-15," and a middle-aged worker with one eye, one arm and a hernia would be coded "C-1-8-9-15."

Applying Code Number

THE code for each applicant would, of course, be determined by the examining physician. This does not necessarily mean that it would be necessary to give the physical examination ahead of the placement interview. In most cases, the interviewer would be able to determine about what code the applicant would come under by the information provided on the application blank and from the interview.

It becomes necessary to re-interview and re-assign jobs only when the code number derived from the physical exam is found to be out of harmony with the physical classification of the job assigned by the interviewer.

At this point, the second factor in the placement program enters the picture; in other words, the physical requirement of the worker's new job. This factor includes a multiplicity of things we must know—whether the work is heavy or light, whether it involves climbing or continued sitting, whether toxic materials must be handled or if muscular coordination is necessary and many other factors.

Every large industrial plant has job classification and job titles. These job titles do not always mean the same thing. A job that one foreman will classify as light work another will justifiably classify as heavy and there will be a wide variation in physical factors for the same job titles from department to department Thus, someone other than the foreman must make the classification but he must work with the foremen to their satisfaction.

Accurate Job Classifications

USING the list previously set forth, each job in each department must be checked to determine how many of the sixteen factors listed a person may have and still be able to handle the job effectively. On many jobs, there will be only one or two factors present. On others there will be six or seven. The coding of the jobs will provide the same type of code as was indicated in the discussion above on physically classifying the workers.

The ultimate question then is simply one of seeing that the physical classification of the applicant and the physical requirements of the job as indicated by the code number are in harmony with one another.

The Recognition of the Fact that There is Need
for a Method of Predicting the Employment Possibilities of Individuals Has Led to the Development of an "Employment Expectancy Rating
Scale."

Employment Prospects

By BERNARD S. NEWER

Syracuse, N. Y.

N O WELFARE department has, so far as is known, assembled its data in such a
manner that it is of much value in predicting the employment possibilities
within a current case load. Such prediction seems absolutely basic to
sound planning in welfare administration.

If the administrator were able, at any time, to know how many in his case load
were, from an employer's standpoint, highly employable, how many moderately
employable, how many slightly employable, etc., it would be valuable information.
In the first place, it would give him some idea of what case loads to expect as the demand for labor increases or decreases. In the second place, within a certain margin
of error for which prediction is impossible, it would enable him to know which
individuals would have the best chances, little chances or practically no chances of
being selected by an employer.

Helps Budgeting

A NYTHING which may help the administrator to make more accurate advance esri-
mates of case loads is of prime importance in the field of budgeting—always a
nightmare to welfare administrators. Obviously, it is basic to sound personnel
administration and to all phases of management.

The usual classification of individuals into "employable" and "unemployable"
is simply a "pigeon-holing" process and, as such, offers little help in the case load
analysis needed for administrative planning. Indeed, to regard persons as either
"employable" or "unemployable" holds danger for the administrator because, as
often as not, it obscures the true employment possibilities of individuals rather than

emphasizing them. Probably, the most striking evidence is found today (July, 1944) when on every hand are "unemployables" obtaining employment. Obviously, the two categories are both static and sterile.

The recognition of the fact that there is need for a method of predicting the employment possibilities of individuals has led to the development of this "Employment Expectancy Rating Scale." The scale presents a method of foretelling the relative employment chances of an individual. Underlying the scale is the basic assumption that there are individual differences in employment expectancy. A corollary to this assumption is that employment chances basically depend on measurable characteristics of an individual. Of course, there are other factors, outside the individual, which have generalized effects on employment chances. "Economic conditions" is an example of this type of factor.

Specifically, our problem is to find out whether we can discover the degree of an individual's employability with reasonable accuracy, and so predict on the basis of his or her measurable characteristics the approximate expectancy of employment. The research we have done represents an attempt at the solution of this problem. The solution involves these steps.

Construction of a List of Characteristics

AFTER considerable research we found that there are sixteen characteristics almost universally considered relevant to employment chances. These characteristics are: Age, Experience, Unemployment (length of time out of work), Nationality, Dependency, Race, Religion, Citizenship, Physical Defects, Wages (weekly), Education, Prison Record, Termination of work (why left last job), Sex, Personality and Home Conditions.

Construction of a Questionnaire

THE characteristic "Age", for example, was broken down into twelve stages, such as "18-20" years, "21-25" years, etc. When we arrived at the specific components of all sixteen characteristics we were able to construct a scale questionnaire in terms of both the general characteristics and their components. This questionnaire provided a means of obtaining values, both for the component parts of the characteristics and for the characteristic itself in terms of the emphasis it has in the total picture of employment chances.

Selection of an Expert Group

THE judges selected were the personnel officers of all Onondaga County (N. Y) employers with over 100 employees and also the employment interviewers of the Syracuse office of U.S.E.S. The employers were divided into a "manufacturers' group" and a "business group."

Interest was shown by Mr. Leon H. Abbott, Onondaga County Public Welfare Commissioner, and he expressed a willingness to have the questionnaire mailed out under his endorsement. In addition, through his assistance, other community leaders' endorsement were obtained. Dr. Robert F. Steadman of the Syracuse University School of Citizenship supervised the study. Dr. Meredith B. Givens, Research Director of the New York State Division of Unemployment Insurance, gave excellent aid in the original construction of the scale.

Circularization of Questionnaire

RESPONSES to the questionnaire were received from 60 business employers, 44 manufacturers and 18 employment interviewers. Tabulation of the results was done separately for each group. Each rater valued each item on a scale from 0 to 10 "0" representing least employability, "10" maximum employability. The scale is known as the "employability scale." Each item in the questionnaire is given its proper location on the employability continuum by means of the same measuring rod. In this way it becomes possible to construct a rating scale based on the psychophysical method of "equal appearing intervals," since every item can be assigned a definite position on the same linear representation of the "employability continuum."

Composite Judgments of Expert Raters

TABULATION and checking of the items were done separately for the three groups: business manufacturers and U.S.E.S. The mean (arithmetic average) was chosen as the best central tendency measure for each item. This choice was based on the fact that the mean is the average which takes into account all values of the sample.

Wide divergence between the means of the three groups would have made it impossible for any single item to be considered representative of general employment practice for an item. However, in as much as great similarity is shown by the computed means (see graphs I, II and XI) an average of the three groups was computed. This is represented by a dotted line on the line graphs, shown.

Results

HE results of the ratings are as follows: (Notice that for no characteristic does the range of scores extend the entire length of the 11 point scale. For each characteristic there is a range of scores different from the range for any of the other characteristics.)

Age (see graph I): The score for this characteristic is highest for the item 26–30 years (8.9); it is lowest for the years "71 on" (0.6). For the group "18–20" the score is moderately high. It increases rapidly and mounts to its peak at "26–30." From this point is begins to decrease.

Experience: The score for this group is lowest for "no experience" (2.1). The scores increase rapidly as experience reaches 1-2 years (7.4). After ten years the "experience rating" becomes slightly lower (8.2). "Experience" indicates the

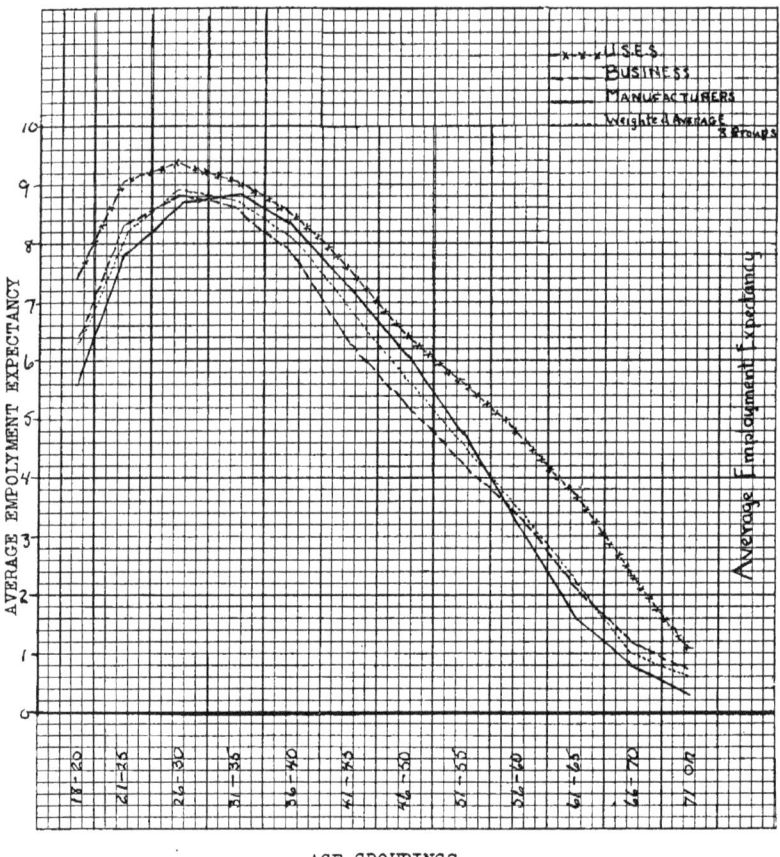

AGE GROUPINGS

CHART I. SHOWING HOW THE CHANCES OF EMPLOYMENT DECREASE WITH AGE (AFTER 30)

amount of time spent in a job, or jobs, for which some specific knowledge or skill is a requisite.

Unemployment: The highest score for this characteristic is for the item "0–3 months" of unemployment (8.3). The score begins to drop rapidly until the item

"10–11 months" is reached (5.0). From 1 year to seven years or more of unemployment there is a steady but slower decrease of scores. Unemployment here means the period elapsing from the loss of an individual's last private employment to the time he is rated.

National Origin

NATIONAL ORIGIN: American-born Canadians and those born in the British Isles have the highest scores. Scandanavians follow with 6.9. Polish, French and Germans have approximately the same scores. The lowest scores go to the oriental countries with a score of 1.7.

Dependency: Married with dependents have the greatest chances of employment (8.8). Next are single people with dependents (7.9). A single person without any dependents is preferred to the married individual whose spouse is working, with scores of 6.1 and 5.4 respectively.

Race: The highest score of 9.7 is obtained for the item "white"; Negro, Indian and Yellow are all low scores: 2.8, 3.2 and 1.8 respectively.

Citizenship: There is a rapid and constant drop from "American Born" (9.4 through naturalized (8.9) and "first papers" (5.4) the alien has a low expectancy rating of 2.1.

Physical Defects

PHYSICAL DEFECTS: With the exception of "normal health," all other scores are understandably low. For example, a person with "weight abnormality" would have a score of 4.3; Vision defect 4.0. The lowest score goes to the person who has syphilis, 0.9. These are only a few of the many under this characteristic.

Education: A person with a technical or business school training has the best chances of employment for this particular characteristic, the scores being 8.8 respectively. The college graduate runs a close second to obtaining work in industry. The lowest score goes to the person who has not completed grammar school. There are intermediate scores between college graduate and grammar school incompleted.

Wages: The person who was earning $26–$30 in the last six months prior to making application for another job has the highest chances of being reemployed, his score for this one item would be (7.3) (see graph II). The scores decrease consistently for both lower and higher wages.

Prison record: For all those who have prison records the expectancy scores are low for this characteristic. A person who had a jail sentence for a misdemeanor has a score of 4.1. Repeated felonies and repeated Federal offenses have scores of 1.6 and 0.6 respectively.

Termination of Work: If a person was laid off, he has the highest chances of being rehired (7.6). While if a person "quit" his chances are lower for this one item with a score of 6.2. If one is fired, he has the lowest chances of being rehired as far as this one item is concerned (score 3.1).

Sex: Males have a higher chance of employment than females with expectancy scores of 8.1 and 6.5 respectively.

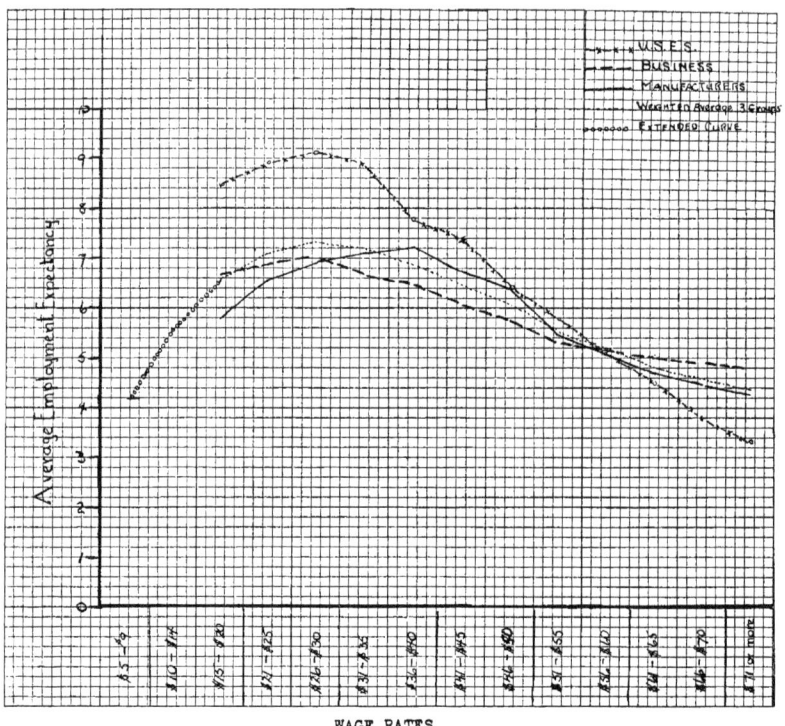

WAGE RATES

CHART II. SHOWING THAT THE CHANCES OF EMPLOYMENT VARY WITH THE WAGES ASKED

Personality: There are 28 items included in this characteristic. Some of these are: alert 8.9, cannot speak English 1.0, expresses self well 9.0, pleasant, 8.9, neat clean clothes, 8.7, sluggish, 1.9, dirty clothes, 2.4 and grouchy, 2.5.

Home Conditions: If a person has a good reputation he gets the highest score for this particular item, 9.4. If he is known to drink considerably, he gets the lowest score of 1.6. If his home is known to be dirty that person would have an expectancy score for this item of 2.8.

Scale in Action

IN ACTUAL application of this scale to a representative sample of the January, 1939 Onondaga County Public Welfare Home Relief case load was made.

The construction of a scale is, of course, an academic exercise until something can be told about its predictive value. Since this could only be done by actual test, the next step was to put the scale into use. The actual application of the test to individuals unemployed at the present time, was, of course, useless from a predictive point of view, as without following these individuals over long periods of time there would be no means of measuring the fulfillment of the prediction. As a consequence 206 individuals were rated as of January 1st, 1939, on the basis of case record information. In other words the scores of the 206 individuals were precisely the scores they would have had if our rating scale had been applied in 1939. Cases for which information was not definite for that time were of course rejected.

Actual Employment Experience

EVERY job held since January, 1939, was recorded for each of the 206 persons.

W.P.A. was considered as half employment since the worker is in a job but the job is not a result of employer selection. The employment criterion selected was the number of months the individual was employed between January 1st, 1939 and May 1st, 1942.

Correlation between Scores and Employment

THE Pearson Coefficient of Correlation between the scores for the 206 individuals as of January 1st, 1939, and the number of months they were employed was found to be $r = +.72$, P.E. $\pm .02$.

The high degree of relationship between scores and employment makes it possible to give popular meaning in terms of employment prospects to every score. These interpretations or "meanings" are simply defined and easily understood. A high score 85.0 to 100 "Excellent Chances" of employment; 75.0 to 84.9, "Good Chances" of employment; 65.0 to 74.9, "Fair Chances" of employment; 55.0 to 64.9 "Below Average Chances" of employment; 45.0 to 54.9 "Poor Chances" of employment; and 44.9 and below, "Very Poor Chances" of employment.

Use of Scale by Onondaga County

SO IMPRESSED was the Onondaga County Welfare Commissioner with our findings that 5000 scale forms were printed to be applied to the Onondaga County Case Load as of January, 1943.

However, along about this time the scale was criticized from the point of view, that if we included such characteristics as Race, Religion and Nationality, the scale could be considered as discriminatory. These characteristics were omitted only

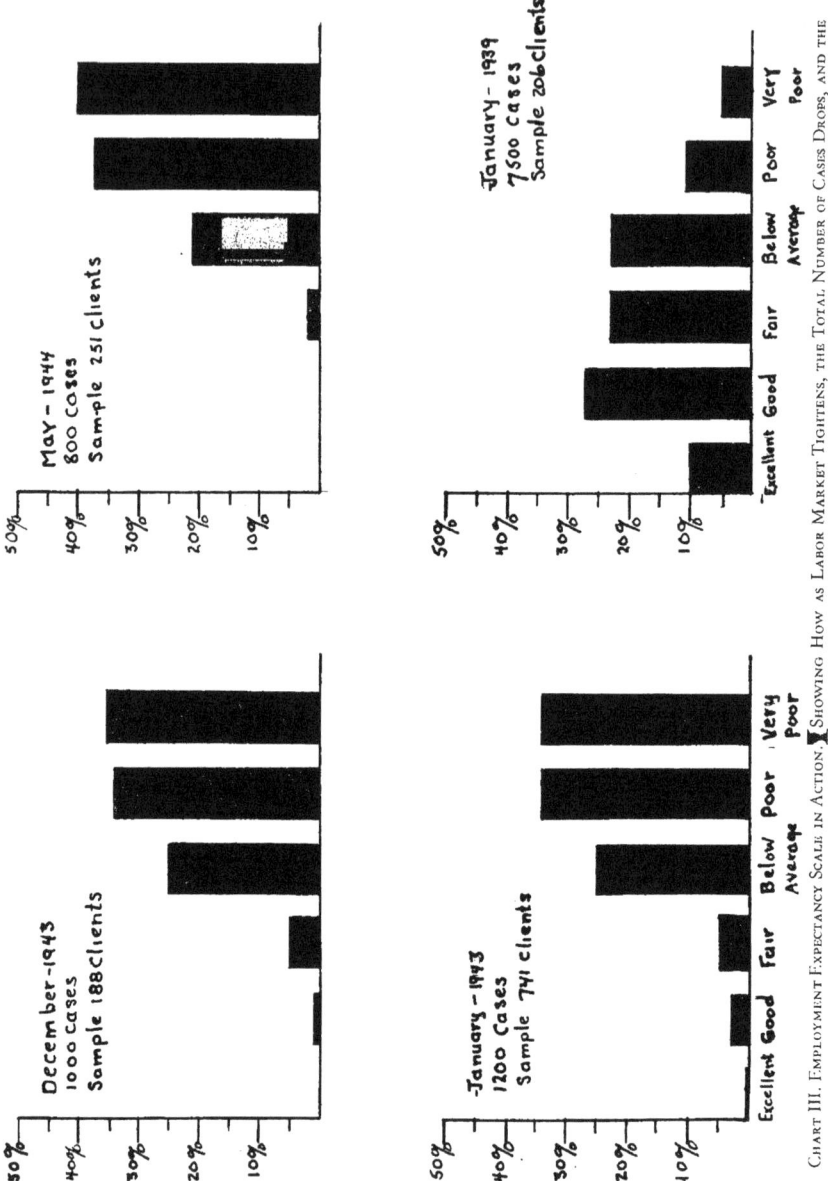

CHART III. EMPLOYMENT EXPECTANCY SCALE IN ACTION. SHOWING HOW AS LABOR MARKET TIGHTENS, THE TOTAL NUMBER OF CASES DROPS, AND THE

after the scale had been retested for its validity without these characteristics. We found that the exclusion of these characteristics did not injure the predictive value of the scale too greatly because their weight in the total score was not large. However, we do feel that, in the final analysis, the inclusion of these characteristics is not a fault of the scale but an acceptance, for predictive purposes, of factors affecting employability. Their exclusion would seem unrealistic especially since changes in scale construction cannot be considered to alter employer selection.

In January of 1943 the scale was applied by 80 case workers to their individual loads. The cases rated in January of 1943 were followed through May, 1944. Our prediction was, of course, that individuals leaving the relief rolls for private employment would leave in a definite score order: those rated with Excellent, Good and Fair chances of employment would be the first to leave. Should our present high employment situation be reversed, those individuals obtaining employment last could be expected to be the first to become unemployed.

If our present manpower shortage becomes more acute, employers will be forced to dig down further among those with lower scores. It must be pointed out, that none of those people who left the relief rolls for private jobs were referred for employment on the basis of the scale. The scale was kept strictly for prediction. Our main object is to show that individuals are accepted for private employment in a definite score order. In other words, individuals present varying degrees of employability.

Predictive Value

WHEN the scale was first applied by the 80 case workers in January, 1943 (see Scale in Action Chart) there were 1200 cases (approx. 2,400 individuals) of which a sampling of 741 individuals was taken (31% sampling). The December, 1943 case load consisted of about 1000 cases or about 2000 individuals. A 10% sample was taken of the December case load. A final sample of the May, 1944 case load was taken. This case load consisted of 800 cases. A 16% sample was taken.

The analyses made after the 80 case workers had rated the clients in their individual case loads, indicated that the scale had great predictive value. The Scale in Action chart shows that in May, 1944 there were no people with Excellent, or Good chances of employment left, while those rated as Fair constituted about 2% of the entire load. A February sampling (not shown) had indicated that there were left on the welfare rolls only about 4% with Fair chances of employment. The people with Excellent and Good chances were all gone by February.

We found that no particular characteristic in itself is the factor which will determine a person's chances of employment, but it is the sum total of all items of the various characteristics which determines that individual's chances of employment.

The scale should be of value to a welfare department not only from the planning aspect but also in the evaluation of the individual client. For the social worker there should be challenge in the client with a high score who does not find employment. Even in times of little employment, the individual with a score of 85 or over should not remain on relief for very long.

Ease of Placement

ANOTHER use of the scale would be in an employment agency. It would be possible, by means of the scale to determine which applicants they can easily place as jobs become available. More effort is needed in the placement of low scored individuals. If this group is to be placed at all they must be sent out repeatedly for interviews. This last is important because it must be remembered that the score is obtained from a scale on which there never was complete agreement on the part of the employers. While the majority of the employers would reject a particular low scored individual, nevertheless, the very fact that he has a low score indicates that his employment is not hopeless but merely difficult to obtain.

A survey of the labor resources of a community could probably be made from a combination of the scores in a welfare department plus the scores of job applicants in the U.S.E.S. office. This of course, would have to be interpreted as labor resources in terms of what the employers want. The actual labor force might be considerably higher than such a survey would indicate. However, from the standpoint of the employer interested in knowing what the community can offer him in terms of what he considers acceptable, it would be extremely useful.

Aid in Community Planning

FINALLY, as a community planning device, the scale would be a method which would help clarify what is meant by "full scale employment." Actually, the term "full scale employment" would seem a misnomer because it is only "full scale" from the standpoint that jobs are plentiful. The employer, however, continues to maintain his own standards and right of selection. There are still individuals whom he refuses to accept into his employ even though the job goes begging. In terms of the Employment Scale even the "Very Poors" would have to become employed in order that we might achieve "full scale employment."

In reality, there can be no such thing as "full scale employment" but actually a degree of employability that is planned to be maintained by a community or Government. That is, how many jobs of various types would we have to have, let us say to maintain the amount of employment we had in May, 1944 (see Scale in Action). The scale, of course, would be a sensitive instrument to determine if the level aimed at is being maintained. It could act as a barometer of employment trends that would give forewarning to prevent disastrous "slumps" and "recessions."

The Debate Has Lasted Long as to Whether or Not Employee Ratings Should be Made Known to Employees. Here is a Tried Plan by Which Employee Progress Reports are Made the Basis of Employee Counseling Looking to the Continued Progress of Employees.

Goodyear Aircraft Employee Counseling

By S. E. Fuller,

Goodyear Aircraft Corporation,
Akron, 15, Ohio

Our program of performance rating and personnel counseling was instigated for the most part by the great numbers and the variety of inexperienced people we were forced to hire from the labor market and the problems that arose when these people attempted to make an adjustment to new duties within a large corporation.

The problem was greater due to the lack of any comprehensive ability and temperament tests at the time of hire. This in itself has magnified the definite need for application of qualified selection tests under normal, non-war conditions. Moreover, the many divergent types of employees and the accompanying variety of cases to be corrected through personnel counseling has emphasized the benefits to be derived from employee ability development programs during peace-time business conditions.

Plant Expansion and Payroll Increase

On December 7, 1941 there were less than two thousand hourly and only several hundred salaried employees on our payroll. This group worked in a building covering eight acres. Eighteen months after Pearl Harbor a modern defense plant sprawled over five times as much acreage, providing a work shop for thirty-three thousand individuals.

At the peak of our hiring program 350 hourly and 100 salaried employees were hired per day and hundreds more visited the employment office daily. There were twenty-five people interviewing hourly applicants and ten placing salaried help.

Payrolls increased so rapidly that it was impossible to lay out parking grounds fast enough to provide space for employee cars. The City Transportation Company could not secure additional busses quickly enough to meet the increased demand for transportation to and from "Aircraft."

Draftsmen and designers were hired before tables could be provided for them, with the result that many original blueprints of bomber wings and tail surfaces were initiated on plywood surfaces supported at each end by makeshift wooden horses. Office employees frequently moved into buildings before heating facilities had been provided, thus necessitating the wearing of hats and coats if occupancy took place during the winter months.

It was a gigantic task providing sufficient floor space and the necessary equipment to get production lines moving, but these items could be manufactured, installed and soon utilized to their best working efficiency once the proper skill of operation and maintenance was applied. It was as great a task securing the necessary personnel and an even greater undertaking presented itself in the training, counselling and adjusting of human beings to jobs and to working in groups so that the best working efficiency of the individuals and the groups of which they were a part could be realized and maintained.

Relaxation in Hiring Requirements

HUNDREDS of defense plants throughout the nation expanded with the same rapidity that we experienced. As country-wide employment statistics soared and sources of industrial man-power dwindled, the armed services continued to drain millions of the most capable men from the labor market and from industrial jobs.

It was not long until labor scouts were combing the depths of the tightened market in an effort to fill employment quotas. Faced with the need for many more employees, selection lost most of its significance and physical requirements relaxed until many ailments which barred the path to acceptance during normal business conditions ceased to be reasons for rejection.

Employment of Many Divergent Types

EFFORTS to reach out further and further into more remote labor markets brought job applicants to our employment office from every state in the Union and a few from remote parts of the world. Many types of people and a wide variety of backgrounds offered us in the minority of cases training and experience which could be applied directly. A good example of our utilizing experiences indirectly was that of a violin teacher trained to be a time study man. It took considerable time to teach him shop methods and procedure, but clicking stop watches with his fingerboard hand, writing job breakdowns with his bow hand, and coordinating these two abilities with a vision sharpened by reading musical notes was an accomplishment of which experienced time study men became envious.

In the salaried division we hired insurance, motor car, piano, whisky and tobacco salesmen, lawyers, ministers, funeral directors, opera singers, models, hobby shop owners, coal dealers, musicians, school teachers and many others, outstanding of which was a man who had spent the previous nine years with the Eskimos.

Reasons for Seeking Employment

PEOPLE with such backgrounds and many others with similar occupational experiences comprised the bulk of employees hired to fill salaried jobs. Many came to our gates because material shortages in civilian goods industries forced them to seek other employment. Others were motivated purely by patriotic reasons or because they had relatives in the armed services. The hidden motive of still others was to postpone induction into the army. Many more individuals were attracted by the lure of money. A good share of the employees were pressured by the United States Employment Service to adjust from non-essential activities to essential war jobs.

Adjustment and Maladjustment

REGARDLESS of the reasons why people came to our plant, thousands were faced with a most difficult adjustment. Many adjusted quickly and in a considerable number of cases the most adaptable were promoted repeatedly to jobs beyond their own expectations. On the other hand many suffered distress in their struggle to find adjustment to an entirely new environment. For all instances where people found an opportunity to release dormant abilities and feel the satisfying surge of unimpeded action, there were just as many cases where maladjustment stunted initiative and mental turmoil ensued.

Those harboring unexpressed desires built up greater emotional instability until release was sought in detrimental ways. With no direction to their efforts, confusion resulted. Wonderments, starting with insignificant trifles, grew to unbelievable proportions. Trying to reconcile antagonistic emotions led to greater confusion.

Employees harboring this feeling of frustration possessed no real anxiety to report for work each morning. Those who were sick intermittantly were usually the ones who didn't like their work. If honest employee admissions had been made, this mental sickness would probably have proved to be the cause of more absenteeism than the common cold. Needing the money but also desiring to escape from the conditions under which it had to be earned, these persons were absent as much as their conscience would allow. While they were on the job, collision of the opposing desires affected efficiency adversely.

Effect of Deeply Embedded Habit Patterns

THE difficulty with some employees coming into the organization was that they had been employed in occupations to which through years of adaptation they had become emotionally adjusted and deeply trained to a particular set of habit patterns. Still others came from distant localities and found adjustment thwarted by homesickness and crowded living conditions.

Some individuals had never been inside a factory office before, or, even worse, had never worked with a group of people in any capacity. On the other hand some had suffered discontentment earlier in their lives when employed by large business organizations and had severed their connections to seek employment to which they were more emotionally suited. These certainly came into our organization reluctautly and with the premonition that a satisfactory adjustment would be most difficult if not impossible. A considerable number of salesmen prophesied that they would not be able to find any appreciable degree of contentment at a desk and would ultimately suffer nervousness and irritability.

Criticism and Faultfinding a Repercussion

THOSE whose minds dwelt on the inevitable, started their first day on the payroll with little hope of making a satisfactory adjustment. Most of their fears gave rise to a reluctance to try making an adjustment. Individuals with such self-assurance of failure were usually the first to find fault with others. Spending much time and energy criticising others unjustly became by-products of their inadequacy to make the change.

Individuals who criticised and talked suspiciously about fellow employees and their boss usually became more and more afraid of them. This led to a vicious cycle of criticism, because the more fearful an employee became toward dealing with others the more he exhibited a tendency to seek criticism as a weapon. The habit of voicing the weaknesses of other people was quite often an admission of the employee's incompetence to cultivate their friendship or to compete with them successfully for a position of leadership. Personality clashes between employees often ruined the efficiency and in extreme cases effected the health of one or both parties. Mental hazards of competition created tensions which in turn frequently led to upset stomachs.

Faultfinding obviously was a camouflage of fear and a bid for attention. Factual, constructive criticism was welcomed, but criticism most always became a clue to something wrong with the individual. This always became a challenge to a Personnel Department representative to delve deeper into the motivating reasons.

Personnel Counseling Needed

WE SOON began to realize that personnel counseling was definitely needed to destroy these seeds of criticism; to make many employees about face and go into action in correction of their own weaknesses instead of wasting time analysing the unworthiness of others. The employee feeling distress on his assigned duties usually desired to change these duties, the boss or his fellow employees, but not himself. Instead of improving his abilities and getting a desired increase in salary, he wanted to reach the goal by changing others. And employees suffering distress in their attempt to adjust from one occupation to a new set of job requirements quite often bred discontent in the employees working next to them.

Seeking release from the complex caused by a collision of opposing emotions these individuals became critical and grasped at the conviction that the boss didn't like them, the job was beneath their abilities, or that they were being exploited, underpaid and generally kicked around. The subconscious mind, taking advantage of their desire to relieve some half-perceived pressure, played tricks with their speech. Complaints of injustices and excuses for their own lack of accomplishment found reception and were transformed into sympathy by fellow employees.

Upon the frequency and intensity of these critical rumblings depends the magnitude of the personnel problem that arose. Many individuals were strong enough to weather the storm and find occupational satisfaction by forceful adjustment. These and others who never found equilibrium but kept their confusion submerged, went unnoticed. But the rumblings of some grew in volume until emotional instability took a firmer hold and then the Personnel Department had a first class personnel problem to solve.

Means of Identifying Personal Characteristics

THE realization that hundreds of salaried employees needed counsel and assistance in their job adjustment problems and that many more possessed abilities which were not being fully utilized prompted us to design a form to be filled out by supervision and utilized as a basis for personnel counseling. This salaried Employee Progress Report proved to be a sound approach to the problem and is currently being used with a considerable degree of success.

The Progress Report contains a comprehensive check sheet for investigational purposes. By means of this we identify inabilities, emotional traits and other factors affecting the employee's effort to make a satisfactory adjustment to his duties or to his group. This detailed investigation uncovers shortcomings and undesirable emotional traits which can be rectified through counsel and training. Wherever undesirable characteristics are identified, plans are made with the employee to help him in their correction.

We stress to all concerned that the program is designed to be of assistance to the employee in developing his abilities and in so doing to bring supervisors and employees closer together in a spirit of cooperation. Encouragement is given to discuss specific plans which will be of assistance in overcoming individual weaknesses due to inexperience or in the further development of outstanding abilities.

Initial Check-Up after 90 Days Employment

IT IS impractical to attempt a comprehensive appraisal of an employee's abilities before three months of continuous service has elapsed. So that maladjusted cases can be identified during this intervening ninety day period, every thirty days supervision fills out and returns to the Personnel Department a less detailed report of an employee's progress. This same procedure is applied to transfer cases involving the change of an employee from one position to another. The form contains items to be checked which are a condensation of those appearing on the check sheet.

Job Evaluation as a Foundation for Progress Report

IT WAS only logical that in designing the Progress Report we should consider judging an employee's abilities on the specified duties to which he had been assigned. The Salaried Job Evaluation Program offered a basis for this approach, since all duties contained in any one job are listed on the job description. This description contains a definition of approximately 200 words covering the general nature of the position and a separate section listing specific duties under the following nine elements: job knowledge, perception, analysis, creative ability, judgment, initiative, responsibility, contacts, and leadership.

The same nine job elements are also utilized as ability elements on the check sheet. By so doing we are able to make a thorough study of each employee's ability measured against the specified duties to which he has been assigned. Identification of factors in which the employee is weak leads to investigation of the causes behind these inabilities. We consider efficiency as a tenth element to indicate the extent to which individual is applying his proven abilities.

The Form

THE ten elements are listed on the left hand margin of the check sheet and each in turn broken down into ability factors. Descriptive statements opposite each factor and extending across the form to the right hand margin furnish guides whereby the supervisor can indicate the employee's degree of ability on the factor being considered. By listing in logical sequence thirty-six different factors, a comprehensive and detailed investigation of the employee's ability is secured.

The initial step in considering an ability factor is to determine which of the descriptive statements opposite it most accurately describes the employee's ability on that factor. Lines drawn perpendicular to the descriptive statements divide the check sheet into zones. These zones are provided to indicate degrees of ability upward or downward from the mid-point of the selected statement. The statements merely offer guides to locating more accurately the approximate zone in which the employee should be checked. A check mark is placed by the person judging the employee's ability in the zone most representative of the employee's current degree of ability. The further the employee is checked to the right, the greater his ability on that characteristic.

Check Sheet Objectives

THE important objective of the check sheet is to obtain all the pertinent facts. The comprehensive investigation may appear to be time-consuming but it does fulfill the necessity of identifying all factors before taking action. Spending considerable time in personal interviews with the employee is encouraged so that all factors can be weighed in the light of the individual's expression of opinion. These precautions most nearly assure the best possible solution before definite action is initiated.

Completion and Discussion with Employee

THROUGH trial and error we have arrived at several practical methods of securing the information we desire and in carrying out the discussion with the employee. The method used varies with the size of the department, types of positions to be considered and personalities involved. Frequently we ask the supervisor to check by himself, the employee's ability and performance. One difficulty to be overcome in this approach is that when working by himself the supervisor is apt to lose interest and hurry through the analysis once he finds that the check sheet requires time and tedious analysis. Others, willing to complete the checking satisfactorily but unable to express in writing what they mean to convey as substantiating evidence, or unwilling to establish written commitments which might be challenged by the employee, sometimes stop at this point.

Another method used is that of asking the supervisor to complete and discuss the form with the employee present. In this case the supervisor is apt to spend most of his time on the employee's good qualities and fail to touch very much upon basic causes of poor performance. The employee's presence seems to block any freedom of expression necessary to identify weaknesses at the root of the inefficiencies. An encouraging aspect of this method is that the supervisor and the employee are brought together and a closer understanding of one another motivated. Inserting a Personnel Department Counselor into this appraisal and discussion improves the quality and amount of information secured through his insistence on a more detailed analysis of the employee's abilities and inabilities. But again, with the employee present it is difficult to influence the supervisor into bringing to light the main issues causing inefficiencies

Independent Checking

IN SOME instances we require that the supervisor check the employee and the employee check himself both independently of one another. Then the two check sheets are put together for comparison in the presence of the counselor, the employee, and his superior. A most interesting conversation based on comparative checks results. Asking for two separate analyses in this manner is time-consuming and in some cases employees are hesitant to complete an appraisal of themselves, especially when it involves the possible admission of inabilities or weaknesses, but overall results of this method are very worthwhile.

A benefit of this method is that the employee, anxious to clear his mind of long held wonderments about his progress, presses the supervisor to action on his part of the plan. Delay between the checking and discussion is, therfore, further minimized. On the other hand supervisors welcome the employee's independent appraisal because it insures a greater degree of fairness and makes the discussion with the employee an easier and more cooperative undertaking.

When we desire complete assurance that proper interpretations are made of the included factors and also that sufficient substantiating statements are included, we request that both the supervisor's appraisal of the employee and the employee's self-analysis be completed in the Personnel Department with the help of a counselor. Besides accomplishing these two main objectives, the counselor becomes well acquainted with both the employee and the supervisor before any corrective measures are actually initiated.

Value of Employee Participation

THE employee's appraisal of his own abilities gives him an opportunity to help reach conclusions concerning duties on which he admits weaknesses and of which the supervisor is not aware. Conversely, the supervisor points out factors needing improvement that the employee may have never realized were of significant importance to spend time correcting. Wide differences in check marks for one factor, reflecting two entirely divergent opinions, offers an opportunity for frank discussion to arrive at the proper level of ability.

This often encourages open discussion on characteristics needing correction and the establishment of definite plans to bring improvement. By the same token low check marks frequently turn out to be based on misunderstandings and false impressions or due to problems beyond the scope of the job such as debts, housing conditions or homesickness which are easily corrected once the supervisor is made aware of them and offers his counsel.

Supervisional Capabilities Judged

ASKING the supervisor to complete the form with the assistance of a counselor presents a means of judging how well the supervisor knows the duties of the jobs under his supervision and also how familiar he is with the abilities of the employees assigned to these jobs. In one case a department manager could not complete the comprehensive analysis of his section heads because, as he admitted, he did not know the employees or the jobs well enough. He requested several weeks time so that he might study his employees and be in a better position to appraise their abilities satisfactorily. This delay caused embarrassment, especially since the section heads had completed their self-analysis and only awaited a comparison with the manager's opinion.

In another case a supervisor stated that his gradings certainly put him on the spot since there were many outstanding weaknesses checked on some of his sheets and he had never mentioned these to the employees. He stated that to mention these now would mean that the employee would ask, "Why haven't you told me these things before?" This implication is typical of what happens when a supervisor gets tied up in details and loses sight of his employees or just does not possess any human interest in the welfare of his subordinates.

Top Heavy Personnel

A supervisor who pointed out that an employee's volume was low, found it disturbing when the employee retaliated with the statement that he did not have sufficient work to do. More than one case of "top heavy personnel" or a need for a redistribution of duties came to light in this manner.

Another supervisor had graded an employee down on creative ability and the employee appraised his own ability in this respect quite high. Investigation, including an appraisal of the supervisor by his department manager, revealed that the employee possessed a good deal of creative ability but the supervisor gave all his employees the impression that he was not receptive to suggestions and was not desirous of spending time discussing any creative ideas.

Overloaded with too much detail work and not possessing the ability to delegate responsibility properly, the supervisor had erected a barrier between himself and his subordinates. Since the department manager should have worked closer with the supervisor to help him pass on details, here was a three party line not clear but noisy and inefficient.

(To be continued in next issue)

Too Many Labor and Personnel People Believe
You Can Learn All about Economics, Industrial
Relations, etc. in Six Easy Lessons. They Be-
lieve in Educational Capsules, Not in Developing
Maturity of Thought and Judgment through
Study with Experience.

Labor Leadership Training

By Donald S. Parks
University of Toledo
Toledo, Ohio

THE professions of labor leadership and personnel directorship have sprung up almost unnoticed in our society and are increasing in importance daily. Thousands of persons trained and educated for these professions will be needed in the years to come.

The glory of a democracy is the privilege of free speech, free competition, free enterprise. To preserve this democracy some sixty-five million people are working at a pace that has not been seen before in our country. The output of our industries has been raised to heights that seemed beyond belief a few years ago.

Trained Personnel Required

UNDER these circumstances, when disagreements arise as to wages, hours, working conditions, and employee representation, it is important that they be quickly settled. It is the duty of union officials and personnel directors to iron out these difficulties under the general rules of collective bargaining. In general this is being done very well and the great industrial machine is kept moving. It is far from perfect, however, and the public has the right to expect that the efficiency of the machine will be improved by the leaders in charge, both labor and management. The needs of people as citizens and consumers, as well as workers and producers, are involved.

After the war the problems will be even more difficult than they are now. *The unions will always be searching for new leaders, the industries for new personnel men and women.* In both cases those young men and women will be picked who have the ability, have studied the problems, and have made themselves proficient.

The University of Toledo offers a basic program preparing for these vocations as well as a number of specialized courses that may be taken as separate units by persons not wishing to complete so full a program.

Certificate in Labor Leadership

To MEET this demand for trained personnel the University of Toledo presents a definite program designed especially for those now engaged in labor relations work and those who wish to prepare for such employment. This includes labor union leadership, personnel work in industry and mercantile establishments, government employment in industrial relations, and work of similar nature.

This program, set up after consultation with distinguished leaders in the field, provides a solid background for such work. The courses selected for the Certificate in Labor Leadership, are, in the opinion of the committee the ones designed to do the most good in the least time. Many other courses are available, either for those who have completed the Certificate Courses or for those with specialized interests.

Basic Problem

This program includes eight courses taken two at a time over a period of two years, September to May inclusive, Monday and Wednesday evenings from about seven to nine-thirty. The program may be extended more than two years if desired.

Persons who complete this program are awarded twenty-four hours of University credit as well as a CERTIFICATE IN LABOR RELATIONS.

The subjects covered are as follows:

(1) English, written and spoken—because every labor leader has to make reports, write briefs and recommendations, and present his ideas orally to various groups. The instructors use text books, examples, report subjects, etc., in the fields of interest to students of labor.

(2) Economics, and Sociology—because to be a successful and wise leader in the difficult times to come, everyone hoping to qualify should understand the fundamentals of the economic system such as prices, wages, and employment; the problems of living together such as race relations, family relations, crime problems, housing problems, etc., that come under the general heading of sociology; and the historical development of our country both politically and from the labor point of view. The general principles of those subjects are taught with numerous examples and discussion of problems that are of special interest to organized labor, and industrial relations personnel.

(3) Government and parliamentary procedure—because if a person is to be effec-

tive in influencing legislation either public such as city, state or nation, or private as in a union meeting, or if he is to join a union-management negotiation, he must know something about these subjects.

(4) Statistics—because the efficient labor leader or personnel manager must understand something of the construction of cost of living index numbers, and the reading of financial statements.

(5) Law—One course will not make a lawyer, but it can give a person an insight into the legal processes and principles underlying contracts, workers' compensation and labor laws.

The above program is a fairly difficult one and will require energy and determination to complete. But it is in no sense an impossible one for a person of ordinary intelligence, it can be broken up into small units and spread over a longer time if desirable. These courses should help anyone who takes up these professions as a life work.

Student Research

THE Personnel Management Class, composed of Senior students at the University of Toledo, as a research problem interviewed (in May, 1944) forty employers, organized labor leaders and public-government officials as to their opinions concerning the following questions:

1. What subjects would you include in an ideal training program for labor organization members, trades, and personnel employees of industry?
2. Who should teach such a course?
3. How long do you believe such a training course should continue?

The students interviewed an average of five persons (three union and two employers or three employers and two union leaders). Interviews of this type provide data for use in curriculum changes by the University, and give the students an opportunity to make practical application of some of the principles studied in such courses as Labor Problems, Personnel Management, and Industrial Relations.

Labor leaders contacted were men and women holding positions of responsibility in the A.F. of L. or the C.I.O. Employers included proprietors, personnel directors, executives of public utilities, and corporation executives. The public reactions came from executives of the U.S.E.S., W.M.C., an executive of the former Toledo Peace Board, and a regional member of the W.L.B.

Similarity of Thought

THE reactions have been tabulated. A comparison of the replies to the question "What subjects would you include in an ideal training program for labor organization members, trades, and personnel employees of industry?" indicated a similarity of thought at several places with emphasis on Labor Problems, Labor Law, Economics, English and Public Speaking by labor leaders. Labor Problems, English, and Accounting are considered important by executives and employers. Reactions by the public were not enough different to justify separate compilation.

The reactions were not guided, the interviewers did not suggest ideas for courses or classifications. In compiling the results I have used the same terminology as the one giving the information and have simply arranged them in vertical columns for comparison.

Although the sample was limited to the City of Toledo, I believe those interviewed were average or better as representative of their groups. From a study of the tabulations, I believe some trends are to be observed.

Subjects to be Included

QUESTION 1: What subjects would you include in an ideal training program for labor organization members, trades, and personnel employees of industry?

Labor Problems, Labor Law, Economics, English and Public Speaking appear to be basic subjects favored by union groups.

Labor Problems, English, and Accounting are favored by the employer groups.

Who Should Teach

QUESTION 2. Who should teach such a course?

Both groups indicate a wish that such a program have as teachers individuals with practical background and experience as well as a thorough knowledge of theory. Class procedure should utilize speakers from the community as well as faculty. Short papers, plenty of discussion and conferences system of instruction seems to be types of presentation that appeals to those interested in such a program.

How Long a Course

QUESTION 3: How long do you believe such a training course should be offered?

There is evidence in this report that long programs will have difficulty in holding interest. It is evident that the time element may deter a large enrollment, and that the best of instruction must be offered to hold interest.

Either the individuals interviewed did not recognize the scope and depth of such a thorough program, or the G.I. type of education is the prevailing trend of the day, for there seems to be a desire to know all concerning this problem in a few weeks.

Supplementary Explanation by Author

IN QUESTION 3, when I refer to G.I. training, I had reference to the quick, short, visual, educational training program. I think that type or types of training have their place, *but in peace time when we are building for constructive, long trend foundational work, I wonder if it can be completed in 6, 8 or 12 weeks.*

In talking with returning veterans, too many of them because of the intensive training courses taken by the military, believe that you can get a new career in a few intensive lessons. It is true you may learn an operation that way, even a job perhaps, but does one get a career that way.

Too many labor people believe you can learn all about the economics system, the industrial organization of today, law, business cycles, etc., all in 6 easy lessons. They believe in educational capsules, not in developing maturity of thought and judgment through study with experience.

Book Reviews

Book Review Editor, MR. EVERETT VAN EVERY
California Personnel Management Association, Berkeley, Cal.

A SUMMARY OF MANUAL AND MECHANICAL ABILITY TESTS

By George K. Bennett and Ruth M. Cruickshank. New York. Psychological Corporation. 1942. 75 pp. Price 50¢

Reviewed by Forrest H. Kirkpatrick

This helpful compilation is the first draft of a report upon tests of manual and mechanical abilities, and is published in duplicated typescript as a matter of expediency. The foreword explains:

> "The present review has as its purpose the objective description of available tests of mechanical aptitude or ability and the summarization of the application of these tests to various types of selection and guidance situations. In doing this, the needs of several groups of people have been kept in mind. One group includes those teachers and administrators who are counselling students preparing for or ready for suitable employment. Another group is made up of those engaged in personnel selection in industry. A third group consists of those research workers interested in the analysis of human abilities for whom this survey will provide reference to some of the background material in this particular category."

The tests are classified as follows: (1) Mechanical ability—paper and pencil tests, (2) Mechanical ability—performance tests with apparatus, (3) Manual ability—mainly performance tests with apparatus. A general description is given in the Introduction, viz:

> "An individual description of a larger number of these tests, standardized to some extent for American populations, is given in a later section. . . . These test summaries include such pertinent information regarding each test and its applications as would be of help in determining whether a test should be examined more thoroughly for use. There are probably some tests summarized which are of limited value, and there are probably a number of other tests listed by titles which, upon further experimental use, may prove of greater intrinsic worth than others now available."

Each test treated in full is clearly and concisely set out, under complete reference headings—author, publisher, age range, date, approximate price, scoring method, testing and scoring times, type of test, and test content. Standardization is given under: Reliability, Validity and Application. A list of articles or references, under the heading Reviews and Research, is given for each test.

One section deals with the prediction of vocational success as related to tests of mechanical and manual ability. Prediction of success in the fields of engineering and physics, and of dentistry, medicine and surgery, is discussed, with some tables of correlations in the use of tests. A short section relates to the use of manual and mechanical tests in vocational selection.

Another section of the review is devoted to problems in the measurement of mechanical and manual ability, in which the effect of practice upon performance, determination of validity, establishment of a critical score, and sex differences are noted. Following the test summaries, the survey is completed by a list of annotated titles of other tests which, for various reasons, it is not thought necessary to summarize fully in the present publication.

A table of general references, other than the bibliography attached to each test summary and an alphabetical Index of all tests referred to, is also included. This publication will be helpful to personnel and employment officers interested in testing.

HAVE YOU SPARE PERSONNEL JOURNALS?

Some issues of the Personnel Journal (as listed below) are required by war industries, but are out of print.

If you have copies of these issues, which you are not now using, will you kindly return them to us, so that we may send them out to the companies requiring them. We will pay full price for them.

Vol. 22, No. 7. January, 1944.
Vol. 22, No. 8. February, 1944.
Vol. 22, No. 9. March, 1944.
Vol. 22, No. 10. April, 1944.

Personnel Research Federation
60 East 42nd St.,
New York, 17, New York

PERSONNEL
Journal

The Magazine of

LABOR RELATIONS AND PERSONNEL PRACTICES

Published by PERSONNEL RESEARCH FEDERATION

Lincoln Building, 60 East 42nd Street, New York City

Volume 23   *Number 5*

Contents for November 1944

EDITORIAL BOARD

Upon Our Ability and Willingness to Give Our
Returning Men a Good Deal—Not a New Deal—
Depends the Preservation of Our American Way
of Life. These Three Papers Indicate the Problems and Offer Solutions.

Returning Servicemen:
I. Personnel's Preparation *for*

By Frank Livingston

Liggett Drug Company,
New York, N. Y.

Attendance at current symposiums indicates the Personnel Directors' vital
interest in the veteran problem. But the phrasing of the questions from the
floor sometimes indicates that an unhealthy percentage of the interest is only
in how to escape our legal and moral responsibilities. This is wrong! For an
honest approach to the problems of the returning veteran must be problem Number
One for all of us.

We should, therefore, prevent by positive advice to management and through
propaganda media, the abuse of veterans by industry and/or the government before
it gains any further headway.

Industry's Moral Responsibility

The very theme and principle behind all Personnel post-war planning should be
the prevention of abuse of the returned veteran by either the government and/or
industry. Abuse can be in two possible, yet obvious ways: Abuse by political
demagogy, which will make community, state or Federal charges of G. I. Joe and
Jane to satisfy the party's crying need of repetitive votes. Then there is the abuse
by industry—which impregnates demagogy—when it circumvents or tries to circum-
vent, its public law responsibilities under the Selective Service Act. An industry's
prime responsibility—and it is a moral one—should be to do everything possible to
rehire returned veterans, regardless of the Selective Service Act, even if we must
create new jobs for them.

A refusal to rehire veterans, with or without reemployment rights, may be genuine or it may be specious, based on the Personnel policy of the firm. But why should Personnel workers recommend that management lean on legislated "outs"? Aren't our Personnel relations really genuine? Don't they support the suggestion that we, for the most part, owe our economic survival to our returning employees?

With that in mind, all Personnel workers should recommend to their management, that they be allowed to make an inventory of future labor needs before the inevitable V-Day that must be ours.

Design for Labor Inventory

THE labor inventory should be based on a study of our Personnel usage and turnover for approximately five years prior to Lend Lease—since Lend Lease was an economic thrust felt by all industries.

Upon completion of the labor usage inventory, the next step should be the compilation of the number of our employees now in the services, if this is not already known.

It is to be expected in war expanded firms, that the peace time needs will be less than the total of the present number of employees, plus the number now serving their country.

So let all Personnel Departments prepare and mail to each former employee in the armed services (including the Merchant Marine) a questionnaire, the basic theme of which should be THE FUTURE. It should contain adequate questions so that the individual answering can indicate what he or she wants to do upon being mustered out. (e.g. Do you want to return to your old job? A new one? What kind? How much training have you for that new job? How much refreshing for the old job? What branch are you in now? Do you prefer to continue in the armed services? Do you want more education? Will you be coming back here to live?)

The questionnaire should be sent to the families of our employees, asking them to forward it for us. The family would have the most recent address of our former employee and it would let the family known that we too are waiting for the G. I. Joes and Janes of our industrial family to "hurry back."

A statistical analysis can be prepared from the resulting questionnaires. It will give each Personnel Department some idea of the former number of employees who are going to look to them for jobs upon returning home.

Adjust Results to Release Problem

AN ACTUAL mathematical survey of present employees as to seniority must also be made and compared with those now serving. If the seniority records indicate that a number of our present employees will be challenging the returned veteran, an established policy of absorption of the veteran and release of present employees should be promulgated. But this *release* should be encouraged first on a voluntary basis. Let's begin with questionnaires to women employees, for instance, asking if they expect to return to their home life, former jobs or select other types of employment in fields usually exclusive to them, when their G.I. Joes come marching home again.

The number of males and females of veteran status that we cannot possibly absorb, should be made known to the proper Federal Agency, perhaps through the present Selective Service Reemployment Service or the United States Employment Service.

Servicemen Who Want Change of Job

THE questionnaires of the employees who say they want other fields could be turned over to the United States Employment Service, where occupational specialists and statistical services, such as exists in the Department of Labor in each state, can begin the compilation of directive data for the post-war planning boards that will control our return to peacetime industrial output.

The USES are statutorily charged with interviewing and placing the returned veteran who is without a job, so we should insist on their being in a position of responsibility and in a cooperative position with us for the acceptance and exchange of data. Or, if we, as Personnel people, exchange information with one another, we can forward the questionnaire to the related industrial group. Even better, if our post-war planning indicates a need for labor, we can make known our needs to fellow Personnel workers and be ready to absorb their overflow.

The protection of the rights and reception of the returned veterans who state they are coming back to us, must be organized under the guidance of experienced Personnel workers.

We should see that the reception of returned veterans should commence with educational releases, in our professional trade and employee journals, on how to behave toward returned veterans, handicapped or luckily unscathed. We should point out that the sooner the veteran returns in spirit to the industrial family, the sooner can the veteran be expected to fall into full production efficiencies.

Handicapped Veterans

JUST as the informational media should commence now, so too should a physical and emotional demands study of all jobs be made in order to absorb the handicapped veteran. This study is necessary so that the emotional and/or physical capabilities of the veteran and the emotional and/or physical demands of the job can be matched. The veteran should not be experimented with. Employment Managers should be sent to recognized training centers so that they may learn how to make physical demands studies of jobs. Once these studies are completed, they should be made a part of the Medical and Employment Department records for mutual counseling.

If our firm is large enough to expect a large absorption of veterans, we should recommend the services of a consulting psychiatrist or a psychologist for two reasons:

(1) Personality changes in the former employee must be made known to Personnel workers and responsible people in management. We must be prepared to assist our former employees and newly-hired veterans over that period of restlessness, which all normal individuals go through after release from a regimented life.

(2) The services should also be used for the training of supervisors in how they can adjust to and assist veterans. How to handle them. How to be watchful for indicative traits that may be preludes to personnel troubles.

Problems of ReadJustment

IT MUST be admitted that many young men will be mentally maladjusted for some time after the culmination of the war. Proper handling of their individual problems by the foremen, and all brackets of supervision, is essential to their welfare. Improper supervisory attitudes can bring on many quits, clashes of personality, and give rise to professional veterans, who will be challenging, both men and women this time, with "What did you do while I was in uniform?".

And the political demagogues are waiting for just this type of "professional" veteran.

A great deal of the success or failure of the accepted post-war Personnel plans will be in the hands of our supervisors, so we must help them to be wary of any attitudes that may be interpreted as unsympathetic. They must be trained to work with, assist and retrain all veterans who come under their supervision. Too much stress cannot be placed on this facet of all our planning.

Where a medical department exists, but the services of a psychologist will not be available, the Personnel Director should suggest that the industrial medicos should exchange experiences, do research, write up their experiences in their professional journals and review the wealth of psychological material written about World War I veteran experiences. In this way, they can give professional guidance to veterans, Personnel workers and supervisors alike.

Job of Personnel Department

IF THERE is no medical department, the work should be delegated to us. And we should be already seeking experience in handicapped interviewing and veteran personnel adjustments. Our trained interviewers, in the smaller plants, should also be entrusted with the training of management in what will be expected of them in absorbing existing techniques for handling the physically and mentally handicapped, as such, and the veteran as a personality.

As Personnel people we could also train some of the already returned veterans to act as Counselors on the operating floors. It works. There is only one weakness, because of the organizing type of personality. He'll want every veteran to join his national group and not all returning veterans are joiners.

We should see that refreshening courses are prepared for our returning employees, regardless of the physical or emotional demands of the job. The decision for formal training or on the job training must be made by each of us in light of our own industry. But a time for "refreshening" must be definitely allowed for, so that our veteran can recapture lost skills or absorb such new techniques as have been developed in his absence.

Within the Hospital Jobs

All Personnel workers, in industries where it can be done, should be informing management of its moral responsibilities under our democratic system, to contact veteran hospitals and see what part of its present products or services can be performed by the still undischarged and hospitalized veterans. Many handicapped veterans will be heartened by doing work and making the same wages as in-the-factory workers for the same services rendered. What can be better than that feeling of usefulness—plus the check from a recognized industry—what better proof for the handicapped veteran that he can be absorbed by industry.

Can't you do something there immediately? Many psychoses are developed in fighting men who are fearful of being so injured they will be economic charges on their families for life. None want to be the "wounded veterans" depending on an apple or a newspaper stand! They'll want to work! So kill the phobia of uselessness by these "within the hospital" jobs—it can be done. Inventory your jobs, then dilute the work and send it out in trucks. Then call for it. Pay the handicapped veterans standard wages.

What greater gesture toward these young men, who have placed Democracy in debt to them, could we Personnel workers make than awakening in management this contribution to G.I. Joe and Jane's usefulness.

No Exploitation of Veterans

And we do not stop here, we go on! For the veterans, our employees, will be always looking to us, their Personnel people, to see that they are accepted into the industrial fraternity of workers and not exploited as "veterans."

We must not, we dare not, let them down. Or we shall have won the Global War only to revitalize and nurture Ism's hydra-headed germs,here at home.

Remember! World War I veterans marched on Washington and dispersed when commanded. If they are organized and march again with their sons of World War II beside them, and their sons' buddies, and go home when ordered, Democracy shall have escaped miraculously, because our sons, fathers and brothers have been trained to kill, to follow a leader and to obey commands pronto and without question. They will come back that way. Some come back anti-civilian by training and remain that way.

When our employees were inducted into the armed forces, their last contact in many cases, was with the Selective Service representative in our Personnel Department. Upon attaining veteran status, if they are going to return to their former employer or seal a new connection, it is reasonable to assumed that they will make their first contact with our staff members.

As a matter of fact, according to more than one administrative member of Veteran agencies, they and the veteran are looking directly to the Personnel Directors for plans that will assure G.I. Joe and Jane a future in private employment.

Torch Handed to Us

THE torch has been handed to you Personnel Directors. The veterans expect you to be ready for them. To have plans ready for their return to the industrial family'' has been heard by more than one Personnel worker, while attending symposiums on the returning veteran.

Consider what fifteen million organized veterans could do, if industry and government should gamble, as it did after World War I, with its responsibilities again, and the anti-civilian veteran follows the wrong kind of leadership. Industry shall lose, of course. But we as a profession, can expect only the worst for not having done our utmost to prevent this over-all exploitation by government and industry in its experiments with ways to get around their legal and moral responsibilities.

The building of good will against such an organized march should commence immediately, and it should be done under the leadership of the Personnel workers.

II. Northwestern National Life Program

A PROGRAM for returning service men that is not a recruiting program but which seeks to help the man get placed in the civilian occupation in which he is most likely to succeed has been announced by Northwestern National Life Insurance Company of Minneapolis.

The program, designed to help the man who may be uncertain about his personal post-war plans as well as the man who definitely wants to rejoin the company's agency forces, is outlined in a printed brochure which has been sent to all fieldmen in the armed forces, with a letter from President O. J. Arnold. The letter says, in part:

Letter to Men in Armed Forces

WHILE self-interest might suggest the company should aim to induce every fieldman now in service to resume his career with NwNL (and the more who desire to return, the more gratifying it will be to me personally), the opportunity to build NwNL's agency manpower to high levels after the war is not the motivating idea behind this program. This is not a recruiting program. The real objective is to see to it that you find the spot where your abilities and interests may be most fruitfully used to your own and your family's best welfare—whether that be with NwNL or in some new field of endeavor."

The program has three phases:

(1) *Vocational Guidance* to help fieldmen in service decide correctly on the most promising type of post-war career fitted to their interest and aptitude. The company will prepare for each man a complete analysis of his earnings prior to going into service, together with a market analysis, analysis of production frequency and average sale and other pertinent data. It has arranged for each returning man to take Vocational Interest tests prepared and analyzed by Dr. Edward K. Strong, Jr., head of Vocational Interest Research at Stanford University.

(2) *Re-establishment with NwNL* for those who return, offering retraining at a Home Office school after an adjustment period of 60 to 120 days. This will be followed by special service compensation during a stabilization period of one year, in recognition of the special service required to re-contact and review the status of their clients.

(3) *Assistance in placement* for men who decide on a new career, with employment agency fees paid by the company.

Exchange of Data

THE company is undertaking an intensive canvass of its operating territory to uncover other firms who will exchange data on their employment needs.

This three-point program also applies to all home office and branch office employees in service, except for the special service commission. Salaries of employees who left for service will reflect increases made in their absence for the type of work involved so that no employee in the armed forces will have lost out on normal advancement while in service. In the case of employees also, the 40-day re-application period in the Selective Service Act is waived and the program will be held open and available to any service man who elects to take advantage of the educational provisions under the G.I. Bill of Rights.

In announcing the program Mr. Arnold said: "In our view, the problem is not merely one of attracting back to the company a group of promising agents. If this were the problem, the company might well limit its offer of re-training and stabilization assistance to men whose past records were outstanding. But NwNL recognizes a responsibility which runs beyond merely getting its good men back.

"The real problem involved is one of seeing to it that all these men whose careers were interrupted by the war are properly re-established in civilian life, whether or not it be with, and for the benefit of, NwNL.

Only 25% Returning to Previous Jobs

RESEARCHES have currently shown that only about 25 per cent of discharged veterans are returning to their former jobs in American industry. While we expect to better this ratio greatly, changes are bound to occur in the thinking, the standards, and the viewpoints of many young people subjected to the radically different environment of army or navy life, the broadening effects of travel, and many other influences new to them. Some will want their old jobs back; some will not; many will be undecided. It is only realistic to recognize, therefore, that practical assistance for these returning veterans should go beyond placing those who clearly want to return to the company, and cover also such assistance as can be rendered and will be acceptable to those who may wish to seek employment elsewhere.

"In thinking about returning life insurance agents, this attitude appears to be doubly important. Not all the life insurance men who were under contract before they entered service were successful men with established careers before them. Many previously successful men may return with a feeling of restlessness or an uncertainty of purpose which may prove distinct handicaps in re-establishing themselves in a business which requires the high degree of self-management and singleness of purpose characteristic of highly successful insurance career men. To welcome a man back to a chance at a failure or mediocre success certainly is not a proper discharge of duty in this case; while to pre-judge the man's chances for success and refuse to restore his contract would likewise be less than a discharge of the company's obligation.

Do Not Welcome Back to Failure

T̤O PUT it briefly, the company wants every returning agent to be re-established in a successful life insurance career; but the company would prefer to help a man in some other career where he will be happy and successful than it would to induce a returned service man into a prolonged and costly failure in life insurance selling."

HAVE YOU SPARE PERSONNEL JOURNALS?

Some issues of the Personnel Journal (as listed below) are required by war industries, but are out of print.

If you have copies of these issues, which you are not now using, will you kindly return them to us, so that we may send them out to the companies requiring them. We will pay full price for them.

Vol. 22, No. 7. January, 1944.
Vol. 22, No. 8. February, 1944.
Vol. 22, No. 9. March, 1944.
Vol. 22, No. 10. April, 1944.

Personnel Research Federation
60 East 42nd St.,
New York, 17, New York

III. War-Damaged Nerves

By Doncater G. Humm

Los Angeles, Cal.

RECENTLY the number of servicemen who are being discharged because of mental breakdowns under war conditions has sharply focussed the attention of personnel men on a serious problem. Various reports of the percentage of men so discharged, ranging from twenty to fifty per cent of all discharges from the services, have been published. As a consequence, employers are wondering to what extent these returned men are going to be an upsetting influence in the post-war period.

This problem makes necessary a frank review and estimate of the situation. If conditions promise to be much worsened, management should know the extent and should also know the preventive measures needed. If the situation promises not to be greatly affected, management needs reassurance.

Optimistic View

WHILE the actual situation probably falls somewhere between these two alternatives, it is likely to be closer to the second than to the first. In other words, it is our opinion that the presence of workers with greatly impaired mental health will not impair the post-war situation as seriously as might be expected.

In order to make this clear, it is well to consider the following questions:

(1) What is normal mental health?
(2) What has happened to cause these breakdowns?
(3) What will be their status in the post-war period?

Let us first consider what is normal mental health. This is a term applied to mental well-being. A person in good mental health is free from mental disorders. As a result, he is able to make a good adjustment to his family life, his social life, and his job situation. He is able to earn his own living; get along with his friends, acquaintances, and fellows; and keep out of serious difficulties with those in authority.

Perfect Mental health Rare

PERFECT mental health is as rare as perfect physical health. Hardly anyone is so free from some quirk of disposition or temperament as never to get crosswise with life to some extent. This tendency of the average individual occasionally to get into difficulties has led to many misstatements relative to the sanity of normal people. As a result, the popular impression is that all of us are a little mad and the mental health of no one is to be trusted. Such sweeping statements are vicious—the more so in that they are so pat.

The fact is that extremely few individuals stand any danger whatever of needing care in mental hospitals and that the great majority of persons will get along acceptably well in spite of occasional and temporary temperamental flare-ups.

The criterion of mental health accepted by most students of the subject is the extent to which the individual is the master of himself.

Individuals who have the temperamental integration so to command, regulate, and control their behavior tendencies as to be able to adjust to life situations without more than occasional outside interference or assistance may be considered to be normal in mental health. Persons who require a great deal of help or regulation may be considered to have impaired or handicapped mental health. Persons who require treatment or confinement in institutions or similar care may be considered to be disabled in mental health.

Definitions of Problem Cases

IT is necessary to use these three distinctions in conditions of mental health for the reason that terms in common use often have one meaning in scientific usage and another in popular usage. Some, in fact, do not have a clearly agreed upon scientific meaning. Some examples may be pertinent.

> Insanity usually is a legal term, referring to the condition of persons committed to institutions because their mental state makes them unable to care for themselves or dangerous to themselves or others. Popularly, it refers to those incapacitated by mental disease.
>
> Psychosis may mean any mental state or condition, but it also refers to the condition of persons with serious mental disorders, such as dementia praecox. Psychopathic may refer to any mental disorder or disease, but it is often used to indicate less serious conditions which do not require commitment.
>
> A neurosis is a nervous disease which is not dependent on pathological change in the tissues, but the term is often used popularly to indicate mildly psychopathic conditions.
>
> A war neurosis is a nervous disorder arising in conditions of warfare. It is sometimes used, however, as a pseudonym for serious psychopathic conditions to which war conditions have contributed little.

An illuminating description of the incidence of various conditions of mental health is afforded by a statement of statistical expectancy. It is particularly valuable in determining what is the usual or customary incidence of such conditions. For that purpose, statisticians agree upon the use of the range of the middle fifty per cent as the range of average occurrence.

Amount of Strain Endurable

FOR convenience this expectancy is presented in a table. The table considers various conditions of mental health, their expectancy in peace time, and the amount of strain persons with such conditions are capable of enduring.

Expectancy of Various Degrees of Mental Health in Peace Time

Condition of Mental Health	Fre- quency	Amount of Strain Capable of Standing
Exceptionally superior	2%	Extreme
Very superior	7%	Very great
Superior	16%	Great
High average or mediocre	25%	Average
Low average or mediocre	25%	Average
Poor	16%	Little
Very poor	7%	Very little
Extremely poor	2%	Almost none

Study of this table and state hospital reports is very illuminating. State hospital reports show that only one-half of one per cent of the population is to be found in institutions for the care of mental disorders. About three times that number in addition, or one and one-half per cent, are in the same mental condition or very close to it.

An additional seven per cent of persons have such poor mental health that they are likely to have upsets with very little provocation. Under severe or prolonged strain, such persons may have serious breakdowns. Still an additional sixteen per cent have poor mental health and are able to endure little strain.

These three groups of individuals have furnished most of those who have been discharged because of war breakdowns. The most seriously affected are very seldom accepted for military duty; the next group are also largely excluded. Most of the breakdowns occur in the group designated "Poor" in mental health.

The reason so many men have broken down under battle conditions is that they are poorly equipped to stand up under strain, especially where such strain is prolonged or very severe. In civilian life, such men have largely been able to get away from situations which became too full of stress; but, in army life, and especially in combat, such escapes are not possible. As a consequence, when the breaking point is reached, they crack up.

Most Crack-ups Recoverable

BY FAR the greater number of these crack-ups are recoverable after a short time. While it is true that the strain of battle will be responsible for the incidence of some serious mental disorders which might not have developed so quickly, these serious cases will be in the minority. The great preponderance of cases arise on the basis of somewhat mild temperamental defects. Most of these will show improvement when the strain is over and they have had time to recover.

These persons with poor temperaments who have broken down under battle strain are in many cases the same persons who were formerly a problem in industry. They are the ones who have made the problems of placement and supervision so important. Considerably in the minority, they yet have been a major source of annoyance. Where their problem has been solved, the solution has usually been accomplished either by such a placement as to give their undesirable traits very little opportunity to operate or by such a skilled handling by competent leaders as to keep the difficulties they originate continuously ironed out.

Number of Cases About the Same as Pre-war

THE same conditions are likely to continue in the post-war situation. These semi-handicapped workers will continue to be problems. Actually, it is not probable that the trouble with this particular group will be greatly increased.

All of this is not meant to minimize the price we must expect to pay for maimed minds and bodies or to minimize the sacrifice of those who suffer these mental and physical wounds. There will be a number of casualties with brain injuries. Some of these will have permanently impaired mental health. There will be some men with extremely poor and very poor mental health who will not have been weeded out prior to induction by the selection service. Many of these will be permanently incapacitated. There may be some of those with poor mental health who also will be permanently worsened.

However, in spite of this dark side of the picture, circumstances may not be expected to be as difficult as one might imagine.

Some individuals are improved in mental health by war conditions. Two helpful factors are the better wages and better general chance for employment to be found in war time as distinguished from peace time. These remove financial worries and contribute to confidence.

Some men are improved by army life. The identification with units of men and the acceptance as fellow soldier do much to remove feelings of difference and break down imaginary social barriers. Other factors such as success in battle, the conquest of fear, recognition, friendships, all contribute in a constructive way.

The principal factor, however, which holds promise that the situation is not insurmountably serious is that of the recoverability of most of the war mental casualties.

Competent Treatment Necessary

AS MENTIONED before, nearly all of those who have been accepted as mentally fit for the army and who yet have broken down under battle strain are those who fall into the sixteen per cent of those we have termed "Poor" in mental health in peace time. In turn, nearly all of these who have not had brain injuries but have cracked up under battle strain stood good chances of recovery. Under competent treatment, most of these battle-strain victims will improve to the point that they will be in about as good mental health as they were before induction.

This does not signify that they will become thoroughly satisfactory employees, but it does signify that they will probably not be significantly more of a problem than they formerly were or than they might have been under a peace-time development.

Such workers will probably be difficult to place and to supervise, just as such workers have always been difficult. However, techniques of placement and supervision have been greatly improved. Industry has profited from its war-time experience. As a consequence, it is probable that these returning workers will, in the main, be better placed and better handled.

Better Working Adjustment Possible

IT is important to keep in mind that every returning worker is an individual. No two will have precisely the same problems. It is up to the personnel man to give each returning veteran the individual attention he deserves. Every one of them should be carefully examined. His assets and liabilities should be carefully assayed. His condition of mental and physical health should be determined. If each one is separately so considered and separately so provided for, the poor temperaments can be used—excepting only those with very serious handicaps.

When every returning veteran has this individual consideration, including some taking into account of how much temperamental integration or normality he possesses, and when he is placed in accordance with his assets and liabilities and supervised in accordance with his idiosyncrasies, there is every reason to expect even a better working adjustment than we knew before the world blew up.

The Debate Has Lasted Long as to Whether or
Not Employee Ratings Should be Made Known
to Employees. Here is a Tried Plan by Which
Employee Progress Reports are Made the Basis
of Employee Counseling Looking to the Con-
tinned Progress of Employees. . (This is the
Second Part of this Paper).

Goodyear Aircraft
Employee Counseling

By S. E. FULLER

Goodyear Aircraft Corporation,
Akron, 15, Ohio

O N THE initial reports it was difficult to get the supervisor to discuss the check
sheet with the employee. Many supervisors had never had people under
their direction before and lacked the confidence to talk to individuals
about their inabilities. Some said that they were in fear of hurting the employee,
thus upsetting his equilibrium and affecting adversely the present condition of the
department.

The most common statement made was that the employee would accept comments on his good abilities only passively and exaggerate and magnify comments made
about minor weaknesses. A number of supervisors requested that the written information substantiating their check marks might be discarded from the discussion
with the employee. Supervision complained that so comprehensive a study was too
great a "broadside" to unload on the employee. This point held some merit and we
took steps to make the statements to the point, not overemphasized and to suggest
rather than criticise.

In spite of these precautionary measures, the surprising reluctance of supervision
to discuss the check sheets with their employees became the biggest problem of our
program. Many supervisors had never had experience directing people's efforts
and either lacked the necessary confidence to present constructive criticism tactfully
or possessed little human interest in the employee's development. Supervision,
moreover, had gone through the trying stages of high turnover and the struggle to
get the quantity of employees required to fulfill all assignments; and with the de-

partment built up to its necessary capacity, hesitated to inject any personnel procedure which, if not presented properly, might revive turnover

Tact and Diplomacy

THE basic reason for this reluctance was the necessity of using an abundance of tact and diplomacy in discussing the employee's weaknesses with him. Fear existed that his sense of pride and personal importance would recoil and challenge the insinuations unless the employee had a real confidence in his supervisor.

Supervisors who had established this confidence found no difficulty in their discussions with the employee. Those who had built up suspicion and lack of faith in their sincerity did not attempt any discussions, or if they did, found it most difficult. In some of the most extreme cases, instead of engaging in a frank discussion with the maladjusted individual, the disagreeable was avoided by suggestive inducements for transfer to another department, sometimes even implied to be promotions but which actually proved to be "unloading" action. "Cutting the department" was used as a reason several times but it bred further suspicion when a new employee was hired several days later to fill the vacancy.

Even with all the preparation which the check sheet offers, we discover occasionally that the incompetence of a supervisor to talk to his personnel satisfactorily makes the anticipated discussions with the employees inadvisable. One completed an appraisal of the employees under his supervision but showed a stern reluctance to initiate the personal interviews. His department manager suggested that these discussions be completed by the Personnel Department.

In the final analysis our most difficult case in the department turned out to be the supervisor himself. A wide experience had qualified him for the position as a keen analyst of production needs, but nervousness, aggravated by domestic troubles and a condition of getting further behind in his work each day made it illogical that he take the rôle of advisor to other people on their inabilities.

Influence of the Over-bearing Type

OCCASIONALLY conceit, argumentative and over-talkative characteristics of individuals lead to group inefficiencies or to resentments toward them which affect adversely their individual application of proven abilities.

A person with a long experience in selling attempted to adjust to analytical work because at the time of his hire there were no sales jobs available. A large vocabulary and a natural ability to talk fluently made him over-bearing to his fellow employees and especially those directing his training. He complained of not being trained properly, but the truth was he lacked the ability to listen.

Trainers found it difficult to show him a new duty because he was more interested in telling them his personal experiences. In the appraisal of his abilities it was pointed out that he had acquired very little job knowledge because of his very apparent lack of interest, but he still voiced dissatisfaction with the attention given him and the insignificance of the duties to which he had been assigned. Transferred to a position where he was required to sell ideas, contracts and products he still created antagonism and we were forced to release him.

Personal Inventories

EMPLOYEES like to know how they are getting along and what the future has in store for them providing they continue to progress. We try to point out in our discussions how close they are to mastering all the necessary duties of their present jobs and in addition to discuss the higher positions to which their present job experience will eventually make them eligible.

Employees take perpetual mental inventory of their present and future. If only a very few conditions of the job are in collision with an employee's motivating impulses, he will not feel the frustrating urge to mull over his status. But when such factors as coldness by the boss, favoritism, lack of appreciation, insufficient salary, overwork, or not being employed at his highest skill start playing leap frog with his real desires, efficiency dwindles. Then throw into his mind a few other wonderments concerning food, clothing and shelter or the desire for a new car and the result is an employee in need of counsel with persons directly responsible for his efficiency.

Employee Argues with Himself

As ONE employee expressed it, "I kept arguing with myself but the more I lined up the pros and cons the more confused I got. It bothered me because just as I felt a solution was in sight, I hilled myself in again. For the first time in my life I began to develop an inferiority complex." This employee's efficiency came back once his ability had been appraised and a discussion followed in the Personnel Department. His immediate supervisor, the department manager and counselor were present. Supervision was not satisfied with his volume. They had kept putting off an interview with the employee to discuss this point. The employee admitted he had slowed down.

He had done outstanding work during the first six months of his employment and had received no verbal or financial appreciation for his efforts. He admitted that he began to wonder why he hadn't received any appreciative word of acknowledgment for his efforts, and, with no salary increase as an indication either, he lost interest. The two in charge of his work admitted they should have talked to him long before. His decreased volume was noticed just previous to their set plans to give him a salary increase. Both admitted they lacked the ability to pass out verbal compliments and didn't do it.

Salary increases came with results measured by output. All parties concerned admitted the case was one of complete misunderstanding. The employee's wonderment was erased and he soon regained his former volume. An increase in salary was initiated once this pace was established.

Pressure and Release

HE first reason for dissatisfaction voiced by a disgruntled employee is usually Tnot the basic motivating factor. Insufficient salary is repeatedly used as a pet peeve but most always this tangent turns out to be a "feeler" to get an audience and relieve some troublesome but submerged and unidentified irritation. If lack of money causes domestic worries, it sometimes proves to be at the seat of the trouble, but most often other factors set up nervous vibrations leading to frustrations.

The correction of a minor misunderstanding, advising or making changes after talking over job conditions, personality clashes, lack of confidence, fear of failure, health, worries, disappointments, financial difficulties, marital troubles, homesickness or just being a good listener to show that someone is interested, quite often takes away the disturbing pressure and stability is realized. Persons who are obviously influenced by deeply imbedded factors should always be sent to a psychiatrist for professional advice and correction.

Problem in Army

ARTICLES appearing in newspapers and periodicals suggest that the army experiences a somewhat comparable problem in adjusting individuals to army duties. It seems adjustment becomes difficult for some because of worries, hunger for affection, homesickness or the disruption of emotional habits developed in civilian life.

When these factors clash with army discipline and the necessity of coördinated group action and thought, nervousness and mental turmoil sometimes result; and in a more advanced stage may lead to melancholia, dizziness, heart palpitations or high blood pressure. The fact that a good share of these cases come to the surface in training camps indicates that the strain of battle or the fear of combat are not necessary prerequisites to an emotional crack-up and an army discharge.

Statements of Availability

HE duties and responsibilities assigned to any individual in our organization in Tno way subject him to the weight of rigid discipline, drill and twenty-four hour per day direction imposed by the army, and, therefore, cases of emotional instability are not apt to appear as frequently. Of the cases that do cause considerable trouble, perhaps, either because of poor placement or neglect in checking the employee's progress periodically to offer assistance, we are partly or wholly to blame that some of these never demonstrate an ability to adjust satisfactorily.

On the other hand it is best that we issue Statements of Availability to some individuals with the recommendation that they seek a more satisfactory adjustment elsewhere. Freezing employees to their jobs has its dangers if adhered to in the strictest sense, especially when such action further frustrates an individual already wedged between conflicting emotions.

No Need of Transfer

AN INDUSTRIAL engineer came to the Personnel Department to request a transfer. He was dissatisfied with his work, thought he could make more money elsewhere and saw no future possibilities in his present department. Moreover, he had developed a tendency to hurry in gathering evidence on a case and had lost the patience to go deep enough into the investigation, all because of a moodiness he had developed. We had completed a check sheet on this individual but had not reached the point of discussing it with him. He completed an analysis of himself and then he and the supervisor got together for a comparison of the two forms:

When the employee returned to the Personnel Department for his second interview, he stated that, "The boss told me things I wanted to know. He told me things of which I did not realize he was aware. On the other hand the discussion gave me an opportunity to tell him additional things which I wanted to be sure he appreciated. I wanted to know how I was doing and how I stood, so that I wouldn't continually wonder about my performance and my future. I wanted to know so that I could enjoy the satisfaction that I was making progress. In addition to this I wanted a plan of action so that I could correct my inabilities and in correcting them get a better job. This check sheet you have asked me to help work out has cleared up the very things that caused my dissatisfaction. I had the wrong idea of my status the whole way through. Things are a lot better than I thought they were. My future isn't as black as I pictured it. The last thing I want is a transfer."

Improving Personal Characteristics

A CLERK who had a good background for his job showed signs of restlessness and his efficiency varied from one extreme to another until at the time of rating he had lost most of his previous enthusiasm for the job. The reasons for this condition came out during the discussion with him. He had always had an intense desire to be a time study man and had hired in on his present job because it was the only logical training ground toward ultimately obtaining time study assignments. He felt discouraged because the training period had passed and he hadn't received a chance at time study work. Months of waiting only aggravated his restlessness.

Due to personal characteristics, the department manager had been reluctant to assign him time study duties, but never told the employee this. Discussion brought out these personal characteristics and plans were made to overcome them. The employee was given assurance that once these were overcome and he demonstrated that he had renewed the efficiency of which he was capable, he could take over time study work. He made rapid strides in the development of the required abilities and eventually was given time study assignments.

The employee admitted that it was by establishing definite plans whereby he might work toward his goal, coupled with the opportunity to talk with someone who took an interest in him, which had helped greatly.

Parental Disagreement Solved

Discussion with a twenty year old boy who had never been able to gain any worthwhile efficiency revealed that he had a good voice and desired greatly to take more lessons to become a professional singer. This desire was thwarted because his father, a minister, desired that his son follow in his footsteps; and to this end wanted to send him to a theological seminary. The boy tried to apply himself to his duties but the parental disagreement and the burning desire to follow music as a career kept his efficiency idling instead of geared up to full speed.

An agreement was finally worked out with the parents whereby he would work until he had earned sufficient money to supplement that which they had available for his tuition to a musical college. With factors working at cross purposes eliminated and a set purpose established, this boy's efficiency picked up considerably.

Fear of Draft

A clerk who had performed his duties efficiently for many months commenced to request hospital passes, complaining that he felt unsettled and a little dizzy. His heart was good and nothing else seemed wrong physically. At times he worked feverishly while at other intervals his efficiency was at zero. Fear of being drafted and a general worry about his nervousness and irritability were obviously surface reasons. He went from a psychiatrist through the model airplane construction stage to a clinic and back to his job again with no one being able to help him.

Rejected by the army for emotional instability he was given a month's sick leave by the company so that he might effectuate a change of environment and realize a complete rest.

Returning to his job he applied himself the first few weeks with the same high degree of efficiency exemplified during the earlier days of his employment, but soon nervous tension developed again to hamper his efforts. A noticeable factor contributing to his instability was the type of duties to which he had been assigned, especially one phase of the job which required that he meet definite schedules. A nervous condition became more distressing as the pressure of his anxiety to meet these deadlines increased.

Taken from his desk job and transferred to one requiring much physical exertion and no deadlines to meet, he has since maintained a record of good job efficiency as well as enjoying satisfying personal stability.

Domestic Worries

AN EMPLOYEE came to us with all indications of nervousness. He wanted a release from his work because the pressure was too great on his present duties. The pressure had as a basis worry over meeting interest payments on a debt, a second child expected and insufficient living quarters for an increased family. A work assignment dealing with details which were far from enjoyable didn't help to take his mind off these problems but aggravated them. He had always enjoyed jostling follow employees about their mistakes or moods and seeing his moodiness they "needled" him in retaliation.

Their "riding" had deeper results than they had expected for he eventually broke down under the strain. A confining work assignment, worries, a need for more money, restlessness and sleeping pills were a part of his admissions. We recommended professional advice and a week of sick leave in addition to his two weeks' vacation. He returned rested and in better spirits. In the interim domestic· worries had been straightened out successfully.

Concealed Physical Condition

THE inaccuracies and poor memory of an employee engaged in analytical work showed up prominently on his Progress Report. After considerable time had been spent with him discussing his check sheet, he confessed that he suffered from a disease which frequently caused a thickening of the blood. While this condition existed his ability to think clearly and his power of retention diminished. In its worst stages it became impossible for him to transpose a column of figures from one sheet to another without committing a great many errors of transposition.

This malady had made the satisfactory completion of his assigned duties most difficult; but until inaccuracies and forgetfulness were questioned he felt that any possible effects of the handicap had passed without detection. His protective efforts had existed for two years. Had his supervisor shared the knowledge of this weakness definite plans could have been made long before to assist him during its treatment by delegating assignments more suited to his condition.

Benefits of Secondary Employee Interview

IT HAS proved beneficial to interview the employee in the Personnel Department after the supervisor has discussed the ability check sheet with him. Since the counselor often assists both the supervisor and the employee in their analyses he is in a good position to pass judgment and assist the employee further. This interview becomes more impartial and assistance to the employee in the correction of weaknesses or distressing factors is on a broader plane. Conditions are often discussed, moreover, which the employee is reluctant to discuss with his immediate supervisor.

These conversations often uncover misunderstandings affecting the employee's mental attitude toward his duties, his boss and his associates. Invariably personal emotional characteristics, frustrated desires and outside influences causing inefficiencies are readily admitted. Individuals kept on their job but who are in need of assistance to adjust properly are interviewed periodically until the factors effecting their efficiency are eliminated. In cases where the only possible remedy is transfer to more suitable work, actual steps are taken to effectuate this change.

Sensing Employee Attitudes

AFTER all persons in a department have been interviewed, besides identifying to the manager individual employee characteristics in need of improvement, we bring to his attention general attitudes causing inefficiencies in the department. Interviewing individuals separately presents a good opportunity to sense employee attitudes toward conditions affecting everyone in the group.

The knowledge that the individual will not be identified as the contributor to any set of criticisms promotes complete freedom of thought. Some of the criticisms which initially seem to be unjustified or misdirected, quite often prove to have some grounds for expression, especially when the same opinion is repeatedly emphasized through successive interviews.

Calculations and Records

SINCE the Job Evaluation Division attaches the given amount of points each element is worth in relation to other jobs, these are easily utilized in calculating the employee's ability and performance points. This is done by assigning a percentage to each of the zones appearing on the check sheet. Since there are several factors under each element, the median check mark represents the percentage to be used. As an example, if job evaluation allows 200 points for job knowledge and an individual receives a grade of 75% for this element, he would get 75% of 200 or 150 points. Since job evaluation does not use the element of efficiency, no points are attached.

The percentage for this is used to calculate the amount of ability actually being utilized. For instance, if an employee earns 1000 points on the first nine elements and his efficiency grade is 50%, he is utilizing only 50% of his ability and is therefore earning only 500 points. The money value of this final figure can be determined by reference to the same scale of point values as is used in job evaluation.

In the Personnel Department both the job evaluation points and the employee ability points for each element are posted on Performance Rating Record cards.

Total ability points and total actual performance points are listed and these in turn converted into a percent of the maximum points allowed for the position. Grades for each successive employee analysis enable the Personnel Department to follow an employee's progress from one appraisal to another.

Conclusions

A CLOSER relationship between the supervisor and the employee has proved that more troubles are "brewed" by the employee's lack of information than most any other factor. We have found that even the most easily adjusted employee will begin to wonder and then become unsettled if he is ignored and not treated as a human being capable of making simple deductions and desirous of being told that his efforts are being appreciated. These wonderments find the most fertile ground for growth in the minds of persons exhibiting real active imaginations. Nurtured for any great length of time they will blossom into personnel problems which might easily be avoided through the existence of a wide open employee-supervisor communication system.

Wealth of Untapped Abilities

A NOTHER fact of which our Progress Reports made us aware was that we had sufficient employees and a wealth of untapped abilities. Our biggest deficiency was methods of managing human beings intelligently. It proved that a remarkable increase in individual and group efficiency can be realized in return for counsel, encouragement and personal interest, especially when these things are given to the employee by his immediate supervisor. Moreover, employees will often double their efficiency once their minds are freed of fear and misconceptions they have built up about their own incapabilities.

The benefits derived from working with human beings suffering emotional instability on war jobs logically assures the continuance of the same intelligent, human approach to this problem during normal business conditions. The value of lubrication to assure efficiency and durability for industrial machinery has always been an accepted principle of good management. The benefits of applying personal interest, counsel and a spirit of helpfulness to the human side of industry to assure the highest degree of personal efficiency and enjoy low turnover is becoming more and more an accepted principle of the same good management.

The Author of This Paper, Who is a Student at the Stanford Graduate School of Business, While Realistically Critical of the Conditions' Under Which He Had to Work, Has Not Yet Been Soured, as Witness the Fact that He Has Been Promoted to a Responsible Executive Position in the Company Where He Is Helping to Improve Conditions.

How Ships Are Built

By F. G.

South San Francisco, Cal.

Because I am employed in a defense plant, and therefore able to report from personal observation, I will deal with this problem subjectively. The shipyard wherein I work is located in South San Francisco. It employs about 8000 people and should give a reasonably accurate cross-section of Employer-Employee problems. It has been in operation as a steel fabricating company for about thirty-five years, and only for the last four years has it been converted to defense work. Its expansion has been no more nor less sudden than similar plants throughout the country. Nor is it more efficiently or less efficiently run than other shipyards. It is, in short, an average shipyard.

Appreciation of War Pressure

There are probably more than twenty such yards in the country with identical problems. I have visited three others and found them faced with such strikingly similar problems that I would easily have fancied myself in my own plant.

At the outset I wish to state that although I will criticize severely, I am also aware of the pressure brought by war time. It would be most unfair to judge entirely by peace time standards, for so many losses and mistakes are admittedly due to the great cry for speed. A speed that is entirely lacking under ordinary conditions.

We are so accustomed to think in terms of the super-efficiency of such plants as the Ford Motor Company or the Chrysler Corporation, that it is easy to fall into an attitude that is nothing less than cynical. Those concerns have had more than twenty years of peacetime work to establish themselves with their well oiled systems and practices. The shipyards have had less than three years in which to get organized. And their products are of such a great size and composed of so many unlike pieces that simple learning, which is a natural product of mere repetition, is not possible. Practically every ship built is a custom-made thing.

And Yet

THE whole program could be better done if the men at the top had time to attend to more details of their organization. Or at least if they would delegate more authority to subordinates.

Let's review, simply, the organization of a shipyard. It consists of these departments or groups—

1. The executive, which includes besides the president and active vice presidents, the board of directors.
2. The active chiefs, Chief Engineer, Superintendent of Yard, of Ways, of Shop and of Outfitting.
3. The numerous departments and their heads, Foremen. The Mold Loft, Fabrication Shop, Assembly Shop, Ways, Erection, Transportation Material, Electrical, Pipefitting, Rigging, Warehouses, and at least twenty more.
4. All the incidental departments such as Maintenance, Fire Department, Hospital, Personnel office, Publicity, Trainee and a number of lesser ones.

It follows, of course, that the problems of the mass of workers, which are felt most acutely at the source, gradually dissipate until by the time they reach the executives, they are so diluted that they seem unimportant. And too, executives want *facts*, which are hard to get when the information is delivered third or fourth hand, for the workers troubles pass through leaderman, quarterman, foreman, supervisor and at last reach the superintendent.

Why Morale Low

GENERALLY speaking, the morale in shipyards is rather low. This, in spite of high wages, labor management committees, and a vast national program to instill morale in the "worker." I think the chief reason for this is the innate desire of men to do things well. I say this and emphasize it because the present condition of the world would lead us to think otherwise. I believe that most men want to see an orderly world, want to live in an orderly society, and want to do work that is orderly. And that's where the shipyards fail.

So great has the emphasis been on speed and production and so little regard has been shown for cost, that it is evident that the "powers that be" never gave a thought to the mentality of the working men who are the spectators of their actions. From the very outset their attitude has been this: We have endless resources, we have unlimited capital, we'll hire a bunch of engineers, we'll hire a whole lot of workmen and put them together and we'll point out that they're working for a "cause." We'll stir the whole thing together and we'll pay high wages and see that everybody has enough and we'll out-produce the whole world. And we have out-produced the whole world.

But the cost has been unbelievable. Astronomical figures daily stun us. This wonderful production is not so wonderful when you stand it next to its cost. And the tax payer is looking more closely to the cost. And he is resenting more and more the way that it is done under the shiboleth "This is War." And the tax payer and the ship yard worker are the same man.

Even if he didn't have to pay, the average man still is adverse to waste. He cannot help but feel a repugnance when his efforts, although paid for, are gathered together and destroyed. One-fifth of the work that is done on a ship, must be undone, and redone.

Assembly Line Hiring

To begin at the hiring end; the worker is at once made to feel like an insignificant stitch in a mighty pattern. He is interviewed, "No I take that back," he is *questioned* by some typist whose only instructions are to see that the hiring form is properly filled. There is no such thing as an interview. The policy is to "hire anybody that is still warm".

The worker is shunted from desk to desk to be finger-printed, photographed, insured, bond deductions, etc. The treatment is strictly the same kind accorded animals when they are being branded. But, let us grant that it is only a maudlin sentimentality that asks for consideration at the employment office. It is highly probable that the exigencies of hiring require an assembly line treatment. While the prospective worker is only too willing to comply with requirements, he is clearly made to feel that here is an organization that knows what it is about and he can fall in line and be given clear instruction. This suits the worker fine. He wants definite instruction.

Once he clears the personnel office however, the definite, clear-cut organization is at an end. From now on the worker takes orders from a leaderman.

Most workers come to work prepared to put in a day's work. Probably less than three per cent are outright shirkers or "goldbrickers." The leaderman will assign the man to help some journeyman who will "teach him the ropes." Let us say the journeyman is a shipfitter and let us follow him for a day.

A Day's Work

HELPER and journeyman are assigned to put some brackets up that support the third deck. The journeyman leads the helper to that portion of the hull where the work is to be done. Here, under the third deck the staging is already in place and a number of brackets are lying about ready to be placed. That's the way the shift earlier left them.

The journeyman tells the helper to wait around until he, the journeyman, can find a welder. The helper waits and the journeyman may be gone from fifteen minutes to an hour. The welder is brought in, it had taken that length of time to connect his wire cable and bring it to the place where the brackets are. Then the three men fit and put in place perhaps four of the brackets. The fifth one offers a slight difficulty that requires the use of a "burner." Now the helper and welder wait while the journeyman hunts up a burner who will burn off some of the steel. They both wait about thirty minutes and by the time the burner is at hand, it is ten minutes to twelve so they delay until noon.

After lunch they proceed and get about three more brackets in place and then discover that someone has placed a load of steel on the remaining brackets. The journey man then hunts up a crane operator who will lift the load so they can get at their brackets. This takes at least thirty minutes. They are able then to continue work until four-thirty and at the end of the day have put in place about a dozen brackets.

Standing Around

THIS must seem like an exaggerated case, but it is not. It is, as a matter of fact, a restatement of one of the better work days. Usually eight or less brackets are installed. Any casual visitor to the yard will be astounded at all the men who seem to just be standing around. The simple truth is that these men are waiting for something or someone. Obviously the answer to this is better organization. But organizers, *real work organizers*, are very, very scarce. Such men must be able to recognize a problem, and to suggest an adequate remedy. One would think that out of the thousands employed in a shipyard, certainly some should be able to cope with such situations.

And in truth, there are good men who do know solutions. But here is where the employer-employee relations break down. The worker does not want to go over the leaderman's head, the leaderman does not want to offend his foreman and the foreman does not want to embarrass his superintendent.

I once explained the situation to a girl who had graduated from Stanford, and was working for us as a draftswoman. She tossed her pretty head and said with some disgust, "But that's so stupid." And I think that points out one of the fundamentals that never quite seem to be learned in college. Simply this: That a whole lot of the world is stupid but it cannot be corrected by simply pointing out its stupidity. It has to be *sold* on the idea that there is something better.

Stuff That Wars Are Made Of

THIS girl, like most college people, was accustomed to dealing with intelligent people who are reasonably honest, honorable and impartial when there is a question to be settled (most college questions are merely academic anyway). She thought that one had simply to explain to the people concerned and when they saw the error of their ways they would take steps to correct them.

Little did she know that when you point out to people the error of their ways you are dealing with the stuff that wars are made of. One is treading on extremely dangerous territory when one presumes to criticise. Almost invariably the criticism is received with this attitude: "Who are you and is your own house in such good order that you can afford to be critical?"

Thus if the helper criticises the journeyman, the journeyman may be outright resentful. Usually the helper does not criticise the journeyman, for he can see the journeyman is trying to get the job done, but is handicapped by conditions beyond his control. In most cases the journeyman tells the helper, almost apologetically, how he has tried to interest his leaderman in the bad condition and the leaderman in turn passed the buck to his foreman who was so darn busy trying to settle another problem, and by this time the lowly helper and journeyman have lost sight of their suggestion.

All they know is that they told the "higher-up" about their problem and nothing came of it. That example illustrates the underlying dissatisfaction prevalent in our yard. Most men say, "Yeh, it's lousy alright, but what can you do about it?" It is this feeling that nobody cares what he, the individual worker thinks, that is the worst thing about the employer-employee relations in our yard.

Labor Management Committee

SO MUCH publicity has been given to the Labor Management groups that almost at once one thinks about the highly praised "Suggestion Box." I do not know how this works in other yards, but in our own this organization is a farce, serving the simple purpose of paying lip service to the Maritime Commission's request that all yards have a Labor Management Committee.

When our vice-president received the Commission's request that such a committee be formed he simply handed the letter to the Personnel Manager and told him to form a committee. The manager went from office to office calling on friends and men he knew, and with no regard as to whether they represented either labor or management simply appointed them on the committee. And so the Labor-Management Committee was formed. For a whole year hardly any one in the yard knew it existed.

Then when outside publicity called it to the men's attention they started asking about it. And it was so poor that criticism was levelled at it. I attended one meeting in which we suggested that the committee reorganize and take an active interest in yard problems. The suggestion was that the yard hold an election, and send from the rank and file of workers elected men to meet with the men who represent the management.

Constructive Program Suggested

A LETTER was read at the meeting, suggesting positive action along the following lines:

We suggest a general reorganization of the entire committee. The members to be elected by the workers of the yard. These members are to be elected in pairs and to represent certain aspects of our program. Thus: two members for welfare, two for production, two for publicity, and two for training. These eight are to meet with a member representing management; preferably the superintendent. This representative of the management should certainly always be present at the meetings, in fact, should preside as chairman. The Maritime Commission, too, should be represented by someone of sufficient rank to speak with authority.

The management member, acting as chairman, could not be expected to handle the correspondence and other book work connected with this office. Therefore a secretary (without vote) should be appointed to take care of this work. The members of the committee will be elected by ballot, which can be distributed with the time cards. The publicity given at this time, and the interest aroused by the local campaigning should make for a great deal of interest in the doings of the Labor Management Committee.

Then, once the committee is elected and established, it is to operate under a simple practical constitution. The objective of which will be to avoid wasting time at committee meetings and to show some tangible results. We have even gone so far as to draw up this preliminary constitution, which we present here for your discussion.

Four Committees

THE four pairs of committeemen will organize subcommittees to work with them and each subcommittee will work to better a certain phase of production.

The *Welfare* Committee to concern itself with: Rationing, Living Conditions, Transportation, Facilities in the yard such as lockers, latrines, restaurants, Morals, Parking, and all other problems of working conditions.

The *Training* Committee to concern itself with: Teachers, Courses, Facilities, The policy of the company about this program, Method of making promotions via training, Orientation of new employees, etc., Safety education.

The *Production* Committee to concern itself with: Simpler procedures and processes, Time saving methods, Tools, Full use of machinery, Prefabrication—use of assembly line principles, Safety practices.

The *Publicity* Committee to concern itself with: Keeping the company informed of the progress of the productive drive, Bulletin Boards, All newspaper work, Bonds, Safety, Posters, Charts, Score boards, etc.

Members Have Job to Do

THE general reorganization will be of no use unless this fact is stressed. The members have a job to do. The meetings of the L. M. C. are not in themselves accomplishing anything, they are held so that the members can report to each other and to the management. The meetings are not to be general bull sessions at which a pleasant exchange of ideas takes place without some action being reported. At the meetings the members should have prepared reports with definite facts to state. The progress of each committee should be recorded. It should be the duty of the chairman to keep the meeting confined to pertinent business at hand. All long winded personal opinions and experiences should be eschewed.

At the time of elections it should be made clear to the nominees that they are laying themselves open to a lot of work and they should be warned not to accept unless they are prepared to deliver.

Discussion of Letter

AFTER the letter had been read there followed a discussion. Most of the members were a little sheepish, for here they were being called ineffectual to their very faces. The Superintendent said he didn't like the idea of not having a handpicked committee. "We might get a bunch of Reds in here". He thought the existing committee was a good bunch of men, who perhaps needed only a little prodding. But we persisted, pointing out the value of a general election. Its publicity would be a morale booster and stimulate the flow of suggestions, etc. Then the Superintendent said he didn't want any campaigning going on in the yard. The men were supposed to work, not run around soliciting votes. (This argument was typical of the type used.)

The Superintendent didn't want any campaigning, yet for a two month period following this meeting there was a campaign in the yard to elect the most popular woman worker, and following that a contest to elect the most popular office worker. Although these contests were to boost the sale of war bonds, their merit was not greater than one that would give us a better Labor-Management Committee. And the vote-soliciting during these contests reach the proportions of a football rally.

Teeth in Committee

As the discussion continued, someone wanted to know how the Committee was going to have "teeth". Here some one said that if a suggestion were ignored by Management, it would be taken up with the Union. That was obviously the wrong thing to say, for at once the Superintendent arose and said if anyone wanted to keep his job he had better not try to take the managing of the company out of the hands of management. And he was right, too. But this simply shows how men can get worked up during a meeting and defeat their own purpose.

It was not a question of putting "teeth" in the suggestions of the committee, it was a matter of the committee forwarding and fostering suggestions and plans that would be beneficial to the company and to the worker. Letters written by workers clearly indicate the attitude that the old committee had, by its inactivity, brought upon our yard. We quote from one:

Employee Reaction

O.K. So what happens? We come to work reasonably awake and with the general idea that we will turn in a good day's work. BANG! The first thing we discover is that there is no particular job planned for us. First, our leaderman must take a mental roll call after which he begins assigning jobs according to: 1. The number of men present; 2. The amount of sleep he had; 3. Whimsy. Then we have a settling down, a planning of our own work. We check blueprints and make sure none of our tools have been purloined. All right, so we put our house in order—now can we get on with our work? Oh, no; not on your life. Now begins a series of delayed bucks which will use up all of our energy and show a minimum of accomplishment. These bucks we will refer to as the "waits." We must "wait" for crane service, "wait" for material, "wait" for a tacker, "wait" for a burner, "wait" for a rigger. We spend so much time waiting we sometimes forget what we started to do.

And, do we have the "waits" because there is a shortage of material, of tackers, of burners, etc.? Oh, No! There is enough of all these. It is simply a problem of timing. If the work is well planned, there are no "waits." This brings us to the point of all this. Who does the planning? We, the poor souls who read the posters and hear the radio? Heaven forbid! The planning is done by the leaderman, the quarterman, the foreman, the superintendents, and other executives whose offices are right next to the pearly gates.

Urges Bosses Bestir Themselves

It seems, then, we should have a program urging these, the members of the planning hierarchy, to bestir themselves. We realize that an undertaking as vast as the shipbuilding program is bound to have growing pains. We know that repeated war-need expansion has created labor problems and supervision problems and safety problems and, yes, even problems caused by a shortage of plumbing facilities. And, frankly, we think that the "big boys" have done a good job. But Brother! **THERE IS ROOM FOR IMPROVEMENT.** We have reached no plateau upon which we can become complacent. What worked last year is no good now. Let's not keep abreast of the times—**LET'S GET AHEAD OF THEM.** That Navy "E" isn't impossible!

Rules and Regulations

THE copy of the Rules and Regulations that is given each new employee has been compared with other booklets of a like nature that are prepared by other companies, and this one falls down in one important respect. It starts out "Putting the worker in his place." Nowhere does it welcome the worker or even seem friendly. Its very title is inimical. If it had at least a suggestion of being helpful, if it did nothing more than tell where the toilets were located, it would change its tone entirely.

We grant that conditions are poor because of a good reason. It is easy to see that the man shortage is not confined to laborers, the important shortage is of organizers and planners. Yet if the efforts of the men were given cognizance and a reason for non-performance given to the men who take the time to make suggestions, their attitude would be changed. The men are certainly intelligent enough to understand when an explanation of this type is given: "Your suggestion is a good one, Mr. Jones, but we cannot act on it now because the Maritime Commission prohibits allocating any more money to this purpose until such a time, etc." "However, please continue in your good efforts and we hope we can find an occasion to use your ideas, etc."

Tossing an Occasional Sop

THE feeling of "belonging" should be promoted. Courtesy is inexpensive and should be used freely. The workers know this too. And when they think the company thinks so little of them that it cannot or will not afford to use courtesy in dealing with its own men, then they feel the company must hold the men in low esteem.

Yet this is but one side of the employer-employee problem. Certainly management has not deliberately suppressed any efforts of betterment. It has discouraged them by great pre-occupation with other affairs. And management has been guilty of "tossing a sop" whenever the criticism was too loud. Good examples of this are the handling of the cry for decent eating facilities. For almost two years after the employment number had increased above the five thousand mark, there was only a small coffee shop to serve the men. The shop was no bigger than a "diner." This concession was owned by one of the bosses and it netted him a neat sum. Finally a larger cafeteria was built.

Dishonest Words

Here is where words become means of being dishonest. This cafeteria serves warm meals. The very words sound appetizing and wholesome. But the truth is that only about one meal of each five is any good. It is always *warm* but it is poorly prepared and frequently unwholesome. Mere heat does not make a good meal. And these meals are not inexpensive. Current inflation prices are charged. While this cafeteria is larger than the coffee shop, it is still not nearly adequate to serve the great number of workers who jam it at every meal time. But on paper and when spoken of as a cafeteria where warm meals may be had, the impression is created that pleasant facilities are made available to the poor working man.

But it suffices to assuage the conscience of management. In truth it must be said here that the workers are somewhat to blame too. They must be told repeatedly not to line up until the mealtime whistle is blown. Yet there is always a long queue started fifteen minutes before the hour. And lest we appear querulous and too demanding, we want to state that we know that conditions are better than they were. But so is everything else. And so long as this is a matter of degree, we point out that it is of the *low* degree that we are complaining.

In the matter of hospitalization of employees, the same was true. We had a hospitalization plan but it gave you no choice of hospitals. No matter where you lived, you had to report to the South San Francisco Hospital. It was later learned, after the plan had been tossed out in favor of a better one that had a roster of about ten hospitals, that the South San Francisco hospital had an "understanding" with the personnel manager of the plant.

There have been many improvements made, of course. No plant could operate for several years without showing some bettering of method. These improvements have for the most part been undertaken by the foremen themselves, who in most cases went ahead and made the changes and then notified the management.

Outsiders Quickly Put Outside

On at least three occasions, management sought to bring in outsiders to help the situation, but on these occasions the outsiders were very poorly received by the present workers. No amount of introducing and extolling of the outsider's ability helped. These men were outsiders who were going "to show us how to do our work."

One of these efforts was carried on by a Mr. X. No one quite knew where he came from or where "he got his drag" but he was suddenly given an office and put in charge of the berthing system. The berthing system is established to keep a check of ship's costs by crafts and by ship's sections. Mr. X was resented at once because his office was nicer than anyone else's and also he was given a secretary. At that time no yard office was sissy enough to have a secretary. (Since women have been swarming through the yard, however, each office has at least two secretaries.)

Mr. X had thousands of work cards printed, and an elaborate system that he carefully explained to the foreman concerned, adding and altering as they suggested, but always, it was "his system." In truth, it must be said that the cumbersomeness of his system far outweighed its value of accuracy. It was given a trial on one hull and ridiculed out. That was the end of Mr. X, his office and his pretty secretary.

Mr. Y was brought in by management to clear the highly complicated problem of material at the outfitting dock. Mr. Y didn't even get to first base. This is no task to be undertaken by an amateur. The outfitting dock of a shipyard is where the final work is done on a ship and it is a gigantic task even to muddle through. The outfitting of a ship's engine room alone costs over a million dollars, so it can be easily seen that the outfitting of the whole ship is nothing one can learn by "reading up on it." Mr. Y quietly disappeared.

Mr. Z appeared to take over the personnel department. He at once reorganized the entire staff (28 people). He had booths built for "interviewing people." He set rigid rules regarding hours of dinner, overtime, etc. He himself could be seen only by appointment, and then if one's business has been first stated in a letter. The letter was required even from old employees. This change was an out and out fiasco. Mr. Z suddenly was drafted. It later came out that his background in personnel work was a course in Personnel Management taken in evening classes at · a nearby Junior College.

Efforts Within Yard

OF THE efforts within the yard, most important were those done by Mr. A. Mr. A., a young fellow of about twenty, was working in the shop as a helper. (The shop has about five hundred men and fabricates all the steel that is assembled into the ship.) After talking with some of the foremen he worked out a plan for a Production Control office. He wrote a long detailed letter to the superintendent and convinced him that improvements could be made. The superintendent gave him free range and asked only that he report frequently enough to keep the superintendent posted and to make no major changes without his permission. Mr. A. talked with all the foremen and made no changes without first discussing the problem with them.

He made many changes in the system of ordering steel, control of the template room, fabrication records and others. But soon there was a growing dissatisfaction among the foremen. It grew from a dislike of change of any kind (most of the foremen were fifteen year men) and from a personal dislike of Mr. A. They seized upon the fact that Mr. A. was Jewish, and after two months of backbiting and under-handed work they forced him out. The method of forcing was simple enough. They would let some factor of which they were aware run down or get out of hand, then when it was hopelessly messed up, they would report to the superintendent and lay the blame directly in the lap of Production Control.

Started "Iaea Ball" Rolling

M R. A. made many far reaching improvements before he left and had the heartfelt gratitude of the superintendent. But the superintendent admitted that he could not buck the actions of his own foremen and it was with reluctance that he had to let Mr. A. go. Mr. A. started the "idea ball" rolling and after him almost every foreman, one by one, altered and changed their department to suit the new and hurried conditions. He was the wedge that showed the worker that management was accessible and amenable to good ideas if properly presented. And the super-intendent too, was discovered to be a progressive fellow. In fact, to the personality of this superintendent, must be ascribed most of the worthwhile changes made in the yard.

By changes, I do not mean in personnel, but in methods and practices. Another fellow named B. also young, under twenty-five, made many improvements. He was fortunate in following A. for he could benefit by his mistakes. B. had great organiza-tional ability and he was soon recognized and promoted to a foreman.

Trying to Learn

I USED to teach school with B. in South San Francisco. We taught evening classes. Most of the students were men and women from the plant who wanted to learn blueprint reading. The students frequently said that they wished the school were located closer to work, so in time we managed to get permission to hold the classes in a vacant room at the plant. Although the state paid our salaries as teachers, and the company had everything to gain by the instructing of men, we had to fight for every advantage gained.

No equipment at all was supplied us. We had to make our own blackboards, tables, models, etc. In time the value of the school dawned on the management. But not as one would suppose, by perceiving its obvious advantage. The value of it dawned when the Maritime Commission issued an edict that no more money was available for the promoting of workers from helpers to journeymen unless they first attended school.

Then the company created a "Training Department." This "department" consists of one man and a secretary. He simply carried on officially the work we had been doing. We had by this time trained about six extra men to work as instructors and had obtained state credentials for them.

Executives Seem To "Happen"

THE interesting thing about job instruction at this plant is that it was not fostered by management, but we undertook to do it ourselves. If the management had had to create and foster a department, it would have fared much better. The point of explaining all these cases is to show that executives are not a collection of smart business men who are in control because they have an insight in the workings of man, but this: Executives are a collection of ordinary men who "happen" to be where they are and who have to be sold ideas just as much as they must sell their merchandise. The employer has to be sold the problems of employees and employees have to be sold the ideas of employers.

And even if Employer-employee relations are worked out satisfactorily, there is still a tough problem of the employee-employee problem. In our own plant there was the "C case." One foreman told another he had one man too many, could the other foreman use him? The man was a good worker. The other foreman agreed and there made out a transfer slip for the man named C. Next day the foreman who had taken C found that none of his gang were working. Upon inquiry, it was found that his gang resented C because he is colored. There are over one thousand negroes in the yard but it just so happens that there weren't any in this foreman's gang. And his men were resolved to let no negroes in. C was finally transferred to still another department. The two foreman each feel the other "did him a dirty trick."

The Blueprint Case

TWO men designed a new kind of blueprint. It was different from the ordinary print in that it was a perspective picture of the unit to be built. The new print proved tremendously popular with the men, it was easier to read and had numerous other advantages. The company spent almost $50,000 on these prints, and they were used throughout the yard. Yet the engineering department constantly fought against the prints. No reason can be ascribed for this, except personalities. The Chief Engineer resented the obvious slam to his department when the yard preferred working with prints that were made by another department.

He finally persuaded the vice-president to put a stopping order on them. This, after all that money had been spent and their usefulness established. The men of the yard petitioned to have the prints put back in use for it expedited their work, and the vice-president reversed his stand. After about two months, the engineer found other means of stopping the prints, and finally he won. The men in the yard shrugged their shoulders and said "Oh well, it's all messed up anyway."

Thus it is easy to see that employer-employee relations are liquid things, flowing first in favor of one and then in favor of the other. The lesson, I believe taught by our yard, if one would choose to learn a lesson, is not one of principle that could be stated in one sentence. It would be a lesson of many facets, as many facets as there are personalities.

Lessons for Young Workers

To one entering the business world, it seems to me first: Make yourself a reputation as a good worker before you put forward any idea for an improvement. Along with being a good worker also establish your reputation as a sound person, not emotionally unstable nor a grind. Be polite, and politeness does not consist merely of saying "pardon me" at the right time. It also consists of the way you smoke, of keeping your nails clean, of being considerate of another's property whether it is their desk or their reputation. Reliability is of great importance. Do not underrate it nor undermine it by such an easy method as tardiness.

In fact, all the old bromides that so frequently are derided as "corny" do still apply, and the virtues of Horatio Alger's characters are still being sought. However, remember, that all these good qualities can be possessed by the simplest soul, so, if you want to get ahead, be sure you have in addition, "some spin on the ball."

In order to confirm the statements I have made here I interviewed about thirty of the people in the plant. The typical question I asked them was if they were happy at their work. Almost all replied they were not and that they were merely marking time until the war was over. Only one said he had any thought about helping the war effort. Practically none knew what they were going to do after the war. Almost all of them would talk at length about themselves in relation to their work or proposed work.

Book Reviews

Book Review Editor, MR. EVERETT VAN EVERY
California Personnel Management Association, Berkeley, Cal.

WAGE INCENTIVES

By J. K. Louden.   New York.   John Wiley & Sons, Inc.   1944.   174 pp. $2.50

This is the best book we have seen on wage incentives if not on the entire field of wage administration.   Few other works on this subject dwell so thoroughly on the fundamentals and seem to be so well adaptable to practical operations in a plant. We find it a practical book written from the point of view of good operations as well as rate structure and wage incentives.   This point of view is not lost sight of in the elaborately developed chapters on policies, wage administration, cost control and union participation.

Throughout the book the author has maintained the most realistic approach we have ever seen in a study of this subject.   There is a great tendency in discussing wage incentives, time study and methods work to become idealistic and to write in generalities, but we found none of that in this interesting book.   The author is production manager of the glass and closure division of the Armstrong Cork Company, and has acquired a name for himself in Eastern industrial circles.

The language and style of the book is essentially intended for business.   The author's statements are direct and pointed as if he were discussing these matters in · his shop office with frequent mention of actual case situations.   Industrial engineers who are concerned with wage problems will find the book very helpful and top-management who frequently deplore their separation from actual working conditions as they pertain to wage and policy matters will go a long way in "putting them back on the right track."   Immediately after the war and during the next few years ahead the subject of this book will very likely become management's number one problem and their major field of interest.   It is this reviewer's opinion that many of the solutions frantically sought over conversion and reconversion nightmares might very easily be found among the many sound administrative principles advanced in this book.

The prominent position occupied today by wage incentives as a means of increasing production for war has been viewed with mixed feelings by those who have worked for years with their use and application.   The general recognition of incentives as an instrument in production and wage administration have made them essentially a tool of industrial management.   The author believes that their sudden renewed popularity must be guarded carefully less the same mistakes and misuses be made that caused time-study and incentives to fall in disfavor a decade ago.

Among the chapter headings, all thoroughly developed, are: A Brief History of Wage Incentives, Wage Incentives Related to Functions of Management, Five Fundamental Types of Wage Incentive Plans, Basic Requirements of Sound Incentive Plans, Comparison of Plans, Policies Insuring Fair and Equitable Administration, Wage Administration, Cost Control, Supervisory Incentives, Maintaining Quality Control, Typical Incentive Installations, Union Participation.   All executives who are concerned in any way whatever in the relationship between production and compensation study this book.   It should be essential reading for personnel directors and we believe the subject treatment is crammed with sound and practical methods toward unscrambling the wartime wage dilemma.

PERSONNEL
Journal

The Magazine of

LABOR RELATIONS AND PERSONNEL PRACTICES

Published by PERSONNEL RESEARCH FEDERATION

Lincoln Building, 60 East 42nd Street, New York City

Volume 23   *Number 6*

Contents for December 1944

EDITORIAL BOARD

The Subject of Workers' Attitudes is of Real
Importance. Although It Involves Some Ques-
tions which Only the Worker Can Answer, No
Worker Can Succeed in Making the Proper Ad-
justment to Factory Life Unless Management
Supplies the Opportunity.

Chronic Absentee
and Good Attendant

By LeBaron O. Stockford

Lockheed Aircraft Corporation,
Burbank, Cal.

IN THE past, most studies of attendance have done little more than record the
percent of working time lost through absenteeism and the frequency of reported
excuses for absence. In sharp contrast, the working hypothesis behind the present survey is that we must study the people who are absent and try to determine
real causes of absenteeism. If there are any differences between the chronic Absentee
and the good Attendant and if these differences can be measured, then a reduction
in absenteeism can be achieved through the efforts of management to control the
various factors creating these differences.

Factual Study

HIS study is an attempt to obtain factual material regarding the economic,
the social and the psychological factors which may differentiate the chronic
Absentee from the employee with a good attendance record. The purpose of the
investigation is to gain additional information about absenteeism so that administrative and supervisory personnel may be able to cope more successfully with the
problem.

This report is based on the study of 200 non-supervisory production employees.
One hundred of these people (the Absentees) had been absent at least 15 or more of
the 132 regular working days in a six months period. The other hundred (the
Attendants) had not been absent once during the same period of time. These two
groups were matched for plant, department, job, shift, sex and seniority.

Conclusions Reached

THE data presented in this report show that there are factors in addition to the
immediate job and working situation which have a bearing upon the employees'
attendance records.

Management has no direct control over all of these factors, but it cannot grasp the whole picture of absenteeism unless it knows what these influences are. It must understand clearly the problems involved in housing, transportation, family stability, economic stability. However, management should certainly center its attention first upon those factors under its direct control: occupational adjustment and attitude. It may safely be stated that those employees who have poor attendance records are, as a group, poorly adjusted toward their Lockheed work.

The attitude of the Absentees is not as good as is that of the Attendants. This reflects, in part, the inadequacy of the placement of the workers. Moreover, as only 17% of the Absentees liked best their previous job which was related to their present job, it is to be expected that only a small percentage of the group would think that their present Lockheed job is the best they have ever had.

Characteristics of the Absentees

    1. A large percentage were placed in jobs wholly unrelated to both their previous training and experience.
    2. For the most part they were given jobs which they disliked.
    3. Their requests for transfer were refused almost as often as they were granted.
    4. Socially and economically, they were comparatively unstable.

This group of Absentees averaged 13 months' employment and none of them had been with the company less than 7 months. It is interesting to note that 50% of them were still in their original jobs.

Characteristics of the Good Attendants

    1. Almost three-fourths of them were placed in jobs which were related to their previous training and experience.
    2. Seventy-six percent liked best their previous job which resembled their Lockheed job.
    3. Only 9% were refused their requests for transfer.
    4. The majority of them have had two or more different jobs during their employment at Lockheed.
    5. Both socially and economically they were far more stable than the average employee.

The subject of workers' attitudes and motives is of real importance. Although it involves some questions which only the worker can answer, part of the problem rests squarely with management. No worker can succeed in making the proper adjustment to factory life unless management supplies the opportunity.

Method of Study

As this is a preliminary survey, all of the possible facts about the employees could not be determined. However, two general groups of data were studied. The first group consisted of company records regarding occupation, age, merit reviews and wage history, and intelligence test scores.

Second, to complete the investigation, the employees were given a questionnaire through which they could (1) supply additional information about themselves and (2), express their own personal opinions and attitudes about absenteeism, their jobs, et cetera. The people in the experiment were asked not to sign their names to the questionnaire, as experience has shown that people are more inclined to express themselves honestly if they can remain anonymous.

The questionnaire was separated into four sections. Each section contained a series of questions about one of the following topics:

> Occupational history and preferences
> Family relationships and living arrangements
> Economic conditions
> Opinion and attitude

Standard statistical procedures were used in the analysis of the data. All results were computed in terms of averages or percentages, so that the degrees of similarity or difference between the two groups could be most easily seen.

The results of this study are presented in two parts. Part A includes a discussion of the attendance records of the Absentees. Part B shows those factors which are definitely related to absenteeism.

Part A—Attendance Records

Reasons for Absence

THE amount of time lost by the Absentees ranged from 15 to 119 regular working days (excluding Saturdays) during the six months' period studied. The average time lost per employee was 29.4 days or 22.3% of the regular working time. According to company records, the following reasons were responsible for absence:

> 18.8 days (14.2% of the working time) illness
> 7.7 days (5.8% of the working time) unauthorized leaves
> 2.9 days (2.3% of the working time) authorized leaves

Of the total time lost, illness accounted for 64%, unauthorized leaves 26%, and authorized leaves 10%. The time lost per employee for authorized and unauthorized leaves was about the same on all three sihfts. However, the employees on the swing shift lost more time because of illness than did the employees on either the day shift or the graveyard shift.

Attendance and Shift

IT SHOULD be remembered that the Absentees were non-supervisory production employees, and their records were being compared with those of a percentage distribution (by shift and sex) of all non-supervisory production employees at Lockheed Plant 1. An analysis of the data for the three shifts showed that chronic absenteeism was proportionately greater on the graveyard shift and proportionately less on the day shift. The graveyard shift, with but 18% of the non-supervisory production employees, had 26% of the Absentees; the day shift, with 49% of the non-supervisory production employees, had only 42% of the Absentees.

Attendance and Sex

CHRONIC absenteeism was found to be more prevalent among women than among men. At the time this study was conducted, 77% of all non-supervisory production employees were men and 23% were women. In contrast, an analysis of the data on Absentees alone showed that 68% of them were men and 32% were women. Men were more inclined to be absent because of reported illness than were women. The women took more unauthorized leaves than did the men.

Part B—Differences between the Two Groups
Social and Economic Differences

PLACEMENT: If similarity of work is a sound criterion, the Attendants were much better placed on coming to Lockheed than were the Absentees. Only 17% of the Absentees (as opposed to 38% of the Attendants) were placed in jobs similar to the type of work they had been doing before coming to Lockheed, whereas 49% of the Absentees (as against only 30% of the Attendants) were placed in jobs wholly unrelated to previous experience.

The fact that the Absentees were more poorly placed on coming to Lockheed is further substantiated through the answers to the question, "Which of your previous jobs did you like best?" The responses of the two groups showed that only 14% of the Absentees liked best a previous job which was similar to the type of work they were doing at Lockheed, whereas 40% of the Attendants liked best their previous work which was similar to their job at Lockheed.

Transfers: The Absentees were not only more poorly placed than were the Attendants, but also they did not hold as many different jobs while at Lockheed. Whereas, 40% of the Absentees had been refused requests for transfers, only 9% of the Attendants had been refused such requests.

Wages: Before coming to Lockheed, the Attendants had a larger weekly income than had the Absentees. However, the average starting rates at Lockheed for the two groups were about the same. After the same length of time with the company, the Absentees had lower "take-away" wages. The difference between the two groups was even greater than these figures showed, for the Attendants had larger bond and savings deductions than had the Absentees.

Reviews and Increases: Employees in the two groups were compared on the basis of the most recent regular merit reviews and those for the previous six months together with the accompanying wage increases. The results showed that at the start of the experimental period there were no real differences in reviews or increases between the two groups. However, at the end of the period the Absentees had made no significant improvement in either scores or wage increases, whereas the Attendants had made significant progress. The Absentees were not penalized, for neither their reviews nor increases were reduced; but the Attendants were given markedly better increases.

The three factors on the merit review sheets in which employees in the two groups evidenced the greatest differences were attitude, dependability and quantity of work.

Occupational Differences

FAMILY RELATIONSHIPS: The Absentees formed a less stable social and family group than did the Attendants. More of them were single and lacked the stabilizing influence of marriage. The frequency of divorce was about the same in both groups. The Absentees were more inclined to board away from home, live alone or with other workers; in contrast, 86% of the Attendants lived at home with their families.

The Absentees were not strongly motivated to maintain good attendance records even though 58% of them (as opposed to 36% of the Attendants) had members of their immediate families in the armed services.

Financial Stability: Among the greatest differences between the two groups was the way in which they answered the following two questions: "Are you able to save or lay aside any money from your wages?" and "Are you paying off any debts or making payments on loans or purchases?"

The results revealed that only 57% of the Absentees were able to save, although 80% of the Attendants were putting aside a portion of their wages. Again, 81% of the Absentees, but only 42% of the Attendants were burdened with debts (excluding house payments, which are actually part of a savings program).

Housing: The data indicated that housing conditions do bear a strong relationship to absenteeism.

The percentage of employees owning their own homes was smaller in the Absentee group than among the Attendants. The Absentees lived farther away from their work (10.8 mile average) than did the Attendants (8.6 mile average). In addition the Absentees were housed in more crowded living quarters. It was determined that, on the average, the Absentees lived in a 3.1 room house, with an average of 2.1 other people. The Attendants lived in houses that had an average of 4.5 rooms which accommodated an average of 2.2 other people. A further statistical analysis revealed that among the Absentees there was a very poor relationship between the number of rooms in houses and the number of people living in them. That is, among the Absentees there were many instances where few people lived in a large house and many people lived in a small house. Among the Attendants there was a more definite relationship between the number of people and the number of rooms.

Transportation: The results of the two questions on transportation showed that the Absentees were more inclined to drive their own cars and were less inclined either to ride with other workers or to enter share-the-ride plans with others.

Personal Differences

AGE: The Absentees constituted a significantly younger group. Their average age was 31 years, as compared to 37 for the Attendants.

Intelligence: The Attendants had a normal distribution of intelligence test scores with an average I.Q. of 100. As a group, the Absentees had a lower intelligence level with an average I.Q. of 95. This difference is reasonably significant.

Fatigue: During the six-months' period studied, 32% of the Absentees and only 3% of the Attendants lost weight. Further 27% of the Absentees and only 12% of the Attendants reported that they felt tired when they arrived at work.

Emotional Stability: If the employee is worried or concerned very much over his family or personal condition, his general actions may be adversely affected. From the answers to the questions, "Have you any especially serious worries created by family, lack of family, social contacts or lack of social contacts?" and "Have you ever wished you knew someone with whom you could discuss your worries confidentially?", it was evident that the Absentees were more inclined to worry, or to fail to answer the questions.

Attitude: The Attendants had a much healthier attitude toward their work at Lockheed. When asked if they liked their present job, 75% of the Attendants and only 50% of the Absentees said "Yes". One-half of the Attendants and only 27% of the Absentees reported that their job at Lockheed is about the best they ever had.

Again, the Attendants were more optimistic about their chances for the future. When asked which of several factors was the most important about working at Lockheed, both groups rated "Being essential to the war effort" as most significant. However, the Absentees ranked "Wages" as second, whereas the Attendants ranked "Security for the future" as their second choice.

Opinion About Absenteeism: It is interesting to point out that 92% of the Absentees and 82% of the Attendants believed that absenteeism hurts the war·effort. In the opinion of both groups, absenteeism is caused most by the following factors arranged in order of importance: illness, home responsibilities, improper job placement, fatigue, and transportation. Both groups agreed that absenteeism is least influenced by: inadequate tooling, job shopping, and poor housing.

In the Scramble for Enough Employees and the Hurried Attempts to Get Reasonable Production from Those Hired Personnel, Work in Many Plants Lacks Cohesion and Continuity, so There is Much Needless Backtracking and Confusion.

Integrated Individualized Training Program

By Natalie Kneeland

Psychological Corporation,
New York, N. Y.

THE forgotten man, the individual employee, towers as a giant in these days of labor shortage. Management has learned the lesson of having to make the most out of what is available. Special pains are taken to determine the assets and liabilities of each applicant, in order that he or she may be placed to best advantage. More attention is given to the follow-up of the individual on the job, so that he will become productive as quickly as possible. The way is being paved for the return of personnel who left to enter war industries or the armed services. Plans for their reinstatement include a thorough searching and trying out of abilities. The employee, as an individual, has come into his own.

Packaged Courses Not Enough

TRAINING *Within Industry* recognized the need for good individual training and supervision when it prepared the packaged courses, JIT, JRT and JMT. Their well deserved popularity is outstanding in the field of training. Provision is made in these courses for the active participation of each class member. However, this does not entirely solve the problem. Unless the members are closely followed up, the trainer has no assurance that the points demonstrated in class are actually applied on the job. In fact, this has been a major criticism of these courses. However, the fault would seem to lie, not in the courses, but in the assumption underlying the criticism, that application will naturally follow, or that professional skill in training or supervision can be mastered in ten or twelve hours spent in class. We know enough about the difficulties in transfer of training to question the first assumption. As for the second, while the feel for and the knowledge of techniques of training can be acquired in such courses, skill in training or supervision, comes about through supervised practice on the job. In other words, real learning starts when the individual tries out for himself, what he has learned. This accounts for some of the difficulties that trainers themselves experience in learning to teach these methods courses. Until a trainer has made them thoroughly his own and has added his unique contributions, he feels unsure of himself. Neither can he learn to teach these courses effectively by the "monkey-see: monkey-do" principle, for such learning results in rubber stamp training, lacking in both inspiration and individuality.

Training Must Be Individualized

THE problem boils down to the fact that training on both supervisory and worker levels, to be effective, must meet the needs, not only of a particular group, but of each individual in that group, and must be followed up personally. The situation is made more acute because of the wide variation in background and experience of personnel, these days. People are working who never worked before. We jokingly say "The're either too young or too old", or "We'll take him, if he's just warm", and then go about making productive workers out of persons whom we would not have even considered interviewing, in the past.

As the cream of the crop is skimmed off, we learn to scrape the barrel. In so doing, unexpected abilities are discovered which, with care and training, can be made to yield valuable returns for both the individual and the organization. It is doubtful that such untapped resources would have ever have come to light under conditions of an expanded labor market. This discovery and salvaging of potential manpower is a bright, forward step in personnel practice and one not to be discarded on the return of full employment.

Situation Will Become More Complicated

IN THE period ahead of us, the situation will be even more complicated. Many will return to their former jobs with skills and newly discovered abilities of great value to their organization. We must be alert to these changes. Others will go through a trying period of transition to normal, civilian occupation. This will demand the utmost patience and understanding of individual needs, on our part. Refresher training will have to take into consideration how much the individual needs to be "refreshed", and how much he can take. Too large or too small a dose of training will be equally disastrous. The starting point for such training must be determined through individual contact.

In the on-rush of new employees, it will be all too easy to lose sight of those who have stayed with us. Their jobs have been of the stay-at-home variety, for the most part, lacking glamour or thrill. In contrast with those with tales to tell, their contribution may appear insignificant and they themselves may be made to feel inferior. Special attention must be paid to this group to prevent this feeling from developing.

We need, then, to supplement ready-made, wholesale, streamlined group instruction with individualized training. This type of training requires a different approach and a special technique. It centers on the individual to be trained, rather than on the content to be taught. It is, of necessity, a continuous process to fit in with the progress of the individual—a made-to-measure model, adaptable and up-to-date.

Types of Interview

Do we have a technique available to cope with this demand for individualized training? Fortunately, the answer is "yes", for the interview, when properly conducted, serves the purpose admirably. We are prone to think of the interviewing technique in terms of its use with workers only, whereas it is equally effective as a means of training those on the supervisory or executive level. Furthermore, it is a flexible tool, with various uses.

Selective Interview

TRAINING begins in the first contact an individual has with his organization, for it is here that he receives that important first impression. The *selective interview*, therefore, is the base note of training. Unfortunately, there is a general feeling that anyone can do employment interviewing, given a little practice, which probably accounts for some of the failure in selection. The technique of interviewing must be learned as one learns any complex business procedure, not by trial and error, but through study and performance under supervision. Practice will improve performance, but not practice alone.

Induction Interview

THE *induction interview* logically picks up where the *selection interview* leaves off. Here the individual worker or executive is made to feel at home, is shown where he is to work and is given necessary information about his job. Here, too, the job is sold to him in concrete terms. Army experience has brought home to us the importance of this induction period. Orientation back to civilian life will need to be as thoughtfully worked out. Transfer from one department to another also calls for careful induction. It is particularly important when the transfer is not of the individual's choosing. Induction at this point is sometimes overlooked because the person is not new in the organization.

Follow-up Interview

THE *follow-up interview* to see how the employee is progressing and to give necessary encouragement and help is a time and error saver, and a morale builder, when rightly handled. Furthermore, it is a means of holding a new employee through the difficult period of adjustment to a new job. Following up older employees on the job makes them feel that they are considered as individuals, not just cogs in a machine, and also helps to keep them from establishing wrong habits or from falling into a rut.

The aim of a follow-up interview is to draw out the employee, rather than to give him information, and in so doing, to find out where he needs help. Such an interview may turn into a corrective interview, but the correction is made at the time it is needed, rather than after the error has become established. The weakness in follow-up interviewing is that it tends to be superficial. Giving a pat on the back is construed as adequate follow-up.

While commendation is important, it does not take the place of really finding how an employee is getting along and what he needs in order to improve. It is a part of, not the whole process, of follow-up interviewing. The follow-up interview is also likely to be overlooked as a frill, when there is a pressure of work. And yet it is at just such a time that an employee needs encouragement and help.

Correction Interview

THE *correction interview* is rarely overlooked, although it is often mishandled. Because of this fact, it is one of the most frequent causes of employee resentment and dissatisfaction, with resulting lowered production. Furthermore, the tendency to concentrate on the correction interview builds up antagonism towards the whole process of interviewing. The immediate reaction to an interviewing situation becomes "What have I done, now?" This negative response can be overcome only by careful handling of correction and proper attention to follow-up interviews as well.

Free Interview

THE *free interview* refers to the spontaneous type of interview called at the employee's request, or one which covers a wider area of exploration than those previously mentioned. For this reason, its training function is sometimes overlooked. And yet, the free interview is one of the most effective training techniques at our command. The indirectness of the approach makes for a good learning situation. The individual has a recognized need to start with, if he comes to the interview of his own accord, or is made to feel he has something to contribute, if the interviewer takes the initiative. Because the discussion is "free", many points come to light which might not appear in interviews that are focused on a given problem. The very process of learning to discuss problems in an objective way with the interviewer is a valuable result of this indirect training.

Apart from its training function, the free interview provides an excellent channel for the expression of individual opinion and supplies information of invaluable assistance to management. Intelligent handling of these interviews fosters mutual understanding and cooperation. An insincere or unsympathetic attitude on the interviewer's part, on the other hand, arouses resentment and distrust, so that the interview does more harm than good. The very informality of the situation is at the same time an asset and a drawback—an asset in that it allows for a free play of opinion, a hindrance to the extent that the interview may not seem of sufficient importance to warrant care or thought in handling.

Personnel Review

THE *personnel review* on production and merit ratings demands special tact and understanding on the part of the interviewer. Since such interviews are ordinarily held only at periodic intervals, and have a direct bearing on the employee's chances for advancement, they carry a good deal of weight in the minds of both the interviewee and the interviewer. However, they are usually conducted by top management or experienced interviewers and consequently, are more likely to be better handled than the more frequent, less formal interviews.

Where Does Personnel Counseling Fit In?

WHAT is the relationship between personnel counseling and individualized training and how does it fit into the entire picture? While personnel counselors employ some of the interview techniques described, they do not ordinarily attempt to cover the whole field of selection, job training and supervision, and follow-up. Personnel counseling usually starts where job training and supervision stops. It is thus a supplement to rather than a substitute for individualized training. It takes over the job in certain restricted areas.

There are various reasons underlying the installation of a counseling program in a given organization. It may be found that foremen or supervisors are too busy with technical details to give sufficient time to personnel problems, or lack the necessary skill in handling people. Some companies feel that an "outsider", not closely related to the job is in a better position to give objective help and will be consulted more readily by employees. The interpretation of what is included under the term "personnel counseling" also differs. Some organizations include under counseling personnel those responsible for the selection of employees, as well as those concerned with follow-up. Plans for the return of the veteran have brought this employment phase of counseling into prominence and are also stressing the importance of individual training and supervision.

The interview is the natural tool of the personnel counselor. If the manner in which this tool is handled by him differs greatly from that of other interviewers, this discrepancy quickly becomes apparent to those being interviewed. Because personnel counseling is so bound up with job training and supervision, it should be considered a part of the whole individualized training program, rather than a separate entity. It should play a duet not a solo—the right hand should know what the left hand does.

Interviewing Techniques Form a Training Pattern

IN CONSIDERING the whole problem of individualized training, we need to recognize the progressive and over-lapping relationship which exists between the different types of interviews, whether handled by employment interviewers, personnel counselors, job supervisors or members of the personnel department. They form a training pattern which starts with the selection interview as the core, and works outward to the personnel review.

The induction interview covers both the introduction of the employee into the department and preliminary or boot training on the job. Follow-up interviews are carried on continuously and correction interviews as the need arises. Other things being equal, the more effective the follow-up interviews, the less the necessity for the corrective type. These three types of interviews deal with on the job training. The free interview, while broader in scope, is so closely related to the follow-up and corrective interviews as to be indistinguishable at times. Just as a follow-up interview may become a corrective interview before it is finished, so a free interview may bring facts to light that would ordinarily be handled in a follow-up or corrective interview. The personnel review sums up the individual's progress and response to training and is an indirect measure of the effectiveness of the other interviewing techniques.

Employer-Employee Relationship Established

THE employer-employee relationship established in the selection interview should logically be carried through the interviews that follow. Too often, there is a decided gap between them, or downright contradiction. An employee may be all set in the selection interview, for a warm reception in the department. Instead, he is rudely inducted, grudgingly received, or even allowed to shift for himself. His induction may be well handled, but there may be no subsequent follow-up, or he may be corrected later, in a way to cause both embarrassment and resentment. Or the case may be the other way around. He may get far better treatment on the job than in the employment office. A poorly handled free interview may destroy the effectiveness of all the others.

Points brought out in a personnel review may be a greater reflection on the poor type of individualized training the employee received than on his inability to learn. Good supervision also shows up in the personnel review. Frequently information given in different interviews, or by different interviewers does not tally.

The Need for Integrated Training

BECAUSE individualized training is handled by many different people and employs various interviewing techniques, the training pattern easily becomes confused, vague or distorted. What is needed is definite integration of interviewing techniques.

This means, first of all, that the techniques be examined to see that they are consistent in essentials. Are they carrying out the same basic principles? Do they "give information, get information and make a friend"? Are the interviewers themselves aware of the interviewing pattern?

Second, training in interviewing should be part of all supervisory training. In this training, the relationship between the different types of interviews should be brought out so that each interviewer sees the part he plays in the total picture. If personnel counseling is carried on as a separate program, its rôle should be made clear. To be realistic, training should include observation and practice in interviewing. Those learning this technique should be warned of the danger of their interviews becoming stereotyped and the need for keeping the "individual" versus the "case" approach. Since one of the advantages of individualized training is the fact that employees come in contact with different personalities, this individual touch should be encouraged, provided the basic principles underlying interviewing techniques are carried out.

Periodic Conferences

FINALLY, some form of follow-up should be installed, to see that the techniques hew to the line marked out. In addition to establishing a form of rating on interviewing techniques, periodic conferences can be held in which situations and problems in interviewing are discussed. Such group discussion brings out a variety of viewpoints and helps to familiarize each member with what the others are doing. It helps to stimulate the apathetic or unsure members and to curb the too venturesome. Holding individual interviews on interviewing is another method of follow-up.

This procedure was used by the writer with members of two supervisory store groups, following a series of meetings on supervision. In the individual interviews it was possible to determine the practical application of information learned and to follow through on problems that arose in the discussion. This interviewing of supervisors on their use of supervisory techniques served, at the same time, to emphasize the value of the interview as a training tool.

Unless definite steps are taken to integrate individualized training, it will continue to lack cohesion and continuity. Planned integration will prevent needless backtracking and confusion. It will give both interviewers and interviewees a sense of direction and completeness. In place of broken ranks, individualized training will present a united front.

The Author Spent Five Months in Research among the Employees of an Oil Company at a Time When there Was a C.I.O. Organization Drive on. This Enabled Him to Get a New Slant Upon the Factors Which Move One Worker Towards a Union and Another in the Opposite Direction.

Who Goes Union
and Why

By WILLIAM F. WHYTE

Department of Sociology,
University of Chicago,
Chicago 37, Ill.

WE WERE discussing the Oil Workers International Union (CIO), which was then trying to organize the Blank Oil Company. Worker Bill Walcutt put his views in this way:

> I have a son and a nephew fighting in the army. I don't think it's right when they are fighting for freedom abroad for us to have a dictatorship here. That's what a union is to me—just a dictatorship. Maybe I'm wrong, but they have to convince me. No, I never have attended any of their meetings. I didn't take no interest.

Worker Lou Jones had this to say:

> In the union, everybody has got an equal right to decide what should be done. Before you make any agreement with the management, it has to be passed by a majority vote of the men. The union is really a democracy.

Jones and Walcutt both worked under the same foreman. They had worked about the same length of time with Blank Oil Company, and their wages were the same. Yet on the subject of unions, they seemed to be talking about entirely different things. Why?

Favorable to Company but Union

Now, just to complicate the problem, let's listen to worker Joe Logan. He said:

This has always been a good Company to work for. They have taken care of their men. In hard times other companies have laid off a lot of men, but if you have been on the monthly payroll with Blank Oil, you could be practically certain that you had a steady job as long as you did your work.

In all my talks with the Blank workers, I never heard a man say anything more favorable to the Company. Yet Joe Logan belonged to the union. Not only that; he probably was more influential than any other man on the Company payroll in the union organization drive.

How can we explain these differing reactions? There are pounds of books and articles discussing the general conditions that lead to labor organization, but the scientist seeking to explain human behavior cannot be content with general explanations which fail to apply to particular cases. Unless he is prepared to say that human behavior is totally erratic and unpredictable, he should be able to discover objective factors which determine the opinions and actions of Bill Walcutt, Lou Jones, and Joe Logan.

Industrial executives, personnel men, and labor leaders have the same interest. They deal not with the labor movement in general but with particular workers in particular plants. They cannot be satisfied with the vague pronouncements of the academic personnel pundits.

To get down to cases, we must sweep aside the orthodox theories that attempt to explain labor organization in terms of wages, hours, and working conditions. It is only when we conceive this as a problem in human relations that we can understand the varying reactions of workers who are all employed by the same company.

Pattern in Human Relations

THERE is a pattern in human relations. As the child grows up, he becomes accustomed to a certain pattern in his relations with others. When a man needs to adjust himself only gradually to changes in this pattern, he feels secure. When sudden and drastic changes are forced upon him, he feels disturbed and insecure. It is against this background that we must understand labor organization.

We have to see the worker's behavior in terms of his social adjustment. Joining a union is one way of regaining social equilibrium when the worker's accustomed pattern of human relations has been upset. To be more specific, we can predict that—

If the worker has become accustomed in his early life to a pattern of human relations that is not disturbed when he goes into industry, he will be strongly opposed to unions, looking upon them, in the words of Bill Walcutt, as "just a dictatorship."

If his pattern of human relations is upset in his work yet he manages to gain a measure of readjustment through building up relations with his superiors or through greatly increased social activity in another field, then the worker will be "on the fence" in the union question.

If the worker develops a pattern of human relations that is seriously disturbed in his job experience, and if he finds no other compensating activity, then he will join the union.

So far we seem to be talking in vague, general terms. Nevertheless, we are dealing with factors which can be observed with objectivity. If we get down to cases, if we learn to know the workers and their jobs intimately, then we can see precisely what is meant by these unfamiliar ideas—and we can see specifically, from case to case, who goes union and why.

Organization Drive Studied

I KNEW the workers of "Blank Oil Company" in "Oil City". I spent two days a week, nine hours a day for five months in hanging around with the men as they worked, interviewing them informally and listening to their conversations among themselves.

I broke in at a time when the Oil Workers International Union was in the midst of an organization drive and the workers were split into contending factions. I began my study with the permission of top management, but the Oil City supervisors were reluctant to let me into their plants for fear that my presence would stir up suspicion and resentment against management. At first some of the workers were suspicious and reluctant to talk, although I assured them that in writing reports to management I would conceal the identities of my informants. However, I continued to hang around until some of the more influential workers began to take me into their confidence and to assure their fellows that I was trustworthy. After that my work was easy.

Oil City was a particularly interesting place for an exploration of labor relations, for it represented in a small scale, and compressed in time, many of the problems of rapidly changing industrial America. In this part of the country the oil industry was very young. It was only a little over fifteen years ago that oil was discovered in Oil City itself. Many of the Oil City workers had had previous experience in the industry, but a large body of them had grown up on farms and had never before done factory work.

Jobs Changing Rapidly

THE workers I knew were most of them engaged in manufacturing aviation gasoline from natural gas. The Company had for years been manufacturing regular automobile gasoline from natural gas in a process which had been reduced largely to routine work, but the workers making aviation gasoline were dealing with much more complex and less easily predictable processes. By the time the Oil City Hi-Test plant went into operation in 1938, the supporting science of chemical engineering was already far advanced and still progressing rapidly, so that it was possible to introduce changes in work procedure with bewildering rapidity.

Aviation gasoline workers needed an adaptability and a technical knowledge that had never been required of them before. They had to operate engines, pumps, a great cracking furnace, large cooling towers, tall fractionating columns, and other complex installations—all of them so closely interrelated that a small change in the operations of one unit could require immediate adjustments in all the other units.

College Men Brought In

UNTIL the recent large scale development of aviation gasoline, it was possible for workers who learned their jobs well to move into the ranks of supervision, to become foremen, plant superintendents, or gain even higher positions. About six years ago, top management decided that, in view of the increasing scientific complexity of the industry, men with college technical educations would be required to fill many supervisory jobs. The workers interpreted this to be a flat rule against promoting noncollege men. As one of them said to me, "It looks like I'll stay in this job until I retire because I don't have a college education."

For American industry this was no new development. In many of our older industries the same rule prevails, but the difference is that the practice which grew up there gradually over a period of decades was more or less sudden in its effects on some of the employees in the Blank Oil Company. As a result, there were many ambitious young workers who had thought the road to advancement was open to the top but found themselves blocked by the lack of a college education. This was an exceedingly frustrating experience and gave rise to much resentment against the Company. It was not easy for them to reconcile themselves to a permanent working class position in the land of opportunity.

Young Supervisors over Older Workers

THIS new development was beginning to draw a line of social distinction between workers and supervisors. In the cases of recently appointed supervisors, the men must take their orders from young men highly trained in science but with little experience in the actual operation of the equipment. Unfortunately, the education which qualifies the supervisors in the technical aspects of their work tends to disqualify them in the field of handling men. They learn in college a "logic of efficiency", a system of organizing entirely in terms of the technical aspects of production—without regard to the human equation. They distrust the "knowhow" gained by the worker through years of experience at his job. They look upon human nature as an obstacle to be overcome in the interests of science and production.

When supervisors of this type are placed over workers accustomed to taking orders from men like themselves, friction is bound to develop. That was the case in the Hi-Test Plant. In any account of grievances, the names of former foremen Ed Jones and Tom Fitch figured prominently.

Jones and Fitch

Jones was a young man who had worked himself through college with jobs in and around the Hi-Test Plant. Shortly after he received his degree in chemical engineering, he was made foreman of the Plant, supervising men who had much more experience than he. As one of the workers sourly commented.

> "You see, we teach them all they know about operations, and then they turn around and boss us."

In the old type gasoline plants, little supervision was required or given, and the men were accustomed to a great degree of independence. Jones and Fitch did not feel that they were doing their jobs unless they were in the plant a good part of the day, giving orders which left very little scope to the judgment of the workers.

Jones and Fitch were also accused of favoritism. There were certain workers in whom they had confidence, and there were others whose ability they did not trust. They would be "down on" a worker over a period of weeks and make him a scapegoat for any operational difficulties. One man quit because he could not "take it", and several others told me that they had great difficulty in keeping from hitting the foreman.

They Pass On

The workers felt that the favoritism was not based upon ability. The foremen encouraged the men to talk about their fellow workers, and "squealing to the boss" seemed to be a good means of gaining his favor. Thus the foremen's behavior not only created resentment against them. It also created distrust and jealousy among the workers.

At the time of my exploration in Oil City, both Jones and Fitch had passed on to other jobs, and Tom Lloyd, the new foreman, was exceedingly skillful in handling his men. However, the frictions engendered by previous supervisors left an atmosphere of insecurity, which stimulated the growth of union organization.

Old Type Superintendent

There was one other general factor in the situation. At the time that oil was discovered in Oil City, the Blank Company was a relatively small organization.

Frank Collins, the General Superintendent of Field Operations, was able to keep in close touch with all the men and meet them frequently on an informal basis.

The result was that the men felt free to talk to the General Superintendent. When they had grievances over local conditions, they would send representatives to the main office to talk with Collins, and they always returned to their jobs satisfied that he would do anything possible for them. Sometimes men who had been fired by local superintendents had persuaded Collins to reinstate them and place them in other plants. Whatever action he took, the men knew that he would listen to them patiently, with a real desire to understand their problems.

Then in the late thirties, with the developments in aviation gasoline, the Blank Company rapidly turned into big business so that it was impossible for Frank Collins or any man to keep up personal contacts with the employees. And then in 1939, Frank Collins died. From all over, by train and car, and at their own expense, the Blank Company workers swarmed into the main office city to pay their last tribute to the man who never forgot them. That was the end of an era.

Clearing Up Laxities

THE man who succeeded Collins as General Superintendent was completely unknown to the workers of Oil City. To make matters more difficult for him he had to begin his work by acting upon certain laxities in local conditions. There was widespread gambling in and around the plants during work hours, and the men were taking company gasoline for use in their cars. There was, of course, a rule against taking gasoline, but the men had become accustomed to look upon free gasoline as almost part of their wages. The new General Superintendent acted abruptly. He fired the local superintendent, the district superintendent, the state superintendent, and seven workers. Four of the workers were eventually reinstated, but, though four years had passed since the shakeup, the employees talked of it to me as if it had just happened. It seemed to change completely their relations with top management.

In the old days, through Frank Collins, they had had a line of communication direct to the main office. With the growth of the Company and the appointment of a new General Superintendent, that line had completely broken down. The men no longer had a means of appealing over the heads of local authorities when they had grievances.

With that general background, we can see that there was an opportunity for union organization, but no such generalizations can tell us why certain men were in favor of the union, others on the fence, and still others opposed. To answer that question, we have to go more into detail upon the nature of the jobs—from a human relations standpoint.

Influence of Farm Background

IN HI-TEST Plant, there were three distinctly different types of jobs. There were the engine repairmen who were called in to service the equipment. There were the engine operators in charge of six large engines in a building about a hundred yards away from the control room. In the control room handling the chemical processes, was an operator in charge of each shift, with two men under him. Related to the Hi-Test Plant and under the same foreman was a chemical plant making the catalyst used in Hi-Test operations. Here there was a catalyst operator in charge of each shift, and he had eight to ten helpers under him.

I found that almost without exception the strongest anti-union men were to be found among the engine operators and engine repairmen, nor was this a matter of coincidence. With the exception of one man (who was pro-union), they had all grown up on farms. Engine operator Walcutt had this to say about his early life:

Early Life Described

We were way out in the country. There wasn't anybody living very close to us. When I was growing up, we all worked twelve to fourteen hours a day on that farm. We had to work hard to make it pay. A farm is just like a business. If you don't work hard to make it pay, you can't keep it going. Us kids just went to school maybe six or eight months of the year. Yes, we went to church on Sunday. There wasn't much visiting between families where I lived. We just stayed on the farm, working all the time. No, there wasn't much talking back and forth when we was out on the farm doing our work. We had no time for that. My father told us what to do and we just did our work.

He went on to comment upon his work. I like that job of operating engines. Yes, the noise is bad, and it has hurt my hearing some, but I got so I didn't mind it. No, there isn't much chance to talk with anybody down there. The supervisors never bother us much either.

That picture holds for other engine operators besides Walcutt. The men grew up under close parental supervision. They were accustomed to a considerable degree of social isolation while they worked. When they went into industry, the foreman could step easily into the place that had been held by their fathers. They worked alone, only one operator being required for each eight hour shift. There was no occasion for conflict with the supervision. The engines operated very much the same, year in and year out, and even such aggressive foremen as Ed Jones and Tom Fitch rarely set foot in the engine room.

Only Stage Setting Changed

FOR these former farm boys, the stage setting had been changed, but from the human relations standpoint, there had been very little change. The men therefore felt very well adjusted in their jobs and looked upon the union as an extremely unwelcome intruder.

For the engine repairmen, the picture needs very little change. They too came off the farms. The nature of their work remained the same, year after year, and they had no problems with the supervision. While they worked on the Hi-Test equipment, they were not directly under the plant foreman. They had their own chief repairman, a man who had spent the first twenty-five years of his life on a farm and had only an eighth grade education. They got along with him with an easy informality growing out of similar backgrounds and interests.

Experience of Non-farm Boy

WHEN we come upon a non-farm boy as strongly anti-union as the former farmers, we discover an additional factor in the situation. Take the case of catalyst operator Martin Shockley who had this to say;

> I don't want to have anything to do with an organization that's run by communists and racketeers. When I have to pay an organization in order to hold my job, I'll just quit. The way I look at it, if my supervisor don't want me to work for him then I ought to get out and work some place else. If the men in here don't like working for Blank Oil Company, why don't they get out and get a job some place else instead of staying here and biting the hand that feeds them?
>
> Of course, my case may be a little different from the rest of the men. My mother has always taught me to believe that Blank Oil Company was the only Company in the world. My father worked for the Company when I was about four years old. That was when Joe Blank was just getting started. My father knew him pretty good then. He had just worked for Blank for a few months when a fire broke out in the plant. In fighting that fire, my father got pneumonia and died. After that my mother got a check every month. It wasn't from the Company, it was from Joe Blank's personal account. That check kept coming until my oldest brother was able to go to work for the Company. Then the check was cut down some, and when I was able to go to work so that the two of us together could carry the load, the check was cut out. In those early days we used to spend some time on Joe Blank's estate. That hasn't happened for years, but he still remembers my mother every year with a Christmas card and a birthday card.

Joined Union for a While

IT IS clear that Shockley enjoyed a relationship with management which was quite exceptional, even in a Company which took pride in its humane personnel policies. As we shall see from two other examples, personal relations with management tend to turn the worker away from unions. However, this early experience did not entirely insulate Shockley from labor organization. In an earlier CIO drive, when he was in the midst of a conflict with foreman Ed Jones, Shockley signed a union pledge card. But then the popular foreman, Tom Lloyd, succeeded Jones, and Shockley was elected as a company union representative, which led to frequent conferences with the management. It was this changed situation, together with his early background, which made Shockley so strongly anti-union.

Not all former farm boys were anti-union, but when we find some favoring organization, we also find that their early backgrounds and their adjustments to the supervision are quite different from those of the farmer-engine operators or repairmen. In Hi-Test Plant there were three pro-union workers who had started life on the farm.

Pro-union Farm Boys

OPERATOR Copeland was thirteen when his father was killed in an accident. He then left home to go into farm labor for several years until he started to work for the Blank Company. He worked under Jones and Fitch.

The father of operator Dixon raised cattle and spent many days and weeks away from home at city markets. Dixon and his brother took charge of the work in his absence. When in his middle teens, he left the farm for a job with the Blank Company. When his plant was shut down, he lost that job. Rehired later, he was again laid off in the depression. On his third try with the Company, he worked his way up into Hi-Test Plant. There he had special difficulties with foreman Fitch who, during one period, made him a scapegoat for everything that went wrong in the plant.

Operator Benson had to leave the farm at the age of thirteen when his father lost the land. For a time he worked at farm labor. He had his introduction to unions on a construction job which had a closed shop. He worked in Hi-Test when Jones and Fitch were still in charge.

In contrast to the experience of the farmer anti-unionists, none of these men was constantly under his father's supervision up to the time of his maturity. Two continued farming for a time after leaving home, but, as farm laborers, their experience was quite different from that of living in a settled family group under the direction of their fathers. It is clear that a man's reactions to unions are not molded by living in the fresh air and keeping close to the soil. Rather it is the pattern of human relations developed in early years which pushes him one way or the other when the conflict arises.

Those on the Fence

THE workers who were on the fence as the labor election approached were particularly interesting because of the conflicting forces that influenced them.

Take the case of Joe Walling. He worked on his father's farm into his late teens. As he put it,

When I was growing up, I didn't think my father could do any wrong. I tried to do whatever he told me. When I went to work, I looked upon the foreman just like he was my father, and I tried to do everything just like he wanted it done. I didn't think the Company could do any wrong. I asked if other men had resented this attitude.

Yes, they did. I didn't realize it at the time, but I know now that they considered me a —— (subservient, self seeking). I didn't even know what that was then, but now that I look back on it, I can see that I didn't have any real friends among the men. I didn't know what the cause of it was. I was just doing the thing that I thought was right to do.

Fired and Rehired

BUT then he was fired by one supervisor, and he told me, "I learned my lesson. I don't act that way any more." However, the influence of those early years was stronger than Walling realized. Rehired by the Company, he became an exceedingly capable and ambitious operator. He was friendly with Jones and Fitch, and was known as the foreman's favorite. One of the workers who was a foreman's scapegoat discovered that Walling had complained against him to Fitch. This "squealing to the boss" stirred up resentment against him among the men.

Probably this would not have disturbed Walling if he had been promoted into supervision, as he had been hoping. However, as it became increasingly evident that no non-college man would make this jump, he identified his interests more and more with his fellow workers and tried to win their friendship.

Favors Union

THAT was the situation when a verbal bombshell landed among the Hi-Test workers. The recently revived company union had been negotiating with management for higher wages. A plea was being made in behalf of the Hi-Test operators, who, it was claimed, had to be especially skilled to handle their complex equipment. In opposing this plea, a management representative argued that the jobs did not require quite as much skill as was claimed.

The workers felt that this was a terrible insult. Walling reacted to it by talking heatedly in favor of the CIO. But then time passed, and the situation changed.

Some of the workers were being transferred to a plant in another area. Walling decided to organize a farewell party for them. He talked to other workers, and, after several telephone conversations, managed to persuade the state superintendent, the state personnel man, and the local supervisors to attend.

The party was a great success. Walling spent some of his time talking cordially with the state superintendent and the personnel man, and in his speech the superintendent paid tribute to Walling for his efforts in organizing the party.

Changes Attitude Again

W ALLING had reestablished his relationship with management, which had lapsed with the passing of Jones and Fitch. Shortly before the labor election, Walling told me that he thought there were "lots of crooked things" about unions. I asked if he had drawn that conclusion from some experience with the Oil Workers International Union. He said not; that he had been reading about it in the newspapers. Joe Walling had certainly read of union corruption before, but he had never before mentioned it to me as we talked about unions. Now, as his personal relations changed, his views changed. While he still expressed some dissatisfaction with Company policy, he reverted back almost to his old attitude, saying "There's no reason the Company couldn't be like a father to the men."

The case of operator Max Decker illustrates the same point. He was brought up on a farm, but his father also operated a sawmill and cotton gin and had little time to supervise the farm work. Decker left the farm for factory work when he was fifteen. That background, together with working under Jones and Fitch, would be expected to make Decker pro-union, and so it did—until he was elected to represent Hi-Test in the company union.

Becomes Company Union Representative

D ECKER and most of the other Hi-Test men looked upon the company union as a weak and ineffectual body, not really an organization at all. They were willing to vote for a representative only because the Company was then negotiating a new contract with the company union, and they felt that if the CIO lost the election and the contract were negotiated without them, some of their interests might be overlooked. Decker accepted his election with grave misgivings.

After he had been meeting with management representatives over a period of two weeks, he had this to say:

> I used to think that the Company was just out to get whatever it could from us. Now, I've been meeting with those men, and I've been studying them. I've come to the conclusion that they are really sincere. You can't be with a group of men for days like I was if they are hypocrites without you have seen that. I think they mean to be good to the men right now. If the company union wins this election, I think they'll just do their level best to make things nice for the men—for a while. I think we would be better off in the company union right now, but the thing is, is it always going to be that way?
>
> I asked how he would vote. I don't know. I'm still on the fence. It wouldn't do for me to come back to these men and try to convert them to the Company union. They would think I was bought off. That's what they're looking for. I just don't know what I'm going to do.

Troubled by Uncertainty

THERE is no question of Decker having been "bought off" by the offer of a cash payment. Management did not operate that way, and such an offer would have been indignantly rejected by Decker, who had in the past sacrificed his own interests out of loyalty to his fellow workers. It is clear that the man was troubled by his uncertainty and would have been much more comfortable with his old convictions. He was trying conscientiously to work for the men who elected him. There can be no question of his sincerity.

Was the representative won over by his own feeling of self importance gained through association with the "big shots?" Decker told me after he returned to Hi-Test that he had not enjoyed the negotiations, that they made him restless and impatient to get back to his plant. He said, "Somebody else can have that job. It bores on me." Whether Decker enjoyed himself or not does not alter the fact that for this period the nature of his personal relations was substantially changed. His attitudes adjusted themselves to that change.

Interests Outside Plant

OPERATOR Nolan was also on the fence. Working for another company, he had belonged to a union. An ambitious young man, he had risen rapidly with the Blank Company, only to find the road to supervision blocked. He had worked under Jones and Fitch. With this background, we would expect to find him in favor of unionization, but there were factors weighing on the other side. He had a relative working as a Blank Company supervisor in Oil City, with whom he was very friendly, though the two men were not in the same line of authority. Then in recent years Nolan had become exceedingly interested in his Baptist Church and had become a Sunday school superintendent. A large part of his time off the job was spent in working with members of his church. He once told me, "I would sooner neglect this job here than I would my church work." While Nolan faced many of the conditions that drove other men into unions, he had, like Walling and Decker, special relations with some of his superiors in the Company, and he also had managed to make his adjustment in human relations through plunging into activity outside of the plant.

Pro-Unionists

SO FAR we have discussed the staunch anti-unionists, those on the fence, and those who, in spite of some early farm experience, were in favor of the union. There remains only one more group: the workers who were such convinced union enthusiasts that they voluntarily undertook to promote the organization.

These men can best be understood against the background of the staunch anti-unionists, who grew up on farms, under constant supervision of their fathers, and with infrequent outside contacts. For the boy who grows up in town or city, the situation is quite different. The father may be away from home a good part of the time. The normal boy associates regularly with group of playmates, his "gang". He learns to lead his friends or to follow the leader. Even in small towns there is inevitably a certain amount of conflict between the authority of the gang leadership and that of the parents.

The boys' gang develops its own tightly knit organization upon an informal basis. The behavior of the boy is controlled primarily by his gang associates, and he becomes intensely loyal to them.

Natural Development of Informal Organizations

MEN of this background naturally develop their own informal organizations among fellow workers when they go into industry. After more than a decade of study and experimentation, the Western Electric Company research staff concluded that informal organizations of workers have a far greater effect upon production of the individuals than variations in native ability or than variations in lighting, rest periods, refreshments, and a number of other material factors. They also concluded that much of the friction between management and the workers arose through management's failure to recognize the existence of informal organizations among the men and to work through these established channels.

Those general statements apply perfectly to the voluntary union organizers. Not one grew up on a farm.

Jess Page went to work at the age of nine in a Southern textile mill, being hidden behind idle machinery with other child laborers when the Board of Directors was escorted through the plant. He had worked steadily since that time in a wide variety of jobs and had been in many conflicts with his supervisors.

Lou Jones grew up in a fair sized town, coming of working age in the early depression years. For months he rode about the country in box cars, looking for work. When he first got a job, the work was unsteady, and he had to make several changes before he finally came to work for the Blank Company.

Frank Lewis was born on a farm, but his father began to follow the oil fields when he was a small boy. At the age of fifteen he went to work himself, having several jobs before he was hired by Blank Oil.

Joe Logan's father was following the oil fields when Joe was born, being away from home much of the time. Joe started work in the petroleum industry when still in his teens.

Supervision that Gives Impetus

OF THESE four, Logan and Lewis worked under foremen Jones and Fitch. While those two supervisors were of course not the only ones responsible for friction among the workers of Blank Company, they will serve as samples of the sort of supervision that gives an impetus to union organization.

While these four had been considerably buffeted about in their work experience, none of them had responded by becoming neurotic or developing persecution complexes. They were among the most popular workers in the plants. They expressed themselves with a sense of humor and made no secret of their convictions.

Nor were they driven by a vindictive desire to gain revenge upon the Company for real or fancied injustices. On that point, we need only remember Joe Logan, who said, "This has always been a good Company to work for," and then went on to say what a good Company it was.

As Walling and Decker had adjusted themselves to the strain of industrial work through developing a line of communication with their superiors, as Nolan had made his adjustment in that way and through his church work, Page, Jones, Lewis, and Logan found their stability in the scheme of human relations through the union.

Outside Agitator Theory

THE intelligent business man has no difficulty in explaining the impetus toward unionization in a company which pays starvation wages and treats its workers simply as tools for profit making. But suppose the company pays good wages, provides for secure employment and rapid advancement, and that its executives, taking a real interest in the welfare of the employees, provide them with a number of insurance benefits in addition to wages. Such a company, according to the orthodox theories, should not have labor troubles. Yet this is a description of Blank Oil Company, which does have labor troubles. How can that be?

To this question, there is one common answer: "outside agitators' must be responsible; the workers can be discontented only if they are misled. The assumption is that men are so susceptible to propaganda that an "outside agitator" can go among completely contented workers and through argument and emotional appeals arouse in them a desire to join a union.

Difficulties of Theory

THERE are several difficulties with this theory. In the first place, some workers react to the same arguments in diametrically opposed manner, which makes it impossible to predict how they will behave from examining the nature of the appeal made to them. For example, it is generally considered a strong argument against unions to say that they are crooked, racketeering organizations. The strong union men have of course encountered this argument, but they dismiss it in the manner of Joe Logan, who said,

> Sure, there is graft in unions. Did you ever know of an organization where there wasn't some graft? Some of the nicest churches have graft in them, and all the schools have graft. But—And then he went on to defend his union.

In the Blank Company there were many men like engine operator Bill Walcutt, who, while professing to have an open mind, refused even to attend union meetings. Then there were many others who were already convinced unionists before the drive started. For them the meetings and organization work simply served to build up enthusiasm for promoting the cause among fellow workers. The outside organizer only has a chance to change the opinions of those who are on the fence. And such men have heard all the arguments on both sides many times before. If their social adjustment is more than usually disturbed, they will be receptive to the appeals of the organizer (who may still alienate them by playing his cards in a clumsy manner). If some of their problems have recently been smoothed out, they will pick flaws in the appeal and conclude, with Joe Walling, that "There is no reason the Company couldn't be like a father to the men."

CIO Lost Election

THE Oil Workers International Union lost the Blank Company election by a very narrow margin. However, all local observers, management included, agreed that if the election had taken place a month earlier, when local conditions were more disturbed, the CIO would have won.

In any closely contested election, it is the votes of the "on the fence" workers which are decisive. But even these voters are not an unknown quantity. On the basis of this analysis, it was possible for me to predict with a high degree of accuracy how they would react to each important change in human relations within the company during the course of the union organization campaign.

It is apparent then that unions c^the public service even under the most benevolently intentioned management. In fact, they can of or eedingly useful to such a management by providing a channel of communication for the adjustment of workers grievances, which might otherwise be blocked by dictatorial foremen and plant superintendents. It is for this reason that some executives prefer to deal with unions rather than with an unorganized body of workers.

Study of Human Relations Backward

ALTHOUGH in the past labor problems have been studied primarily in terms of wages and material conditions of work, it should be clear now that they are also problems in the adjustment of human relations. It is only through advances in that field that labor-management cooperation may be obtained.

Unfortunately the first hand study of human relations, of the relations of particular people at particular times and places, is still the most neglected of the social sciences. Mayo, Roethlisberger, and Dickson made the pioneering study in industry with their Western Electric experiments. Arensberg and Chapple have developed some of the theories I have used in explaining the behavior of the Blank Company Workers. And now the recently organized Committee on Human Relations in Industry at the University of Chicago, under the chairmanship of W. Lloyd Warner, and the research direction of Burleigh Gardner, is vigorously acquiring and applying knowledge in this field. The beginning has been made. Let us hope that it has not come too late.

At present it is difficult for people to think about a labor dispute without immediately trying to decide which side is to blame. The search for a scapegoat destroys the possibility of adjustment. Such punitive thinking leads only to open conflict. It is only through increased scientific knowledge increasingly applied that we can solve the difficult problems of adjusting human relations.

one common a.
be discon_____

We Have Always Thought that the Current and Widely Used System of Foreman Training Conferences Is Psychologically Wrong, and a Useless Waste of Time—Being Also an Insult to the Intelligence of Foremen.

Vitalizing Supervisors

By Pvt. Joe J. King

Formerly of Farm Security Administration,
Seattle, Wash.

HELPING to establish sound working relationships in governmental agencies is one of the most challenging jobs now confronting federal personnel officers. Not only is this true in the war period with its emotional stresses and strains resulting from war uncertainties, but equally important is its tremendous significance in the post-war period when returning war veterans must be helped to adjust to civilian job requirements.

Blanket Criticism

THE need is apparent. Everett Van Every, reviewing the new book, *Employee Relations in the Public Service* in the September, 1943, *Personnel Journal*, boldly stated: "The authors go along in the same vigorous style that we were accustomed to ten years ago. The study is literally charged with as fine a presentation of what constitutes good personnel relations in the public service as anything I have ever read. But how little of it is actually in practice! How few of our government agencies are actually carrying out the very principles of employee relations they so enthusiastically endorse! . . . . our public service agencies seem to me to be poorly administered when it comes to employee relations." Similar criticisms are appearing with increasing frequency in many magazines and journals.

If these blanket criticisms are true, the important consideration is what is being done to meet them. In the specific case of Farm Security Administration in the Pacific Northwest, something is being done. It all started last fall when we suddenly recognized that FSA "talked" a splendid employee relations program and "practiced" the opposite. Since that period of awakening we have slowly evolved a program of helping supervisory officials fulfill their responsibilities, not only of promoting efficient production, but also of developing healthy employee relations.

Base of Program

THE basis of the program in Oregon-Idaho-Washington is a realistic attitude toward employee relations. In our judgment the present FSA organization of 320 employees will always be subjected to emotional strains and disturbances. Each human being consists of three selves:

1. What he thinks he is.
2. What he thinks his supervisor thinks he is.
3. What he thinks his associates think he is.

Any one of these three selves can become tangled up with the selves of working associates. All sorts of unpredictable human misunderstandings can and do rapidly develop.

In addition to this, each human being has four fundamental needs: Work, Faith, Love, Recreation.

The order of importance of these needs will vary with the individual. Misunderstandings based upon emotional stresses and strains can easily and do readily develop among FSA workers.

The important need, therefore, is for supervisory officials to have the ability to evaluate a situation when a working relationship is becoming strained. What is the emotional cause of the strained relationship? Are the individuals unable to understand the situation? What are the human factors which are contributing to the tension?

Once it was recognized that FSA employee friction often results from emotional tensions which are not job connected, the next step was to convey this point of view to the rank and file of supervisors. There seemed to be four possibilities: written materials, lectures, individualized teaching, and conferences. The first possibility was impractical because the average supervisor is reluctant to read "required" materials. Lectures were ineffective because they lacked audience participation. Individualized teaching was out of the question because sufficient time, energy, and money was lacking. Conferences, therefore, proved to be the only method available.

Call Them In and Tell Them Off

FSA had already experimented with conferences. To begin with, FSA officials had prepared elaborate conference programs, called the subordinates into the conference, and laid down the policies. Very soon the subordinates described the conferences as a process "to call them in and tell them off." Thereupon the supervisory officials reversed the conference procedure, they did not prepare complete programs. Instead, they asked for suggestions from the subordinates and hesitated to assume leadership. This resulted in the human tendency for supervisors to defend their position against what seemed to them to be attacks upon the supervisors' ability to do their jobs. It was not long until these conferences intensified the friction and tension between superiors and subordinates.

Out of these trials and errors a conference technique has been developed which seems to be effective. Prior to the conference each subordinate is asked to prepare a statement on the weak points and the strong elements in his work unit. At the conference each subordinate has an opportunity to read his statement *without interruption*. After this is done in the general meeting, each subordinate is routed into the offices of the regional director, assistant director, program analyst, and personnel officer for individualized visits on the subordinate's particular problems. The regional director, it should be noted, assumes his direct responsibilities for supervisory relations. When the individual visits are completed, the group returns to a general session. There the regional director approves or disapproves the recommendations of the subordinates.

Lessons Learned

Out of these conferences all of us have learned a few simple rules which are helpful in maintaining sound employee relations. First, the supervisor should never interrupt a subordinate who is explaining or describing his work or problems. Let the subordinate talk freely and make suggestions without fear of ridicule. Second, the supervisor should always attempt to understand the human characteristics of the subordinate. He should endeavor to evaluate the emotional forces which are influencing the subordinate in the particular situation. Third, the supervisor should never argue with a subordinate. Fourth, the supervisor should never hastily criticize a subordinate. Finally, and of major importance, the supervisor should always treat the subordinate as *a particular individual in a particular situation at a particular time*.

Application of these rules in day to day FSA working relations is having a salutary effect. For example in September, 1943, a FSA regional bulletin was issued on the subject of transfer of FSA Civilian Employees. The last part of the bulletin read: "In every such case the Farm Security Administration will object to the release of the involved employee, giving the Civil Service Commission complete information as to why the employee should be retained in the Farm Security Administration. In such cases, the Commission will be able to make a judicial decision as to whether it is for the benefit of the total war drive that the employee remain in his present position or be transferred to another position. The decision of the Civil Service Commission is final . . . the personnel office has the responsibility of carrying out the above stated policy. Any question with reference to it should be referred to the personnel officer for clarification. All cases will be concurred in by the administrative officer involved, the personnel officer, and the regional director."

Bluntly Worded Bulletin

THIS bluntly worded bulletin had the psychological effect of stimulating employees to want to leave FSA. It was a morale destroyer. It was a disruptive influence upon working relations. Consequently, in December, 1943, the bulletin was rewritten: "When a release has been denied by FSA, an employee may seek further consideration of his case by means of appeal to the Regional Civil Service Commission officers. . . . If an employee appeals, our policy is to submit complete information and justification for our action and to abide by the final decision of the Commission. Each FSA employee should understand that the particular and unusual circumstances surrounding his individual case will be frankly and objectively considered by the Administration. If you wish to have your case considered, first talk with your immediate supervisor and then write the Regional Director outlining the particular circumstances with a copy to the supervisor."

In this rewritten bulletin each FSA employee was assured of particular attention to his particular needs at a particular time. He was told in straightforward terms that he was an individual and would be treated as an individual. The bulletin received excellent response and had a quieting effect upon employees who otherwise were restless.

Dealing with Deferments

ANOTHER example of our revitalized employee relations program is the matter of deferments. Because FSA employment was never classified as highly essential, our draft-age male employees suffered an unusually large amount of emotional stress and strain. Last fall many of them quit FSA to enter employment where a deferment could be obtained. At that time we lacked a clear cut approach to the employee who happened to be troubled by this particular problem.

Today, however, FSA supervisors know how to meet the problem. They counsel individually with the draft-age employee, indicating that FSA will do what it can to obtain a deferment, but they also indicate that if a deferment is not forthcoming, the individual must follow his conscience concerning service in the armed forces. If he stays on his FSA job until the Selective Service System calls him, he will receive re-employment rights after the war. The supervisor sits down with the individual and helps the individual work out his personal solution to his particular problem. It is an effective approach. It is resulting in closer working relations than in the past, and interestingly enough, it is helping to keep men at their FSA jobs and aiding to cut down labor turnover.

Consult Workers about Desires

STILL another example is on the matter of reduction of force. Last summer FSA in the Pacific Northwest suffered a sharp cut in budget, necessitating a painful reduction in personnel. The reduction was made without individualized conferences with the persons involved. The result was a high degree of emotional tension and resentment. In January the agency had to go through a similar reduction in personnel. This time, however, each affected individual was carefully and conscientiously consulted on his personal desires and feelings. There was a minimum of misunderstanding because each individual knew that his particular situation had been analyzed.

In conclusion this should be said, FSA in the Pacific Northwest is no longer leaving its employee relations to chance. It is encouraging its supervisors to cultivate their understanding of human behavior and human relations. It is repeatedly saying that in order for supervisors to get their subordinates to work together effectively they must understand the forces which motivate human beings. Above all, FSA is emphasizing that sound working relationships are not administered from a personnel office. They are developed and maintained by the entire membership of the organization, when each individual comes to strive for tolerance and sympathy toward his supervisors and subordinates alike.

Long Ago We Suggested to a Large Company with 25,000 Employees in One Plant that the Thing Should be Organized in Small Groups. They Did Not Do So, and the CIO Got Them, and They Still Have Plenty of Troubles.

Small Group Plan

By Carey O. Pickard

Reynolds Corporation
Macon, Ga.

THERE are certain observations I have made in the field of personnel during the past three years which I believe should be put down in writing for the benefit of others.

For instance, on a number of occasions I have noticed that many people holding responsible positions, both in our industry and out, seem to have the idea that to control attendance percentages (the word absenteeism is passé), turnover or any other situation requires a propaganda program based on flags flying, drums beating, poster displaying, and perhaps some chest-thumping. I am convinced that any person responsible for operating a personnel department, or anyone else, who operates only on the basis of such ballyhoo and believes it is getting results is not only kidding himself, but also is earning his salary under false pretenses.

Bally-hoo

OFTEN I have seen instances which convinced me of the value of one constantly growing belief: There is only one way to accomplish outstanding results in any undertaking at an industrial plant, and that is by an organized division of employees into small units and individual contacts by the proper persons forming a part of such groups. Of course, the plant-wide propaganda and ballyhoo can accomplish *some* results, but I'm speaking of outstanding results. To cite an instance, when we put on a Red Cross Campaign over a year ago, the usual plant-wide appeal was made. One production department employing 1,600 people promptly turned in over $1,600— or an average of $1.00 per employee. Another production department employing approximately the same number of employees turned in only $800—or about 50 cents per employee.

Bear in mind that each department received the identical plant-wide appeal. I told the $800 department head that he should be ashamed of his department's contribution as compared with the $1,600 department. He went back to his production building, got his people organized into units, and the next morning turned in an additional $500, although he had considered the campaign over when he got the first $800.

Regular Attendance

ATTENDANCE in one of our larger production departments usually ran as low as 87%, while in another major department, attendance averaged 96%. Both departments received the same benefits from plant-wide appeals through the weekly plant newspaper, bulletin boards, posters and the like. The department with the high attendance average had worked out a plan of keeping records of small groups, and personalizing the on-the-job attendance plan. In fact, this department was the only one in the entire production organization which had a well organized plan based on the small group theory. In other words, it had a departmental plan which was broken down by groups or units small enough to make each person in the group feel that the program applied to *her* instead of everybody but her.

Recently, a monthly publication devoted exclusively to attendance in war plants quoted the following statement of Mr. James T. Mangan, Director of War Promotions, Mills Industries, Inc., Chicago, Ill.:

"The key to this control is the *individual foreman*. He's struggling with it right now. Posters, charts, drives and the like won't mean a thing unless the *foreman* carefully and thoroughly makes all of the necessary moves. These moves are:

A. A personal talk with each absentee and a thorough discussion of all causes and excuses offered.
B. The personal stressing of accountability. An absence from work is *a sin of war*, unless completely justified.
C. The written record of the explanation by the employee.
D. Praise the model employees for their attendance records.
E. *Personal salesmanship by the foreman.* He should sell his employees one by one.

It's all up to the foreman."

Top Management on Record

I AM not acquainted with Mr. Mangan, but I am convinced that he has stated the only real answer, not only to the problem of poor attendance, but to any undertaking which any service organization in an industry wishes to pursue with outstanding results. There are many problems in industry which are just as costly as poor attendance or high turnover, whether it be in war or in peace. The same fundamental principle applies to all such undertakings.

As to the effectiveness of the plan, this to a very large measure, depends upon top management. Does the General Manager's backing consist of only the statement that he is interested in attendance percentages going up, or War Bond sales being high, or Red Cross quotas being met? Or does it go further and cause the foremen and supervisors to *feel* that if they put forth considerable effort—and some *time*—on the plan *every day* it will be looked upon with favor? Or do they feel that the General Manager has merely gone on record in favor of the plan, but in reality is only interested in getting out production? Farsighted top management knows that more production will be accomplished by the broader viewpoint.

Attendance Boosted

IN OUR plant, top management came to the conclusion that a plan devised and executed by production supervisory personnel in each department, sub-divided into small units, was worthy of time and effort to increase attendance. It authorized, in fact urged, all departments to use the plan vigorously. Within a short time after the plan was used in all departments, attendance rose from the previous average of 92.1 to 95.9.

The real in-plant job of the personnel department is to inspire supervisory personnel to action. But the first step which should be taken in any particular undertaking is to assure yourself that you actually have the backing of top management. After that, the job of putting over a well organized plan based on the small group theory becomes a pleasant task.

Book Reviews

Book Review Editor, Mr. Everett Van Every
California Personnel Management Association, Berkeley, Cal.

FACTS ABOUT FOREMEN

By Staff. New York, 19, N. Y. Labor Relations Institute. 1944. 42 pp. Price $1.00 to $1.50

Because an Institute Field Staff survey revealed that as few as 38 percent of foremen know exactly what their jobs consist of, this manual on how to make supervisors actually, as well as nominally, a "part of management", begins with a recommendation that a specification or requirement's sheet be drawn up for every foreman's job. A sample job description and a questionnaire for determining which points should be covered in describing each supervisory position, are included.

Job analysis for such positions is important for several reasons, according to the report. The procedure adds dignity to the foreman's job, and acquaints executives, employees and fellow supervisors with each foreman's requirements and responsibilities. It also facilitates the preparation of a practical organization chart—protecting the foremen from the hazards and confusion of reporting to more than one boss.

The report stresses the value of policy manuals for supervisors, and tells what topics should be covered. Announcement of new company policies to workers without giving the foremen at least a week's notice is condemned, as is circumvention of the supervisor as the "first court" in handling grievances. The report also suggests ways and means of building foreman morale and improving the selection and training of supervisors.

DEMOCRACY AGAINST UNEMPLOYMENT

By William R. Stead. Harper & Brothers. 1942. 288 pp. $3.00

Discussions on War and Unemployment is one of the best ways of understanding our present war economy, and what is yet to come. Wartime production is superimposed on our existing economic structure, resulting in tremendous overexpansion. The rôles of plant construction, confusion in planning and scheduling, shortage of skilled workers, lack of machine tools and equipment, managements' reluctance to give up normal procedures, strikes and labor disputes . . . all of these are accounted for in our present war activity. The author believes that the acceleration of the present war forecasts an even greater dislocation of our industrial system than was earlier anticipated, and he refers to a rather serious postwar crack-up that may easily reach major proportions.

What government controls are, why they are necessary, how Germany and later England were obliged to use them . . . these together with the kinds of regulatory and control devices we are now experiencing, account for the need to keep our war expansion within bounds.

If you would know how far we may have to go in this country to keep within the framework of what we call our "present system", you will need to know what wartime controls are yet to come. Stead tells us what these are. His chapters on Government Controls, the Expansion of World Trade, and the Extension of Economic Democracy should be required reading for the thinking business executive. Men who are charged with the administration of private enterprise through the war years ahead had better make such reading a business necessity.

Stead tells us further on that unless the spectre of unemployment and want are at least reduced, it is likely that the people of the earth will abandon democratic institutions in a desperate search for economic security. He advises against dropping our guard and opposing the necessary improvement and political evolution of our American democracy which has marked this country's industrial progress so far.

This is not a book to be put aside until after the war. It is more than a discourse on unemployment. It might well be called a study of the economic forces threatening management, labor and the public interests of America.

HAVE YOU SPARE PERSONNEL JOURNALS?

Some issues of the Personnel Journal (as listed below) are required by war industries, but are out of print.

If you have copies of these issues, which you are not now using, will you kindly return them to us, so that we may send them out to the companies requiring them. We will pay full price for them.

Vol. 22, No. 7. January, 1944.
Vol. 22, No. 8. February, 1944.
Vol. 22, No. 9. March, 1944.
Vol. 22, No. 10. April, 1944.

Personnel Research Federation
60 East 42nd St.,
New York, 17, New York

PERSONNEL
Journal

The Magazine of

LABOR RELATIONS AND PERSONNEL PRACTICES

Published by PERSONNEL RESEARCH FEDERATION

Lincoln Building, 60 East 42nd Street, New York City

Volume 23   *Number 7*

Contents for January 1945

We Are Used to Thinking of Reconversion as a
Machine Problem But There is Also a Problem
of Human Reconversion Because There must be
a Vast Number of Job Changes, Migrations and
Improved Standards of Performance Required of
Workers.

Reconversion
of Personnel

BY FRANZ A. FREDENBURGH

Loft Candy Corporation
Long Island City, N. Y.

GEARING personnel practices to the necessities of wartime has been a full-time
responsibility challenging the initiative, ingenuity, and patience of every
executive charged with the administration of personnel programs. Not only
have standards to be revised, techniques modified, services extended, procedures more
clearly defined, and activity intensified but staff retrained to appraise every personnel
action with a keener appreciation of the importance of correct action in every instance. Mistakes have been, and still are, costly in terms of curtailed production,
while mishandling has lost personnel difficult to replace and costly to recruit.

Transition *from War to Peace*

INDUSTRIAL relations departments must now prepare to face problems of reconversion in adjusting their personnel practices to an ever fluid and rapidly shifting
labor market. The transition from a war to a peacetime economy and the attendant
problems of restoring our civilian industrial machine have been cast into high relief
by the spectacular events taking place on the fighting fronts and by production cut
backs and the cancellation of war contracts.

Attacking such problems admits of two choices: that of discussing the pleasant,
uncontroversial phases of the issues at stake, or the more daring approach of calling a
spade a spade at the risk of offending the sensitivity of one's hearers.

As personnel counselors to the returning veteran you are confronted with one
of the most challenging and stimulating of human relations experiences. At the
same time you face one of the most difficult and complex problems of our times.

May I submit that you bear well in mind that you cannot successfully counsel an unwilling counselee; that *rapport* is fundamental, yet so elementary that it is sometimes overlooked or underestimated.

The basic principles of successful human relations hold wherever counselor and counselee meet. Make it your first order of business to understand your counselee before you try to advise with him concerning his occupational and personal adjustment.

Present Themselves Properly

Your problem is doubly complex, for you must not only recommend alternative courses of action; you must assay the increasingly exacting standards of business and industry in the matter of personnel selection in a freer labor market; but even more than this you must make your recommendations practical and workable.

I urge you to counsel your charges in the refined techniques of presenting themselves for employment to the best possible advantage, emphasizing their assets and outlining their specific qualifications.

Nothing is more disheartening to a personnel interviewer than to be confronted with the job applicant who has no conception of his qualifications, his limitations or his capacities, who is willing to do anything but has no idea what direction his aptitudes should take him.

It is not enough to have analyzed and identified these characteristics; the counselee must understand, appreciate, and accept the implications inherent in his psychograph.

You can help your counselees by advising them to prepare resumés of their qualifications and experiences to supplement the routine records which will be made available to everyone.

Counsel them to hold their aspiration threshold to a level consistent with their business experience and to discount appropriately the commercial value of their marks and stripes, which, when victory is won and patriotic fervor has subsided, will be valued somewhat less highly than now, regrettable though it may be.

Problems with Veterans

Employer-experience with veterans who have not met the exacting standards of military discipline and assignment and have accordingly been discharged, has not been too happy. These men, we appreciate, are not typical nor do they indicate what we may expect in the veteran as a job-holder after demobilization. However, there may be some value in noting that employer-experience with this type of veteran as a job-holder in today's labor market points plainly to the fact that he must undergo a period of readjustment from the rigors and tensions of war which tend to make him temporarily, at least, maladjusted to satisfactory job-holding and incapable, temporarily, at least, of job satisfaction.

He has inflated evaluation of his military experience translated into commercial values; he is dissatisfied with the slow and even pace of civilian employment, and he expects a rapid upgrading somewhat inconsistent with usual business practice.

This is not in criticism of the veteran—he has gone through more travail than those of us on the civilian front can hope to fully comprehend—rather it is a commentary on his plight and his need for intelligent counsel and sympathetic understanding.

You have a real job to do in orienting the veteran to the limitations of our civilian economy which has looked so green from afar off.

Personnel selection and occupational counseling both stem from the same roots, yet one is the virtual antithesis of the other.

Personnel selection emphasizes *man* selection; occupational counseling emphasizes *job* selection. If the two are well matched we obtain *job satisfaction*.

As counselors you will attempt to recommend the best available job opportunities consistent with the aptitudes, interests, and personal preferences of your counselees.

Personnel interviewers, on the other hand, are concerned with selecting the *one best man* from among what surely will be a vast reservoir.

While both counselor and personnel interviewer are concerned with the individual, the difference in purpose is *emphatic*, and one which counselors are prone to overlook.

The Labor Market

In order to appraise personnel practice with some degree of accuracy, it is fundamental to consider the current labor market into which the non-essential employer has had to dip more deeply than others.

Well over 11 million men—the most employable of all employables—have been withdrawn from what is normally a highly competitive market.

Yet in spite of this, the number of employed persons is today higher than ever before—some 53.3 millions as compared to a peacetime high of some 40 millions.

Into this labor market have poured literally hundreds of thousands of persons who were never before regarded as employable.

Large numbers of these workers are youngsters of teen age who would normally be unable to qualify for employment because of employers' standards as to age, aptitude, work habits, and quality of workmanship. Others are mothers and wives of service men, and unattached young women, who in normal times would have had marital ties. Many of these persons have been induced to work out of patriotic fervor; others because of higher than usual wage rates, or other extraordinary circumstances. Normally they would not appear in the labor market in such numbers as they have in time of war. Many of them would be regarded as |unemployable because of self-imposed restrictions as to hours of work, absenteeism, and other personal consideration. Others would not be employed in normal times because of overageness, inaptitude, poor work habits, and quality of workmanship.

Minority Groups

A SUBSTANTIAL number of workers have come from minority groups such as Negroes, aliens, and the limited handicapped, who are normally barred from certain types of employment because of tradition and employers' standards or other cause, but who are now able to obtain employment due to the tightness of the labor market.

Finally, the so-called "unemployables" comprising the loafers, the ne'er-do-wells, and certain types of the more extreme handicapped, have found employment today when normally they would be unable to obtain consideration.

All of these groups thrown together have produced a labor force of tremendous dimensions, although momentarily sorely inadequate.

The non-essential employer has not only found it expedient but mandatory that he continually lower his hiring standards, as the labor market has tightened. Not only has he offered employment to all kinds of applicants; he has actively solicited their consideration. He has found it necessary to overlook incompetence, insubordination, poor work habits, and the many shortcomings of the ill-qualified, not only at the time of hire, but on the job as well. He has unwillingly but necessarily submitted to personnel practices upon which he has frowned.

Readjustment Due

IN DUE time we may anticipate a sharp readjustment in the labor market. As was typical of our experience after the last war, we may expect certain classes of persons to remain in the labor market who were not there prior to the war.

It is very possible that more women may remain on production lines than before. Employers' experiences with women in certain types of fine precision assembly work, formerly closed to them by tradition, have been so satisfactory that it is likely they will remain on the job.

The future of the hundreds of thousands of adolescents who have found new avenues of employment formerly closed to them is fairly clear. Employers' unfavorable experiences, restrictive labor legislation, and school attendance laws, will tend to drain off the bulk of these young people from the labor reservoir.

Minority groups have a fair chance to hold some of their gains where they have proved themselves not only employable but well adjusted and productive. The unemployables will doubtless revert to the dole and substandard living.

Reconversion and Transition

THE inescapable fact remains that with the return of some 11 million men to the labor market, and with the gradual, if not sudden, recession of industrial output to a peacetime level, we may expect and must gird ourselves to face a labor market in direct and striking contrast to today's situation—a market glutted with able and willing workers, competing with one another for the available jobs.

Unemployment has decreased from 8,600,000 in 1940 to about 1,000,000, an abnormally low figure. In prosperous post-war times we may reasonably expect at least 2,500,000 unemployed persons after all readjustments have been made.

On the authority of economist Julius Hirsch[1] we have the prediction that a deflationary trend is probable within 8 to 10 months after hostilities cease.

A gap must be expected between the wholesale cancellation of war contracts and the resumption of production for peace. There has been scarcely any realistic, practical action on the political horizon to guarantee that the war's end will not mean wide-spread unemployment.

Size of Problem

JOHN F. FENNELLY, executive director of the Committee for Economic Development,[2] has pointed out that the much-bandied-about term "reconversion" carries with it the implication that the main problem before us is that of physically restoring peacetime production, whereas this is probably a much smaller problem than is popularly believed.

The immediate problem lies with 8 million workers—some 15% of the total civilian working force—who are currently employed in industries which will have a physical problem of reconversion.

Obviously, no reconversion will be necessary for most farmers, for food and clothing industries, for public utilities, for wholesale, retail and service establishments and for most of our raw-material producers.

Employment has changed very little in these fields. Agricultural employment has dropped from 11,000,000 to 9,600,000 since 1940 but it seems reasonably certain that the farms will be able to support about as many people after the return of peace as they did in 1940.

Manufacturing employees have increased by well over 50 per cent in the war years, and most of the newcomers are making things not used in peacetime.

Approximately half of the eight million persons employed in industries subject to problems of reconversion are now employed in shipyards, for which little use is likely to exist after the war, and in the aircraft industry, which probably can be converted only gradually and to a limited extent to meet peacetime demands.

The remaining 4 million are largely accounted for by such typically civilian industries as machinery, automobiles, office equipment, radios, and a host of other consumer durable goods.

What Public Will Tolerate

THE reconversion of such civilian industries, together with the shutting down of many of our shipyards and aircraft plants, will inevitably cause serious unemployment, particularly in areas where such activity has been concentrated.

The real magnitude of the problem, however, becomes apparent only when we realize that it is not alone what plans may be made but whether or not the American public will tolerate our, or perhaps I should say YOUR, present plans for an orderly demobilization.

When the war ends, the pressure of the veteran to get home, regardless of economic considerations, and of his family to have him home, will be very difficult to resist or to counteract in terms of intelligent counsel.

Finally, our pre-war level of national production will be grossly inadequate, if we are to avoid mass unemployment after the war, as the result of an increased working population and of technological advances since 1940.

It is estimated that from 7 to 10 million new jobs must be made available above the number existing in 1940 if we hope to avoid wide-spread unemployment.

The only sound way to do this and at the same time maintain our standard of living is through industrial expansion and increased output of goods and services.

Construction Industry

THE construction industry, for example, if properly stimulated, may provide a partial answer to the problem by providing a substantial number of jobs for some time to come.

Although the industry itself can begin operations just as soon as men and materials are released from war purposes, the key to the opportunity for jobs in construction during the post-war period lies in detailed planning that requires months to complete. Unless these preliminaries are disposed of before the war ends, construction cannot begin at the time when it will be most needed.

In normal times about two-thirds of all construction is privately financed and one-third consists of public works. We may properly expect private industry to hesitate in making large capital commitments but there is no reason why the various agencies of government, Federal, State, and local, should hesitate.

Planning Manpower Requirements

IT is not generally appreciated that there are some 3,500 businesses in this country that employ more than 1,000 persons while there are 2 million establishments which employ 100 workers or less. These latter employers provide almost half of all jobs.

A satisfactory level of post-war personnel practice implies that the problems of reconversion must be conceived in terms of an orderly and sensible evaluation of borh the current and the potential labor force.

The current labor force must be appraised in terms of *individuals* whose value to their employer can be best measured on the basis of job performance, personality characteristics, promotional potentialities, and length of service.

Major personnel policy establishing an operating framework for such an evaluation program leading to a sound reconversion of the labor force from a wartime to a peacetime level involves many imponderables for all employers, but especially for the employer who anticipates chiefly a reconversion to more competent employees. Foremost among these problems is the matter of policy respecting the separation or other disposition of recent hires in order to make way for the reabsorption of veterans to whom employment has been guaranteed. Next, is the matter of what if any policy shall be adopted respecting preferential consideration to veteran job applicants who may be better qualified than present employees for given jobs but for whom no jobs are available unless certain present employees are separated from their assignment and perhaps from employment.

The same problem presents itself with respect to war workers released from essential employment and available for general employment. There is also the former employee who went into war work, perhaps leaving his non-essential employer in a tough spot at the time, who wants to return to his peacetime employment.

Traditional Practices

UNION contracts, traditional company practices, recent technological developments, competition, social approval, governmental regulations, and the ideals of top management respecting these gigantic problems are fundamental considerations in clearing the way for definitive and effective action and sound personnel practice.

Despite the temptation to wait to see what the other fellow will do, and to estimate the influence and effect of public pressure on personnel practices, forward-looking Management is giving careful consideration to these problems and formulating policy in advance of the necessity of making spot decisions in the face of specific problems demanding immediate solution.

Post-war planning with respect to manpower is no less and is certainly at least equal in importance to planning production. The magnitude of the problem is no excuse for avoiding consideration of it.

As an initial step in this direction top Management must set the stage by giving the personnel executive opportunity to be informed of and to relate proposed production schedules in terms of manpower requirements. Forward-looking Management is giving the personnel head a seat on policy-forming committees in order to insure a well-informed approach to problems of manpower and employee relations.

Initial Steps in Planning

ORGANIZING for intelligent post-war planning of manpower requirements implies that certain fundamental and anticipatory steps be undertaken.

The first of these is the evaluation of present personnel beginning somewhere close to the top of the business and then straight down the line.

The term diagnosis has a variety of meanings. At one extreme it means mere description of an individual's behavior or performance. In this sense it is synony-

mous with survey. At the other extreme diagnosis refers to the complete understanding of the individual and his conduct.

The *Personnel Audit* is diagnosis by measurement of performance. It provides a
workable means for collecting with precision data on those less tangible manifestations of human behavior which lead to a practical diagnosis of present effectiveness
on the job—*proficiency*—and suitability for transfer, demotion, or promotion-*capacity*
—particularly where assignments involve greater responsibility and the exercise of
authority. The Personnel Audit is an effective means for systematically making
judgments analytical, representative, impartial and unbiased with respect to individual proficiency, capacity, and capability.

Job Analysis

O F NO less aid in planning for, and in anticipating personnel changes involving
promotions, transfers, and demotions is that effective instrument which the
Occupational Research Program of the United States Employment Service[4] has
done more to further in recent years than has any other agency—JOB ANALYSIS.

Job analysis has done yeoman service in industry during the war. Not only
has it served as an important aid to inexperienced personnel interviewers; it has
helped collate similar jobs into job families; it has helped in the development of
trade and aptitude tests; in determining the suitability of jobs for women, for the
physically handicapped, and the relative importance of jobs one to the other.

Moreover, it has aided in revising hiring requirements, realigning job tasks for
the job breakdown; in shortening training periods, and in outlining training courses.

Job analysis is no less important in planning for post-war manpower requirements. It will point the way to where handicapped veterans may be used; it will indicate where hiring requirements may be legitimately tightened and where factors
such as special skills, personality qualifications and other pertinent considerations
may be recruited for in the interests of a more scientific selection of qualified personnel.

Adequate analysis, description, and classification of all jobs, plus an audit of
present personnel places in the hands of the Personnel executive scientific tools for
evaluating his personnel requirements and for establishing manpower schedules in
line with proposed production schedules.

The Handicapped

H AVING assayed the question of who and how many new employees can be absorbed, the next step is fairly obvious. It is that of utilizing adequate selection
techniques for the purpose of measuring the skills, aptitudes and interests of job
applicants, in order to match the men and jobs.

An individual's ability to perform a given job successfully is dependent upon
many factors. The skilled personnel interviewer wants the facts about a candidate's

skills and aptitudes *as they are at present* and an estimate of characteristics indicative of his future potentialities for successful adjustment to a given job assignment.

Some employers have been quite successful in utilizing handicapped persons as a result of job analysis and refined selection techniques, plus the pressure exerted by a very tight labor market. Their experience has led them to conclude that such workers are efficient, careful, industrious, loyal, and are not prone to absenteeism.

The successful adaptation of plant personnel practice to the utilization of the handicapped involves careful planning, specific information, and adequate follow-up, in keeping with better personnel practices for the selection of all personnel.

As counselors of veterans let me urge upon you the importance of supplying the employer with an ANALYSIS OF THE PHYSICAL QUALIFICATIONS of your applicants—especially the handicapped—a definite specification of *physical restrictions* as to walking, standing, sitting, kneeling, lifting, pulling, pushing, use of hands, feet, sight, speech, and hearing, as well as a list of *environmental restrictions* as to outside, inside, hot, cold, dusty, noisy, oily work, etc.[5]

For his part, the employer will require, if he is to do a satisfactory job of matching the man and the job, a comparable list of the *physical demands*, and *working conditions* of the jobs for which he plans to select personnel.

Orientation

HAVING successfully matched the man and the job, the next step, in keeping with sound and successful personnel procedure is that of orienting the new employee to the job. The problems of adjustment are not all solved by careful selection, no matter how faithfully an individual's skills, aptitudes and interests may have been gauged. He must be adjusted to his surroundings, his fellow workers, his supervisors, his tools and materials. Job satisfaction is largely dependent upon satisfactory adjustment to these several conditions of employment. Job adjustment is a product of the many activities of the work day diffused into a total state of satisfaction, or dissatisfaction, as the case may be. The average new worker is assailed by doubts and uncertainties which temporarily influence, frequently nearly paralyzing, his efficiency and job performance. He is in a peculiarly sensitive frame of mind. The introduction of the new employee to his job becomes a matter of considerable strategic importance. Escorted to his assignment by a representative of the personnel office whose reassuring manner reinforces confidence, reflects courtesy and tact, and bespeaks loyalty and enthusiasm for the company, does much to assist him to adjust more rapidly to his work assignment.

Full-blown orientation programs frequently include a movie or talk on company history, and a lecture on company policy, rules and regulations, so that the new worker feels informed and at home almost at once.

Fringes of Adjustment

WHERE mental attitudes and lack of recent work experience are so likely to place the veteran on the fringes of satisfactory adjustment rather than in the middle of it,⁶ it is particularly important that he begin his employment under the most favorable of circumstances. His war experiences may have made him self-conscious; he may be sick of having been the target of a thousand questions about his experiences. While anxious to re-establish himself and do his work well, he may be fearful that he will not acquire job skill as quickly as expected.

Conferences with foremen and supervisors on the techniques of absorbing veterans, the appointment of fellow workers to take the responsibility for assisting the new workers to adjust to the job, and to act as friend; and the actual training of the new employee for the specific job, all have a part in successful orientation.

Follow-up Plans

SOME method of following up and evaluating the assignment and adjustment of new employees is equally essential to sound personnel practice. Like many other activities relating to human relations in industry, it is not easy to measure the real effectiveness of selection and orientation techniques.

It is important, therefore, to check on the suitability of assignments and to make adjustments, if required, before difficulties arise, rather than afterwards. It cannot be taken for granted that once assigned, an employee may be assumed to be adjusted to that assignment, successful or even satisfactory in it. ·

Follow-up is essential in order that personnel interviewers may have ample information on how the new hire performs and how satisfactory he is in the opinion of the supervisor who is directly responsible for his production.

Not infrequently a new worker who is getting on reasonably well, is satisfactory to his superviser, and should remain where he is, develops a real or imaginary grievance which interferes both with his productivity and his adjustment on the job. An inexperienced worker may discover, for instance, that a worker next to him, and doing identical work, is earning substantially more than he is. He may want to give up his job immediately unless he has an opportunity to discuss his problem with someone in authority to learn that he, too, can earn the same rate of pay, when his production and experience is equal to his co-worker.

Personnel Counseling

THE assignment of personnel supervisors or counselors to re-interview new hires periodically for the purpose of checking up on their adjustment, recommending transfer or reassignment in the event of unsatisfactory adjustment, and for the purpose of maintaining progress reports and performance ratings, is sound practice and an effective instrument in promoting efficiency.

Finally, personnel counseling to smooth out any kinks which may have crept into the situation, or may be apart from it but are influencing the efficiency and adjustment of the employee, finds an important place in present-day personnel practice.

Counseling implies an intimate, personal relationship between counselor and counselee. It is not giving advice but rather it is giving assistance. In the role of counselor, the interviewer hears out the personal problem of the individual, whether it is a gripe against a supervisor's method of handling a situation, or a complaint against company policy, or a disagreement with another worker. The function of the counselor is to help the interviewer marshal all the facts, help him weigh them, and then suggest alternative courses of action which may be open to the individual in the specific situation.

Ideally the counselor should function in a staff rather than in a line capacity—in an advisory rather than in an authoritative manner. He is then in a strategic position to see both sides of the story more objectively and to recommend to the line officer, who exercises authority in the matter, an impartial solution to the problem.

The recognition of the employee as a human being and much more than a cog in the industrial machine has not only humanized personnel practice, but has reaped rich rewards in terms of increased production and greater efficiency. A happy employee is a good producer, other things being equal.

Six Point Procedure

ᴏᴘ management, having recognized this fundamental principle, has given into Tthe hands of Industrial Relations Departments responsibility for the maintenance of employee morale and good employee relations.

My report, then, for post-war personnel reconversion presents a 6 point procedure:

1. A personnel inventory or audit of present incumbents;
2. Adequate job analysis, description, and classification;
3. Refined selection techniques to measure skills, aptitudes and interests for the purpose of matching the man and the job;
4. Orientation of the new employee;
5. Follow-up on the job, and
6. Personnel counseling during encumbency.

Paper delivered before the Third Class of the Separation Classification School, Fort Dix, New Jersey.

Bibliography

1. CONROY, THOMAS F., "Hirsch Discounts Talk of Inflation," *New York Times*, September 3, 1944.
2. FENNELLY, JOHN F., "The Shift from War to Peace Economy, "*New York Times Magazine*, September 3, 1944, p. 11.
3. "Industry Leaders Describe Approach to PostWar Jobs," *New York Times*, October 12, 1944.
4. "Ten Years of Occupational Research," *Occupations*, The Vocational Guidance Magazine, XXII: 7 (April, 1944) Entire
5. "A Plan to Help You Employ Disabled Veterans and Other Handicapped Persons Productively and Safely," Chicago, Illinois: American Mutual Alliance 1944, pp. 22.
6. LOUTTIT, C. M., "Personality Problems," in *Clinical Psychology*, New York: Harper & Bros., 1936 Chapter XII, pp. 4535.

Vocational Guidance Counseling and Occupational Service Helps Workers to Become Self Sustaining in the Right Jobs and Helps Employers to Secure Capable and Efficient Employees.

Vocational Guidance
in Minneapolis

By A. O. Pearson

Division of Public Assistance
Minneapolis, Minn.

WE FEEL that in the future the importance of vocational guidance to postwar planning and to any public welfare agency's program will become increasingly important. Especially will this be true when the agency is called upon to help in the rehabilitation of returning veterans. On the basis of the present size of the armed forces, it is estimated by responsible authority that about 83,000 Minneapolis men will be released from military service at the close of hostilities. Past experience has shown that the majority of men who experience difficulty in making adjustments to peace economy and who are ineligible for state and federal benefits, eventually become the responsibility of the Division of Public Relief.

The Division of Public Relief is the only agency that is equipped, prepared and ready to assume the responsibility for this segment of our city's population. The majority of these men are in their youth. Many have never established a vocation and if the experience of the last war is repeated, very few will go back to schools and colleges to complete their education.

The Vocational Guidance Service will be in a position to give assistance to this group by way of helping them to make a vocational choice that will be compatible not only with their interests but with their abilities and aptitudes, thus insuring good vocational adjustment as well as employment security.

83,000 Returning Servicemen

ALSO, we are considering the more than 7,700 Minneapolis youths who become available each year for employment of some kind. About five-sixths of them seek work in unskilled fields. These young people face the necessity, before leaving school or very soon thereafter, of deciding what occupation they will follow. Then each year among those already employed, another army of people, many young and many well along in life, find it necessary to choose new occupations. To these groups in the relief population the Vocational Guidance Service can provide expert assistance in making sound occupational choices.

File of Occupational Information

THE Division of Public Relief is looking forward to the readjustment of the working population to peace time employment. This is being done by establishing and maintaining a readily accessible file of information about the job aptitudes and potentialities of a segment of the population which found difficulty in adapting to the employment conditions of 1930 and the years following. If a public works program should again prove necessary, placements could then be made on a scientific basis.

The question might be raised as to whether a public relief agency has the right to enter the vocational guidance field. To that question we would raise another, namely, has the community the moral and legal right to deprive a recipient of any service which might add to his permanent well-being. Those who find it necessary to apply for public assistance frequently have social problems which have contributed to their indigency. For that reason we believe Vocational Guidance should be as much a part of a relief agency's program as the actual granting of assistance. Our agency's experience in vocational guidance has been extremely profitable to the client and to the community and very satisfying to the agency. In the final analysis we believe that is the best evaluation of its effectiveness.

Six Years Experience

THE Vocational Guidance program which is being carried on by the Minneapolis Division of Public Relief really dates back to the WPA program of 1938 and 1939. During that period there were 18,000 persons at work on WPA. There was a high turnover in persons being laid off. Layoffs were for such reasons as "not suited to the job", "inability to adjust", "insubordination", "cannot do a fair day's work", "disciplinary reasons" and many others.

At the time this was occurring there was a general feeling in the community that relief clients were unwilling to work. A survey made by the Minneapolis Relief Department in 1939 revealed that ninety-eight percent of all WPA work assignments were being accepted and only in rare instances could a client's failure to remain on the job be attributed to his unwillingness to work.

Misplacement Discovered

IN 1939 the agency was operating a WPA survey project under the direction of one of its supervisors. The supervisor found that a number of clerical people on the project were not competent workers. They were slow, they made many mechanical errors and they had a low rate of production. At the request of the supervisor these persons were tested by the University of Minnesota Testing Bureau. The Bureau revealed these persons had little or no aptitude for clerical work and should have been classified differently and assigned elsewhere. The whole matter of classification and assignment was discussed with WPA officials.

WPA reported that it had been their experience that a high percentage of persons employed on their program were incorrectly classified. Many still registered at the employment service in their former skills which were now obsolete. Many professional and skilled people were registering as common laborers hoping that by so doing they would get an immediate assignment since there were relatively few skilled and professional assignments being made. Likewise many clients had "adopted" the skill which they thought they had obtained while employed on the old CWA and ERA programs. United States Employment Service classifications, therefore, could no longer be depended upon.

Many Cooperating Agencies

IN AN attempt to work out a solution to the problem, the agency secured the counsel and help of other interested groups such as, University of Minnesota Testing Bureau and Psychology Department, the State Department of Education, the Minneapolis Public Schools, the United States Employment Service and the Works Projects Administration. It was suggested that the agency initiate a vocational guidance program for the purpose of testing all relief clients before referring them for replacement.

As a result the Minneapolis Division of Public Relief set up a Vocational Guidance Clinic in September, 1940. WPA assisted by furnishing part of the clerical and professional staff while the University of Minnesota Testing Bureau and Psychology Department, the State Department of Education, the Minneapolis Public Schools and the United States Employment Service agreed to act as an advisory committee. The purpose of the committee was to give publicity to the community for vocational service, to secure employers' action and to promote vocational guidance service within the United States Employment Service.

The primary objective of the Vocational Guidance Service was to help clients find employment and become self-supporting, thereby reducing the relief rolls. This was to be done by ascertaining the abilities and aptitudes of relief clients to determine whether or not it was possible to place them in private industry either with or without training and to make available to employers persons, who with a limited amount of training could be used on skilled or semi-skilled jobs; also, to select individuals for training programs who had aptitudes and potentialities for such training.

Getting Community Support

THE stated purpose, therefore, was quite simple and there was an advantage in having it so. First, the program had to be interpreted to the agency's Board which was being asked to finance the project. Second, the program had to be interpreted in terms the client could understand. Third, it was felt that only by stating the purpose in simple terms would the community as a whole be able to understand vocational guidance and give it its support.

A section of a building which had been used by our agency was turned over for use as the Vocational Guidance Clinic. The staff consisted of a unit supervisor in charge who was a social worker, a personnel technician, interviewers, testers, receptionists and clerks. A total of 18 persons were employed at the peak of its activity.

It was recognized early that for the program to be effective it must be integrated into the total case work program. There was a natural interdependency of the Vocational Guidance Clinic and the social case worker. The clinic was dependent upon the worker for the selection of the clients to be tested, for the case history information and for the follow-through to see that recommendations of the clinic were carried out.

In the beginning the only trained person in the Clinic was the Personnel Technician and it was necessary for her to train those persons who were to be working in the capacity of interviewers and testers.

Name Changed

THERE were certain definite reactions to the Vocational Guidance Clinic when it was first set up. The client for whom the service was initiated was suspicious. He associated the name "clinic" with hospitals and the test batteries with mental examinations. Many, at first, resisted in the belief that their sanity was being examined. To overcome this resistance some of the social workers used the well known pressure method of withholding relief until the client appeared at the clinic.

In the early days of the program the clinic frequently found angry, silent and uncooperative clients waiting to be tested. These clients had little confidence in the tests given. One of the methods used to overcome the clients' resistance was to change the name to Vocational Guidance Service. Also, it was felt that a more intensive job of interpretation had to be given to the client by the social worker.

Employer Reaction

EMPLOYERS at first questioned the value of the service but were willing to be shown. Their interest was in proportion to their individual knowledge of present day methods of personnel testing. A great deal of skill and tact was required to sell them the program. Types of tests had to be explained as well as the meaning of test scores. When the confidence of the employers was gained referrals were accepted without question.

Initial eligibility requirements of the clients who were to use the service were at first very high. It was limited only to those male heads of families on relief who were under thirty-five years of age, had completed the eighth grade and were in sound physical, mental and emotional condition. This group was readily placed into industry and the eligibility requirements had to be lowered. Later, as the need for women in industry increased the service was open to all women under thirty-five years of age. Early in 1942 the program was made available to all relief clients sixteen years of age and over.

In September, 1942, it was open to all agencies, industries and individuals, not on relief, on a fee basis of $6.00 per person. In addition to private industry and individuals, every case work agency in the city has made some use of Vocational Guidance Service. Services have been given to boys and girls in correctional institutions and to persons who are on probation to local, state and federal authorities.

Placement of Those Limited

As the case load diminished from a high of twenty thousand families when the program was initiated (thirteen thousand on relief and seven thousand on WPA) to an all time low of less than fifteen hundred as of May 1, 1944, the residual load in the agency more and more was made up of the aged and the physically and mentally handicapped. The present emphasis, therefore, has been on those who heretofore have been considered unemployable. There was a need to intensify the counseling processes. Many unattached women, widows who had not worked outside of their homes for ten to twenty-five years, found it difficult to accept the idea of employment. Others, both men and women, had made an adjustment to relief and were opposed to losing relief security. Some had lost confidence in their ability.

Repeated interpretations and counseling in cooperation with those employers who were able to give guarded and limited employment resulted in a high percentage of placement for this group. As an added incentive, the agency's policy permitted a twenty percent increase in relief allowances to those gainfully employed but needing a supplement to their budget, thereby materially assisting those whose earnings did not fully cover their relief budgets.

Post-War View

Along with the drop in our case load there has been a corresponding reduction in the over-all staff. Whereas the Vocational Guidance Service once was staffed by eighteen persons, now the staff consists of but four. Currently this staff is completing a survey of the entire case group that have received its service. Hollerith cards have been punched showing such information as name, address, case number, date and place of birth, sex, marital status, education, disability, year relief was first granted, relationship to head, number of persons in the household, veterans' status, social handicap, employment classification and recommendation of Vocational Guidance Service. We believe there will be a great value in such information especially to the United States Employment Service, our own agency and others concerned with occupational classification in the event there is a resurgency to relief after the war period.

Results and Conclusions

THE program has been able to obtain its objective insofar as getting jobs for people and removing them from relief rolls. From the beginning of the program in 1940 to January 1, 1944, three thousand persons have been tested. Ninety per cent or 2700 have gone off relief to accept jobs. Ten per cent or 300 still remain on relief Of this number, 194 are men and women over fifty-three years of age; 32 are mothers with small children receiving aid to dependent children; four were boys and girls under sixteen years of age. With the exception of the Aid to Dependent Mothers and the four youths, all were severely handicapped by physical or mental difficulties.

The Vocational Guidance Service does not wish to leave the impression that solely through its efforts many of these persons were reclaimed by industry. There is no doubt that the man-power shortage due to the speeding up of war industries had much to do with many of these persons being called back into employment.

That the program promised the means whereby potential and existing skills and aptitudes were uncovered and subsequently utilized in industries cannot be denied. The scientific method of placement replaced the trial and error method based essentially on previous employment experiences. Placement, when made on the basis of tested skills, aptitudes and preferences resulted in a more satisfactory work adjustment to the client and a better job performance.

Saving to Taxpayers

HERE was an obvious saving to taxpayers by cutting the relief roll far below the average of comparable cities in the state of Minnesota. The three major metropolitan areas in the state—Minneapolis, St. Paul and Duluth—had, over a period of years, showed a similar trend in both the increase and the decrease in their relief loads. From 1942 through 1943 the reduction in the number of family persons on relief in the three cities named showed a decrease in favor of Minneapolis. For the period in question the City of Minneapolis had .414% of the total population as family persons on relief. St. Paul showed .824% of their total population while Duluth showed .984% of its total population. The agency likes to believe that the difference is primarily caused by the work of the Vocational Guidance Service in getting so-called unemployables off relief and into industry.

Much thought was given to the work which may be done with the handicapped. It was found that women with low IQs on occasion had a high degree of arm and finger dexterity and were readily absorbed by those industries needing assembly workers. Those who showed no unusual capabilities and whose abilities conform with their mental rating were found to make exceptionally good laundry workers. The program was sold to laundry management on this basis and many women were so placed.

C & S Tool Company

IN THE fall of 1942 the Vocational Guidance Service began to concentrate on the physically handicapped who remained on relief. At first the "selling" of these handicapped people to management met some resistance as it long had been thought that the handicapped were unemployable except in special areas of employment. In this respect, however, the experience of the agency with the C & S Tool Company of Minneapolis was an outstanding exception to the rule. The senior partner of this firm, Mr. Castner, had opened a small tool plant in the basement of his home. In the beginning he had had no personnel problems. Later he obtained a war contract and found it necessary to expand. He now has on his payroll seventy men and women all of whom are physically handicapped.

Thirty-five of the handicapped were tested and referred by Vocational Guidance Service. Without exception they were men with no machine experience but had been selected in terms of general ability to learn measured dexterity and measured performance for machine work. The firm provided stools for those who could not stand. It furnished platforms to put machines within reach of the men without legs and assigned one-armed men to such jobs as punch press operation. Mr. Castner said that the policy of employing physically handicapped persons did not stem from a sentimental interest in the physically handicapped persons. Rather it was based on his realization that a physically handicapped person with special abilities and interests is a far better production worker and possesses much higher morale than the physically able person who lacks the necessary abilities and interests.

Employers Now Value Program

THE Vocational Guidance program has received very favorable publicity and there has been an increase in the general feeling of community good will directed toward the agency. At the present time there are over one hundred employers who are cooperating closely with Vocational Guidance Service in the interest of obtaining more manpower. The Vocational Guidance Service has demonstrated to employers that a public agency can assist them in obtaining competent labor. Through discussions and conferences with Vocational Guidance Service many employers have become acquainted for the first time with social factors which influence job adjustment. Some employers began to seek out the agency, not only for obtaining additional labor but to request the agency to assist in matters of absenteeism.

"Let Dogs Delight to Bark and Bite,
For God Hath Made Them So;
Let Bears and Lions Growl and Fight,
For 'tis Their Nature Too." Isaac Watts.

Psychology *of* The Reprimand

By Ralph R. Brown

Business Management Institute
Pittsburgh, Pa.

PLANNING and timing are as necessary to the reprimand as to other supervisory functions. The act of criticizing a subordinate is a serious matter—the how, when, and where should not be neglected. Too frequently, however, the supervisor hastens to criticize an employe before he has his facts or his temper in hand. It is not uncommon to see a supervisor spot an error, grab up the evidence, and rush out to castigate the offending employe.

The Big Lug

TO THE supervisor, it is simply the exercising of his responsibilities and the demonstrating of his authoritative control. To the employe, however, it may be something different—"the big lug ought to get his facts straight before he blows off his mouth!" Or, "It will be a cold day before I try to protect that guy again!" In most instances the final result is the creation of additional problems in morale and efficiency.

It is reasonable to assume that the employe does not enjoy making mistakes. There is seldom anything deliberate about an error. Why, then, does the supervisor work himself into such a heat? Obviously, it is not the error. It is often an expression of a fundamental psychological drive—something which is common property of the human species. It is the will to power. When handled properly, it gives us the ambition and the joy of competition which constitute the very essence of progress. When out of control, however, it leads to all sorts of trouble, both for ourselves and for others.

Possible Causes of Error

No, IF the employe makes an error, the cause can usually be traced down.

He did not know WHAT was expected. Perhaps the full details of the job were never explained; perhaps they were explained but forgotten (due to poor memory or because there were too many details to remember). Perhaps the policies or conduct expected were never explained, or perhaps were forgotten.

He did not know HOW to do what was expected. The instruction may have been inadequate, or perhaps there was insufficient practice. The instructions may have been too complicated to remember, or perhaps the employe did not pay sufficient attention to the instructions as given.

He COULD NOT DO what was expected. The job may have required more skill or training than the employe possessed. Perhaps the employe lacked the educational background or the necessary experience. He may have been ill, fatigued, nervous, or worried. He may not have had time to perform the required tasks, or perhaps was prevented from doing so by some other authority. Perhaps he did not possess the necessary intelligence.

He WOULD NOT DO what was expected. Perhaps the job was too unpleasant, or was not in line with the employe's idea of company policy. The job assigned may have been against his personal principles, or perhaps he was just angry with the supervisor. Perhaps he wanted to be transferred to another department, or maybe just wanted to have some fun.

There may be other sources of error, but I believe the above classification covers more than 90% of the territory. None of these errors calls for correction by table-thumping and shouting, nor by sarcasm, no matter how cleverly delivered. In most instances, if not in all, such measures give a negative rather than a positive result. Nothing is to be gained by convincing the employe that he's a dope or a sluggard.

Lincoln Quoted

The futility of such tactics has been emphasized by many authorities and was particularly well expressed by Abraham Lincoln as follows: "...assume to dictate to his (man's) judgment, or to command his action, or to mark him out as one to be shunned and despised, and he will retreat within himself, close all the avenues to his head and heart; and though your cause be naked truth itself, transformed to the heaviest lance, harder than steel, and sharper than steel can be made, and though you throw it with more than herculean force and precision, you will be no more able to pierce him than to penetrate the hard shell of a tortoise with a rye straw. Such is man, and so must he be understood by those who would lead him even to his own best interests." (Quotation from Lincoln's Temperance Address; taken from *The Psychology of Dealing with People*, by Wendell White, The Macmillan Company, 1937.)

In their attempts to correct such behavior disorders as insanity, neuroses, and criminality, psychologists and psychiatrists do not find it necessary or advisable to indulge in loud shouting or bulldozing. The cure of such disorders must come from a clear understanding of the fundamental factors involved. The therapeutic principle is one of insight—not force. Many supervisors would find it to their advantage to use this principle in the control of their organization.

Advantages in Using Checklist

IF AN error is sufficiently serious to warrant discussion, it is deserving of consideration in an atmosphere conducive to calm judgment and easy exchange of ideas. Why not sit down with the employe to discover together the factors which are responsible for the difficulty? It will pay off in time and errors saved in the future. The check-list shown below will serve as a guide to this discovery. The supervisor will find in its use the following advantages:

1. Assures calm and reasonable discussion of the factors involved.
2. Assures a fair and impartial hearing to the employe.
3. Assures collection of all facts before decision is made—prevents snap judgment.
4. Provides information essential to proper adjustment on present job.
5. Provides information essential for transfer, demotion, or dismissal.
6. As records accumulate, information becomes available covering the most common sources of irritation within the department, thus furnishing the basis for the establishment of more effective policies and procedures.
7. Supplies information concerning training needs.
8. It is one of the most effective means of building Morale.
9. In the case of older employes who are losing their grip, this approach may be used to advantage in bringing to light the advisability of transfer to a less exacting or complex job. Through an objective discussion of the problem, such an employe can be made to see the advantage and necessity of facing facts and adjusting to them.

No supervisor can neglect to give serious consideration to his technique of reprimand. If clumsily and indiscriminately applied, the reprimand can backfire with a terrific explosion. If handled intelligently, however, it is an effective instrument for increasing morale and efficiency.

Reprimand Check-List

Check Primary Source of Trouble:
  A. *Did not know WHAT was expected*
  Full details of job not explained.. ——
  Details explained but forgotten .... ——
  Sufficient explanation not given of policies and conduct expected........ .... ——
  Policies explained but forgotten.. ——

B. Did not know HOW to do what was expected
    Improper instruction . . . .
    Insufficient practice . . . .
    Too complicated to remember . . . .
    Did not pay attention to instructions . . . .
    Other (record)

C. COULD NOT DO what was expected
    To much skill and training required . . . .
    Lacks background of education . . . .
    Lacks background of experience . . . .
    Illness . . . .
    Fatigue . . . .
    Nervousness . . . .
    Worry . . . .
    Insufficient intelligence . . . .
    Did not have time . . . .
    Not permitted to perform duties required . . . .

D. WOULD NOT DO what was expected
    Duties too unpleasant . . . .
    Angry with supervisor . . . .
    Just didn't feel like it . . . .
    Against personal principles . . . .
    Not in line with company policies . . . .
    Wants to be transferred . . . .
    Wants to be discharged . . . .
    Not part of the job . . . .
    Nobody else follows rule . . . .
    Wanted to have some fun . . . .
    Job was too monotonous . . . .
    Preferred to do another job first . . . .
    Didn't see any sense in it . . . .
    Preferred to do things the old way . . . .
COMMENTS:

Oh Lord, give me the *patience* to endure the things I cannot change.
Give me the *courage* to change the things I ought to change.
And, above all, give me the *wisdom* to know the difference.

Human Relations
in Business

By L. C. Hart
Johns Manville Corporation
New York, N. Y.

A s EVERY one engaged in personnel work quickly comes to realize, we in management are dealing continuously with that most delicate and sensitive mechanism known to science, the human personality. In many respects it is unpredictable. We must, therefore, be ever on the alert to detect, in advance if possible, a change of thought, an emotional reaction or perhaps a temporary lapse of consciousness, in order to deal intelligently with any one of the many psychological situations which is likely to arise. Such phenomena are frequently so spontaneous and illogical that we are not given the opportunity to "reason why."

System and Leadership

N EVERTHELESS, the issue must be met effectively if we are to attain those objectives of management; intelligent performance, profitable results and mutual contentment. Failure to meet such issues squarely frequently results in personal frustration, unnecessary inhibitions or inferiority complexes.

In all management, the primary need is to maintain *balance* between the two phases of managerial work, *system* and *personal leadership*. Both are essential. Neither can accomplish much without the other. Necessarily, for each peculiar type of business, there has been developed a systematic operation. Organized routine, however, exists for only one purpose—to make personal leadership more effective.

The risk faced by every person with managerial responsibility is that of over-emphasizing one side of the work at the expense of the other. One may devote so much of his time to "paper work" that personal contacts become inadequate. Another may concentrate so much on personal contacts that he cannot find time to keep abreast of his routine duties. Partly, this risk arises from temperament. Each man tends to stress most heavily the type of work which he likes best and which he knows he can do best. But the real task of every manager is to do a *balanced* job.

Management means *control* and control means *action*. The natural functions of all management are guidance and control. Management succeeds not by what it has accomplished in the past but by its ability to control what is happening at present and what is going to happen in the future. System is essential but is effective only if it leads to action. The record of what has happened is merely history. As history it may serve bookkeeping purposes. If it stops at this point, however, it misses its major function as a tool of management.

What to Do Next

THE real question facing all management is, "what to do next?" Any management routine which ends with this question, either unasked or unanswered, is a waste of precious time.

The heart of management is CHANGE. Management effort must constantly be exerted in two quite different directions. On the one hand, there is the necessity of getting the known methods used consistently by all subordinates. On the other hand, there is the equal necessity of creating and establishing still better methods. Weak, unimaginative management concentrates almost its entire attention on the first of these two types of supervision and thereby misses its greatest goal. Management that is content with unaltered repetition always fails. The failure may be delayed and gradual but it is nevertheless inevitable.

Handling the Boss

ALL good management, in its most obvious and most elementary form, centers around the making of changes. This means changes in personnel. But the prime responsibility of management is to get better performance from existing personnel, which can be done largely by making changes in methods and procedures, shifting personnel in accordance with the best determinable functional aptitudes. This latter is attainable only as the result of a keen understanding of human relations, intelligent appraisal of aptitudes and sympathetic understanding of personalities. It is with this phase of management, *personal leadership*, which this study deals.

In my opinion, however, management is not confined only to the direction of subordinates but involves, also, relationship with superiors, associates and those sections of the general public with whom we come in contact and over whom we have no administrative control.

Let us consider first our immediate superiors and higher executives. "Handling the boss" intelligently is truly a science and an art in which, unfortunately, too few persons are adept. The science is "knowing how" and the art is the "technique of execution." To be efficient in this phase of human relations, the individual must be a constant student of the temperament, moods, methods and ambitions of the "boss." He must direct his efforts and pattern his operations in accordance with the known wishes and the desired objectives of his superior. I do not imply by this statement any semblance of "apple polishing." No real executive respects a "yes" man.

But I do mean that there is always a proper time and method or avenue of "approach." Gage the proper time and select the logical method as the result of intelligent study, thereby eliminating or circumventing the numerous obstacles so likely to be encountered when the "approach" is made in careless or haphazard fashion. Intelligent planning and execution accomplishes amazing results in obtaining executive approval of known desirable proposals.

Public Relations

L ET us consider the next relationship of management with the general public, in view of the fact that the methods and techniques applicable in public relations follow a close parallel to relationship with all superiors. In neither of these types of contact does management possess the authority or the rights of administrative control.

Managerial contacts with the public usually involve interviews with visitors at the office. They may be customers of the company or applicants for employment but in all cases they are invariably potential customers. With this thought kept constantly uppermost in mind throughout every interview, a manager is reasonably certain to perform his job of public relations effectively. Many interviews may be kept entirely on a friendly basis, depending upon circumstances, and therefore not difficult of handling. It is with the antagonistic type of caller, however, where extreme tact and intelligence are vitally necessary. Perhaps the most difficult individual to "handle" is the disgruntled customer whose patience has been exhausted and who, as a last resort, makes the effort to call at the office for a final showdown.

Deflation

I N DEALING with an angry, or emotionally upset individual of this type, there is, in my opinion, only one dependable technique which provides reasonable assurance of a mutually satisfactory outcome. That technique is nothing more nor less than inducing "deflation" into an emotionally "inflated" personality. Argument at this stage is dynamite. It raises his "guard" and tends only to increase "inflation" and produce inevitable explosion. Temperamental "deflation" can usually be induced by permitting the individual to get everything "off his chest" and is gradually encouraged by sympathetic listening. Until the period of "deflation" has completely run its course, one must "spar for time."

It is surprising how easily proficiency can be acquired in this art of sparring with a little practice. Sometimes nothing more than a confused or amazed expression on the face during the tirade is all that is necessary. As deflation progresses, opportunity is offered to encourage the process through the injection of simple and inoffensive expressions and statements, such as, "Is that so?" "How?"—and the most disarming of all, "Why?" It is strange how difficult it is for an angry person to answer the question, "Why?" if it is injected at the right psychological moment. He finds himself immediately on the defensive and impelled to justify his own position.

This method of conciliation can be employed without the necessity for capitulation and without making any commitment which might jeopardize the position of the company from the standpoint of financial exposure or moral responsibility. After deflation has run its course and one is dealing with a perfectly normal, sane personality, there is ample opportunity for intelligent and logical appraisal of facts and a mutually satisfactory adjustment.

Subordinate Personnel

UNDOUBTEDLY the most fascinating phase of human relations is the technique of handling subordinate personnel. This does, at least, present the best opportunity for management to make a truly valuable contribution to employee welfare, as well as to serve mankind in general. In my opinion employee relations start with the first interview of an applicant and provide excellent opportunities to build company goodwill, regardless of whether or not actual employment results. It has been my policy for many years to see personally every applicant who calls at my office. If that is impossible at the moment, an appointment is made for a subsequent interview.

First impressions are not necessarily accurate but with experience one comes to recognize the degree of potentiality which exists in applicants. The amount of interest engendered during the early part of the interview naturally dictates the length of time which should be devoted to the individual. If it is perfectly apparent and obvious that the applicant would be a misfit in the organization, a reasonable amount of time can still be devoted to a sympathetic explanation of the circumstances and the applicant properly "anesthetized" so that the "turndown" may be as painless as possible. By this method goodwill for the company is induced because of the sympathetic hearing granted by the manager.

It may be that that interview represents the one and only contact which that applicant may have with the company over a long period of time. He appraises the company by the nature of his treatment and with the proper goodwill attitude will always think of the company favorably and constitute an ally. When one considers the number of applicants who must necessarily be refused employment by one company within a year, it is apparent how important the cumulative effect of this goodwill building can be.

If, on the other hand, the applicant immediately shows signs of fitness with some likelihood of ultimate employment, it is more than ever necessary to start the foundation at once for healthy employee relations to follow. Since no employer-employee relationship can ever develop successfully without mutual confidence and complete understanding, the manager at this point has within his power the opportunity to sell his company to the future employee in a manner which is bound to engender enthusiastic loyalty and healthy esprit de corps.

Checklist

IN THE actual conduct of administrative work in the handling of personnel and as a self-guide or checklist, I have found the following reminders extremely helpful for frequent reference:

Three-quarters of management problems lie in the field of human relations.

In appraising people, whether applicants or employees, make due allowance for all the facets of personality, including moral, social, political, cultural, religious and commercial attributes.

Recognize always the difference between intelligence and book-learning. Culture is absorbed and assimilated by exposure to people; rough edges are knocked off our natures and a well-balanced education is attainable without the benefits of college training.

Encourage and nurture suggestions from others. (Creative vs. synthetic imagination.)

Our employees are largely what we make them. Releasing a recalcitrant employee is the short and easy road but it is not the solution. The real job is to locate his weaknesses and help him to correct them.

The only justifiable purpose of a reprimand is to make it constructive and then, *never in the presence of a third party*.

The error made through ignorance calls for training—not blame

Begin every corrective interview with a question, thereby avoiding false accusations and embarrassment.

Keep eyes and ears open for personality traits and habits in others for comparison with your own; assimilate virtues; correct irritating traits and bad habits.

Criticize Methods—Not Intentions

CRITICIZE methods—not intentions. To criticize intentions will hurt an employee's self-esteem. It implies a question of his loyalty, ambitions and sincerity.

Long range judgment is greatly preferred to impulse. Anticipate problems so that a planned course of action is always available—in advance of the interview.

Human conduct is sometimes predictable. Employee attitudes do not generally spring up by accident. There is usually some basic reason for wrong or unhealthy employee attitude. Seek out the reason before determining the remedy.

Consult frequently with employees. The most dangerous policy in handling subordinates is to ignore them. An employee whose efforts go long unnoticed is justified in feeling that his task is unimportant.

Do not keep an employee static on a job which he performs well, or above average, merely because he is hard to replace. Recognize his performance by promotion to greater responsibilities.

Find the proper niche for each employee in order to promote full self-realization and self-development. Change misfits.

In difficult cases of maladjustment, look for the source of the trouble. An inferiority complex or a repression of initiative may result from some remote childhood influence or environment. (Example: Fear of harsh words.)

Praise Work—Not Worker

Do not be hesitant about giving praise—but praise the work, not the worker. Do not spread praise too promiscuously but save it for the unusual job. A large percentage of people suffer from inferiority complexes and inhibitions. They need praise to overcome these temperamental deficiencies just as they need food for physical sustenance.

Maintain close observation over the "self-starters" who generate their own steam. They may need a tight rein occasionally but never spurs. They are fully self-confident, frequently cocky and occasionally require rigid control.

The best compliment in the world to a conscientious employee is to ask his opinion on some phase of the business or the progress of his work. It is the most subtle form of praise without indulging in flattery.

Always be sincere.

Assign responsibility instead of merely giving instructions. Always "What" but only occasionally "How."

The handling of grievances or personal troubles sympathetically and with patience is a most potent form of mental wage or remuneration.

Study constantly your employees. Learn their habits of work and thinking. Adjust your "handling" of individuals to their respective temperaments.

Compare an employee's performance with a *standard*—not with other employees.

"The ability to handle people is an acquisition—not a gift," says Burton Bigelow.

Acknowledgment is gratefully extended to such students of human relations as Dr. Richard S. Schultz, Dr. Verne Steward, Dr. James R. Kave, Messrs. Carroll Belknap, Burton Bigelow, George Lightowler and many close associates in my own company over the period of the last 30 years.

Reprinted from The 1944 Proceedings, National Office Management Association, 25th Anniversary Conference.

Each Department Should Work Up a Plan which Most Nearly Fits Its Particular Needs. The Executive in Charge Will Be More Interested in His Own Creation than in Something Forced Upon Him.

Absentee Control Plans

By Carey O. Pickard

Reynolds Corporation
Macon, Ga.

W E HAVE had all the varying degrees of attendance percentages from very poor to excellent, but it is definitely believed that the excellent percentage we are now maintaining is "the real McCoy." Our attendance average for the entire plant for several months has been in the neighborhood of 97%, even though four-fifths of our 5,000 employees are women, many of whom travel long distances (as high as 150 miles daily) and work on the swing and graveyard shifts We have had no openings on our day shift in almost 2 years; new employees must take one of the night shifts regardless of personal inconveniences.

Ballyhoo No Good

T HE first major premise to consider is a fundamental principle which must *never* be overlooked. Discard any theory that outstanding results will be accomplished merely by banners waving, flags flying and ballyhoo. Get saturated with the theory that excellent results begin with real backing from top management and run all the way to the lowest supervisor; thus you pave the way for *small group* handling which is most certainly essential.

Keep the above two principles in mind in every move you make and your work will not fail to produce outstanding results; otherwise it may.

It is not necessary for every department in the plant to use identical internal plans. In fact, a certain amount of freedom of action for each department should be encouraged. We *never* suggest that any department follow exactly in the footsteps of another, regardless of how good a record the other department has made. Experience has proven that, given the privilege of taking any portion of the other department's plan which appeals to the Department Head, an even better record can be made by the department which designs its own internal plan.

Our plan is simple, but like anything else which produces results, it requires considerable work spread out over many of the supervisory personnel. Its simplicity lies in the fact that it can be started with only one department and gradually spread out to all departments one by one.

Records Kept

Two kinds of records are maintained: (1) Those kept in a central clearing house where all departmental summaries are received. (2) Departmental records which keep the Department Head and all employees informed daily as to the individual attendance of the employees in the department.

Every day each department turns in a form to the Personnel Department absentee clerks, reflecting the total of employees who should be present and a list of those absent. The form lists, by columns, eight types of absences. The absentee clerks charge the department with absences for any reason except the following: authorized leave of absence, vacation, plant accident or death in immediate family. Separate records are kept for each shift of each department.

For attendance purposes each week ends on Friday. By Saturday afternoon the various departments begin to call to find out their percentages and to get their standing as compared with other departments. The department which wins first place usually strings a large piece of paper across the production room, or puts up a big placard on the wall announcing that they won first place and usually takes a "crack" at the department which had first place during the previous week. This "advertising" remains up until the next week's percentages are received. A sense of rivalry prevails.

Attendance Score Board

Each of our production departments has a Department Head (classified as foreman 1st class) who is entirely responsible for the operation of all shifts in his department. Published percentages never give a breakdown of the various shifts, and therefore the Department Head tries to keep all shifts making good records so that his departmental average will make a good showing. Each week our plant newspaper has a box on the front page called "THE ATTENDANCE SCORE BOARD", and lists the past week's score by Division Heads in the order of accomplishment. Those departments not making 95% or over are printed in small letters. Here is the score board as it appeared recently on the front page of our weekly newspaper.

ATTENDANCE SCORE BOARD

Department	Division Head	Average
Primer	John Brake	98.
Fuze 6	Jim Robertson	97.65
Detonator	J. B. White	97.64
Tracer	W. G. Paskowsky	97.4
Fuze 106	Frank Liebert	97.28
Fuze 6	Bill Moses	97.27
Maintenance	B. M. Van Buren	95.9

PRODUCTION AVERAGE: 97.3

Only departments having 100 or more employees are listed

The following departments did not make an average of over 95%:

Department	Division Head	Average
Cafeteria	Tommy Watkins	95
Fuze 106a	R. A. Lowe	94.8

On Monday, or not later than Tuesday, of *each* week, the Personnel Director receives a tabulation from the Employment Manager of all departments by shifts, and prepares a memorandum for the signature of the Vice-President and General Manager addressed to each Department Head whose average was above 95%, praising him, his foremen and employees for their good record. No mention is made of any particular shift unless one of the three shifts has a very poor showing as compared to the other two shifts. This is done so the Department Head can use it in encouraging the delinquent foreman to get his average up. A typical weekly memorandum to a Department Head is as follows:

"Last Week's Attendance Record November 30, 1944
"I was pleased to learn that your department is continuing to maintain a very fine attendance record with 97.2% for the past week. It is noted that your second shift had a slump, but I feel sure that it must be only temporary, and that within a short time your departmental average will give you top place among the major departments in the plant. My best wishes to the foremen and employees who are responsible for the fine record being maintained by your department."
Vice-President and General Manager"

To Maintain Interest

THE record system and procedures followed in one department are as follows: The attendance system of this department was conceived on the theory that the success of any program is brought about through participation of every individual. To get the interest of the individual, the following steps in the program have been instituted:

1. Small competitive unit lines or groups, of ten to twenty employees under a supervisor.

2. Attendance absentee cards.
3. Recording daily line or group attendance, by supervisor.
4. Posting weekly attendance sheets.
5. Competitive daily attendance percentage black board—three shifts.
6. Poster bulletins.
7. Personal contacts.
8. Periodic "pep" talks by shift foreman or Division Head.

Cycle of Treatment

To show the use of these steps, let us take the complete cycle of an absentee, and see how this employee is treated and governed, so that the individual's attendance will improve.

Let us assume that Mr. X is employed on Line 1, one of the small competitive unit groups within the department. Upon arriving at work the day after the absence, Mr. X finds in his time card rack an absentee card on which the individual writes in the reason for the absence and signs his name. Upon reaching the production room, the employee has a personal interview with the foreman, who discusses the problem and the reason for the absence until both are completely satisfied.

Here we get the much needed *personal contact* between the foreman and employee by making Mr. X's problem the foreman's problem. After the interview, the foreman signs the card if he accepts the employee's excuse as true. If he thinks the employee's excuse for absence is false, then he writes "not accepted". If this employee has two or more days with "not accepted" excuses, the foreman will write a warning slip, pointing out his poor absentee record. If an employee gets two warning slips on the same reasons, he will get a suspension of a week or more, whatever penalty the foreman then thinks he should have.

After Mr. X gets his card O. K.'d by the foreman, he takes his card to Line 1 supervisor, who records absence and reason on daily line attendance sheet, which information is available to all line workers. The percentages are also recorded. At the end of the week the sheets are turned over to the shift foreman, who calculates the shift overall attendance. In turn, the three shift reports are forwarded to the Division Head, who posts the daily line attendance sheets and the division weekly overall attendance. Each employee on all three shifts has an opportunity to see his own attendance record in black and white along with his fellow workers, whether good or bad. If an employee sees his record beside another employee's record, results are improved with time.

Intershift Competition

To create intershift competition, there is posted in the production room in view of all workers a daily attendance percentage board. The purpose of this procedure is to bring before the workers in the division the daily attendance percentage of each shift and of the overall division, which is also compared with other departments.

The daily progress, up or down, as the week passes by, shows the shifts doing better work in attendance and the comparison of the three shifts. This gives both the shift foreman or Division Head an opportunity to stimulate more interest to the lagging shift by calling the employees together for a "pep" talk of ten to fifteen minutes. During the talk, create the "right thinking" and the individual's need to participate in the attendance program. The production lost during this time is doubled in the future.

Finally, the success of the program on any shift, or for the division as a whole, is "advertised" and stimulated through posters, bulletins, newspaper writeups and cartoons which are placed on the wall in the production room.

Another System

ANOTHER system used in another department, and just as effectively, is as follows: This department has an independent attendance program, which, if enforced 100%, works exceptionally well. This program consists of several steps and includes some personal contact with the individual worker. To begin with, it has four definite rules governing the consequences of absenteeism. These are enforced to the letter and without partiality. These rules are posted on the department bulletin board, as follows:

1. One unexcused absence per month is permissible.
2. Two unexcused absences per month will result in a written warning.
3. Three or more unexcused absences per month will result in a suspension.
4. Continued unexcused absences or excessive absences will necessitate a separation.

In conjunction with this procedure, a monthly sheet is kept on the bulletin board, and each unexcused employee during the month has her name put on this sheet marked for the day on which she is absent.

A careful study of each employee's past attendance record is made before we excuse her. For instance, if a person calls in and says, "I am sick today and just can't make it," this does not mean that that person is an excused absentee. Often such cases are marked up "unexcused" when, after a little investigation, we find that either the employee could have worked, or her past record is so bad that we can not continue excusing her. *At present we seldom ever have two or more unexcused absences marked up against one person in a month's time.*

Yearly Record to Date

WE ALSO have listed on a large sheet of graph paper on the wall each employee's name with the number of days missed from work *this year* up to date. We believe that when confronted with a bad record the majority will try to improve.

To build morale, an effort is made to create a little competition between shifts inside the department. . This is done primarily by using the room bulletin boards. These are changed often to keep from getting dull and routine. A slogan board is kept on which a new slogan is posted daily. These vary from the witty and humorons to the deeply serious.

To stimulate a little competition within the department on a single shift, the department is broken down into several groups which are as evenly divided as possible and group records are kept on file. An attendance award (made of wood and cardboard) goes to the group having the best record each week, and it remains on the work table of that group until it is won by another group the next week.

We try to get each person to confide in her supervisor her domestic troubles, and, if at all possible, we do something to help her. In general, a great deal of personal contact is made, and in this way the supervisory personnel learns to know each employee in the department almost as well as if he or she were a brother or sister.

Work Out Plan in Best Department

IN ORDER to apply our plan, it is recommended that one of the better departments be picked for a starter and perfected along suitable lines. After it is felt that the plan is operating smoothly in that department, call a conference of all Division Heads in the major departments (the foremen need not be present) and have the model Department Head explain the plan he used.

It should be stressed that no department is required to use the identical plan, but instead should use its own ingenuity and work up a plan which would more nearly fit its particular needs. The Department Head will be more interested in his own creation than he would one which he was forced to adopt.

Book Reviews

Book Review Editor, Mr. Everett Van Every

California Personnel Management Association, Berkeley, Cal.

PERSONNEL MANAGEMENT IN WAR INDUSTRIES, Volume II

By John W. Riegel. Ann Arbor. University of Michigan Press. 1944. Litho'd Paper Covers. 148 pp. $3.50

Many personnel executives are making the mistake today of thinking of their current wartime problems as something wholly apart and distinct from peace-time operations. They seem to feel that today's problems are so entirely different from those they have experienced before the war and that they will confront when "normal production is resumed." Certainly we will not be able to say that production has returned to normalcy for a long time to come. Our whole economic and social structure in this country, in the world for that matter, will need recasting for at least time to crystallize and assume whatever shape and development fate has in store for us. My point is that we cannot casually refer to "normal times" from our present position and trust that revision will be reasonably soon, prompt and accurate. A war economy doesn't end that smoothly and dependably. It is as full of variables and the unexpected as war demands themselves . . . and business and industry must not lose sight of what it means to "return to normal."

The text material of this volume, which is the second part of a summary of conferences held at the University of Michigan on wartime personnel problems, does not develop the point raised above, but the reader is left pondering over his future problems, and what changes he may expect in his day-to-day struggle to keep up production and personnel control when conversion or reconversion sets in. If anything, the reader is left weighing and contemplating the differences he will encounter when hostilities cease. The war has surely brought personnel practices and techniques into sharp focus with the usual day-to-day situations—but in reality, our wartime personnel problems are the same problems in different surroundings. Outside of the emergency aspect of war production the difficulties encountered in handling war workers are not much different from those we find in what so many of us like to refer to as "normal times."

John Riegel's conferences, of which this study is the summary of the last three of twelve meetings, are crammed with pertinent information and prevailing practices that every personnel manager will find helpful. . . . The first chapter tells how employees can be brought to accept production standards, and why no incentive program is worthwhile that does not have the support of the workers to the extent that they understand and participate in it. Other chapters relate how shop stewards are trained in the incentive program; how one company had the union elect time-study stewards who were later trained by the company to deal in technical questions.

Methods improvement, production standards and incentives are thoroughly discussed in this report. The chapter on "Experience With Incentive Plans" is a valuable treatise on about all the fundamentals including such important aspects as union plans, indirect workers, women's base rates, industrial engineers, spoilage, etc.

The chapters on Supervisory Training, Disciplinary Problems, Preventing Griev-ances and Placement of Veterans are excellent thumb-nail studies. Each of these chapters is an outline for a book and the treatment is surprisingly complete. The effectiveness of the volume may be due in part to the conference style of writing which affords a direct and brief statement of facts supported by specific company experiences. Recommended for all personnel managers.

SENIORITY PROBLEMS DURING DEMOBILIZATION AND RECONVERSION

By Frederick H. Harbison—Industrial Relations Section, Princeton
University. 27 pp. Price $.75

One of the foremost problems confronting labor and management during de-mobilization and reconversion is that of seniority. This report deals clearly and succinctly with the approaching questions of veterans' seniority in industry as well as permanent and temporary employee rights accumulated during the war years, and suggests plausible solutions and policies.

Dr. Harbison's brochure gives the background and growth of seniority systems since 1935, years in which the systems received their greatest impetus. Today "Seniority" is an accepted feature of industrial relations in American industry but the concept as we have known it appears to be changing under the impact of war and has become subject to federal legislation and court review. The passage of the Selective Training and Service Act, setting forth Veteran re-employment rights to-gether with the pressure of public opinion, indicate for the future modified seniority systems of a more flexible nature to be workable in the post-war period.

Seniority is inevitably the responsibility of both labor and management and changes must be made by joint determination. In the complicated post-war period both management and unions will benefit by a flexible administration of the seniority principle which gives less emphasis to legislation of detailed rules and more attention to fundamental questions of policy.

For efficient post-war industry, Dr. Harbison suggests that possibly the fairest and most democratic solution seems to be to treat civilians and veterans alike. Claims to post-war jobs "by virtue of seniority" should be limited to those persons, civilians and veterans, who had pre-emergency permanent employment status and who accumulated seniority during the war period. The opportunity of others to qualify would then be based on factors not related to length of service. This should result in higher employment and job performance standards.

For a clear analysis of the above position as well as other important problems entering the industrial seniority picture, we recommend this report to all personnel executives.

MAKING AND USING INDUSTRIAL SERVICE RATINGS

By George D. Halsey. Harper & Bros., N. Y., 1944 (Aug. 23). 149 pp. $2.50

Reviewed by J. Bernhagen

The development of Service Ratings since their origin in 1916 is covered in this book which gives the best proved current practices in efficiency and merit ratings and which also outlines the construction of rating forms as well as methods of successful application.

The author shows that Service Ratings have two distinct purposes, namely:

(1) To serve as an aid in training and supervision
(2) To furnish evaluation of employee job performances and thus aid in making sound administrative decisions—promotions, transfers, salary increases, layoffs, etc.

In answer to the long standing criticism that efficiency or service ratings are subjective—or just personal opinion—Mr. Halsey replies that all judgments relied on by management for personnel decisions are subjective. The alternative to the use of well designed and well administered Service Rating plans is continued dependence on unguided judgment.

More and more industry has come to realize that an opinion, formed from a well constructed and administered service rating plan, is the best and fairest basis for all personnel decisions, including the setting of salaries. No one can justly complain about honest efficiency ratings fairly applied. Service Ratings of employees give executives a uniform method of training, making and recording judgments of character, accomplishment, and needs of each person supervised. Executives are thereby better able to reward and train their employees.

Service Ratings consist of (1) a decision as to what qualities of performance, aptitude and attitude make up the optimum person or job performance for each position, and the relative importance or weight of each quality, and (2) a systematic rating of the degree to which each separate quality is shown in the person's job performance. This is prepared by a supervisor who has close personal contact with the work of the person rated.

Making and Using Industrial Service Ratings

Consequently, a Service Rating may be defined as "an orderly, systematic and carefully considered analysis or evaluation of an employee's services, based on both observation over a considerable period of time and a study of all available objective records of performance and behavior.''

It is true that service ratings have not always been fair; there is a possibility for favoritism or injustice. However, Service Ratings also have the possibility, with proper administration, of being made absolutely fair whereas many salary plans based as they so often are, on partial and non-uniform criterias of job performance, are inherently unfair and often can not be made otherwise even by conscientious and skillful administration.

Ratings should not be condemned because of misjudgments they reflect. To a certain extent, the more errors there are, the greater the need for rating because it provides opportunity for correction through pooling of judgments of several raters and through the review of the rating with the supervisor. While Service Rates are not infallible in measuring the efficiency of employees, they are a medium for assisting supervisors in making more systematic judgments. They assure that employees are judged by different supervisors according to uniform standards.

Since no system can operate itself, it is important that the successful Service Rating Plan have the support of top executives actively interested in the reviews; supervisors should understand and approve the plan; and the Rating Form should be thoughtfully and skillfully designed to suit the work judged. It is necessary that clear, specific and detailed directions be given to persons administering the plan and that ratings should be used skillfully and sympathetically.

In form, Service Ratings have been of two general types: (1) Rating of personal qualities and, (2) Job descriptions—or a statement of the efficiency of the person's job performance. Very often a combination of the two types of analysis proves most feasible.

To industrial management which is confronted with conversion and post-war seniority and veteran re-employment and placement problems, this book offers constructive suggestions toward fair personnel policies and decisions.

PERSONNEL
Journal

The Magazine of

LABOR RELATIONS AND PERSONNEL PRACTICES

Published by PERSONNEL RESEARCH FEDERATION

Lincoln Building, 60 East 42nd Street, New York City

Volume 23   *Number 8*

Contents for February 1945

Wake Up America

WITH this issue of the Personnel Journal, being prepared early in the New Year, we find ourselves in a rather anomalous position. Much of the material we publish, and have published, we heartily disagree with. But partly because we publish ideas that are currently thought good, and partly because our columns are open to all points of view, we have presented them.

Our main protest is against the mechanistic view of human relations in industry that has been increasingly creeping in, in the last ten years. This, of course, is due to the mechanistic trend that has been evident in psychology for the past twenty years.

By "mechanistic" we mean the business of sizing up employees by psychological tests of intelligence, personality, temperament, interests, etc., as suitable for employment or promotion by industry, or as fit only for the garbage dump of Federal relievers, if they do not pass the unpsychological psychological tests to which they are subjected by our best companies.

Based upon a worker's past experience, and some guess as to how well he will fit into the present organization of a company, his life is determined by some employment interviewer, whose very inferior position in the industrial or government organization plainly marks him or her, as inferior in the eyes of top executives.

Though it is highly important that a company get into its employee ranks, right from the beginning, the most suitable employees, it is current practice to pay employment managers, so called, the lowest rate of executive salaries. Hence poor hiring, and poor labor relations.

In the early days of the Russian revolution the psychologists were nearly thrown out. They used their methods to show that a man was good or no good. But in so far as the communistic theory was that all men "are equal" (that sounds familiar), the psychologists were told to go back and find out the positive abilities of those they discarded.

In other words, if the theory holds, if a man has deficiencies in some respects he has strengths in other respects—and it was up to the psychologists to find these out and fit the man into a job where he could use his good qualities to the best advantage of himself and the country. That was the Russian idea.

That also was the basis upon which America was built, though no one stopped to theorize about it then. Today with psychology bogged down in psychological tests, and potential workers put through the grinder of employment procedures, designed primarily to exclude, rather than admit, we are drifting away off our original pattern, and are shutting out very, very many good workers from our industries.

Perhaps the matter may be summed up by pointing out that the internal organization of many industrial companies is so poor, that through their employment departments the companies try to screen out all workers who do not look as if they can stand the gaff of the rotten administration they will have to work under.

Mayo points this up in his report. Without excluding people because of their supposed limitations, you can get excellent work out of an almost unselected bunch of workers, if you provide them with the proper working environment. So one of the things to do is to fuss less about fancy hiring methods, and compulsory tying of workers to their jobs, and devote more attention to organizational problems.

This means study. Mayo comments upon current industrial relations policies, in which companies set up pension schemes, and other welfare projects, all in the vague hope that somehow they will help smooth labor relations. Millions of dollars have been spent on this kind of hooey, and no one knows whether it has been any good or not.

Mayo calls this a "Blunderbuss" technique. As far as we know a blunderbuss is a short gun that shoots wild.

It is high time that American industrial companies quit using blunderbusses in their industrial relations, and start to use intelligent methods in their dealings with their employees. In doing so they should certainly veer away from the mechanistic concepts of the psychologists, and the compulsory concepts of legislators, and take note of the findings of the social psychologists and the sociologists, on how to get people to work together in accordance with their fundamental natures.

The Editor

"When We Look Through the Many Records of Attendance and Absenteeism in the East and West We Are Struck by the Invariable Persistence of the Human Desire for Active Association in Teamwork with Others."—Elton Mayo.

Teams *of* Workers

Digest and Review
BY CHARLES S. SLOCOMBE
Personnel Research Federation
New York, N. Y.

THERE are those who seem to think that, by and large, there is something, or perhaps there are many things, wrong with our present system of employer-employee relations, in industry, in business and in government offices.

That we fall very far short of utopian ideals in these matters is evident to all. Yet the question remains as to whether we want a utopia, and whether we would like it if we had it.

EnJoying Company

IT is interesting therefore to come across the recent study by a Harvard team, headed by Elton Mayo, pointing out one of our lacks in industrial organization. Mayo and his associates went into Southern California to see what they could find out about high labor turnover and absenteeism in the aircraft industry in that part of the country.

They came out with the basic idea that if things are arranged properly so that workers work in, and identify themselves with, teams or groups of workers there is little absenteeism or turnover, except that caused by unavoidable circumstances, such as serious illnesses, etc.

It would almost seem that they think that if workers could be put together in the right teams, and kept there, there would be no problems of turnover, absenteeism, grievances, wage growls, etc., in the war period or after. Workers would get up bright-eyed in the early hours of the morning anxious to go to the factory because they would enjoy so much the company of their fellows, and would find the work not at all boring or fatiguing.

That would be utopia indeed. It is perhaps an exaggeration of Mayo and Company's point of view. But it seems to be the trend of their thinking. Let us get down to what they actually found.

They went to Southern California, particularly the region around Los Angeles, to see what this absenteeism labor turnover complaint in our aircraft factories was all about.

Restless Population

THEY found an apparently restless shiftless population of workers, who had come from all parts of the country, motivated by patriotism, the promise of high wages, or the lure of California's well known publicity agents. Some had plenty of previous factory experience, others had none. Waitresses—if that is what they are called—from diners and one-arm lunch joints, and young housewives whose experience was limited to putting diapers on their babies, all joined in the procession to build fighters and bombers.

Selective Service took supervisors and technicians, and at the same time the Army and Navy demanded more and more bombers and fighters to be built by salesmen, hash-slingers and diaper washers. Plant payrolls grew from 3000 to 50,000 in a few months, all filled with this motley assembly.

Yet somehow the planes were built—how nobody has yet said.

As a matter of fact, though personnel policies and practices in the aircraft industry seem away ahead of those in most other war industries, they are, by academic standards, elementary in the extreme. The fact that the companies have met their war schedules in spite of this leads one to wonder at times whether all this elaborate personnel business we talk so much about is necessary, or whether it is just a fad.

The only answer to this seems to be that even the best informed know very little about the science of personnel administration, or how to get it used by line executives, and that those companies who use the most of it get better results with less friction and trouble than those companies, businesses and government agencies who regard it as unnecessary

Hiring and Quitting

MAYO and his group in Southern California make no pretensions about having found the final answer to the problems facing the aircraft industry or general industry in war or post-war times. They do, however, present the results of a study of causes, and show that only by getting to the roots of a problem can it be dealt with, even if for many years to come, it cannot be solved.

During eight months the aircraft companies hired 173,800 new workers—in the same period 175,700 quit their jobs and went somewhere else. In addition to the numbers quitting their jobs, often without notice, in one typical company, employing about 40,000, an average of 1500 a day failed to show up for work, and were classed as absentees.

Also almost a quarter of a million girls, who went into all war industries in the area, didn't like their jobs and quit to go back to domestic work, war or no war.

Uninformed about Jobs

Most of these people quitted within a few weeks or months of their being hired. In Mayo's terms it is evident that when they went into the factories they did not find the other employees with whom they had to work friendly or congenial. In many cases, of course, their previous conception of the job they would be put in did not in any way correspond with the job they found they had to do. Hence the high degree of quitting after a short time.

Yet the turnover rates of the aircraft industry was less than the average for essential industries in Los Angeles County, during the period studied.

Relating back to the Mayo and Company's concept of the necessity of arranging for the formation of congenial groups of workers as a basis for stability of work habits—meaning lower absenteeism, labor turnover, and increased production—there was found to be an additional factor.

Absenteeism and turnover are causes and symptoms of unsatisfactory working conditions and relations between employees. They certainly prevent the formation of the work groups which Mayo and Company regard as important.

Internal Turnover

The additional factor, partly caused by and related to these factors, was found to be the internal turnover within plants, in which employees were transferred from job to job, and from department to department, sometimes due to promotion, often due to the constant changes necessitated by absenteeism and labor turnover, and often due to changes in production schedules, shortages of materials, etc. In one plant studied a count was made, and it was found, quoting from the Mayo report, that·

REPORT QUOTED

In a large plant, of approximately 40,000 employees, producing attack bombers and transports, the loans of employees between departments for the year ending January 23, 1944, amounted to 1,204,900 hours, the equivalent of about 150,000 man-days. Since loans are typically for less than a day, this figure represents over 150,000 moves. For the same period the same plant had 65,114 transfers and 31,104 clear-outs, or terminations. Out of 8,572,969 man-days of work scheduled, 523,540, or 6.1%, were lost through absences.

The situation in this plant, which is sufficiently typical, for the year ending January 23, 1944, may be summarized thus:

	Number of Changes	Percentage of 1943 Average Personnel (41.179 = 100%)
Clear-outs	31,104	75%
Transfers	65,114	157%
Loans (approx.)	150,000	360%
Total changes	246,218	592%

These figures take no account of movements of workers within a department occasioned by (1) absences and (2) work changes. It is impossible to estimate the number of these changes with reasonable accuracy. Nevertheless, the figures suffice to show that changes of actual work within a sufficiently typical plant during 1943 amounted to approximately 600%. This is quite a different figure from that for terminations alone; in this plant, for instance, clear-outs were 75%. This report will show that the dimension of the figure for total changes nevertheless has a bearing on turnover (terminations) and absence rates.

Turnover, Absences, and Organization

IN ANY plant the organization of teamwork cannot ordinarily be effected except upon the basis of organized operations. Although success in the attempt to induce in workers an attitude of spontaneous cooperation is a complex matter and involves far more than merely organized operations, it is nevertheless difficult to believe that, except in special situations, this basis is not a prime necessity. Indeed, any industrial research we know points to organized operations as the necessary condition for large-scale industry.

Since the aircraft companies faced constant changes of schedule which reached their peak before October, 1943, the loans and transfers of workers mentioned above were inevitable. But this is, as we have indicated, already a species of turnover within the plant that easily becomes transferred beyond the factory gates. There is no question that stability of working conditions—the job to which a worker is accustomed, at which he has become skilled, his daily association in work with those who have become his friends when he has "made the team"—leads to stability of attendance.

In the east coast study of absenteeism we found that in well-organized departments a majority of veteran workers had not been absent in a year or had been absent only once. These workers, as well as those absent 2, 3, 4, or 5 times in a year, were obviously not "turnover." Such groups as these display a high resistance in normal conditions of work to casual absences or quitting.

—287—

New Workers Quit Quickly

he highest incidence of absences and terminations is among those who are new to the work or to the plant, and who have not worked themselves into relationship with the job and with their fellow workers. In a well-organized mid-western plant doing essential war work for the Army and the Navy, the highest number of terminations in the first seven months of 1943 was by workers with from one week's service to one year's; after this point, the number leaving the company declined sharply. In these months, total terminations at this plant were 2,817; those with under 6 months' service comprised 70.1% of the total.

With such evidence of the effects of organization on absences and turnover, we could not restrict ourselves to the study of one of them. They were our starting points, and both of them were symptoms of disorganization, symptoms that organization of operations had not yet been achieved, or that workers had not been successfully organized into teams. (*end quote*)

Absenteeism vs. Turnover

The report then shows a most interesting chart, for comparative purposes, of absenteeism and turnover in an East Coast sheet mill. During 1943 the turnover rate almost steadily declined to zero, but the absenteeism rate steadily increased.

It would seem from this that if the organization of working relations in a company is about as usual, or "normal," that is with certain inevitable defects, due to our lack of complete knowledge of personnel administration, then if you crack down too hard with inappropriate methods to reduce absenteeism, you just get increased quitting. If you slacken up a bit on disciplining for absenteeism your labor turnover drops off.

Either solution is not very satisfactory. The only solution which seems satisfactory is an improvement in internal organization, of employee groups and working relations. When we speak of these we do not mean labor relations as ordinarily thought of, that is as between the employer and employee unions, but rather aiding in the organization of better relations among employees themselves. We again quote from the report:

Our studies have not been extensive enough to let us say to what extent the relationship between labor turnover and absenteeism found can be called "normal." We do know that if both absenteeism and labor turnover had risen sharply, the rise would have indicated a serious problem of some kind; if both had fallen sharply, a brief inquiry would have shown improvement in internal organization. The more usual movement of absenteeism and turnover in a sufficiently orderly situation seems frequently to be as in the sheet mill cited above.

Attendance Records

WE NOW turn our attention to the part of the report dealing with the study of absenteeism. Mayo and company finally got down to the study of this problem by different departments in different companies, and a comparison of departments within one company.

Roughly, according to our interpretation of their figures and charts, they regarded an employee as not being a bad actor if absences averaged less than six per year. If there were more than that the employee was regarded as an irregular attendant.

In the worst department they reported, only 37% of employees were found to be regular attendants at their jobs. In the best department found, 90% of the employees were regular attendants, according to this standard, and the majority of these did not lose a day's work a year.

Limitations of time and research personnel made it possible for Mayo and company to select only two of the best work groups for close study. Briefly their findings were, and we quote:

REPORT QUOTED

OUT OF a total of 55 workers, 50, or 90%, had excellent attendance records; of this 50, 37 had a rate of well under 2 absences in 12 months. Only 3 had records giving them more than 10 absences annually. The turnover in the whole group was small, especially by comparison with other departments in the plant. Those who left included, for instance, 4 minors returning to school, 2 women who married, and 1 worker who was discharged for habitual alcoholism. The assiduity of attendance in the whole department, we were told, was such that on numerous occasions employees had come to work so ill that they had to be sent home.

One of the two work centers, B, happened to be separated from the other, and could be made the subject of close study. Eighty-four per cent (16 out of 19) were absent at the rate of fewer than 6 times per year; 10, or 53%, had perfect attendance records.

Beavers

THIS small group was known in its plant for the fact that the persons in it "worked like beavers." The foreman of Department IV said that their efficiency (output per man-hour) ran at 100% to 105%, whereas the average for the plant was about 80%. The group itself was thought by others to be somewhat clannish; members of it quite definitely thought of themselves as a team and, as such, in some degree different from other workers in the plant. "Just for comparison," one of the workers said to us, "go down and walk through Department CD some time. See the difference among the welders there." This man had at one time been a welder in Department CD, but was transferred to Department IV to prevent his departure from the plant by reason of an inarticulate dissatisfaction. He worked happily in Department IV, although he was probably earning somewhat less.

The foreman of Department IV rarely visited the B work center; his senior assistant foreman visited it once daily. The work was actually in the charge of a "leadman," Z, a college man with considerable experience in steel mills, who did not rank as a supervisor. He was formally responsible for taking care of only the minor, hour-to-hour interruptions in the operations of his group; the actual working out of much of what he did was not specified by management but left to his own initiative. In many ways he was "just another worker" with the extra job of servicing his fellow workers.

How the Leadman Worked

THE team relationships in this department did not occur by chance; the persons responsible were the leadman, Z, and the senior assistant foreman, who gave Z his support. In conversation both expressed a strong conviction that the achievement of group solidarity is immensely important in the long run, if not immediately, and actually necessary for sustained production. On separate occasions both men went beyond this to express pride in the human aspect of their administration; they were alike confident that absenteeism could not become a problem in B work center.

How exactly was this fortunate situation brought about? Z gave most of his time to facilitating the work of others; he and his company reaped the reward. He saw the problems of maintaining balance among technical efficiency, organization of operations, and spontaneity of cooperation far more clearly than many of his superior officers. His chief activities were, first, helping individual workers; second, "trouble-shooting"; and, third, acting as contact man for the group with the "outside world" (i.e., the departmental foreman, time-study men, inspectors). His activities are worth examination in detail, because to such a great extent they were determined by himself rather than by the direction of management.

First, the Individual Worker

THE help Z gave an individual was both technical and personal or social. Any mechanical difficulty received his whole attention. If he could not himself solve the problem, he secured the appropriate aid from engineers or others. Since the technical organization of his department was in charge of experts, however, his chief attention was demanded by the personal needs of his workers. Z listened to a new employee, introduced him to his companions, tried to get him congenial work associates. After an employee had worked a few days, Z got him a pass and took him to the assembly line to see the part he had made installed in the complete machine.

In addition, Z listened to any personal problems preoccupying the mind of a worker, new or old. He said that line supervision, and probably top management itself, is not in these days sufficiently aware of the new demands that the war situation is making of management in respect to the human aspect of administration. In these days, he said, people have "many more things on their minds" than they used to have and "strong-arm methods don't work." By way of example, he cited the case of a worker who seemed to have one personal problem after another, about all of which he complained. Z remarked that the main thing this worker needed was to "get his troubles off his chest to his boss"; if he could do this, he was one of the best producers in the whole department and got on well enough with his fellows.

Second, "Trouble-shooting"

THE department was likely to get low-priority materials. Occasionally there were shortages of material. Z worked actively to anticipate such troubles if possible or to get attention for them when they arose, and thus contributed directly to the production record of his department.

Third, "The Outside World"

REQUESTS for raises went through Z to the foreman. Z also handled inspectors, efficiency men, and the like; he acted for his group both as buffer against and as effective link with the plant, the "outside world."

It is interesting to observe that his chief self-imposed task was that of securing for the individual worker an effective and happy relationship with his fellow workers and his work. The result of his effort in his work center was an effective group, a team, and not a few effective workers scattered sporadically in a disunited collection of individuals, such as we had found in so many other departments. (*end quote*)

With their stress on teamwork as essential in industrial organization and production, Mayo and company obviously had to consider the size of teams—how many people can you put together, and how the groups can be related to each other so that they are cooperative rather than snarling up the works because of jealousies and antagonisms. We quote their findings in this respect:

REPORT QUOTED

How Large Is a Team?

WHAT number of people can naturally associate themselves together in work? Many arbitrary or empirical answers have been given to this question. The Army, for instance, places it at from 8 to 14 according to function; certain industrial psychologists say 5 without any convincing reason for doing so. We found that we had in our hands some evidence of definite interest in this connection. There seemed to be three types of groups in our studies: the "natural" group, the "family," and the "organized." These distinctions are empirical and tentative, but they indicate something in fact that demands further inquiry.

The "Natural" Group

IN THE records of 69 work centers given earlier in this report, there are 12 with a regular attendance record of over 80%. Since one of these consists of only 1 worker (we do not know the "company" reason for this), we shall ignore it. The other 11 groups are all small, several of 2 or 3 workers, the highest numbers are 6 and 7. The regularity of attendance does not occur independently of supervision, for one department had definitely more good working teams than the two others and this accords with the reputation in the plant of the department's foreman. But regular attendance may occur in the most unlikely places.

Actually it is evidence in support of the claim that human beings like regular association with others at work; such association will happen in the natural order of events without explicit attention from management to the organization of human needs, unless some interference prevents. *In the absence of an internal plant organization deliberately designed to foster the habit of daily association, almost anything may operate as interference.*

In Southern California the possible interferences are very numerous. This point should be borne in mind by every executive and supervisor. It should also be remembered that in the fall of 1943 the aircraft companies had existed at their peak size for only a short time. Particularly under such conditions it is not surprising that the "natural" group remains small in size.

The "Family" Group

THE "natural" group, if not too much discouraged, may develop in size, by way of a move toward organization almost as equally automatic and unguided by supervision as the formation of a "natural" group. One Work Center is an example. It consisted of 30 workers of whom 80% had a regular attendance record. Of the 30, 8 were veterans, 5 with almost perfect attendance records, only 1 at all doubtful. Twenty-two were relative newcomers; of these, 17 had almost perfect attendance records, and only 3 could be classified as irregulars.

Our term "family " is purely arbitrary as description; it is intended to denote a situation in which a core of regulars may, if they have prestige, determine, almost by inadvertence, the group attendance.. Wise parenthood, we are told, builds on the principle that "example is better than precept." This is all that the word "family" is here intended to denote: a situation in which the behavior of newer members is determined by the example set them by those who have been there longer. This situation is, of course, more common in the industrial centers of the East than in California; yet it occurred there in this Work Center. Its significance for management is limited to situations where a "natural" group can be held together long enough to act as a core for a larger group.

Our researches have given us little insight on how long such a period must be. Our estimate is that, except under conditions of emergency or unusual stress when even large teams may be achieved almost overnight, the minimal period necessary for the formation of teams of the size of which we are speaking, and without explicit attention from management to the organization of human needs, may be between six months and a year of continuous working together.

The "Organized" Group

Natural and "family" groups achieve their integration, not by direct action of management, but spontaneously and because management establishes around the workers a "climate" of the technical and operating aspects of organization such that groups can grow. The relationship of management to such growth is thus indirect; whereas in an "organized" group it is direct. This type of group we have already discussed in the description of the B work center of Department IV. It differs from both other types in that someone—leadman Z—with the respect and confidence of the workers and with the support of management as indicated by his selection as leadman, *has set himself deliberately, with intelligence and skill, to achieve a group integrity of association* and to order the relations of his own integral group with other departments in the plant. Given sufficient experience, intelligence, and skill in management, the problem of number therefore does not arise.

For the first type of group, the number limit seems to be in the neighborhood of 6 or 7; we have given an instance of the second type numbering 30; but there is no reason why the third type should not extend over an entire plant and include persons of widely different backgrounds. The desiderata are the group integrity of small groups, and, beyond this, an integral relationship among all groups. But this is the proper task of administration and management.

The Irregulars

To learn something of the irregulars we attended exit interviews in several plants, specializing in two, a large plant and a small one. We also interviewed persons working on the line, chosen at random, and in this the supervisory staffs were of great assistance. As a further step, we encouraged exit interviewers and supervisors to discuss the problem with us, especially when "off duty," and we benefited by their experience. The interviews with workers, of which in certain instances we have full records, numbered several score.

These interviews were of the type known as "undirected." That is to say, the person interviewed was encouraged to talk of anything at all; the choice of topic and the manner of its development were left entirely to him. We also accompanied groups of new workers through the whole process of induction and assignment to jobs, and kept in touch with these persons for some weeks afterwards.

The first observation from these interviews must be the wide range of persons employed—young and old, with mechanical experience and without it, persons with family problems, and solitary individuals. Among them were many who became "turnover" because for them their work was only a part of their total life, all the demands of which they had to keep in balance. For instance, many of the younger women had husbands in this or that branch of the services and tended to follow them from station to station. Other women were compelled to be absent from, or give up, industrial employment by reason of young families that ran into trouble of one kind or other when left without direction during the day or night.

The Glamour Girl

Offices of the War Manpower Commission told us that in 1942 and 1943 the airplane was the "glamour girl" of industry. The in-migrant with a family usually took a job before he had found a home; in very many instances, probably the majority, this job was in an aircraft plant. He then discovered that he could not get suitable quarters for the family near the plant; sometimes he had to live as far as twenty miles from his work. Subsequently he found work less distant from his base. Frequently, we were told, in-migrants made three moves before settling down It is to the credit of the aircraft companies, in this situation, that they stood so well in figures of comparative turnover.

The second observation must be that native Californians seemed to be in the minority, and many of the in-migrants from other states compared the somewhat casual social attitude of Californians unfavorably with that characteristic of the smaller and more closely knit communities from which they came. . This was the more true the greater the difference.

One girl from Oklahoma had been told by her mother that "she would soon be back." She probably would have returned to Oklahoma had she not happened to find and settle in a community of Oklahomans, which eased for her, as for others, the process of social acclimation to California. When we saw her, she had married an Arkansas man who lived in the small Oklahoman community, and was developing a satisfactory work and home life. Her attendance was regular, in spite of the fact that she was not strong.

Inconsideration Leads to Quits

This story and, in effect, the majority of those we heard lead to the further observation that, although (as we observed in the beginning of this report) we have no evidence that the seething population movement in California finds a direct reflection in labor turnover, the restless background nevertheless makes workers, especially in-migrants accustomed to the routines of a stable community, more than usually sensitive to supervisory attitudes. This sensitiveness works in two directions: on the one hand, any inconsiderateness leads more promptly to departure from the plant; on the other hand, workers respond more eagerly to any show of personal consideration. These statements need illustration.

As an example of the first, we have seen a supervisor, without really hearing a worker's complaint, take out a card and say, "Of course, if you want your certificate of availability. . .", thus indicating by his behavior that he will not listen to the worker's point of view. In some instances, such a worker is speaking for his associates, an incipient "team," so that much greater damage is done than the foreman realizes.

The other result is illustrated strongly by the situation in Department IV; here we found many workers who had, in effect, walked off their jobs in other parts of the plant; but when induced to try Department IV, had remained there. It is perhaps significant of the development of this team, in contrast with the isolation of the "irregulars," that workers from Department IV in interviews tended to say "we," whereas most others said "I."

Irritable Impatience of Supervisors

THE third observation is that the material collected from exit interviews differs from that collected from interviews arranged with workers on the line. The exit interviews showed that, although the worker concerned might occasionally have been presenting a case to the supervisor for an incipient team, more usually he was a disappointed person whose attempt, probably clumsy, to get permission from his foreman to transfer had been summarily cut short. The inevitable emphasis during the emergency on production and operations and the lack of interest displayed by management in team organization combined to foster in supervision an irritable impatience with matters that seemed to the supervisor personal to the worker.

On the Way Out

THE material collected in interviews with line workers, many of them of high standing for performance and teamwork, showed that the majority of them had, at one time or other, been "on the way out" as described in the paragraph immediately above. Circumstance, in the form of a sympathetic foreman or an exit interviewer, had saved them for the company and had aided their subsequent adjustment. It is important to realize that, whereas an exit interview is often too late to "save" a good but isolated worker, leadman Z of Department IV made a point of thoroughly interviewing the individual *on induction*, when he was beginning work. Furthermore, Z was careful to see that the job and the compansions on the job were suited not only to the worker's technical capacities but also, so far as might be, to his personal idiosyncrasies. The results Z obtained thus are astonishing.

In general, we were forced to the conclusion that the workers clustered at the right side of the charts, the irregular attendance group, were not a group at all, but a collection of unrelated individuals; it is in this collection that one finds the greater part of absenteeism and turnover.

We must not be understood to imply that the aircraft companies gave no thought or care to developing an organization to attend to the personal well-being of their workers. Indeed, such organizations have been developed to an extent that amazed us. We were astonished by the excellence and variety of the personnel programs—welfare, recreation of every conceivable sort, saving schemes, facilities for shopping, plant-provided transportation, day nurseries.

One executive said to us half-jestingly that the management of his company had "put in everything but bullfights." All this activity was unquestionably wise and undoubtedly had effect. It probably is at least one reason why labor turnover in the aircraft industry, though high by comparison with peacetime, yet ranks low in California by comparison with other essential industries in the period studied.

Blunderbuss Personnel Work

B UT all this activity occurred, as it were, in a void; it was not pointed at a particular problem, it was a "blunderbuss" technique. *No palliatives external to the work situation can remedy a fundamental defect of organization.* In respect of the human organization of these plants, much remains to be done. Personnel counselors and exit interviewers can do much to clear a worker's personal preoccupations. But counselors at present are rarely sufficiently trained to be thus effective. Consequently, once again the findings of research point back to administration of working groups as the critical factor in determining the extent to which teams will come into existence in an organization.

Human Desire for Active Association

I NDEED, when we look through the many scores of attendance records that we have of East and West alike, we are struck by the invariable persistence of the human desire for active association in teamwork with others, and our conclusions from the various experiences cited may be simply stated:

First, the desire of individuals for association in work with others is deep-seated in humanity, and is sure to find some form of expression.

Second, there is thus no question for industry as to whether there shall, or shall not, be working groups. The important question for management is whether, in a particular situation, the attitude of these groups is:

    a. *Hostile.* This attitude is fortunately rare and usually evanescent.
    b. *Wary of wholehearted cooperation.* This, unfortunately, is the usual attitude. Our own and other inquiries show that workers often are on guard against the engineer or newcomer. The behavior of the members of such groups is often as though they sought to maintain themselves in the *status quo*, rather than to contribute their efforts wholeheartedly to the changes which the promotion of the purpose

of the larger organization of which they are a part may require. As such groups develop their self-identity rather than their identity with the rest of the organization, they become what are sometimes called "cliques," and in extreme cases may tend to the openly "hostile" attitude named above.

c. *Cooperative and friendly.* This attitude finds illustration both in the experimental test room at the Hawthorne plant of the Western Electric Company and in the Work Center B of Department IV described in this report. In both instances, management, or supervision, has worked for the result and has got it.

Group Formation Should not Be Left to Chance

THIRD, it is clearly unwise to leave the method and form of group formation wholly to circumstance or chance. In such a situation, which is unfortunately usual, the team formation is fortuitous and may exclude, capriciously, many workers who should "belong." A consequence of this exclusion is that such workers constitute a ragged edge or fringe who become discontented and provide a population for absentee or turnover statistics. The neglect of the problem by management seemingly does not greatly matter in small organizations or in peacetime; but this is only seeming. Company C enjoyed an enormous advantage over Companies A and B in respect to the problems of absenteeism, labor turnover, and labor shortage; the management had worked for and earned this advantage. Leadman Z in Department IV also had worked for what he had achieved in his work center.

Trouble Caused by Management

FOURTH, and for this report perhaps the most important of our conclusions. It is possible in a situation characterized by constant and almost chaotic change that the natural processes of group association may be almost wholly defeated. Something of this has been true of the scene in Southern California. Management under the pressure of dire necessity has moved individuals and groups by so-called loans and transfers to such an extent that, as we pointed out earlier, the labor turnover within a plant was greater than that at the factory gate. In this situation it was probably impossible for management to act otherwise. Our only comment would be that management does not seem to have been aware of the probable consequences of such action.

This fourth statement is entirely in accord with the first above. In other words, the desire for association in work is deep-seated and sure to find expression. This expression, if the deep-seated desire is defeated, will take the form of exaggerated absenteeism and labor turnover, so that management by its inattention to the organization of teamwork in the factory is in a significant way responsible for the conditions for which it blames workers. (*end quote*)

The above is a digest and review of the most recent report of the Bureau of Business Research of the Graduate School of Business Administration of Harvard University, dealing with

"*Teamwork and Labor Turnover in the Aircraft Industry of Southern California*", by Elton Mayo and George F. F. Lombard. *This is obtainable from Harvard University, Soldiers Field, Boston, 63, Mass. Pp. 32. Price $1.00.*

We strongly recommend it. *Anything that comes out from under the leadership of Elton Mayo is bound to be worth study, and this is no exception to that rule. Limitations of time, funds and research personnel obviously handicapped the study. Also the pervading notion on the part of company executives that in publishing the results of studies of labor relations you may never disclose the unsatisfactory conditions found, but only report on the best conditions found, limits seriously a full treatment of the subject. That, every researcher in industrial relations knows.*

However, operating under these handicaps, Mayo and company have done an excellent job, and one which every personnel man should study seriously, both in his war-time work, and in consideration of his plans for the future.

The chief lack in the report is the fact that Mayo and company could not—owing to the limitations mentioned above—give more than generalized suggestions as to how management could play its part in helping in the formation of congenial work groups and teams.

That, however, does not stop intelligent personnel men from doing something about this on their own. For war or post-war, if you can cut your irregular worker attendants from 63% to zero, and your labor turnover from 75% to near zero, you will find that you can do it only on the basis of the theories put forward by Elton Mayo and company.

Some People are Optimistic as to What Will Happen at the War's End. Others are Pessimistic. Perhaps it is Too Soon to Think About These Things.

20 Million Jobs
on the Auction Block

By Victor Riesel and Paul Sann
New York, N. Y.

D o you want to buy a war plant? Or a 420-family housing project? Or a 30-ton press, a carrier pigeon, or 12 million zippers? You can buy all these— and sundry other items—from Uncle Sam, who is now the world's largest second-hand dealer.

He has billions of dollars' worth of government-owned war production facilities for sale, and in a comparatively short time he'll have another 40 billion dollars' worth to put on the market, including choice items like the $100,000,000 four-motor bomber plant at Willow Run. And Willow Run employs 40,000 men and women; other plants going on the block employ millions more. Where will all these breadwinners go when the hammer falls?

The Lengthening Shadow

T his is the lengthening shadow which V-E (Victory in Europe) Day has cast over many of America's communities from coast to coast.

Recently, on a tour of the nation's industrial centers, the writers were startled to see workmen tearing down a new federal housing project in Niagara Falls. This 24-building community, which had sheltered 383 families, had been built after Pearl Harbor to ease the housing shortage created by the influx of workers. Now it was being taken apart for shipment to Kansas. Niagara Falls' employment boom was over.

Fate of the housing project is typical. Everywhere, the government is setting in motion the complex process of dismantling the colossal war machine that had turned the tide in Europe. This involves not only the sale of mammoth war plants, but the disposition of thousands upon thousands of seemingly trivial items—the by-products of total war.

In Washington, for example, among the "remnant goods" listed for sale by the Treasury Department we found flocks of carrier pigeons, demilitarized dogs, fly swatters, billiard balls, collapsible buckets, 100,000 bolo scabbards, 300,000 white helmets for drum majors, nearly a million pounds of talc, 300,000 reams of yellow telegraph blanks, and half-a-million mosquito bars.

The Lone Ranger

A CARLOAD of nickel-silver alloy spurs was conveniently unloaded when the sponsors of the *Heigh-Ho Silver* radio program bought them up for distribution to the Lone Ranger's countless admirers.   But no such happy deliverance is in prospect in such arsenal cities as Buffalo, Detroit, Cleveland, Akron, Pittsburgh and Philadelphia.

Here it isn't simply a matter of selling surplus properties.   We found bankers, union leaders, and chamber-of-commerce officials concerned with the infinitely more difficult problem of converting to civilian use the war plants which are going on the block, thus assuring a livelihood for their dispossessed war workers.

In all these cities, there was anxious discussion of the CIO's prediction that on V-E Day-plus-one some 4,000,000 workers will be thrown out of their jobs, and that on V-E Day-plus-30, as many as 10 million will be unemployed.   Ominous as this may sound, the far more conservative AFL warns that when the war against Japan is over too, "there will be a deadly depression in which a total of 20 million Americans will be unemployed unless steps are taken immediately to forestall such a catastrophe."

As for the interval between the ending of the war in Europe and the war in the Orient, the AFL calculates that a peak unemployment of 11 million will be reached. Boris Shishkin, the Federation's economist, says: "We don't seem to be prepared to enter the era of peace with employment maintained anywhere near the maximum achieved in wartime.

"Shortening of hours, elimination of overtime, cut in employment, and the demotion of workers to lower-paying classifications will cut payrolls from $80,000,-000 to $48,000,000—enough to knock the bottom out of the civilian market after V-E Day.

What a Guess!

WE HAVE already passed the peak of war employment.   Immediate sharp declines are ahead.   No comprehensive program is ready to be put in operation to hold employment at high levels, and to assure stability in transition.

Shishkin recalled that, immediately following World War I, the brief boom was followed by a collapse that threw 6,000,000 men out of their jobs and shrank payrolls 44 per cent.   This, Shishkin noted, is mere child's play compared with what is coming.

These dire predictions were partially corroborated by the United States Office of War Information. In a secret report circulated among a select group of national business leaders, the OWI foresaw that "dislocations in civilian life after V-E Day are likely to be widespread and, in some quarters, serious," and that "very difficult situations may develop in some areas where the arms cutbacks will have the heaviest impact."

The report estimated that 5,000,000 persons would be changing jobs right after V-E Day.

CIO leaders told the writers that cutbacks had already cost the Buffalo-Niagara area 15,000 war jobs. True, most of the displaced workers were able to find other jobs (almost invariably at lower pay) but the time may be approaching when no other jobs will be available there.

Detroit Uneasy

IN DETROIT, the Michigan Unemployment Compensation Commission is prepared to spend about eight billion dollars a week in jobless benefits. The Commission's blueprint calls for the care of 400,000 idle when the cutbacks come.

Detroit is handling a greater volume of war production than any other industrial area in the world. A quarter-of-a-million workers have swarmed there to help man the assembly lines. And Detroiters are wondering where these outsiders will go when the change-over is made from war-boom to normal peace production. Will there be jobs in communities whence they came? Or will they stay in Detroit? And if they do—

People of Detroit are afraid and justly so, that if the nation's key industrial city fails to get its own post-war house in order, there will be chaos in other urban centers too. Both union and industry sources do not hide their concern over the possibility of serious labor strife if widespread unemployment occurs.

There is much anxiety, too, over possible strife between extremist white and Negro elements when lay-offs force out white workers with little seniority while veteran Negro employes keep their jobs under labor-management contract terms. Many observers regard the Detroit race riots of 1943 as a preview of what may lie ahead.

Leaders of both groups are convinced that only the presence of nearby army units and Detroit's specially-trained anti-riot police squads has kept peace in the city this past year. Even now, rabble rousers and such subversive organizations as the Ku Klux Klan are laying the necessary groundwork to exploit these animosities.

Cleveland Also Uneasy

CLEVELAND is uneasy too—without a race problem. "The city will have an unemployment problem in spite of everything that's done," said Mayor Frank J. Lausche. Its population has jumped 40 per cent since 1940. Sixty thousand workers came in 1943 alone.

As in the case of other large cities, Cleveland must also absorb its returning soldiers—130,000 in its case. Army discharges, totalling about a million-and-a-half now, are increasing at the rate of 100,000 a month. B. C. Seiple, director of Cleveland's employment service, is far from over-confident about prospects for the immediate future.

"There may be a lot of unemployment here for a short time and some for quite a while," he said, noting that many women and older workers will be forced out of industry in the re-employment process, and that the in-migrants may have to hit the road again.

KKK Revival

THE Klan is also a problem in the Cleveland-Akron-Youngstown area, just as it is in the rural counties along the Indiana border. The Ohio Klan Kleagle was calling public meetings even after Pearl Harbor; informed newspapermen believe that the Klan is simply sitting out the war in anticipation of a KKK revival such as the nation witnessed after the 1918 armistice.

Growing fear that postwar America faces a revival of the Ku Klux Klan and an even greater rabble-rousing organization specializing in racial intolerance was recently expressed by Dr. H. S. Mekeel, professor of anthropology at the University of Wisconsin. In an address delivered before the annual convention of the National Committee for Mental Hygiene, Dr. Mekeel called for a campaign to publicize and combat this threat to minority groups, which he expected would come under the guise of "nationalism."

Across the border in Pennsylvania, Pittsburgh faces this grim fact: The government has become the chief, and sometimes the only, customer of such firms as Westinghouse Electric, the Aluminum Company of America, United States Steel, Jones & Laughlin. Even Heinz, with its 57 varieties, is producing primarily for our armed forces and lend-lease.

Can Pittsburgh Hold Up?

CAN Pittsburgh's industries hold up when the government steps out? The answer we got from the best-informed industrial sources there can be summed up this way: Pittsburgh will hold up only if the other big production centers hold up. For, as a supplier of the basic raw materials which other cities turn into glistening products for automobile showrooms and department stores, her prosperity depends on the country's orders.

The orders depend on the jobs that supply the people's purchasing power. And the jobs depend on the ability of government, industry, and labor to channel into useful civilian productive fields all the Willow Runs, big and small, in the land.

Victor Riesel is labor editor of the New York Post, whose column "Labor News and Comment" is widely read. Paul Sann, on the staff of the New York Journal-American, is a specialist in relief and housing problems.

Reprinted by special permission from Magazine Digest, Toronto, Canada.

While Proper Job Placement Has a Distinct Therapeutic Value Many Individuals Need Psychological and Psychiatric Help Before They Are Ready for Effective Employment.

How People Differ
from One Another

By Percival M. Symonds
Teachers College, Columbia University
New York 27, N. Y.

A PERSONNEL man having responsibility in the guidance of people should know something about the way in which they differ from one another. One should also know something of the range of such differences so that he can judge to what extent the person before him may be considered normal or whether he deviates so far from the average that he must be considered deficient, pathological, or superior. For the purpose of this discussion three dimensions of individual differences will be recognized: (1) variations in mental capacity; (2) variations in individual adjustment; and (3) variations in social adjustment. These three dimensions are frequently confused.

Abilities

THE first has to do with the abilities of a person—how much he can do, how difficult the tasks are that he can do, and how quickly he can do them. A person who is a fortunate deviate in mental capacity is frequently called bright, or a genius, while the unfortunate deviates would be called dull, or if the deviation were more extreme, a moron, imbecile or idiot. People distribute themselves over a wide range of ability. Most persons tend to be average or normal. If we think of this scale in terms of I.Q. (Intelligence Quotient) we find that approximately 50% of people have I.Q.'s between 90 and 110. Relatively few people are superior,—possibly 25% have I.Q.'s of over 110. In the same manner relatively few people have inferior ability and roughly 25% have I.Q.'s of 90 and below.

Personal Adjustment

THE second dimension has to do with the quality of an individual's personal adjustment. We may think of this variable as having a different kind of distribution. A large majority of people would be considered well adjusted. A smaller number would have various degrees and kinds of less satisfactory adjustment. It is not possible to state in terms of per cent those who might be considered well adjusted or those with different degrees of less adequate adjustment as this is a matter that depends largely on definition. Measures of personality are still in an experimental stage and it is doubtful if there will ever be any one measure which will cover the various meanings of personality and adjustment in which we are interested.

Social Adjustment

THE third dimension of social adjustment is similar in shape to the second. Most people are good citizens and are acceptable to their neighbors. Only a few tend to break the laws or violate moral and social standards. These we call delinquent or criminal.

There is very little relationship between mental capacity and adjustment. Probably those with higher intelligence tend on the whole to be better adjusted but this relationship is so low that numerous exceptions will readily come to mind.

Boris Sidis entered Harvard College at the age of twelve and when he was fifteen lectured before a group of Harvard professors on the Third Dimension. He died in poverty and made a failure of his life. This is an illustration of a gifted person who made a poor personal adjustment. On the other hand, it is not uncommon to find dull persons who are capable of managing their affairs, running small businesses successfully, and maintaining happy and successful family lives. The problem child in school is not always the dull child, neither is a dull child necessarily a problem child unless his teacher feels that any child who cannot keep up with the majority of his classmates in his studies is a problem. Many dull people are forced into poor adjustment because people expect more of them than they have the capacity to give.

Delinquents and criminals on the average tend to have less than normal intelligence. However, one finds in penal institutions men who have better than average ability although these would be in the minority. The relation here is so loose that one could not possibly assert that a given dull child would have delinquent tendencies. Neither could it be asserted that any given delinquent would be subnormal in ability.

By and large, there is a close relationship between social adjustment and individual adjustment. Delinquents and criminals in general have pathological tendencies. They are frequently neurotic or psychopathic. Indeed modern criminology has become aware of the fact that many criminals are mentally sick and need hospitalization rather than incarceration.

Variations in Mental Capacity

THE accompanying table indicates the distribution of abilities as measured by the Revised Stanford-Binet Intelligence Test. About one out of a thousand persons will have an I.Q. of 150 or over and these individuals are in the genius or near-genius class. Genius and I.Q. are not necessarily identical and it is possible to have geniuses along specialized lines who might be below an I.Q. of 150 on an intelligence scale. However, if one is thinking of general intelligence when speaking of genius it would refer only to those who are in this very small group. Those who have I.Q.'s between 115 and 150 are considered superior or bright in varying degrees.

Roughly speaking, about one person out of a hundred has an I.Q. of 135 and over. The various degrees of brightness have not been as carefully defined as the varying degrees of dullness, partly because the problem of segregating them has not

TABLE I

INTERPRETATION OF I.Q.'s ON THE REVISED STANFORD-BINET FORMS L AND M

Range of I.Q.		Per cent	Range of Adult M.A.
above 150	Near genius	0.1	22.50+
130–149	Very superior	3	19.50–22.49
115–129	Normal	14	17.25–19.49
85–114	Dull	66	12.75–17.24
70–84	Border line	14	10.50–12.74
60–69	Moron	2	9.00–10.49
40–59	Imbecile		6.00–8.99
20–39	Idiot		3.00–5.99
0–19			0.0 – 2.99

Taken from: R. G. Bernreuter & E. J. Carr, "The Interpretation of I. Q.'s on the L–M Stanford-Binet", *Journal of Educational Psychology* 29: 312–314, 1938.

been so important. Individuals with I.Q.'s from 70 to 90 are usually classified as *dull*; those with I.Q.'s between 80 and 90 are sometimes called the dull-normal. Individuals with I.Q.'s of 75 and over are usually kept in the regular school classes although they may have difficulty in progressing from grade to grade each year and by the end of elementary school may be one or more grades retarded.

Lowest Grades

THOSE with I.Q.'s between 60 and 75 are spoken of as border-line feeble minded. These individuals cannot make satisfactory progress in regular school classes and large school systems organize special classes for these children. As adults they can only do the most humble and routine and repetitive kinds of work that put little demand on their capacity to meet new situations. Below an I.Q. of 60, three different degrees of feeble-mindedness are recognized. The moron is a person with an I.Q. of 40 to 60 and mental age of from 6 to 9. They correspond in ability with children in the first grades of elementary school. They can barely read and write and can undertake tasks only of the most simple kind. Those with I.Q.'s of from 20 to 40 and mental ages of from 3 to 6 are commonly termed imbecile. They have a mental capacity of a child of the nursery school or kindergarten age. They cannot read or write and their mental capacity is extremely limited. Idiots have I.Q.'s up to 20 and mental ages up to 3. Their mentality is undeveloped and in a very infantile or primitive stage. They require complete care for all of their needs.

Individual Adjustment

IN THE second dimension of individual adjustment we come to problems with emotional disturbance and disturbances in behavior. The mildest kind of these disturbances is known as the neuroses and the psychoneuroses. Neuroses are disturbances primarily of a physical or neurological origin. Psychoneuroses are disturbances in which there is a mental factor. The neurotic person has mild adjustment difficulties. He is known as the peculiar individual with idiosyncrasies and mild emotional disturbances. Such an individual can manage himself adequately and can maintain his place in society. He can carry on with his work and is able to establish a home. However, the neurotic individual may have difficulties which to a greater or lesser degree impair his efficiency and make him difficult to get along with. Most persons are to a mild degree neurotic.

Frightening Term

A LARGE number of men, both those who have been accepted in the Army and those who have been rejected, have been designated as psychoneurotic. This technical term may be frightening but actually it does not indicate anything very serious. These same men were psychoneurotic before they entered the Army. They were known in their communities as the ne'er-do-wells, persons who hung around street corners, who would be difficult to get along with in factory or church, who would be peculiar or tempermental. Many persons who have contributed much to the world have been neurotic, even to a high degree. Beethoven who is recognized as one of the world's great composers was a very erratic and temperamental individual. A psychiatrist, L. E. Bisch, once wrote a book entitled, *Be Glad You're Neurotic*, (McGraw Hill Book Co., 1936) in which he emphasized some of the positive values of neurotic peculiarities. Every problem child in a school is to a degree neurotic. Consequently to be called neurotic or psychoneurotic is not an alarming thing.

Psychosis More Serious

A PSYCHOSIS represents a more severe form of mental deterioration, disorganization, and disintegration. An individual who is diagnosed as psychotic is more emotionally withdrawn from the world of people and events about him. He may be more excitable or more depressed. Usually the psychotic individual is so disordered in his mental functioning that it becomes impossible for him to continue as an acceptable worker, family member, or member of society. His mental life may be characterized by extravagant and unreal fantasies.

Psychiatrists are still not entirely clear concerning the nature of psychotic states. There are still differences of opinion as to whether these states are inherited or are a result of life experiences. The belief in the constitutional inherited basis of psychosis is dwindling, however, as research shows more clearly how these states can have a functional or psychogenic origin. Another matter not entirely cleared up is the extent to which psychosis represents an organic or tissue change and to what extent it represents an extreme form of mental or functional change. Naturally it is recognized that any learning change also represents a change in the nervous system but this may or may not be of a pathological nature.

Psychological or Physical

CERTAINLY there are some psychoses that are caused by tissue change,—the presence of tumors in the brain, inflammations of nervous tissue, the invasion of bacteria, or pathological functioning of the glands. On the other hand, it is clear that some psychotic conditions are also the result of learning from life situations leading to a more serious form of poor adjustment than would be represented in the neuroses. Probably most psychotic conditions represent a combination of both the organic and the functional. Most persons who are psychotic have to be cared for and many of them are cared for in institutions. On the other hand, there are numbers of people with psychotic tendencies who are ambulatory. More popular expressions to indicate psychotic states are the words *crazy* and *insane*. The latter is also a legal term used to denote those individuals who have been recognized as mentally disordered by law.

Another term frequently used needs careful definition. Peculiar and troublesome people are often called *psychopathic*. This term is carelessly used to represent a variety of conditions of mental disorder. There is a tendency today, however, to define it more strictly. Current usage would restrict the use of the term *psychopath* to those individuals who are lacking in feeling, particularly the moral sense. They are individuals without conscience and without guilt. They have wild standards of social conduct and are not governed by the controls which guide the conduct of the majority of citizens. These individuals may have uncontrolled aggressive tendencies or may commit violences against property and persons without regret or without feeling. Many criminals are psychopathic. The term would also apply to a number of cranks and uncontrollable individuals who make undesirable citizens.

Rather than attempting to describe the various types of psychoses and neuroses a list of nine forms of mental disorder and poor adjustment will be given:

Neurasthenia

THIS is an old term but is still used to describe various states of personal discomfort. Of particular importance are the feelings of inferiority and inadequacy which beset large numbers of persons. Studies conducted by the writer would indicate that a very large majority of people are disturbed in their personal relations and feel inadequate in the work and tasks for which they are responsible. This kind of maladjustment was popularized by Alfred Adler in his discussions of the feelings of inferiority and ways of compensating for them.

Hysteria

THE hysterias are one of the major types of psychoneurosis. Of particular importance are the conversion hysterias in which unacceptable emotional tendencies are converted into physical symptoms. These may be aches, pains and discomforts in the joints, muscles and tendons of the body, or in various organs. Hysterias may affect motor functioning in various forms of paralysis or motor disturbances. Stuttering would be one example of a conversion hysteria, or the conversion may be in some sensory organ, and various disturbances of vision, hearing, and other senses may have a functional origin.

Anxiety States

THESE anxiety states may have their expression in various somatic disturbances as in disorders of the alimentary system, breathing, functioning of the heart, or in the various secretions. Each of these represents an action of the sympathetic nervous system as it becomes overstimulated through fear. Anxiety may exhibit itself through phobias which are directed toward specific objects or persons or situations, or anxiety may show itself in behavior disturbances,—disturbances of sleep for instance, as in sleep-walking, nightmares and night terrors, which are definitely anxiety disturbances. Or anxiety may exhibit itself in vague anxious states as in worry, or so-called free floating anxiety.

Obsessional

A FOURTH group of psychoneuroses are characterized by *obsessional* and *compulsive* tendencies. These individuals take on stereotyped and repetitive behavior. They tend to be rigid in their beliefs and methods of thought. Many times these individuals tend to be over-clean, neat, orderly and systematic. To a mild degree such tendencies are considered valuable but they may interfere with a man's usefulness if they become extreme.

Paranoid Tendencies

THIS fifth group includes tendencies to become suspicious of other individuals and to ascribe to other individuals motives and intentions which are purely fictitious. Paranoid tendencies depend on the well known mechanism of projection in which an individual projects out into other people tendencies of his own which he finds unacceptable and which he does not wish to admit as belonging to himself. Tendencies toward megalomania and over-estimation of personal worth may also be included in this group. Many persons have these tendencies to a mild degree but they are also characteristic of certain psychotic conditions when they tend to separate a person from effective functioning in the world about him.

Schizophrenia

THIS represents one of the major psychotic conditions. Schizophrenia comes from a Greek root meaning *to cut* and stands for a variety of pathological conditions in which an individual is split off from the world about him. In its simplest form it shows itself by withdrawn tendencies and tendencies toward isolation from other persons. Such an individual may spend time in daydreaming and have bizarre fantasies. More generally, however, schizophrenia is characterized by emotions which become seriously disordered and disoriented.

Manic Depressives

ANOTHER psychotic group includes the *manic* and *depressive* tendencies. These two tendencies are frequently linked together because in some cases there is a cyclical tendency in which a person alternates from a manic phase to a depressive phase. In the former the person becomes highly excitable, perhaps optimistic and buoyant, and occasionally violent and destructive. In the depressive phase the individual becomes melancholic, moody and depressed. Activity is lessened and an extreme state of pessimism results. In some cases the alternation from one of these states to another takes place with rapidity over a period of hours or days. In other cases, however, one may maintain the manic or the depressive phase for weeks, months, or even years.

Psychopathic tendencies have already been discussed and need not be further described at this point.

Sex deviations. A number of perversions of the sexual drive are socially unacceptable and because of this produce grave psychological problems to the individuals whose sex drives take these socially unacceptable forms. It is usually found that a person with sexual deviations has had unfortunate affectional experiences in infancy and childhood.

Social Maladjustment

L IKE mental adjustment most persons are socially well adjusted and only a relatively small number of individuals are socially maladjusted. There will be no attempt here to make a classification of the various types of delinquent or criminal tendencies.

Following is a list of some of the minor signs of personality disturbance: 1), seclusive, 2) moody, 3) suspicious, 4) effeminate, 5) deceptive, 6) markedly nervous, 7) temper tantrums, 8) strikingly immature, 9) a "show-off", 10) a "day dreamer", 11) "peculiar", 12) precise, 13) marked fears, 14) believer in systems. (The first eleven items in this list have been taken from a blank entitled *Data On Student* which was prepared for use in secondary schools by the Selective Service System and was printed under authority of the Budget Bureau ✳ 11-4340.)

The employment interviewer, as he conducts an interview with a client, should be alert to the presence of any one of these fourteen signs of personality disturbance. Many of them would be exhibited during an interview. The presence of even a trace of one of these signs should be taken seriously for experience shows that the chances are good that such a trend occupies a prominent place in the individual's personality structure. There is a common tendency among all of us to excuse or pass off as inconsequential some sign of an unfortunate personal characteristic on first acquaintance, and it is commonly believed that such a sign may be a spot or chance occurrence.

Not Accidents

C LINICAL experience, however, leads one to believe that these manifestations are are not accidents, but are the expressions of deeper underlying personality trends. The following list of physical signs should also be noted:—asthma or hay fever, tics or twitchings, heart trouble, severe stomach or bowel trouble, fainting, fits or convulsions, chronic ill health. The interviewer may ask his client directly and rapidly such questions as: "Have you ever had asthma?" "Have you ever had hay fever?" "Have you ever had tics or twitchings?", etc. An affirmative answer to these questions may be considered a sign of possible neurotic tendencies. It is not intended that in asking these questions one is usurping a physician's role, and the interviewer should merely note affirmative answers and interpret them as indicating the possible presence of neurotic tendencies.

Use of Tests

M ORE and more in vocational guidance it becomes important to take into account the whole person in helping him to make a vocational choice. It has long been known that abilities and interests are important factors in making a wise vocational choice. Intelligence tests are now well known and their value is generally accepted. During the war work has gone on apace in the development of more specialized aptitude tests. One important development along these lines has been undertaken by the U. S. Employment Service under the War Man Power Commission.

A series of aptitude tests more varied than any that have previously been available are now being experimented upon and worked through under the direction of C. L. Shartle. Interest inventories for vocational guidance have long been effectively used. Among the more important are those by Strong, Kuder, Cleeton and Brainard. By far the most important of these is the Strong Vocational Interest Blank available for both men and women. Keys for the Strong blank are available for scoring for 35 occupations, 6 groups of occupations, and 3 non-occupational interests for men, and 19 occupations for women. However, the Strong blank is very difficult to score by hand and although it can be scored by machine, it becomes somewhat expensive.

Help Before Job Placement

THE employment interviewer must take other factors, however, besides ability and interest into account in helping a person make an occupational choice and helping him in his placement. Personality and adjustment factors are recognized as important in vocational effectiveness and the interviewer must become increasingly sensitive to the presence of personality disturbances and should work out a philosophy with regard to the vocational placement of these persons. It is extremely important for the vocational counselor to recognize that many of these individuals should not and cannot be placed in work positions where their personalities may be disturbed and distorted.

While job placement has a distinct therapeutic value, many individuals need more intensive psychological and psychiatric help before they are ready for job placement. It is the duty of an employment interviewer to recognize these individuals and to take the necessary steps to see that they receive the help which they need in order to rehabilitate them for effective employment.

Abstract of some remarks made at a class of U. S. Employment interviewers, conducted by the Department of Education, State of Connecticut.

When Victory is Won, Management Will Face
One of the Greatest Tests in History. Preparation Now May Well Determine the Survival of
the Free Enterprise System After the War.

Industrial Relations Reviewed

By John Paul Jones, Jr., SKD 1c. USNR.
Brooklyn, N. Y.

W
HEN victory is won, management faces one of the greatest tests in history
with the return of millions of servicemen to industry. From the safe van-
tage point of the United States Navy (which has little or no labor problem)
the writer feels free to briefly review some long standing criticisms of certain general
systems of industrial relations now in operation throughout the nation, and to present
a theory of revision or modification of these systems to assist in enabling management
to properly meet this crisis.

Industrial Relations Defined

A
NY discussion limited to the specific subject of personnel problems concerning
both management and labor must necessarily begin with a definition of terms
since the descriptive expressions used to designate the same division of personnel
work vary widely from industry to industry. It is the writer's intention that the
term "industrial relations" refer specifically to that portion of management activity
concerned with maintaining a friendly cooperative balance between plant management and its employees.

Industrial relations, therefore, does not include the specific functions of employment, safety, recreation, morale, plant protection, public relations, or many other
activities which are generally lumped under the all embracing heading of "personnel". We are concerned here only with the direct relationship, through conference
and negotiation, between management and labor in the duscussion of grievances and
employee requirements of management. The writer's use of the term "industrial

relations" rather than "labor relations" is simply one of preference rather than prejudice.

Four Points of Criticism

THERE are four important focal points of criticism in a survey of the most common methods of handling labor problems within industry. They are the indefinite departmental method, the public-industrial relations combination, the foreman plan, and the direct negotiation by the plant executive. All four contain elements which materially weaken the effectiveness of one of the most important factors of industrial progress, the maintenance of balance between company policy and employee demand

Indefinite Departmental Method

HE indefinite departmental method, most common in small units of larger corporations, places the responsibility for the handling of industrial relations in the personnel department without specifically assigning these duties to any particular individual or group of individuals. Often it is the part time job of one of the members of the department in addition to his regular duties. Fortunately both for management and labor, this system is gradually dying out under the impetus of wartime tension and the consequent increased need for specific handling of these problems.

For true efficiency, the functions of general personnel (employment, safety, and so forth), public relations, and industrial relations should be handled by entirely different groups of management employees. Even though the divisions must dovetail in many respects, each is a full time responsibility and must be recognized as such.

Public-Industrial Relations Combination

THE second method, the public-industrial relations combination, is one of the most frequently found and strategically poor combinations in industry. The chief reason for this contention is that the type of personality splendidly suited to public relations work too often is by the same characteristics utterly unfitted for the delicate task of maintaining the balance between employer and employee. A public relations man must of necessity be an extrovert, a good mixer, and something more than a fair politician; and it is exactly these personality traits in a man which employee representatives distrust, in many cases with excellent reason.

There can be little doubt that this common anachronism has caused more trouble and friction in many otherwise well working industrial relations programs than almost any other factor extant in the field. It is a frequent complaint of employee representatives that the public relations man is given too much to patting the union secretary on the back with one hand while slipping him an industrial mickey finn with the other. While the writer does not imply that all public or industrial relations men are insincere, it is very often true that they depend on their political instincts rather than their sense of integrity in handling the frictions which naturally arise in the course of the job.

The Foreman Industrial Relations Plan

Some industries during the past few years have slanted their industrial relations program more and more toward the goal of using their foremen in the bulk of the labor relations work of the company. While it is true that the foreman has a most important role to play in the maintenance of good relations between employer and employee, it is foolish and even dangerous to expect that he can carry the full load. To the men immediately under him, the foreman is, in effect, the employer.

The plant superintendent is often a remote person to the employees, but the foreman, assigning work, filing reports, and responsible for maintaining the necessary production on the job is the epitome of the employer to the worker. How then can this man be expected to handle labor problems, many of which arise as a direct result of his own necessary actions in carrying out policies handed down from his superiors?

An intelligent, well informed foreman is one of the greatest assets to a successful industrial relations organization, but foremen training courses directed toward the basic theme that the foreman should be the complete arbiter and conciliator of the men under him are a waste of valuable time, and a large majority of foremen will support this view. They will assert that in most cases they have no power of decision, this being reserved for the department head or higher supervisory authority, and that furthermore a foreman has no desire to stick out his neck to his men if he cannot be assured that higher forces will back him. In most cases this reluctance is justified. It is not fair to the foreman, with all his other responsibilities, to place him in such precarious balance with the men subordinate to him.

Industrial Relations by Plant Executive

The direct handling of industrial relations by the plant executive is the fourth and last target of criticism and is, in some respects, the most important of all. Many organizations have taken the function of industrial relations out of the personnel group and placed it in the hands of the executive of the plant. This is due in a large measure to the fact that major labor questions within an industrial organization must have the final decision of the man in charge, and often the executive feels that he must personally handle all negotiations in order that the company may be fairly represented.

Nothing could be farther from the fact, and there can be few worse choices of industrial negotiator than the very man whose policies, by company direction, are usually placed in opposition to the employee demands. No one is more suspect to employee organizations than plant management, and consequently any conference or negotiation under these circumstances begins with the employee delegates certain in their own minds that the man with whom they must deal is there exclusively to insure that the company gets the best of the bargain. Unfortunately this presumption is usually correct.

Management Must Represent Owners

MANAGEMENT must represent the owners (usually stockholders not including the employees) and as such must protect the interests of the owners. But it is undeniably true, though obscure to many executives, that the interests of the stockholders are better served by carefully considering the problems and requests of their employees and not prefacing joint conferences with the assumption that the employees are bent on the destruction of the business. While there are undoubtedly as many racketeers in organized labor as there are insincere men in industrial relations organizations, the basic spirit of the American democracy is a sense of fair play. Labor is not generally stupid and cannot be accused of deliberately desiring to kill the goose that lays the golden egg, but inherent suspicion of the motives of management sometimes encourages union or employee representatives to carry their demands even further than their own undisturbed reflection would permit under the stress of bargaining with the men who control their immediate livelihood.

Calm and Dispassionate View

UNDER the stress of his primary responsibilities, the plant executive is often unable to view calmly and dispassionately the demand of the labor group within his organization, and his nearness to the problem, especially his responsibility for a smooth working industrial relations program. Since the company has no control over the organization and demands of employee groups, it is necessary that the company accept the task of meeting these groups and ironing out with them in the best possible manner the mutual problems confronting both groups.

The American working man is an independent individual, and the company or executive failing to respect and recognize this truth is completely liable for unfortunate results of employer-employee relationship. Unless management is willing to consider some changes in the traditional outlook on and handling of plant labor problems, there can be no great improvement over the present unsatisfactory condition which exists in many organizations today.

A change in the organization of the industrial relations department depends, of course, on whether the present program is now satisfactory, and whether this same program will be sufficient to handle the increased load inevitable after the war. If it is apparent that this is not the case, then steps must be taken to remedy the situation.

Separation of Function

THE basis of the proposed revision in industrial relations organization is the complete separation of this function from any other job in the plant. The first foundation stone of the new program is the man who will be placed in charge of the organization, and here, of course, lies the rub, for many men who have previously been responsible for the relations work will either not be able or will not desire to adapt themselves to the requirements necessary to fill the revised position.

Is there a man in the present personnel organization who can meet to a large degree these following qualifications? He has initiative. He is trusted by the employee organization. He is generally known to be intellectually honest. He is capable of hard work. He is not snobbish nor class conscious; and he is a man to whom, after proper preparation, a very responsible job could be entrusted.

If such a man is already in the organization, he is the logical choice. If there is no such individual available and company policy prohibits the bringing in of an outsider, the executive must determine which of his available personnel is best fitted by training, background, and general adaptability to fill the proposed job.

Frankness Essential

ONCE the man is chosen, the executive should bring him together with representatives of the employee group and discuss with them the proposed system, bearing in mind that if the man is not acceptable to the employees the plan fails its purpose before it begins. The executive must determine that he will insist upon complete frankness from the industrial relations man, even though it hurts! And the executive must convince both the employees and the industrial relations man that every demand, grievance, and controversy must receive the most careful consideration and that recommendations from the industrial relations department shall be made to the executive on the basis of actual merit and not from a fear of or desire to please the company management.

It cannot be overemphasized that the industrial relations man *must* be given the responsibility of his job. If he is made to feel that his job is in jeopardy if he recommends action contrary to the personal opinions of the executive, the industrial relations man might as well be out picketing the union for all the good he is doing his company or his job! This honesty of exchange among the employees, the industrial relations department, and the executive is vitally necessary to the success of the program, and if management refuses to consider the importance of this tenet they must face the consequences of their indifference when returned servicemen, already wary of reported home front dissension, gather in industrial groups to demand, fairly or unfairly, a share of the high wages and other privileges granted to war time workers.

Distrust Not Dispelled

THIS fundamental distrust existing between management and labor has not been dispelled by the war, and it can never be improved unless both sides agree that open discussion and unbiased research rather than constant opposition is as fundamental to good labor relations as it is to a working democracy. And again it must be pointed out that the responsibility for the inception of this relationship rests with management. If honesty, not blind and foolish idealism, but hard, clear cut honesty is adopted as the keynote of management in its relationship with employees, labor will, you may be assured, follow not far behind.

No Wild Eyed Idealism

IT IS the factor of unbiased research which protects the executive from the element of wild eyed idealism or personal bias on the part of the industrial relations representative. Once the decision to change the program is made and the man is selected for the job, the program he is to follow must be carefully worked out and the necessary tools be provided.

One does not manufacture without tools, and it is similarly unreasonable to expect the human side of production to be mastered without equipment. Yet this is attempted time and time again in organizations where executives and personnel men try to settle these important problems by relying solely on personal opinion and belief.

Weeks and even months may be necessary for the gathering of the pertinent information and background necessary to the proper conduct of the new industrial relations program. The amount of assistance needed will vary in proportion to the size of the plant and the various industrial factors involved such as the number of job jurisdictions or the type of employee organization in effect. The industrial relations man must familiarize himself with the current labor laws and regulations both state and national, and a running file should be established of decisions applicable to his industry given in state and federal courts and boards.

Necessary Familiarity

HE MUST become thoroughly familiar with the provisions of the "G.I. Bill of Rights", the Civilian Relief Act, and the provisions of the Selective Service Act relating to the job and seniority rights of the returned serviceman. He must acquire a thorough knowledge of company policy and union contract regarding promotion, seniority, job rights, and other restrictions or benefits peculiar to his own plant. He must acquaint himself with the wage scales prevalent in the region on comparable jobs, company assets, wage scales within the company in other units, working hours permissible and customary, and all other necessary general information.

If there is a foreman training course in labor relations contemplated, the industrial relations man must be prepared to handle its instruction, be able to give a concise and clear account of the company policy in labor relations, and be able to answer intelligently questions on all phases of pertinent labor legislation and practice. To properly handle this phase of the program, he must become acquainted as far as possible with the foremen and department heads and their particular problems. He must gain the confidence of the foremen and group leaders and urge them to bring before the industrial relations department any problems arising between themselves and their men which cannot be settled on the job.

Free Access of Shop Stewards

HE SHOULD instruct them to allow shop stewards and other accredited representatives of the employee organization free access to the industrial relations department whenever necessary, and in every way strive to promote cooperation in this field between the foremen and their men. Finally, the highest degree of cooperation must be established between the foremen and the industrial relations department because the foreman is the first and closest link between employer and employee and as such is immensely important in the successful operation of the program.

All this data must be correlated and made easily accessible for immediate reference and consultation. When all this is done and the necessary subordinate organization set up, the industrial relations department is ready to take from the shoulders of the executive the responsibility of hundreds of minor decisions and conferences, and relieve him from the time consuming, laborious research necessary as a background for a fair analysis of problems requiring major decisions.

Relations with Plant Executive

IT IS not suggested that the program can function without the guiding hand of the plant executive, for the major problems will always need the final word from the first representative of the company. But if the industrial relations man is well chosen and is given the thorough background outlined here, he can be trusted to protect the company and integrate the company with the employees far better than under many existing programs. A fifteen minute conference two or three times a week between the executive and the industrial relations man can put the front office up to date on every phase of the new program without ever seriously interfering with the executive's own tremendously important job.

Remodel Now if Necessary

MANY organizations may have industrial relations programs which are functioning as perfectly as possible now and will continue to do so after the war. But if the program is not satisfactory now, it is better to remodel it now rather than after the strain begins.   If the industrial relations program is taken out of the indefinite category and placed alone and on a well defined basis as the immensely important industrial factor it is, the resultant organization will be able to cope with many of the vital and pressing problems arising with the return of the serviceman to post war industry.

When victory is won, management faces one of the greatest tests in history. Preparation now may well mean industrial survival after the war.

Book Reviews

Book Review Editor, Mr. Everett Van Every
California Personnel Management Association, Berkeley, Cal.

INDUSTRIAL OPHTHALMOLOGY

By Hedwig S. Kuhn, M.D., St. Louis. The C. V. Mosby Company. 1944. 294 pp.
Price $6.50.

Reviewed by Crawford W. Adams, M.D.

This volume clearly illustrates and offers a practical solution to the problems which relate to efficient vision in all modern phases of production. Visual defects in industry, based upon a good physiological classification and their correction by means of modern medicine, surgery, and occupational therapy, reveal the solution to this vast problem.

The author because of her keen interest, and experience, as well as her location in a densely industrialized region is well qualified to discuss the industrial hazards and their solution to the ophthalmologist. The chapter on industrial eye injuries caused by solid bodies and their treatment is meticulously discussed by Dr. Albert Snell. The most recent developments relating to the eye in industry are presented in the final chapter of ''Industrial Ophthalmology''.

The appendix covers very thoroughly toxic hazards, an industrial eye program, and a method for appraisal of loss of visual efficiency. This book is an excellent guide for all Ophthalmologists and plant nurses who contact industry.

PERSONNEL
Journal

The Magazine of

LABOR RELATIONS AND PERSONNEL PRACTICES

Published by PERSONNEL RESEARCH FEDERATION

Lincoln Building, 60 East 42nd Street, New York City

Volume 23   *Number 9*

Contents for March 1945

EDITORIAL BOARD

It is Said that Many Veterans and Present Workers in War Industries Intend to Go into Business
for Themselves Rather than Become Employees.
It Should be Pointed Out to Them the Difficulties
and Hazards of So Doing.

Starting Your
Own Business

BY NATIONAL ASSOCIATION OF BETTER BUSINESS
BUREAUS

Cleveland, Ohio

THIS booklet, "Facts Veterans Should Know *Before* STARTING A BUSINESS",
is prepared for and dedicated to service men and women, three million of whom,
according to estimates of the United States Department of Commerce, may elect
to go into business for themselves during the first three or four years after the war.
To this number will be added war workers and others who may start new businesses
or reopen many which were closed.

Loans under G.I. Bill

IT TAKES money to start a business. This money must be provided by the veteran.
The Government under the G.I. Bill of Rights does not make a gift to a veteran
to start a business; neither does the Government make the veteran a loan. It does
provide assistance if, and only if, the veteran can comply with definite and rigid
requirements. For example, assume the veteran is qualified by experience and
ability to manage a business. If he can induce a bank, insurance company, manufacturer, wholesaler, supply company, or individual to loan him money to go into
business, at an interest rate of no more than 4%, he can apply to the Administrator
of Veterans' Affairs for a guaranty by the Government not to exceed 50% of the loan,
with the guaranty part of the loan not to exceed $2,000. To illustrate, if the loan
is for $6,000, the veteran can apply for a guaranty of $2,000 of it. If the loan is for
$3,000, the veteran could apply for a guaranty of only $1,500.

A loan for the purchase of business property includes any business, land, building, supplies, equipment, machinery, or tools to be used by the applicant in the operation of a business.

The Administrator of Veterans' Affairs will approve the application if, after investigation, he finds:

1. That the ability and experience of the veteran, and the conditions under which he proposes to operate are such that there is a reasonable likelihood that he will be successful.
2. That the proceeds of the loan will be used to pay for real or personal property that the veteran needs and will use in the operation of a business
3. That the purchase price does not exceed the reasonable normal value, as determined by proper appraisal.

Responsibility of Borrower

IF THE Administrator of Veterans' Affairs approves the application for a guaranty, the entire loan (including the guaranteed amount) must be payable in full in a specific period of time. The Government will pay interest for the first year on the guaranty part of the loan. As the guaranty part of the loan is limited to not more than $2,000, the Government is limited to pay 4% interest for one year on this amount, or $80. In the event the guaranty part of the loan is half this amount, the amount of interest the Government will pay is $40, or 4% interest on $1,000, for the first year. This represents the only cash or money outlay contemplated by the Government to aid veterans in starting a business.

Unquestionably the guaranty part of the loan will be a valuable inducement for a lender to agree to make the full loan. However, the veteran should frankly face the fact that he must get a responsible party to be willing to make him the loan at 4% interest. This may be difficult. First, the lender must assume at least half of the risk and second, the interest rate is low in comparison with the speculative risks involved in financing new businesses. A bank or lending institution, as the custodian of funds of its depositors, must be guided by these considerations. In addition, the loaning activities of banks are regulated and subject to investigation by banking authorities to assure that all possible protective safeguards for the funds of depositors are in force.

Thus the decision of a bank or lending institution to make the loan may have to be based, in addition to the character of the applicant, his experience and ability, and the fact that the government guarantees one-half up to $2,000, on what security the veteran can put up to cover the loan.

Two Important Facts

TWO important facts the veteran should fully understand are: 1. If the debt or interest is not paid and it becomes necessary for the Government to make any payment on account of the guarantee, the veteran is obligated to repay such amount and the Government will hold him or his estate responsible. 2. Under the G.I. Bill, a veteran can apply for a guarantee of loans for (a) purchase or construction of a home (b) purchase of farm and farm equipment and (c) purchase of business property. However, the *aggregate amount guaranteed shall not exceed $2,000* whether the loans are for more than or only one of the above purposes.

Opportunities and Risks

THE time for starting a new enterprise is very important and any one thinking of doing so should consider carefully general economic and business conditions. Among these, he can consider the possibilities of (1) new businesses to take the place of those which have discontinued, and (2) having expanding production and distribution in excess of pre-war levels.

How about the risks? Business is a hard competitive struggle and the yearly mortality is high. Nearly as many businesses discontinue each year as start up. In the ten-year period from 1932 to 1941, both inclusive, approximately 3,600,000 enterprises discontinued business, whereas during the same period there were approximately 3,700,000 new enterprises. In normal times more than 1,000 new concerns open their doors each business day and about an equal number close. Mortality rates in the first year of life are high. In retailing, 1 out of 3 new concerns do not survive the first year and 2 out of 3 close their doors within 6 years. In wholesaling and manufacturing, 1 out of 5 concerns discontinue in the first year and 2 out of 3 close within 9 years.

Short Life of Small Business

A STUDY of retail stores in 207 Indiana towns showed that 25% of the retail stores closed their doors in the first year of life, another 18% in the second year, another 10% in the third year, an additional 7% in the fourth year, another 5% in the fifth year, another 5% in the sixth year, and 3% in the seventh year, leaving only 27% still in business after seven years. Another study showed that of slightly more than 10,000 enterprises established in Poughkeepsie, N. Y., between 1844 and 1926 a total of only 47% lasted for three years or more and almost 80% were out of business within ten years of starting.

Similar studies made in other parts of the country show essentially the same facts.

Many and varied reasons are given for failure. But practically the only one recognized in the business world is lack of experienced and intelligent management. In the final analysis, management makes or breaks the business enterprise. This fact can not be stressed too strongly. To repeat it in another way, management ability is the simple reason for the difference between success and failure in the business world.

Poor Management

SOME types of risks, such as floods, storms, fires, etc., can be insured against. But other risks of business depend entirely upon the experience and the ability of the management to cope with them. So, although many reasons are given for failures, these usually represent the *occasions* for the failure rather than the *causes*. Had the management been efficient, it would have anticipated and controlled them. For example, the United States Department of Commerce made a study of 487 business establishments which went into bankruptcy in New Jersey. Of the total number of businesses studied, 23.5% kept no books, 29.4% kept inadequate books, and 39% never took an inventory. Although many of those who failed blamed the failure on a business depression, an analysis of the data indicates that business depression was the occasion rather than the cause of the failure and that inefficient management was the real cause.

The following, taken from a study of 570 cases of businesses that became bankrupt, shows the causes or occasions for failures as expressed in the opinions of the owners of the bankrupt businesses and as expressed by the creditors of the businesses: (Many listed several causes.)

500 Bankruptcies

Causes or Occasions of Failures	Owners' Opinion Percentage of Enterprises Affected	Creditors' Opinion Percentage of Enterprises Affected
Business depression	67.7	29.1
Inefficient management	28.2	58.7
Insufficient capital	48.2	32.9
Adverse domestic and personal factors	35.1	28.1
Bad-debt losses	29.8	17.6
Competition	37.9	9.1
Decline in value of assets	31.6	5.8
Dishonesty and fraud		33.7
Excessive overhead expense	24.0	8.9
Too rapid expansion	10.5	7.2
Losses from speculation	11.6	5.8
Poor business location	14.6	2.7
Buying too much on credit	9.5	3.9
Excessive interest charged on borrowed money	11.1	2.1
Unfavorable changes in trading areas	11.2	1.9

Study of 570 cases of business that became bankrupt from "Business Principles and Management" by Bernard A. Shilt and W. Harmon Wilson, published by South-Western Publishing Co.

Books Essential

ALL of these reasons for failure expose the poor quality of management. For example, insufficient capital is given by the owners of the business as one of the causes of failure in 48% of the cases and by creditors in approximately 33%. Yet this is entirely due to management not properly analyzing the financial requirements of the business. It is poor management which is responsible for concerns either starting up or expanding without sufficient capital.

Certainly a business can not know where it stands if it doesn't keep books and the number of concerns that either keep no books or keep inadequate books or who never take an inventory is extremely high. It shows up repeatedly in various studies of bankruptcies and failures.

Experience and Ability Essential

FOR all of the above reasons a veteran considering starting a business should determine if his education qualifies him for the business, what experience he has had to qualify, and what management ability he possesses. *Experience in business and managerial ability* are two prime requisites for the veteran to make a success in business. If he doesn't have experience, the best course is for him to get it by working for some one else before going into business for himself. Actually, failure to do so would be evidence of lack of managerial ability.

Management ability also includes full knowledge of financial requirements, both as to invested capital and working capital. Those contemplating applying for a Government guarantee of a loan should note that the application cannot be approved unless the Administrator of Veterans' Affairs finds *that the ability and experience of the veteran, . . . are such that there is a reasonable likelihood that he will be successful. . .*

Schemes to Avoid

THE great amount of war savings in this country, together with the problems which will be faced by millions of people during the reconversion period, offer the swindling fraternity unusual opportunities for their schemes and promotions. Veterans will be high on their list of prospective victims. Many will have ready cash in mustering-out pay, in savings, or invested in war bonds. Only a few have had business experience and are aware of the many schemes which the unscrupulous endeavor to promote at all times and among all prospective victims. The swindler will try:

1. To rush veterans into taking hasty actions.
2. To prevent veterans from making investigations.
3. When this is impossible, to discredit what the swindler knows in advance will be the outcome of such investigations.

Better Business Bureaus have records of over 800 schemes of various sorts. Not all of these relate to business "opportunity" schemes. For the purpose of this booklet, therefore, we are confining the discussion to those types of schemes which the veteran, looking for an opportunity to go into business, should avoid. A few highly speculative "opportunities" are also included. The list is not intended to be all-inclusive.

Absentee Farming

THE offering of land in a distant state on a cooperative arrangement to raise fruits or nuts, has its share of racketeers. Some sell land at exorbitant prices, minimize the hazards and quote misleading figures.

Advance Fee

IF YOUR business needs financing, don't fall for an unscrupulous promotor who offers to arrange a loan if you first pay his expenses. Front-money operators may offer to incorporate your business and assist in selling stock. But, when advanced fees have been paid to them or their associates, service usually stops or is found to be worthless.

Business Brokers

SOME business brokers, in acting as agents for sellers of businesses, are irresponsible, unfair to prospective purchasers, avoid all liabilities, and are interested only in collecting a fee. Do not be rushed into a deal. Get all verbal understandings in writing from the seller. Put the deal in escrow with a third, reputable, disinterested party. Before you sign an agreement to purchase, have all papers checked by your attorney and all books and records showing earning capacity, past profits, inventory, equipment, obligations, etc., checked by an accountant.

Buy-Back Contracts

BUY-BACK contracts, like money-back guarantees, are no better than the guarantors. They are frequently worthless promises made by dishonest promoters.

Cash Bond

THE advertising of attractive jobs by swindlers who request applicants to deposit a cash bond, is a vicious scheme that has swindled thousands.

Fur Farms

ANIMAL breeding promotions or fur farms are sometimes designed only for the promoters' profit. They appeal for your investment through biological statistics which appear mathematically sound but which neglect to include the natural hazards incidental to such enterprises. Many include worthless offers to buy back the progeny at high but fictitious prices.

Home Work

LUCRATIVE home employment is often advertised in help wanted columns when the real and only purpose of the promoter is to make a tremendous profit on "Home Work" equipment which he has to sell.

Job Investments

INVARIABLY large earnings or a better than average weekly salary are offered to those who will "invest" in the business of a promoter who misrepresents.

Listing Fee

THIS is a variation of the Advance Fee Scheme. The fake business broker gets you to pay a fee for listing your name with him for finding the type of business you wish to engage in. Listing fees are sometimes disguised as expenses for advertising or circularizing prospects.

Loan Sharks

LOAN SHARKS" take advantage of borrowers by imposing very unfair if not illegal terms. Some get as high as 400% interest.

New Promotions

DECIDE whether you can afford to lose before you invest in any new enterprise. A large number of new enterprises fail.

Partner Wanted

PARTNER wanted propositions are sometimes nothing but deceptive frauds to get your investment in a supposedly profitable business claiming the need of new funds. In a partnership, each partner is responsible for all the debts of the firm. *Know* your partner.

Patents and Inventions

INVESTMENTS in new inventions, patents, or patent litigation ventures are usually risky speculations and sometimes frauds.

Territorial Rights

SHOULD a high-pressure promoter lure you with the right to sell his product in exclusive territory, reserve your decision until you possess the facts. Some promoters misrepresent their products to get quantity orders and often sell several people the same territorial rights.

Vending Machines

SOME promoters of coin-operated vending machines for nuts, confections, etc., exaggerate probable earnings and otherwise deceive.

Inasmuch as the foregoing business opportunity schemes represent the activities of an unscrupulous minority of schemers masquerading under the good name of business, it is fitting to emphasize that nearly all business is fundamentally honest and anxious to help the veteran.

You can protect yourself by making sure you deal only with legitimate business, reliable persons, and responsible concerns. This you can be sure of doing by following the slogan of Better Business Bureaus, namely, "BEFORE YOU INVEST—INVESTIGATE". Before committing yourself, it will be useful to get the answers to the following questions:

1. What are the facts? Do they agree with the representations?
2. What are the promises or predictions? Are they reasonable?
3. What is the past record of the seller or his agent? Is he worthy of confidence?

Read Before You Sign and Keep a Copy

PRACTICALLY every business transaction involves a contract in some form. It does not always need to be in writing, although that is advisable in any important transaction because oral agreements are sometimes difficult to prove or may not be enforceable. You should not sign a contract without reading it and understanding its terms.

A complete understanding serves to guard against ill-advised undertakings, as well as fraudulent or unfair schemes. If you do not understand certain terms, phrases or fine print in a contract, delay signing until you have found out what they mean. The reasons are obvious. Your signature to a contract means that you have agreed to all its terms and provisions. Furthermore, the written document usually speaks for itself, holding participating parties strictly accountable for the performance of their mutual promises.

Sources of Additional Information

THIS booklet, as stated in the introduction, covers only a few important "FACTS" that are not generally known. If helpful to the veteran, its purpose will be fulfilled. If the risks, disappointments, and schemes of business appear to have been emphasized, it is only because there is a lack of general and widely circulated information on these phases and because of the availability of extensive data on other phases, such as the rich rewards and satisfactions for those successful in business.

There are many thousands of worthy opportunities to start in business and the warnings are given only in an attempt to avoid disaster. The country needs growing and successful businesses and there is plenty of room for experienced and intelligent management. Service men and women can profitable study the success stories of individual businesses, most of which originally started as small concerns not so many years ago.

The following agencies, listed alphabetically, are all interested in helping the veteran. Some have national headquarters and in such instances, their headquarters addresses are listed. In most cases, however, there are regional, field, district, or local offices which may render more direct and personal service. The service man or woman can profitably contact these agencies, state his or her problem in some detail, and be assured of valuable help on the problem of establishing and managing a business. Communicate with each one, checking off the list as you do so.

☐ Committee for Economic Development
285 Madison Ave.
New York 17, N. Y.

☐ Bureau of Foreign and Domestic Commerce
United States Department of Commerce
Washington 25, D. C.

☐ Educational Institutions offering courses and providing information on business administration and research and Libraries.

☐ Local Chamber of Commerce.

☐ Local Veterans Service Center. (Sometimes called "Information and Reception" or "Information and Referral".)

☐ United States Armed Forces Institute
Madison 3, Wisconsin.

☐ Veterans' Administration
Washington 25, D. C.

☐ Veterans Personnel Division
Selective Service Systems
Washington 25, D. C.

An extract from a pamphlet produced by the National Association of Better Business Bureaus, 212 Cuyahoga Building, Cleveland, 14, Ohio. Copies of the booklet may be obtained from them.

There is No Greater Contradiction than that
While the Foreman is Colorfully Pictured as a
Versatile and Indispensable Manager His Au-
thority Has Been Modified and Side-Stepped, His
Pay Differential Narrowed and His Viewpoint
Often Blindly Disregarded.

Let *the*
Foreman Manage

By Ellsworth S. Grant

Allen Manufacturing Company
Hartford, Conn.

THE war has affected industry in many revolutionary ways, the most disturbing of which may be the precipitated crisis of the foreman's relationship to management. This crisis, sown during the rapid rise to industrial bigness and cultivated by the labor ferment of the last decade, is today dramatized in the growing power of the three-year-old Foreman's Association of America and the wave of supervisory strikes. Management is making the overdue discovery that for years it has extolled the virtues of foremanship but done little to protect them.

Government Straddling Issue

To put the present turmoil in proper perspective, it must be remembered that unionization of supervisory employees is not new; in fact, it has existed in the printing trades since 1889, and it is found in the building trades, on railroads, in the maritime industry, and in the mines. Recently the trend in the mass production industries has been toward separate and independent unions like the Foreman's Association, since the C.I.O. has frowned, publicly at least, on membership along-side of non-supervisory workers. Meanwhile the government, unsure of the significance of foreman unionization, is straddling the issue by permitting supervisors to unionize but refusing them collective bargaining rights. The chaotic results, though they have fixed employers in the middle legally, have nevertheless served to arouse them to self-analysis and action.

There is no greater industrial contradiction that while the foreman is colorfully pictured as a versatile and indispensable manager, his once supreme authority has been gradually withdrawn, modified or sidestepped, the pay differential between himself and his subordinates greatly narrowed through organized labor's wage gains, and his viewpoint as well as his position blindly disregarded in formulating and communicating company policies. It is the same kind of paradox that traditionally exists between the candidate's promise and the officeholder's performance. In all holiness the foreman is sworn in as part of management, and in all practicality he is treated as part of the rank and file.

Foreman the Glamor Boy

BY DEFINITION the word "foreman" means the first or chief man. The title "foreman" is promiscuously used to cover every type of supervisor from the straw boss, setup man or group leader who directs the work of a handful to the general foreman, manager or superintendent who may have jurisdiction over hundreds of employees. If used to refer to a supervisor in full charge of a department or section thereof, who handles a number of workers with the help of assistant foremen and group leaders, and who reports to the general foreman or superintendent, it can be truly stated that in modern industry the foreman stands on the production line as management's closest representative to the worker. He is variously dubbed as the "cutting edge" of management, the "sergeant of production", or "management's right hand". Certainly, to most workers, he is the company.

If one could accept the glamorized version of the foreman's job, he would have to believe that there was no limit to its variety and complexity. The war has undoubtedly added many hurdles and headaches, but it is impossible that one man can possess so many qualities and skills and carry so many responsibilities as are currently claimed for the foreman. In the first place the ideal of what a foreman should be is a long human distance from the fact of what he can be. Similar personal and job demands, varying only in degree, are made of every manager in the industrial hierarchy up to the president, and not even the best fulfills all of them to perfection. In the second place, once the amount of the foreman's responsibility and authority is determined, specific limitations can and should be applied to his position.

Foremen Blame Management

BASICALLY the foreman's job is concerned with production and people. His primary function is to get people to produce with maximum group efficiency and minimum individual dissatisfaction. All his other functions are related, and subordinate, to that task. So much emphasis is usually placed on his technical knowledge of materials, machines and methods—his "know-how"—that frequently the foreman's ability to handle people is taken for granted. The modern concept, giving human relations their rightful place in the industrial sun, holds that the foreman must know his men as well as his machines. If he is a first-rate mechanic yet unskilled in leadership, he cannot be expected to manage.

Knowing what is expected of them, how do the foremen themselves react to their present status? In a limited survey one out of two who were questioned felt unhappy and frustrated, not because of labor or government but because of management. They blamed management for the lack of clear lines of authority, for having more than one boss, for failing to provide adequate training, for being left out of policymaking, for being paid wages only slightly better than their subordinates. Perhaps the most revealing fact was their reference to management as a group distinct from themselves. They could not admit identity with something of which they were supposed to be part; they were unable to say "we".

1,500,000 Foremen

SPOKESMEN for the belligerent Foremen's Association, in answer to management's claims about the importance of the foreman, argue that the world in which he could function as a manager disappeared "with the successful organization of mass production workers" beginning in 1935. Now, in their opinion, the foreman occupies no more favored position than the average employee. As a result foremen have become increasingly worried over not only the status of their job but its permanence.

Two other factors intensify this concern: the advance toward job security which their subordinates have achieved through labor contracts; and, the knowledge that industry has been compelled to treble its supervisory force in wartime to over 1,500,-000, many of whom face demotion or worse when peace comes. To the War Labor Board panel investigating the grievances of foremen principally in Detroit the F.A.A. president remarked: "If you ask me what foremen are complaining about, I say they want the right to hold their jobs."

The Bulldozer Disappears

IT is true that the ascendancy of industrial unions in the turbulent thirties changed the climate in which the foreman supervised. The appearance of the shop steward and union committeeman signified the establishment of a new authority right in the foreman's department. Previously, many a foreman had bossed a business within a business without fear from above or below. He hired and fired at will; he drove and discriminated in the best bulldozing tradition. Now he quickly found he could no longer rule as he pleased; his personal power was circumscribed by mass organization and law

This competition for authority shook the whole structure of management and its function, forcing the supervisor and his superiors to change their attitudes, to devise new techniques, to take different actions. In many cases the foreman lost ground at the hands of both management and labor; the one defied his authority, the other spiked it by allowing the steward to bypass him in the grievance procedure and by placing the total responsibility for labor relations at the top of the organization.

But even organized labor's rise does not tell the entire story of the foreman's decline. Both are effects of a greater, more irresistible cause—centralization of industry. Mass production is impossible without industrial bigness; it is the price which America must pay for the highest standard of living in the world. Yet the human danger of bigness in business is separation—between manager and worker, planner and doer, office and shop. The general result is, on the surface, order and efficiency but, underneath, a social atmosphere that is impersonal, materialistic and frequently undemocratic.

A gulf of enormous human proportions keeps management and labor apart, when fundamentally there is every economic reason for both to be one in purpose. In such an environment foremen are apt to differ from workers only in that their obligations grossly outweigh their rights. They stand just as far away from top management. They constitute a one-way street, taking but not giving, performing but not participating. They are foremen in title only.

Many Leaders Necessary

NEVERTHELESS, to be efficient, the modern corporation requires many leaders instead of one. As a company grows, it is necessary to divide managerial responsibility and its twin authority into several levels of supervision, starting with the foreman and ending with the president. Out of this division develops staff and line, similar in many respects to military organization, in which one part does the planning and the other part the operating. All these managers are essential if the big boss is to maintain as close control over the blood and bone of his business as his grandfather did alone.

Under this system the foreman becomes head of a part of the whole, a link in the chain of management, the big boss's direct contact with the worker. His department, instead of being a shop in itself, becomes integrated with every other department, and all are held together by the decisions and rules made at the top. His authority and responsibility are cut from the cloth that fits a manager and not a petty tyrant.

Actually under the functional type of organization the supervisor has greater need for the qualities and skills, in addition to the status, of leadership than when he could call his job a throne and his department a domain.

Ford's 9,000 Foremen

WITH the fact of the supervisor's relationship to management so prevalently incompatible with the theory, is it any wonder that foremen in the mass production industries want to unionize? The N.L.R.B. has declared them to be "employees" within the meaning of the Wagner Act. They have seen the fruits of collective action. In fact, many of those promoted to the supervisory force during the war were union members only yesterday when they belonged to the bargaining unit. Ford's 9000 organized foremen in themselves add up to a large plant. And they have seen, especially during wartime, the deterioration of the foreman's position in respect to pay, security and recognition. In the words of an authority on personnel administration, also a vice-president of General Foods: "After the foreman was selected for his job he was lectured blue in the face regarding his importance as 'the key man in industry', and then in too many instances no confirmation was given this lip service by appropriate and genuine recognition."

What is the answer: encourage foremen to join unions; resist bitterly their unionizing activities; eliminate foremen entirely; or make it unnecessary and undesirable for them to unionize?

Why Not Abolish Foremen?

THERE is a minority among executives which is willing to have foremen and most of their functions eliminated. These people, many of whom believe human relations in the company is a one-man job or no job at all, argue that the foremen is nine-tenths technician and can never be trained as a personnel man or executive. Let him, they urge, be responsible for output and quality only, and leave labor relations and the rest to the plant manager or the personnel department. As evidence of the foreman's inability to handle human relations problems they point to the wartime development of employee counselors.

This argument is self-destructive because on the one hand it assumes that the foreman cannot become an executive in the full meaning of the word, and on the other it concedes that he is an executive insofar as he has charge of a department's production. In other words, it leaves the foreman still in the middle—neither fish nor flesh. Furthermore, if the foreman's position were to be abolished, industry would have to create a new level of management to supervise the rank and file. There has to be a first line of management to maintain efficiency and morale.

For this same reason all of management including foremen stand to lose in the end if foremen continue to unionize. If supervisory unions eventually succeed in gaining collective bargaining rights, their interests will inevitably drift toward the unions of production workers—man and women whom they are supposed to manage. And it is hard to understand how unionized foremen will be able to represent both management and labor at the same time. They must be one or the other. Yet it will not do for manufacturers to fight supervisory unions as in the past they often have other unions; experience shows that the best way to strengthen labor organizations (aside from granting union security) is to resist them.

Foremen Must Be Made Employers

To save its foremen, industry must first decide they are "employers"—in both the functional and legal meaning of that word. Next, it must make them think of themselves as employers, as managers, as company representatives. It cannot accomplish overnight this task of changing attitudes of mind that have been built up for so long on what the foremen have observed and felt to the contrary. A talk from the president and the survival of weekly foremen's meetings will not suffice. Top management must first redesign much of its own attitude and approach, then practice it day-by-day in countless small, frequently repeated actions. No one executive like the personnel man or the plant manager can be delegated to perform this metamorphosis; every level of supervision needs to be convinced that foremen are management and to treat them as management.

Six Basic Points

Specifically, a policy that lets the foreman manage should, regardless of the company's size, cover the following basic points:

(1) sound selection
(2) continuous training
(3) adequate compensation
(4) proper status
(5) two-way communication
(6) individual treatment and recognition

Part of industry's neglect of the foreman involves the vital matter of proper selection and promotion. More attention seems to have been given the selection of non-supervisory employees, probably because there are more of them, and because the appointment of foremen is usually left to some one operating executive. For years men have been promoted out of the ranks to supervisory jobs on the primitive basis of "greatest seniority", "best worker", or "boss's favorite". As a result there are many foremen in industry who function well as technicians but not as managers. These men totally lack executive capacity or are mentally too hardened to learn. Today it is imperative to have a sound, objective method of supervisory selection, placement and promotion. At the same time the incompetent and static foremen should be removed as fast as good personnel practice permits.

Most Training Is a Crazy-quilt Pattern

Foremen training must be tailored to the company and the foreman. Because of the unrealistic tendency to regard the foreman as everything from engineer to father confessor, there has been considerable overzealous and misguided thinking about his training needs. The subject matter of many supervisory training programs is a crazy-quilt patched with business administration, government control, social psychology, leadership, and what not. The theory of such eclectic education is apparently that the good foreman should know a little about a lot. Before setting up a foreman training program it must be recognized that the foreman's job has a definable beginning and end.

As one personnel man keenly observed: "The essence of such training is the imparting of specific information necessary to the successful accomplishment of the agreed-upon responsibilities. The nature of the training is the rifle, rather than the shotgun, method of hitting the target." The programs of Training Within Industry are an outstanding example of this approach.

The purpose of supervisory training is to develop better managers through the basic methods of the lecture, the conference, the direct contact. The latter, emphasizing personal example and follow-up, is perhaps most consistently neglected by the foreman's superiors. As for content, why not ask the foremen themselves what they desire most to learn? In a survey at the Radio Corporation of America 80% of the foremen gave first choice to human relations. The next three topics, selected by a much smaller percentage, were production control, company policies and instruction. Under the number one topic were stressed understanding and treatment of the individual workers, delegating responsibility to subordinates and preventing grievances. These same foremen, commenting on training techniques, preferred practical case illustrations of general subjects like psychology, down-to-earth discussion, visual aids such as movies and slides, and short, intensive, voluntary courses.

Proper Pay

ADEQUATE pay for the foreman is that which is commensurate with his position as determined by job evaluation. The foreman with real managerial responsibility should be paid a salary substantially (15%–25%) higher than the total earnings of his highest-paid subordinate. Wherever possible the foreman should participate in an incentive plan based on more production at lower cost.

To give the foreman proper status in the organization, first the boundaries of his job must be sharply drawn, and secondly he must be delegated specific authority sufficient to carry out his specific responsibility. Obviously, the amount of authority is determined by the scope of the job, which in turn depends on the size of the company. The more levels and divisions of supervision, the less authority for each. There are clear indications that the trend toward centralizing functions in staff departments is being reversed and that the foreman is getting back many of them, not for the purpose of restoring his throne, but in order to facilitate departmental teamwork, individual treatment and leadership.

Essential symbols of authority are a desk and a telephone, a place to talk with employees privately, and a clerk if necessary. The foreman should unquestionably have the right to accept or reject job applicants selected by the employment office, and he should be the first step in the grievance procedure.. When a time study is made, a piece rate set or a new job evaluated, the foreman should be consulted and his approval obtained. He should be able to recommend pay increases for his employees. Under no circumstances ought he to be bypassed by a subordinate or a superior.

Foremen Included in Consultative Management

Two-way communication goes hand in hand with proper status. The principle behind keeping the foreman informed and enabling him to inform you is consultative management. Numerous channels of communication exist: regular meetings on company time, supervisory letters, memos, questionnaires, daily contacts. Policy changes, orders and other information are often given out without advance notice or sufficient explanation. It is essential that all company policies and practices be clearly set down and put into a foreman's manual.

Better still is to have the foremen assist in the preparation of such a manual by analyzing their duties in relation to standard policies and practices and calling to top management's attention any omissions or discrepancies. In this way they will gain a fuller understanding of their position and its place in the organization.

In addition, it is wise to have foremen represented during contract negotiations (or at other management meetings which directly concern them), not only to present the supervisory viewpoint but also to keep all foremen fully and quickly informed. A few companies have even established representative supervisory committees to discuss and recommend policy.

Complaints—Doubts—Failings

A major aim of the Foremen's Association is a formal grievance procedure. The War Labor Board panel in Detroit seemed to conclude, in weighing the relationship between foremen and higher executives, that "management should do less talking and more listening". It is patent that foremen are human beings with problems, complaints, doubts, failings. Their lot is to be bawled out when they fall down but rarely given credit when they come through. They deserve to be treated with at least the same amount of individual consideration from their superiors as they in turn are expected to give to their subordinates.

Good job relations between foreman and superior consist of praise when due, solicitation of the foreman's ideas, consultation before the deed, full admittance of the foreman into the superior's confidence, fair and sincere dealing day in and day out. Periodic merit rating is one tool to bring the foreman and his superior closer together. Perhaps the major factor is a foreman's performance in the executive makeup of the superior to whom he reports.

Isolated as he is because of his staff function, the top executive is inclined to forget or minimize the fact that the foreman knows the average worker better than any one else. Moreover, he is responsible for carrying out all company policies and getting the average worker to accept them.

Rooted into the Foundations of Management

For these simple reasons alone the foreman is rooted into the foundation of management. For these reasons alone he has a valuable and continuous contribution to make to company progress. It would seem that unionism appeals only to foremen in companies where top management consistently frustrates their desire to belong to management. To doubt the foreman's ability to handle this responsibility is to lack faith in management itself; to fail to make him part of management is inviting great trouble and expense.

Foremen do not want an easier job but the chance to do a better job. Yet to an increasing degree the foremen, as well as the worker, is demonstrating loss of pride in his work and of confidence in his boss. Industry's answer must be to give the genuine foreman his proper place on the team, to back him up, to show him the goal, to let him manage.

The Labor-fixers and Confidential Consultants Who Have Tried to Surround Our Work with an Air of Mystery and Intrigue belong with the Witch Doctors. This also Applies to the Bally-hoo Artists and Social Service Welfare Workers.

Personnel Problems
after Victory

By Forrest H. Kirkpatrick

Radio Corporation of America
Camden, N. J.

It seems clear that the first few years after this war will find us in the grip of major economic problems. The Committee for Economic Development has stated that our postwar employment goal must be fifty-six million to sixty million workers with a gross output of goods and services to support such employment estimated at one hundred thirty-five billion dollars, plus ten billion dollars for military goods. Such a goal must be contrasted with the top prewar year of 1940 when we had forty-six million employed workers, with gross output at ninety-eight billion dollars, plus two billion dollars for military goods.

A World of Superlatives

Economic stability will depend upon our success in offsetting decreases in demand for some products with increases in demand for other products. Some economists have said that we shall be living in a world of superlatives—a world of record-breaking "highs" and "lows." They call attention to 1941, when Americans were driving twenty-nine million automobiles. At the end of this year the number of automobiles will be down to twenty-three million or less. If employment after the war is higher than in 1940, Americans may want to drive considerably more than twenty-nine million automobiles—probably thirty-three million or thirty-four million.

On the other hand, we are told that in the last four years the machine tool industry produced thirty times the output of any prewar years. We are also told that the electronic industries have increased production of radio and radar so much that a small percentage of the present work force could produce the equivalent of the 1941 production.

Whether we agree with all such statements and statistics or not, there is general agreement that the reconversion and readjustment period after V-Day will be freighted with many problems. Taxes and tariffs, government-owned war plants, surplus military stocks, renegotiation of war contracts, continuation of price and wage controls, planning of demobilization, and the care of the handicapped and dislocated are some of the problems.

Job Security and Wages

OF MAJOR importance will be the handling of personnel and labor relations in the years just ahead. There are some explosive elements in this area and they come from the two important issues of *job security* and *wages*—issues which are assuming greatly increased importance in the minds of many employees as the progress of the war brings us closer to the inevitable lay-offs and shorter work week. The recent hearings before the War Labor Board on the modification of the "Little Steel" formula showed that labor unions seem to be suffering from a case of "conversion jitters." To them a war-contract-cancellation policy that fails to take into account loss of earnings due to overtime, incentive bonuses, and similar schemes is regarded as a calamity.

In these war years millions of men and women have changed their homes, seeking employment and wartime wages. Fear and uncertainty on the part of many of these migrants is likely to develop into panic as cancellations and cutbacks are announced. Many will gradually return to the farms and rural areas from whence they came. Others will remain in the industrial centers where they are now employed and others will be compelled to make quick shifts from the "one-industry" towns where they are now employed.

Flavor of Unreality

SOME have enjoyed comparatively well-paid jobs in shipbuilding and aircraft plants, but others have been confined to comparatively low wage fields like textiles. But workers seem to sense that there is a flavor of "unreality" about the present situation. They know that there will undoubtedly be cut-backs, lay-offs, shorter hours, and some unemployment. Job insecurity may become a national as well as a personal hysteria.

Recently Detroit faced one of the most serious labor threats of the war—serious not only because of the potential number of workers involved, but also because of its effect on the war effort at a crucial time. All of Detroit's major war plants were threatened with shut-down when a strike of about 4,000 maintenance workers, members of the Maintenance, Construction and Power House Council, UAW-CIO, was called. At that time Louis G. Miriani, Chairman of the Regional War Labor Board, stated that in his opinion, this situation was the result of typical feeling on the part of labor and was going to get worse. This means that the current mood of many American workers is on the side of dissatisfaction with their lot and it is due principally to the uncertainties of postwar adjustment.

Wage Bargaining

IN BARGAINING about wage rates after V-Day, labor and management will confront a combination of common and opposing interests that will be more disturbing than in any other period of our history. Both labor and management will want to expand markets, for employment will depend on sales as truly as do profits. The sales of any product depend, in turn, on keeping its unit price so adjusted to the prices of other goods as to attract buyers.

As a rule the lower the selling price in relation to other prices, the larger the sales. But prices must cover costs if prices and employment are to be assured. In most industries, labor charges are the largest item of expense next to materials. So if unions seek to maximize incomes of the total membership, which not all unions do, they will have to consider what effect such wage demands will have upon unit costs, unit selling prices, physical volume of sales and employment.

To find what wage rates, between the admittedly too low or too high, will be most advantageous to labor will tax the shrewdest judgment. The wage rates most advantageous to the employer are no easier to determine. An employer might suffer from rates so high that they would force an advance of selling prices sufficient to reduce sales drastically. Very low rates on the other hand cannot suit an employer who must get an adequate supply of competent labor in competition with other industries. Unfortunately sober analysis of common and conflicting interests is seldom the sole factor in collective bargaining on wages. Anger, obstinacy, personal ambition and politics—both union and party politics—sometimes have a large part in fixing demands and swaying the final decision.

Degree of Unemployment

THERE is disagreement and uncertainty, of course, as to the extent of postwar unemployment. Estimates have run as low as one million and as high as fifteen million. These conflicting estimates are bewildering unless one realizes that the "postwar period" will have many phases. There will be a period after "V-E" day, another after "V-J" day, and then the swing into full peacetime economy. Men now doing work that will continue in peace probably will be best off. Those engaged in work that ends with the war must change jobs and will be in a weaker position. One is often reminded of the conversation from "Alice in Wonderland."

"I don't see," said the Caterpillar.

"I'm afraid that I can't put it more clearly," Alice replied very politely, "for I can't understand it myself to begin with, and being so many different sizes in a day is very confusing."

The main problem of unemployment, of course, will arise when war production is virtually eliminated with the final termination of hostilities in Japan. At that time we shall have almost complete demobilization and reconversion. The measures instituted during the months following the defeat of Germany, however, will substantially affect the magnitude of the unemployment problem in the later period. Such measures may also determine a pattern for business, labor and government to follow in later months.

Social Policy Will Determine Labor Force

THE significance of our social policy will have much to do with the size of the total labor force, and consequently the unemployment residual. This is indicated by the possibility that several million withdrawals from the labor market might occur if we have a program of government subsidies for expanded educational opportunities, increased old age coverage and higher benefits, and more liberal family allowance or income tax reductions for dependents, thus making it possible for some women to return to the household who otherwise would not do so.

In some instances the reemployment of war workers in industries producing civilian goods will call for training. There is some expectancy that many industries producing war goods will return to production which will not utilize the single skills of many war workers. Many industries, and especially local plants of large industries which have shifted their operations during the war, may not return to the manufacture of prewar lines. A large segment of present-day workers may have to undertake less skilled work, or relocate where a single skill may be in demand, or be retrained in new skills needed by local industry.

Will Unions Disintegrate?

SOME personnel men feel that the period of transition and readjustment may also bring the disintegration of unions and a general decline in membership. I do not look for this to happen in the next four years. Let us keep in mind that, in the past, American labor has scored its greatest gains during the process of readjustment after great wars. Usually the prices of labor have declined less rapidly than the prices of commodities at retail. During postwar depressions the slighter fall of wage rates from wartime peaks, has been more than offset by large unemployment. But when business picked up again, the slow subsidence of wage rates compared with living costs has brought about a substantial rise in "real wages." Whether this bit of economic history will repeat itself after V-Day remains to be seen, but I am inclined to think it will.

Workers will certainly be reluctant to see their rates cut, and the strength of their unions will presumably be used to resist reductions. The labor argument is that "unemployment compensation" for corporations is a fixed fact under present legal procedure, while unemployment compensation for wage-earners during the reconversion period will be wholly inadequate. It seems certain that we may look for an even more militant attitude on the part of unions in the years just ahead and on just such points.

Labor leaders contrast the "human side of reconversion" with items of "depreciation," "obsolescence," "reserves," "tax refunds," and similar devices which they maintain the laws permit corporations to apply to their finances. Quite naturally they would like at least to maintain present wage standards, which they do not consider entirely adequate. Yet they are worried lest government and corporate policies may ignore their desires and needs.

Carry-over of War-time Policies

THERE is the strong probability that wartime developments in settling labor disputes may come to be almost folkways. We may be working under a new frame of reference that we do not yet recognize. It might be useful, therefore, to take stock of the practices which have come to be accepted in large part through War Labor Board sponsorship. Among the most important policies are:

(1) Equal pay for equal work regardless of sex, color, or race.
(2) Minimum wage rates to eliminate substandards of living.
(3) Maintenance of membership and its latent corollary of union responsibility.
(4) Job classifications and integrated wage rate schedules.
(5) Premium pay for shift work.
(6) Arbitration as the capstone of union-management relations.

Moreover, it requires no bold prophet to suggest that three other policies, already perceptible, might take on a more definite shape in the immediate future. These are: (1) extension of collective bargaining to include group insurance and employee benefit plans; (2) recognition of the right to collective bargaining an the part of organizations of supervisory employees; and (3) development of guaranteed annual wage plans.

Differentials Wiped Out

IT is clear to all of us, I am sure, that the economics of war have served to wipe out pay differentials as between men and women, or white and Negroes, who do the same work. Not only has this become national policy, but to an important extent—it has become national reality. It must be anticipated, therefore, that a movement to re-emphasize or re-establish differential pay will meet with considerable resistance. Hence, most personnel men take it for granted that equal pay for equal work is here to stay. If correct, this will doubtless be an important factor in personnel planning—influencing the composition of the postwar work forces. And plants that have been able to classify jobs in terms of "female jobs" and "male jobs" will soon have to give attention to a more realistic job classification and evaluation program. Likewise we must plan for better measures of work performance and efficiency.

In every War Labor Board award where the Union-management dispute involved the writing of a contract, the board has provided for the arbitration of unsettled grievances. In doing so it blazed no new trail, for many firms and unions have a long history of arbitration. But the Board has brought arbitration to every industry and type of enterprise in the land, and it has found arbitration to be among the least controversial of its standard recommendations. It seems certain, therefore, that in the future an employer will find little if any public support if he refuses to write an arbitration provision into the union contract.

Specific Problems

WISE planning for the handling of specific personnel problems in the years just ahead—especially at the time of war contract cutbacks and cancellations— is one of the major responsibilities of every personnel officer at this time. . Such personnel problems as the following will present themselves:

(1) Job priority to returning veterans. (Unions are far from reconciled to the absolute job priority given to veterans by the Selective Service Act.)

(2) Seniority in lay-offs and promotions, especially where an "ability" clause gives management discretionary rights in selecting employees for a lay-off, a re-hire, or promotion.

(3) Down-grading of employees and resulting reduction in their rates of pay.

(4) Lay-offs of employees belonging to minority groups. (Certain problems will also come when employees belonging to minority groups are retained because of "ability" or seniority.)

(5) Reduction of hours in work week with the consequent 20% cut (approximate) in take-out pay.

(6) Transfer of supervisors back to production work and the resulting squeeze on the seniority rights of production workers.

(7) Absorption and adjustment of returning war veterans. Some will come back with physical handicaps, others with mental and emotional maladjustments, some will be looking for the "big money" that war workers earned, others will have a "hero complex."

(8) Unionization of professional, white collar workers, and supervisory employees.

(9) Work loads and rate setting for efficient peacetime operations when there is sharp price competition.

(10) Fraudulent or questionable claims for workmen's compensation benefits at time of cut-backs and lay-offs.

Friction Can Be Reduced

I AM not so optimistic as to believe that friction, dispute and tension involving these situations can be entirely eliminated. They can be reduced and diluted by careful planning. Sound procedures must be worked out in advance for each situation. These must be properly implemented with accurate records and operating techniques. Employment estimates can be made, personnel policies can be clarified, procedures for lay-off and down-grading can be determined, jobs can be classified and evaluated. The importance of adequate and complete personnel records cannot be stressed too much.

Study of Jobs Available

A DETERMINATION of the jobs available in each plant or industry of course can be made by careful study of proposed production schedules. Such data and procedures as the following are needed.

1. Number of jobs that will be available after V-Day on the basis of planned civilian production and estimated war production.
   (a) By departments and job classifications within departments.
   (b) Total number of jobs available in all departments.
2. Number of employees who will be available.
   (a) Number of employees, if any, now working on civilian production . . . by departments and job classifications.
   (b) Number of employees now working on war production . . . by departments and job classifications.
   (c) Total number of employees available from all sources.
3. Comparison of the total number of jobs expected to be available with the total number of employees who will be available.
   (a) Re-examination of planned production and job creating possibilities if more people than jobs will be available after V-Day.
4. Number of jobs expected to be available after V-Day . . . by departments and job classifications . . . final determination.
5. Number of employees who will be transferred to civilian production and Number of employees expected to be surplus.

Serious study of current practices, policies and trends in the field of personnel management will make clear, however, that there are many constructive forces and influences at work. These are of varying value and import. None can be disassociated from the total social scene or from the climate of opinion in which personnel management lives and moves and has its being. It is obvious that, in the last few years, management has lost to government, and to a lesser degree to labor unions, the leadership of its employees. The older pattern of relationships between employer and employees has been challenged by a new philosophy imposed by public opinion and by Federal law. This represents a change in relationship that has tremendous significance and wide implications.

In the near future we may be seeing an entirely new responsibility pushed toward management, and in most instances, being intelligently accepted, namely, that one of the principle objectives of a business enterprise is to provide steady work opportunities for all employees. This, too, carries tremendous significance and many errors. "Full employment" is a phrase which postwar planners have been using to excess but it is ambiguous and cloudy in meaning.

A Labor Flat

In a recent Brooking's study concerned with national income, the author made the assumption that there would be a "reasonably full employment" in 1947. He then went on to point out that this would mean that "something like three million would normally not be working." Included in this large group would be "some unemployables, those out because of protracted illness, the seasonally unemployed, and those in the process of shifting from one job to another." It seems certain that there would be a "labor flat" due to such factors as those outlined above, even at times of maximum employment.

But a number of other questions might be raised in connection with the meaning of this term. Is full employment based upon a forty-hour week? Or, if there were substantial unemployment at that number of hours, would an attempt be made to secure "full employment" by reducing the working week to thirty-five hours or even less? Does full employment mean a worker at any job? Or does it mean that workers are located in those jobs where they can make their maximum contribution to production—and how can this be determined? Depending upon which of these two assumptions is made, the aggregate volume of production would be widely different and so would the real incomes of our people.

Are we to consider our labor force fully occupied if part of it is engaged in make-work projects, such as a new WPA? Would employment on extended public works projects be considered as desirable as work in private employment? Does full employment mean a job for everyone who wants to work? What about those persons who were past 40 before the war and who had difficulty obtaining jobs? Recently they have been considered as a welcome addition to our labor force. What about after the war?

Moreover, what time period shall be used to determine whether or not there is full employment? At certain times of the year there is a large volume of seasonal employment in agriculture, retail stores, textile trades and others. At other times many of these workers are unemployed or work only part time. Are we referring to the utilization of labor supply for a period of a year? If we are, what constitutes full utilization—fifty-two weeks, fifty weeks, or some lesser number?

"Full Employment" Wrong Term

In talking of "full employment" may we not be setting up a goal which is unattainable under a dynamic and progressive economy? How meaningful can this phrase be if at the same time it is believed that as many as 3,000,000 persons would still be unemployed? Would there not be many disappointments over the failure to achieve such a goal if people come to believe that it is attainable? These questions suggest the use of a more moderate description of our goals. A more usable and less misleading phrase might be "high level" or "maximum" or "optimum" employment, which would not give rise to the unrealistic conceptions concealed in the phrase "full" employment.

There are signs on every hand to indicate that industrial management has a broader, wiser, and more helpful concept of personnel problems and responsibilities than ever before. This gives us courage as we look to the years just ahead. Most of us see many difficulties but we also see great opportunities if intelligence and integrity give supporting strength to the work that falls to personnel and labor management.

Watershed of Social History

IN THE whole social scene, we seem to be moving toward a new era, the structure and functions of which are only faintly perceivable. It seems to be a period in which "human resources" will be counted at a much higher value in business and industrial life. In this era the industrial worker will move in a new sphere of importance and influence. He will have recognition and security beyond the dreams of earlier crusaders for social justice. We seem to be standing on one of the great watersheds of social history.

Certainly it is clear to the men in this audience that there is need for exercising sound judgment and for thoughtful planning as we build into the future. Prejudices and patterns of other years must be put aside quickly. Loose and flippant personnel work must go. The problems we face will demand something better than informal and careless methods of dealing with employment, placement, training, grievances, and wage rates. First rate methods and men are needed in this field! Personnel techniques, personnel policies, and the whole status of personnel administration must assume greater importance in the business and industrial world. Our work—now somewhat haphazard and confused in purpose and techniques—must be redesigned and must gradually be lifted to a higher level of professional competence and management acceptance.

We Know Little about Social Factors

SOMEDAY—and I think it will be soon—all industrial leaders will be stirred by the sharp realization that human factors in business and industry are more important than any others and that we know very little about them. Then they will face the fact that personnel administration must be provided with adequate support—financial and organizational—and that a new generation of men must be recruited for this work.

Now we realize that the "labor fixers" and "confidential consultants" who have tried to surround our work with an air of mystery and intrigue belong with the witch doctors. The bally-hoo artists and welfare workers, who have tried to make personnel work seem like a social service activity are "on the wrong bus".

Armed Truce Poor Aim

FORTHRIGHTNESS, realism, intelligence, competence, and a durable faith in man—these qualities belong to personnel management now and in the future. Our work is a professional service, set toward the best utilization and development of the human resources. It must not be regarded as simply a means for maintaining an armed truce, a channel for pious preachments or a program of sentimental welfare.

Our first task is to do all we can to help in the winning of this war—for freedom, for justice, for decency, for fair dealings with all men. And in the winning of that war to work also for the winning of a war within our own industrial organization—for freedom, for justice, for decency, and for fair dealings with all men. This may sound a bit idealistic but if we lose our reach toward the "things that exceed our grasp" we shall never learn how to be master craftsmen. With such faith—personnel problems after V-Day will be handled by men who see opportunities in difficulties—rather than difficulties in great opportunities.

From a talk before the Pittsburgh Personnel Association.

Management Has a Moral Responsibility in Dealing with the Health Problems of Employees. It Must Pay a Heavy Price if It Shirks This Responsibility.

Industrial Medicine

By J. J. WITTMER, M.D.
Consolidated Edison Company of New York
New York, N. Y.

IN ONE sense the electrical industry with which I am connected is as new as radar, that device by which, in the pitch-black dead of night our boys have sunk battleships beyond the range of the camera or the human eye. In another sense it is older than the Pyramids. The *art* of generating electricity, like the art of practicing medicine, constantly acquires new aspects, but the underlying principles remain unchanged. The year does not pass in which we are not startled by the invention of some new electrical device, or by a miracle-working advance in the practice of medicine. But the discovery of new laws, new principles, is not so simple. And I speak of principles because *it is only by the recognition of basic principles that management can discharge its responsibility for personal relationships.* It is only by a grim, steadfast adherence to *principles* that the industrial physician can discharge his responsibility to his employer, his patient and himself.

Moral Responsibility

I AM a doctor, not a sky-pilot, a physician, not a philosopher, a healer, not a preacher. But as a doctor, a physician, a healer, I believe that the industrial doctor shares with management a *moral* responsibility to society which is quite apart from material, economic or financial responsibility. Fortunately it is true that a man's success as an industrial doctor varies directly with his success as a practitioner of medicine. The more clearly he recognizes the moral nature of his obligation, the better he will serve the industry of which he is a part.

Actually, of course, there are no "industrial doctors," except in the sense that a doctor becomes competent to solve the medical problems that are inherent in industry. The best industrial doctor is simply the doctor who is most competent in the practice of medicine and has been able to apply his practice to the industrial field. The moment he forgets that fact he ceases to be a good industrial doctor. Similarly, the moment a corporation forgets that it has a moral obligation to discharge in the personal or medical care of its workers, it will start failing as a unit of industry.

You can shirk a duty. You can evade a responsibility. But you can no more avoid a moral responsibility without paying a price than a bare handed splicer can handle "hot" wires without a stinging, painful or mortal shock. I stress this point because I believe it is the heart of the problem of personal relationships in industry. Once an industrial executive, doctor, nurse or laboratory worker recognizes that he has a moral obligation to discharge, he has reached the halfway point in the solution of his personal or medical problem.

Electricity Not New

In the Consolidated Edison System we have what I am told is one of the most efficient electrical machines in the world. Extracting energy from tre mendously high pressure, high temperature, steam, it generates 50,000 kilowatts and then passes along to low pressure equipment steam which has still enough life in it to develop another 50,000 kilowatts which is enough energy to light a dozen Empire State buildings. Every possible refinement, such as the generator's hydrogen cooling system, is incorporated in this machine, which makes older units look like relics of the horse and buggy age. But the electrical principles on which that machine is based were not discovered this year, last year or the year before. They were enunciated by men of science more than a hundred years ago, or roughly half a century before electricity first lighted the sidewalks of New York.

Long before that electricity in some degree had been utilized or harnessed by mankind. Electric shock therapy made its appearance, not recently, but in the century before Christ, or earlier. Electric lightning bolts were first controlled in the most ancient times of which we have record. Thus the royal physician at the Court of Artaxerxes recorded experiments in which the Persian king, twenty-four hundred years ago, used iron swords to subdue the fury of electric thunder storms.

In our own time we have seen startling advances in medical practice but the beacon lights which should guide our progress were erected by prophets and philosophers centuries before Christ. As the evolution of society progresses we understand these beacon light principles more clearly but principles themselves remain unchanged. Thus the concept of the brotherhood of man was understood in Palestine long before the Christian era. I repeat, therefore, that whoever participates in management, whether executive, physician, or supervisor, must discharge moral responsibilities as well as regular routines.

Without treading on the toes of the private practitioner I may say that the industrial doctor occupies an advantageous position in his treatment of his patients. He is in a position to recommend diagnosis and treatment in many cases where the private physician is held back by the "pocketbook" aspect of the case. Thanks to his intimate connection with his corporation's supervisors he is in a position to know that a man's health is below par long before the patient's private physician is aware that he is sliding down.

Early Diagnosis and Treatment

I NEED not tell you that *early* diagnosis and *early* treatment afford the surest means of arresting or curing a physical or mental ailment. Not infrequently the *timing* of the diagnosis spells the difference between work or unemployment, health or sickness, life or death. In addition, the industrial physician in every instance should have the opportunity of recommending to his corporation's principal executives procedures which can go far toward improving employe health. I refer to procedures involving periodic examinations, medical department attention to absenteeism, medical approval of materials used by employes, etc. It is not only the industrial doctor's opportunity, it is his *duty* to advise management in matters relating to employe health.

Here we come to the nub of the question. Aside from a corporation's medical department, where does the responsibility for employe health rest? To say that it rests with "the supervisors" is not enough. Where a problem is charged to everyone it is handled effectively by no one. Let me say with all the fervency at my command that primarily management's responsibility rests with the corporation's principal officials—with board chairmen, presidents, vice presidents, and department heads. Only when they have recognized *their* responsibility, can we be sure that minor supervisors, down the line will discharge theirs. Make "management's responsibility" read "executive responsibility" and you have the answer to the problem of personal relationships. The private practitioner is not in constant touch with his patients, supervisors and executives. The industrial doctor has the golden opportunity of placing his views before them and seeking if not insisting upon their help in preserving employe health. Only in seizing this opportunity can the industrial doctor discharge his obligation to himself.

Relations with Superiors

THE help of supervisors, all the way down the ladder from president to section foreman, is indispensable to the physician seeking early diagnosis and early treatment of his employe-patients. It follows then that he must *know* the supervisors, become acquainted with them, obtain their confidence and "sell" them on the crucial importance of referring below-par workers to the medical department. One of the principal doctors in my own corporation recently spent three months in the field doing that very thing. To do their job competently industrial practitioners must have first-hand knowledge of conditions under which employes work. Through personal contacts they must obtain the confidence, the willingness of supervisors to "play ball" with them in watching over employes' health.

The more important a man's job is, the more he feels impelled to retire into an ivory tower and let "someone else" handle supervision questions. I am well aware that executives must delegate matters to their assistants, but the primary responsibility still rests with them. Ivory towers must be torn down if management is to do its job. They have no place in an industrial system which recognizes its moral responsibility for the well-being of its employes. Is this visionary? Impractical? Private enterprise will not survive if management does not recognize and discharge its moral as well as its material responsibilities.

The world owes no man a living but here in the United States, thank God, it owes every man the *opportunity* of making a living—and that is where private enterprise comes in, that is where management comes in, that is where we come in. It is our duty as executives, supervisors, personnel men and physicians, not just to hire and fire but to do our utmost to see that our employes' well-being is so preserved that they can do their work properly and discharge their obligations to themselves, their families and their community.

How Far Should We Go

How far should we go in our effort to preserve employe health? Is a preplacement examination enough or should we have the most elaborate medical set-up we can devise? Should we begrudge funds for this purpose or is the sky the limit? There is no rule-of-thumb answer to this question. Every industry and every corporation has its own needs and must find its own answers. Here again *executive* responsibility looms large for in every case the responsible executives advised by competent medical men, must determine the extent to which their corporate funds will be employed. The ceiling on expenditures for industrial medicine is reached when results equal costs—results in work-hours saved, improved job performance, loyalty, and a host of other advantages. Participation by employes in furnishing the funds is, in my opinion, not without advantages to industrial medical programs: An employe who helped pay his own way is freed from any "free clinic" thoughts which might injure his relations with the company and his respect for himself. Labor and management are partners—not servants and masters—in the conduct of private enterprise.

In planning its medical program management must remember that whatever spiritual endowments a man may have his body is a machine and must be treated as such. Like a machine—a boiler which must be taken out for overhaul—it runs down at times, develops squeaks, rust spots, sluggishness and the threat of breakdown if deterioration is not halted. Management must remember that the cost of helping men over their health hurdles is less than the cost of replacement. Put it crudely. If you lose your man you lose your investment in this man. Healthy bodies are just as necessary to industry as smoothly working machines for what good is the finest machine if you haven't a healthy man to run it. As I have suggested it is fortunate for all of us that the practical necessities of private enterprise run parallel to the procedures dictated by humanitarianism. ,

All Should Have Annual Examination

IF EARLY diagnosis and treatment is the surest way of preserving employe health, how can we be sure that timely diagnoses are being made? We can do this in two ways. First, by winning the confidence of supervisors, and selling them on sending below-par employes to the Medical Department for examination. Secondly by annual voluntary examinations—examinations for everybody, from top flight executives to rank and file workers. Especially should pressure be placed on supervisors to undergo annual examination. I say "especially supervisors" because the company has a larger investment in them than in the average employe; because a sick supervisor can raise cain with other employes; because by having himself examined the supervisor sets an example for others to follow. Furthermore I recommend a medical examination for anyone, executive or workman, who has more than three sick absences a year. Over a period of three years most of your employes will be covered in this way.

An industrial doctor who is working closely with supervisors will come in contact with employes who have started the down-hill slide. He will find out what is physically wrong, cure or arrest the troublesome condition and in many cases restore his patient to health. Vigilance is necessary for it is generally admitted that for every man absent from his job two other men are working at decreased efficiency because of a chronic or dormant medical condition. Thus men suffering from chronic nephritis, diabetes mellitus, generalized arteriosclerosis, chronic arthritis and anemia of various types over a period of years will gradually lose efficiency and finally break down. In many cases, the reduction of their efficiency can be halted and a final breakdown avoided by early diagnosis and care.

Returning Veterans

THE industrial doctor owes an even greater obligation to returning veterans than to employes who have not risked their health, their skins, their lives to save his. All returning veterans, without exception, face problems in readjusting themselves to their work, their families and their community, but returning veterans impose no medical problem which the industrial physician is not called upon to solve every day in the year. Peace as well as war produces broken bodies and broken minds. It is the physician's God-given opportunity to mend these injured bodies and mangled minds. War increases the responsibility but his technical problem is unchanged. Further I suggest that we discard thoughts of "post-war" problems. The end of the war has already come for veterans returning to our ranks. If there be a problem —and I see no special problem for physicians—it must be solved *now* not tomorrow. And God help the industry, corporation or doctor failing to go the limit in helping these returning boys. Here again moral obligations take precedence over the legal, financial or economic considerations involved.

From a paper presented at the Postgraduate Course in Industrial Medicine at the Long Island College of Medicine, Brooklyn, N. Y.

The Desired Objective is to Get the Employee to Work Out His Own Problems, To Think Independently and Objectively about His Difficulties and to Lead Him Toward Self-confidence and Self-guidance.

What *is* A Grievance?

By Schuyler Hoslett

Kansas City Quartermaster Depot
Kansas City, Mo.

M ANY organizations strictly differentiate between "personal" and "on-the-job" problems and the responsibility of counselors regarding each. Under this policy, the counselor is expected to give information on such matters as housing, transportation, and rationing and render a certain amount of assistance regarding personal problems originating outside the plant, referring the most difficult cases to outside agencies. But the solution of problems "directly connected with the job" is deemed a distinctly supervisory responsibility.

Job-Related Grievances

I F THE employee has a "job-related grievance," the procedure prescribes that he shall present it to his immediate supervisor for a decision as to adjustment. Should this decision be unacceptable to the employee, he may appeal it to progressively higher levels of management, reaching the top official for final decision in some cases. Thus, in large organizations, five or six levels of review may be involved. In all of this, the counselor has no official part to play.

The question immediately arises, "What is a problem 'directly connected with the job' or a 'job-related grievance?'" The need to work on a different shift because of home responsibilities, excessive absenteeism of a divorced man who is trying to rear his children alone, failure to get along with fellow workers because of nationality, dissatisfaction with wages because of extraordinary family demands—all these can be approached either as personal or job problems, in one case a suitable subject for discussion with the counselor, in the other strictly a supervisory responsibility.

Actually one does not know at the beginning of an interview just what the real problem is, if the difficulty is discovered through skillful counseling it may very likely be an amalgam of personal and on-the-job factors. Extremely important is the fact that when an employee comes to the counselor to discuss some non-work related problem there may be several important contributing factors in the background concerning supervisors, fellow employees, working conditions, or other aspects of organizational policy and control.

Aiding Employee to Work Out Own Problem

HERE may also be personal factors other than those stated by the employee which will be brought out in the course of the conversation, if the interview is well conducted. The employee himself may not be explicitly aware of these contributing factors until he is led to talk them out. Thus there is no simple dichotomy in initially distinguishing between personal and job factors—they are frequently interrelated and interacting.

The desired objective is, of course, to get the employee to work out his own problem, to think independently and objectively about his difficulties and to lead him toward self-confidence and self-guidance. This cannot be accomplished without giving the employee an opportunity to talk at some length about those things which trouble him, in the process of which he not only obtains some satisfaction through the catharsis provided, but begins to think through to his own plan of action.

In some instances the factors originally stated may even be unrelated to the real problem. Without a very "permissive" relationship, which may be difficult to develop in one or a few interviews, the employee tends to give the "easiest" answer for dissatisfaction rather than the "real" one. Regarding job grievances, for example, an employee may complain of poor lighting and ventilation when he is actually upset by his inability to get along with a supervisor generally well-liked by the other employees. Since it is more upsetting emotionally to reveal the latter fact, particularly since it seems to reflect on himself, he talks about more-or-less unrelated factors until led to make a more discerning evaluation.

Mixed Personal-Grievance Problems

UNDER the grievance policy outlined above, it is conceivable that employees might be criticized by supervisors for taking "mixed" personal-grievance problems to the counselors. At the same time the non-job related factors involved seem to give the counselor a legitimate interest in these problems. While management may attempt to state and publicize just what problems are to be taken to counselors, how can a written statement distinguish in advance between grievance and personal problems when the employees themselves cannot until they have had an opportunity to discuss them?

Perhaps the counselor has a useful function to perform in connection with "mixed" personal-grievance problems, as well as "pure" grievances. While it is not intended that a counselor be more than a staff aid to the operating official, the discussion of so-called grievances with employees and later with the supervisors concerned, perhaps in an objective manner without mentioning employee names, certainly does not overstep the line dividing the staff and operating responsibility.

Talking Grievances Out

IN ANY event, one observes a tendency for employees to bring grievance complaints to counselors. Where such action is contrary to a formal grievance procedure, theoretically the employee is referred immediately to his supervisor; yet it is just this opportunity for discussion with an "outsider" that the employee may most desire. If the counseling is first-rate, it is more effective for the counselor to talk to the employee about the grievance, discuss it later with the supervisor, and refer the employee to the supervisor for a decision, if required. Should the decision prove unacceptable to the employee, he might present the case to higher levels of review in the usual manner.

With effective counseling, this method eliminates some grievances at the start through "talking them out" and gives the supervisor the benefit of unbiased, professional advice, possibly tempering his decisions in particular cases and tending to improve his total performance.

The writer is indebted to Mr. Joseph Biter, Employee Counselor, Kansas City Quartermaster Depot, for some of the ideas used in this paper.

Book Reviews

Book Review Editor, Mr. Everett Van Every
California Council of Personnel Management, 442 Flood Building, San Francisco, 2, Cal.

TECHNOLOGISTS STAKE IN THE WAGNER ACT

Published by American Association of Engineers—Chicago 3. 1944. 260 pp.
$2.00

This is one of the courageous studies of our time. It shows the professional men—the engineers, chemists and architects—caught in a wave of organization frenzy, whipped by hysteria and yet faced with realism of economic and professional pressures.

Engineers and technical men have to eat. They want economic security, but they also want professional pride and personal prestige—and they want it conventionally in the manner that has come to be accepted as professional standards. But in recent years inroads have been made against these standards. Even radical, left-wing proposals have shocked the carefully sired professional heads, but shaking themselves, turning their packs or ignoring developments will not eliminate the liberal proponents. The labor organizer has picked the professions as fertile field—and he means to organize them solidly. The AFL and CIO have been carefully studying the technologists for many years—and this book is merely an awakening to the fact that they have been scrutinized, examined—if not hypnotized.

This thought-provoking study is not anti-union. It does not object to collective bargaining or the principles of unionism. And furthermore, what is not generally known, the American Association of Engineers was itself in its earlier days, a union in the strictest sense. Older engineers will remember those days, and few trade unions today are more aggressive organizers than those fellows who organized the engineers. But the influence changed after years of activity and the leadership of the American Association of Engineers swung around to conventional engineering ethics and standards—and that leadership prevails today. What this book pleads for is not a stand for or against unionism, but an awakening to how unionism, as sponsored by the National Labor Relations Act, affects engineers, chemists, and architects. If technical men do not throw off their apathetic and indifferent attitude to what can easily be a sudden surprise to many, they may someday find it necessary to carry a machinist's card before they can continue as an engineer or an architect. By way of assurance that we are not unduly alarmed, witness what has happened to pharmacy as a profession in many parts of the country. The professions are dotted with trade union conquests—nursing, pharmacy, engineering, chemistry, some medics and lawyers. The objection is not in collective bargaining of their own choosing—but rather in a kind of professional retreat that serves no good union purpose and defeats sound professional exercise and practice.

The book is an excellent study of how the National Labor Relations Board works. It shows by illustrative cases just how the Board defines "appropriate units", how it weighs the desires of workers for "autonomy", and how it appraises labor organizations that would represent workers in bargaining.

Various technical societies are considering plans to "organize" technologists in the manner prescribed by the Wagner Act. Quite definitely they do not intend to foist upon technologists the coercive tactics of bargaining that are an essential feature of the program of labor unions. When technical men are brought into heterogeneous labor unions their interests are not capably promoted. The technical engineering societies hope to substitute sponsorship for labor union representation, and institute methods of collective bargaining consistent with principles of professional conduct. This means, however, that such a plan must essentially look toward substantial improvement of the economic status of professional engineers, chemists, etc, or it will be considered an evasion of the Wagner Act.

Chapters are devoted to Scope of the Act, Discretion Vested in the Board, Concerning Representation, Desires of Employees, Employers Interference and Domination, Protection from Discrimination, The Appropriate Units, Selecting a Representative and The Actual Process of Bargaining.

This book is recommended to all engineering societies—and to all technical men. It should also be read by employers so they may understand the dilemma in which technologists now find themselves.

PERSONNEL
Journal

The Magazine of

LABOR RELATIONS AND PERSONNEL PRACTICES

Published by PERSONNEL RESEARCH FEDERATION

Lincoln Building, 60 East 42nd Street, New York City

Volume 23   *Number 10*

Contents for April 1945

Earnest Cooperation of Management, Labor, and
the Government and Public Response to the
Necessity for Action Will Make Possible Satisfactory Dealing with the Many New and Difficult Problems that Will Face the American
People.

Postwar Job *of* Employment Service

By Charles Farmer

United States Employment Service,
Washington, D. C.

THE United States Employment Service does not create jobs, but it will have an
extremely important function to perform after the war is over. Even in the
postwar planning, much valuable information is being provided from the Employment Service records and statistics on industrial and occupational trends and
other valuable labor market information.

Military officials, Congressmen, Government and private planning commissions, industrial and trade associations are carefully analyzing our experiences
during and after past wars in order to profit by the mistakes made then, and to define
the many problems to be solved in demobilization and the change from the manufacture of military supplies to civilian production. Plans are rapidly taking shape
for turning America's "G.I. Joe" back to plain John Doe and providing peace time
jobs for millions after the war is ended. All realize their responsibility for the
planned and orderly release of military personnel and their reorientation into civilian
life.

1500 *Local Offices*

IT is to be assumed that the United States Employment Service will carry a responsibility in staffing peace time industry, mercantile firms, and service establishments. New business establishments, both large and small, will spring up
all over the United States by the thousands and they will look to the United
States Employment Service for assistance in finding qualified workers. With a
chain of more than 1,500 offices located throughout the United States, the USES
will be the best source of available workers of all types.

The Problem

IT IS estimated that fifteen (15) million service men and women will return after the war, either to take up their old jobs, to find new work opportunities, or to enter schools to complete their education. Approximately twenty (20) million men and women now in war production jobs will eventually find that a shift to peace time employment is necessary if they wish to stay in the labor market.

It is assumed that many of the eighteen (18) million women workers will return to their duties of home and family, after rendering a very patriotic war service to their country. Thousands of older workers, who were retired but took up work again to aid in the war effort, will again retire from the active labor market. Other thousands of teen age youngsters and those in their early twenties will again resume their education after doing their bit in the war effort. A "Back to School" movement is expected and it will be encouraged by employers as well as school officials.

With these groups leaving the labor market the need for post-war jobs will be reduced somewhat; however, good authorities estimate that 55 to 60 million jobs must be provided if we are to have full employment after the war

The Adjustment Period

IT IS to be assumed that after the defeat of Germany there will be a considerable cutback in production of some war materials. Since we do not know when Germany will quit, it is impossible to plan definitely for the change to civilian production to off-set all unemployment caused by necessary time for retooling and plant changes. Sufficient war production must continue to guarantee swift and sure victory over Japan. The period between the two victories will be one of trials for personnel officers. As victory approaches, turnover tends to increase. Even talk of planning for civilian production has caused increased turnover in the war essential plants. The urge for a change from a war job to a berth in civilian employment will be even greater after Germany's surrender—yet the ship yards, the munition and aircraft plants must be staffed. We must finish the job and bring Japan as well as Germany to her knees.

Contact Centers for Millions Covered by Social Security

WITH the proposed expansion of the Social Security Program, practically all of the working population will likely be covered. This will mean that perhaps 55 to 60 million or more workers will come under this program. It does not mean that 60 million people will be registered with the employment service for jobs. It does mean, however, that the majority of the unemployed who are employable, will have an application at their United States Employment Service Office in order to qualify for Unemployment Compensation benefits. The Unemployment Compensation law requires that all claimants for U.C. benefits be registered for employment.

With the proposed expanded Social Security Program in effect, it would mean that practically all able-bodied men and women who were unemployed and eligible for Unemployment Compensation benefits and who wanted to find jobs would have their work experience, educational background and capacities for various types of employment, carefully recorded and on file with their local employment offices. This information is available to employers needing workers.

Objectives of the United States Employment Service

THE main objectives of the Employment Service will be:

1. To provide fully effective employment service facilities such as recording the work abilities of applicants, placement of workers, counseling, and employment information in all communities.
2. To facilitate prompt re-employment of demobilized veterans and war workers displaced as a result of production cutbacks.
3. To facilitate the transfer of workers from labor surplus to labor shortage areas.
4. To provide statistics on employment opportunities and labor supply which can be used in national, state and local planning.

Organized Functions in Local Offices

EACH of the 1,500 local United States Employment Offices in the country is organized to meet the needs of the community it serves. All offices have uniform procedure for gathering labor market information, such as industrial and occnpational trends, statistics on the number of unemployed, work abilities of registrants by occupation, statistics on veterans employment, handicapped workers, and agricultural workers. While general policy is set from Washington, sufficient leeway is allowed states and local communities to permit their offices to function to meet the needs of the community. A small three to five man office may be sufficient to meet adequately the needs of a rural community in a county seat town, while a metropolitan center such as New York City may need fifteen offices with a personnel of 1,200 to 1,500. Most offices in metropolitan centers and even in cities of 100,000 are organized to allow for specialization of functions.

Interviewers are selected on the basis of training and experience to deal with specific occupational or industrial groups of workers. Likewise placement officers are selected to deal with specific employers because of their familiarity with certain industrial fields of employment. In some cities complete offices are set up to service special industrial or occupational groups of workers.

Regardless of the type of office most of them will provide the following services:

Reception and Registration of Applicants

ALL offices will provide general information to callers at the desk or counter. Persons seeking employment will be directed to the proper section or interviewer where a complete and accurate work application will be taken. This application will contain identifying information, information on age, height, weight, physical fitness, educational background, work experience with details as to specific job duties, wages received and length of service on each job the applicant has held during the past few years. The application card will be coded occupationally and filed or made immediately available to the placement officers.

The occupational file of applicants available for employment is kept active by moving the card from the active to the inactive file when an applicant is placed in employment or when he notifies the office that he has found employment or fails to respond to a call-in card or phone call to discuss employment. It is moved back to the active when he is seeking work.

Files are maintained on an occupational basis, behind guides indicating the occupations by codes. By use of this system it is possible to locate any available workers in a specific occupation instantly and to evaluate the abilities of each for a specific employer's job order.

Selection and Placement of Workers

LOCAL offices will attempt to supply workers to all types of production, commercial and service establishments as well as workers for domestic and personal service.

Placements will be made on an individualized selection basis of workers in jobs suited to their particular experience, abilities and interests.

Employers as well as workers will be encouraged to use the employment service facilities on a voluntary basis.

Field contracts will be made by placement officers to employer's establishments to study their needs, to secure orders and to build up good working relationships Studies of specific "hard to fill" jobs will be made and a real intelligent effort made to meet the employer's requirements.

Technical Assistance to Industry

THE local offices will be equipped in most cases to provide technical assistance to industry in establishing in-plant training and in installing and improving employee selection techniques.

All offices use a standard occupational dictionary. The dictionary contains brief descriptions and codes for approximately 30,000 job titles in many different industries. The use of this dictionary by all United States Employment Service offices, numerous government agencies and many private employers makes possible uniform understanding of job requirements on a nationwide basis.

It is not uncommon for employers to use the codes and job descriptions from the dictionary in ordering workers. This necessitates a complete analysis of the jobs in their plants setting up codes for each occupation as indicated in the dictionary of occupational titles. An order to the Employment Service set up on this basis assures complete understanding of the duties to be performed and needs only individual requirements, wages, etc. to be complete. Many United States Employment Service offices will be glad to lend an analyst to assist an employer in such a study which is mutually helpful and leads to improved service because of valid information on each order.

Employment Information and Counseling Service

LOCAL offices will provide a greatly expanded employment information and counseling service both to veterans and non-veterans. Considerable emphasis will probably be placed upon facilitating transfers across occupational, industrial, and geographical lines.

Tools for Service

THE local offices will utilize many tools developed by the Headquarters Occupational Analysis Division. These include Job Analyses, Job Families, Occupational Dictionary of Job Titles, Batteries of Aptitude Tests, and Area and Industry Statements on Labor Market Information, Army and Navy Aides for Conversion of Military Experience to Civilian Occupations.

The Area Statements present in summary form, labor market information pertaining to the principle employment centers of the country. The summaries are designed to serve only as a broad guide to employment opportunities in which non-resident veterans and war workers might display an interest and is intended for use of the personnel of the United States Employment Service in their counseling and placement activities. The statements indicate the nature of the local industries, the number of jobs expected to develop, the occupations in which openings are immediately available, entry wages and scheduled hours of work, as well as the names of major firms in various areas of the United States. Additional information is also provided on the general housing and living conditions in each area.

The Industry Statements present in summary form basic descriptive and labor market information pertaining to a number of major industries. They are designed to assist local office personnel in the counseling functions. The local office program will attempt to guide workers between labor market areas and to prevent aimless shifting into areas where no employment is available.

Counseling Service

THE local offices will undertake a service program of counseling for occupational adjustment. This service will be available to all who have need for it, whether veterans or non-veterans, and including inexperienced, overage, technologically displaced, and physically handicapped workers. The service will assist the worker to discover, analyze, and evaluate his potential abilities and interests; to relate them to the requirements of occupations and to the demand for workers in such occupations, to formulate a plan for training or work experience or both, and to adjust to unfamiliar training or work experience.

The physical capacities of handicapped workers, and the physical demands of jobs which the workers may perform will be related to each other for satisfactory placement of handicapped workers.

Approved batteries of aptitude tests will be available in local offices and will be administered in connection with counseling and placement programs.

Clearance from Surplus to Shortage Areas

ONE of the prime services supplied by the United States Employment Service is that of facilitating the transfer of workers from labor surplus to labor shortage areas.

Through knowledge gained from labor market information on a nation-wide basis, definite areas or communities have been designated as labor surplus areas and others, where the need for workers is much greater than the supply, as labor shortage areas. Through the nation-wide chain of employment offices, the exact needs for workers in these shortage areas have been made known. Orders for workers to meet the needs were spread to the labor surplus areas.

Hundreds of thousands of workers with a wide variety of skills have been recruited and transported to shipyards, aircraft plants, munition plants and vast construction projects. Without this machinery for making known where workers were needed, the skills needed, and where pools of labor could be located, the war effort would have been greatly retarded. Information was not only furnished as to the need for and location of workers, but also, information regarding working conditions on the job, living conditions, housing, living costs, hours of work, wages, and permanency of the work, was made known by the interchange of information through the United States Employment Service offices.

Pools of workers were recruited by the employment office personnel in widely scattered labor surplus areas. Employer representatives interviewed, weeded out, and hired them on the spot in the local employment offices. Transportation and meals in transit were arranged and workers were rushed to war essential jobs.

This same type of clearance of information on available jobs and where workers may be found will be available to both employers and workers after the war. Many job seekers may be stranded in over-crowded war production centers and will need information as to the availability of jobs in civilian plants. Fruitless, costly wandering in search of employment can be prevented through proper use of the clearance facilities of the chain of United States Employment Service offices.

Special Service to Veterans

Facing the problem of assisting thousands of world war veterans who return to civilian life each month, the United States Employment Service has established a special veterans counseling and placement service in offices throughout the country. The employment service has especially trained personnel in its offices whose duty it is to see that veterans are given special attention in regard to counseling, registration and placement. Veterans applying at local employment offices for jobs may need the services that other agencies can give them before they are prepared to make a choice of occupation or to enter into the occupation of their choice. To assist the veteran to recognize this need and to direct him to the proper agency is one of the responsibilities of local office personnel serving veterans.

Many veterans ask for information not directly related to employment and they are directed to the proper agency to obtain the information. A complete list of organizations in the community which may render any service to veterans is usually maintained in the local employment office together with exact locations, phone numbers and services offered. The policy is to call and make definite arrangements before a veteran is referred for service or advice. This avoids much inconvenience and waiting time. Close cooperation is maintained with all veteran service agencies in order that office personnel may be kept up to date and qualified to advise veterans.

The applications for work and the placement of veterans on jobs are steadily increasing month after month. Figures from Headquarters office of the United States Employment Service indicate that for the month of September 1944 ,a total of 91,276 work applications were taken on veterans in United States Employment Service, offices throughout the country. Placements for the month totaled 80,444 including 12,492 placements of disabled veterans. In addition to the veterans placed, 7,573 were directed to the Veterans Administration for service; 1,667 were directed to State Vocational Rehabilitation agencies; 1,372 to the Selective Service System; 1,473 to training agencies and 8,796 to various other agencies for service.

Handicapped Workers

Studies of occupations for the handicapped, begun by the United States Employment Service several years ago, have been continued. Offices are now better equipped to aid the handicapped worker than ever before. During the past few years a new technique has been developed—selective placement. Designed specifically for the placement of the handicapped, it has been tried and proved to be sound and efficient. It is based on a careful analysis of the physical requirements of a job, an appraisal of the physical capacities of the handicapped worker, and a matching of the two. The result is a productive, safe placement.

Because of the huge wartime demand for workers, and because of the ever-mounting number of disabled veterans and civilian workers, the public has become increasingly aware of the necessity for finding suitable employment for the handi-capped. The task is two-fold: to have jobs available for such workers, and to place workers in the jobs. The first is the responsibility of industry; employers must be able and willing to supply the jobs and to hire handicapped workers on the basis of their skills and capacities. The second is the responsibility of the United States Employment Service, to know where the jobs are and how to select and place handicapped workers in them successfully, so that they become productive wage earners. The employment service offices in most cities have especially trained personnel who know the selective placement technique and how to apply it to bring about satisfactory placement of handicapped workers.

The placement of disabled persons both veteran and civilian, has recently reached a high peak. According to reports from Headquarters office of the United States Employment Service, the placement of disabled persons in September 1944 was 40.6% over the month of August 1944. This increase in placement was attributed to new techniques being used to fit such persons for jobs and a series of recent con-ferences, sponsored by the United States Employment Service offices, at which co-operation of industrial, commercial and service employers was enlisted.

Strong Employment Service Needed

A STRONG and effective public employment service is a necessity if the gradual demobilization and reconversion of the war economy is to be accomplished with minimum dislocation and suffering. A nation-wide public employment sys-tem will have to carry the load in providing job information for veterans and war workers, in preventing the development of stranded areas, in contributing to the enormous training and retraining program required for transferring veterans and war workers to useful peace-time occupations.

The task of the Employment Service in the transition period is reasonably clear. First, it must serve as a labor exchange. Second, it has a large responsibility for job counseling. Third, it must assemble basic information on occupations and labor demand. Finally, it must operate nation-wide clearance machinery to facili-tate the transfer of workers.

Reproduced with permission from the Official Publication of the Society for Personnel Administration—"Personnel Administration."

The Fact Must be Faced that Unions Are Not
in Business to be Reasonable. Since a Great
Number of Employees Probably Always Will
Consider Themselves Down-Trodden, Any Labor
Leader that Becomes Too Friendly With Man-
agement Will Soon Be Out of a Job.

Labor Relations Code

By Richard H. Wood

Princeton, N. J.

Although it has become obvious that organized labor is a power that must be reckoned with, there still appears to be considerable confusion in the minds of many management representatives concerning how to deal with this power. The purpose of this article is to suggest a foundation upon which management may build satisfactory relations with its employees in general, as well as with their union representatives, if any.

Hitting the Saw-dust Trail

Two things should be emphasized at the outset of this discussion. First, by "satisfactory" labor relations is meant not only pleasant relations, but also relations which, over a period of time, will be worth attaining purely as "good business". The tremendous power of organized labor can be used to impair seriously the earning power of even the strongest company, especially through the use of strikes and slowdowns. Conversely, the influence of labor leaders can be very constructive in the matter of having disputes settled peacefully. The approach to labor relations suggested in this discussion is designed to promote the use of labor's power toward constructive rather than destructive ends.

In the second place, satisfactory relations with employees or their representatives can be built only over a period of time. Sound labor relations consist not of sudden fine pronouncements nor of other similar forms of hitting the saw-dust trail, but of day-to-day dealings, over a period of time, in which representatives of management and labor learn to treat one another as they, themselves, would like to be treated.

Where mutual trust between the parties is lacking, management, because of its position of leadership, should clearly make the first overtures toward peace. It should not be expected, however, that such overtures will produce immediate and lasting results. Employees do not soon forget the slights and wrongs which they have suffered over a period of years. There follows a check list against which management may test its labor policies:

Fairness

THE first suggestion is that management must be scrupulously fair in its dealings with labor. It has been said that peace grows only in the soil of justice. While, of necessity, the ruthless cutting of wage rates is becoming a thing of the past, does the company still "chisel" whenever it gets a chance? This usually turns out to have been penny wise but pound foolish when the slowdown or strike is over.

Does management interpret its contract with the union in a fair and liberal (not soft) manner, or does it perform legal ju jitsu on the words of the contract when in a tight spot? If so, the union soon turns up with yet a smarter lawyer. The very great emphasis which unions generally place on seniority can be traced very largely to the fact that the promotion, demotion, lay-off, and re-hiring practices of industry have been, either willfully or because of neglect, far from fair. This emphasis on seniority is becoming a serious threat to the efficiency of many business concerns. The causes and results of the current trade union attitude toward seniority should be pondered by those who still doubt that it is "good business" to be fair in dealing with labor.

Frankness

NO DEMOCRACY, much less the "Industrial Democracy" prevalent in industry to-day, can function properly unless all interested parties have the facts. The reason for this is that democracy, if it is to achieve its best results, must be based on cooperation; and people tend to cooperate to the extent that they participate. Unless management treats its employees and their representatives as though they are trustworthy, those representatives will not be trustworthy, and their power will tend to be used destructively. Does management make a guessing game of its dealings with the union? If so, the union will fear the worst, and often do the worst. Does the company tell its employees that it cannot afford to give them a wage increase, while refusing to let their representatives examine its income accounts?

There are two important truths which must be taught to employees, in the interests of all concerned. The first of these is that a company which is in competition with other companies must keep its prices competitive if it is to stay in business, and if it is to continue to provide jobs for its employees. The second of these truths is that bankruptcy will eventually overtake that firm which is unable to keep its costs, including its labor costs, from getting very far above those of its competitors.

But how on earth can any company expect its employees to believe that their jobs will be threatened by a wage increase unless the facts are on the table? Labor may very well wreck much of industry, to its own detriment, as well as to the detriment of the community as a whole, unless labor is shown, frankly, what it is doing. It would appear that the trend toward full and frank disclosure to employees of the facts of corporate life is bound to grow. Meanwhile, the less spectacular every day problems of industrial relations will, for similar reasons, be solved with less waste to all concerned if management will give to the representatives of its employees the reasons for its actions, with perfect frankness.

Firmness

ONE of the least productive things management can do when dealing with labor is to indulge in "chest-beating" regarding "Management's prerogatives". However, when the representatives of management are sure that their position is fair, and when they have been frank with their employees concerning the reasons for taking a particular stand, lack of firmness can be disastrous. This is not to say that management should be so inflexible that it closes its eyes and ears to any new evidence that may be presented by the union; or that it refuses to make a counter-offer where it is discovered that there is some merit in the union's demands.

However, it does mean that management cannot afford to let itself be "pushed around", or it will cease to be respected. Labor leaders are often forced to make demands which they know should not be granted, but which they have been forced to make by some of their unreasonable brethren. For example, when a work stoppage has occurred (often in spite of the best efforts of the union leadership), and the union, under pressure, is forced to put on a "show" in demanding that the strikers be paid for the time they refused to work, does the company give in? If so, not only does the management lose prestige in the eyes of its employees, but it greatly reduces the power of the union to prevent strikes in the future, since striking in such a case tends to become a "heads I win, tails you lose" proposition.

Does the management agree to "mutual consent" arrangements with the union in matters where efficiency demands prompt action at all times? If so, instead of being able to take necessary action in a crisis, the company may find its hands tied. It is to the interest of all concerned that management handle its labor relations with a firm hand.

Treating Employees Like Human Beings

UP TO this point we have been concerned very largely with a discussion of how management representatives should approach the problem of dealing with the representatives of their employees. However, if a reasonable attitude is to be promoted in collective bargaining, the great majority of employees in the plant must feel that they are being treated like human beings. Without this background, relatively reasonable employee representatives are likely to be replaced, before long, by less reasonable individuals.

Does the company's promotion policy give the employees an incentive to do a good job in order to advance themselves? Is the very fundamental human desire for security also given adequate consideration? Is every effort being made to combat the boredom so likely to result from the routine processes of modern industry? For example, is it thoroughly explained to employees what they are doing, and why they are doing it? Also, are employees given a pat on the back when they have done a good job?

Industrial relations is primarily human relations, and any company which thinks of its employees as anything less than human beings simply will not be able to raise the efficiency of the organization above the level of mediocrity.

Not in Business to be Reasonable

ONE approach to industrial relations which has been proposed to this discussion obviously will not end all of management's labor difficulties. The fact must be faced that unions are not in business to be reasonable. Since a great number of employees probably always will consider themselves down-trodden, any labor leader who becomes too friendly with management will soon be out of a job.

If we face the facts, therefore, management's job in many cases is to make the best of a bad situation. Any well-conceived attempt on its part to better the situation, however, may be viewed as a means of self-preservation. Business must learn to cooperate with the power of organized labor if the present structure of capitalism in the United States is to survive at all.

Collective Reasoning

THERE is one especially good reason for believing that this attempt can be increasingly successful, provided management acts wisely. "Collective Bargaining", in the great majority of cases, can really be Collective Reasoning. By far the greater part of the time spent by management in dealing with employee representatives does not, or at least should not involve "horse trading". On the contrary, the proper solutions to the every day problems of industrial relations are beneficial to both parties.

Even in negotiations over new contracts or general wage increases, which appear on the surface to involve wide differences between the parties, the interests of management and labor are very largely mutual. Both parties are benefited by a high and steady level of production because this would tend to bring with it high and steady employment, high real wages, lower costs of production, and general business prosperity.

The best way to put this mutuality of interest to constructive use is for management to make every effort to promote a reasonable attitude on the part of its employees and their representatives, while preserving the functions which it must retain for the good of all concerned. These objectives can best be attained if management is fair and frank, yet firm, in its dealings with labor; and if employees and their representatives are treated like human beings.

How Many Americans, a Branch of the RFC
Asked, Could Not Only Speak Burmese, but
also the Dialects of Eastern India, the Shan
States, and Assorted Hill Tribes of that Theater
of War? Sixteen Were Found.

Talent
Tabulators

By Cyrus Tanner

Toronto, Canada

T HE "turn of a card" gave America half a million key men to help her win
the war.
These cards have nothing to do with games of chance. Quite the contrary;
their function is to eliminate the possibility of chance, to choose from 130,000,000
people the comparatively small handful with special skills, queer distinctions, individual abilities needed for particular jobs which nobody else could do quite as
well.

French with a Southern Accent

F OR example, several weeks before the Americans clinched the Allied foothold
on the western invasion by landing in force and unexpectedly in the Riviera,
the United States Office of Strategic Services needed a number of Americans who
spoke French with a "southern accent"—southern French—idiomatically enough to
avoid suspicion. Apart from that, the only special qualifications needed were the
ability to operate a radio sending-and-receiving set expertly, to repair their equipment with spare parts consisting of old tin cans and rusty nails—and the courage to
risk summary execution if caught by the enemy.

Strategic Services took their requirements to the National Roster of Scientific
and Specialized Personnel, the "alma mater" of special operatives. Within half
an hour, the names and addresses of a dozen who fitted the exacting requirements—
some of them doubtlessly socialite playboys of former days who knew the battle-
ground as the "cote d'azur," were furnished.

—375—

How? Not, it must be admitted, by any occult, mysterious or even faintly romantic method of search. It was a purely mechanical—and therefore exact—transaction. Chief asset of the National Roster is a large battery of mechanical "thinking gadgets" which delve into the impersonal history of thousands of men and women possessed of special capabilities, and come up with the right one every time!

Census of Specialists

HERE's how it works: Many months ago, America took a special census of her specialists in every field. No facility, no accomplishment, no experience, the questionnaires insisted, were too trivial or too fantastic to be mentioned. Every one of these was noted on a special card. So today, when the army, navy, air force, a war industry or essential business makes a special request, all that the National Roster has to do is "run through" their half million cards and sift out the best candidates for the job.

The "machines with brains" do the work. Every card has a number of punched perforations indicating each special qualification. When the cards are run through a bank of machines, the requirements which the machines are set to "detect" are segregated.

From their very nature, most of the requests made of National Roster are queer. One, for example, was for a "cement structure expert who speaks the major Hindu dialects, knows something about public health measures to combat epidemics, and has lived in the Far East."

With no more clues, it is not difficult to deduce the nature of the job for which such a man was needed. Or is it? Then there was the War Department's demand for "an American who is an expert in flood control, is between 40 and 50 years of age, is accustomed to handling native labor, and has a working knowledge of soil analysis."

The machines rattled over these non sequiturs without a murmur, and emerged with more than one such paragon among versatile specialists.

Physician with Knowlege of Slavic

SOME of the functions of these mechanical classifiers of specialists are far removed from war, and hence give an idea of the value of these machines in postwar life. For example, when a epidemic broke out among Eskimo and Indian workers on an Arctic island where a United States air base was being built, the National Roster found the right man in time to bundle him aboard the next air liner to a Pacific coast terminal where he was transferred to an army plane bound for the island.

Could a physician be found in America who had a working knowledge of Slavic languages? The office of Strategic Services needing a few to work in the Baltic underground, asked the question none too hopefully. The Roster's educated machines probed among its cards—and produced no fewer than 11.

Equally outlandish was the query of the Office of Economic Warfare for a couple of agriculturists who knew both the language and the flora of certain Pacific islands freed by American forces. Their fields and crops destroyed by battle, the islanders needed quick and expert aid if they were to become immediately self-supporting.

Service for Burma

How many Americans, a branch of the Reconstruction Finance Corporation asked timidly, could not only speak Burmese, but the dialects of Eastern India, the Shan states, and assorted hill tribes of all that embattled theater of war?

"Sixteen," replied the searching fingers of the Roster's machines.

When one of the fighting services or government departments is not keeping Roster's machines busy, their "keepers," under the direction of George A. Works, former dean of students at the University of Chicago, practice "trial runs" of qualifications which will be most in demand immediately after the war. Already two "job studies" have been completed, one of chemists and the other of chemical engineers, and now the machines are doing spare-time work on agricultural scientists.

Postwar Value

When the last "left-handed physio-therapist who speaks Tamil fluently and is immune to sunburn" returns to America and returns to his normal occupation in a small-town hospital, the Roster's battery of super-human machines will not shut up shop. Re-converted industry is expected to be the Roster's biggest peacetime customer, along with higher education authorities.

Postwar demand for specialists will be high, and tens of thousands of trained experts in scores of skills and sciences will be released by the army and navy. During the demobilization and rehabilitation period, industry will find it of great advantage to utilize Roster facilities to find the right person to fill the right job.

"I Do Not Expect to Suggest Anything Very New To You. Everything that Can Be Said About Supervision Has Been Said Before. But There Are Some Things We Know that We Need to be Reminded of Frequently."

Self-analysis Check List

By Rowland English

University of Wisconsin
Madison, Wis.

M EN and women, rather than methods and machines, make the most difficult problems in an office. It takes a long time to select, train, transfer, and promote employees and to build up a good organization—a group of people who are well-adjusted to each other, who work efficiently, and whose morale is high. Keeping such an organization running smoothly is the never-ending task of the office manager and the supervisors.

Filing Under Miscellaneous

E VEN the newspaper cartoonists have discovered the beautiful but stupid little file clerk who files nearly everything under Miscellaneous and the flippant little stenographer who does not know much about punctuation or punctuality. Neither seems very important to her; in fact, she does not seem to know the difference between the two.

The cartoonists have not discovered, but you and I are well aware of, the conscientious worker who does everything well, but who is supersensitive, whose feathers are easily ruffled, who constantly has the mistaken idea that his supervisor and his fellow workers "have it in for" him. Each employee poses an individual problem.

People cause most of our headaches in an office. Yet the biggest problem that we have with people is with *ourselves*. Do we give enough attention to this problem? Can we not profitably spend more time in self-analysis?

If I were an office manager or supervisor, I would ask myself a number of searching questions. I would try to see myself as others see me.

In raising such questions, I do not expect to suggest anything that is new to you. Everything that can be said about supervision has been said before—and doubtless has been said better than I shall say it. But there are some things we know that we need to be reminded of frequently.

Giving Recognition to Employees

EVERY worker wants recognition. He wants to be treated considerately. He wants to have his supervisor show an interest in him and in the work he is doing. When the supervisor caters to these wants, it gives the employee a sense of importance. It raises his morale. So I would ask myself these questions:

Do I know each employee by name? Do I greet him pleasantly? Is my attitude toward him always friendly, without being too familiar? Do I know what training and experience he has had? Do I know his hopes and ambitions? Do I study his capacities and interests? Do I try to place him where he will be most useful and most satisfied? Do I see that he gets the training he needs? Do I show a genuine interest in his work and in the progress that he is making? Do I stimulate him to put forth his best efforts?

Do I encourage him to ask questions and to come to me with his problems—not only problems arising in his work, but his personal problems as well? Do I invite him to make suggestions for improving methods, cutting costs, raising quality, and bettering working conditions? Do I introduce each new man to his fellow workers, make him feel at home, and get started right? Do I lead my men, or do I try to drive them?

Giving Orders Properly

ORDERS will not be followed correctly unless they are properly given. So I would ask myself:

Are my orders crystal clear, and are they complete? They should be definite, and they should leave nothing to the imagination. I should not expect the worker to be a mind reader.

Do I give my orders slowly and distinctly enough to make them sink in? Otherwise, even though the instructions are clear and complete, they will not be understood. When in doubt as to whether orders are understood, it is a good idea to ask the employee to repeat them.

Do I give my orders in a courteous and considerate manner, or am I too dictatotial? In an emergency when things have to be done in a hurry, a direct order is appropriate—such as, "Hold it!" But when there is more time, an indirect order often gets better results. People resent being "shoved around". They will do their work more cheerfully and co-operatively if orders are given tactfully.   For example, we may say:

"Will you ask Mr. Jones to come in."
"I wish you would take this to the Purchasing Department, Mary."
"Please see why this machine isn't spacing properly, George."
"Could you complete this report by Monday night, Miss Smith?"

Explaining Why

WHEN I tell a worker *what* to do on an unfamiliar job, do I also tell him *why* it needs to be done, and why it should be done the standard way?

Telling why takes time, but it saves time in the long run.   The worker who knows why is more interested in what he is doing, takes more pride in his work, works more intelligently, and is less inclined to "cut corners".   If, for example, a clerk is making out a form in triplicate, the extra sheets seem to him like unnecessary "red tape".   If he smears up the carbon copies with erasures, leaving them rather illegible, he does not see why that should make much difference.   But if he knows to whom each copy goes and why it is needed, that puts things in a different light.   He sees a reason for doing the work accurately and neatly.

Praising Judiciously

PRAISE is one of the most effective tools that the supervisor has, if he uses it judiciously.   Consequently, I would ask myself:

Do I fully realize that my employees will put forth greater effort and do better work if I give them praise when they deserve it?   Do I realize that I have fallen down as a supervisor if the employees say, "You never hear from him except when something goes wrong"?   Do I want praise?   Praise should not be given too freely.   It should never be given insincerely.   It should be given when a man has done something especially well or has accomplished a hard job.

Do I praise a man in the presence of others, as a general rule?   Praising a man publicly builds up his self-confidence.   Moreover, it makes other workers want to earn similar recognition.   Occasionally, a man may be found who has to be handled differently because he has such an inflated ego that public praise goes to his head. He should be praised sparingly, and in private.   When commending him for something that he has done especially well, the supervisor can point out something else he has done that failed to come up to expectations.   If he is still too conceited, it may be a good idea to give him a difficult assignment that he cannot handle without the supervisor's help.

Criticizing Constructively

CRITICISM should be given fairly and constructively.   So I would ask myself these questions:

Do I criticize a worker only when he deserves it, and after I have obtained all the facts?

Were the orders that I gave him clear and complete?
Did he understand them?
Was he capable of carrying out the orders, or did I expect too much of him?
Did he carry out the orders?

What does he have to say for himself? An employee should always be questioned and given a fair hearing before he is criticized. Suppose, for example, that I have instructed my assistant to have a report typed by Friday afternoon. The deadline has been passed, and the report has apparently not been completed. If I were to criticize him for his apparent failure to carry out my orders, without first questioning him, I might learn, to my embarrassment, that the criticism was undeserved. Is it not better, then, first to ask him, "You remember that I asked you to have that report on the P-34 parts ready by this afternoon? Have you completed it?" His reply may be, "Yes, it is on your desk," or he may say, "Yes, I remember that you did, but I understood you to say afterwards that I should finish the report on the B-24's first."

Do I always make my criticism constructive? Do I show the worker how to improve, or do I merely find fault? Do I criticize in a straightforward manner, or do I "beat around the bush"? Do I remember that the main purpose of discipline is not to punish the worker—although punishment may be necessary—but to prevent a recurrence of the mistake? My aim should be to get the worker to do what I want him to do and to avoid doing what I do not want him to do.

Do I, whenever possible, accompany criticism with some words of praise? If, when I criticize a worker's mistake, I commend his general good record or praise him for having done some task unusually well, he realizes that I am fair—that I recognize his good points as well as his weaknesses. Instead of feeling beaten and resentful, he will be anxious to improve. Do I cool off before I criticize, and control my temper while talking to the employee? Do I realize that if I criticize angrily I shall defeat the purpose of the interview?

Do I give criticism in private? A public reprimand is almost always inadvisable. It humiliates the employee in the presence of his fellow workers, whose respect he wants to keep. It makes him resentful: he is likely to feel that your act in "bawling him out" publicly is a greater offense than the one he has committed. Moreover, your action may arouse sympathy for him, and ill will towards you, among the other employees. And, too, neither the supervisor nor the worker can be natural when there is an audience. What is needed is a private, man-to-man talk.

There are, of course, rare cases where a man is so "thick-skinned and cocky" that he does not respond properly to private criticism. It may be advisable to reprimand such a man publicly—but the supervisor should think twice before doing so.

Fairness

To GAIN and hold the confidence of his employees, the supervisor must be a "square-shooter". Here we face a battery of questions:

Am I impartial, or do I play favorites? Do I treat everyone fairly, even if I do not like him personally? Am I careful to avoid granting special privileges to those whom I like best? Do I assign work and overtime impartially? Do I recommend the best qualified workers for promotions, transfers, and increases in pay—so far as seniority rules will permit? Do I avoid favoritism in making lay-offs? Do I handle grievances properly?

When an employee comes to me with a complaint do I listen sympathetically and patiently, and give him ample time to state and restate his case? Before deciding what action to take, do I get all the relevant facts and weigh them carefully? Do I make a prompt decision? Do I give the employee the reasons for the decision and convince him of its fairness? Do I follow up to see that the adjustment is properly carried out? Do I give credit where credit is due? Do I say "We did it" and not "I did it" when I have accomplished something with the help of others?

If a worker makes a helpful suggestion do I give him the credit that he deserves, or do I claim the credit myself? Do I keep my promises? Employees lose respect for a supervisor who fails to keep his word. Am I careful to make a promise only when I am sure I can carry it out? Do I make a note of each promise so that there will be no danger that I may forget? When an employee confides in me, do I keep his confidences?

Do I set as high standards for my own conduct as I do for my employees? Or do I expect the workers to follow my orders, but not my example? If I make a mistake, do I have the courage to admit it, or do I try to saddle the blame on someone else? Do I take responsibility whenever I should, or do I "pass the buck"?

Planning

In ORDER to get work done properly and on time, the supervisor must plan the work well in advance. Planning takes time, but it saves much more time than it takes. So I would ask myself: Do I plan my work thoroughly? Having planned my work, do I work my plan, or do I just muddle through?

Delegating Work

By DELEGATING work to others the office manager or supervisor frees himself from handling many matters of detail and has more time to do well the planning, deciding, training, and supervising that are his most important duties. A real executive works through other people. Therefore, I would ask myself: Do I try to handle too many details myself, or do I delegate details to others so far as possible? If I have to answer "No" to this question—as most of us will if we are honest with ourselves—I would follow up with some further questions.

Why do I not do more delegating? Is it because I am afraid that others will not do the work as well as I can? If so, the remedy is to be found in training and developing my assistants—in giving them a chance to act, to achieve, to use their initiative. They will make mistakes, but they will learn from those mistakes under my guidance.

Is it because I am afraid that I will build up my assistant to such an extent that he will be able to take my job? That is a foolish fear if I am in the right sort of organization. If I am working for a company that I cannot count upon to play fair, I had better look for another job. If my employer is fair, I have much to gain and nothing to lose from developing a capable understudy. He can fill my place if I am sick or on vacation or away from the job for any other reason. And when a vacancy occurs higher up in the organization, I will be available for promotion. Many a supervisor has failed to win promotion because no one else was available to fill his place.

Making Decisions

Someone has defined an executive as "a man who makes many decisions, some of which are right". Every supervisor is an executive in the sense that he is one who gets things done through other people. A weakness often found in supervisors is the tendency to put off an important decision because of the fear of being criticized for making a mistake in judgment. One who has that tendency is certain to be criticized, and fairly criticized, not for making an unsound decision, but for failing to decide promptly. So I would ask myself, do I procrastinate in making decisions? I am not suggesting that a supervisor should make snap judgments. Before deciding he should, of course, get all of the needed facts and weigh the facts. He should then decide, then act, then follow up. But he should go through these essential steps as promptly as possible

Making Suggestions

A tactless suggestion usually brings a negative response. So I would ask myself, when I make a suggestion to my chief, or to a fellow supervisor, am I diplomatic? If I say, "We ought to do so and so", I should not be surprised if he merely listens, thanks me (perhaps), and then does nothing about it. He does not like to be told what he ought to do, any more than I like to have an employee tell me bluntly what I should do. A better way to approach him is to say, "Do you think it would be a good idea to do so and so?" His opinion is being requested. He is not being told what he should do.

A variation on this method is to suggest to one's chief two or three ways of making a needed change and ask him which of these ways he thinks would be best. It is sometimes appropriate to suggest the arguments for and against each of the courses of action. His good judgment will choose the best way to proceed.

—383—

Yes-Men

A supervisor who always agrees with what his superior in the organization says is a "yes-man". If someone asks my opinion, he does not—if he is the right sort of man—want me merely to echo his views. He wants to know what I sincerely think, rather than what I think he wants me to think. So I would put this question to myself, Am I a yes-man, or do I give my opinions sincerely and courageously? It takes courage to state one's views candidly when they differ from those of one's chief. But the candid, courageous man will be respected more by others and will be able to keep his self-respect. Moreover, he will be more helpful to his organization. He should, of course, be tactful in expressing his ideas, and he should not be too stubborn in defending them. If the decision goes against him, he should carry out that decision loyally.

Co-operation

Co-operation is simply working with others. The co-operative man goes out of his way to be helpful. The only way to get co-operation is to give it. This question must be faced, therefore, in my relations with others, do I co-operate wholeheartedly?

Open-Mindedness

Most of us have a tendency to resist new ideas and proposed changes, especially if their adoption would upset our established routines. I should confront myself with these questions: When someone suggests a new idea to me, do I consider it solely on its merit? Am I constantly trying to make improvements in methods, or am I satisfied to do everything in the established way without trying to find a better way?

Self-Improvement

Some mistakes are excusable, but it is inexcusable to repeat a mistake. Consequently, this question should be raised, Do I learn from my mistakes, or do I make the same mistake twice?

No one ever knew everything about anything in the field of business. Each one of us can learn something every day, if he will. These questions, then, require answers:

Do I try to improve myself? Specifically, Do I take, and complete, courses? Do I study books on office management and supervision? Do I read trade and professional journals? Do I join, and regularly attend, the professional associations in my field? Do I take an active part in the discussions at supervisors' conferences? Do I exchange experience with others who have similar duties and problems?

Taking Life too Seriously

MANY of us have a tendency to take our work and ourselves too seriously. Such an attitude makes life more difficult for us and for our associates. Let us, then, face these questions: Do I take myself too seriously, or do I have a sense of humor that eases the tensions that develop? Do I have an exaggerated dignity, or do I act naturally? Am I cheerful in the face of disappointments? Do I allow myself to become upset by petty irritations, or do I exercise self-control? Do I worry about my problems, or do I self-confidently take obstacles in my stride? Do I make work a grind, or do I make it a game?

In Conclusion

I AM not so blindly optimistic as to expect that anyone will rate 100% on such a self-analysis check list as I have briefly sketched this evening. It is a target to be aimed at. We cannot expect to hit the bull's-eye every time. But by constant practice we can improve our score.

In presenting this summary I am painfully aware of my past mistakes in dealing with other people. It has doubtless reminded each of you of your own shortcomings. Only when we are aware of our faults and make an all-out effort to correct them can we do a better job of supervising office personnel.

Summary of a talk delivered before the Milwaukee Chapter, National Office Management Association.

Religion, Politics, and Nationality Have No Influence on the Efficiency of Workers. Prejudices about These Matters Leading to Lack of Cooperation Should Therefore Be Discouraged in Business and Industry

Prejudices *in* Industry

By James J. Jackson
Woodbury, N. J.

How often in industry we hear reference made to a man's religion, politics, or nationality. Much of the friction that is found in industry may be traced to one of these three things. Some of the people that take their religion, politics, or nationality rather seriously bring them to work with them, and try to make the workplace a battle-field on which to fight for those things in which they believe, but which have nothing to do with the production, transportation, or selling of goods.

Everyone Entitled to a Belief

Everyone is entitled to a religious belief. People have undergone great hardships in order to follow their own methods of worship without being molested. In fact, much of the credit for the settlement of this country is due to people who came here to avoid persecution and to worship as they saw fit. So intense were their desires in this respect that they were willing to settle in a wilderness and to risk their lives daily.

The matter of politics is one that is often taken quite seriously by some of our most patriotic citizens. Everyone of voting age, particularly, should be interested in the subject. In a democracy every person is entitled to vote as he wishes. Not only should he be allowed to vote, but he should be encouraged to do so at all elections.

Many of our supervisors and workers were born in foreign countries. Others are the children of parents one or both of whom were natives of another nation before coming here. Whether or not these people who were born in other countries have taken out citizenship papers, they and their children have racial characteristics that are somewhat peculiar to their people. Even though they may have become American citizens in every sense of the word, we usually think of them—unfairly no doubt—as being of the same nationality as were their ancestors.

Industrial Ability not Affected

IT IS only natural that people who are devout adherents to a religious faith should think that followers of a different belief are wrong in their ideas. Political feelings sometimes become intense and are often the source of argument. Wars or disagreements of some kind between countries may be the cause of hatreds between descendants of citizens of the two nations. Differences on such matters have often been the sources of trouble in industrial concerns.

But, the ability of the man in industry is not affected by his religion, politics, or nationality.

It is one of the duties of the executive to see that religious or political beliefs or nationality controversies do not enter into the relations between individuals or departments under his supervision. These matters are foreign to the real problems at hand.

Religion

RELIGION can, however, be taken a little too seriously in some cases. A rather amusing situation arose some years ago in which a political election was settled on a religious basis. It so happened that a new real estate development resulted in a town growing up within a year's time. When the time came to elect a mayor, it was found that practically all of the population was about evenly divided between two religious groups which had got into difficulties with each other in regard to church sites. The feeling between the two factions was so intense that each mayor gave up and resigned after a short period in office until finally no one wanted the job. A very capable young man, Mr. W., was drafted, however, and was almost unanimously elected. When an outsider asked him why he had gone into politics, he replied: "I didn't want the job, but I am the only one of the —— faith in town, and no one knows what that means, so they elected me." Fortunately for the administration of the affairs of that town, the neutral man has been able to prevent the matter of religious beliefs from becoming serious again.

Cases have been known in which the matter of religious beliefs entered into business to such an extent that there was continual bickering between two departments. Each department would consist of followers of but the one faith and any other person could not be employed there. The "buck would be passed" back and forth between the two departments, and everything that happened was the fault of someone from the other section. The whole performance was very similar to that of gang fights between two groups of boys from opposite sides of town. Once in a while a stone would be thrown, and possibly a stone-fight would take place.

None of Your Business

SUCH tactics do not have any place in business. Religious beliefs, when they are the cause of friction, are better left at home. It is far better to practice tolerance of the other man's religion and ignore the fact that he has different beliefs. It would seem better to forget the whole matter, because it has no connection with business except for the influence it may have in raising the moral standard of the individuals. Perhaps, it was well expressed by the young chap who applied for a job, and the prospective employer questioned him as to his religion. The applicant suspected that he would not get the job if he told his religion, so he merely said, "None of your business."

Politics

PEOPLE can become too enthusiastic about party politics. A case in point was observed with some interest immediately after the returns of a recent important election were received. The wife of a company official did not approve of the results. She commanded her poor, hen-pecked husband: "Dick, you go down there to that factory tomorrow and fire every —— in the place." It must be said in fairness to Dick that he did not discharge any employees because of their party affiliation, but he did make things uncomfortable for certain men for a few days. Perhaps he was able to satisfy his wife's desire for revenge on those who did not vote to please her.

Politics, like religion, has no place in business, when the merits of the workers are to be considered. True, legislation which may be favored by one or the other of the political parties may have a very definite effect on business. Laws passed in regard to tariffs may bring favorable or unfavorable results to certain industries. Changes in the tax rates or additional taxes, or wages and hours legislation, or any other attempts of governments to regulate industry may affect the degree or success of an enterprise. But, these are matters that cannot be blamed on some chap who operates a lathe in the machine shop. Rather, if the man votes the wrong ticket, in the opinion of some people, it must be because his father made the same mistake before him, he read the wrong newspaper, or he talked to the wrong party-worker! In any case, he exercised his right as he saw fit, and no one is in a position to criticize him for it. At any rate, his ability to operate the lathe is not affected by his politics.

The politics of an employee, no matter in what capacity he serves, is something that should not concern anyone else. Each person is entitled to his own opinions. It is advisable, then, to keep quiet on the subject during working hours and let the matter be settled elsewhere.

Nationality

IN THIS connection, an incident occurred soon after World War I, when there was a boundary dispute between two European countries, that demonstrated the feelings of men who were natives of one of the countries involved. All of the men in one department of a plant were of one nationality. It is so happened that a junior executive tacked up in conspicuous places in the department some fire regulation placards printed in several languages. One of the languages was that of the people on the other side of the dispute from that of the men employed in the department. Later in the day the executive noticed that the section showing the regulations in the language of the hated nation was neatly cut out of the placard. The explanation was that the employees would not work there if that language had to be shown. Needless to say, when the employment department sent down a man of the hated nationality to work there, he did not return after the lunch period. The nationalism of the group was finally broken up by replacing those who left with neutrals in the particular dispute.

Hans and John found a solution to their problem when they were placed side by side at a work-bench soon after the start of World War I. Each had a great deal of sympathy for his mother country, and the homelands of the two were on opposing sides during that struggle. Hans and John fought the war each day as they worked, but their weapons were not injurious. They knew how far to go with their kidding and became fast friends. In other words they adjusted themselves to the situation and they remembered that they had both left the mother country and that they had adopted a new homeland. Their case was an example of Americanism that it would be well for other new citizens to follow.

Should Be Forgotten at the Workplace

ADMITTEDLY, the impressions made on the mind of the individual by his religion, politics, and nationality are too deep to be easily forgotten. Those who are members of some religious organization are usually trained in the beliefs of their church from infancy. Most children hear politics discussed at home, read about it in the newspapers, hear it on the radio, and argue it with their schoolmates. Natives of other countries are taught loyalty to their flag, and they learn to love their homeland as our American children do. "Just as the twig is bent the tree's inclined" applies to all three, and, after the person has acquired a belief in or love for a certain religion, kind of politics, or home country, it is difficult to change that person's opinions.

Adjustments Can Be Made

RELIGIOUS beliefs, political affiliations, and nationality connections can be forgotten in business. There was a situation soon after the first World War in which it was thoroughly demonstrated that this could be done. It so happened that a young man, who had just returned from military service, and who had reported to work for his former employers, found himself assistant superintendent of a division of the plant in which most of the employees had been immigrants from one of the nations on the other side during the war. The young man found himself reporting to a superintendent and supervising the work of foreman who often resorted to a language that he did not understand. Furthermore, the young man learned that the religion and politics of his associates were different from his. The stage was set for fireworks, if any of these things had been made an issue.

It so happened, however, that the superintendent prided himself on his Americanism and taught his employees that their value depended on loyalty to the employers rather than any other connections. That young chap spent several very pleasant years amidst surroundings that would have been very unpleasant if religion, politics, and nationalities had not been ignored. This example is a rather extreme case, but it demonstrated to the writer that such matters can be forgotten in business.

Such matters should be forgotten, because they have nothing to do with business. This writer, in over a score of years in business, has never seen a case in which a man's religion or politics has made him more valuable to his employers. Furthermore, a man's nationality has no bearing on his value to industry except for the possibility that racial characteristics may have some influence on his ability to do certain types of work. But, generally speaking, the church to which Ed goes, his party affiliations, and the language that his parents speak have little do do with his ability to operate a punch press, to mine coal, or to fire a railroad engine. In like manner, these things do not affect Harry's efficiency (That poor overworked word!) as a production clerk, billing clerk, or traffic clerk. If these things do not affect the value of an employee at his work, they should be forgotten.

Costly Disputes

DIFFERENCES in religion, politics, and nationalities are sometimes the causes of costly disputes, although the real causes may never come to the surface. Suppose the bookkeeper were to keep accounts on his books headed: "Costs of differences in religious beliefs," and "Costs of political disagreements," and "Costs of settling boundary disputes in foreign countries." Perhaps nothing could be more ridiculous, and yet, if the exact figures could be obtained, they might be very interesting, and they might supply valuable information. The trouble is that the correct information is impossible to obtain.

No, there are no headings on the cost ledgers that correspond to those mentioned above; but, when the costs are really there, the company has to pay them. Although these costs are hidden, the total cost of the product or service that the company has to sell is increased, and the margin of profit is decreased, or the losses are increased. If these costs could be brought out in the open, they might be eliminated, or if their seriousness were realized, more effort could be made to train people to forget their personal affairs during business hours.

Summary

THE matters of religion, politics, and nationalities are delicate subjects that have nothing to do with business.   They should be ignored in the workplace because they have no bearing on the merits of the worker, and, when allowed to become the cause of disputes, they are also the causes of hidden costs.

Suggested Educational Background and Essential Qualifications for Those Wishing to Take Up Industrial Relations Counseling Together with a Selected List of Readings.

Tomorrow's Counselor

By H. W. WEDAA

New York, N. Y.

THE need for counseling in industrial relations has been accentuated by the pressure of conditions created by the war.

Much has been said and written about the technique, function and duties of the counselor, and such delineation of duties are generally accepted by the more enlightened and progressive leaders of industry and labor.

Background and Qualifications

VERY little, however, has been written about the educational background and requirements of the counselor. It is the purpose of this paper to attempt to set forth what appear to be the undisputable qualifications required of any individual who desires to engage in a field of endeavor which is destined to become more important as we proceed into the future.

During the war industry was faced with the difficulty of finding ways and means of adjusting and adapting individuals to a new environment. Individuals who had not previously been employed by industry and who had not previously been subject to industrial discipline.

Difficult and delicate as this problem proved itself to be, a greater task yet lies before us in assisting our returning veterans to not only adapt themselves, but also to become successful members, in every respect, of industry and the community.

What, then, are the requirements of tomorrow's counselor?

Insight and Practical Experience

As a person who must deal objectively with subjective forces, the prime requirement of the counselor must be that of insight into the motives and forces that causes human behavior. The requirement second in importance, is that of having worked with people under the stress and strain of the discipline imposed by a rigid industrial economy.

The last mentioned requirement is relatively easy to acquire by anyone who does not feel it below his dignity to do and perform tasks uncommon to the socalled educated person. It is, however, part of a counselor's basic education to have associated with the workers on a work level, because, only through such association does one acquire a real understanding of the psychology of the workers.

A mental conception of the worker's problems, without this work level contact and association with the workers' problems, is valueless.

The quality of sympathy is often stressed as being basic in the requirements of a counselor. This, however, is a fallacy that too often negates the usefulness of the counselor. An outpouring of sympathy, contrary to popular belief, does not alleviate or constructively assist an individual in the overcoming of imaginary or real grievances. Sympathy is not always a helpful force and may be harmful.

The quality that will be most helpful to a counselor is that of *responsiveness*.

Being responsive to the plight of an individual brings out constructively the quality of sympathy and places the counselor en rapport with the real problem faced by the distressed individual seeking counseling. Such subconscious rapport between minds usually provides the ability on the part of the counselor to correctly analyze and diagnose the real cause of distress, and it has been well said that recognition of the cause is nine tenths of the cure.

Foundation SubJects

What are the subjects or learning that will contribute to developing the insight and understanding that will make of the counselor, the constructive and effective counselor in industrial relations, that the future will demand.

The below mentioned subjects:

1) History
2) Sociology
3) Economics
4) Politics
5) Comparative religion
6) Psychoanalysis
7) Psychology

should provide a foundation of the mental equipment of tomorrow's counselor.

History

HISTORY, as the branch of knowledge that records and explains past events, as steps in human progress, has intellectual value in that it furnishes our mind with a vista of the events and forces which contributed to the upbuilding of our complex civilizations and cultures.

The objective movement of mankind is here revealed in its aspiration and progress through family, tribe, nation and world organization and helps us to view events in their relationship and in perspective, creating tolerance of ideas, new and old.

Sociology

SOCIOLOGY is the science of the constitution, phenomena and development of society as a social organism. Through a study of the age old pattern of society it seeks to discover how the interaction of individuals in groups, through collective action, affect and modify the current social structure. Social organization and institutions being in a state of constant flux require an unflagging attention to major and minor movements constantly arising to challenge the mores, folkways, accepted social institutions or the status quo.

The task of sociology is the study of the interrelationship of all the social sciences.

Economics

ECONOMICS, the science which explains to us the method of finance, production and distribution of economic goods is highly contributory to an understanding of the forces that motivate the daily conduct of individuals, governments and nations in their interrelationship.

Our present method of making a living can best be understood against the background of the past. Economic history affords such an understanding and provides an invaluable understanding of people who have been subject to removal from countries subject to semi-feudal, feudal, semi-capitalistic or modern capitalistic institutions.

Vestiges of the thinking process inculcated into the mind by the educational process of such social institutions are to be found in generations far removed from the original influence.

Our present economy is, like every other social institution, the product of the evolutionary process and subject, as such, to the impact of evolutionary forces.

Political Science

POLITICAL science studies the form of organized state or government. The relationship between individuals and government, the state and the nation and how the contemporary state evolved. Political science defines government by law, the framework of government, types of government, how governments are choosen and the distribution of power. It is a study indispensable to an understanding of our environment.

Comparative Religion

COMPARATIVE religion provides us with insight into the deeper crevasses of man's mind in that it traces the history of man's concept of the origin of the Universe and conceived governing powers. The fears and hopes to which mankind have been subjected through the ages, and systems of ethical codes, derived from such fears and hopes, are the subject matter of comparative religion. Religion in one form or other is today the compelling influence in the lives of the great majority of mankind.

Psychoanalysis and Psychology

PSYCHOANALYSIS and psychology are interrelated in that they study the provinces of the mind, the conscious and unconscious or subconscious aspects thereof.

The conscious mind may be defined as the receptive part of the mind and the subconscious as the storehouse thereof. The interaction of the subconscious and conscious mind in its effect upon the personality is the subject matter of psychology and psychoanalysis.

Psychopathology resulting from the pressure of modern living is becoming more clearly understood by the psychiatric profession and no individual engaged in personnel work or counseling can afford to neglect this important phase of modern knowledge.

The subject matter of evolution and anthropology should by no means be overlooked

All the social sciences are the field of the forward looking personnel director and counselor, and in the degree to which he devores himself to such study, does he become successful in this most important future endeavor in the field of industrial relations.

Bibliography

History

"Whither Mankind," Charles Beard.
"An Outline of History," H. G. Wells.
"Europe and Europeans," Carl Sforza.
"The Rise of American Civilization," C. Beard.
"The Epic of America," James Truslow Adams.
"History of the American Working Class," A. Bimba.

Sociology

"Man's Rough Road," William Graham Sumner.
"Man and Society," Emerson P. Schmidt.

"The Making of Society," V. F. Calverton.
"Law and the Social Order," M. R. Cohen.
"Labor an Social Organization," McCabe and Lester.
"What the Negro Thinks," R. R. Moton.

Economics

"Development of Economic Society," Modlin and de Vyer.
"Economics and Social Institutions," Luthringer Chandler and Cline.
"Economic Behaviour," Members of the Department of Economics, New York University.
"The Outline of Man's Work and Wealth," H. G. Wells.

Politics

"The Economic Basis of Politics," Charles Beard.
"Foundations of Modern World Society," L. A. Mandler.
"Modern Political Philosophies," L. Wasserman.
"An Economic Interpretation of the Constitution of the United States," Charles Beard
"The Folklore of Capitalism" Thurman Arnold.
"World Politics," E. P. Dutton.

Comparative Religion

"This Believing World," Lewis Browne.
"The Worlds Saviours," C. H. Vail.
"The Golden Bough," J. G. Frazer.

Psychology

"Psychology, Briefer Course," William James.
"General Psychology" D. B. Klein.
"The Nature of the World and of Man," H. H. Newman.
"An Outline of General Psychology," Fryer and Henry.
"Basic Teachings of the Great Psychologists," S. S. Sargent.
"The Story of Man's Mind," G. Humphrey.
"Understanding Human Nature," Alfred Adler.
"The Mind in the Making," J. H. Robinson.

Psychoanalysis

"A General Introduction to Psychoanalysis," Sigmund Freud.
"The Basic Writings of Sigmund Freud," A. A. Brill.
"The Meaning of Psychoanalysis," M. W. Peck.
"Men Against Madness," Lowell S. Selling.
"The Human Mind," Karl Menninger.

Credit Note: The article in the March, 1945 issue of the Personnel Journal by Ellsworth S. Grant, titled "Let the Foreman Manage" was reproduced from *Connecticut Industry* through the courtesy of its Editor.

PERSONNEL
Journal

Index to Volume 24

May 1945–April 1946

Managing Editor—CHARLES S. SLOCOMBE

Business Manager—HAZEL HIMSWORTH

Circulation Manager—J. SLOCOMBE

Published by

PERSONNEL RESEARCH FEDERATION

60 East 42nd St., New York 17, N. Y.

Index

ARTICLES

CONTRIBUTORS

BOOKS REVIEWED

Book Review Editor—EVERETT VAN EVERY

· PERSONNEL
Journal

The Magazine of

LABOR RELATIONS AND PERSONNEL PRACTICES

Published by PERSONNEL RESEARCH FEDERATION

Lincoln Building, 60 East 42nd Street, New York City

Volume 24   *Number 1*

Contents for May 1945

Though This War is on Its Way to Being Over, and We Are Not Supposed to Have Another, Both the Army and Navy Have Recently Released Long Lists of New Inventions They Would Like to Have.

Inventors
in Overalls

By Thomas A. Dickinson
Toronto, Canada

A POMPOUS vice-president of a large industrial plant approached a grease-smeared, overalled mechanic who was working at his lathe. Then, while the nearby operators looked on, he pinned a bright Badge of Merit on the worker and praised a mechanical gadget the man had devised "which will speed up our production and, in its small way, help towards winning the war."

Tom Gerlach, a lanky engineer with a sense of humor, who works for another company, happened to be in the plant for a conference with the superintendent. After witnessing the ceremony, he asked the vice-president: "What do those badges cost you?"

"They're sterling silver," answered the official proudly. "They cost $5.00 each."

Maybe They Cost $100,000

MAYBE they cost $5.00," said Tom, "and then again, maybe they cost $100,000. . . ."

Tom Gerlach is patent director for the 13 divisions of Consolidated Vultee Aircraft Corporation. Not one Vultee employe has ever received a silver button for an invention—because Gerlach happens also to be chief administrator of the most generous company-employe patent plan known to exist.

The often-proved theory on which Gerlach works is this: a practical invention that speeds up war production or improves the products of a defense industry is worth far more to a company—and to the nation—than its dollars-and-cents value; the men most likely to come up with a practical new gadget, short-cut, or process are the ones who actually work in the industry and handle its tools every day. But when the reward is a silver button, the inventor—and all potential inventors working around him—will not only be discouraged from "thinking up things," but will conceal from the company any good ideas they may have.

This was what Gerlach meant when he said the Badge of Merit "might cost $100,-ooo." As an example of how the Vultee system works, there is the case of Morris Brown, a 54-year-old toolmaker at Vultee's Plant No. 2 at San Diego, Calif.

In his home workshop Brown developed a new "bucking-bar"—that's a bar that is held against the back of a rivet while the pressure-tool is flattening the other end He took it to the factory to see if it could be used in airplane building. Tests made by his fellow workers proved it to be simpler and faster than anything yet in use. It eliminated the need for vital man power on many types of jobs, and the American aircraft industry was experiencing the greatest man power shortage in its history.

Badges Don't Pay Rent or Buy Food

A FOREMAN's enthusiastic report brought the superintendent, engineers, and executives from the front office. They, too, wanted a demonstration. Brown hesitated. In his 30 years of work in many companies, he had received many a merit badge, none of which had ever paid rent or bought food. He told the executives bluntly: "I developed this at home on my own time. If you want it you'll have to buy it from me."

The demonstration impressed the experts, who asked Brown how much he wanted.

"A million dollars," Brown replied without hesitation. His hearers gasped, then tried to explain to Brown why his demand was "impossible." Brown was adamant. Finally Gerlach was called in, and did not gasp.

"Sure," he said, "your invention must be worth a million, if it's as good as everyone says it is. And we'll help you get it. It wouldn't be worth as much as that to one company, but it might be if all the manufacturers in America can use it."

Patent Royalties Do

G ERLACH patented the bucking-bar and had Brown agree to let a tool manufacturer turn out his invention on a mass production basis. To date he has not received his million dollars, but his royalty cheques are becoming increasingly large. And, more important, the time and man power saving tool is being made available to all war industries by the Zephyr Manufacturing company of Los Angeles.

When Brown's success became known among the employes, a power plant engineer, W. A. Clegern, came to Gerlach. He had many ideas for improving aircraft engines, but until now had hesitated to disclose them, fearing he would not gain by his inventions. He showed Gerlach his plans for a new-type exhaust unit for supercharged motors which, when tested, promised to increase a plane's speed by 10 to 20 miles an hour. Plans have been made to use Clegern's invention on all Vultee's aircraft, and he has since turned up with other plans of even greater promise. Both he and the company have profited tremendously.

Research Men Included in Plan

NOT only "home workshop" inventors but members of Vultee's own research department, who, after all, are paid to develop ideas for the company's use, come under the patent plan. For example, there is the case of the "flight recorder."

This remarkable new radio-recording device enables engineers on the ground to determine the cause of test-flight accidents by providing a continuous and accurate report of the performance of vital parts of a plane in flight. Although this instrument was developed through three years of research at Vultee's expense by three staff electronics experts, Harvey D. Giffen, Thomas B. Thomson, Jr., and Willard C. North, the trio are eligible to receive royalties over and above their salaries as research engineers.

Other members of the research staff who have derived "dividends" from Vultee's patent plan are Dr. G. G. Havens, R. D. Ford, H. R. Jenks, and G. A. Gordon. They are the creators of *Metlbond*, a new adhesive which forms metal joints stronger than riveted ones, and *Conolite*, a low-pressure laminated plastic of extreme lightness and durability, to be moulded into airplane parts. Financed by Vultee, Dr. Havens and his associates are now manufacturing the two products in their own plant at National City, Calif.

Even ideas that are not patentable are rewarded by substantial cash payments, based approximately on the saving they effect for the company over a six-months period. Inventions that are both patentable and money-saving benefit by both plans. Fred Einer's tool for collapsing and removing the self-sealing fuel cells of military aircraft, now in use by service mechanics all over the world, brought him $1052 in cash as a "money saver." And royalties are beginning to roll in from other manufacturers who are turning out the tool in large quantities for the United States Air Force.

Generosity of Plan Criticized

GERLACH's department has a representative in every branch of the company, to act as a consultant for employes who feel they have patentable ideas that the aircraft industry in general can use. They also advise employes about gadgets that have no possible connection with aviation. For example, J. M. Druliner, a Vultee engineer at Nashville, invented a "collator" which would collect and assemble sheets of paper in a predetermined sequence. Gerlach's representative filed the patent application and arranged to have American Type Founders, Inc. manufacture the device on a royalty basis.

"We have often been criticized for the generosity of our plan," says Gerlach, "but that is mainly because of other manufacturers who feel we are setting an unprofitable example. As a matter of fact, we have found the patent plan to be one of our most profitable enterprises. True, our income from any one patent is not tremendous, but the income from all our patents is increasing daily—and most of it is money we wouldn't have if we didn't give our inventors an even break."

Graphic Rating Scales with Numerical Scoring
Have Serious Logical Difficulties and Practical
Inadequacies—Flaws which More than Offset the
Advantages Claimed for Them.

Merit Rating Criticized

By Thomas Arthur Ryan

Cornell University,
Ithaca, N. Y.

CURRENT books and periodicals devoted to personnel management techniques commonly present a strong case for the use of some form of graphic rating scale for progress or proficiency ratings, usually a standardized form which permits a total numerical evaluation of each worker. While the aims and advantages claimed for these rating techniques are highly laudable, the present writer sees little evidence that these aims are approached or that the supposed advantages really appear. In fact there are certain basic difficulties with these methods which indicate a need for intensive effort to discover new and quite different approaches, or, at least, drastic modifications in the way in which these ratings are employed in current practice.

Taken on Faith

FEW would question the importance of keeping track of the development and potentialities of workers for purposes of promotion, establishing differential pay rates based upon merit rather than upon seniority alone, or evaluating employment practices by checking upon the performance of men hired by these methods. The question to be raised is whether the methods now in use have any reasonable degree of demonstrated accuracy for these purposes.

We are asked to accept the rating scale technique largely on faith, since there is no way of testing its validity directly. The rating scale is ordinarily used in situations where there is no other way of obtaining an estimate of the worker's characteristics except, possibly, for records of his production. It is apparently believed necessary to know more than the productivity of the worker, else the rating scale would not be proposed. As a result of the impossibility of direct validation we are told what the rating scale is *expected* to do or what it *ought* to do, with little or no support for these claims.

Supposed Advantages

IN THE following discussion we shall consider these supposed advantages of the graphic rating scale in some detail. We shall try to show that these claims are by no means easily acceptable, in fact, that some of them are logically contradictory. Throughout this discussion we shall assume that the merit rating system is satisfactorily administered, with proper instruction and training for the raters. The difficulties we shall discuss are inherent in the technique itself, even when it is administered under the best possible conditions. How often these conditions are met is another question, although some may admit that these rating scales are only too seldom used according to the plans of those who designed them.

Although it is not always explicitly stated, the graphic rating form in so frequent use apparently aims to secure several advantages over unsystematized procedures which have been prevalent in the past and continue to be common. These expected advantages might be listed as follows:

These Advantages Listed

ONE. Requiring the rater to consider a number of different 'traits' or aspects of the man rather than a single total evaluation without any explicit analysis.

Two. Defining these traits for the rater so that there is less likely to be disagreement upon the meaning of terms.

Three. Emphasizing that individual differences involve a number of levels along a continuous scale of each quality. Thus it prevents such vague terms as 'dependable,' 'skillful,' 'honest,' being applied to a worker, and requires instead an estimate of the *degree* of dependability, skill, or honesty possessed by the individual.

Four. By giving examples or definitions it is hoped that the raters will agree not only upon the general meaning of the trait under consideration, but that they will also be able to use a common standard for determining the various levels of the trait. If this purpose is attained, 'average skill' would mean about the same thing to various supervisors. (Not all graphic rating forms make the attempt to define levels of a trait, and some even fail to define the traits themselves. We are considering here the more carefully worked-out rating techniques, and all of the possible advantages which might accrue through the use of all known precautions in composing the form. There are methods for "correcting" for errors due to failure to secure common standards of raters. These will be discussed later.)

Five. By deciding upon the relative importance of the various traits considered in the rating, and by assigning point values to each level of each trait, it is possible to produce a total score which would represent the over-all value of a particular employee and would provide ready comparison with other employees.

Incompatibilities

IT is not usually recognized that the first and last of these expectations are incompatible with one another. If we are successful in getting the rater to consider a number of distinct traits and phases of the worker, there are several difficulties and a definite fallacy involved in applying a total numerical score to the result. The fallacy consists in the assumption that it is possible to substitute one trait for another. The use of a total numerical score means that worker who is weak in skill can make up for that failing by getting an especially high rating in such a trait as dependability. Perhaps such compensation is possible within limits, but

TABLE I

HYPOTHETICAL RATINGS OF THREE WORKERS WITH EQUIVALENT TOTAL SCORES

TRAIT	POINT VALUES* OF RATINGS FOR:		
	Worker A	Worker B	Worker C
Skill.....	10	5	5
Cooperativeness....	5	10	5
Capacity for future development.......	0	0	5
Total....	15	15	15

* It is assumed that all three traits are of equal importance (i.e. each is allotted the same number of points).

in cases where there is considerable divergence between the traits of a given individual his total numerical score may not represent at all his relative value to the company. In the above example we shall for simplicity suppose that three men are each rated on three traits. They all receive equivalent total scores but one would scarcely say that they are equivalent for purposes of transfer, promotion or even for establishing relative pay.

H. M. Johnson has pointed out this fallacy in connection with aptitude test-batteries which take into account several distinct aptitudes (1). As an example, he describes the score which he might receive as an operatic tenor, based upon several component abilities. It is possible, he says, that his score for aptitude in this profession might be fairly good in spite of the fact that he is totally unable to produce a high note, and would therefore never have any chance of succeeding as a tenor.

Johnson's discussion was written primarily for psychologists. The point has received little consideration in discussions of merit rating which are aimed at the practical administrator, in spite of the probability that the fallacy is even more important in ratings than it is in the field of aptitude testing. In rating we are not even limiting ourselves to aptitudes but are considering all phases of the man, including a variety of traits which come under the broad heading of personality and character.

Weighing of Traits

OF COURSE, there are some arguments which could be advanced to justify the procedure of totalling points or scores based upon several distinct aptitudes or even several disparate traits like those included in a merit rating form. First, it might be asserted that if a particular trait is so important that the worker is no good without a high rating in that trait, the trait will be weighted in proportion to its importance. Thus Johnson would not be able to get an extremely high score as an opera singer because ability to produce a high tone would be weighted very heavily in the total score.

Unfortunately, there may be a number of traits, all equally important, and such that a low rating would indicate almost certain failure on the job. No system of additive point scores could take this situation into account. When we are dealing with aptitude tests the process of validation would be such that these possibilities would be examined. If there were minimum requirements on each trait these could be established through an examination of the validation data which would be secured in developing the test. It would be possible to discover *critical scores* which would be taken into account before any composite score is determined. These critical scores would appear in the correlation tables which are used in analysing the validation data. If an addition procedure is finally adopted for combining the test scores, it can be based upon observed correlations with job performance, and the weighting based upon the closeness of relation between test performance and job performance. If the additive procedure is successful, it must mean that some degree of substitution of traits is possible—that the work can make up for his deficiencies in one aptitude by having an extra amount of another.

Opinions Cannot Be Validated

THESE devices for overcoming the difficulty do not exist when we are dealing with merit rating. There is no way of weighting the various traits according to their importance, except by taking the consensus of opinion of those engaged in developing the rating scale. There is no way of validating these weights by a comparison with some independent measure as there is when aptitude tests are properly validated. Since there is no independent measure of the value of the worker, there is no way of determining whether a low rating on a given trait is indicative of certain failure in the job or in jobs to which the man might be promoted.

Thus, when we are discussing merit rating, it may be claimed that the system of weights attached to the various traits takes their relative importance into account. It may also be claimed that a worker can compensate to a certain extent for deficiencies in one trait by his higher degrees of other traits. These are only claims, however, unsubstantiated by any concrete evidence. In fact it is not possible to test these claims by any means known to the writer.

Halo Effect

THE logical difficulty which has been discussed here at some length seems to be the most fundamental difficulty with merit systems based upon a point system. If the first four of the advantages we have listed as possible attainments of a carefully designed rating procedure are secured in any degree, we should abandon the attempt to summarize the results in a numerical form. The only case in which the numerical summary could be justified would be that in which the raters do not actually rate distinct traits. Discussions of the 'halo effect' have pointed out the tendency of raters to rate men similarly on all traits. If the halo effect is extremely strong we might find that the rater does not really rate distinct traits at all. His separate ratings may be no more than repeated ratings of the worker on a single scale—a scale of the supervisor's belief concerning the worker's value to the organization.

If this were the situation, a numerical total score might be justified as being somewhat more reliable than the individual ratings The advantage would be so doubtful, however, that we should seriously question the value of the rating technique. We lose most of the advantages which might be expected of the graphic rating method if the halo effect is strong, and it no longer has much usefulness. Would it not be better to ask the supervisor to make a single careful rating of the over-all value of the man and let it go at that?

Ewart, Seashore and Tiffin, in an analysis of a large number of ratings made in one industrial concern, found that there was a very strong halo effect (2). It was so strong that ratings on one trait correlated with ratings on others to the extent of about .70, on the average. He suggests, however, that the result does not necessarily hold if the raters are given better training on the use of rating forms (3).

Total Point Score Unjustified

THUS we are faced with two possibilities. If the halo effect is as strong as Tiffin found it to be in his statistical study, few of the advantages which are claimed graphic ratings are left. In such a case no elaborate rating system is justified. If on the other hand, the halo effect is only moderate in size, as it may be under careful training of raters, we may secure the advantages of a more complete analysis of the individual and possibly some of the other benefits listed above under headings 1–4.

We cannot in this case, however, justify the use of the total point score to summarize the results.

If the reader is still inclined to believe that substitution of traits is justified as a working hypothesis, in spite of the preceding discussion, we should like to point out other difficulties that still appear after this assumption is made. Another aim of the graphic rating method is to help the raters to adopt common standards of judgment. If this were fully successful, a man in one department who is rated at the 'average' level in a certain trait would be equivalent to a man in another department rated at the same level. Students of the rating data do not believe, however, that this condition is met in practice, since they usually provide methods of 'correcting' for the raters' differences in standards.

No One Knows the Facts

WE SHALL not discuss the details of these techniques of correcting for constant errors of the rater in this paper. They may be found in numerous presentations of rating methods (4). These methods, regardless of their details, all have a common basis. If one rater differs from another in the average ratings for all men in the department, it is assumed that this difference *must be* an error due to differences in standard between the supervisors. Before men from the two departments are compared, their ratings must be corrected for this constant difference between the raters. To put it another way, these methods assume that if the raters differ it must be due to a difference in leniency or kind-heartedness. The possibility that the men in one department are actually better than those in the second department is not taken into account.

It is equally unjustified to make the opposite assumption that the difference of raters is due to a real difference in the quality of their men. No one knows which is the case, and the facts, if they could be found, would probably indicate that part of the difference is due to difference in leniency of the raters, and part is due to real differences between men in the two departments. Either the 'corrected' or the 'uncorrected' ratings, or both, may be in error by unknown amounts. What we have said here concerning differences in average scores is equally true of differences between raters in the *spread* of their ratings—another difference which is usually taken into account in 'correcting' the ratings.

Thus, even if we are willing to make the assumptions necessary for using point scores for rating, there is little chance that we could compare ratings which are given by different supervisors with any degree of confidence. It is even questionable whether men rated by the same supervisor could be accurately compared if they happened to be working upon different jobs. The same rater's leniency may vary with the type of work and we should be faced with the same dilemma we met in comparing results of different raters.

Reliability Low

So far we have said nothing of the problem of reliability of the ratings. The direct study of the repeated ratings of a supervisor shows that they often have poor consistency, and the correlations between successive ratings by the same rater are moderate at best. As Tiffin points out the reliabilities are such that a point system of rating based upon a range of four or five hundred points is absurd because differences in the last place and even in the tens place are likely to be the result of chance variations rather than real variations between the persons rated. This difficulty with reliability could be overcome by using only five to seven rough groupings for the total score rather than attempting to use a finer scale, and it might also be improved by better training of the raters. Improving the reliability of the ratings would not, however, overcome the objections to a point system which we have discussed in preceding paragraphs.

What is the solution of this problem? As we indicated at the beginning, there is a real need for intensive search for other modes of approach to the problem of evaluating employees. So far these other methods are not available. Until they are, however, the writer believes that little is accomplished by elaborating and complicating the rating methods. Instead, he would recommend proceeding on a much simpler common-sense basis. The following suggestion is presented as one possible way out, not as a final solution of the problem.

Three Levels Suggested

For the lack of any better and more reasonable suggestion, we could assume that experienced supervisors ought to be able to distinguish on an *absolute* basis three levels of over-all value of men in their departments. If the men are engaged in quite distinct types of work, they would have to be divided according to occupation and rated separately and with reference to that occupation. In addition it seems reasonable that they should detect extreme degrees of certain specialized traits even though they do exhibit the halo effect and unreliability when they are asked to rate all men in the department on each trait.

The result of these suggestions would be a form like Figure 1 with certain changes dictated by the industry or the occupations involved in a particular application. The form which is reproduced in Figure 1 is not meant as a final version, and revisions of the instructions are probably necessary for use in any specific organization. The general approach is the thing which we are mainly interested in presenting at this time. It should be emphasized that this proposed form does not include anything radically new. In fact, it is basically a return to procedures of evaluation which are older and simpler than current rating techniques. It is an attempt to secure some of the advantages of a standardized rating technique without depending so heavily upon the assumptions required for the graphic scale-point method of evaluation.

FIG. 1. SUGGESTED FORM OF EMPLOYEE APPRAISAL

INVENTORY OF PERSONNEL

Department...................... (This should be a single job or group of similar, related
Jobs .... jobs. Jobs requiring unrelated skills or training should be
considered independently).

1. *Outstanding men:* List names of the men who are doing an exceptionally good job, and whose all-round value to the department is very high. Consider their present ability and skill, not what you think they might develop later. Men placed in this group should be in about the top ten per cent of men in this line of work *anywhere*, not only in this shop. If you are doubtful about any man's belonging in this group, *do not include him.* List these men in order from top down, if that is possible.

2. *Poor workers:* List the names of all men who are doing an exceptionally poor job, and whose all-round value to the department is very low. Consider present ability and skill, but do not include those who are poor because they do not have sufficient training or experience. These will be listed separately. As in the top group, if you are doubtful about a man belonging in this group, do not include him. The men in this group should be those who would be considered as about the bottom ten per cent of men in this occupation *anywhere*, but they may include more or less than ten per cent of your own men.

3. *Average workers:* List all men who have not been included in the first two groups except those who are not fully trained or who lack experience. As you list them consider each one to make sure that he does not belong either in Group 1 (exceptional men) or Group 2 (poor workers).

4. *Trainees and inexperienced workers:* Include here all those who have not finished the normal training period or who have not worked long enough to show what they can do. Mark those who show promise with a *G* and those who do not appear to make normal progress with *P*.

SPECIAL QUALIFICATIONS AND ABILITIES

Listed at the left are a number of special characteristics which may be important considerations in promotions or transfers. List, for each of these qualifications the names of those men in the job you are considering who are outstanding in this quality, and those who are especially poor in this respect. The names listed are not necessarily the same names you have given in your over-all estimates of the value of the employee on page 1.

QUALITY*	OUTSTANDING MEN	POOR WORKERS
1. Dependability (Does he follow instructions without close-follow-up?).............................		
2. Ability to get along with others (Is he respected and trusted by fellow workers?).....................		
3. Specialized technical knowledge of the job.........		
4. Ability to instruct others in his job..............		
5. Interest in his work and in the department.........		

* Other traits to be added to meet the needs of a particular organization. Instructions to be revised after conferences with supervisors and experience in application of the forms.

Inventory of Personnel

THE writer believes that this "Inventory of Personnel," while it still has flaws which cannot be entirely eliminated, is more defensible than the graphic rating scale. It obtains an over-all estimate of the value of men in a job from the supervisor, which, in view of the halo effect, is all we can confidently expect of the graphic rating technique. It requires the supervisor to make only broad groupings, which, in the light of the known reliabilities of the graphic scale are the only groupings justified. (If three groups are felt to be too broad, the same technique could be used with four or five categories instead of the three major groups illustrated in Figure 1). The method obtains these broad groupings without resort to dubious point rating scales.

The method also allows us to obtain useful information upon special traits without forcing the supervisor to rate all workers on each trait. He can thus designate those who show noticeable excellence or deficiency without being asked to make ratings on these traits where no information is available.

Paper Work Reduced

LAST, but by no means least, this procedure should reduce the amount of 'paper work.' While the supervisor has to write names instead of check-marks, he is not overwhelmed with a rating form for each man. One form can serve for all the men on a job or a related group of jobs, so long as sufficient space is provided for listing the names. At the same time, the supervisor is required to consider each man because the form requires that each man must be listed somewhere.

Obviously, the inventory method here described cannot fit all requirements any more than any other single procedure can. It is felt, however, that it has advantages, both logical and practical, over the graphic rating method for a great many of the purposes for which the graphic method has been employed.

Use of Evaluators

IF IT is still felt that the graphic form of recording supervisor's judgments is desirable some of its difficulties could be avoided by other methods of handling the information they contain. The rating forms might be sorted by inspection into three or four categories. With some training for those who do the sorting it is possible that the method could be made quite reliable, and it would not be necessary to make the assumptions required by a point system of evaluation. The evaluators could take into account both the average level of the ratings for a given individual, and any marked deficiencies on single traits. In this way a rough qualitative analysis of the forms might produce a more adequate evaluation than would be possible by the point system.

Even this procedure would not, however, settle the question of whether to 'correct' for the rater's tendencies to rate higher or lower than normal. That problem can never be settled until there is some more objective criterion against which the ratings may be checked. If we had such a criterion, the ratings would no longer be necessary.

Summary

THIS article has supported the thesis that the graphic rating scale with numerical scoring has serious logical difficulties and practical inadequacies. These flaws are so serious that they more than offset any advantages which are claimed for these rating techniques, especially since there is little more than common sense argument to support these claims.

There is a serious need for research to develop new and fundamentally different methods of evaluating workers for promotion, transfer, or validation of employment techniques. Until this development is carried out, the writer has proposed to return to simpler procedures which require fewer doubtful assumptions. This simpler approach was illustrated by a suggested form for recording information in an "Inventory of Personnel." Such an inventory is aimed at securing some of the advantages of currently popular rating techniques while making the task of the rater as simple as possible, and making fewer baseless assumptions.

References

(1) H. M. JOHNSON, Some neglected principles of aptitude testing, *Amer. J. Psychol.*, 1935, 47, 159–165.

(2) E. EWART, S. E. SEASHORE, AND J. TIFFIN, A factor analysis of an industrial merit rating scale. *J. Applied Psychol.* 25, 1941, 481–486.

(3) J. TIFFIN, *Industrial Psychology*, New York, 1942, p. 245.

(4) J. P. GUILFORD, *Psychometric Methods*, New York, 1936, p. 274.

Most Workers Did Not Bother to Vote about Staggered Vacations. Of Those Who Did the Majority Were in Favor. But the Non-voters Were Not Indifferent, as Indicated by Their Criticisms.

Experiment *in* Democracy

By GEO. H. CLAYTON

Park Vale Works
General Electric Company
·Leicester, England

IN RESPONSE to the Government's request many industrial firms have abandoned the traditional custom of closing their works for the Annual Holiday during the first week in August. Instead, a system of "staggered" holidays has been adopted during the war in order to avoid if possible a break in the flow of production, and to relieve the strain on transport services which would result from the usual peace-time rush at August Bank Holiday Week.

Staggered Holidays

THE most usual practice in those factories which have adopted "staggered" holidays is for a proportion of the workpeople to go each week during the five month's period from May to September. This rota system has been fairly successful as a means of spreading holiday travel more evenly throughout the season, but it has not worked so well from the industrial point of view. If a steady rate of production is to be maintained, holiday rotas must be planned, with a view to avoiding fluctuations both in the total labor force and in the relative strength of the different departments and sections of the factory.

Managements have found that it is not possible to achieve this aim in practice for a variety of reasons. For instance, husbands and wives want to spend their holidays together; mothers want a week during the school holidays to be with the children; girls want to delay making a choice of dates until they know when their boy friend in the Forces is having his seven days leave; and finally, many workers have no wish to change their customary habit of taking their holiday in August.

Difficulties Involved

IN CONSEQUENCE, as the rotas are being compiled production suffers in order to satisfy a series of individual needs, with the result that many managements who have tried the rota system are of the opinion that the interests of production would best be served by retaining the practice of closing during the August Bank Holiday Week.

Apart from the transport and other problems resulting from the war, much can be said against the old custom. The annual holiday should provide the industrial worker (and indeed every other kind of worker, not forgetting the housewife) with an opportunity to relax and enjoy themselves so that they return home thoroughly refreshed in body and mind, yet the conditions under which the thousands of people who normally go away in the first week of August spend their holiday are calculated to produce exactly the opposite result. They begin by waiting for several hours at a railway station; and then travel to their various destinations in an overcrowded train.

It is however doubtful whether any nation-wide scheme for spreading holidays to avoid the congestion of peak periods would be well received by the people as a whole. But a local experiment of this kind is being made in the City of Leicester which is of interest as an example of democratic planning on a small scale; and if the result proves to be successful it is possible that similar experiments may be made in other parts of the country.

Meeting Held

AT THE instigation of the Ministry of Production a meeting took place at Leicester in December 1943 between Employers, Trades Unionists and Representatives of local authorities to consider whether it would be desirable to have a recognised Leicester Holiday Week at some period other than the first week in August.

This was purely an informal discussion, and it was decided that the representatives should talk the matter over with their constituent bodies, and hold a formal meeting at a later date. The suggestion aroused interest and a second meeting was held in the Town Hall in January 1944, when it was arranged that representatives of all Employers Organisations and Trade Unions would jointly plan a ballot among all the people engaged in each industry, to obtain their views on the following questions:

    1. Are you in favour of a week other than August Week for a permanent City Holiday?

2. If so, which do you prefer; the third full week in July or the fourth full week in July?

The main industries of Leicester are Hosiery, Boot and Shoe Manufacture and Engineering, and ballots were, of course, taken by every industry, in both Federated and Non-Federated Firms.

The only direct experience I possess of the working of the ballot concerns the Engineering Industry, in which each firm organised a separate ballot according to an agreed procedure. A ballot paper was issued to every employee during the week ending January 22nd, 1944 and all personnel irrespective of age, and including management and staff were entitled to vote.· Representatives of both management and workpeople were appointed as scrutineers, and were responsible for submitting a summarized result of the voting to the local offices of the Ministry of Production.

Majority Favor Change

THE Engineering industry voted for a change by a 79% majority, and the result indicated that there was a preference for having the holiday in the fourth rather than the third week in July. The combined ballot results showed that 60% of the total voters in all industries were also in favour of a change, and again in favour of the fourth week in July.

But in spite of the nature of the collective result, in certain individual trades there was a majority vote against changing the Summer Holiday. This fact was taken into consideration in interpreting the results; and at a joint meeting of the parties concerned it was recommended on a resolution that the question be submitted to individual trades to make mutual arrangements with their workpeople for holidays in 1944. The outcome of this was that the whole of the Engineering industry adopted the new scheme, while all other industries took their holiday as usual in August Bank Holiday Week.

Only Partly Successful

AT THIS stage, therefore, it can be said that the experiment was only partly successful, but at the meeting which considered the ballot results, it was felt that the problem deserved further examination. It was recommended that any future discussions should be held under the auspices of the Leicester City Council

In September 1944 a conference of leading Employers and Trade Union officials covering all the industries in Leicester, held several meetings to *discuss holiday plans for 1945*. This was done with the knowledge and ready consent of the Mayor who was kept informed of the proceedings.

The opinion of the Conference was that the substitution of an alternative holiday week in place of the first week in August was desirable to enable workpeople to travel under comfortable conditions and obtain more suitable holiday accommodation. A preference was also expressed for one agreed holiday week for all the industries in the city rather than different weeks for different industries, as the latter arrangement would lead to difficulties in the case of families with members working in more than one industry.

Another Conference Held

THE conference also dealt with the question of the spacing of Bank Holidays throughout the year, a matter which was not included in the previous discussions. The general opinion was that it would be a good thing to have a week-end break during the rather long period between August and Christmas instead of the Bank Holiday on Whit-Monday. · This issue was considered in relation to the proposals for changing the date of the annual holiday, and a sub-committee was appointed to draft a set of recommendations: This committee was composed of an independent chairman, one representative each from the engineering, hosiery and boot and shoe industries, a representative of the Leicester Trades Council, and the Secretary of the Leicester and County Chamber of Commerce, and the following revised proposals were put forward as an experiment for 1945:

1. The summer holiday to be transferred from August Bank Holiday week to the second full week in July.
2. The Whitsuntide holiday (seventh week after Easter) to be cancelled and transferred to the fourth week-end in September.
3. Christmas and Easter holidays to remain unchanged.

The question of school holidays was not forgotten when these proposals were formulated, as parents naturally want to spend their holidays with the children; the Director of Education stated that only about 1% of the school children would be affected by the scheme, which it was suggested should apply to the City of Leicester and any area within five miles radius of the centre of the City.

A ballot was held among the workpeople in the area during the week ending 9th September, on a straight issue; uniform ballot papers were distributed throughout all the Leicester industries, asking for a direct "Yes" or "No" answer to the question; "Are you in favour of the suggested alteration of Leicester holidays as a trial for the year 1945?"

The particular works in which I am interested adopted the following procedure· a locked ballot box was placed in a prominent position in the works, and remained there for a whole week.

A notice was posted on the works notice board outlining the recommendations made by the conference and stating when the ballot would be taken and how it would be supervised. The ballot box was opened in the presence of the Convenor of

Shop Stewards and the Personnel Manager who acted as scrutineers, and were responsible for notifying the result to the Engineering and Allied Employers District Association.

Results of Ballot

THE detailed result of the ballot for the whole area is worth noting, and the exact figures are given below:

Total ballot papers issued:	101,236
Total votes recorded:	57,751
Votes in favour of the scheme:	41,855
Votes against the scheme:	15,896

Thus only 57% of the whole "electorate" troubled to vote, and in one particular factory with which the writer is well acquainted only 43% of the workers (the total pay roll is approximately 1000) were sufficiently interested to complete a ballot paper.

Among those who recorded their votes, approximately 72% were in favour of the change, and the sub-committee in charge of the ballot considered the majority to be large enough to justify putting the scheme into operation. A letter was therefore sent to the Mayor asking him to notify the result to the Parliamentary and General Purposes Committee, with the further request that arrangements should be made with the authorities concerned to enable the experiment to be carried out.

As Leicester has decided to try out the new holiday scheme, the employers and trade unionists who originally planned it are to meet again in October, 1945 to consider the results.

Disappointing

AT THIS stage it would be unwise to prophesy success or failure for the scheme as a whole; but as a democratic experiment it would appear to be somewhat disappointing. The low percentage of voters points once again to the truth which is revealed year after year in the results of Parliamentary by-elections and Local Government elections—that only about half the men and women of Britain are prepared to make the effort to think ahead for themselves how they shall live.

But in spite of this lack of response on the part of the electorate when an opportunity occurs to plan for the future, the reaction is often very different after the event. When an issue has been decided and the results of that decision become apparent, people then begin to voice their opinions in no uncertain terms.

This sequence of events may sadden the administrator, but it restores the faith of the true democrat, and in Leicester, the low level of voting on the holiday ballot was followed by some lively criticsm of the scheme and comments on the validity of the ballot, some of which were expressed in letters to the local press.

One citizen wrote "41% only of those who could have voted desired the change; the remaining 59% are apparently expected to accept the Committee's assertion that a majority!, (41%) exists to justify the change. Incidentally, a number of workers refrained from voting, not out of apathy as the Committee asserts, but from sheer disgust . . . ", and a worker in the boot and shoe industry asked "May I register a protest at the way the holiday ballot was taken?"

"It was stated that the ballot would be strictly secret. In point of fact in our factory the boss handed out the forms and later proceeded to collect the marked section from each individual without so much as a tin box to put them in".

Criticisms

Aɴᴅ another citizen expressed an opinion on behalf of the Forces, "When our boys and girls come home from the war they will find that they will have to take their holidays at a period decided by persons whose interest lies in their home or their home towns; who, through no fault of their own have been directed here under the National Service Act and who will return to their homes as soon as they can. Surely our own absent voices have a full right to be heard!".

After all, there is not really so much indifference, and perhaps when the experiment has been tried and the opportunity again occurs for the people to make their wishes known, some who did not bother in 1944 will make their contribution to the final decision in 1945.

So far as the writer is aware, Leicester is the only town in the country where the community has made an experiment of this kind; and in a statement to the Press, an official of the T.U.C. drew attention to the fact that "if we all reached the same conclusion as Leicester we might find new difficulties". This point should certainly be borne in mind, if the people of any other district decide to plan a similar scheme.

With Some Turnover Apparently to Be Expected
Despite the Success of this Program, Methods for
Reducing the Time Lag in the Adjustment of
New Employees Are as Important as Methods for
Reducing Terminations.

Reducing
Labor Turnover

By Sgt. Sidney Margolius
Camp Ross
Wilmington, Calif.

B UILDING planes pays better, there's a romantic air about a girl welder, young-
stets come out of school into an unreal world where pay is wonderfully high
and jobs are for the taking. Any excuse becomes a good-enough reason for
leaving a job. Altogether, a "white collar" organization has its hands full holding
on to its employees in wartime.

Put that white-collar plant under civil service, making wage competition with
defense plants out of the question, set it down in the heart of gaudy Southern California's booming new industrial center, make it largely dependent upon transient
personnel like service wives for its labor supply, and a high rate of turnover would
seem perfectly natural and excusable. That is, if you want to accept it.

Preliminary Studies

L T. Col. Samuel Glazier, Ordnance Officer at the Los Angeles Port of Embarkation,
refused to accept it. Perhaps a girl could make three times more in tips as a
waitress than she could as a posting clerk keeping track of 400,000 spare parts being
floated to a hundred Pacific bases, but the colonel is rather stubborn about the idea
that it's more urgent to keep 'em rolling out there.

When personnel statistics for the Ordnance Office indicated that the organization (somewhat under 200 people) was suffering from the general high rate of
separations, Col. Glazier and his control officer, Capt. Carl J. Allen (civilian-bred in
administration at General Electric's huge Nela Park establishment), launched a

continuing study of turnover. On that foundation has been built an interesting localized program that has reduced the turnover rate steadily and convincingly.

Since last June, when the office reached a peak turnover rate of 20.7 per cent, the rate has steadily decreased (except for a rebound in September reflecting the return to school of some of the Port's younger employees), until in January the turnover figure had been whittled to 3 per cent. That January figure compares with the office's average of 11.3 per cent for the six months of June to November inclusive.

How this performance was accomplished may provide some useful ideas for administrators elsewhere. It illustrates the possibilities of attacking turnover on a local-area basis; on the ground, as it were, not only from the front office of a firm or plant.

Assessing the Damage

FIRST of all, a study was made which demonstrated for local administrative executives the damage that a high number of separations does to their organizations. Not only are replacements difficult in the painfully tight labor market of today but, section heads were shown, it is 30 days before a worker in a job such as posting clerk is fully capable of handling her share of the work load. The time lag before a worker is wholly adequate for her duties is less of course in such general classifications as stenographer, but does average 30 days in more specialized and unique operations.

It was further pointed out that not only is there this long period of adjustment before the new worker functions at full capacity, but her adjustment is a drag on her co-workers. Approximately half a supervisor's time for several days must be devoted to instructing the new worker. In addition, the work of older, experienced workers is interupted by the need for coaching the newcomer and answering her questions.

Result: a backlog of work accumulates; there develops a tendency to acquire more new employees who must further be coached, necessitating added supervisory employees, etc. Supervisors were shown in terms of the actual experiences of their own departments how such conditions tend to reduce employment standards in order to secure necessary personnel in a tight labor market, sowing in turn the seeds for a future crop of separations.

From the Bottom Up

THE approach to the study was to query directly and anonymously personnel at all levels: worker, supervisor, section and branch chief. The mission was to secure estimates of time lost by terminations, to collate remedies and expedients locally used in the several sections for minimizing the problems of personnel dislocation, and to ascertain in those cases where turnover was high the supposed reasons.

Why They Leave

IT was generally agreed at both supervisory and operating levels that the official reasons tendered by separating employees frequently are not the actual reasons.

Here is a comparison of reasons for resigning given officially by 45 separating employees, with reasons suggested by other employees, including supervisors, to explain why co-workers left. The official reasons, in order of frequency, were:

1. Released due to absenteeism or inefficiency—13.
2. Dissatisfied with positions or working conditions—8.
3. Illness, including pregnancy—7.
4. Followed husbands—6.
5. Obliged to move because of family or family illness—5.
6. Return to school—3.
7. Return to teaching—2.
8. Transportation—1.

The unofficial reasons, in order of importance as weighted by employees, are:

1. Transitory personnel, following husbands or returning to school.
2. Insufficient civil service rating.
3. Monotony of the type of work.
4. Resentment of supervisor, or feeling of unfair treatment.
5. A so-called negligent attitude towards the job on the part of younger employees, especially those just out of high school, induced by the employee's awareness it is so easy to get another job, perhaps at even more money than civil service pay.

Why They Remained

WHAT was happening in many cases, of course, was that when an excuse presented itself, employees were leaving for the unofficial reasons. Furthermore, those released for absenteeism, and in many of the cases of release for inefficiency, might be considered as separating on their own account. Absenteeism is simply the reverse side of the terminations coin. It has become an axiom during this period of manpower shortage, that when separations go down, absenteeism goes up. Absenteeism, looked at from any angle, is a kind of part-time termination.

In an effort to halt turnover in civilian war industries, the idea of cash rewards has been broached. These suggestions fall into two types: attendance bonuses and added seniority; cash bonuses after the war. Both J. A. Krug, WPB chairman, and General Somervell, ASF chief, are advocates of the plan for giving cash bonuses after the war to employees who remain on the job.

But a cash reward is not authorized for an army installation. The non-cash devices that finally succeeded in effectively paring the rate of turnover month by month consisted of these three devices:

1. Motivation
2. Work simplification
3. Rearrangement of supervision.

Motivation

GIVEN two armies of equal strength and equipment, what makes one more successful than the other? The quality of its indoctrination. That has been dramatically proven in this global struggle. Our own Army currently is putting more and more stress on the indoctrination and orientation of troops, as the most important factor in developing morale.

The Ordnance Office put this lesson to work on a local basis to fight the turnover rate among its white-collar personnel, with a program that stresses the employee's work as a direct and important contribution to the war effort. The program was based on these two premises:

"Our job right now is to restore the sense of urgency." (General Somervell's statement as applied to the problem of job turnover countrywide.)

An employee might be able to earn more in some other place, but nowhere can he or she identify more readily with the job of backing up the troops, including a husband or brother, than in the task of helping get the weapons of war over to those men.

Daily Newspaper

AS AN initial device in implementing this program, a small one-page daily newspaper-bulletin is published in the office. It performs these functions: it gives the employee a quick scan of the news in the form of a digest of headlines; it explains incidents in the war in direct relation to the employee's work; it connects up directly such monotonous operations as posting or tabulating with operations on the battlefield and boys and men who need these weapons; it offers sound advice from the best authorities on adjustments to rising prices and consumer problems in general; it gives the local news of the office; it serves as a medium of infomation for lost and found items, apartments and rides needed; it conducts polls of opinion among the employees on such topics as whether or not home-fronters shoud be given full, reaslistic reports of the horrors of the war; it introduces newcomers to the office at large; it tells every chance it gets of wounds suffered or honors won on the fields of battle by employee relatives.

It takes one minute of reading time, and 16 sheets of onionskin to produce daily. It has been singularly successful

There is a fine weekly newspaper for the entire Port, and Port-wide bulletins and news reports issued daily. But nothing is as popular in any newspaper as the local news, and no other medium can as closely pin the war effort down to a girl posting the progress of a shipment of spare parts. The success of this experiment would seem evidence that in publishing house organs, the smaller the area covered by the publication, up to a reasonable point, the keener the interest of the audience. An "area" house organ of this type does not duplicate a firm's plant-wide publication; it *can* tie in very neatly.

Port-wide Orientation

ANOTHER method of indoctrination has been a local orientation for new employees, that brings down to a local basis the all-important rôle of the staff in the winning of the war. A comprehensive program on a Port-wide scale has already done much to orient the new employee by the time he or she finally arrives in the Ordnance Office to go to work. But another investment of time is made to develop a sound relationship with the new employee at the very beginning and in the local area of her work-life. She is taken on a "Cook's tour" of the Ordnance Office, introduced to other people and what they do is simply and briefly explained, people in other sections, not merely in her own section, whom otherwise the employee might not meet for months. The initial paragraph of the prepared script suggests the tone and purpose of this planned first impression:

"This office is where you, as an American, are going to play an important rôle in the task of getting ammunition, guns and other equipment out to our men on the fighting front. Because your job is so important both you and we want you to be as efficient as possible. You've got to be good to win a war, especially against the Japs, and you'll be more efficient if you know what our mission is in this office, how we accomplish that mission, and where *you* fit in on the team."

Flow Charts

EVERY document issued, every announcement made to employees of the Ordnance Office now illustrates and bears upon this recurring theme. For example, a set of flow charts is presented with this preface:

"This pamphlet is published to give personnel concerned practical assistance in achieving the maximum efficiency each of us desire so that we may collectively win this war as soon as we can, and save as many lives as possible."

The mission is clearly stated; consistently adhered to.

At the outset of the program, some executives, both officers and civilians, thought that a realistic presentation of the war news and its impact upon the men overseas might upset some of the girl employees, many of whom had husbands and close relatives in the armies overseas. The feminine home-fronters settled the question by overwhelmingly voting in a special poll held in the office, for a completely realistic report of the war news and its significance to them.

As part of the policy of motivation, administrators who conduct initial interviews with prospective employees try to determine in advance the applicant's intention of staying on the job, pointing out the key rôle of the installation in the war effort, and the obvious fact that transient employees slow up a flow of work that must not be slowed up. This technique not only helps weed out transients, but impresses upon newcomers at the outset the importance of the job.

Rearrangement of Supervision

SEVERAL rearrangements of supervision were installed that would be of no special interest to non-military installations. One policy that did have good success and is worthy of report is the channelization of the flow of work and, equally important in a less tangible way, the flow of queries, complaints and rectification of information. In one large section of posting clerks, other sections of the office formerly had made contact directly with these girls in various matters of work relationship. Too many interruptions and not a few raw feelings developed from this situation. The turnover rate in this department was high.

Two assistant chief posters were designated. The work flow and come-backs now are routed through them. They not only serve to maintain an even distribution of the work, but act as shock absorbers for any complaints.

Too much channelization, especially that for its own sake, leads to over-organization, delays in procedure, red-tapism generally with its evils which are intolerable in time of war. "Functional channelization", such as this example, is valuable.

A supervisory device that has been adopted to assure empoyees fair evaluation of their perfomances consists of a chart, listing at the side the names of personnel in each section, and along the top edge the various duties handled by the section. In the squares thus formed, the employee is rated by a symbol as excellent, good, satisfactory or unsatisfactory in each duty. Thus a supervisor can tell at a glance in how many duties each employee has been trained, in which she has shown facility, and the general quality of her performance.

Work Simplification

A SEPARATE paper can be written on the relation of employee attitudes to work simplification, to efficiency of procedure. It is the thesis of the Ordnance Officer's program that motivation is the coefficient of capability. Ask a worker in the name of the war effort to do a job which for one reason or another she may come to feel is unnecessary or inefficiently-conducted, and she loses interest in the task and learns to distrust the appeal to her patriotism.

Here are two examples of work simplification that aided job satisfaction considerably.

In one department, the need for interrupting operations to make folders slowed down the work of the posting clerks with resultant dissatisfaction, particularly during moments of pressure. Now the jobs in the section have been broken down so that one girl makes all folders for all the posters.

In another section, the girls had to type form letters to go to overseas theaters with the reports they prepared. The letters were a bothersome detail, aggravated by the fact that no erasures are permitted on such overseas letters. Consequently, what was a brief letter might be typed up as many as six or eight times. The simplification was an obvious one: permission was secured to mechanically reproduce the letters, leaving space for the only isolated and minor changes that ever occurred in these letters.

Suggestion Campaign

SIMPLIFICATION has become one of the most important programs of the Ordnance Office, and its effect on personnel attitudes is very welcome. The main drive of the office now is full employee participation in developing more efficient methods and correcting administrative deficiencies. Every effort is made to cooperate and tie in to the Port-wide employee suggestion campaign, and to have employees receive as much recognition and cash as possible for their ideas.

Are supervisors sensitive about suggestions from people under them for improving operations of their own departments? Sometimes they are. Colonel Glazier met this problem at the very outset, and in interesting fashion. He put the responsibility for seeing that personnel produce suggestions upon the supervisors themselves. He established that it was the mark of a good supervisor that his or her staff was interested enough in, and understanding enough of, the job to come up with ideas for doing it even better.

Minimizing the Product

WITH some turnover apparently to be expected despite the success of this local program, techniques for reducing the time lag in the adjustment of new employees and the burden of training them, are as important as methods for reducing terminations. Personnel are pretrained before entering the Ordnance Office by a Port-wide training program. To further ease adjustment, each Ordnance department has developed a policy file—a simplified operating procedure—which is given each new employee to be as much a part of his or equipment as a desk and typewriter. Another device is a pre-prepared list of typical questions and answers dealing with the work of each unit, which most new employees are prone to ask. The purpose of giving such a list to the employee is to eliminate hesitation on the part of new workers in requesting information, especially if they already have been shown how, and to provide an accessible, understandable guide. The list also reduces the burden of questions on the part of older employees.

Some new employees ask questions they can answer themselves. They are merely seeking reassurance. It is no solution for a supervisor to say, "It's because they don't think," when devices are available to answer such doubts, while conserving the supervisor's time and energies.

We Have Always Felt that There Are Many
Objective Standards of Which Records Can Be
Kept That Would Give a Proper Picture of the
Work of Supervisors. These Would Also Aid
in Defining Their Jobs.

Charting Supervisory Efficiency

By George G. Flood and Murray A. Lewis
Los Angeles, Calif.

THE war, with its attendant economic upheaval, created a situation, which necessitated rapid expansion of industry to produce urgently needed war materials. The demand for workers was enormous, and within a short time reached an unparalleled level. Every type of individual, no matter what his previous background or lack of one, was exhorted to participate in the all-embracing war effort.

Housewives, who had never worked in industry before, students, fresh out of school, or the aged, the physically handicapped—all were utilized in this tremendous undertaking. Time was of the essence, consequently radical measures had to be taken to prepare and mould this heterogeneous assemblage into an active working group.

Partially Trained Supervisors

ALL training facilities were harnessed, and every sound and scientific principle of personnel practice was exploited in an effort to prepare these people for production. To train for skilled operations would have consumed an inordinate length of precious time. Industry, therefore, had to devise such means as would permit the breakdown of skilled jobs into simpler operations, so that utilization could be made of individuals with limited or no experience.

The necessity for rapid promotions, stemming from this industrial expansion, resulted in the elevation of many individuals to supervisory positions, who were only partially skilled technically, and in many cases otherwise inadequately prepared to assume their responsibilities. Particularly, they lacked the ability to handle people.

The inadequacies of supervisors were reflected in general dissatisfaction among employees, increased labor turnover and absenteeism, lowered morale, and other conditions which seriously impaired production. The need for specialized training to partially compensate for these deficiencies, became apparent. Supervisory train-, ing programs were developed to teach supervisors how to handle people, how to adequately instruct their employees, and how to achieve greater efficiency through analysis of work methods. These elements fundamentally represent the Training Within Industry program, which comprises Job Relations Training, Job Instruction Training, and Job Methods Training. The value of these training programs was recognized by many industrial leaders. One weakness, however, was manifested in the absence of objective techniques to evaluate the extent to which the supervisors were practically applying the principles stressed in supervisory training courses.

Day-by-Day Relationship

IT is a recognized fact that the day-by-day relationship between an employee and his supervisor represents the bulwark of an organization, and has far-reaching effect upon the stabilization of a force, and the maintenance of high morale and production. The success or failure of a business organization frequently is attributed to the manner in which this relationship is consummated and the extent to which it is maintained.

In many instances, productivity and the working success of a group is more directly affected by the considerate and personally helpful qualities of a supervisor, than the technical knowledge and ability to organize he possesses. Therefore, it is important to exercise care in selecting a supervisor, in consideration of his skill and ability in handling people, and his faculty for assigning tasks and directing his responsibility with a minimum of friction, as well as for his technical attainment and organizing ability.

Much of the unrest, deleterious morale, absenteeism and labor turnover in industry can be attributed directly to poor supervision. It is believed that management generally admits the validity of this observation; and may also admit the difficulties involved in identifying labor turnover, absenteeism and low state of morale with the particular supervisor who may be directly responsible for such conditions. Obviously, it is difficult for management to maintain consistent contact with and review of the efficiency of the many supervisors employed in a large plant.

Because of the important rôle a supervisor has in maintaining and increasing production through the efforts of those he supervises, it would appear feasible to chart or record a supervisor's "efficiency" just as carefully as industry charts production control records. It is believed that the technique which we have evolved would satisfactorily furnish a visual, factual, and compact record of the supervisor's performance, which could serve as an objective basis for judicious action by management.

What Might Be Charted

A SINGLE chart would suffice to graphically present pertinent data. By means of a line or bar graph, it would be possible to chart rates of absenteeism and labor turnover. Morale is a measurable element; and the charting of morale is most conveniently expressed in terms of absenteeism and labor turnover, making allowance for extremely unfavorable or unhealthy working conditions indigenous to certain operations.

Substantiated complaints relating to supervision made to employee counselors, or direct to management could be appropriately categorized. For example, grievances concerning favoritism might be grouped under one heading. Another series of complaints might relate to the attitude of a supervisor when disciplining his employees, adversely affecting the state of morale. When a predetermined number of substantiated complaints are received which relate to the same condition, a "demerit point" could be entered on the appropriate supervisor's chart.

The number of mistakes of major importance made by employees under a supervisor's direction, also is a pertinent point, which could be shown as a "demerit point." To some extent, it reflects the competence of the supervisor in the rôle of an instructor.

The number of approved suggestions, relating to work-simplification, elimination of overlapping functions, consolidation of duties, etc., could be noted as "merit points."

Production record of the unit over which the supervisor has responsibility, can be easily portrayed by means of a line-graph.

This three-fold division of graphically representing a "supervisor's efficiency" is concretely illustrated in the attached chart. To emphasize the personal implication involved, it is suggested that each chart or record be identified under the supervisor's name, as well as the title of the section, branch, or unit he supervises.

Abnormal Conditions Revealed

WHEN any one, or a combination of these indicies attain a point or a frequency of occurrence which represents an abnormal condition, management should consider it essential to counsel with the supervisor responsible. Continued failure to co-operate or improve his conduct through self-analysis implemented by counseling, could provide a basis for disciplinary action leading to reassignment, reduction in rank, or termination of the supervisor.

MR. JOHN DOE, Supervisor,
Shop #38, Wing Assembly.

PRODUCTION

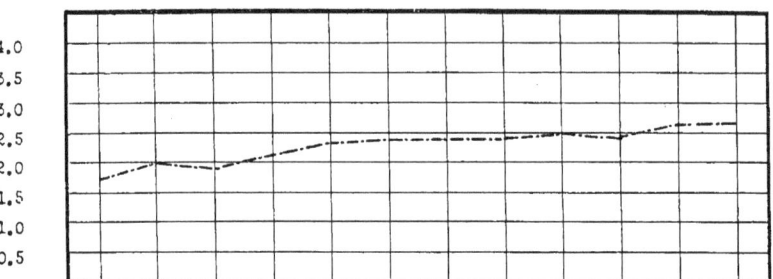

MERIT AND DEMERIT POINTS

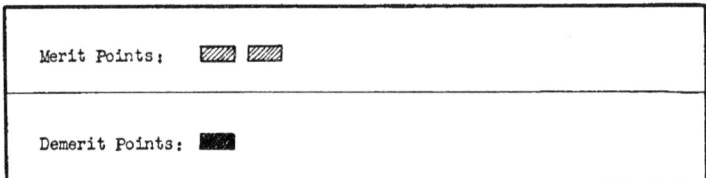

Merit Points:

Demerit Points:

ABSENTEEISM AND TURNOVER

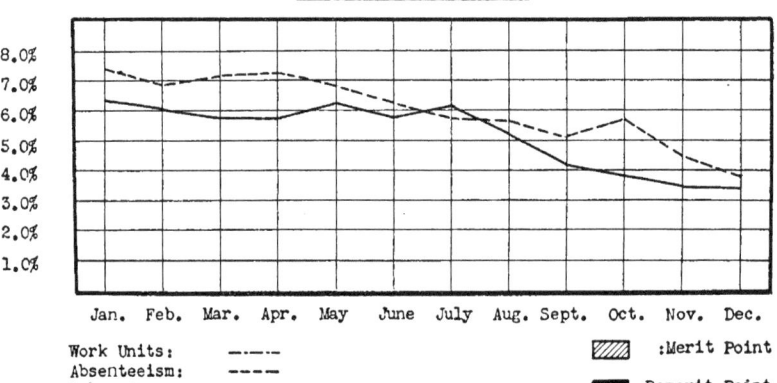

| | Jan. | Feb. | Mar. | Apr. | May | June | July | Aug. | Sept. | Oct. | Nov. | Dec. |

Work Units: —·—··—
Absenteeism: —— ——
Labor Turnover: ————

▨ :Merit Point

■ :Demerit Point

The statistical data maintained would substantiate the disciplinary action taken. Conversely, this statistical data would be of considerable value in taking action leading to promotion and reassignment of the good supervisor. And the knowledge that such data is maintained and employed in the manner suggested, certainly would have the salutary effect of injecting a spirit of competition among supervisors to improve morale. Furthermore, this procedure would focus the attention of the supervisor on the absenteeism and turnover rates, consistent with a share of responsibility which he should bear in this direction.

Personnel Job

IN ORDER to obtain the maximum usefulness of such a system, it would be necessary to assign responsibility for compiling and maintaining the data to some group or body detached from a direct line of command. For the purpose of retaining complete objectivity and freedom from erroneous interpretations, it is believed that this represents a personnel function, or one which should be directly under top management. It is important that these charts be posted in a conspicuous place, and that the supervisors are made thoroughly aware of all of the elements which are taken into consideration in charting and recording their "efficiency." It is equally important that supervisors are informed of the manner in which the statistical data will be utilized, and the effect it may have on their demotion and promotion.

It is believed that this technique, if properly inaugurated, publicized, and supported by management, can prove effective in localizing and correcting causes of employee dissatisfaction. The cost of installing and maintaining the various charts involved would be more than off-set by increased production resulting from enhanced job interest and generally improved morale. Even if application is made on a small scale, for the purpose of correcting certain conditions within an organizational division of a plant, the general publicity afforded such a program would have a salutary effect throughout the organization.

If this limited analysis results in corrective action involving reassignment or separation of poor supervisors, the knowledge that the same technique would be applied to other sections of the plant when necessary, would provide an initial stimulus for other supervisors to intelligently evaluate working conditions existing in their organizational units. This would lead to corrective action, emanating from self-analysis, providing a firm foundation in the structure of better management.

A Boat Will Drift with the Current but There Is
No Way to Row Upstream without Getting the
Oars Wet.

Management
as Minority

By Leonard V. Smoot
Ft. Thomas, Kentucky

D URING the past several years the relations between management and labor
have steadily deteriorated. A few short sighted individuals insist that
nothing can be done to correct this incipient trend, that it is the result of
forces working in human beings upon which no control can be imposed; while others
insist that it is the swing of the pendulum which will reverse itself eventually. To
take such a defeatist attitude is unfortunate for either or both management and
labor.

There is every indication that the relations will get much worse before they begin to improve, and it is possible that both management and labor will suffer untold
persecutions. The majority will win out eventually although it may suffer immeasurably before victory is attained.

Management a Minority

M ANAGEMENT must realize that in order to maintain itself it must do so by the
same methods that any minority group is perpetuated. No minority on earth
can survive by force or coercion or even by stealth. It survives merely because the
majority finds it of use or because its existence does not interfere with the majority
rights. Once the minority violates either of these conditions its doom is sealed.

Management has assumed the rôle in this highly industrialized age of furnishing
the facilities for labor to produce commodities which management again tries to
sell. If through ignorance or greed or carelessness it fails to perform its functions
its usefulness is doubtful. If its failure can be traced to misunderstanding between
labor and management, it is difficult to believe that all of the fault lies with either

the one or the other. Although both are at fault the very fact that management represents the minority group imposes upon it the necessity to act to remove the cause of trouble.

Management and labor can not iron out the trouble by mediation. The formal conferences between representatives of labor and management do not get to the root of the difficulty. Their arguments are superficial and their decisions are erratic. Even though the present trend is toward this type of negotiation, it is doomed to failure. Management will be forced to concede at an ever increasing rate until its function is completely voided. The demands of labor are like those of a spoiled child who asks for more each time he is granted his wish.

Collective Bargaining Not a Solution

THERE is no doubting the fact that management is being lulled to sleep by the thought that the solutions to its problems is collective bargaining. It is positive that it can sit quietly on its side of the fence and await developments on the other side at which time duly appointed representatives will meet at the fence and settle the problems by remote control.

There is evidence that management has welcomed collective bargaining so that it can blame any grievance of labor on the representatives of labor. If the representatives fail to develop the question fully and to obtain a settlement satisfactory to their constituents, more's the pity, but management must not be blamed for the inability of the labor representatives to get a satisfactory settlement. This is not all one-sided but management does enjoy a distinct advantage.

Bargaining and contract making is a highly specialized field in which management is a professional, but labor is yet an amateur. Management has been winning most of the decisions in collective bargaining, but labor is improving its technique. As the tricks of the trade become more apparent to labor groups the decisions will be reversed.

Problems Become Abstract

THERE are advantages to be gained by collective bargaining, but only on a temporary basis. The problems of labor become abstract as they are dealt with by specialists, and all abstract problems can be solved in an abstract way. Most of the problems are very remote to the representatives of both groups, but an abstract solution is seldom satisfactory for a concrete problem. It is doubtful if an abstract solution is a solution at all.

The solution to all problems involving human beings must be prompt, it must be personal, and it must be just. There is not the remotest possibility that a representative can ever present the problem accurately, or for that matter maintain a personal interest in the solution unless he himself is involved. For this reason, if for no other, collective bargaining will not solve the problems of labor.

The deterioration of labor relations began when management retired to its own side of the fence and left no representatives of its own on the other side. This began not with collective bargaining, but with the gradual reduction of supervisory personnel to the level of mere order givers. At one time, not too long ago, supervisors and foremen were truly the representatives of management. As such they stood with management on all questions of policy and practice, but because they were close to the workers they could recognize most of the complaints at their very beginning and eliminate them before they became a grievance.

But supervisors have no such power today; they do not represent management, and they are forbidden to hold any brief for labor: that is the duty of labor representatives. Management is a closed clique, small indeed, and far removed from the actual workers. The supervisors and foremen have nothing whatever to do with policy making, yet they are expected to carry out to the letter the policies made by remote management. Often the policies which have been made abstractly are entirely contrary to what any supervisor should do. By carrying out such contrary policies he alienates the workers from him and likewise from management, because to the workers he is management regardless of his actual status in the business.

The Supervisory Problem Again

IT SEEMS that management must revise its policy to restore the supervisors and foremen to their previous level. The deterioration has not been so great that this can not be done. But it must be done promptly.

Supervisory personnel, being a part of management, should enjoy the confidence of management and not await the formal announcement of new policies through the labor contract.

The right to choose workers for a particular job should be the prerogative of a supervisor, and not the function of a superior supervisor who can shift men about from one department to another at his own discretion.

A supervisor should have the right to discharge a worker for sufficient cause. He should also have the power to reward a worker for unusual services.

A supervisor should be permitted the dignity of his position, and the differential in pay between himself and his workers should be sufficient to maintain that dignity.

Supervisors should be chosen for their position because of their qualifications rather than their politics. Their qualifications would be obvious if proper records were kept. Every man in a group knows who would make the best foreman, but management does not.

These recommendations are not meant to be exhaustive, but management can not survive indefinitely unless it does something to restore the confidence of the workers in management.

A boat will drift with the current, but there is no way to row upstream without getting the oars wet.

The Post-war Competitive Market Will Not
Suffer the Parasitic Behavior of the Untrained
Unenlightened Mismanager. Companies Will
Have to Purge Themselves and Re-design their
Organizations.

Emergency
Administration

By Walter M. Mirisch
Lockheed Aircraft Corporation
Burbank, Calif.

O ne more significant development in American war industry commands our
careful attention

We hear on all sides how schedules are now being leveled off. Production quotas have in most instances been attained and we now seek to maintain those
peaks that have already been reached. However, it is stated in many quarters that
our full production potential has not been fully realized due to the fact that economy
has been tossed to the winds in our efforts, and full utilization has not been made of
our available machines, materials, and manpower. In short, that subsidization has
in innumerable instances led to a relaxation in the characteristic American drive for
greater efficiency.

Relaxation

T he following discussion seeks to explore one particularly virulent form of this
relaxation and the ill-effects it may presage for post-war industry if it is allowed
to continue.

It has often been said that new goups and classes have been spawned by the
war-time stimulus to industry. In the main we have been acquainted with the shop
worker who is today earning more money in a week than his supervisor earned in a
month a decade ago. However, let us now focus our attention on the new-type,
mid-line industrial administrator—for through his portals pass the heart and brain
of American genius. The top executive transmits policy through his office while

workers seek to transmit their ideas and views to top management through his agency.

Five years ago our present industrial administrator was a broker, a salesman, the proprietor of a small business or a minor clerk within the plant. The curtailment of civilian activities and the unprecedented expansion of defense industry channeled him to his present niche in the industrial picture. Continued increase in the size and scope of plant units have quickly brought many of these men to positions of responsibility and importance. Some plan and schedule production; some organize systems and methods; they place, review and administer personnel; they conduct the meat of industrial relations, directly in the work situation.

We may properly ask what training and experience qualify these men for their important functions. Surveys have shown that many of them are inadequately equipped to exercise the authority that rests in their hands. This is often due to a lack of appreciation of technical problems and manufacturing operations, and a deficiency of organizational and administrative ability.

Limited Executive Capacities

IN THE first instance this acts to limit their executive capacities and they tend to shift responsibility on important issues. In the second they tend to act as an extreme force for conservatism. Becoming entrenched in positions of control and prestige, exercising supervision or influence over the activities of great numbers of people, this peculiarly war-time administrative phenomenon is rapidly becoming a vested interest.

As such he tends to be unfriendly to innovation and unduly suspicious of the manifold creative efforts that industrial mobilization has unleashed. Perhaps this is because he does not understand them or perhaps because he fears they might threaten the security of his safe, comfortable position. Certainly, in most cases the poorly trained administrator is probably unaware of his inner motivation. His actions are more overtly determined by a desire to escape responsibility, by a deficiency of technical knowledge or a lack of appreciation of technical problems. He is not trained in the more advanced managerial tools, cannot work with them, and resists the suggestion of them. In many cases he has been above taking E.S.M. W.T. courses and though he abstractly believes the program a fine idea for those below him in the organizational picture, he resists proposals culled from their training made by those who have sought to broaden the base of their job knowledge.

Mid-rank Administrators

THE mid-rank administrator is in a particularly strategic position to exercise his influence. He is the funnel through which ideas flow from the bottom to the top of the organization and vice versa. It is within his province to make decisions on matters of major potential importance. A large west coast aircraft producer was able to salvage (through Work Simplification) a set of recommendations which had been gathering dust in a department manager's office for over a year and which ultimately yielded a savings of $750,000.00 per annum to the Company.

Much has already been said and written about the wastefulness of war industry and there is probably some truth and some excuse on both sides of the question. However, it should be instructive to pursue the matter of waste as a consequence of the psychological makeup of the ascendent war-time industrial administrators.

Cost control has received but little heed from men acting on the theory that the more you spend the more you produce. Line administration, with little intrinsic appreciation of the industrial cost concept has often seemed ignorant of the fact that efficiency is often consonant with cost. Aimless studies are made; useless statistics are collected while really significant items are ignored.

Covers Collect Dust

In the engineering department of one large concern a quality control study was authorized by department managers. After a year and a half of work on this subject a detailed report was prepared and submitted. The report went from the office of the sponsor of the project to that of a colleague with the notation, "What shall we do with this now?" The report had cost roughly $8,000.00. Nor is this an isolated example; similar happenings occur every day.

Time studies, methods, research, absenteeism, have all been variously explored by a certain company with conclusive evidence that the covers on these researches have not even been disturbed. One administrator undertook a large and costly reporting plan to present certain material, already available in another form, because a hazy "management might like to have it." "It would be a nice thing to lay on their desks every morning." The administrator had no request for the material, nor any clear idea as to what it might be used for.

Many managers cannot see the waste of man power. They feel they need all the people they can possibly secure under them. For the more people the manager places under him, the wider the petty bureaucracy reporting to him, the better is his own position fortified. The more impressive is his prestige standing in the plant community. He seeks to make himself so important a part of the line or staff that he will be irreplaceable when the day of reckoning comes. And well he might be if he succeeds in constructing a maze of red tape, winding octopus-like through his department, branch, or company with himself at the core.

Work Simplification Does Not Always Work

In many respects the Work Simplification programs instituted by many companies have been directed toward correcting some of the inefficiencies and abuses to which reference has been made. The idea was that Work Simplification would constitute a bridge over which ideas could cross from the lower ranks to the upper while over-stepping the mid-administrative waters that might have bogged new ideas down in their conservatism. However, where the Work Simplification programs have fallen into the hands of the inept administrator they have themselves been subverted and have failed to realize their potentialities.

Recently one of America's leading industrial engineers ventured the opinion that this problem constitutes one of top management's major difficulties. Many top managements have literally lost control of many phases of their businesses due to tremendous war-time over-expansion. Weeding out self-interest, bureaucracy, and rank conservatism is no small matter. Yet the situation is not entirely hopeless. The consulting engineer, previously referred to, has conferred with some of America's most important industrial executives and their appreciation of the malignant organism, so destructive to enterprise and initiative, offers at least a glimmer of hope.

The post-war competitive market will not suffer the parasitic behavior of the untrained, unenlightened, mis-manager. Those companies that do not purge themselves and re-design their organizations on the sole basis of ability and enterprise will find themselves at the competitive mercy of those who do. If none do, it is the consuming public that will suffer.

Purge Needed

THE accomplishment of a purge will itself be no easy matter even if the ax is swung from the very top. In most instances there has been tacit collaboration and log rolling among this type of official and he has probably sunk his roots deep in the organization. It may require surgery to remove them.

These statements are not intended to be construed as a blanket indictment of war-time management. Far from it for American productive results convincingly give the lie to any such condemnation. However, they do seek to throw light on an influence that has progressively acted as a drag, restraining or threatening full potentiality. The stronger it becomes entrenched the greater the handicap it will become and the more difficult to dislodge.

The conscientious, experienced, capable industrial administrator with the interests of his company and his community before him will have no trouble recognizing the "drags" about him once he has the time to carefully survey his organization. Let us hope he has the strength to cope with them.

PERSONNEL
Journal

The Magazine of

LABOR RELATIONS AND PERSONNEL PRACTICES

Published by PERSONNEL RESEARCH FEDERATION
Lincoln Building, 60 East 42nd Street, New York City

Volume 24   *Number 2*

Contents for June 1945

Psychiatry and Industry

W̶E MAKE no apology for including in this number three articles on psychiatry in industry. It is a high sounding title, which we have found many
top executives cannot even pronounce correctly.

Yet it is a fact pointed out by Dr. Burlingame that over 60% of discharges by
industry are not due to the inability of employees to do their jobs, but to the physical and emotional environment in which they are expected by industry to work.

That was true thirty years ago, and is still true. Dr. Burlingame does not believe in molly-coddling workers, but he does believe in an intelligent understanding
of worker problems. This cannot be obtained from home-grown personnel men, as
they exist in most industry today.

As pointed out by Drs. Millet and Hayward, this problem is going to increase
in intensity with the return of large numbers of servicemen, whose psychology has
been deliberately—and well—distorted to make them good fighting men. The problem of psychological reconversion involved here, when the war is over, is far beyond
the abilities of most present personnel men.

We therefore strongly recommend that each company either take on its staff
a qualified psychiatric medical practitioner, or enter into a consulting arrangement
with one, for advice and consultation, and the referral of individual difficult cases.

The Editor

The Fighting Forces Have Turned Civilians into Fighters—a Marvellous Psychological Change, Done Not by Amateurs but by Experts. When It is All Over Industry Has the Job of Converting Them Back to Civilians—and This Cannot be Done by Amateurs.

Psychology
of Fighters

By John A. P. Millet, M.D. and
Emeline P. Hayward, M.D.
N. Y. State Committee on Mental Hygiene,
New York, 10, N. Y.

MANY men now in the Armed Forces will, after demobilization, show certain personality changes. If these changes are not understood and taken into account, these men may fail in bridging the gap between military and civilian life. If such failures in re-adjustment should rise in proportion to the rise in neuropsychiatric casualties, which may be expected as the tide of invasion reaches its high water mark, they may well constitute a socio-economic problem of no small significance in our national life.

Peace-time Standards No Use

WAR is a highly abnormal state, and the man who adjusts himself to the life of a fighter does so by ridding himself of certain normal reactions. His normal self protectiveness, for example, which would make him flee danger, is replaced by a combination of idealism and discipline. The good soldier is not a "normal" person by peace time standards of a non-militaristic state. Any soldier, therefore, may have a hard row to hoe in adapting himself to the postwar world, whether invalided out of service, or not.

In some men the long period of hard fighting under the constant threat of death or mutilation, alternating with periods of tense and anxious waiting of unknown duration, has induced a chronic state of tension. In response to the demands of military life, many will have developed hairtrigger reactions to anything which threatens or seems to threaten them. In such a state a man shows marked irritabil-

—43—

ity, quick temper, and restlessness. His sleep may be broken by terrifying night-mares.

Sudden noises produce an exaggerated reaction, and may even throw the man to the ground in a reflex attempt to hide in a fox hole which isn't there. The major-ity of these men can regain their poise and equanimity if they have peace at home, adequate recreation, and an occupation consistent with their abilities.

Will Fighting Instincts Continue

CAN a man who has been systematically taught to release his fighting instincts under the exigencies of war, put those instincts back on the shelf when he doffs his uniform? To this question no general answer can be given. Some men will be able to do so and some will not. Peace time life offers a healthy natural outlet for the fighting instincts through competitive sports and business and professional activities. The majority of men now in the service came from and will return to a life wherein these outlets may be enjoyed constructively. If the world to which a man returns makes a resumption of these activities possible, his fighting instincts will not need to find direct expression in actual hostile combat.

On the other hand, those men who left a life of limited opportunities present a totally different picture. They may feel justified in carrying their fighting tech-niques into civilian life in an attempt to wrest forcibly for themselves the benefits which the community refuses them. It will take wise, courageous planning in the direction of franchise, wider educational and work opportunities, and adequate housing, to enable the soldier whose pre-war life was circumscribed by restricted opportunities to re-direct his combative drives into constructive channels.

Psychological devices, which an individual may have perfected for the purpose of withstanding the otherwise intolerable strains of modern warfare, may rebound and cause difficulty in re-adjusting to civilian life. One such device is the free play of the imagination in day-dreams. It is relaxing to a man who is over-fatigued, yet keyed up, and whose living conditions are extraordinarily primitive and uncomfort-able, to dream dreams of home. As in all day-dreams, the less pleasant elements are left out.

Day Dreams

MEMORIES of the endless disputes with father, the mother's nagging, the shabbi-ness of the furniture, recede, to be replaced by the warm, comfortable picture of father smoking his pipe, mother bringing a pie out of the oven, and the cozy feel-ing of warm bed-clothes. The strength of these day-dreams will make for deep disappointment when the man returns and finds the same defects in the house and the family which annoyed him before he left.

Another source of disillusionment stems from the remoteness from civilian life which comes over a soldier as he goes through the difficult period of adapting himself to army life. He forgets that civilian life in all its trivial details continues even when he is away. On returning he finds that time was not standing still while he was fighting. Mr. Brown who was just a clerk now owns a haberdasher store, the cute girl down the block on whom he never could make an impression has married a 4F, and he feels a burning resentment that these people have gone on with their lives as if "they didn't know there was a war going on".

This resentment is fed by those newspapers and radio commentators, who exaggerate civilian earnings and play up minor outcries against rationing as if they represented the national attitude. In order to counteract such feelings, the community, in its services to the demobilized man, must offer concrete evidence that he is being given credit for the hardships he endured, not merely in terms of a cash settlement, but through arrangements for him to find a secure and productive existence.

Fighting Man vs. Civilians

A MORE serious jolt awaits the man who has come from a fighting unit where life is risked recklessly for the safety of the whole group or any individual in it. In his home town he finds that every man is for himself and little more than lip service is paid to the welfare of the group.

Many a man will feel strange with civilians, will feel that they don't speak the same language any more, and will find when he is in a group of friends that he is lonely and not sure of making himself understood. Recreation centers for ex-service men seem to be the logical suggestion to meet this, yet they have the disadvantage of widening the already existing gap between the men and the civilians, making it more difficult for them to adjust themselves to each other.

More constructive help might be expected in community centres, where the returning veteran could find experienced counsellors, a variety of interests, and an opportunity to make new friendships. In such centres opportunity could be provided for him to discuss his problems freely with interested and experienced counsellors, a varity of interests, and an opportunity to make new friendships. In such centres opportunity could be provided for him to discuss his problems freely with interested and experienced counsellors, and to talk out his grievances, real or imaginary, in an atmosphere of good will, friendliness, and understanding.

Decision Making

WITH some men the major problem of demobilization will lie in learning again how to make their own decisions. They will have to get their minds out of uniform. All men who remain long in service learn to leave decisions and planning to those higher up. Having finally adapted themselves to this state of affairs, some with much greater difficulty than others, they are apt to find that the ordered routine life has its compensations.

Inability to make decisions and uncertainty where to turn, therefore, are common reactions in men recently discharged. In some instances, they are confused by the ready availability of too many jobs and need an opportunity to discuss their vocational future with a counsellor who can encourage them to look at all the angles of a given opportunity. The counsellor should anticipate the veteran's desire to have major decisions made for him and should avoid fitting into the role of advisor when he senses a too strongly dependent attitude.

Some men will show a pronounced fear of the future. With the memories of the recent depression still fresh in their minds they will block themselves from starting anything because of the relative insecurity inherent in any occupation. These men, too, will need wise counselling to make them realize that only by developing their skills can they insure their futures and that no job in itself can offer a guarantee of continuous employment. A strong, nation-wide program to make maximum employment possible coupled with an intelligently run program will implement the counsellor's advice.

Advice on Realities Necessary

In advising about occupation, counsellors will find men who wish to make plans that are beyond their abilities. Some will want jobs which require special training which they are not intellectually equipped to undertake. Great tact and ingenuity will be required to make such men aware of the realities and to steer them in a direction which has hope of success. Aptitude tests are often helpful as a means of dissuading men from unsuitable undertakings.

Every effort should be made to help men distinguish realistically between the background of a job and the job itself. The man who wants to start a business of his own will serve as an example. Has he the ability, courage and resourcefulness needed for success? Or is he merely seeking a situation in which no one can tell him what to do? If the latter, he may risk time and money only for a failure.

The man who is discharged with a disability presents, beside the problems mentioned above, some special problems of his own. In many the natural desire for independence is blocked by the realization that his disability may interfere with his doing the kind of work to which he is accustomed. He may be unable to visualize what other kind of work he could do, were he trained for it. To avert this possibility a very active advisory program is needed to prevent some men from slipping into a frame of mind which would further encourage dependence on a pension. Occupational advisors should also take some responsibility for convincing employers that a disabled man is not necessarily incapacitated for all types of work.

—46—

Nervous Cases Difficult

Many men are being discharged with nervous ailments of one sort or another. These men are in a more difficult situation than those with physical handicaps, because, beside the specific disability, they have the added burden of feeling ashamed of the condition. They feel that it was a sign of weakness to have become sick, that if they had been "real men" they could have "taken it". The popular belief that nervous symptoms indicate weakness of willpower is very strong, and is one of the misconceptions which the counsellors must combat in order to persuade a man to accept his new opportunities, or, when necessary, to continue psychiatric treatment. Many of these men feel that by becoming sick enough to be withdrawn from active duty they have let their buddies down. Their feelings of guilt may be so strong as to make them believe that everyone they meet looks on them with the same contempt which they feel for themselves. These men need to be assured repeatedly that everyone has a mental as well as a physical breaking point and that there is nothing disgraceful about having reached either. The counsellor's attitude toward neuropsychiatric casualties and toward physical casualties should be the same.

Where Specialized Help Is Necessary

Certain symptoms indicate that the man needs specialized help. These are, a tendency to repeat the same anecdotes over and over again, depressions or "moping", over-sensitiveness, an emphasis on the disability which is out of proportion to its severity, persistent preoccupation with bodily discomforts, states of unaccountable fear or anxiety, tenseness and restlessness which do not disappear within a few weeks, panics, indecision, nightmares, sleeplessness, violent reactions to sudden noises, memory difficulty, extreme irritability, bad temper, drunkenness The man should be referred to a psychiatrist or a psychiatric clinic for treatment of any of these disorders rather than be encouraged in the all too common idea that "no one can help him but himself".

There are certain specific points which it is wise to remember. Every man reacts differently, and what is helpful for one may not be helpful for another. Any plan must be worked out directly with the man himself, following as far as is feasible the man's own ideas as to what he wants. In dealing with a disabled veteran, one should treat him in the same way as one does a healthy man. In helping him to make his plans, however, one may not ignore his specific disability. This should be taken into account only insofar as it produces real incapacity. The man can be assured that others have succeeded in making a life for themselves with similar handicaps. A consistent expression of optimism and confidence is necessary, to counteract the man's natural feelings of discouragement when he learns that he must start life all over again.

Certain attitudes should be avoided in dealing with disabled veterans. One should not argue with them about things that anger them, nor insist on knowing all the details of a man's experiences when he shows no inclination to discuss them. Over-effusiveness or an overly sympathetic attitude is distasteful to an adult man whether or not he is disabled.

Family Help

IT is desirable to explain to relatives how they can help the man. Many points mentioned above apply at home as well as in the counsellor's office. Relatives can help further by reducing causes of friction at home, such as endless discussions of trifling inconveniences, and by encouraging the man to return to the group activities he used to enjoy. It is damaging to self esteem and to the chance of recovery if men are treated as invalids or as people not wholly responsible, yet it is important that they should not be nagged or crowded into doing things which they find distasteful. Families can be of assistance also in getting the man to take advantage of benefits for veterans, and especially to continue any treatment needed for mental or physical disabilities. He should not be encouraged to become a ward of the government or to involve himself in litigation for compensation beyond that which has been allowed him. Such attitudes on his part can prevent him from ever getting on his feet. Compensation awards will be made whenever there is a justification for them, but, whether or not they are made, the man needs to be encouraged to take responsibility for his own future.

Families who are puzzled by the reason for the discharge should discuss the matter with a physician or a social worker before signing a waiver. There are times when it is not in the man's best interest that he be brought home from an Army hospital, and the Army's routine request for the family to accept him may need to be refused.

Do Not Give Harmful Advice

THE counsellor has a great responsibility. It is hard enough for one person to help another even when the background is known that has made him what he is. In the present situation the counsellor will have only a brief contact, and the most astute may give advice which is not only valueless but even harmful. Good will is not enough and every counsellor should feel it a duty to improve his service by constant study and self-criticism. No one knows all the answers and team-work is essential. The counsellor can not do his full duty unless he picks the brains of others and pools what he can give with services of other organizations.

In conclusion it can be safely said that all veterans are going to need friends. Men with emotional disturbances, particularly, should not remain secluded from people. Opportunities for recreation must be developed to the fullest extent.

Competitive games, for example, are often particularly helpful. Nothing, however, is of greater importance than the acceptance of responsibility for plans, which must be the first step towards building a future. Before a man is ready to make such a plan effective he must be helped to achieve a realistic evaluation of his disabilities, and of the opportunities afforded him for overcoming them.

He must feel accepted by his new group, so that he can identify himself with civilians. In his turn he must accept membership in this new group before he can be assured of successful performance. It is this last mentioned need which he may find it hard to meet. This fact gives to professional counselling its greatest challenge.

Report of a Survey by Ten New York Psychiatrists as To How Psychiatry and Allied Sciences Might be Used by Industry in the Solution of Personnel Problems.

Psychiatry
and Industry

By Lawrence S. Kubie, M.D.

College of Physicians and Surgeons,
New York, N. Y.

IN THE spring of 1944, a group of ten physicians who practice psychiatry in New York City accepted the invitation of Mrs. Anna Rosenberg and the local headquarters of the United States Employment Service of the War Manpower Commission to join their staff in a study of problems of placement in industry. The immediate goal was to see what help psychiatry could bring to the solution of difficult placement problems.

Impression Not Diagnosis

EACH psychiatrist worked with a group of between twenty and thirty interviewers. Case seminars were held, in which an interviewer presented the information that was available on a particular job applicant—to wit, a biographical summary, a job summary, and as much factual data as could be obtained as to the nature of the applicant's contacts with fellow employees, with bosses, and with the employment interviewers. This data was used as the basis for a general discussion by the counselors, the psychiatrist acting as moderator, summarizing the findings, and giving his own impressions as to the nature of the psychopathological problem that underlay the employment difficulty.

One must say "impression" rather than "diagnosis," because the applicant himself was never seen by the psychiatrist, and because the data had not been assembled by a staff trained in the gathering of psychiatric histories. Consequently, although some records were remarkably informative, in others there were significant gaps. This depended partly on difficulty in approaching the individual applicant, and partly upon the native acumen and previous training of the interviewer. Despite these limitations, a fairly dependable impression could usually be reached; and the psychiatric evaluation of the applicant often clarified what had otherwise been a perplexing riddle.

One found many schizoid personalities, many depressive equivalents, many phobias, a few outspokenly psychotic and paranoid persons, a number of mixed conversion states, psychopathic behavior disorders of various kinds, and occasional hypomanic states. In short, one ran the gamut of the unrecognized, untreated, ambulatory psychopathology of our population.

Four Types of Job Applicants

IT SOON became clear that differences in the nature or severity of the psychopathology divided the applicants into four general groups. One group could be cured if treatment facilities could be made available. In another, even with no attempt to cure their neuroses, the applicants could be successfully placed by finding special job situations for them, in which their neurotic needs and fears would not be unmanageably stimulated. It became evident that, for this particular group, the formulation of general rules to guide interviewers and counselors in the placement of applicants with different types of neurotic difficulty was a matter of great practical importance. A third group were so sick that they could be employed only in some form of sheltered workshop; and a fourth were too sick to be employable at all.

These two last groups seriously impeded the work of the agency by taking up a disproportionate share of the time of the workers, particularly as such applicants turned up again and again. Furthermore, these unemployables disturbed the relationship of the agency to industry, because when such applicants were sent out repeatedly, personnel officers tended to lose confidence in the agency's recommendations.

The work is to continue; but in the meantime these preliminary experiences have led us to attempt to formulate in a general way some of the principles that underlie the relationship of psychiatry to employment problems. We are presenting this in the hope that it will lead to further work in the field.

Allied Sciences Must Be Used

IN ANY practical application of psychiatry to sociological problems, several allied disciplines must be utilized: to wit, clinical psychology for psychometric tests and aptitude evaluations, employment counseling, psychiatric social service, and many aspects of education. Separately, each of these can do only part of the job; together, they can make a major contribution to the problems of employment in industry. Yet if this is to happen, the allied scientific and sociological disciplines must develop a better integrated relationship to one another, and the code of industry with respect to its responsibility toward industrial man power must change.

The war has taught that certain types of work, certain forms of risk, certain aspects of responsibility and discipline are all potent forces in making and breaking men's spirits. It has taught, further, that one man may thrive on another man's poison. All of this is equally, if less dramatically, true in the industries of peace. If society recognizes the full implications of this, then a consideration of the quality of human life must take its place beside cost-accounting at the council tables of industry.

Seven Things To Be Done

AT THIS council table, psychiatry and its allied disciplines can make several contributions: (1) by screening out those who are totally unemployable and providing for their shelter, care, and treatment; (2) by allocating to specially chosen tasks, or to sheltered workshops, those who can remain well only under special working conditions; (3) by evaluating individuals both as to their special technical aptitudes, and as to their special personality quirks, and by allocating them to jobs for which their aptitudes fit them, and which are at the same time consonant with their personalities; (4) by applying therapeutic principles to the individual worker who is maladjusted and by using therapeutic principles within the industrial setting; (5) by using social-service procedures to assist workers in coping with those out-of-plant problems which affect both their total psychological adjustment and their plant efficiency; (6) by studying the incidence of neurotic disturbances in different types of work, and under different working conditions (*e.g.*, the effects of hours of work per day and per week, of the two-day week-end as compared to the mid-week holiday, of speed-up systems, and so on); (7) by comparing the efficacy of different systems of job training, and so forth.

Undoubtedly, many other ways of applying psychiatry to problems of labor in industry will develop as experience grows. Whether either management or labor will welcome the help thus offered will depend partly on the way in which such a service is established, but even more on how the recommendations of the psychiatrist affect the vested interests of each group, under varying conditions in industry as a whole, and in the labor market in particular.

How to Set up Industry Service

OUR next task, therefore, is to consider how a psychiatric service in industry must be set up, if it is to be accepted both by labor and by management, and if it is to persist through fluctuating economic conditions.

In the first place, it is clearly essential that the representatives of the psychological sciences should be in a position the impartiality of which can never be questioned. They must be like the expert who is retained by a court, rather than the expert whose testimony is hired by one side of a legal controversy. Therefore, they should never be employed either by labor or by management. They should function, rather, under the auspices of some body whose disinterestedness is generally accepted, such as a joint labor and management council, with joint financial support and joint supervision. Alternatively, they might function under the auspices of a local, state, or federal labor-relations board.

In the second place, all potential objections of organized labor must be taken into account. For instance, certain older unions bear the scars of old struggles with "company doctors" whom they suspected, justly or unjustly, of using medical examinations as an excuse to get rid of union organizers and union members. The coöperation of such old-timers in labor activities can be won only by placing beyond any possible doubt the impartiality of the psychological and psychiatric group.

Union Problems

FURTHERMORE, workers and unions in general tend to prize highly the principle of seniority. Under this principle, length of service gives an employee an increasing certainty of tenure of his position; and any procedure, however scientific, that cuts across this principle will inevitably engender opposition. If an individual laborer has a high seniority rating in one department, and if it should be found that in the course of the years he has become ill-adapted for the work that he is doing, whereas he could work happily and effectively in another department, it would be impossible to persuade the man of the wisdom of making such a change, unless his seniority status could be protected. Furthermore, since he had always looked to his union to protect his seniority, any union that espoused a scientific procedure which jeopardized seniority ratings might soon face rebellion in its ranks.

These objections can be met only by organizing in such a way that indicated changes can be made without endangering seniority rights, and by first convincing union leaders and their members that in the long run proper placement and early psychiatric advice and help are worth more to them than any absolute inflexibility in the application of the seniority principle.

Employer Attitudes

ON THE side of management, we face the fact that the attitude of employers toward any such innovations as this will vary with conditions in the labor market. Under conditions of full employment, when jobs are plentiful and labor is scarce, and when the job must hunt the man, management will be eager to salvage every possible laborer, to shuffle men about so as to fit them into jobs where they are most effective and to supply them with all the care that is necessary in order to help them to function as productively and as healthily as possible. Under these conditions, there will be no incentive to misuse the psychological disciplines simply as a means of getting rid of "inferior" workers.

—53—

On the other hand, when there is any degree of unemployment, when the man must hunt the job, when the competitive struggle grows sharp between different concerns in the same industries, when narrow margins of profit force individual concerns to a close scrutiny of costs, then inevitably the attitude of management must become quite different. Employers of those types of labor which do not require extensive experience or training will at such times have much less objection to an active turnover of labor. They will find the rough-and-ready, trial-and-error method of employment more economical than any elaborate method of evaluation and classification. Thus, in general when many job-hunters are available, industry has less incentive to be patient with those workers who need laborious steps of re-education, retraining, and emotional rehabilitation; and the interest of an individual employer in the psychological disciplines will tend to narrow down to those devices which can function as a watchman at the door to screen out those he does not want. A large labor surplus outside each plant creates stability within the plant; and all the employer needs is some one to relieve him of the less desirable workman.

Flexibility of Plan Necessary

EMPLOYERS with a sense of civic responsibility deplore such an attitude; but since profits are the catalysts of industry, a trend in this direction becomes inevitable whenever jobs are scarce, and before undertaking to organize a psychiatric service for industrial and employment problems, the psychiatrist and his psychological allies must weigh carefully such facts as these. They make it obvious, for instance, that any plan that is adequate for a period of full employment would be likely quickly to fall into disuse during periods of unemployment. Therefore, it is of prime importance so to plan the utilization of the psychological disciplines in industry as to give them at least a chance of persisting through periods of economic contraction as well as periods of economic expansion.

Many ways of approaching this goal might be considered. A tentative suggestion to this end can be made. In the first place, as already indicated, conflicting interests such as these can be reconciled only if such services are made the joint responsibility either of a whole community or of an entire industry. At any time an individual concern can set up a pilot test of such a service; but the service is not likely to endure long if it remains the individual responsibility of an individual plant. If, on the other hand, it is the responsibility of an entire industry or community, it has a fair chance of survival.

Possible Community Center

IT WOULD then be possible in a small community to set up a center in which all industrial operations and processes that are carried on in that particular community would be represented. In larger communities, there would have to be more than one such center. Alternatively, if it was organized on an industry basis, then each industry could set up such cross-sectional centers at key points throughout the country for the industry as a whole.

These centers could perform, either for the community or for the industry that set them up, the functions that replacement training centers and redistribution centers serve in the armed forces—that is to say, they could be portals of intake at which new men were evaluated both as to craft aptitudes and as to emotional quirks; and they could be used for the retraining, reëvaluating, reclassification, and reassignment of men.

Different Plans Could Be Tested

As far as each individual is concerned, the use of such centers would be voluntary; but their existence would mean that for men who had lost their jobs, whether because of ill-health, absenteeism (the AWOLs of civilian life), poor performance, or because of changing economic conditions, an opportunity would be available to find out both what they were best fitted to do under the new economic conditions, and what to do about past difficulties, before undertaking a new haphazard job placement. It is conceivable that sheltered workshops could be set up as accessories to these cross-sectional centers, to serve as neurosis-treatment centers for more individual psychotherapy where this is needed.

If labor and management are ever to develop an adequate over-all psychiatric and psychological service in the employment field, then it would seem that pilot tests of some such scheme as this should be undertaken, both in typical industries and in typical industrial communities.

For helpful criticisms and suggestions, grateful acknowledgement is due to Mrs. Anna Rosenberg, Regional Director, War Manpower Commission; Miss Ann Lehman, Senior Employment Consultant for the Handicapped, United States Employment Service, War Manpower Commission; Mr. Richard C. Brockway, Chief of Division of Placement, War Manpower Commission; Mr. Herbert Feis, economist; Mr. Anthony W. Smith, C.I.O.; Mr. Leo Huberman, Director, Education and Publicity Relations, National Maritime Union; Dr. Sydney Margolin; and to the nine physicians who collaborated with the author in this undertaking: Dr. Viola W. Bernard, Dr. I. T. Broadwin, Dr. Emeline P. Hayward, Dr. Olga Knopf, Dr. Bela Mittelmann, Dr. Z. Rita Parker, Dr. Nathaniel Ross, Dr. Dudley D. Shoenfeld, and Dr. Bettina Warburg.

Reproduced from Mental Hygiene, with permission of the publishers, The National Committee for Mental Hygiene.

Dissatisfaction and Poor Morale Are Often Due
Not so Much to An Employee's Inability to Do
the Job as to His Inability to Adjust Himself to
the Conditions Under Which He Must Do It.

You Can Drive
a Horse *to* Water . . . .

By C. C. BURLINGAME, M.D.

Hartford, Conn.

THE old adage from which the title of this paper was taken seems to me appropriate to a discussion of personnel relationships in industry. The concentration on the drives in industry during the past decades is due for a reëvaluation, particularly in view of the multiple problems that face industry in the post-war period.

It is not my purpose here to wave the banner of psychiatry; I should prefer to speak as one practical man to another, seeking ways and means of applying in industry the principles of psychiatry, through developing an approach to the problems of personnel relationships based on an understanding of human nature and human personality.

Social Incompetence

I WAS myself a pioneer in industrial medicine, and in 1915 I became the first psychiatrist to venture into industry when I went with the Cheney Silk Company on a full-time basis, and eventually became their personnel manager. During that time, we established the fact that psychoneuroses and emotional attitudes on the part of employees toward their employment, their foremen, their fellow workers, and the machines in the great textile industry were responsible for a greater loss in dollars and cents than accidents and contagion.

In 1922, my contemporary, Dr. Elmer E. Southard, of Harvard University, in the course of a survey sponsored by the Engineering Foundation, found that 62 per cent of the cases observed reached the discharge status through traits of social incompetence rather than through occupational incompetence. Dr. Southard's conclusions, like my own, were that "what might be termed dissatisfaction, both on the part of the employer and the employee, arose not from the employee's inherent inability to do the work, but rather from his failure to adjust himself to the conditions under which he was to work."

Emotional Drives

THESE are but two examples of early research in industry that have been carried on for the past thirty years, and the final findings all agree on this point: You can teach a man to operate a machine, you can give him good working conditions, you can give him security in his job—*but* it is the man's own emotional drives that determine whether the man will become a real success from his own standpoint.

Thus, if we are practical, we must study the factors that will develop a man's emotional drive to the end that he may be a coöperative member of a producing team. We must face realistically the fact that both management and labor share the problems of production-for-profit; and since the employee serves the employer in order that the employer may better serve industry, the well-adjusted employee pays dividends.

Workers, like all other human beings, have psychological and social, as well as economic, needs; and the worker who is most profitable to himself and to industry is the one who finds in his work a means of self-expression and a satisfaction of his needs for group relationships. If you din into a man that he is unimportant and that his contribution is ineffectual, he will become irresponsible; if you overinflate his ego, he will "swell up like a poisoned pup" and become a nuisance. The real problem—and this is the key to all constructive thinking—the real problem is to make a man feel as important *as he really is* by making him as important as he is capable of being.

Spotting the Screwballs

TO THE extent that a man feels *essential*, he will become a responsible and productive citizen and worker. The great function of psychiatry in industry is to point the way more directly toward the realization of this goal. I have no intention to-night of presenting you with a treatise on psychotherapeutics. Diagnostic techniques—or what is popularly called "the best ways of spotting the screwballs"—and the whole subject of neurological organic disorders, psychoses, neuroses, and maladjustments are subjects for the consideration of your industrial doctors. But I do intend to outline those broader considerations of policy which will grow out of an industrial philosophy that takes into account the human drives fundamental to mental health in any industrial organization.

It *is* necessary, however, to define clearly the functions of the psychiatrist or the medical man who heads the medical department of an industrial organization. In the interests of a sound program of mental health, he should be first of all a *doctor*, maintaining zealously at all times the confidential doctor-patient relationship with all members of the organization. He should be only secondly an officer of the company. When the reverse is true, industry has only a medical technician, doing an obvious technician's job. The real profit to industry comes from the service of a *doctor*, whose professional standards and ethics are respected and taken for granted both by management and by workers.

Not a Medical Policeman

THE physician in industry, who should possess a psychiatric point of view, must have two main functions. One is administration in the matter of placement—and here it may be well to utter a word of caution that he must be careful not to become a "medical policeman," whose job is merely "to keep the screwballs out," for in that case it may become a game with prospective workers "to fool the nut pick." Again in connection with placement, he has the all-important function of seeing to it that no man is placed on a job that is injurious to his health or beyond his physical or mental capacities.

To repeat, the function of the medical man in industry in connection with placement is not that of a medical policeman, but of assisting a man to get a job he really can do; of protecting the health, life, and limb of those already on the pay roll; and of preventing any new employees from bringing contagion into the plant and thereby menacing the health of those about him.

When the workers know that the various health examinations, routine checkups, and frequent medical reviews are for their own protection—as in the case that the man working next to them on the assembly line might have something "catching"—they will back up the doctor's program with respect and coöperation. But the doctor must be the friend and not the disciplinarian.

If the man in industry with a psychiatric point of view has avoided the pitfall of being regarded as a medical policeman in the employ of the management, and has maintained the confidential patient-doctor relationship, he will have a golden opportunity to serve the worker, to serve the management, and to serve the industry as a whole through the psychiatric point of view.

Purpose to Clear the Tracks

I AM inclined to believe that it is unnecessary to present this psychiatric point of view as something separate and apart from the rest of industrial medicine and of employment practice, as only too often a man will run from a psychiatric consultation which he will welcome under another label. If the industrial medical man will bear this in mind, he will be able to observe and to diagnose neuropsychiatric symptoms without arousing suspicion, resentment, or alarm.

The purpose of psychiatry in industry is "to clear the tracks" for active, vigorous enjoyment of the job to be done, in the interests of maximum efficiency and minimum loss; it is certainly not its purpose to bandy about the terminology of psychiatry to the point where the entire personnel is bent on psychoanalyzing their inmost thoughts. If that happened, we should have something to worry about! Let our psychiatric services emanate from the doctor-patient relationships, and let us be wary of establishing an attitude whereby the worker takes time from the assembly line to go in for a good cry on the psychiatrist's shoulder in order to ease an emotional problem.

Avoidance of Paternalism

THIS kind of set-up in industrial psychiatry is too near paternalism to make me feel comfortable; for I am strongly "agin" paternalism in business, or government, or anywhere else except in the home, and then only up to adulthood. Paternalism is bad both for worker and for management, because it is against the inherent dignity of man. I am not against bigger and better holidays, or against bigger and better things for everybody. But I have reached the conclusion—from a not inconsiderable experience—that we are actually living in a world of struggle; and if we acknowledge that fact, we must also acknowledge certain fundamental premises in human relationships.

One of those premises involves the idea that life is not a bed of roses. It is a kind of game—and a tough one at that. There are people who consider it to be a game like bridge, played in a comfortable parlor in which the players nod to each other amiably, saying, "May I play a heart, partner?" To which they receive the response, "Pray do."

Life is a Struggle

MOST of us realize, however, that life is more like a football game, and that we are liable to get a boot where the back forms a sort of mound, and be commanded to get up into the line and carry the ball! And I doubt whether any group of people have taken the hurdles of life better than those raised on "football techniques"; certainly, few have enjoyed the game more. So I believe that we should train our people to survive in a world of struggle, and not overprotect them to the point where we deprive them of the strength that is their rightful heritage, and that can be gained only through the development of moral, intellectual, and social muscles.

Actually, there is no fundamental difference between dealing with children and dealing with adults; both must be given a chance to stand on their own feet and to fight their own battles. For that reason, if for no other, industry should keep out of the private emotional problems of employees. When such problems do arise with individual workers, they should be handled on a man-to-man basis through an individual approach—never as an organizational policy, or through an employer's bureau.

If the emotional problem is related to the job, or has a specific relationship to other workers or to the industry, it is the job of the management to delve into the circumstances and find the cure. But if the problem arises out of community or domestic relationships, industry would do well not to step in except on invitation from the worker, and then only on an unofficial and co-worker basis, advising and helping as a good citizen of the community might advise and help another good citizen. In other words, dealing with the emotional problems that arise out of community or domestic relationship should not be considered by the employer as a formal function of industry.

Avoid Welfare Aura

INDUSTRY must get away from all "wellfare aura." No one can buy a man's emotions with welfare work. Attempts to do so are like trying to bring up children on a lollypop-reward basis—they will all want bigger and better lollypops. This does not imply that industry should ignore the basic drives of a man for the psychological and social factors necessary to a productive life which I mentioned earlier; it means that the things that have to be done should be so handled that men will better understand the members of their "team," and will be enabled to make a better producing team. Such things cannot be done even indirectly as a means of buying good will or morale—which are not "buyable."

Any permanency in the development of constructive emotional drives among workers is based upon employment justice, which must be so clearly expressed that the man on the street will be able to understand it readily.

War Psychology Analyzed

THE war has shown us that we can produce at capacity for an almost indefinite time. Industry has been able to mobilize its workers for sustained, concentrated work over a period of increasingly long hours. American patriotism, to be sure, has been one source of motivation—but there is another source, equally potent. War workers have met long hours, difficult housing conditions, food shortages, and other major obstacles to morale and have continued to carry the ball *because the purpose of industry has become the purpose of the worker; he has associated himself with the process and considers himself essential to the total effort.*

Here lies the answer to our major industrial problems. The future of our way of life depends upon the continuation of full production on a sustained basis now and after the war, and industry must take the lead in giving its people that conception and, with it, a vision of what the industrial team has as an objective.

There is no use in trying to solve the problem through a group of phrases and catchwords such as "labor management," "partnership in industry," "profit-sharing methods," and so forth. It is the fact that counts. If the war has taught us anything, it has taught us that *the forces that have brought management and labor together* have been enlightened mutual self-interest. *The cement that has held them together* has been a mutual understanding of the aims, objectives, and goals of that particular industry. The *drive that has sustained production* has been a worth-while goal which the worker could see and was interested in reaching.

The industry of the future, to be successful, will be merely a continuation along these same lines, with the emotional drive of winning the war replaced by appropriate peace-time objectives which will seem worth while in the eyes of the worker. It will not be sufficient to return to buying a man's time at so much an hour to do so much work in a mechanical, unimaginative way; in the post-war period, a man is going to want to know what the industrial team's objectives are, and why. I do not believe I am romanticizing when I say that he is increasingly going to want to know what his particular industry is trying to do, and he will be increasingly restive if he is merely told to "do that" or "do this."

Emotional Desires Not Separate

THERE should be none of the "welfare idea" in such a policy; it should be based squarely on human drives for psychological and social, as well as economic, needs. If psychiatry has taught us anything, it is the fact that there are no lines of demarcation separating a man's various emotional desires. Industry's actual job, of course, is to see that his vocational urges are met, but that need is inexorably bound up with others, and unless the worker sees purpose and essential service in the job he is doing, agitation and unrest will follow. The progress of industry will be determined by our ability to preserve the individual while adjusting him to the central effort.

Twenty-five years ago, I said that "the man who comes along and finds a way *to complicate* industrial tasks so as to use more of the worker's capacity without reducing production will make a great contribution to both worker and management." And I repeat that statement with added emphasis to-day. Monotony, coupled with the failure to absorb a man's capacities, and the inability of the man to comprehend industry's goals are dangerous factors in any industry.

In the days of the artisans, there was a direct incentive "to get out production." The worker took pride in his own craftsmanship and struggled of his own free will to make his cabinet, or his shoes, or his table the finest that could be made. The development of the assembly-line technique has brought a sense of frustration to many workers which has been a potent factor of unrest.

—61—

Interest in Assembly-line Work

IN THIS regard, an interesting experiment is now under way in one of the country's great industrial plants. In connection with an experimental rehabilitation program, this management is instigating trial methods in machine training. In this project, visual performance charts have been pictorially designed to show how each screw and bolt made in the assembly line fits into the final product. The new worker, viewing these charts before starting his first machine experience and referring to them as he proceeds, is thus made aware of the essential significance of each seemingly isolated procedure. Certainly this is a step in the direction of giving purpose and interest to assembly-line work, and the results of such experiments may prove highly valuable to increased production.

I refer to an orderly presentation as part of a training program that is something over and above the practice of showing the worker a complete typewriter, or a complete bomber, or any other finished product, with no real education to orient him in the production scheme.

Incentive Provided

IN THE type of program to which I refer, the trainee is given sufficient knowledge of the other steps and processes so that he can see opportunities for his own orderly progression to higher and higher responsibilities in the industrial team. This is done with the implication that, within practical limitations, his own abilities and his own ambitions determine his own future.

The psychological soundness of such an idea is that a man is given incentive to go ahead—he is *incentive-driven* to develop his own resources for the ultimate profit both of himself and of industry. Through such an effort as this, industry *can* make a man feel as important as he really is because industry will have the means of letting him become as important as he is capable of being.

Experiments in present-day industry extend to other psychological factors as well—for example, in the use of color on machines and work tables. In one large industrial plant, machines employ five or six different colors—such as red for the handles that start the machinery, blue for those that stop it, and so on. On work tables, designs of various colors and shapes are employed on those parts on which the precision work is done. All of these studies that industry is carrying out seem to be a step in the right direction of understanding and utilizing the basic drives in human nature for the ultimate good of all through making the job more interesting and a bit more inspiring.

Dollars and Cents Loss

TO SUM up, I would stress the fact that emotional attitudes of employees toward their employment are responsible for a greater loss in dollars and cents to industry than are accidents and contagion, and that dissatisfaction and poor morale are due not so much to the employee's inability to do the job as to his inability to adjust himself to the conditions under which he must do it.

I would also repeat the statement that the function of psychiatry in industry is to seek out and correct those symptoms of maladjustment in order to save the employee in the broader interests of industry and progress; but that this neuropsychiatric service would best remain a rôle unheralded, although actually it will constitute an irreplaceable service to industry.

General principles to follow in the interest of mental health, as I have stated them, are the avoidance of paternalism, a hands-off policy regarding the employee's private and family problems, reduction of the "welfare aura," and the development in its place of a clearer understanding of the individual's need for psychological and social, as well as economic, satisfactions in his relation to his employment. We will be able to meet those needs, and at the same time increase production, when our workers become *incentive-driven* through realizing the *mutual aims* of workers and management.

Whatever means industry may use in following such principles, it *cannot* fail if in the end it succeeds *in making the purpose of industry the purpose of the worker*, so that the worker associates himself with the process and considers himself essential to the total effort. If industry can do that, then I will amend the old adage: "You can drive a horse to water—and even make him drink!"

Reproduced from *Mental Hygiene*, with permission of the publishers, The National Committee for Mental Hygiene. From a Paper presented at the Eleventh Annual Meeting of the Texas Society for Mental Hygiene.

The Destinies of Management Labor Community
Family Life Stockholders and the Content of
Happy Living Is Now So Closely Interwoven
that the Concerns All Have Quivering Effects
Upon Each Other.

An Appreciation Index

By GERALD ELDRIDGE STEDMAN
Gatlinburg, Tenn.

As I WENT about my interviews in 187 war plants in 12 cities during 1944, searching material for many technical articles concerning engineering, shop practise and tooling, I experimented extensively to develop an "appreciation index," using a form of investigation devised to poll a comparative rating as to city or plant, based upon flash answer to the question: "Tell me, is this a good place to work in? In your opinion, is it a place where workers seem happy in their factory work and the wages they get . . . or not?" Answers were rated positive or negative without attempt to give weight to vehemence of reply, but rather, by gaging total attitude expressed.

Appreciation Index

IN ESTABLISHING the "appreciation index" of each city, persistent care was used to win such interpreted answers from 100 people. These were selected for their broad public contact . . . cab drivers, street car conductors, policemen, ministers, social service workers and teachers, meeting most of them personally on my regular rounds, but phoning others to reflect representative balance.

The results of this study, for the 12 cities under investigation is shown in the "appreciation" of column "A": (Column "B" explained later)

	"A" %	"B" %
St. Louis	68	71
Kansas City	62	63
Tulsa	72	70
Dallas	42	44
Houston	66	62

Denver	71	73
Los Angeles	38	42
San Francisco	52	47
Detroit	18	20
Milwaukee	70	68
Chicago	42	44
Evansville	78	92

War worker immigration, climate, management-labor problems, size, racial proportions, political characteristics are all reflected in this index. But it does represent employee and public attitudes which make it easier or harder for individual manufacturers in various cities to do business from the many standpoints of labor difficulties, absenteeism, production per manhour, employment problems. It reflects to some considerable degree the character of management thinking and industrial relations within each city. It signals the resistance which any forward-thinking individual management may face in attempting to establish cordial worker relationships in areas where callous practices of other industrial managements have tended to produce strife, bitterness and unhappy worker attitudes.

Any inquisitive observer who has traveled at all during this war period will be quite forcefully struck with the way this "city appreciation index" agrees with his own comparative impressions. The index has close parallelism with other economic indices established to measure production efficiencies within such areas.

Index Also Used in Plants

LIKEWISE, I sought to establish this "appreciation index" among individual plants visited. My interviews constantly take me into most plant departments and to machine-side. My habit was to ask this same question of twenty machine operators or floor workers of various departments in each plant, making sure I covered five such plants in each city. Accumulating the interpretation into an average measurement, based upon the 100 answers among five plants in each city, the results are shown in the foregoing Column "B". These indicate again a closeness of agreement, when approached from these two angles.

In the case of Evansville, having had as yet no opportunity to visit the other four plants, the rating shown is that produced from 100 answers secured within the plant of Servel, Inc., Evansville's largest industry. I have so far rated 104 individual war plants by this method and find that Servel, Inc., so far leads all others. Its influence upon the public attitude is reflected by Evansville's leadership in the Column "A" rating.

How was this healthy condition achieved, and what is being done to maintain it? Of this, I write.

Mr. Ruthenburg Quoted

LOUIS Ruthenburg, Servel President is widely known for his industrial statesmanship. He has always recognized management's stake in employee and public attitudes. Before the National Metal Trades Association at Cleveland in 1935 (reprinted in 'Vital Speeches of the Day''), Ruthenburg early emphasized what he then called a self-evident fact that: "Modern managements recognize distinct and special responsibility towards its stockholders, toward the sector of the public which is or may become customers or clients, and toward the people on its payrolls. Responsibilities toward the first and second groups cannot be effectively discharged unless responsibility toward the third group receives adequate attention."

In 1935 he added a fourth consideration—the development of right attitude in the community itself toward industrial management purposes and intent. His influence played a commanding part in the organization of the Evansville Cooperative League, which has accomplished much in the development of that spirit of unity and cooperation which has come to be Evansville's unique reputation as a community of folks willing to work together. This appreciation assures that there will be minimum dereliction caused by discordants produced by individual factors beyond control, who otherwise might pull athwart the common intent.

Evansville Under War Conditions

E VANSVILLE is not particularly favored in climate, with flood threat and smog. It is the commanding center of a 400 mile area. Its transportation facilities are varied. It is densely populated. Its government has left considerable undone in public health measures. Over 95 per cent of its citizens are native born. The majority of its families before the war were rooted there in generations of happy home life; sturdy German and English stock with hereditary traits of skill, solidity and thrift. Presumably destined as "ghost town" in early war production; business leadership soon made it a critical war area with an influx of 30 per cent newcomers. Its war rating is now unusually high and diversified. Mayor Reichert states that 40% of its industries have received the Army-Navy "E" award. The National average is 5%. Servel is the dominant industrial factor, but there are other prominent manufacturers there, such as Mead-Johnson, American Fork and Hoe, Bucyrus Erie, Sunbeam Electric, Hoosier Lamp, Chrysler, Briggs, Republic Aviation Corporation and Missouri Valley Bridge and Iron Company (LST builders).

Influx of Furriners

P ROBLEMS in public attitude have been aggravated in many cities by the influx of "furriners" who cannot gain an "old home town" feeling overnight. Nor can their loyalty for any employer be developed synthetically. There is that period of gestation before appreciation can be born, under even most favorable circumstances. Yet, the Servel "appreciation index," evenly divided between interviews among old and new employees (the latter among workers of the Servel P-47 wing section plant), is in close agreement in a relative 98–86% relationship. This tends to substantiate the conclusion that the company had previously generated right industrial relation practises which, extended to the 4,000 additional new workers, have caused them quickly to develop relatively as great appreciation for Servel working conditions. It is testimony of astute management abilities.

Fundamentally, I presume, this fine Servel and Evansville appreciation rating has stemmed from Ruthenburg's insistence that: "Ye shall know the truth and the truth shall make you free." Nothing is concealed from Servel workers. They know where the money goes. They know the company's post war plans in detail. They know management purposes and intents. They are not held in the dark. There are no sources for malicious rumor, wrong conjecture or bitter supposition. All the beefing is of a healthy nature.

Servel industrial relations are under the able guidance of H. O. Roberts, Personnel Director, with a staff of 72 people including the medical staff. Searching for prime reasons that have most contributed to Servel's good industrial relations, I spent considerable time interviewing Roberts, and I quote him:

Personnel Manager Explains

THERE is no fine line of demarcation between employee and public attitude. Management's stake in either is its stake in both. Ten years ago, coming to Servel ahead of my family, I engaged a temporary room from a charming old lady who, when I said I had arrived to work for Servel, replied, 'Oh, Mr. Roberts, I am so sorry to hear you say that because it is such a terrible place to work. They treat their employees so mean.' While this may have represented the feeling of only one individual in Evansville, I thought it was probably indicative of what was in the minds of many other Evansville citizens.

The duality of the industrial relations task was rather strikingly emphasized to me right there. We immediately inaugurated a ten year program designed to place our internal house in order while, simultaneously, using every earnest means to regain community respect and good will.

We had the essential ingredient, without which all such programs will fail . . . *the inspiration and leadership of top management.*

Sound human relations, either public or employee, are not created overnight They require constant attention. They develop gradually. Once attained, they are not self-perpetuating. Management must be constantly alert to avoid mistakes by any representative who, in a short time, can destroy the good will which has required years to build.

Well defined policies, thoroughly understood by everyone in management and adopted by each person as a personal policy in day-to-day contacts with employees are the foundations of sound industrial relations. Other than that, the job of building and maintaining happy relations is primarily one of sharing complete information with employees.

Heron's Understanding Unit

THE various parts of our ten year program were not started immediately. They have represented the cumulative results of our own experience as well as those of other companies. We have relied on the leavening effect of the 'old timers' in the organization. And we emphasize the importance of developing multiple numbers of what Alexander R. Heron, in his book 'Sharing Information With Employees' calls 'the understanding unit;' a sufficiency of positive cells scattered through the organization to create and maintain positive and healthful attitudes, (end quote).

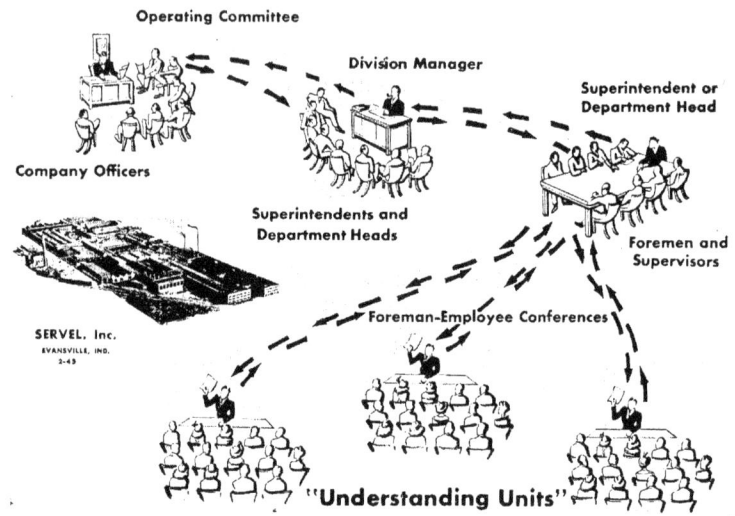

The UNDERSTANDING UNIT in Industrial Relations

Some important features are detailed, of the master objective to which Servel is constantly striving, and which as a long-term program, now shows such evidences of success without in any manner being considered finished. Their mention does not infer any particular order of importance.

Ten Year Program

HOUSECLEANING—Literal as well as figurative. Orderliness and cleanliness essential to good housecleaning came to have real meaning and recognition among all employees. Studies of operations were made to improve efficiency. Plant layout was changed for greater productivity. The wage payment system was overhauled and an incentive system was adopted which protected the employees. Work groups were reduced in size, giving better control and improving morale. Employees were rewarded in direct proportion to output, with guarantee features.

A personnel division was created to coordinate and administer industrial relations. Policies were overhauled or formulated where lacking. Employee services, such as credit union, hospitalization, mutual aid medical care, suggestion award system and others were provided wherever there was a need. Labor relations counselors and consultants were scattered around the plant to talk to employees and assist them with their problems. The policy of the open door with supervisors and management became a real thing. Labor relations became preventive as well as curative.

An intensive safety and health campaign was inaugurated. Modern hospital facilities and a full-time medical and safety director were procured. Frequency of accidents has dropped from 12.95 in 1935 to .083 in 1944. Severity has dropped from 1.15 in 1935 to 0.07 in 1944. Servel has become a safe place to work and everyone knows it. The "S" safety flag of the National Safety Council is flown, with a white star recently added for renewal.

Production schedules were regularized to provide greater year-round employment, eliminating peaks and valleys of income for the worker. This involved storage of the product in "off" sales periods. Labor turnover was greatly reduced. People wanted to work at Servel. Labor supply became more adequate. The Army-Navy "E" flag with three stars attests recent production records.

Keeping Employees Informed

POLICIES and procedures were published through the use of employee handbooks, standard practice bulletins, bulletin boards, posters and other media. There was no secret about what the company was doing, but rather an educational campaign was conducted to show and explain to employees these things of vital concern to them.

An educational department was organized with a full-time educational director. Close tie-in is maintained with schools and colleges. A library was provided for the convenience of employees and as a distributing center for magazines, reports and digests, etc.

A plant publication, "Inklings," was started with the assistance of employees. In addition to the usual plant patter, it serves as a medium for management to talk to employees. It keeps them informed about matters of mutual interest.

Regular conferences between top management and supervisors were started These helped to create the realization that all supervisors are an important part of management with a common stake in its welfare.

Formal foreman conferences were held, stressing the symbol "Triangle of the Job," consisting of economic and technical sides and the human relations base.

Open Forum Conferences

EMPLOYEE conferences with immediate supervisors are held on regular schedule. These are open forums, where any problem or question can be presented by employees. If the foreman doesn't have the answer, he gets it. Recently the story of

"Servel as a Place to Work" was presented by each superintendent or department head and all employees were given copies of the booklet. More recently, a sound-slide film on the company's post war plans has been shown to all employees. Other movies and sound-slide films are shown to stimulate sales of bonds, reduce absenteeism, maintain morale.

Recreational and social activities were started and co-ordinated by an employee organization known as the Servel Employees Association. A board of directors elected by employees annually guide the activities of this organization in coopera-tion with management. Their chief source of income is from stores located around the plant to serve employees. Picnic grounds, lighted ball park, tennis courts and recreation building were provided jointly by the S.E.A. and the company. Clubs of ten, fifteen and twenty year employees were formed. Departmental social clubs became very popular. The head of this department of employee services has been honored with the presidency of the National Industrial Recreation Association.

Annual get-togethers of employees and their families are held at Christmas time. Family picnics for each department or division feature the summer season. This year, close to 100,000 people will have used Servel picnic ground facilities

Open House for Public

OPEN house for the public was inaugurated. Mrs. Smith and her friends were invited to come in and see for themselves what a "terrible" place to work was Servel. She has changed her opinion greatly since that day ten years ago when Roberts first saw her. Upwards of 15,000 people of the community each year visited the plant prior to the war.

Product displays are arranged for employees and their families. Twelve thousand people recently viewed a Servel war product exhibit, together with an Army Air Force display of captured enemy material, in the recreation hall.

An annual letter in understandable language, under Mr. Ruthenburg's signature as president, gives employees "Facts About the Business." Distribution of the income is explained in detail by the use of simple charts. These are then discussed in employee meetings where blown-up charts are used. A unique new type of annual report will soon be given to both stockholders and employees. This cannot yet be described.

Letters to Employee Homes

LETTERS are sent to the homes of employees occasionally when the subject is con-sidered of vital interest to them and their families. A special effort is made to keep in touch with employees in the armed forces to keep them informed about com-pany affairs, especially those affecting their post war plans. A survey among them indicates that $99\frac{1}{2}\%$ desire to return to work at Servel after the war. This is a fine tribute to Servel as a place to work.

Adequate feeding facilities were provided and a program of industrial nutrition was carried on by the Servel sales promotion and advertising department in cooperation with its medical and employee services departments. This program became nation-wide through the cooperation of gas utilities and radio programs. Better health and reduced absenteeism were the immediate results obtained from this project. The main cafeteria is provided with a public address system for announcements, news and musical programs.

The inevitable fact is that any plant in any city is going to gain some sort of "appreciation rating," whether it wants it or not. Public and employee attitudes are not static, dormant states, rather they are vibrant, growing emotions which turn into weeds of bad relations if let alone or into useful crops of flowering appreciation among these "understanding units," if truthfully nurtured. Too many companies feel that relations can be left alone. However, like the ground of a fallow field, neglect causes a rubbage growth of wild rumor, misunderstanding, bitterness with eventual harm to all. It is easier to use methods to cultivate good relations than to ignore the consideration. Bad relations are very expensive.

Servel has established an excellent communication system for the organization, delivery, control and favorable registry of plant information. It guards carefully the proper flow of right impressions from management outward through the supervisional structure into the convictions of. employee and family. And it encourages reflow of idea from them back to management. There is this two way stream of information pouring in orderly and enlivening grace throughout all Servel plant affairs. This "information sharing" is largely accomplished through regular conduct of plant meetings, each refining and advancing the information, each doing its part automatically in training those responsible in methods for its effective presentation to the succeeding group. Regularly scheduled meetings are:

8 Sets of Meetings

A MONTHLY operating committee meeting of top management where plans and program relative to all phases of the company's business originate.

The weekly staff meeting of the vice president in charge of manufacturing, known as "Baker's Meeting", wherein Servel's well known Bill Baker gathers superintendents and department heads around him to discuss engineering, production, personnel and shop problems, schedules, procedures.

The monthly management meeting in which top management and division heads huddle with superintendents and general foremen. Each division head is given an opportunity to speak to this group and enlighten them on things of interest in his particular division. Current announcements are also made in these meetings

Department superintendent weekly meetings are held, involving all members of each concerned department staff of foremen, assistants and group leaders.

The Board of Butchers

FORMAL foremen conferences are preceeded by one week by a preview session attended by superintendents and department heads. This is jokingly referred to as the "Board of Butchers" where all subjects for broad dissemination are hacked, remolded and made ready for most effective presentation to the supervisional, staff and employee components of the Servel organization.

A series of two formal foreman conferences are conducted by the industrial educational department each month. Each subject usually requires a series of five daily meetings with that number of supervisional groups, or approximately 10 sessions each month to cover the 350 top foremen and staff men. Two way flow of information is encouraged in these forums. Here, too, the foremen gain training in group presentations down the line.

Regular foreman meetings are held by foremen with their assistants and group leaders, dedicated to "passing the ripples of information along." No curb is placed upon free discussion of any grievance, beef or squawk. Servel operates on the principle that "expression deflates, repression inflates."

Foreman-Employee Meetings

REGULAR foremen-employee conferences are held once each month. This is the last link in the group communication chain. These are entirely on company time. Here the company shares completely all information with its employees and in turn, picks up from them suggestions to be carried back to management, received through minutes of every meeting. The foremen encourage everyone to speak his mind. These meetings last about one hour. Group attendances average 35 to 50 employees.

It is by such persistent, long-range programming that Servel has achieved its high "appreciation index" among employees and community; the right attitude thus attained having been very profitable to all concerned.

There is, perhaps, no other consideration that merits such attention by the typical manufacturer, for certainly management's stake in employee and public attitude has a mighty bearing on the social responsibilities which industry faces in the more integrated era ahead. The destinies of management, labor, community, family life, stockholders and the content of happy living and satisfaction of all is now so closely interwoven and interdependent that the concerns of all have quivering effect upon each other. No manufacturer can longer ignore human relations without being thrown for a loss . . . a loss to all.

"I Have to Stay Away from the Plant a Few Days a Month to Restore the Self-respect My Boss Takes Away from Me," Wrote a Machine Operator Who Was Absent Twenty Percent of the Time.

Foremen
and Absenteeism

By E. William Noland
Cornell University
Ithaca, New York

WE HAVE too much foreman dictatorship in our plant now. It causes a considerable degree of ill-feeling among the workers, particularly the old-timers and those in the higher skills", wrote a worker whose absenteeism record was one of which neither he nor his employer could be proud. A detailed investigation by the writer of the causes of absenteeism in a New York State industry, extending over several months and eliciting the responses of nearly five hundred workers, either by interview or questionnaire, revealed their attitudes with regard to various spheres of their living. The study disclosed that while the foreman's rôle was only one aspect of the overall absenteeism picture, its importance as an aid to any substantial attack on the problem was unmistakable.

The Foreman as an Appreciative Leader

MANAGEMENT should mingle with the workers and get to know them; during business hours they should come down to the level of the employee, learn his name, and stop and give him encouragement. Do not delegate this authority to the labor-management and other small committees. Plant X executives are not in the plant enough—they spend too much time at the office desk," wrote another whose answers to the one hundred twenty-nine questions submitted to him in a questionnaire bore clear evidence that in his thinking management's key men were the foremen.

"I've been working for Company X eighteen years and have missed six days in that time. Four of them came when my wife was ill several years ago. All this time

I've been blessed with foremen who have always kept me feeling good about my work," said a middle-aged man who criticized severely the seeming propensity of the "younger generation" to take job responsibility lightly. "But it's the foreman's job to understand and redirect their whims!" he added. These are only three of many similar comments volunteered by workers; and almost without exception those who saw such an urgent need for improvement in the foreman-worker relationship were in the high absenteeism category.

Restoring Self-respect

ONE worker, who averaged more than 10 days a month away from his job, insisted that he was never ill physically, but simply "dreaded to face that . . . foreman who doesn't give a fellow credit for having any brains at all." Others insisted that their foreman "knows his stuff" but "lords it over his men until they have no urge to cooperate and do a good job." "I have to stay away from the plant a few days a month to restore the self-respect my boss takes from me," wrote a machine operator who admitted being absent 20 percent of the time.

The correlation between absenteeism and the opinion of the workers concerning the extent to which the foreman displayed appreciation for work well done was 0.67. 89 percent of the workers in the highest absenteeism bracket (i.e., absent more than 10 days a month) felt that the foreman *never* showed such appreciation. On the other hand, 67 percent of those who were in the low absenteeism categories (i.e., absent less than 3 days a month) found that the foreman *always* was appreciative of good work. Furthermore, most of those in the low categories actually had been absent less than *1* day a month.

The Foreman as a Fairminded Supervisor

IF YOU like your job you've got to court the boss to keep it. If he doesn't like you, it's too bad—you get shifted to another department. It's bad for your morale and makes you feel you don't care whether you're on the job all the time or not." This complaint came from a man of forty-two who had worked for the company nine years and who was absent from 4 to 6 days a month because "my foreman doesn't do anything to help me move up in my job. He's the one who has to get the promotions for me." "My boss always acts as though he has a better way to do things—as though you might get his job if he let you try your way," wrote another whose poor attendance record put him indisputably in the category of major offenders.

"My foreman always listens to my suggestions and tries out the ones he thinks will work," stated a woman worker, mother of two grown children, who had been working for the company fourteen years and whose absence had averaged no more than a day a year during that time. "It gives you an interest in your work that you wouldn't have otherwise. Perhaps that is why I want to be here all the time!" she decided.

Of those workers with the poorest absenteeism records, 56 percent felt that getting on with the foreman was 'very difficult'; 33 percent more felt that it was 'difficult'. On the other hand, of those with the best absenteeism records (i.e., less than 1 day a month), 53 percent felt that getting on with the foreman was 'very easy', and 34 percent more felt that it was 'easy'.

Those Over Them

THE workers who got on best with those 'over them' in the plant had the best absenteeism records, and vice versa. 99.4 percent of the Regulars (i.e., those workers who were absent on the average less than 1 day a month) felt that the treatment they were receiving from those 'over them' was at least 'fair', and 59 percent labeled it 'very fair'. On the other hand, 78 percent of the Delinquents (i.e., workers whose absence amounted to more than 10 days a month) felt that their treatment at the hands of those 'over them' was either 'unfair' or 'very unfair'. All this is significant in a discussion of the foreman-worker picture.

The correlation between the opinion of the workers concerning the fairness of their treatment by the foreman and their opinion concerning the fairness of their treatment by those 'over them' in the plant was .81. This seems to indicate that the workers closely identified the foreman with those 'over them', which further accentuates the seeming contribution of an "understanding" foreman to absenteeism reduction.

Non-acceptance of Suggestions

SEVENTY-ONE percent of the Regulars insisted that the foreman not only listened to the workers' suggestions but tried them out. Only 7 percent of this group felt that the foreman paid no attention to suggestions. On the other side, however, none of the Delinquents believed that the foreman tried out suggestions, and eight-ninths of them claimed that the foreman paid no attention to *any* suggestions they made.

While in general workers were not interested in learning what management was doing but felt it was out of their "sphere of influence", 73 percent of the Regulars were 'very much' or 'quite a bit' interested in knowing the functions of management. The remark of a woman worker that "I don't think it's any of my business what the top office does and I'm not particularly interested. Anyway, my foreman ought to tell me what I need to know about management," in addition to being typical, reflects further the reliance that workers place or would like to place in their foreman.

The Foreman as a Teaching and Placement Functionary

I'VE been here three years and have been on four jobs in that time. If the foreman had done a good job of teaching me on my first job, I would still be there. It's pretty hard to really get interested in a job and work at it steadily if you don't know how long you are going to stay at that job," wrote a young worker who was absent from 7 to 10 days a month.

'88 percent of the Regulars felt that their instructions when starting a job had been 'very clear'; 78 percent of the Delinquents felt that their instruction had been 'not at all clear'. "Give us better instruction when we start a job—we'll do a better job then—we'll satisfy the boss better—we'll like and will be made to like our jobs more—and we'll be more regular in attendance at work" was the sequence of logic given the writer by an interviewee at Plant X—and the responses of the several hundred workers who turned in questionnaires indicated that this worker had reflected the attitude characteristic of the vast majority of those who were having trouble sticking to their jobs faithfully. This seemed to be true especially of relatively young and new workers, many of whom had found their first job during the wartime boom.

74 percent of the Regulars said that they were not aware of any needless shifting of workers within the plant; only 3 percent of this group felt that there was a great deal of such shifting. On the other hand, only 11 percent of the Delinquents thought that there was no or very little needless shifting.

The Foreman as Collector of Reliable Data

I DON'T think that most of us know how important absenteeism is," one worker insisted several times in a two-hour interview with the writer. "The foreman is the key man here. He is in the best possible position to 'sell' the worker on the need for regular attendance," he continued.

"Cutting down absenteeism calls for a close checking on its causes and some disciplinary measures. That is the place where the foreman plays an important rôle. As it is now around here often the foreman doesn't even ask you why you were absent, and when he does he usually starts with the assumption that you were sick and says something like 'John, what's the story about yesterday—not feeling well?' Then it's a very simple matter for the worker to nod or mutter a casual 'yes' and go his way. You've got to make the worker feel that he is going to have to give a satisfactory and legitimate account of himself when he returns to his job after having been absent. It's one of the best ways to teach his responsibility and at the same time a composed understanding of his real importance in the industrial production picture."

This description, furnished by a young man who was forced to quit college during the depression, seems to parallel the opinion of the majority of the workers at Plant

X regarding the proper role for the foreman to play as a truant officer. "We aren't made to feel at home around here," declared one man who had been with the company sixteen years. "The foreman is the liaison officer between the worker and management—if he can't make you feel that you are an important cog in the wheel, then no one can," wrote another on the margin of his questionnaire opposite the item on the best way for management to handle the absentee.

Summary

THE workers in this New York State industry saw in the foreman the person who could make a most substantial contribution to the reduction of absenteeism. According to them, the foreman

(1) should recognize that his job involves dealing with human beings as well as being a superior technician, and that regular work habits (which include good attendance) on the part of workers is contingent upon a generous dose of "rapport" between him and those he supervises;

(2) must realize that an important aspect of harmonious foreman-worker relationship is that which has to do with adequate instruction by him when a worker is beginning a job;

(3) will find it helpful to encourage and listen carefully to suggestions from his workers. In fact, the smart foreman finds it effective to make employees feel that certain innovations come from them, when in reality such changes are strictly his "brain children";

(4) can make a genuine contribution to plant efficiency by "fitting the worker to the job" and thereby eliminate much needless shifting of workers from job to job;

(5) holds the key to the collection of reliable absenteeism data, without which absenteeism control is a lost cause;

(6) is "guide, philosopher and friend" to all his workers, especially the "wayward" ones.

There Has Been Too Much Concern in Recent
Discussions about the Quantity of Manpower
We Need Now and After the War—Too Little
Discussion about the Quality of Manpower We
Need.

Manpower *and*
The Future

By Donald Tyerman,

(formerly) Editor of the "Economist,"
London, England

THERE is one important topic of discussion just now which is common to both
Britain and the United States. This topic is manpower. In the United States,
it would appear, current discussion centers upon the desirability or otherwise
of tightening the control of labor for war purposes. .In Britain, that question was
settled perforce long ago, and the central allocation of manpower has been complete
for at least two years. The current question is the extent to which the purposive
allotment of labor to specified occupations of high national priority will continue
to be necessary when the war is over. The methods by which this could conceivably
be done, while at the same time relaxing the war-time regimentation of the individual worker and employer, are being subjected to continuous examination and
argument.

Two Lessons

AMONG the several lessons in economics learnt during the war by the democracies,
two are of outstanding importance. One is the evident fact that national
wealth is composed of real resources of materials, plant and labor, and not money.
The other is that, in the last resort, the limiting factor in both productive and war-
like enterprises is manpower, regarded both quantitatively and qualitatively. The
basic budget of a nation in both war and peace is its manpower budget. Both Britain
and the United States are self-consciously aware that a major task of social organization when the war is over will be the maintenance of high or full employment,
both for reasons of social necessity and productive capacity. The British Govern-

—78—

ment's White Paper on Employment Policy definitely placed the drafting of a regular manpower budget as the executive foundation-stone.

Stress Word "Productive"

THE matter can be stated quite simply. The first requirement of national health and wealth is the regular productive employment of the people. Emphasis should be laid upon the adjective "Productive". The test of a successful employment policy is only in the first instance the provision of jobs for all. In the final analysis it must be productivity or output per head, and it is significant that the discussion in Britain has lately tended to shift very markedly from the general concept of full employment to the particular yardstick of output per man hour.

Reports, articles and speeches from all political quarters are making much play with the notable differences between British and American industrial productivity, which was only masked before the war by the high rate of unemployment in the United States, by the higher proportion of the American population engaged in agriculture and by the shorter working hours in American industry. Even so, the national income before the war was something approaching one fifth higher in the United States than in Britain, and if the rate of unemployment, the ratio of agriculture and the length of hours in industry had been similar, the difference would have been at least a half.

Managerial Ability Needed

THUS the manpower debate in Britain has several sequences. There is first the determination to avoid chronic or periodic unemployment on a mass scale, which was the subject of last year's White Paper, and leads to controversy about direction and allocation as applied to individual work-people. There is secondly what can in general terms be called the problem of management, the solution of which, in the spheres of both government direction and business organization, involves two essential requirements.

The first requirement is a sufficient supply of properly trained technical, executive, professional, administrative and managerial manpower. The second requirement is methods of making use of these technicians and managers in the most fruitful way, without impairing the opportunities which must be left intact for the exercise of their individual enterprise and initiative. In other words, there is a growing demand in Britain for a "managerial revolution" of a kind somewhat different from that popularized in the social analysis associated with the name of Mr. James Burnham.

At the moment, however, it would be untrue to suggest that this qualitative aspect of the manpower problem is uppermost in British discussion. The quantitative problem is still too evident. It has been deeply impressed upon the British mind during the war that fewer than 50 million inhabitants is a small population for the requirements of a great nation, and this population is likely to age and then to diminish in the not distant future.

For the moment, during the war and the transition to peace, the task will be to find enough men to do the jobs at hand, the more obvious physical tasks of re-building and re-equipment. This is the kind of manpower budget which is and will be imperatively required, whatever political snags may be involved.

Output per Head Important

B UT in the solving of these immediate problems it will be increasingly realized, as is already happening, that the qualitative aspect properly treated can itself offer a solution to the merely numerical difficulty. In the last report the decisive factor will be not numbers, but output per head, and it is at this point that organization, management and skill will determine the issue.

PERSONNEL
Journal

The Magazine of

LABOR RELATIONS AND PERSONNEL PRACTICES

Published by PERSONNEL RESEARCH FEDERATION

Lincoln Building, 60 East 42nd Street, New York City

Volume 24   *Number 3*

Contents for September 1945

It is Estimated That One-third of All Army
Jobs are Directly Related to Civilian Occupa-
tions, One Third Are Indirectly Related and All
Are Related in Some Way.

War Department
Views Demobilization

By Major Bradley Nash
Special Planning Division,
War Department,
Washington, D. C.

T HE task of providing employment for the twelve million to-be-discharged
servicemen and women may be considered at the very top of the list
of essentials. The importance of this task will increase as the rate of discharge
from the services continues to grow. Obviously, it is not possible to definitely set
forth at this time the rate of return of our overseas troops, or the rapidity of release
of the forces stationed in this country.

The War Department has announced its intention of discharging in the vicinity
of two million men during the next twelve months, an average of 160,000 a month.
However, their return is not likely to be in an even flow, greater or less numbers
will arrive as shipping becomes available and is released from other assignments.

Job Great

W HEN Japan is finally defeated, the pressure for employment will greatly increase; men will return from overseas more rapidly, since much more shipping
will be available, preference being given to the return of troops, the need for rede-
ployment having ceased to exist. Not only will men return from overseas, but they
will be released from camps and installations in this country. In addition millions
of war workers will attempt to find employment in their normal peacetime occupations. The task before us is a great one and will require all the energy and skill of
which we are capable.

Although the legal responsibility of the War Department ceases when the
serviceman receives his discharge papers, nevertheless, the War Department is most

eager to assist the potential employers of veterans as well as the various interested civilian agencies in any practical way, prior to the soldier's discharge, so that the veteran may have every opportunity to recommence his civilian life under the most favorable circumstances.

New Personnel Record

THE War Department has tried very hard to relate the training and experience which the soldier has had in the Army with his post-war employment opportunities. I would like to call to your attention the new and considerably revised Form 100 which each soldier is given at the time of his discharge, and a copy of which is also available at the regional office of the Veterans' Administration which is nearest his permanent address. This is an exceedingly useful document and as many of you may know from your examination of copies of the earlier form, it undertakes to portray the civilian and military experiences of the soldier from the point of view of occupational skill and training.

Now the new form is much more complete and it allows for more detailed and careful description of just what each man has been doing. In addition, the form does something which I have tried to emphasize elsewhere in my remarks; it directs particular attention to skills acquired in the Army.

This military experience record is placed ahead of the civilian and is the first to catch the eye. The way in which this form is now set up has received favorable comment from a number of personnel directors of large and small business organizations as well as government employment officers. I consider particularly interesting the statement of potential conversion of acquired experience which is also set forth in Form 100.

This lists the wide variety of civilian jobs which can be performed by the former soldier who has had this or that type of military experience. It means that almost automatically, a man can be directed into several types of employment with the knowledge that he has had sufficient experience to perform the work in question.

Relation of Army to Civilian Jobs

IT is estimated that about one-third of all Army jobs are related directly to civilian occupations, one-third are indirectly related, and all are related in some way. Even artillery and infantry assignments such as artillery mechanics (light or heavy) and reconnaissance non-commissioned officers, have thirty to seventy-five related civilian occupations each.

The Army and War Manpower Commission have jointly set up a classification dictionary which lists military occupations and the civilian jobs related to them. This dictionary also shows what additional job training, if any, is needed to convert each military skill to a related civilian specialty, and also the physical activities

—83—

and working conditions of the related civilian job. The list of military occupations is long, including 1,028 job titles they extend from:

> "Anti-aircraft Artillery Observer, Instrument" and "Anti-aircraft Fire Control Observer, Flank Station" through "Camouflage Technician," "Enlisted Bombardier," "Small Arms Weapons Mechanic" and over a thousand others, to "X-Ray Technician," "Yard Foremen" and "Yardmaster."

These one thousand odd military jobs are related to nearly 17,500 civilian jobs covering 130 industries.

Rifleman's Job

LET us take the Army job of rifleman as an example and examine its related civilian occupations and the additional training required for them. The task of the rifleman is at first sight about the least similar to a civilian job that one can find anywhere—but it has 49 related civilian occupations. Here is the Army definition of the duties of a rifleman:

> "Loads, aims, and fires a rifle or automatic rifle to destroy enemy personnel and to assist in capturing and holding enemy positions.
>
> "Reduces stoppages as they occur by operating bolt and cleans, oils, and fieldstrips weapons.
>
> "Must be familiar with use of all hand weapons, including rifle, automatic rifle, rifle grenade launcher, bayonet, trench knife, rocket launcher, and hand grenades.
>
> "Must be trained in taking advantage of camouflage, cover, and concealment, recognizing and following hand and arm signals, and identification of enemy personnel, vehicles, and aircraft. Must be familiar with hand-to-hand fighting techniques. Must understand method of defense against enemy weapons, must know how to read military maps and use a compass."

Related Civilian Jobs

ONE would not say that this is the approved vocational training for a young man trying to find his place in industry, unless he intends immediate participation in black market activities, but here are some of the related civilian occupations:

> Cigar-Machine Oiler, Shape Greaser, Star-Gage Operator, Heat-Treating Bluer, Proof or Final Inspector, Shrink-Pit Helper, Bench-hand or Bench Assembler, and Sub-Assembler, and so on, until 49 jobs are covered. Or take the work of the Army Refrigeration Mechanic. When he returns to civilian life he is fitted to perform a score of duties ranging from bus mechanic and pipe fitter or plumber, to vacuum cleaner repairman. The light machine gunner will find that his experience is related to that of the surveying chainman, chamfering machine operator, shape greaser and so on.

Appreciate Acquired Assets

I HAVE mentioned several times elsewhere, that the really quite extensive period of time which many soldiers have spent in the Army, has resulted in the development of these new skills and trade experience to an extent that would not be possible if the term of service had been for a few months. In many cases these men have advanced well beyond the experience possessed by them in their civilian careers.

It seems to me that one of the most important things that we can do is to bring the employer, as well as the veteran, into full realization of these newly acquired assets. I think that many business men may appreciate this fact, and our personnel officers in the War Department have estimated that as many as 90% of the members of the Army have received direct benefit in the service from the point of view of trade experience, not to speak of the other gains such as health, spirit of cooperation, et cetera.

While 90% is the estimate of these personnel officers, a survey among a small group of discharged servicemen themselves indicated that only a third believed that their Army experience had added to their capacity to secure employment superior to that held before entering the service. It is my belief that a clearer understanding of the relationship between military training and experience and qualifications for civilian jobs will lead to more general utilization of this training and experience.

Surveys by War Department

THE War Department has made some quite extensive, and I think successful efforts, to determine the post-war plans of the soldier. The Information and Education Division of the Army Service Forces had conducted a half dozen attitude surveys which inquire into the lines of employment which the serviceman intends to follow. They have asked his intentions as regards farming, starting his own business, continuation of his education, work with the government, community where he will live, and many similar questions.

Nearly two-thirds of the Army's male personnel have fairly definite expectations as to what they will do when they leave the service. This is not to say that they have already lined up specific jobs or even that they have definite plans for getting into the field they expect to enter, but they have pretty well settled in their minds whether they will try to go to school, start a business of their own, or do some particular type of work for an employer. Another sixth of the men have tentative plans for their post-war occupations—have leanings toward doing a particular kind of work, but do not feel sure of their plans—and the remaining sixth are either undecided or inconsistent in their expressed plans.

Only 40% Want Old Jobs

I THINK these studies are most interesting because they show in broad outline the magnitude of the problem of absorbing these millions of soldiers into useful civilian life. These studies indicate that only ⅔ of the enlisted men who worked for employers before they entered the Army seem quite likely to return to their old jobs; another one-fifth are seriously thinking of doing some other kind of work, although they are still considering going back to their old jobs; but the remaining two-fifths say definitely that they do not wish, or they know that they could not get, those old jobs back.

Also, a preliminary analysis of the Air Corps enlisted personnel shows that in this one segment of the Army alone, about 140,000 men are seriously thinking of trying to get jobs in commercial aviation after they leave the Army, perhaps four times as many men as the job opportunities likely to become available in the first five years after the war, even with an optimistic expansion of commercial aviation. And this does not take into consideration others who may complete for these jobs, that is, personnel from other portions of the armed forces, civilians now working in aircraft plants, and others.

I do not point out these things to be discouraging, but simply place it on the record for all of us to understand and appreciate; the job of fitting the veteran into our industrial and commercial structure will be a demanding one upon our facilities. I suggest the urgency of careful and prompt planning to meet the many problems which you will be confronted.

Expectations of Higher Job Status

Inquiry into the civilian occupational backgrounds of the men surveyed, to obtain perspective on their plans, reveals that nearly four-fifths of them had worked as employees before they entered the Army. Ten per cent reported that they had been in school, and eight per cent said they had been self-employed. Slightly over two per cent of the men surveyed had entered the Army before the war emergency. These men have not been classified by civilian occupational background since some of them were professional soldiers and since none of them would have re-employment rights under the Selective Service Act.

One notable characteristic of the aspirations of the soldier is the hope or expectation that he will enter on a higher employment status than the one occupied prior to his Army service. Of course, this complicates the problem of predicting what the men are most likely to do when they leave the Army for undoubtedly some men have allowed their aspirations unduly to color their expectations of post-war employment.

Twice as many persons wish to enter administrative and professional occupations than were so engaged before the war, and a somewhat less proportion applies to those hoping for employment in skilled occupations, while roughly half as many soldiers desire to return to clerical and sales occupations and semi-skilled and un-skilled occupations as were thus employed before entering the Army.

Eighty-five per cent of the pre-war administrative and professional personnel are likely to return to their familiar fields, and about seventy-five per cent of those formerly enjoying skilled occupation will do likewise.

Some Migration Expected

OF EVEN greater interest to California and the Pacific Coast are the migration plans of the soldier. When the War Department study was made a few months ago, about 80% of the enlisted men in the Army thought that after demobilization they would return to the same state in which they had lived for the most of the five years of their life just prior to entering the 'Army. About nine per cent thought that they would live in a different state—that is, be migrants. 11% of the men were undecided.

Of course changing economic opportunity among the states in the post-war period will help determine the amount and direction of migration; however, as California well knows from its earlier migration experiences, information as to economic opportunity is not always readily available or understood by the migrant previous to his actual arrival at the destination he has selected for himself.

But note that two out of every five migrants expects to come to the Far West. The main stream of Negro migrants will be from the South to the Northeast. The net result from all these movements will result in considerable migration to the Pacific Coast states.

Mainly Those Not Returning to Old Jobs

SOME indication of the characteristics of proposed migrants may be learned from the fact that the least migratory enlisted men are those who were married before entering the Army, the most migratory, those married since entering the Army, while the unmarried occupy an intermediate position between the two. Also, enlisted men who have been in the Army for the greatest length of time, especially those in the Army over two years, are most likely to migrate after the war. Some of the expected migration of the returning soldier simply represents migration resulting from returning to a home which has migrated during the soldier's absence.

The influence of economic opportunity upon migration is indicated by the fact that a much larger proportion of men who do not expect to return to their pre-war employer can be expected to migrate, than among those who plan to return to the same employer. Two-thirds of the veterans who hailed from California declare themselves certain to return to their home state and another 25% believe they will do so but less certain. Less than 2% are certain to return to a different region.

Can Become Embarrassing

OF COURSE, these westward migratory plans are a true compliment to California and its sister states bordering the Pacific Ocean, but I know that all of us here today are fully aware that such intentions are not an unmixed blessing, and unless careful preparations are made, the compliment can become embarrassing. The establishment by your state government of the State Reconstruction and Re-employment Commission shows that you are aware of this.

A representative of the Sacramento Chamber of Commerce was in my office in Washington a few weeks ago and also pointed up your particular problem by stating that that city already had indications of a contemplated movement of veterans to it which substantially exceeds the number of men which left that city to join the armed services. Of course, we cannot rely entirely upon the unemployment compensation privileges which Public Law 346, the so called "G. I. Bill of Rights" extends to the veteran. Those are defensive measures only. Your alertness in recognizing the problem and the adoption of steps to meet it are the important points.

Study of 300 Discharged Veterans

I SHOULD like to describe to you a brief study of the actual experience of 300 discharged veterans who have already had a considerable number of months experience in private life. These ex-servicemen, who served overseas for an average of one to one and a half years, and in this country for another year or two have had little or no difficulty in finding employment under prevailing conditions. This was the case despite the fact that all these individuals were discharged for some medical reason, either physical or mental.

However, only 16% are properly classified as unemployable, or have not sought work. 73% have had little or no difficulty in securing a satisfactory job and only 11% have had real difficulty. 52% have held one job, 22% have held two jobs, and 13% three or more jobs. It is not believed that this mobility is particularly related to their war experience, but rather to the fact that the job first accepted by the veteran was too heavy or otherwise inappropriate for the man in question.

It is interesting to note, in support of statistics which I have quoted earlier, that only 34% returned to their former employer and more than half of these looked elsewhere before returning. 58% did not return to their former employer, and 8% had no job before entering the Army. About one-fifth of the group who returned to their old employers were put to work at some other kind of labor than that which they had done before entering the Army.

USES One Point of Call

IT is interesting to note that half of the veterans seeking jobs made the USES one of the points of call, and it is clear that this agency will be utilized by the vast majority of veterans who do not return to their former employers.

It is also interesting to observe that these 300 ex-servicemen were practically unanimous in favor of joining veterans' organizations, either existing organizations, or those to be formed by veterans of this war. The reason that I consider this interest in veterans' associations noteworthy will be seen when the reasons given for such action are examined. 67% state that veterans' organizations should provide personal help and counseling in job placement, case work, and mutual aid. 54% mentioned social activities and recreation, and 51% the need for protecting or gaining veterans' privileges.

All this emphasizes the interest of the veteran in securing regular and adequate employment and points out that if such employment is not forthcoming in a normal way, he will expect to seek relief through agencies organized by himself and his former comrades in arms.

From a paper presented at the Fourteenth All-day Conference of the California Personnel Management Association.

"This Committee Believes That Action and Planning in All Industries during the Reconversion Period Should Look Toward a Policy of High Wages Accompanied by More Than Corresponding Increases in Purchasing Power."

After *the* WLB— What?

BY WILLIAM S. HOPKINS

Stanford University,
Palo Alto, Cal.

T HE committee which has the belief, as stated above, is not a committee of the CIO or the AFL or of the Government. These are the words of Mr. R. E. Flanders, President of the Federal Reserve Bank of Boston. It is the Committee on Economic Development. The last fact—increases in the purchasing power of wages—relates to the very critical problem we are facing now in approaching postwar prices and inflation. The statement is that there should be continued wage increases. That is what it really means if prices remain high or move upward. Even if prices fall, a wage decline should lag behind the decline in prices. . I am sure the AFL and the CIO would agree with President Flanders on that statement. I will confess it is a little surprising to me, however, to find that positive statement coming from the Committee on Economic Development.

What Is WLB's Policy

T HAT is the position at least of one group in business. Certainly it is the position of labor. There is no saying now what the position of the government agencies will be. It seems possible, perhaps we can say it is probable, that the War Labor Board policy might at least be similar to that C. E. D. proposal.

As a member of the Regional War Labor Board, I am not speaking on behalf of the Board and I am not speaking officially. If any of you have cause to come before the Board, I won't expect you to use it against me.

The War Labor Board's policy is clearly unformulated. There isn't any. There has been a good deal of inference from different opinions of the National and Regional

Board, but I think it is perfectly clear that there is no formulated policy as yet. However, regardless of what policy it may formulate, it is quite probable that its policy will not have a fundamental influence upon the reconversion period.

Board's Days Numbered

THE Board, as you know, is created to last for the duration of the war and six months thereafter. In all likelihood, during the six months thereafter it will have a rapidly declining influence. In general, I think it is safe to say that the Board's days are numbered. I don't know just what the number is, but it is approaching a position of declining importance.

Its policy then may not be of tremendous significance over a very long period of time. The question then remains, if there is no continuation of that Board and if there is no substitution of peacetime agencies set up in its place, and it is probable there won't be, at least immediately, what is the policy and where is it coming from?

I think there is a strong probability that there will be very little government policy in determining the postwar relations. The important facts of the War Labor Board's history are the facts which have taken place during the last two years, and perhaps those during the next six months. The fact that it will be declining in importance doesn't mean of course that there is any decline in the significance of the things it has done during the period when it did have the authority.

Standardization of Wages

SEVERAL things have happened which are more or less the result of policies of the Board which will have a definite effect upon economic labor relations in the postwar period. One of those, which I think is perhaps among the most important in its effects, is the standardization of wage rates which has taken place. It had to take place if the Board was going to do anything about stabilizing wages

There was an inevitable tendency towards standardization. That was apparent even before the bracket theory was promulgated, and, as some of you are aware, the bracket system has enabled a good deal of upward movement in individual cases. The substandard principle has produced still further upward movement among the lower wage rates with the realization of a greatly increased standardized level for individual job classifications.

Wage Rates Sticky

WHEN substandardized wages have been increasingly geared to job description and the subsequent classifications, we say these wage rates have become "stickier" than they were before the war. Fewer personalized rates and more classified rates is certainly the characteristic of the wage structure of this nation today. Classified rates are much more difficult to move downward than to move upward.

They have a tendency to remain fixed even without War Labor Board controls. Of course one of the reasons has been the increased extent of labor unionism during wartime period which I think is a natural influence for stabilizing these rates. Secondly, there have been other stabilized and more or less standardized practices which are still moving into the scene.

The so-called fringe issues, those things the Board called fringes, have turned out to be the Board's principal work although it was originally concerned with wages. Vacations with pay for non-whitecollar workers which were comparatively rare prior to the war, but which are acquiring an increasing standardization, show not only increases in the number of instances with paid vacations, but the present system is being extended. The general Board policy of one week after one year, two weeks after five, is becoming more increasingly accepted everywhere. A large additional group of these so-called fringe issues, most of them familiar to you, are becoming generally accepted.

There are a great many others. You have been dealing with them probably. These fringes acquire a greater stability as the result of the increased trend of the union movement.

Unions Due for Jolt

THIS increase in strength among the unions, in membership, in wealth, and I might add, in brains, in ability to negotiate and in ability to conduct its affairs, of course, is something which undoubtedly will take something of a jolt in the postwar period. The closing down of a great many of the purely wartime operations will undoubtedly result in a considerable decline in union membership. What will happen in the others is, of course, hard to forecast.

The wealth and financial resources of the unions enable them to put up a better fight to maintain the standards they have achieved. It is, of course, well known and undeniably a substantial figure and the increase in the skill, the intelligence in handling of the union affairs, is likewise conspicuous. That, I might add, has been greatly fostered by the mere existence of the War Labor Board and the other government agencies dealing with labor during the war. They have had to put research staffs in the unions. They have had to employ experts of various sorts.

They have employed quite a few of the people away from the staff of the War Labor Board just as the employers have hired others and put them in as experts to conduct their labor relations business, to present their cases before arbitrators as well as before government panels. These things will undoubtedly lead to stronger policy on their part and perhaps to the possibility of much more intelligent leadership.

Hundreds of Labor and Employers Experienced

Now there is another influence or effect which the War Labor Board has left upon the scene which you might not have thought significant. There is a National

Board, Twelve Regional Boards, about fourteen special commissions of the national board and all of these are composed of industry members, labor and public members. I don't know just how many industry members have served on all of these boards, but they certainly run into several hundreds. They have come and gone, of course, but they represent a good cross section of leadership in industrial relations work on the part of employers and leaders among unions, both nationally and locally.

Two or three hundred from each side have had this experience in dealing with the other side across the table in the War Labor Board sessions. Of course, the Boards themselves have large numbers of panels. One public member, one labor member and one industry member, and there, too, they have had the experience of dealing with each other in a capacity which was comparatively new. That is where they have had to solve their problems and come out with the solution; it means that hundreds of leaders on both sides have had to learn to get along.

They have learned how the other side operates. They have, incidentally, in many cases, ganged up on the public members. They found that they can get together on a great many matters, a great many issues. They have been involved in a great many questions beyond the immediate disputes such as national policy, working together and coming out with a remarkably large number of unanimous votes.

All that is to the good and it is all going to be to the good in postwar relations. These individuals are going to know each other better, are going to understand each other better, but, of course, there is that which isn't all to the good.

Flaws and Grievances

THERE is something that isn't quite roses in the picture because they have also found flaws in each other's armor as they sat around the table. They have accumulated grievances. Many parties before the Board have accepted the Board's decision very reluctantly. Very few have not accepted it at all, they are a surprisingly small number.

Most of them have accepted it in a spirit of good grace, but with reservations for that postwar period when there won't be a War Labor Board and plenty of them have accepted the Board's orders, unpopular orders, but said, "We do this now because there is a war on and because we don't want to have trouble now, but as soon as the war is over we are going to rectify it."

So those reservations which have been made by parties on both sides—by industry as well as labor, reservations that they are going to work this out in some other way when the war is over and the War Labor Board controls are withdrawn, can lead to a great amount of disturbance.

The Big Question

THAT is what lies back of this C. E. D. proposition. There can easily be a record-breaking wave of labor disturbances after the war. Whether this will be for the better or not I cannot forecast because I am not a crystal gazer. The chances, however, that they will really break loose are equally great. It depends a great deal upon the point of view and the attitude with which these matters are approached. It depends a great deal as to whether those who have learned to get along with each other in the experiences of the War Labor Board will be able to continue getting along.

Certainly an outspoken union busting campaign will lead into worse and worse trouble. I don't think there is any question about that. The only way to avoid the breakdown of the whole labor relations structure is to go into some sort of intelligent and cautious bargaining and I think it should begin now. It should have begun before this and in some cases undoubtedly it has. It is going to have to be bargained out. It is either going to have to be bargained out or fought out and if it is fought out, it is going to be disastrous for everybody.

Weakness of Employers

REMEMBER what I said a little earlier. The unions are stronger than they were before the war. They have greater wealth and greater brains at their command. The industries may be in some ways stronger but they are going to be temporarily weakened, at least, by the very process of reconversion and the desire on their part to get into as much as possible of the postwar business and not to be frozen out. Many employers are not going to feel that they can afford a long period of inactivity or lockout. They will want to get to work on their peacetime construction as rapidly as possible. Whether that means the maintenance of these high wage scales depends a great deal upon the particular industry involved.

The Committee for Economic Development is urging frankly the maintenance of high wage scales and I think the primary reason for it is the prevention of this postwar turmoil which is so very, very possible. The maintenance of the wage scale may prevent the conflict which came after the first world war with the announcement of substantial wage revisions. You undoubtedly remember that we concluded the first world war by going into a hectic 3 year period in American history. At the end of that three years the unions were very much weaker. They were much weaker when they went into it than they are now. The results of a unionbreaking campaign, if one were undertaken this time, might not be so successful from the union point of view, or the breaker's point of view, as it was in 1921.

Unions May Accept Decreases

I THINK that with the decline of the War Labor Board, more and more is to be placed on bargaining out the disputes. There are going to be a good many incidents in which the unions are going to accept wage decreases if they are bargained properly. I don't know how substantial such decreases will be. A lot depends on the war with Japan, what happens between now and the end of this war.

These points are nevertheless fairly clear in general and are very clear to anyone who has been sitting in on these disputes, seeing the way they have been solved frequently to the satisfaction of almost everybody concerned. A great many of them, as you know, are compromises and I suppose a compromise can be defined as "a settlement which pleases nobody." That is the type of thing which can build up to many a postwar difficulty unless it is carefully thought out and worked out.

Cannot Leave It to Government

Much depends on the industrial and individual situation, but the general position is being taken that this problem cannot be left to the government to solve. We cannot leave it to the government very much longer—as we approach the end of the war with Japan. The government may possibly, if things do go badly, have to come back with a peacetime Labor Board which probably none of you would like. That may be the only alternative if things do go as badly as they possibly can go. The way to do that is to bargain these things out over the table.

From a paper presented at the Fourteenth All-day Conference of the California Personnel Management Association.

The Atmosphere of Many American Factories is Filled Not Only With Dust and Soot But Also with Suspicion and Fear and Distrust and Even Hatred.

Our Class Struggle

By Boris M. Stanfield

Minnesota and Ontario Paper Co.,
Minneapolis, Minn.

T ODAY's popular slogan is: "High Wages and Low Prices that Would Guarantee New Investments." I don't see any other way of solving this almost insolvable problem except by paying the greatest attention to productivity. We don't pay enough attention to it. Higher productivity may result from technological progress, from perfecting organizations and from morale building—a factor that is too much neglected now a days.

Two men of the same skill dealing with the same machinery will produce—it is a well-known fact—different results, depending on their attitude toward their job and the organization to which they belong.

Class Struggle and Confusion

W HAT I find in American labor-management relations is an existence of actual struggle, sentiment on the one hand, and confusion on the other. The ideology of class war is popular only among certain groups, but these groups are influential out of any proportion to their small size. While labor as a rule, and management as a rule, do not adhere theoretically to the doctrine of class war, the daily life of an American enterprise is characterized by class struggle because the atmosphere of an American factory is filled not only with dust and soot, but with suspicion and fear and distrust, and even hatred.

This is a tremendous obstacle. We can look confidently to the production problem. We know that our economists were wrong, not only when they did not foresee in 1929 that the country was on the brink of a catastrophe, but also when in

1940 they underrated so terrifically the productive capacity of this country, demonstrated by the magnificent miracle during this war.

May Lead Us Nowhere

BUT, as I see it, this great technical progress may lead us nowhere. It may be wrecked on the rocks of unsettled human relations in American business, especially in American industry.

How, if there is any chance, can this problem be solved? Drifting—aimless drifting—is so characteristic for management behavior and policies with regard to labor. While labor is demanding more and more, and is in a state of insecurity and confusion, because it doesn't know how much more it can ask without breaking the system of private enterprise, which they would like to see continue in existence, management is haunted by a nightmare of being robbed of its managerial prerogatives in the course of labor-management negotiations.

Is it possible to produce something to convert this state of conflict and suspicion into loyalty and solidarity? I believe it is possible, but certain conditions are required to make it possible. First, the theory and slogans of class struggle must be replaced by propaganda and teaching where all the time of the opposite idea, of class cooperation. This idea must be sold to people with the same enthusiasm which Communists have shown in advocating class hatred and class war.

Management Initiative

MORALE building must be done by management initiative. We can't expect labor, poisoned as it is by distrust and feeling, to start it. You, ladies and gentlemen, know that any labor man who dares, as a rule, to say in a union meeting a good word about management, is usually hissed down and declared a company stooge. There is a feeling of that sort. Management must start, management must take upon itself the initiative, be prepared to encounter difficulties, and yet proceed consistently with a firm faith that it will succeed in the end.

What does it mean for management to start? It means first of all to apply to labor-management relations the same principle that has covered all other phases of managerial work—a scientific approach. Any demand of labor should be considered, not as a battle to be fought and won, but as a problem to be interpreted and solved as sensibly, as practicably as possible. This one thing, this ability to prove to labor its requests, demands, are treated as a problem, would, in itself, produce before long a beneficial change in the whole mentality of labor with regard to management.

Anticipate Labor's Problems

MANAGEMENT, too, should anticipate labor's problems and needs. It is pathetic, as I observed in my studies, to see how management gives in finally under-pressure and threats, and then has to carry the expense, while the union gets all the credit for what costs so much to management. This can't go on without poisoning more and more the labor-management relations, and deepening and widening the wedge between them.

Let me call your attention to one of the neglected factors that should be included in this program, and that is, while we think of American labor as being mostly interested in material satisfactions, we have neglected too much for our own good what you may call the ego of our laboring man, that is a defense for self assertion, for recognition, for appreciation. Every one of us knows that next to hunger and love, the ego is the third most powerful instinct that appears in the earliest childhood, and disappears only with death; and yet, in the treatment of our employees we frequently neglect it.

Don't Humiliate Men

WE OFTEN humiliate our men. We are being punished for it right now. From my observations, many wage demands are camouflaged protests of hurt egos, against bruised self-respect of the laboring man. Paternalism unfortunately will not do much good in this country where people are proud. Management often feels that labor is ungrateful, whereas labor is just proud.

The next step in my program is child and adult education. I find that while we are all very enthusiastic in this country about training vocationally, training draftsmen, automobile mechanics, and so forth, we haven't enough interest in educating citizens, building characters. I find that a great majority of our common laborers are relapsing rapidly into specific and general illiteracy after they have left school.

A dangerous state of affairs, because that is how these millions of people fall an easy prey to irresponsible demagogues, of which we will have plenty when the war is over and the truce between labor and management will be called off. No money is too much, no expense in the budget of enterprise should be considered too great in fighting this dangerous state of illiteracy

Train Leaders

AT THE same time, my program requires training of leaders. You know as well as I do that this vogue of personnel management has led to a tremendous amateurism, and a dangerous racketeering. The only protection against this is spending money, by the enterprises, together and separately, on training managerial and union leaders.

Executives, in my observation, are too often absolutely ignorant, just as much as they are conceited, when it comes to the treatment of labor; they don't know, they assume they know, they have to learn elementary facts about the mentality of their own men, to avoid great disillusionment.

Next, I will say, that because unions seem to be with us to become a part of our new conception of democracy, they are as yet recognized only but the law of the land, but not by the people at large. This is a message to unions that I feel I should mention here.

The unions are playing with fire when they rely exclusively upon legislative protection, and neglect the growing indignation of people who don't understand their irresponsible policies oftentimes. But I maintain that management, in its attitude toward the unions must realize that it is of vital interest for management to have honest, responsible and democratic unions. Management should take an active part in helping unions to become better. It can be done by personal influence and taking unions into their confidence, making union leaders, labor leaders voluntarily act as agents of good will.

Soviet Influence

THIS is something that I feel is essential if we are to avert the greatest trouble after the war. Since 1917 there is the Soviet Giant, the Soviet nightmare to some, the Soviet Heaven to others, that will not leave us alone after the war as it has been haunting us before. It seems that this Soviet pattern is going to stay. It is spreading; it may not spread as rapidly as some of us think, fear or hope; it will undoubtedly undergo substantial changes, because the Soviets don't stand still.

Nevertheless, from now on, as soon as the war is over the Soviet pattern, this Soviet Utopia of which we know so little, but which many millions of people in this country believe to be the seat of happiness—this Soviet will be a challenge to us. That means that the principle of private enterprise that has been for generations glorified as such, considered a natural, immutable law, will have now to prove that it can work and meet the challenge, or else be subjected to drastic and maybe violent changes. If we realize that this challenge can be met, it will be met. All that the unions are doing now is pioneering for good or evil. And so we will have to meet this challenge.

Abundance Plus

IT MUST be met and it can be met if management takes the initiative in pioneering on the new frontier of human relations in industry, with the idea that I have heard from Mr Wallace in Washington just a week ago. He told me it is not just abundance we have to work for, but abundance-plus. I asked what "plus" meant, and he said "Spiritual values."

Let me put a more specific, more concrete meaning into this word "plus." Service, an idea that is rather alien to American enterprise built on the glorified principle of rugged individualism. Yet we begin to feel more and more that without this idea of service, private profit becomes unwarranted. It was not so a generation ago.

That is where this idea of trusteeship or service will strengthen the position of American Enterprise. The Soviet pattern may spread over a good part of the globe. America, however, will produce her own pattern that will not only bring about peace and jobs, as the Soviet pattern did, but will add something that the Soviet pattern was unable to produce so far, namely, dignity of the human being, human freedom.

From a paper presented at the Fourteenth All-day Conference of the California Personnel Management Association.

There are Four Measuring Instruments by which the Value of Any Personnel Function May Be Determined—Testimony or Opinion, Simple Arithmetic, Statistics, and Cost Accounting. The First Is about the Only One Generally Used.

Results *of* Personnel Work

By Herbert G. Heneman, Jr.

On leave of absence from
University of Minnesota,
Minneapolis, Minn.

P ERSONNEL administration is generally regarded as an applied science. Facts, principles and techniques are selected from the natural and social sciences, collated, and adapted for use in the field of manpower management.

Progress in personnel administration depends primarily upon four factors: (1) the state of the arts in the natural and social sciences; (2) the professional personnel viewpoint, i.e., the conception and perception of possible applications of the techniques and findings of the natural and social sciences with respect to increasing the efficiency of the personnel function; (3) the use of the scientific method in the evaluation of these techniques in practice; and (4) at present, to a lesser degree, the assimilation of independent findings arising from industrial experience. These factors essentially predicate the state of the arts in personnel administration, and their inter-relationships are equally vital as a determining force.

Disjointed Admixture

T HIS article will attempt to demonstrate that the current state of the arts in the personnel field represents a disjointed admixture of the four factors, and certain actions will be suggested that might reduce this lack of balance which currently hinders progress in the applied science of personnel. Emphasis will be placed upon the need for proper perspective of the personnel function and for verification of results at the operating level. It will be contended that critical evaluation must stem from within individual plants rather than from academicians and research groups. Finally, cost accounting will be suggested as the most promising simple tool in verification and its use shown as an essential to personnel budgeting and manpower control.

Distortions in Current Practice

A s an applied science, progress in personnel is dependent upon progress in the natural and social sciences. But, progress in the natural and social sciences does not maintain an even pace, and progress within each of the several disciplines occurs at an uneven rate. This alone would account for a portion of the disjointed condition of present-day personnel administration. In addition, personnel must await the findings of the mother disciplines before the techniques can be utilized. For example, the measurement of personality factors would be of great use to applied personnel, but until such time as the psychologists can provide a solution, the applied science of personnel must do without these techniques. It is obvious that there will always be a certain amount of distortion solely because personnel is an *applied* science.

This distortion is amplified by the current dearth of professional personnel administrators with the applied personnel viewpoint. This viewpoint, difficult to reduce to writing, enables the possessor to make skillful judgments in the application of knowledge revealed by other disciplines for the purpose of utilizing manpower most efficiently. This viewpoint consists of the ability to see how the findings of each of the several basic disciplines can contribute to the art of personnel management, and, also, the ability to combine the findings of the several disciplines into new tools or techniques useful in personnel work.

In addition, the applied personnel viewpoint implies the ability to perceive the role of personnel management as an integrated part of general management with the aims of personnel work subordinated to the goals of the total enterprise; it implies long range perspective, social and personal ethics, and the quality of unholding professional ideals regardless of the expediency of the moment. The applied personnel viewpoint is more similar to that of the scientific management philosophy, however, than to a philosophy of social welfare, humanism, or altruism.

Lacks in Perspective

L ack of perspective in personnel administration is not always perceived. There are countless psychologists, economists, college deans, business men, and others who call themselves personnel administrators, when in reality they have little, if any, conception of what the term means. The broad panorama that constitutes the new science of personnel eludes them; their perspective is faulty. Thus, the dean of men in College X who advises Joe Doakes to take chemistry instead of music, the personnel manager who "knows how to handle people", the rough and tumble type of union leader—these have one feature in common. Though they call themselves personnel administrators, they are usually personnel workers engaged in one phase of the work with a lack of perspective that often hinders rather than makes for progress in the field. This lack of the applied personnel viewpoint is responsible for much of the current distortion. To such persons, the phrase, "most efficient utilization of manpower", has little real significance. Personnel workers are technicians. Personnel administrators should be applied scientists.

There is a third factor of even greater importance that hinders—almost stifles—progress in the field. That is the almost complete disregard of industrial personnel managers in their daily work for one of the basic ingredients of the scientific method; namely, the function of *verification*. Indeed, the present state of the arts in the field would justify the designation of personnel as applied witchcraft rather than an applied science.

Unless this condition is rectified, further progress will be almost impossible, for no matter how much progress is made in the natural and social sciences, how profound the applied personnel viewpoint, and how many techniques are adopted, without controlled experimentation in the industrial arena based on observation and verification, progress in personnel will be negligible and accidental. For example, the psychologists may perfect and standardize (probably upon college freshmen) a new test. Personnel workers may use it in industry, but unless they re-appraise its value in the new situation, they are acting blindly with possibilities of regression almost equal to those of progression.

This amazing lack of concern with the *results* of their efforts explains, in part, the apparent paucity of independent experiments by personnel workers within their separate industrial establishments. It is urgent that the personnel journals be filled with case histories of controlled industrial experiments, like the medical and psychological journals, for example, instead of the many opinionated articles currently found in personnel magazines.

Can Verification Be Accomplished

THE current need for verification of existing techniques is great and urgent, and the importance of the task, fairly obvious. The functions of administration, i.e., planning, directing, coordination and control, can be accomplished best only if knowledge replaces whim and fancy. The personnel administrator cannot evaluate policy without possession of the facts. That much is basic. In addition, the possession of facts decreases industrial strife and, hence, improves labor relations; unsatisfactory techniques can be discarded and labor costs, patently reduced. These are basic objectives of industrial personnel administration. The present lack of verification in industrial personnel practice tends to defeat these objectives. Here is the focal point where current practice suffers its greatest breakdown.

This breakdown is so complete, the consequences so dire, that the task of verification of current practice cannot be left to a few university professors, consultants, and other so-called experts. A wholesale attack upon the problem must be made by all personnel administrators. This is only logical, for the problem of verification of results in personnel administration is not a metaphysical exercise, but it is of importance to each personnel administrator in his own bailiwick, confronted by unique problems perhaps, but aiming always at lower unit labor costs.

Further, these men in industry have, in many cases, a background of knowledge, in their own industry far better than that of the social scientists for the purposes of the first attack upon the problem. The assistance of the scientists may be desirable, of course, but the burden must of necessity fall upon those in industry.

The Tools of Verification

THREE simple tools are available to aid in measurement. These include simple arithmetic, statistics, and cost accounting. One simple tool, testimony, while widely used at present, should be discarded. For example, someone sells a firm on the idea of installing a "human relations program". When the program has been installed, the results are appraised by statements from department heads and others who testify that "my foremen have new confidence", or "it has worked wonders", and other such generalizations. Maybe the program was successful—but equally important is the possibility that it was not. Testimony does not give definitive answers. Further, even if testimony gave the right answer, and on the basis of chance that should happen fifty per cent of the time, the vital question of whether the cost of installing the new program was offset by subsequent decreased labor costs remains unanswered. Testimony, as a tool, is the slovenly way, and has little, if any, place in modern personnel administration.

Simple Arithmetic

SIMPLE arithmetic, on the other hand, has a surprising number of uses: various ratios and formulas, refined labor turnover and absentee rates, or, combined with visual aids, such things as Gantt charts and other visual control devices—these are illustrative. However, it might be argued, for example, that all firms measure turnover, and that they are already employing simple arithmetic as a basic tool.

Every craftsman uses some simple tools in his trade, a hammer, a trowel, a wrench, and the like. But there is a vast difference in the way a carpenter handles his hammer from the way a novice would use the same tool. Many firms measure labor turnover—a few use refined rates. But what usually happens? Suppose the separation rate shows an increase. They immediately plan to expand the recruiting function. In such cases, they are abusing the simple tool. The next step after the discovery of increased separations should be a follow-through process to determine specific reasons for the increase. In many cases, the specific causes can be appraised through the use of simple arithmetic, and, once discovered, corrective measures can be instituted.

The above discussion may seem so simple and so obvious as to be out of place in this article; but the fact remains that the tool of simple arithmetic is misused more than it is used in industry today. Most personnel workers are novices in the use of this elementary tool, but once they acquire proper perspective, simple arithmetic will become a valuable aid in verification.

Statistics

SIMPLE arithmetic is not always enough. In seeking cause and effect relationships, personnel administrators must be cognizant that any experiment may yield figures wherein *chance* plays a major role. If the experiment were repeated, it is possible that a different course of action might be indicated. The effect of these chance factors can be appraised through the use of simple statistical techniques such as analysis of differences between means, correlation, and so forth. Description and use of these techniques is beyond the scope of this article, but there is an abundant literature covering the subject. In most cases, reading alone is insufficient to acquire a mastery of statistical tools; however, courses in elementary applied statistics are generally available. It is hoped that those who teach such courses to the practical personnel worker will lay maximum stress on *how* tools are applied, with a minimum of the customary erudite derivations of formulas.

The third simple tool is cost accounting. This is, in many respects, the most useful and potent of the tools of verification. Current practice in personnel suffers greatly from not using cost accounting in the process of critical evaluation. In fact, the wedding of cost accounting and personnel administration is long overdue.

Cost Accounting: The Primary Means

THERE are many situations in industrial personnel administration where use of statistical tools provides inadequate verification. This is because of the need to relate actions to profits in industry. Two simple examples will be used to illustrate the point. Assume that Company Z is considering hiring operators to make a certain commodity. On the basis of selling prices of competing concerns, Company Z can afford to pay no more than five cents per piece for direct labor. Now assume that the company gives tests to prospective employees that indicate that men will produce from 40 to 50 units a day; women, from 55 to 60 units. This illustrates tool number one, simple arithmetic, in action. On the face of the matter, it appears that the company would be better off to hire women operators. However, it is possible that the apparent difference between the sexes is due to chance factors that are operating at the time of the experiment. Tool number two, statistics, can give the answer.

Assume that statistical analysis reveals that a difference of that magnitude could come about only once in one hundred times by chance. Company Z has almost decided to hire the women operators. But before they do, they apply tool number three, cost accounting. Employees work eight hours a day, at a legal minimum wage of forty cents an hour. Total cost of a day's labor is $3.20. The total daily return using women operators is 55 to 60 units at five cents per unit, or from $2.75 to $3.00. Clearly, Company Z cannot afford to hire either male or female operators. And note that cost analysis was the decisive factor.

Another illustration. Company Y institutes a training program that yields labor savings of $1000 per year (revealed by cost analysis). Should the program be repeated on the next group of similar operators? If the cost of the training program is $2000, the answer is obvious. This is the type of analysis that companies could and should, but generally do not, make. The above examples, deliberately simplified, reveal the vital role that cost analysis should play in policy determination. That cost accounting is not extensively used in evaluation of personnel policies and practices is indicative of the primitive level of current personnel practice.

Cost Accounting in Personnel Administration

MOST industrial firms use cost accounting extensively. One of the standard cost break-downs is that of direct and indirect labor costs. Consequently, it might be argued that current cost practice furnishes adequate labor cost control. This is true in some respects. Direct labor costs are available by sub-assembly part, final product, department, and the like. In this respect it is adequate. But there has been a fundamental change in management philosophy, and the old divisions of management into Production, Distribution, and Finance are being replaced subtly by new realistic functional concepts.

The two basic functions may be thought of as Materials Management and Manpower (or personnel) Management. Within each are various sub-functions. Under manpower management might be listed job analysis, selection, training, industrial relations, and so forth. The names are unimportant, but the concept of these functional groups is important, for improved administration will depend on functional controls. For example, selection of personnel is a function common to Production, Distribution, and Finance. Better operations will result if it is conceived as a single function and not as being a separate sub-function of production, a sub-function of distribution and a sub-function of finance.

How It Could Be Used

CURRENT cost accounting practice does not provide a measure of the effectiveness of these newer functional groups, or of their sub-functions. But the same basic figures (job tickets, etc.) that yield labor costs of product X can be used to evaluate the separate personnel functions. Thus, it is not proposed that current cost accounting techniques be suddenly and completely revolutionized. They serve a useful but *different* purpose from the role suggested in this article.

As a beginning, after the cost accountants are through with the job tickets, the tickets could be loaned to the personnel department as basic data for cost analysis by personnel function. It is granted that such evaluation might be rather crude at first. That is to be expected. But with experience would come refinements—the path of progress stems from such crude beginnings. Eventually, handy yardsticks of evaluation would emerge, similar to the current ratio in balance sheet analysis, for example. And slowly but surely would come that most valuable tool of control —budgeting. Imagine the advantages of being able to budget selection costs, or composing a manning table using specific costs. The use of cost analysis as an evaluation technique could open new vistas of industrial personnel administration, replacing haphazard, indiscriminate practice with more precise judgments based on facts.

Basic Progress from Infancy

THIS avenue of approach offers greater possibilities of basic progress in personnel with attendant reductions in unit labor costs, than the practice of bounding from one current fad to another like a shuttlecock in flight. It offers each firm a chance to recoup costs of personnel research in reduced labor costs. It offers results in terms understood by general management and labor unions alike. Personnel administration has reached that stage of infancy where much more research is needed, not from the top down, i.e., from the natural and social scientists, but from the bottom up, i.e., from the industrial personnel workers in their individual plants. Research is meaningless without evaluation, and the use of such simple tools as arithmetic, statistics, and cost accounting can provide a beginning in the direction of sound progress in personnel administration.

Summary

WHILE industrial personnel administration is generally considered an applied science, industrial personnel workers almost completely disregard one of the basic components of the scientific method, i.e., verification of results, in their daily work. This results in slipshod practice in the individual concern and effectively throttles progress in the field. Further progress can be expected only with wholesale application of the tools of measurement, such as simple arithmetic, statistics, and primarily cost analysis, to current practice in each of the personnel functions. Such critical evaluation would result in decreased unit labor costs, reduced strife between labor and management, and would mark the beginning of effective and intelligent direction and control of manpower.

During the Acute Manpower Shortage Period
of the War We Had to Hire Whom We Could Get,
and Had to Invent Many New Ways of Keeping
Workers on the Job. Now the Situation Is
Easing It is Time for Us to Review Our Practices
with a View to Improvement.

Reconversion Problems I

By Harold R. Bixler

Mutual Life Insurance Co. of New York
New York, N. Y.

O F BASIC interest in the planning and the solution to personnel problem in the reconversion and post-war period is the present outlook regarding the labor-economic situation. According to information made available recently by J. A. Krug, Chairman of the War Production Board:

Pent-up Demand

THE production of durable civilian goods, which this year will amount to about $7,000,000,000, will more than double one year hence, reaching an estimated figure of $16,700,000,000, which is 30 per cent more than the level produced in the peacetime year of 1939. Expansion will not be confined to durable goods for civilians. If workers are released from munitions plants at the rate now expected, the service trades will also expand. Transportation, public utilities, retail trade and service activities will hire workers to maintain adequate working forces, so will non-durable goods manufacturers, such as textile mills; as well as the construction industry.

There is a backlog of industrial plant expansion and renovation. At the same time it is expected that foreign countries will be in the market for United States goods of all kinds—foods, clothes, industrial equipment, raw materials. This pent-up demand is a foundation on which the country can build a strong transitional economy in which decreases in war output will be offset by increases in the production of civilian-type goods and services.

Within the limits permitted by the war against Japan, the United States must now get rid of regulations against industrial and production limitations which technically put ceilings on initiative, imagination, and resourcefulness. Of 650 orders and schedules in effect on April 1, 1945, 156 have already been revoked, and an additional 83 will be revoked in the next six weeks. Of the 51,200,000 employees now employed, 44,600,000 are in jobs which will not be affected by cutbacks, while 6,600,000 employees may have to seek other jobs.

Jobs Not Directly Affected by Cutbacks

Agriculture	7,750,000
Transportation and utilities	3,800,000
Construction	600,000
Mining	800,000
Trade and service	11,400,000
Manufacturing	
Iron and steel	800,000
Machinery	2,000,000
Other (mostly soft goods)	7,700,000
Government (excluding war agencies, arsenals, and navy yards)	4,400,000
Miscellaneous	5,350,000
Total	44,600,000

Jobs Most Likely to Be Affected by Cutbacks

Aircraft	1,600,000
Ships	1,300,000
Ordinance and Signal equipment	1,800,000
War chemicals	300,000
Federal war agencies	1,600,000
Total	6,600,000
Total employment	51,200,000

War Production Chairman J. A. Krug, predicts a sharp new cut in munitions production soon, with a resulting jump in unemployment. He said, however, that within six months rapidly increasing civilian production should be able to begin taking up the slack of cutback war workers and discharged soldiers. Mr. Krug posed the paradox of unemployment in some fields while other industries were falling short of meeting requirements because of manpower shortages—notably textiles and lumber.

He said wage adjustments probably could do more to solve the shortages than any other measures, and revealed that if needed production could not be obtained otherwise "it may become necessary to ask for a modification of the wage and price ceilings for a number of low-wage industries."

War Manpower Commission's Views

THE views of the War Manpower Commission, as expressed this week by Stephen Sheridan, Area Director, are more restrained than those of some of the other government authorities. They state that within a few months, the volume of unemployment will start rising and unless planning and action is speeded up to meet the situation, the more distant outlook may become grave.

Six months after V-E Day the volume of unemployment will be probably greater than at any time during the past two years. By then cuts in war production will be substantially larger, and a sizable number of veterans will have returned. The real problem involves the average duration of future unemployment, and this depends upon factors unmeasurable at present.

Congress of Industrial Organizations

PETER K. HAWLEY, C.I.O. Labor Member of the Regional War Labor Board said the hope for 60,000,000 post-war jobs "positively was not in the cards now," and blamed lack of planning by "reactionaries" in responsible government offices for failing to act to prevent future disaster.

American Federation of Labor

EDWARD A. NYEGAARD, A. F. of L., who is Regional Chief of the Office of Labor Production, War Production Board, criticized the lack of planning especially for reconversion to civilian production. He said he felt only "pessimism for the future" and asserted that many industries were wholly unprepared to reconvert, and others don't want to at present.

C.E.D. Research Committee

ONE of the most constructive studies of this subject has recently been completed by the Committee for Economic Development under the guidance of Mr. Charles A. Myers, Industrial Relations Section, Massachusetts Institute of Technology, as Executive Secretary of the C.E.D. Research Committee. This report provides most valuable assistance in formulating a company's Post-War Personnel Policy, and is well worth study by each of you who has not yet seen it. It confirms that the major personnel problems now confronting us fall into the following four classifications:

Rehiring of Veterans

PREPARATION—Analyzing the present work force and estimating the labor requirements. Many firms have found it desirable to make detailed analyses of their present work force and estimates of post-war employment, covering any or all three of the following phases: (a) Post-war questionnaire to all present employees, including those in military service. (b) Estimate of probable labor requirements based upon the company's anticipated post-war production volume. (c) Labor inventory indicating the probable post-war employment status of each individual.

This should show the number of employees in military service who expect to return to the company and resume their former positions; those who will return and whose military experience might qualify them for better positions; and those who have indicated they will not return to the company after the war. They should also show among the present "temporary" employees those who intend to leave at the end of the war; those who can be terminated without personal hardship; those who will continue to need work; and special cases involving outstanding merit or ability.

Avoid Fumbling

PARTICULAR *problems* involved in the rehiring of veterans are the following: (a) What changes have taken place in the veteran's former position? (b) What retraining and re-orientation of him will be necessary? (c) How best to measure and evaluate his new skills acquired in military service? (d) What salary should be established for the position at the time he returns? (e) Where can the disabled veteran be best placed in the organization? (f) What arrangements can be made for those for whom it is agreed that there is no future in the organization? (Office Boy who returns as a Major) What written understanding; termination allowance; placement assistance? (g) Is the veteran entitled to the promotional opportunity which he lost while in military service? (h) What follow-up should be made to be sure that all the veterans are readjusted to their positions?

You may very well have a considerable number of skilled employees coming back disabled as far as heavier work goes, but physically and mentally capable of work. Can you place them? They may well turn out to be valuable employees if you can fit them into the right position without too much fumbling. Of course, putting them into an unsuitable position in which they will fail, is going to be bad for their morale and bad for your office efficiency.

Disabled vs. Normal Workers

A MOST *important comparison of the absenteeism, safety, and productivity of disabled vs. normal workers* has recently been completed by the Center for Safety Education at New York University in cooperation with the National Conservation Bureau, which shows the following:

Productivity Better for Disabled—24% of the companies
Same for Both Normal and Disabled—66%
Poorer for Disabled—10%

Safety Better for Disabled—57% of the companies
Same for Both Normal and Disabled—41%
Poorer for Disabled—2%

Absenteeism Better for Disabled—55% of the companies
Same for Both Normal and Disabled—40%
Poorer for Disabled—5%

Transfers and Demotions

NEARLY every organization will have to shift some of its personnel, if only to re-employ those returning from military service. In some companies a considerable number of transfers will accompany the decline of wartime operations and the return to peacetime products.

In all these cases, probably the same types of personnel problems will arise, including the following: (a) How best to evaluate the new skills acquired by the employee, either through longer service in the same position, or in a "temporary" higher position? (b) What right does the transferred employee have to his previous "permanent" position? (c) What importance in relation to seniority will be assigned to such factors as ability, performance, marital status, number of dependents, and residence location? (d) Is it better to lay-off newer employees than to downgrade or demore them to lower rated positions?

Salary Changes

WHAT salary reductions will be necessary in relation to demotion?
Perhaps typical in the field of office employees are the results of a *survey* completed some months ago *among 25 selected life insurance companies* which showed that the wartime work week increased 13%; 52% of the companies expected to return to the former work week; 52% expected to reduce salaries in relation to reduced work week, modify or drop cost of living bonus, and eliminate overtime pay; 68% expected to pay the same to women as to men for equal work; 52% of the companies anticipated it would not be necessary to change salaries because of downgrading; 44% intended to make salary increases in relation to new skills; and 56% had prepared termination allowances for any lay-offs.

Lay-off of Employees

A CONSIDERABLE volume of lay-off is inevitable, particularly in the sharply expanding war industries such as ordinance, aircraft, and ship production. Cutbacks have already curtailed some munitions production. Other industries such as automobiles, refrigerators, and washing machines will very likely have substantial lay-offs during their reconversion from war production to civilian goods. Even companies with little or no conversion problems, such as machine tools and equipment, will probably experience a drop in epmloyment.

Important Questions to Be Planned

AMONG some important personnel problems in this classification are the following: (a) What will be the relative importance in determining the first lay-offs, of length of service, efficiency, knowledge and training, physical fitness, family status, and dependents, and place of residence. (Proposed order of lay-off of typical and industrial firm—married women, part-time employees, probationary employees,

employees less than one year's service). (b) Will shifts and overtime work be eliminated? (c) To what extent should hours of work be reduced in order to avoid layoffs? (d) What steps should be taken to retain "key" personnel on payroll during temporary reconversion shutdown? (e) Should leaves of absence or advance hiring commitments be given to those who will be needed in the near future after reconversion? (f) How much notice of lay-off should be given employees? (g) How should termination or exit interviews be conducted? (h) What termination or separation allowance should be granted? (i) What efforts should the company make to place employees with other employers?

Employment Office in Reverse

MOST companies apparently will attempt to assist such employees in securing other suitable work. This could involve contacts with any local offices of the Committee for Economic Development, War Manpower Commission, U. S. Employment Service, other companies engaged in similar activities, good employment agencies, agencies offering free placement services; referral for civil service opportunities, National Roster of Scientific and Specialized Personnel; and the various local professional organizations dealing with personnel, business, and office management. Individual reference could also well be made to the various sources of occupational guidance and study, including a wide variety of publications on related subjects.

From an address before the Joint Conference of the Boston, Providence and Worcester Chapters of the National Office Management Association.

(To be concluded in October, 1945 Personnel Journal)

The Primary Factor in Hiring during the War Was the Urgency of Clearing an Employee Through the Personnel Office and Placing Him on the Job as Quickly as Possible, Little Consideration Being Given to Thorough Selective Job Placement.

Personnel *and* Job Analysis Data

By Joseph E. Zerga

Walt Disney Productions,
Burbank, Cal.

FOLLOWING the defeat of Germany certain types of industrial organizations experienced war contract cutbacks that have necessarily affected the employment situation in this country. It has become increasingly evident that an increase in unemployment is unavoidable for a short period of time due to the necessity of industry retooling for civilian production after being on a war production basis. The amount of general unemployment that will follow the defeat of Japan is, of course, dependent upon governmental and industrial postwar planning.

Assuming, however, that plans have been laid to absorb any unemployment following the defeat of Japan, there will still be millions unemployed until the retooling of industry (3, 8) (numbers in parentheses refer to references at end of paper) has been completed and such plans have been put into effect. Consequently, whether or not there are plans for maintaining a maximum of employment there will still be unavoidable unemployment.

War Experience

AT THE start of the war the rapid expansion of war industries resulted in a clamor for all types of skilled and semi-skilled labor, with the result that the demands for such types of labor far exceeded the available supply. To cope with this problem industry initiated a program of job simplification. Thorough investigations were made of all skilled and semi-skilled jobs having critical labor shortages, and from the results of such investigations simplified jobs were developed. Although this program meant the establishment of more training schools and a tremendous expansion of plant space and facilities to absorb additional employees, it did solve the problem of critical war shortages in skilled and semi-skilled occupations.

Now, with the gradual transition of war industry to civilian production, one of the immediate problems is that of employee selection for jobs essential to civilian production. Inasmuch as postwar civilian production is not expected to approximate present war production, industrial management (3, 8) is becoming increasingly cognizant of the problem involved in employee selection. Some organizations are prepared to cope with this problem, but the majority are either unprepared or are hurriedly assembling all types of information regarding their employees and jobs.

Four steps

THERE are four steps directly concerned with the accumulation of employee-job information: (1) The determination of the general types of information required; (2) the determination of the sources from which such information may be obtained; (3) the organization of the information obtained; and, (4) how such information may be used. Each of these steps will now be considered in their respective order.

The two general types of employee-job information that are a necessary prerequisite to employee selection are: (1) Personnel records (6); and, (2) job descriptions (1, 9, 10, 12). The information contained in the personnel records of most industrial organizations is inadequate for the purposes for which it was intended. This is primarily due to the fact that mass hiring for war production purposes permitted the obtaining of only a sketchy outline of an employee's work history, educational background, etc.

The primary factor at the time was the urgency of clearing an employee through the employment or personnel office and placing him on the job as quickly as possible, little or no consideration being given to selective job placement. It may have been the intent of the employment or personnel office interviewers to recontact the employee at a later date for the purpose of obtaining additional information, but this opportunity seldom presented itself. As a rule, these records were filed away and seldom reviewed or used for reference purposes.

One Company's Experience

THE Pollak Manufacturing Company (11), Arlington, New Jersey, represents a typical example of industry's efforts to remedy this type of situation. In 1944, this company was using a half-dozen different types of personnel forms, resulting in duplication of information, erroneous information, and wasted effort. The solution to this problem was the development of a single-sheet personnel form calling for brief answers on the part of the department foreman. This form covers such items affecting the employee as: leave of absence, termination, merit increase, reclassification, transfer, employee job rating, etc. The form, filled out in triplicate, is distributed as follows: one copy to the industrial relations office for personnel administration purposes, a second copy to the plant superintendent's office, and the third copy is retained by the foreman. This type of a procedure enables the company to maintain close control over its employees.

Most industrial organizations have, in addition to the usual personnel form or forms, brief records covering an employee's progress in terms of wage increases or decreases relative to job transfers, upgrading, etc. These records, usually 5 x 8 in size, are generally maintained by the wage administration department and the various operating departments within the plant. Such records, while serving a useful function, are also inadequate for employee selection purposes. Although an employee's progress from job to job may be readily perceived from the various job titles or classifications appearing on such a card, it is still necessary to determine what the basic skill qualifications are for each job and their relationship between jobs (1, 12). The determination of such skill qualifications can be made only through job analysis (9, 10, 12), and the relationship of skill qualifications between jobs can be made only through job evaluation (1, 12).

Review of Personnel Records

NEEDLESS to say, personnel records should be periodically reviewed as they are the primary quick-reference source of employee information. As far as job analysis is concerned, it is not a difficult task to prepare job descriptions for each of the separate jobs existing in an organization. Three or four experienced job analysts can, within a few months, completely cover all of the separate jobs in the average-sized (400-700 employees) industrial organization.

Surprisingly few organizations have satisfactory job descriptions, i.e., descriptions that give a true and complete verbal picture of the jobs. The greatest sources of confusion in the preparation of job descriptions are definitions as to what constitutes a *job* and what types of information should be obtained about jobs. Stead and Masincup (7) present the following definitions of a *position*, *mob*, and *occupation*, to show their relationships: (1) "A 'position' is an aggregation of duties, tasks, and responsibilities assigned to one individual; (2) a 'job' is a group of positions that are identical in all respects; and (3) an 'occupation' includes a group of jobs sufficiently similar in respect to their duties, responsibilities and working conditions to warrant like treatment in personnel processes."

Proper Job Descriptions

THE types of information that are to be included in a job description should cover the following topics: 1) The common name or title of the job; 2) the number of employees working at this particular type of job; 3) the department or departments in which the job is to be found; 4) the necessary physical requirements of the job; 5) the experiential requirements of the job; 6) the knowledge or abilities required for the job; and 7) the tools and equipment required for satisfactory performance at the job. It is absolutely essential to have, in addition to the preceding information, a complete verbal job description (10). The value of the job description depends entirely upon its degree of similarity to the job and its completeness. Industrial organizations should, depending upon the types of jobs, products, and needs of management, supplement the job description with information believed to be pertinent to a clearer understanding of the jobs and their relationships to one another and to the employees.

The best source of information for the preparation or revision of job descriptions is the employee. It is also necessary to consult the department supervisor or foreman for the purpose of verifying or obtaining additional information that may not be obtained from the employee. The small amount of an employee's time that is utilized for this purpose will ultimately pay large dividends to management.

Job description information may be conveniently summarized and placed on 5 x 8 cards, or some other technique may be developed for quick-reference or comparative purposes.

Uses Made of Records

THERE are a number of significant reasons why an industrial organization should maintain up-to-date personnel records and reliable job descriptions.

First, it provides an impartial basis for selective job upgrading, transfers and terminations (5).

Second, it enables management to quickly review, and compare available employee skills with critical job shortages. Since the start of the war there have been numerous instances of the under-utilization of employee skills by industry. This has resulted from the necessity of filling critical job shortages with little or no regard to selective job placement and has been one of the primary contributing factors to excessive labor turnover and absenteeism.

Third, it facilitates inter-industry cooperation by providing a basis for the exchange of employees. For example, two or more companies within an area might be reconverting to civilian production, and, through a cooperative exchange of employees it might be possible for them to not only fill their job requirements but also greatly reduce unemployment

Fourth, it assists management in planning for job simplification or combination in terms of what a job consists of as related to the type of employee skills available within the company.

Fifth, it provides a basis for the development of a job evaluation and merit rating (4, 5) program.

Sixth, it provides a basis for the establishment of equitable wage rates and ranges.

Seventh, it facilitates the development of an employment testing (2) program.

From the preceding discussion it may be concluded that an industrial organization that has complete and reliable information in regard to its employees and jobs is in a position to not only cope with most employee-management problems, but minimize the possibility of such problems developing.

References

(1) Industrial Relations Counselors, Inc. *Job Analysis and Its Allied Activities: A Classified and Annotated Bibliography.* New York: 1932. Pp. 59.

(2) Industrial Relations Section. *Employment Tests in Industry and Business: A Selected, Annotated Bibliography.* Princeton: Princeton University, 1945. Pp. 46. $.50.

(3) ———. *Readjustment of Manpower in Industry during the Transition from War to Peace.* Princeton: Princeton University, 1944. Pp. 112. $1.50.

(4) Knowles, A. S. *Merit Rating in Industry.* Boston: Northeastern University, College of Business Administration, 1940. Pp. 36.

(5) National Industrial Conference Board. Studies in Personnel Policy No. 39. "*Employee Rating: Methods of Appraising Ability, Efficiency, and Potentialities.*" New York: 1942.

(6) ———. Studies in Personnel Policy No. 59. "*Personnel Practices in Factory and Office, II.*" New York: 1943.

(7) Stead, W. H., and Masincup, W. E. *The Occupational Research Program of the United States Employment Service.* Chicago: Public Administration Service, 1942. Pp. 219.

(8) Tead, O. (ed.) Management problems of conversion (annual conference papers, 1943). *Adv. Mgmt.*, 1944, 9, No. 1, 1–67.

(9) War Manpower Commission. *Guide for analyzing jobs: Analyst's Workbook.* Washington: U. S. Government Printing Office, 1944. Pp. 20.

(10) ———. *Training and reference manual for job analysis.* Washington: U. S. Government Printing Office, 1944. Pp. 104.

(11) Wood, C. A. Multi-purpose personnel form saves time and effort. *Personnel*, 1945, 21, No. 5, 310–312.

(12) Zerga, J. E. Job analysis: A resume and bibliography. *J. Appl. Psychol.*, 1943, 27, 249–267.

Book Reviews

Book Review Editor, Mr. Everett Van Every
California Council of Personnel Management, 442 Flood Building, San Francisco, 2, Cal.

PERSONNEL RELATIONS, THEIR APPLICATION IN A DEMOCRACY

By J. E. Walters. New York. The Ronald Press. 1945. 547 pp. $4.50

The term "democracy" is experiencing an interesting evolution. After the last war we thought of things democratic as meaning governmental affairs and matters of state. We hardly thought of democratic principles as applied to our daily work in the business sense. And if we did discuss such applications several decades ago it was usually done in the classroom or as eloquent presentations before banquets, etc. But during the past ten years we have seen a profound increase in the tendency to account for economic and social advances as if they were democratic processes at work.

If what we mean by democracy are the rights and privileges of a people to have a direct voice and a direct opportunity to shape their own opportunities concerning their welfare, far below the level of governmental operations and extending down into the working lives of individuals, then it may be supposed that a business text on personnel relations is justified in devoring much of its theme and point of view to "their application in a democracy."

This the author does, but not in a mere descriptive sense. We find the book divided into three logical parts: (1) personnel relations presented from the management point of view when the management of personnel relations is being considered; (2) from that of representatives of government when personnel relations under government cooperation and regulation are discussed; (3) and from labor's standpoint when the aims, history and actions of labor unions are reviewed.

The author is aware of the irritation his book may arouse, but he need make no apologies. Walter's books on personnel management have been standard business reading and college texts in schools of business administration for many years. This somewhat new approach to justifying some of our present labor relations problems may be surprising to some readers and to students of conventional text material It probably is no satisfaction to some readers to have the author imply that what we get today in work restrictions, strikes, lock-outs and fringe concessions should be considered, to some extent at least, as democracy at work.

He does not say so in just those words, but that is the lasting impression and one the reader feels confident to judge for himself. In warranting his discussion of the labor movement, for instance, Walters says that no country can be democratic without considering the dignity of the individuals who compose it; and no people can constitute a real democracy without considering the dignity of that part of the public in or dependent upon organized labor.

The chapter on "Labor Unions in a Democracy" is a fine historical presentation and excellent analysis of how the labor structure is formed. Part II which follows is devoted to "Management of Personnel Relations" and is an especially fine treatise for executive management. The chapter on Wages is a complete and adequate background for a sound understanding of wage administrative problems and our cutback era ahead. Chapter 7 is a model study on Personnel Ratings, reporting many successful company experiences and the actual forms used. Other chapters that are a complete study in themselves are Job Evaluation, Personnel Training and Education, Minimum Wages & Maximum Hours, Government Relations & Personnel Research.

Walters' book is a sound presentation of the principles and practices of the entire field of personnel management and labor relations. If today we were to be limited to but one new book on personnel administration, this would be it.

PERSONNEL
Journal

The Magazine of

LABOR RELATIONS AND PERSONNEL PRACTICES

Published by PERSONNEL RESEARCH FEDERATION
Lincoln Building, 60 East 42nd Street, New York City

Volume 24   *Number 4*

Contents for October 1945

EDITORIAL BOARD

The Subcommittee Believes That the Activities Described Cover Fairly Completely the Steps That Have to Be Gone Through in Placing a Man on a Job in Modern Large-scale Industry. It Also Offers a Checklist for Medium and Small Companies.

Veterans' Placement

From Report on Rehabilitation

National Research Council,
Washington, D. C.

EVERY employee who has been honorably discharged and applies for re-employment must be made to feel the depth and sincerity of the Company's welcome to him. Before his employment interview takes place, he should be greeted by plant officials, his former supervisor, associates in his department, etc.

Reception of Employee

EACH operation shall appoint a person who will have the special responsibility of receiving the ex-serviceman when he first calls at the works and of arranging all other details in connection with his reception. This interviewer shall be carefully selected and receive training in procedure to be followed, requirements of the Federal Veterans' Administration and state rehabilitation centers, and other matters affecting his duties.

Application Form

AT THE time of his application . . . a friendly, informal, helpful attitude is shown toward assisting him in the process of re-employment. Two forms are provided, the usual application blank and a separate sheet covering special wartime information. The information given on these blanks becomes part of the factual record relating to the veteran's education, past experience, and military experience, including any special training received while in service, time of overseas duty, rank, type of discharge, etc.

Preselection Interview

THE first screening takes place at this level. Information on the application blank is checked for purposes of verification and further review, as may seem indicated. On the basis of his contact, the employment interviewer rates the applicant on factors of personality, health, education, work history, and social background, and this is recorded in profile form. In addition, the applicant is given an over-all rating which serves as an index of the interviewer's opinion of his potentialities as an employee. .

Veterans' Coordinator

IN MOST instances the employment interviewer will not be in position to evaluate fully the military record of the veteran or to offer advice as to the many steps in the demobilization or readjustment procedures as directed by the military or Selective Service authorities and the Veterans' Administration. These and other matters falling under the scope of Section VIII of the Selective Service law can best be interpreted by the specialist in veterans' affairs. It is obvious that liaison between the military agencies and industry will be increasingly necessary as the complicated and involved government demobilization machinery gets into action. By virtue of his close contacts with the man on the job and with all others in the plant interested in his welfare, the coordinator's service will be sought for special problems in this area, and he will also serve as counselor in long-range plans affecting the veteran as an employee.

Placement Tests

PLACEMENT tests are used to supplement other information about the veteran's aptitudes, skills, job information, personality, and vocational interests. These tests are given by the educational department.

Counseling

IN THE vocational counseling interviews with the Industrial Psychologist, Educational Director, or Coordinator, the veteran is given assistance in evaluating possible job opportunities in relation to his physical condition, aptitudes, skills, and experience. Special training plans make it possible for the veteran to learn a trade or prepare himself for a better job.

Job Interview

HAVING before him the recommendations of the medical examiner, the veterans' coordinator, and the benefits of any special classification techniques, the employment interviewer is then in a position to fit the individual into the specific job for which he is best suited and for which there is a requisition. The matter of specific job interests and skills is of prime importance, for at this level the most difficult aspect of placement takes place. If the interviewer is not alert to all cues, a misplacement may result, with consequent dissatisfaction on the part of all concerned. With a given set of worker characteristics, the interviewer must select a job which will offer maximum advantage to both the worker and the job. With careful thought and investigation, it might well be that several possibilities for placement will be disclosed with corresponding seniority and pay. Unless the worker comes with a highly specialized skill, in most instances it will be well to give alternate placements due consideration. The problem is always to select that job which will best fit the veteran as an individual and which is commensurate with his interests and abilities.

Medical Examination

WE HAVE been given to understand from military authorities that the employer will not be notified of the reasons for a serviceman's discharge. Except where the defect is obvious, the man himself may not be specifically informed unless his condition required special consideration over an extended period.

It will be the duty of the plant medical authority to determine as fully as possible:

The exact nature of the applicant's disability.

The exact scope of his capabilities.

This information shall be indicated on a special pre-employment examination report and forwarded to the plant personnel manager who will compare this record with the job requirements schedule developed for available jobs.

Interview with Foreman

WHEN the job has been selected, a contact is made with the foreman who supervises the work. It is not good policy to descend unannounced upon the foreman, but an appointment should be arranged, if possible, at a time when his undivided attention can be given to the applicant. In this way it may be possible to reduce to a minimum the number of instances when there is time for only a perfunctory interview. After the applicant has been introduced to the foreman the interviewer or coordinator will be able to determine whether or not he should remain in the contact. Since the foreman has full knowledge of the steps in the employment process, he can assume that the applicant is considered fitted for the job recommended on the interview slip.

It is the foreman's responsibility to evaluate the individual in terms of the specific job opening. The final decision as to the applicant's acceptability should, and must, rest with the foreman. It is particularly important that this contact be skill-fully handled, for the applicant at this point gains his first impression of the potential work environment and social structure within which he may spend the full span of his working day. If the foreman is overly sharp, matter-of-fact, or caustic, the appli-cant will assume that he can expect that kind of treatment as a worker. On the other hand, if the foreman looks upon him as a man in whom he has a friendly, human interest, then the impression is gained that this will be a desirable place in which to work. It is, therefore, most important that foreman-applicant contacts do not be-come routinized or mechanical

Showing the Job

THE foreman or his designated assistant will want to show the applicant the job opening under consideration, and probably will proceed to a discussion of this without any considerable effort at that moment to become better acquainted with the man. A suggested procedure might be for the foreman to proceed to the job location, introduce the applicant to a worker doing a similar job, and conduct a discussion-demonstration with the aid of the man on the job. Brief mention can be made as to the significance of the job operation. . . . Time and effort should be given to enlist genuine interest and enthusiasm on the part of the applicant in the product. In this manner, the individual is made to see that he is not just drilling a hole . . . but is performing an operation that will permit assembly . . . of the completed product Blueprints or pictures of cutaway models of the product can assist the foreman in more accurately describing and fitting in the job operation. An explanation of the other types of work going through the department will also assist the applicant in gaining an over-all picture of the importance of His job and His department.

Induction Interview

AFTER the foreman has given his approval for hiring the applicant, the routine procedures of making up employment records are carried out. The applicant will be finger-printed, photographed, issued a temporary badge, given booklets describing shop rules and insurance plans, and sign allocation forms for income tax and bond deductions. The wage structure pertinent to his particular job will be discussed thoroughly to forestall any future feelings that wages were misconstrued at the time of employment. At this point, it might be well if the interviewer indi-cated to the new worker the location of time clocks, rest rooms, the cafeteria, person-nel service offices, and his own department on a floor layout drawing of the plant. Some type of brief running comment on other departments might serve to give the worker a feeling of belonging to the plant, not just the department. Returning veterans will need to be brought up to date on company policies, new production methods, and any information which is available on postwar plans and prospects.

Orientation

THIS step is handled by the veterans' coordinator, who will go into more detail on some of the things sketched briefly during the induction interview. A trip through portions of the plant, pointing out those facilities of practical interest to a worker, would be helpful. Some men might like to listen in on a training session. The safety director is introduced, and a brief discussion on the need for observance of safety principles fits in here. A copy of the last issue of [the plant magazine] will familiarize the worker with a few of the people and events that transpire at [the company]. An introduction to the personnel manager, or any other executives, might be in order, if it can be handled in a natural fashion. Arrangements for share-the-ride, rationing, etc., are discussed if the need arises. At the conclusion of the orientation session, opportunity is allowed for some discussion, so that the new employee will bring into the open any questions he may have concerning his job. He will have a clear understanding of working hours and the time when he is to report for work.

Safety

RECORDS to date indicate that physically handicapped persons are relatively safe workers, particularly those who have been incapacitated for long periods of time. In the cases of the returning veteran with a new handicap, the situation may be entirely different. Consequently, placement must be made taking into consideration that the person is not accustomed to his new condition and that his state of mind may be depressed as a result.

For his own safety and the safety of others, he should receive some form of attention not only from his supervisor and doctor, but from the safety engineer as well, on approximately a weekly basis for the first six weeks and monthly thereafter, depending on the doctor's opinion of the employee's condition. During such checks, the safety engineer should review the setup with the supervisor. Thought should be given to the individual's working position, limitations and interferences, whether or not any mechanical features provided are effectively aiding the individual, etc. In contacting the individual, it is recommended that we refrain from any actions that could be interpreted as "helpful pity."

The safety engineer should record events, illnesses, accidents, progress, etc., on a form which should be readily accessible to the doctor or the personnel manager.

With respect to occupational analysis charts, . . . it is advisable to clear all such analyses through the safety engineer for his opinion in view of his familiarity with the plant in general, the over-all features of this program, and the physical requirements of the specific job involved.

The safety engineer should likewise be of direct assistance to the personnel manager in the placement of individuals. In all matters of doubt, the plant doctor should make the decision.

Training

PRE-PLACEMENT training shall be given to all employees returning from military service who come within either of the two classifications enumerated below, and shall include practical instruction and necessary related classroom work, safety, and company policies.

Handicapped Employees

INDIVIDUALS with handicaps shall, whenever necessary in the judgment of the medical department, receive training to prepare for definite occupations. If the aptitude and interest shown in the school indicate that the employee is better suited for other work, training should be modified accordingly. The period spent in the training school should continue long enough to assure giving the individual confidence in his ability to fill the occupation in question. In more extreme cases, the facilities of outside schools, institutions, or agencies should be employed to assure the utmost possible rehabilitation.

Specially Qualified Employees

ALL returning employees who, through training or experience in the military forces, have acquired ability which appears to qualify them for positions above the rank of their former position, are to be referred to the director of training, who will determine what training is to be given and recommend placement. Every effort shall be made to utilize the individual's capabilities fully.

Follow-up

COMPANY 1: Follow through periodic consultation with the man, his supervisor, the doctor, and the safety engineer to determine the success of the placement and the disposition of remedial measures suggested by the doctor. The handicapped person must be given the benefit of the doubt at all times, permitting changes from shift to shift, department to department, until ample time has elapsed to permit complete acclimatization. This may require several placements before complete adjustment. . . . As checks are made by the doctor, safety engineer, and supervisor, they should send their comments to the personnel manager. . . . It would also be appreciated if the Central Officer were notified on approximately a monthly basis of the number of contacts made, changes, and progress that is developed during that period.

Company 2: It is to be expected that almost all returning servicemen will need time to learn how to settle down to a steady job. Because it is most important that the new employee gets off to a good start, it is during the break-in period that friendly, reassuring contacts with foremen can have an especially beneficial effect. Through their experience and through the information made available in training programs, foremen . . . have become aware that full and satisfactory adjustment to the job is necessary before any re-employment or rehabilitation program can be considered complete. In their contacts foremen make it a point to become acquainted with their men, to learn something about their personal history, interests, hobbies, social activities, athletic skills, etc. The basic principle is to approach each employee as a distinct individual, unlike anyone else, with full realization that problems related to the home, to health, or to getting along with people both within and outside the plant, all may have a determining influence on the success or failure of a man's work adjustment.

Nervous or worried veterans will need special understanding and occasionally opportunities for personal interviews. Many of the problems of these men which at first seem difficult will respond to the continued interest and willingness on the part of the foreman to "talk things over." When foremen know each returned serviceman as an individual, they will be alert to symptoms of worry or changes in behavior which indicate that problems have arisen. When the usual on-the-job contacts are not effective in bringing about desired changes in attitude and behavior, foremen may need to use the special facilities available through the Personnel and Medical Departments for consultation and follow-up. Much can be done in a preventive way by keeping open the channels of communication established between the veterans' coordinator, the Employment Office, and other consultants of the Personnel Department.

Advisory Conference

THE Advisory Conference has for its main purpose the correlation of all information concerning the placement and job adjustment of veterans. Maximum improvement in all personnel functions is made possible by pooling the results of experience at regular intervals, and then making these results available to all supervision concerned with veteran placement and follow-up. Conferences are attended by the Personnel Director, Plant Physician, Veterans' Coordinator, Employment Manager, Safety Director, Psychological Consultant, and occasionally others in supervisory capacity by invitation.

Individual case records are taken up in detail at these conferences, and the employment experience of the veteran is reviewed in light of the data available at the time he was hired, his job adjustment, and the outcome up to the time of the last contact. If termination ensued, all steps leading up to the exit interview are fully presented and discussed. From a full and impartial discussion of this kind, all members of the group receive the benefit of an interchange of information which in effect is also an in-service training experience with respect to personnel practices in general. By this means employment interviewers are given an opportunity to study the effectiveness and outcomes of their selective procedures, the veterans' coordinator sees his efforts in perspective, foremen gain a deeper insight into the over-all employment picture, and all concerned share an experience which is constantly put to use again in the service of future applicants.

The above is an extract from the report of a Subcommittee on Rehabilitation of the National Research Council.

The Subcommittee made extensive studies of what leading companies and communities are doing.

The result is a very full and informative report which every company should study to check its methods.

Orders, accompanied by remittance made payable to the National Academy of Sciences, should be addressed: Publication Office, National Research Council, 2101 Constitution Ave., Washington 25, D. C. The price of this report is $0.25.

During the Acute Manpower Shortage Period of the War We Had to Hire Whom We Could Get, and Had to Invent Many New Ways of Keeping Workers on the Job. Now the Situation Is Easing It Is Time for Us to Review Our Practices with a View to Improvement.

Reconversion Problems II

By Harold R. Bixler

Mutual Life Insurance Co. of New York
New York, N. Y.

THE war has brought about a number of changes in the employment of women in the United States. Some of the problems arising out of these changes are at this time of particular concern to management and labor and to the general public, as recently indicated by Miss Frieda S. Miller, Director, Women's Bureau, U. S. Department of Labor.

Before the war in 1940, there were 11,000,000 women working in the United States, and another 2,000,000 seeking work. One out of every four women of working age was employed and one out of every four employed workers was a woman. At the July, 1944, peak employment of women, 18,500,000 women were working and another 500,000 were seeking employment. Out of every three civilian workers, one was a woman

The war has enlarged the number of women in occupations in which formerly they were considered exceptional. The most marked changes have taken place in manufacturing industries where in March, 1944, 5,500,000 women were employed, 141% more than in 1940. Of these newcomers more than one-half came from home housework and one-third directly from schools. Significant is the increase in married women who entered the labor market. Although the number of single women employed increased 32% between 1940 and 1944, the number of employed married women increased 75%. Their membership in trade unions has increased from 800,000 to an estimated figure now well over 3,000,000.

80% Plan to Continue Working

ON THE basis of information already obtained, the Women's Bureau estimates that 80% of those now employed plan to work after the war. "Obviously their employment as well as that of returning veterans and of men in the labor market, and of the young people who join them as they complete their education, hinges upon an active economy in which there is opportunity for every individual to use his capacities and abilities in the production of goods and services.

Three-fourths of the representative women workers interviewed by the U. S. Department of Labor were members of households, and of these, 90% contributed regularly to the family upkeep, at least half of them contributing one-half or more of their take-home earnings. The casualties of war increase rather than decrease the financial need for women to work. The decisions and choices involved in the changeovers from war to peacetime production will fall with special impact upon women workers. Many of the decisions represent a choice of personnel policy, while others involve choice of social policy or legislative action. All have broad social implications."

Hiring New Employees

SOME organizations will be able to employ more people after the war than either before or during the war. The major immediate expansion in employment, however, will probably come in the non-manufacturing industries, particularly the distribution and service trades. It will be essential to utilize the important personnel techniques based upon an experience gained during the war period which include the following:

Job Analysis and Specification

WHILE some executives may still cling to notions established from hearsay or chance acquaintance about whom they should hire and whom they should reject, the use of a realistic, business-like job specification has now become established practice in leading organizations.

Based upon the original analysis and classification of individual positions with relative salary ranges established for each position, the job specification is necessary to specifically outline the various qualifications of the employee required for the work. This generally includes at least the physical, mental, and training or experience qualifications; and a statement of the regular, periodic, and special duties involved in the position.

Recruiting

I KNOW full well what a great relief and pleasure it will be for many of you to be able to recruit your employees from a better labor market—in contrast to some of the methods necessary to attract employees during the war period. Does this kind of an advertisement strike a familiar note to you? (An Indianapolis firm ran an ad for stenographers):

> "You can be cross-eyed, pigeon-toed, table-legged and anemic . . . or you can be a ravishing beauty. All we want to know is, lady, can you type and take shorthand? Age requirement, 21 to 91. Ability, yes,

should have a little. Physical condition, strength enough to get you to the cashier each week to collect $35. Seriously, this is a very pleasant job with an old-established firm and now we're not kidding. May we hear from you, please?''

The net result was a total of 51 applications in four days and the employer was able to pick qualified stenographers needed.

Another Story

Here's another one somewhat of the same type, as taken from a Baltimore newspaper, not so long ago:

"Wanted—Office help. No serious work expected. Abundant water coolers, elevators, pencil sharpeners and other labor-saving devices. Charming companionship, both male and female.

"Delightful and stimulating conversation at all hours. Late arrivals in the morning will not be questioned. Early departures in the afternoon taken for granted. The flimsiest excuses for absence accepted, from a slight head cold to a desire to do a little shopping.

"No experience needed. Wages will be paid while new employees are being instructed by old employees in how not to do a great deal. Comfortable chairs provided with desks adjacent to serve as convenient foot-rests. Elastic noon hour readily stretched into an hour and a half. Ample opportunities for catching a nap.

"Excellent telephone facilities so that employees may keep in touch and make dates with friends and acquaintances employed elsewhere. Newspapers, magazines, comics, and other light reading material for those who find time hanging heavy on their hands. Convenient hide-outs where employees may conceal themselves if they suspect they are about to be wanted.

"No obligation to answer when a button is pressed. Soda fountain within a stone's throw. Excellent light for applying makeup. Use of cigarettes at all hours taken as a matter of course. Superiors accustomed to waiting on themselves. No consideration given to gray hairs or other evidences of advanced age. No scoldings, lectures, or reprimands. Permissions freely granted to go out during the day to investigate other positions that may appear to offer greater advantages. Mistakes overlooked or willingly pardoned.

"*By an employer who can't quite meet the competition of war industries* but who just likes to be surrounded by a rollicking, laughing, carefree bevy of girls and boys, *and knows that all he can do is to wait for his revenge when things get back to normal.*"

We assume that your recruiting policy will naturally take due advantage of all the local sources of labor supply, including the U. S. Employment Service, Veterans' Agencies, Schools, Newspaper and Radio Advertisements, relatives and friends of employees, as well as other voluntary applicants attracted to your organization for any reason.

Selection

NO PHASE of the selection procedure takes the place of a friendly and realistic interview. Many concerns are now even more than ever interested in testing procedures, as a practical aid in the selection and placement of applicants. A variety of tests are available. Consult the Psychology Dept. of your nearest University about these.

Causes of Failure on the Job

ADDITIONAL interesting experience has been gained during the war period in the use of tests. The Humm-Wadsworth Temperament Scale for example, in over 2,000,000 applications, indicates the *importance of the handicaps of temperament* in the following analysis of the causes of failure on the job:

Cause of Failure	Approximate Per Cent
1. Temperament (mental health)	80%
2. Unsuitable intelligence	6%
3. Lack of skill	6%
4. Lack of physical fitness	6%
5. Miscellaneous causes	2%

The importance of the various phases of selection which indicate character traits is again emphasized in the results of the analyses of 4,000 cases of discharge and termination of employment of office workers among 76 organizations. Contrary to normal expectation, 85% of these 4,000 individuals were discharged primarily because of lack of character traits, while only 10% were discharged because of lack of specific skills:

Office Employees—4,000 Cases of Discharge—76 Companies

Character Traits		Lack of Specific Skills	
Carelessness	14.1%	In Shorthand	2.2%
Non-cooperation	10.7%	Typewriting	1.6%
Laziness	10.3%	English	1.6%
Absence for Causes other than		Dictaphone	1.3%
Illness	8.5%	Arithmetic	1.3%
Dishonesty	8.1%	Office Machines	.9%
Attention to Outside Things	7.9%	Bookkeeping	.6%
Lack of Initiative	7.6%	Spelling	.6%
Lack of Ambition	7.2%		
Tardiness	6.7%		10.1%
Lack of Loyalty	3.5%		
	84.6%	Unclassified	5.3%

Occupational Selection and Contentment

THE mutual need for the best selection procedures is also emphasized when considering the "occupational contentment" of individuals. Apparently, not all people attempt to make, or in the final result are successful in making, the correct occupational selection, as would be indicated by later "occupational contentment."

While most of us are, in general, familiar with the desires of individuals who wish to change their kind of work because of apparent lack of interest or opportunity in their present connection, it is interesting to note the results of an actual survey on this subject, made sometime ago by "Fortune" Magazine. In answer to the question, "If you could go back to the age of eighteen and start life over again, would you choose a different career or occupation?" the following answers, by age and sex, were given:

	Total	20-40	Over 40	Men	Women
Yes, a different career. ...	41.0%	39.0%	43.0%	44.8%	37.0%
No.	39.2%	40.3%	37.9%	37.9%	43.5%
Depends on circumstances.	15.2%	15.9%	14.6%	15.9%	14.6%
Don't know.	4.6%	4.8%	4.5%	4.4%	4.9%

This shows that over one-half of the people checked in this survey would choose a different career, or are uncertain, and that a large proportion of them are in the age group of 20 to 40 years, contrary to the normal thought that such a change in career might be desired chiefly by the older individuals who had been completely unsuccessful.

It is interesting to note also that fewer women than men indicated a desire to change their present occupation. The women, I am sure, will be glad of this proof that the recognized woman's prerogative of changing her mind is not always exercised in this important connection.

Placement—Induction and Orientation

IMPROPER induction is often the cause of turnover among new employees. Leading companies these days are careful about: (a) Introduction to the company, through the Personnel Department, including the use of prepared information covering company policies and operations. (b) Introduction to the job, including the use of organization charts and instruction manuals. (c) Introduction to people, including the immediate supervisor and other associates on the job.

Training

IT SEEMS hardly necessary to emphasize the importance of proper training of the new employee. This story, however, might help:

Interviewer of Job Applicant: "You are asking for high wages for a man with no experience."

Applicant: "Yes, but you see it's much harder to handle a job when you don't know anything about it.'

In addition to the special and safety training for the job, industry and business now makes wide use of the three step "Training Within Industry" Program, originally prepared and conducted by the War Manpower Commission. This involves: (a) Job Instruction Training—Teaching the employee how to perform the job as it now exists. (b) Job Methods Training—Teaching the employee to analyze and to simplify the job as it now exists. (c) Job Relations Training—Teaching the supervisor how to best handle employee relations.

Performance Rating of Employees

PERFORMANCE or merit rating of the individual employee has now become accepted practice in the leading companies. This involves periodic evaluation of the performance of the individual as measured in terms of the various factors which are the basis of satisfactory fulfillment of the position.

Uses for merit rating include making wage adjustments, developing and training employees, improving the supervision, making promotions and transfers, making lay-offs or discharge, and for special purposes such as leave of absence, company loans, educational refunds, etc. Perhaps the *essence of factor merit rating is that it enables the supervisor to deal individually with the specific weakness and strengths of the employee* in relation to his overall performance on the job.

Supervisory Relations

IT IS logical for most employees to want, just as all employees are entitled to expect, close and friendly supervision on the job, particularly employees newly hired, and older employees promoted to new positions. Since we can rightfully assume that no employee accepts employment to become a failure, we must see to it that it is not the supervisor's fault if any individual proves to be a failure on the job. Close supervision is essential to insure satisfactory performance in the present position and proper development for future advancement.

The supervisor's great opportunity lies in his ability to change unfavorable employee attitudes by convincing the individual of the handicaps which he faces unless such traits are corrected. Periodic discussions with each employee will normally provide the supervisor with ready opportunity to emphasize how important to job performance the previously mentioned character traits are, and to make recommendations for the purpose of inducing the employee to improve unfavorable attitudes which affect his job status.

Loyalty

IT IS well to consider briefly the trait of loyalty from the viewpoint of the new versus the old conception. Quite contrary to the normal consideration of loyalty as an inherent part of satisfactory employment relationships, is the feeling by some individuals that loyalty need not be considered as important or necessary. Such people feel that, even though they should be loyal to their country, or to their religion, or to their family, they need not necessarily be loyal to their employer, since the employment relationship is based upon a cold "give and take" of work for pay.

Fortunately, this viewpoint is apparently not shared by very many office employees. I feel that we all agree that loyalty must be an inherent quality of satisfactory employment relationships, rather than something specifically purchased by the employer "across the counter." It exists only to the degree of employee satisfaction resulting from the application of company policies and the consideration of each employee with regard to his individual circumstances and viewpoints. There is, therefore, great satisfaction in recognizing the strong spirit of loyalty which many individual employees have shown in their past employment relationships, particularly during the war period.

Discipline

IN ANY consideration of the supervisor's responsibilities in personnel relations, there is usually some reference to discipline. Most management representatives agree that the *prompt, definite and fair application of the discipline which suits the individual case* will usually prevent unfavorable performance on the part of the employee from developing to an unacceptable degree.

Proper supervision requires the friendly and fair application of company policies to all employees, without individual discrimination, and any failure to maintain the proper supervisory relations for the ultimate benefit of the employee and the company, will proportionately reduce the respect for the supervisor, which each employee under his control should have.

The employee himself certainly expects his supervisor to train and educate him for development in the present and future positions within the company, and not to accept substandard performance on the job, to the employee's own occupational detriment.

Recognition

EMPLOYEES who satisfactorily fulfill the requirements of the position should, of course, receive prompt and suitable recognition frequently enough, and in such a manner as to make them individually realize that their efforts are appreciated. Such recognition cannot and need not always be in the form of a promotion or an increase in salary.

The supervisor should make a point of expressing verbally his appreciation of good work done. We strongly recommend that, if such a procedure is not being followed at present by each of you, employees within your respective groups be encouraged to ask, "How am I doing?" at least once or twice a year, and be answered specifically on the basis of some type of rating or progress system.

Provide for this purpose a rating form to be used periodically by supervisors, to measure the performance of individual employees in terms of the essential qualifications which apply to their work. It is assumed, of course, that outstanding performance will be recognized by salary increases, and by promotions whenever such opportunities are available.

Employee Morale

IMPORTANCE of Employee Morale—Today there is a wide recognition of the correlation between a high level of employee morale and the successful operation of a business. This recognition is based upon two related types of evidence: (a) That the employee with a high level of morale generally does a superior job; (b) That the degree of success achieved by a company bears a definite relationship, over a long period of time, to the collective attitudes of its employees.

In *contemplating the stresses and strains expected to accompany reconversion and post-war activities* in industrial relations, it is not surprising, therefore, that many of the *country's foremost executives and labor leaders are eagerly searching* for basic information about this highly complex and elusive subject. They believe that general factual data about employee morale and particular information about the attitudes of their employees will help to achieve greater industrial efficiency through more harmonious labor relations.

The National Industrial Conference Board recently completed a survey among 200 executives and labor leaders regarding their definition of employee morale, and the importance of various morale factors. Among these many factors more or less familiar to you, it is interesting to note that both the executive and the labor leaders agreed upon job security (including employment stabilization) and compensation (base pay) as the first two in importance.

Cost of Labor Turnover

APPARENTLY, not yet have many companies calculated the high cost of labor turnover. Important, therefore, is it that 47 companies in the Los Angeles area recently cooperated with the Merchants and Manufacturers Association, to show that the total cost of turnover averaged more than $188 per employee during 1944. At The War Manpower Commission estimate of turnover of $8\frac{1}{2}\%$ per month in the industries surveyed, a firm employing 1,000 employees sustained an average monthly loss of $15,980. (Multiply yours accordingly!)

Individual estimates of turnover cost ranged up to $430 per employee, including not only the cost of separation, but the expense of recruiting and training replacements. Estimates of time required for average replacement for routine office workers was two and one-fifth weeks, for specialized office workers, 4 weeks.

Nearly half of the total separating employees reported on in this survey were employed for less than three months, and nearly 90% were employed less than a year. The conclusion of the group was that it would be much more economical, obviously, to spend $1 for the prevention of such separation than $2 as a consequence of it.

Four Ways of "Not Doing Work"

FROM a "worm's-eye viewpoint," a personal observation of the performance of individual employees during the war period clearly shows four ways of "not doing work," with the related personnel techniques required for improvement:

(1) "Don't be there"—Analysis and Control of Absenteeism.
(2) "Don't know how"—Training and Education.
(3) "Let the other fellow do it"—Performance and Merit Rating.
(4) "Don't want to do it"—Development of Employee Attitude and Morale Studies.

Conclusions

FROM all of the above, it seems to me that we may safely conclude that the major personnel objectives during the reconversion and post-war period are:

(1) The best possible readjustment of the veteran to the organization.
(2) The best possible utilization of the higher skills and experience developed by the "temporary" employees.
(3) The best possible occupational guidance and placement assistance for those employees whom it is necessary to lay-off.
(4) The development of cooperative attitudes by new employees for their maximum efficiency on the job, and their direct contribution towards the competitive ability of the enterprise with which they have become associated.

From an address before the Joint Conference of the Boston, Providence and Worcester Chapters of the National Office Management Association.

(Continued from September, 1945 Personnel Journal)

War-workers Who Will Be Dismissed and Mil-
lions of Veterans Returning to Find Peace and
Quiet May Find a New Kind of Warfare—the
Battle for Jobs, Homes and Security.

American
Migrants

By Princeton Surveys
Princeton University,
Princeton, N. J.

A s war production ends, millions of Americans will face the need to find peacetime jobs. Gathered into war centers from every part of the country, they
may not find work, either where they are or from where they came. Unless
preparation is made, there may develop an army of families migrating in search of
employment.

It is hard to guess their numbers. Business conditions will determine how many
will quickly find steady and satisfying employment and how many of those with
lesser skills and resources will join the bands of permanent American nomads in agriculture, industry and transportation.

Four or Five Million Leave Homes

It is already estimated that after V-J Day, four or five million Americans will leave
their homes every year in search of work. Of these, at least two million will be
permanent migrants. The living and working conditions of migrants *in agriculture*
were dramatized in John Steinbeck's *Grapes of Wrath*. His locale was California, but
a migrant land army of 700,000 to 1,500,000 roams over three-fourths of the states.
The Consumer's League last year found thousands of *Joads in New York*. Ninety-five
per cent of these workers are native white Americans. Their conditions have improved very little during the war when standards for other workers have generally
increased.

No one has yet dramatized clearly the plight of migrants who work in logging
camps, in railroad track or general construction gangs, who are itinerant carpenters,
mechanics, plumbers or those who follow other trades. There are, nevertheless,
hundreds of thousands of them.

Recruited by "rumors" of work somewhere else, by handbills promising employment or by unscrupulous labor contractors, migrants travel from place to place either in their own ancient jalopies or in contractors' trucks of equally dangerous vintage.

Society Pays

MIGRANT children receive little schooling, and are often pressed into child labor. Migrant homes are too frequently chicken-coops, stables, tents, abandoned freight cars, primitive camps or even the open road. Wages are below industrial standards and wage collection and wage payment laws offer little protection. Medical care is meager and epidemics are prevalent. Sanitary facilities are often lacking. Migrants receive no workmen's compensation when injured, no unemployment compensation when jobless, and no social security when aged. The seasonal nature of their work results in the most irregular employment. Society pays for these chaotic conditions in heavy relief costs.

The plight of farm migrants was recognized in 1935 when the Farm Security Administration was charged with aiding and rehabilitating them. It constructed two types of camps: one, to provide temporary shelter and minimum sanitary facilities for families who remain in an area for short periods; and two, to provide permanent camps with shelter facilities and some permanent homes, each with a small garden. The latter were established where the work season ran from six to nine months of the year and represented a beginning toward stabilization of at least a part of the migrant army. Even at its peak, however, this program reached only a small fraction of farm migrants and when World War II came, the FSA facilities were taken over and expanded by the War Food Administration.

Foreigners and Prisoners Fare Better

THE approach of war brought some temporary relief to migrants. Many of them went into the armed services and into war plants. To relieve war labor shortage on the farms, land armies of women, older men and young people from nearby cities, prisoners of war and Mexican and Jamaican workers were recruited. Housing, transportation, medical and labor standards for prisoners are determined by the Geneva convention and for foreign workers by international agreements. *It is more than ironic that standards for both our "good neighbors" and for our enemies are far higher than for our own countrymen.*

Under the War Food Administration program, camps are operated today on 273 sites for migrant and seasonal workers, 43 of which are permanent. They can house a population of 150,000 and are located in 29 states. It is assumed, however, that the WFA, like other war agencies, will be liquidated when the emergency is over. Certain of its functions have post-war implications which need review now from a long-term outlook.

The plight of our migratory workers on the farms and elsewhere is not a war phenomenon. It was merely dramatized by the war and by contrast with standards offered foreign nationals under stress of labor shortages. It existed before the conflict and will remain afterward. Its causes are basic—low wages, irregular recruiting and employment and their corollaries, child labor and poor living conditions.

Institute Meeting at Princeton

THE highly complicated problems connected with post-war migrant labor were the subject of an Institute on Migrant Labor Problems held at the Nassau Tavern, Princeton, N. J., today (June 26, 1945) under the sponsorship of Princeton Surveys and the Industrial Relations Section of Princeton University. It was the first such institute to be held in the East.

The Institute was participated in by officials of national labor, civic, health and religious organizations. John F. Sly, Director, Princeton Surveys, and Douglas Brown, Director, Industrial Relations Section, served as co-chairmen. Chief among the speakers were Mrs. Eugene Meyer, Washington Post columnist, and Paul S. Taylor, Professor of Economics, University of California.

Mrs. Meyer noted that the "state governments" are aware of the many migrant problems, but added that "what we mainly need is coordination of our health, education and welfare departments at the Federal level, preferably under a Cabinet officer." As to migratory problems brought on by people travelling for war production jobs, "we achieved a monumental record of production in the nation's military defense but made a shameful record in the nation's social defense." She added:

Battle for Jobs

WE ARE now facing another mass-migration of proportions such as has probably never taken place before in human history. Soon the war-workers will be dismissed in vast numbers and twelve million veterans who will be returning to find peace and quiet, may find instead a new kind of warfare, the battle for jobs, homes and security. It may be a period of such turmoil as the nation has not seen at the height of the war effort unless we devise orderly methods of readjustment to peacetime employment. It will be the greatest challenge our nation has ever met, not excepting the perils of the war itself."

She referred to "one of the real dangers of the migratory problem"—that of the return of the Negro soldier to the South. "When they return," she declared, "they are not going to put up with the unemployment and political disenfranchisement, the lack of educational and health facilities they had to endure in the past.

Either we move quickly to see to it that the South overcomes its economic handicaps, and its meagre social provisions for the Negro, or we shall see another Negro migration from the South into the slums of the North, which will make the one that took place after the last war look like a mere trickle. If we allow this to happen, the results would be disastrous for the Negro and for the nation."

Strikes and Friction Caused

D R. TAYLOR declared that unless migrants received the protection of State and Federal labor and social laws accorded other workers, neither migrant families, their employers, nor the communities to which they move would be safe from strikes and friction.

He urged the formation of a permanent citizens' committee to promote public education and intelligent action; appointment by President Truman of an Inter-departmental committee of Federal Agencies with possibly the U. S. Department of Labor being responsible for leadership; encouraged a Congressional Committee, per-haps the Senate Committee on Education and Labor, to undertake serious investiga-tions of migrant problems.

Dr. Taylor declared that States which have not already done so, should enact legislation to assure collection of wages, to regulate the labor of women and child workers, and to provide workmen's compensation, particularly in agriculture.

Federal Action Advocated

A RGUING that there is no reason to safeguarding the movement of commodities without safeguarding the movement of humans, Dr. Taylor urged enactment of laws to give the Interstate Commerce Commission power to supervise trucks and other vehicles which haul laborers commercially across State lines.

The Institute endorsed H.B. 613, a bill now before Congress pertaining to the regulation of private employment agencies; arranged for a permanent organization of the Institute and adopted the following statement of principles:

The Institute on Migrant Labor Problems accepts the basic principle that no per-son shall be denied the exercise of his full human rights and privileges because of occupation or location.

Migrant workers and their families, both in agriculture and industry, including transportation, do not have the same opportunities for adequate and safeguarded employment; for social, health and welfare services; for education; for decent hons-ing; and for full participation in community life. These disadvantages and discrimi-nations have long given rise to migration problems to which too little attention has been given by the public and governmental agencies.

As the end of the war approaches with its resulting reconversion and demobiliza-tion, the magnitude and character of migration problems reach proportions which may be explosive. This demands attention and action by the public through govern-mental and citizen groups.

Two Ex-Marines Were Placed Near an Area
Where a Noisy Riveting Machine Operated and
Dived Under the Bench Each Time It Started.

Veteran *as* Individual

By Cyril M. Rappaport
New York, N. Y.

Most companies that expect any sizeable number of veterans to return to them
have already set up reemployment routines for their benefit. Procedures
for physical examination, testing, interviewing, counselling, placement,
followup, and for whatever else the management has deemed advisable, have been
carefully explored and installed. Yet, in spite of what almost amounts to loving
care in many instances, turnover among veterans—especially internal turnover as
evidenced by transfers and change in work assignments—remains high. There
probably is no pat remedy for this, but the situation can be better understood by
approaching it from what is actually the basis of all personnel work—human
understanding.

Marines Dive under Table

Most veterans return from an environment highly divorced from anything civilian. Soldiers who have been through long months of combat, soldiers who
comprised the rear echelons in foreign countries, soldiers whose work experience is
colored by the Army way of doing things, are just not familiar with the way civilians operate. Yet, these men have been civilians, and must be reintegrated into
civilian patterns of everyday working life. A few of these men have been through
psychologically devastating experiences. Many more of them have not. The factor
which personnel men must forever hold in mind is that these men, whatever their
military experience and background, went into service as individuals and came out as
individuals, and must be treated as individuals.

Almost any personnel man can think of instances where veterans were misplaced, such as the two Marines who were placed near an area where a noisy riveting machine operated and who dived under the table each time they heard it. The routines and procedures may operate perfectly in effecting such placements, but a little individual attention and common sense would have helped.

The personnel instrument that lends itself most readily to the understanding of the veteran as an individual is, without doubt, the interview. Without going into the technique of the interview, suffice to say that a well conducted interview can throw more light on the veteran as an individual than any other personnel tool. The interview supplemented by psychological tests is even better, but it may not be advisable to subject all veterans to tests.

Orientation Program

THE interviewer of veterans must be a capable person—his job is far more than to "get information, give information, and to make a friend." His job includes the formation of a relationship between the veteran and civilian life in general as well as between the veteran and his job.

Many companies use the shop tour as part of the orientation of all employees, or as part of the welcome of veterans who were former employees. This is probably one of the best types of orientation procedures used, when supplemented by the usual employee handbooks. A well conducted shop tour can be a gentle reintroduction to civilian life, for it shows how people act to earn their livings. It shows the normal pursuits to which the veteran is returning. The interviewer who accompanies the veteran on the tour is doing a wise thing—for he can then inquire about his reaction to the various activities he sees going on about him. The veteran who evidences strong discomfort at being in a noisy place won't work well there—though his buddy who has been with him from the date of induction may be perfectly undisturbed by such surroundings.

It is the *individual's* reactions to his surroundings that count. Those reactions are tempered not only by the military experience, but by the civilian experience which preceded entry into service. Thresholds of tolerance to noise, attention to detail, can be studied by mass statistics, but when it comes to placing a man to work at a machine in the midst of surroundings created by the necessities of a particular manufacturing process, we are dealing with an individual, who brings with him a certain background which shapes his reaction to his surroundings.

Few Sheltered Shops

MOST employers can not afford to run sheltered workshops which adapt conditions to the individual, but must try to find individuals who are adaptable to conditions. Of course, some working conditions can be changed, but the gross situation can not. The shop tour lends itself to the evaluation of the veteran in terms of the gross situation he must meet daily.

It will probably be the interviewer who, on the basis of what he has learned from talking to the veteran, must decide whether or not it would be advisable for the veteran to return to his old job, or to another of "like seniority, status, and pay," or to a better job. Part of his decision will be based on the veteran's civilian history. Part of the decision will undoubtedly be based on the veteran's military experience and training.

Usually, it is the interviewer's estimate of what the veteran's reaction to a job situation will be that determines the working conditions of the veteran's first job assignment. If he is wrong, a series of transfers usually result until the veteran finds tolerable working conditions—or until he walks out. Might it not be a better idea for the interviewer to walk about the shop with the veteran, before he is placed, and get from him his reactions to the various types of surroundings? Might it not be a good idea for the veteran himself to have a beforehand idea of what his work will be, of what his surroundings will be for eight or more hours a day?

Working conditions consist of more than light, sound, machines, walls, windows, and assembly lines. Working conditions include the people who work.

Social Relationships

THE interviewer who handles veterans would do well to remember that the Army is a very social body. Most veterans have met many men, and worked with and under many men. However, these men were not civilians engaged in civilian occupations. Now the veteran will have civilians, men and women, as part of daily life. In addition to judging the veteran's reaction to the physical working conditions, it will be the job of the interviewer to judge the veteran's reactions to his associates.

Would an ex-MP, used to guarding lonely stretches of road by himself, do well as part of a fast moving team of assemblers who work under a group production bonus? Or would an ammunition passer, used to working at high speed as part of a gun crew, be likely to do better?

The interviewer must be highly cognizant of the importance of the social working conditions as well as the physical working conditions before making a placement. In this connection, it might be well to point out that the Army, like personnel men in general, is not infallible in its assignment of personnel—and the ex-MP who guarded lonely stretches of road may or may not be just the man to form a useful part of the fast moving assembly team, while the ex-ammunition passer may well do best in some kind of an isolated job. Again, judgment must be on an individual basis, buttressed by all available data, civilian as well as military.

Foremen Must Be Specially Trained

ANOTHER phase of the social working conditions consists of the veteran's relationship to his supervisors. An awake management will extend an effort to make

its supervisors aware of what it means to supervise men who have been in the Army
Leadership in the service is a prized and rewarded quality. A foreman who tries to
drive a veteran, rather than lead him, probably will not be hauled in front of a grievance committee—it is likely that he will be handled in a highly individualized, personally violent fashion by the veteran concerned.

Management must undertake to train foremen to realize that they have an
additional responsibility on their hands when it comes to the veterans working under
them. They will be an important factor in helping these men to return quickly to
productive civilian pursuits as useful, self-reliant citizens. Such training is probably
best accomplished by devoring one or two conferences of the regular foremanship
training program to veteran's problems.

By all means the foreman should be made to realize that veterans per se are not
freaks, are not psychopaths, but are men like themselves, but men who have been
through a rather special set of experiences which will require more human understanding on their part. Foremen should be cautioned against treating the veteran as
a highly privileged character, exempt from all rules and regulations. Such treatment
brands the veteran in the eyes of his fellow workers, and is not at all likely to be welcomed by the veteran. Special concession to the veteran in terms of his limitations,
yes—but favoritism on a general basis, no. Above all, foremen should be urged to
regard the veteran as an individual man among men, with a somewhat different background from most men he is used to dealing with at present, but nevertheless one
of them.

Just why is the foreman so important in the veteran picture? Precisely for the
same reason that he is important in the creation and maintenance of the social working conditions of his department. The foreman's methods of handling his people
effects them all, but the effects on the veteran returning to his first civilian job are
more concentrated—from them the veteran is likely to gain his first impressions of
what his return to being a working civilian means. In the large sense, it is highly
desirable that the veteran's first impression be a good one.

Veteran Coordinator

After the foreman has become acquainted with the veteran problem in general,
what tools can be given him to help deal with the individual veteran? The
interviewer who finally decides that a particular veteran is to work with a particular
foreman is that tool. He is the man who knows most about the veteran. His is the
job of acquainting the foreman with the veteran's history, with his shortcomings,
with his strong points. He, having already created a friendly bond between himself
and the veteran, should work towards creating a similar bond between the veteran
and the foreman. In short, the interviewer who placed the veteran should also do
the followup work.

In plants where foremen supervise lesser supervisors, such as lead men or group leaders, the training in foremanship and in dealing with veterans obviously must not stop with the foreman, but should extend down to the veteran's immediate supervisor.

The two thoughts prsented above, that veterans should be handled as individuals, and that instruction in the handling of veterans as individuals should be passed on to supervisors, should be held in mind by personnel executives when examining their placement routines for veterans. Procedures that tend towards mass consideration of veterans should be reexamined in light of their neglect of individuals. Supervisory training courses that omit stress of the veteran as an individual should be reexamined in light of whether or not they are actually producing any favorable veteran-management relationships. Management must remember that the backbone of the industrial labor market will one day consist of men who have been in the service. Their reception by, and their return to civilian life must be such as to foster and promote those values by which our industry functions in a democratic state—and in a democratic state all men are individuals.

According to This Study the Main Desire of
Women War-workers Is to Go Home, Make It a
Home and Look After Their Children.

Rosie *the* Riveter

By Staff of Women's Personnel

Grumman Aircraft Engineering Corp.,
Bethpage, Long Island, N. Y.

WILL "Rosie the Riveter" be content to return to the unsung tasks of the home: washing, mending, picking up toys, and binding little Willie's cuts? Or will she want to continue bringing home the bacon, leaving the frying of it to Grandma? What sort of answer will she give Jim, who, when approached for money, responds, "What did you do with the quarter I gave you last week?" Will she return a curt answer, or has her war experience given her insight into Jim's problems and a new sense of the value of money and the difficulty with which it is earned? With the sound and fury almost dead and Jim doffing his uniforms—please, God, forever—what can we expect? A nation of women all bent on Cash and Careers, or will a war-torn Rosie accept woman's traditional lot of Cooking, Cleaning, Children, and Church?

Thumb-nail Sketch

OUR aircraft company decided to sound out its women workers, who made up a quarter of their total personnel, and perhaps find some answers. One third of its six thousand women were interviewed by the Women's Counselors, and the results tabulated. In an effort to make the interviews as genuine as possible, we 'skipped' any questions that did not elicit a ready response. That this does not make for statistical accuracy we freely admit, so in lieu of a scientific survey we herewith present our prognostications and predictions for the future based on our findings. Multiplied many times, our little group is probably a pretty good sampling of all those "Rosie the Riveters" who were so suddenly and dramatically torn from their normal vocations and thrust into the furnaces of war.

Local Girls with Little Race Hostility

A THUMB-NAIL sketch of Rosie would reveal that her roots are far-flung; every nationality, color and creed being represented, with a minimum of racial antipathy. She may be from eighteen to sixty-five, but our largest group is between twenty-six and thirty-five, married, and generally has two children. One third of our mothers have a child less than twelve years of age, which means that somehow a child-care problem has had to be tackled. Another third of our women are childless, among these large numbers of war brides who must await their Jim's return to have their families. As further evidence of war's dislocations, nearly a fourth of our women are living with parents, temporarily. While Jim is over there fighting, Rosie, with the children, has gone home to Mother, and she speaks feelingly of that future day when she can again have her own little home.

Ninety-three per cent of our women are local, living in the two 'home' counties where most of them were born, and we can truthfully call this a 'family affair' when we learn that forty-seven per cent of our workers have relatives working side by side with them in the various plants. Seventy-two percent of our women had a member of the immediate family in the armed services, and ninety-six percent had a blood relative. Do you wonder that they had a real incentive—and we don't mean the bonus—to turn out planes, planes, and more planes?

Here, then, is Rosie of the PRESENT. We see her on a windy corner waiting her driver. He is late and the wind whips through her faded slacks, and the sleet stings her face. Behind her lie home cares and anxieties that she may not completely shake off all this day, and before her are ten hours of riveting and factory noise and discipline. A figure of fun? Decidedly NOT!

Let's leave her here in the cold, dark morning and explore that ghost of Rosie of the PAST—that dim, shadowy, pre-Pearl Harbor Rosie.

Little Previous Business Experience

E IGHTEEN percent of our women either had no business experience at all or had not been employed for periods ranging back twenty years. Thirteen percent were housewives, and seven percent were girls just out of school. Sixteen out of every hundred reported that they had been 'domestics'. Some were skilled household servants, formerly employed in the elaborate houses that dot the North Shore, but most of then were 'run-of-the-mill' maids, mother's helpers and part-time workers. Twenty-two percent reported 'office' or 'sales'. Twelve percent had previous factory experience. The remaining fall under the categories: trade, restaurant, laundry, institutional, and telephone, and in that order.

It becomes immediately apparent that our pre-Pearl Harbor Rosie didn't have much of a business past. Only four percent reported anything remotely resembling a professional or executive career, and this includes those women who managed a shop or business of their own.

Miscellaneous Jobs

To sum up: our Rosie waited on you at the 'Five and Dime'; did your nails and hair; ironed your shirts; served you at your favorite restaurant. She was your next-door neighbor, whose over-the-fence gossip has been missing these past three years. She was your office file clerk or stenographer. She made your clothes, and occasionally designed them. She trimmed your hats; she was Mrs. Jones' maid, or succession of maids. She stitched the button-holes on that once elegant pre-war suit—the one that was so becoming. She made your wallets and pocketbooks. She was that police matron who was bringing up a family on a small pension because her husband was killed by a thug. She is the ghost of a giggling school girl, with nothing on her mind but her curls.

In short—Rosie once did everything, with one glaring exception—she did NOT work on a farm, even though ours is a great truckfarming community. Only one woman reported that the land had been the source of her living.

From the smoldering embers of a world conflagration let us try to evoke Rosie's 'Spirit of the Future', about which there is so much speculation.

Spirit of the Future

Rosie at present is restless and uncertain; and she tells us (in our survey) with only two exceptions, she doesn't want to go back to her pre-war occupation. Domestic work! Ye Gods! Anything else BUT! And this is particularly true of the colored worker. Not that Rosie won't be glad to go home—but of this, more later. She just doesn't want to go back into *someone else's* home. You home-makers, Better DO SOMETHING about this! There's really rancor here, and all the long hours, heavy work and ear-splitting noise of war work hasn't erased it. A special word to you mistresses of large estates. Your cooks, waitresses and personal maids will probably come back to you, but, almost without exception, they complain that you expected too much service, day and night. How about it?

Your laundry? Rosie doesn't want to do that either. Remember the good old days when it was returned to you quickly and neatly done? Hubby's shirts crisp and shining? Think that those days are coming back? Maybe so, but not if Rosie can help it. That work was too heavy, even compared with riveting; the heat un-bearable in summer; and shop conditions, generally poor. Of forty-one laundry workers, only seven guessed they'd "HAVE TO" return to it.

The Factory fares even worse. Of one hundred and eighteen women with former factory experience, only fifteen wanted any part of it. A few enthusiastic Rosies would like to go on building planes, especially under the conditions our girls had here, but they do not expect to have the chance and are prepared to step aside for the returning veterans with a good grace.

Only Telephone Girls Like Previous Jobs

OF FORTY-THREE former restaurant workers, only four expressed any desire to return. As to that sign: 'Be nice to the waitresses—We can always get another customer,' "No thank you", says Rosie. Why? "Tips are too uncertain." "You have to take too much from the customers." Maybe that sign will stay up, even after the war.

Ah, Mr. Executive, are you rubbing your hands in anticipation of any number of highly efficient office workers at reasonable wages? You, Mr. Store Manager, expecting flocks of docile and polite salesgirls? Maybe you'll get them anyway, but Rosie turns thumbs down right now. Of two hundred and twenty-six office and sales persons, only thirty-nine want to assume their former jobs.

The trades needn't expect a sudden influx of applicants, either. Many a skilled needle worker or milliner exhibited her hands, saying, "How can I ever do fine work again?" Truthfully, it is hard to imagine, for these women, after three years of heavy work, display hands that are rough as the files they handle

Telephone operators are one of our exceptions to the general rule, but they have doubts of their welcome. "They like to train new girls," one woman told us. "I'm too old," said another. "They don't think you're good if you drop out for a while," said a third. So Mr. Telephone Company (you really should feel flattered), here they are, ready and willing, but only after the last rivet is shot.

So it goes, all up and down the assembly line. Rosie doesn't want to do whatever it was she did before the war. "For pity's sake," we hear you say, "whatever does she want to do?"

Improve Herself and Go Home

ROSIE has two main desires. One is to improve herself. She is not very satisfied with anything, right now. If she must go on working, she wants to be fitted for something that pays better and will be more satisfactory than whatever she did before the war. She wants to take courses in beauty culture, physical education, nursing, office procedures, dress designing, and what have you. Two women announced that they were enrolling for courses leading to the degree of 'Beautician to a Mortician'. Now, don't laugh—it was a new one on us, too.

But above and beyond all this desire to improve herself there is the one clarion cry—"Rosie wants to go HOME." She's tired of this dual rôle and double responsibility. Given her choice she'd want no part of bringing home the bacon, but would welcome the chance of frying it. The younger unmarried woman can hardly wait, now that V Day has come, for the return of her sweetheart. She, too, wants to marry and STAY HOME!

Those Who Must Work

THE only women who will fight to stay in the labor market are 'must works' and the older women, whose family responsibilities are ended and who have had to live on the bounty of relatives. These older women (and good, hard workers they are, too) know the joys of money of their own for the first time and will struggle to remain in the current. The 'must works' are the "My husband (or father) has been bedridden for the past seven years and I must work at something," or, "My husband's income has never been adequate and I've always had to work," or "I'm not married, and not likely to be, and I'll have to support myself somehow," and, more recently, "My husband was killed in action, and I can't give the baby what his Dad would have wanted him to have unless I work."

These, and many another Rosie, will have to keep on toiling. They know they will never again make so much money, but they are wistful, not resentful, about it. If that is the price of peace, they are more than ready to pay it.

What about the war job? What has it taught Rosie? From her own comments we feel she has learned much and will be a more desirable wife, neighbor, and all-around good citizen for this experience. She should be more able to understand Jim's stand on her useless expenditures now that she knows what it takes to earn the cash. She has learned of the deep responsibilities of the bread-winner; the need for self-control and self-abnegation in business life. One woman told us she had learned to gauge the cost of an article by the number of hours she had to work to pay for it.

Business Boring

MANY women commented that they had never realized that going out to business could be so boring. Said one, "I used to envy my husband his contacts with people, but after two and a half years of this, I'll not complain any longer of staying home. At least at home you are your own boss and can do things your way." Our Rosie has learned to get on with all sorts of people, to find the values hidden under differences in speech and ways of living, to take jokes and teasing, as well as orders. At times she has learned too much and too fast about men and the susceptibility of some, but she has also learned the patience and friendly helpfulness of others. She has learned how to put up with scornful disapproval of the skeptics and to live with others without succumbing to coarseness.

One foreign-born mother of a girl in the plant, after quoting a somewhat profane remark of her daughter's, explained, "Since she work in the plant she use those man words." But more than one has mentioned the tremendous widening of her social experience and increased understanding. Good or bad, there is plenty of both, the plant has definitely enriched Rosie's life pattern.

Money Well Used

WHILE the job lasts, Rosie had plenty of uses for the extra money she made. It doesn't all go for clothes and permanents. She has paid off the mortgage, refurnished the old house, bought land to build on when Jim gets back, replaced her bad teeth with a store set, thrown off the crushing load of debt left from the depression era, and put aside a nest-egg for the boy who went straight from high school to the war and may want to buy a filling station or start in business when he gets back. She is putting by for the household conveniences she will be able to install after the war, and for the baby's education, determined that he shall have the best of everything.

She wants the *home* she goes back to to be a good one, worth staying in, and she sees her present employment as the chance of a lifetime to pay for the things she would not otherwise have in it. But stronger than anything else is the urge to *be* in it, to have time for all the things that go to make a real home, to be with the children and control the standards by which they are growing up, instead of leaving them to strangers.

So Rosie would prefer to go back to her traditional sphere; and should you throw "Cash, Careers, Clothes and Cavorting" at her, you're apt to hear a chorus from millions of feminine throats—"A fig for your fat pay checks—A pox on your independence—And as for your so-called masculine prerogatives—well, now that we know what they cost—YOU CAN HAVE 'EM BACK!"

Estelle Meeker, Lorraine Abel, Elizabeth Junken, Lois Blagden, Ruth Johnson, Milfred McKeown, Hedwig Ellsley.

Some Simple Ideas Developed in Foremen Training Courses in a Small Company.

Motivation

By Guy M. Wilson, Faye Burgess and
Walter Dunn
Raytheon Manufacturing Co.,
Newton, Mass.

THE "slow down" is the natural response to the "drive" of the industrial foreman. In other words, drive as a regular technique ends in failure. It may not be a slow down; it may be an increasing percentage of terminations. Of course there may be successful driving by some foremen, particularly if people need their jobs badly.

But the foreman who is also a good student of human nature will find a better way. He will realize that the most successful drive of all is that which comes from the worker himself. True motivation can not be found in external pressure; it must come from within.

Scale of Motivation

OF a scale of motivation were made it would run somewhat as follows:
100—thorough understanding of the work and its value
—acceptance of the particular job as suitable and desirable
—reasonable hope of getting ahead
—proper recognition and encouragement
—respect for superiors and desire for approval
—pressing need for money
—response to a speed-up man or a pace setter
—fear of ridicule
—fear of scolding or other penalties
—fear of loss of job
0—threats and warnings

The upper end of this scale, the end with the large plus values, contains the positive forces for motivation, the things that build one up and stimulate a maximum of effort. The items at the bottom of the scale are low in value; some of them may be negative. A response to threats may be a desire to get even and may result in a monkey-wrench in the machinery.

No more Slave Labor

A FOREMAN who has a perpetual grouch, who doesn't like people, or who tries constantly to "take it out on others", has no place in modern industry. The days of slave labor are over, or should be, in America. Labor is free in proportion to understanding, choice, and cooperation.

Realizing that true motivation must come from within, the foreman tries to understand the worker and then find suitable work for him. He arranges temporary assignment and try out if necessary. He wants the worker to be satisfied.

The foreman takes time to instruct carefully for any job to which the worker is assigned. He takes time to induct the worker into the job, developing its value and importance in itself, or because of its connections in a total process.

Then the foreman tries to put himself in the worker's place, and to treat the worker in all respects as he himself would want to be treated.

Some may object that "soft" treatment will not work in a factory. These same people would probably insist on severe discipline in the home and in the school, where the trend for years has been toward humane and considerate treatment, and where also, it should be noted, discipline has grown better and better because of the cooperative spirit engendered. Considerate treatment need not be "soft"; it needs only to be fair. Faults and infractions are not to be overlooked, but they should be so handled that they are not repeated. The result is that they gradually disappear.

No More Cracking Down

THERE are homes today in which there is no punishment; children understand and try to cooperate, and under such circumstances there is no call for punishment. All that is needed is better instruction and better foresight in terms of child behavior.

There are schoolrooms in which there are teachers so considerate and understanding, that there are no disciplinary problems. There is understanding to the point of cooperation in the making of the few general rules needed. The teacher is merely a friendly leader in the group.

So it should be in a factory. Time should be found for induction, for instruction, and for an explanation of the day-to-day problems and goals. If this work is done well enough, there is no necessity for cracking down on the workers.

Even animal trainers know the truth of the above statements. Horses resent ill-treatment; they respond to good treatment. They try to understand. A dog will try so hard to understand and to do what his master wants.

Humans behave according to known laws of which the law of motivation is one of the most fundamental. This law requires that we use the right appeals in order to get favorable responses; it recognizes the fact that wrong appeals will in the long run fail.

The approach to the right use of the law of motivation is simple:—what motives appeal to you? Then no doubt the same motives will appeal to others. This is a good start. But since individuals do vary, you must study your group, wait for their leads or suggestions, and always make sure that the appeal is of the right kind.

Examples of Cooperation

For example, on an unbalanced team, the 1st position operator is slow and holds up the work of the whole team. If you wait for your leads or suggestions to come from within the team, you will probably get leads like this:

> The slow operator will ask to be placed on another team that she can keep up with. The other team members might suggest possible changes with an operator on another team. Most operators know the entire floor, and therefore what each operator is capable of doing.

If you take their suggestions and try to make the change satisfactorily, the group will understand and will be happy about the change, for the suggestion came from "within".

It is worth much to the foreman to have the idea prevail among his workers that they should feel free to make suggestions and that all suggestions will be considered. Increased cooperation is the immediate result. Even if the foreman is doubtful about the value of a suggestion, it may be well to permit a person or a team to try it out for a while.

Arranging Quota

You as a foreman want to give a team a definite quota. How should you do it? How can you bring the team into it cooperatively? You decide to talk it over with the team. They like the idea. They suggest quotas higher than you had thought possible. You hold back. You compromise as a starter on a figure lower than they propose. They exceed this figure and again suggest their higher figure. "All right", you say, "if you reach that figure you can go home. That is worth a cut off."

Thus you restrain your "authority". You leave it to the team. Cooperation is increased; morale is raised; and production goes up;—all of this with less effort, less wear and tear all around.

Motivation is one of the basic laws of behavior. When all the facts are known, behavior is predictable. Humans react to fairly well-known laws. Most people at times recognize some of these laws. Everyone, for instance, knows:

    —that good understanding aids effort

    —that praise and commendation are appreciated

—that good treatment secures friendly and favorable responses
—that recognition is highly valued by a person
—that loyalty and concern secure loyalty in return
—that people like to see a plan, a stake to work toward.

Also,—

—that abusive treatment is resented, even if deserved
—that unjust treatment drives people away
—that scolding and nagging are detrimental in the long run
—that "my authority" should not be the chief reliance for control
—that fear is negative, not positive; destructive, not up-building.

The above are not inclusive, but typical. For the purposes of this discussion on motivation, they provide a ready-reference summary for the interested foreman.

Book Reviews

Book Review Editor, MR. EVERETT VAN EVERY

California Personnel Management Association, Berkeley, Cal.

EMPLOYEE COUNSELING

By Nathaniel Cantor—University of Buffalo. New York. McGraw-Hill Book Co., Inc. 1945. 167 pp. $2.00

Reviewed by Orrin Arnold

"Insight into human relations," the key words in the preface of Mr. Cantor's book, is the theme which is carried throughout every chapter of this well organized treatise of an old problem brought out in a new way. Far from claiming any panacea into gaining an insight into human relations, the author points out that insight into human relations is not found by measuring-instrument methods such as aptitude and intelligence tests, fatigue studies, etc. Counseling by and through the interviewing method as recently developed comes much closer, he believes, to shedding light on what happens when employees engage in industrial activities.

Dividing his book into three parts, namely, The Problem, The Approach, and The Organization, Mr. Cantor claims the problem to a considerable degree is due to the fact that industrial and personnel managers have not been concerned with human problems in the plants but with problems such as absenteeism, upgrading, training, etc. The economic problems have been dealt with, but the persons having the problems have remained unrecognized. Therefore, recognition of the employee as a dynamic, living, feeling individual who chooses and thinks for himself appears a partial solution to this problem. The solution however is far more than mere recognition. Chapters on the Development of the Counseling Program present a good picture of what industrial management has been thinking and doing in recognizing that there is a problem.

Part Two, The Approach, digs right into the heart of the basic psychological needs of the industrial employee. Here the reader definitely feels the author is not simply writing but is sharing an "insight into human relations." Chapters entitled "The Psychology of Adjustment," "The Function of the Consultant in Operation," and "Knowledge and Skill in Counseling," present actual case histories which, when read in their entirety, give the impression that counseling is effective listening.

Part Three, The Organization, deals with the counseling staff and the Counseling Program in an organization. Here many practical tips are suggested for the installation of a counseling set up. Any executive who wishes to keep abreast in industrial relations will find this book a stepping stone in the right direction.

THE ELEMENTS OF ADMINISTRATION

By L. Urwick. New York. 1944. 132 pp. $2.00

Reviewed by S. A. Abrahams

This book outlines in compact form the fundamentals underlying the principles of administration and organization. It is based on a series of lectures delivered by the author under the auspices of the London Branch of the Institute of Industrial Administration at the Polytechnic, London, England.

The author gives recognition to the fact that the art and science of administering the social groups, large and small, which are increasingly characteristic of our civilization, has emerged as a truly technical skill. In some respects this situation is the summation of the ideas and principles previously expressed by many students of scientific management. A re-statement of F. W. Taylor's three principles forms the basis for "A General Discussion on the General Principles of Administration."

Urwick stresses the underlying principle on which the whole field of administration rests and identifies it as Investigation. He shows how Investigation enters into process with Forecasting, and the effect is Plan or Planning. And in a rather technical manner we are shown how Forecasting has its own fundamental principle, namely, Appropriateness. This latter factor enters into process with Organization, and the author illustrates this situation by citing the first thing one does when he looks ahead and anticipates developments for the future, is to try to provide the means, human and material, to meet the future situation which he foresees. This Urwick calls Coordination.

Finally Planning finds its principle in Order, enters into process with Command, and the final effect is Control. In all a thoroughly complicated piece of theorizing that leaves the reader whirling about, but there is nevertheless something realistic about the subject treatment . . . something that makes the reader want to "try out" the plans proposed.

These principles are further elaborated and examples stated as to how they have been incorporated in business administration. The importance of Planning in business administration and a discussion of its application are particularly emphasized and well done. Authority and its delegation came in for considerable treatment and especially with the idea of encouraging the desire for Responsibility. The author calls Leadership the Unity of Management and describes its functions within an organization.

Further analyses provided for the types of relationship within an organization, outlining the degree of supervision exercised, as well as subordinates' responsibilities. Many of the fundamental principles in handling personnel, such as selection, placement, remuneration, promotion, initiative, morale, equity and discipline are discussed. Here we find Control and its relationship to the whole management picture well covered.

While the author thoroughly covers the fundamentals of administration he confines his material to a rigid textbook style. Business needs a book like this that can be used as a handbook for junior and senior executives, and perhaps even more in the field of supervisory relations and training.

HUMAN RELATIONS IN INDUSTRY

By B. B. Gardner. Chicago. Richard D. Irwin, Inc. 1945. 307 pages. Price $3.00

Reviewed by Harold B. Baker

This is another of the books stemming from the epoch making studies in employee relations at the Hawthorne Plant of Western Electric. Dr. Gardner has brought together many of the points scattered throughout the longer reports on this research and has added material from his studies in other plants to make a readable and instructive book on human relations in a factory.

The discussion centers around the factory as a social system with individuals and small groups being and interacting within the entire structure. The forces and factors which operate to influence the status of the individual and the complex interrelations of persons, positions, and groups are well described.

In its intended use as a college text on employee relations, the book will give the students a realistic picture of the way in which the human element is involved in nearly every industrial situation and problem. This picture is presented with authentic atmosphere and plant terminology (e.g. Big Boss, on top of a job, rate-buster) which give it a practical training or industrial orientation aspect.

In a subject in which the various points are so interrelated, it is inevitable that there will be differences of opinion as to the logical arrangement of material. For example, the reviewer would have placed some of the material in the chapter on The Industrial Relations Organization (IX) in the one on The Individual in the Structure (VIII). Although the book is rather limited in coverage to serve as the basic text in an employee relations course, it certainly deserves wide spread usage as a supplementary text. As such it fills a long felt demand for a reference book on these important problems.

Persons engaged in personnel work will find the book worthy of reading and study, not only for the overall personal relations picture it presents but also for the astute observations it contains on the relationship of the personnel department to the line supervisors and the workers.

Emphasis is given to the task of the personnel department in assisting the individual to adjust to the group. A brief statement on personnel counseling is given with most of the attention devoted to the interviewing technique as developed at the Hawthorne Plant. Dr. Gardner has well shown how the human factors complicate matters of wages, incentives, merit rating, job timing, and promotions to mention some of the outstanding points to which he has directed attention.

PERSONNEL
Journal

The Magazine of

LABOR RELATIONS AND PERSONNEL PRACTICES

Published by PERSONNEL RESEARCH FEDERATION

Lincoln Building, 60 East 42nd Street, New York City

Volume 24 .*Number 5*

Contents for November 1945

Many Men in the Armed Forces Have Had Their First Taste of Personnel Work There. They Think of Continuing in the Work After Discharge. Here an Attempt Is Made to Tell Them How.

Getting *into* Personnel Work

Compiled by THE EDITOR

The Editor is constantly receiving inquiries from men in the armed forces asking how they may get jobs in personnel work in industry after their discharge, and what institutions they might best go to for courses in the subject.

We open with an unofficial statement from a prominent personnel man in the War Department. Then follows some material from the United States Armed Forces Institute, and finally from the National Roster of Scientific and Specialized Personnel.

Unofficial War Dept. Comment

As to information about jobs in business, industry, education or government for men who have had a taste of personnel management in the army or in war agencies, my guess would be that no single government agency in Washington has all the information needed to reply informingly to all inquiries. There are as you know the National Roster of Scientific and Specialized Personnel, the United States Employment Service, the United States Civil Service Commission and the Office of Education. Professional psychologists wanting information about job opportunities may turn also to the Office of Psychological Personnel in the National Research Council.

Some Colleges Listed

As to opportunities for training in one phase or another of personnel management, I confess to continuing prejudice in favor of the University of Minnesota and the Ohio State University. For women the revived program at Radcliffe looks good. Jay L. Otis is doing a swell job of industrial psychology in Cleveland with headquarters at Cleveland College. Purdue University is stepping out briskly as you know. Keep an eye on Wayne University at Detroit, where Roger M. Bellows has gone to organize an institute of business research in collaboration with several prominent industries. Douglas Brown in the graduate college at Princeton University continues to push inquiries in the field of industrial relations, construing that field broadly.

Universities of Harvard, Columbia, Pennsylvania, Penn. State, Michigan, Chicago, Northwestern, Washington University at St. Louis, University of Washington at Seattle, and the several institutions in California are among those which will offer advanced instruction, but I don't know enough about details to have any judgment as to which places will be the strongest in what lines.

Special Warning

I HAVE a few strong hunches. One of them is that a lot of army officers not only in this field of personnel management but in many other fields of specialization are slated for a solemn period of disillusionment. Some of them have performed exceedingly well in the Army or Navy but know so little about industry that employers could scarcely afford to pay them more than $1800 to start, which is about one-fourth of the salary they expect to be offered.

United States Armed Forces Institute Courses Available to Enlisted Men Related to Personnel Work

COLLEGE level correspondence courses offered by United States Army Forces Institute, Madison 3, Wisconsin:

C526 Elements of Economics I
C527 Elements of Economics II
C569 Statistical Methods in Education
C646 Social Problems
C651 Municipal Personnel Administration
C545 Personnel Management
C547 Labor Problems
C548 Introduction to Statistical Method

Self-study textbooks available through USAFI

EM783 Personnel Management and Industrial Relations
EM295 Labor Problems in American Industry
EM763 Economics, Principles and Problems
EM490 Industrial Psychology
EM917 Educational Psychology
EM939 Measurement and Evaluation in the Secondary School

Arrangements can be made through USAFI to secure correspondence courses from cooperating universities at half-price.

The "USAFI Catalog" and "Information Bulletin" and an Information-Education officer should be consulted.

High School and College Credit, USAFI

A. USAFI Form 47 (Revised Sep. 1944) (Application for Educational Achievement)

Members of the Armed Forces on active duty interested in seeking credit at civilian schools for basic or recruit training, for courses completed at service schools, or for other educational experience while in the service, should secure and fill out completely USAFI Form 47 (Application for Credit for Educational Achievement). This application may be obtained from the Information-Education Officer, the Educational Services Officer, the Marine Corps Special Services Officer, or by writing to the Institute.

USAFI Form 47 must be sent direct to the civilian school. The Institute does not grant or recommend credit for in-service training and experiences. Granting of credit is a function of the civilian educational institution.

Veterans of World War II no longer on active duty may apply for school or college credit by writing direct to the school or college of their choice, and by inclosing with their letter a certified copy of WD AGO Form 100, (Separation Qualification Record); or Notice of Separation from the U. S. Naval Service, NavPers 553; or Notice of Separation from the U. S. Naval Service—Coast Guard, 553; or U. S. M. C. Report of Separation, NAVMC 78-PD, or by requesting a transcript of in-service training from the Special Services Branch, Headquarters U. S. M. C., Washington 25, D. C. In the case of naval commissioned or warrant officers, the Officer's Qualification Record Jacket (NavPers 305), a certified copy thereof, or a statement from the Bureau of Naval Personnel covering the data desired should be submitted to the school, college, or employer.

B. USAFI Examinations

If you use USAFI Form 47 you may be asked to take the USAFI General Educational Development Examinations or one or more of the USAFI Subject Examinations. General Educational Development Examinations, on both the high school and college level, are designed to show your general level of educational achievement. Subject examinations measure your ability in a given subject or subject field.

You may not wish to apply for high school or college credit, but you may wish to take the General Educational Development and Subject Examinations for your own information. If so, make application to the Institute on USAFI Form 68, (Application for Institute Test or Examination).

National Roster of Scientific and Specialized Personnel

I AM writing to describe to you the cooperative arrangement now in effect between the National Roster of Scientific and Specialized Personnel and the armed services.

This arrangement is designed to assist professionally qualified dischargees in locating suitable employment in civilian life as rapidly as possible. A supply of postcard forms, a copy of which I have enclosed, has been made available at the separation centers, hospitals and other discharge points of both the Army and the Navy. Each professionally qualified person being processed for separation who indicates that he wants assistance in locating employment is given one of these cards with the suggestion that he complete it immediately and mail it.

Use of Qualification Card

WHEN the Roster receives one of these cards, it is first checked against our registration files to determine whether or not the applicant is already registered. If he is, his registration papers are pulled and a summary of his training and experience immediately prepared. If the applicant is not registered with the Roster, appropriate documents are sent him and upon completion, the summary of his training and experience is prepared.

The Roster now has on hand a large volume of orders for technical personnel from industrial employers, colleges and universities, and non-profit research laboratories throughout the country. Additional orders of this kind are being received daily.

Summary Sent to Employees

FOR each applicant, a copy of the summary mentioned above is submitted to three or four employers seeking personnel with his qualifications. If the employer, after examination of these summaries, is interested in any of the applicants referred to him, he may then proceed to get in touch with the applicants directly. All negotiations from that point on are carried on between the employer and the applicant. The Roster only asks that a report be furnished of the outcome of the negotiations.

I might add that this service is available generally to professional and scientific personnel in addition to veterans. However, special attention is given veterans' applications.

An increasing number of these postcards is beginning to arrive in our office and the procedure based on our experience to date seems to be working quite satisfactorily. We hope in the very near future to launch a publicity program on these procedures so that their existence will become more generally known to employers and to professional personnel.

Copy of Card Used

Filled in cards or application for cards should be sent to National Roster of Scientific and Specialized Personnel, War Manpower Commission, Washington, 25, D. C.

1. Designate professional field (from list below)..
2. Are you registered with the national roster?...

3. On what date will you be available for civilian employment?..... ... .
4. Give preferences as to location and kind of employment : ....
....
....
5. What is your present military rank?.... ....
6. Name (print)..
   Service serial number.................... Date of birth............................
7. Address after discharge.... ....
....
8. Temporary address (other than separation center)..... .. . .
....
9. Signature.... .. ..

PROFESSIONAL AND SCIENTIFIC FIELDS

ACCOUNTING

ADMINISTRATION AND MANAGEMENT
  Management and Industrial Engineering
  Personnel Administration

AGRICULTURAL AND BIOLOGICAL SCIENCES
  Animal Sciences
  Anatomy
  Bacteriology, Immunology and Pathology
  Biology (inc. Zoology and Entomology)
  Forestry and Range Management
  Genetics
  Nutrition
  Pharmacology and Experimental Therapeutics
  Plant Pathology, Horticulture, Agronomy
  Physiology

ARCHITECTURE AND PLANNING
  (inc. Landscape Architecture)

FOREIGN LANGUAGES

SOCIAL SCIENCES
  Actuarial Science
  Anthropology
  Economics
  Geography
  History
  Political Science
  Psychology
  Sociology
  Speech Pathology
  Statistics

PHYSICAL SCIENCES
  Chemistry
  Geology
  Geophysics
  Mathematics
  Meteorology
  Physics and Astronomy

ENGINEERING SCIENCES
  Aeronautical Engineering
  Agricultural Engineering
  Architectural Engineering
  Automotive Engineering
  Ceramics and Ceramic Technology
  Chemical Engineering
  Civil Engineering
  Electrical Engineering (incl. Illumination)
  Heating, Ventilating, and Air Conditioning
  Marine Engineering and Naval Architecture
  Mechanical Engineering
  Metallurgy and Metallurgical Engineering
  Mineral Technology
  Mining Engineering
  Petroleum and Natural Gas Engineering
  Radio Engineering
  Refrigeration Engineering
  Safety Engineering
  Transportation and Traffic Engineering

The Story Below Is of Intrinsic Interest. It also
Provides Pointers on Problems of Personnel Con-
trol in a Wide Variety of Companies with Widely
Scattered Small Units.

Personnel Control *in* AAF Weather Service

By Colonel Theodore R. Gillenwaters

AAF Weather Service
Asheville, N. C.

Personnel control is one of the top functions of management, be it business management or that intensified, hard-to-define form of management called "command" which a military organization must have. One of the top men on any
commanding officer's staff is his personnel officer—in Army parlance his G-1. A
personnel officer not only must keep detailed, readily accessible records of the men of
a command but he must anticipate personnel needs and plan in advance to meet them.
His ultimate objective, like that of the personnel director of a civil enterprise, must
be the effective, economical and complete utilization of man power. Though somewhat less spectacular than bomber strikes and amphibious landings, personnel control was hardly less important in bringing defeat to Germany and Japan.

Specialized Technical Work

An outstanding example of personnel control in the Army is furnished by the
AAF Weather Service which grew from about 600 men in 1940 to nearly 20,000
men in 1945 operating a globe-girdling service of great technical competence. Personnel control in Weather has included some unique considerations and practices
which stemmed from the specialized, technical nature of the weather business. It
also has included the general principles upon which all such control is based. What
the Weather Service did in the way of adapting business practices to a military situation and in improvising practices of its own based on the best business experience
placed it in the forefront of the Army. It was my privilege to play a part in development of personnel control in the Service, and it is my belief that our use of both
standard and novel practices should be told.

The instruments of personnel control in the Weather Service ranged from that old Army standby, the morning report, day-to-day basis of all Army personnel statistics, through certain general AAF practices to several special Weather practices including a manpower "yardstick" developed early in 1945 to solve a trying and multiform problem. In fact, as we move into the post-war world our personnel control system may come to be based on the yardstick because it provides flexible criteria by which personnel can be procured, relieved, assigned and evaluated.

Every Pilot Given a Forecast

TO UNDERSTAND the personnel problem of the Weather Service it is necessary to understand the nature and scope of the work the Service performed from Pearl Harbor to V-J day—and beyond. The development of aviation and the growth of mechanization in ground warfare intensified to a degree unknown before 1939 the need for current and forecasted weather information in all military planning. The bulk of our effort was directed toward increasing the efficiency of air combat, but our general mission was to furnish weather information and advice to the Ground and Service Forces as well as the Air Forces.

No military plane goes into the air in war or peace until the pilot has been given a forecast covering the route and duration of his flight. The exact time and place of any landing—be it on the coast of Normandy or the coast of Honshu—was determined in a substantial part by climatological information and weather forecasts. Think of these facts in relation to the innumerable and complex air and ground operations of a military campaign and the role of a military weather service will be clear. Our motto, *Coelum ad proelium elige*—choose the weather for action—is particularly apt. Moreover, accurate meteorological information had as many applications throughout the war to logistics as to outright combat.

World Divided into Weather Regions

THE organization and operation of the Weather Service was dictated by the nature of the air masses moving across the surface of the earth and by the uses to which current and forecasted air mass information was put. Current weather could be analyzed and future weather anticipated in an area only if hundreds of simultaneous observations covering a continent or an ocean were gathered together quickly and accurately. Observations at stations far from any landing field might govern route forecasts for vital air transport runs or bomber strikes from bases hundreds of miles away.

Accordingly every available area in the world was dotted with weather stations, many of them only observing posts through or near which no air traffic passed. In addition, weather reporting ships far at sea radioed vital weather information and especially equipped aircraft were flown on weather reconnaissance missions over water areas and over enemy territory. These meteorological and operational compulsions helped both to define and to complicate our personnel problem.

The world was divided into weather regions each under a regional control officer. Within each region was a field administrative unit to which the men who operate weather stations were assigned. All weather regions in North and South America were assigned in turn directly to our headquarters in Asheville, North Carolina. And those regions in theaters of operations overseas always were subject to certain technical controls directed from Asheville. From a personnel man's viewpoint, Asheville was the world headquarters. We were specifically charged with providing personnel trained and equipped for combat to theater commanders. We not only had to keep a sensitive finger on the personnel problem in our domestic weather regions at all times but we constantly had to anticipate demands from overseas. In point of fact, our basic organization was somewhat similar to what it had been before the war and it will continue on a smaller scale. The meteorological compulsions remain. Air masses do not distinguish between war and peace.

Character of Men Stumbling Block

OPERATIONAL and geographical problems to one side, perhaps the greatest stumbling block to efficient personnel control in the Weather Service was the character of weathermen themselves. I say this in no disrespect, for I believe that most of them would agree with me, however wryly. Weathermen are technical experts. Many of them are scientists. Technical experts and scientists sometimes do not differ much in temperament from artists—and rightly so. Weather forecasters in particular must be men of imagination as well as men of unusual intellectual capacity and judgment. They are uninterested in the maintenance of management records whose application to the business of forecasting clouds and precipitation is not immediately apparent. Their apathy for such things is congenital.

AAF weathermen fall into three occupational categories: forecasters, observers and technicians. Forecasters may be officers, warrant officers or enlisted men. The officer forecaster can be generalized as a college graduate who specialized with distinction in mathematics and physics and has completed a rigorous cadet course in meteorology comparable to a year of university graduate work. The enlisted forecaster can be generalized as having completed two years of college and a course in meteorology, identical in its practical aspects with that completed by weather officers. (Since most enlisted forecasters are men of exceptional ability, it is not surprising that many of them became weather officers themselves via officer candidate school.) The weather observer can be generalized as a high school graduate who has completed an intensive course in weather observing and codes. Technicians, experts in meteorological and electronic equipment maintenance, possess qualifications midway between those of enlisted forecasters and observers. Men of this timber are, as often as not, inclined to excessive individualism.

Temperament and Administrative Inexperience

TEMPERAMENT combined with administrative inexperience among our predominantly youthful officers created some difficult problems. However, if our men had been more phlegmatic the Weather Service would have suffered though our personnel management problem might have been simpler. It was a source of pride to those of us in executive positions that we were able to institute a system of personnel control in a technical service which worked smoothly and was in the vanguard of Army practice.

The tremendous war-time expansion of the Weather Service was a personnel man's headache from the beginning—probably more of a one than the expansion problem of any other Army organization because of the mental level required of the men who were to observe and forecast the weather around the world. Training in meteorology would have been wasted on men not mentally qualified to absorb it and absorb it rapidly. Consequently, from Pearl Harbor until the middle of 1944, our personnel men were far too concerned with the procurement of carefully screened manpower to afford much interest in the refinements of personnel control. Our first problem was hiring, not management. Studies of manpower utilization based on an eight-hour day were academic when men were working twelve hours or more with no prospect of relief, whatever the studies might reveal.

Training Program

FORTUNATELY we had begun to expand during the growing tension of 1940. At that time not only was there an increase in training in our enlisted categories but we established a program of training exceptional young engineering and scientific graduates as cadets in meteorology to be weather officers. Until then all but one or two of our officers had been regular Army pilots who had been trained in meteorology at Massachusetts Institute of Technology and California Institute of Technology. In the fall of 1940, we sent nearly 150 cadets to MIT, CIT, the University of Chicago, the University of California at Los Angeles and New York University for a nine-month course. And we continued to send cadets to those five universities in increasing amounts until the middle of 1944 although the course itself was later reduced to 33 weeks. Late in 1942 our quotas exceeded the capacity of the five universities and we induced the AAF Technical Training Command to establish a Weather Training Center at Grand Rapids, Michigan, for cadets—and for enlisted men as well who previously had received their training at Chanute Field, Illinois. The Grand Rapids Installation was in existence for nearly a year.

Meanwhile, in the fall of 1942 the problem of finding suitable men for the cadet course became almost impossible of solution. We actually had about 450 weather officers in the field and about 800 cadets in training when Headquarters Army Air Forces decided that we would require some 5,000 weather officers by early 1944 and possibly an additional 5,000 by the beginning of 1945. This decision was something of a bombshell. There were not 10,000 qualified men or even 5,000 available. But we solved the problem.

10,000 Trained

OFFICERS of the Weather Service—and I am more than proud to say that I was Chief of the Personnel Division at that time—together with the members of a body called the University Meteorological Committee which represented the institutions which had been training cadets translated a scheme suggested by President Gordon Chalmers of Kenyon College into a plan and then into a working program. We decided to select young men of demonstrable intelligence and by intensive schooling provide them with the proper educational background to qualify as aviation cadets in meteorology. We set up two pre-meteorology courses to feed them into the cadet course. One was designed to provide for men who could be prepared for the advanced course by six months of intensive preparation. The second was designed to provide for men who could be prepared for the advanced course by twelve months of intensive preparation.

By the winter of 1943 we had the plan in operation so geared that beginning the following October we could produce 1,500 new weather officers every three months. We did not train the entire 10,000 and as it turned out some of those we did train proved to be temporarily surplus. (But I do not think we should be too strongly censured for over-estimating in the dark days of 1942; there were good reasons for our over-estimate which later disappeared.) It was not until we had procured and trained these thousands of officers—and the thousands of enlisted men whom we were training at the same time as forecasters and observers—that we could think more than superficially of personnel control. But we came a long way after the middle of 1944. The coming of peace naturally means shrinkage but our control methods persist.

Personnel Control—Early Stage

Personnel control in the Weather Service commenced with the weather regions. And, as must all such control, it commenced with a column of unexciting figures. Each field administrative unit made up, as do Army units around the world, what is called a "morning report" covering the weather stations scattered across its control region. For the benefit of those unschooled in Army practices let me say that a morning report is a daily statistical history of an administrative unit: So many men assigned, so many attached, so many on detached service or temporary duty, so many on leave or furlough, so many sick or AWOL and so on, plus any editorial comment that may seem appropriate.

These morning reports—there were seven for the continental U. S.—were consolidated by our Personnel Division in Asheville into a master morning report for the command, copies of which were forwarded to the War Department. The morning report system made it possible to keep records practically up to the minute for a service with units scattered across the land, and it was the basis of all personnel statistics. But the morning report system did not provide a control, it only provided a basic running record upon which controls could be based. In such a headquarters as ours which had to plan and operate an intercontinental service of its own as well as meet demands from other commands overseas we needed more elaborate means of keeping track of personnel, of assigning personnel and of planning future personnel needs.

To a degree a means was provided by use of AAF Form 127, which was made up as of the end of each calendar month. Form 127 was an elaborate statistical summary of the manpower of the Weather Service. It showed the number of assigned men by rank and by military occupational specialty. It showed how many of them were available for duty, how many had been detached to other commands for special advanced training, or to perform special functions for which their weather training was a prerequisite.

The routine by which a master command form 127 was prepared was similar to that by which the morning report was made. The form 127 provided a special check of our actual strength against our strength as authorized by Headquarters, AAF. It controlled our personnel relationship with the rest of the AAF which was a very necessary function, but it actually did little for us.

To Meet Short Notice Demands

FROM the above it should be no surprise that the Weather Service began to devise checks of its own beyond what was required by the War Department and Headquarters Army Air Forces in order not only to keep close track of its men but—more to the point—to know how personnel distribution could best be achieved, especially the filling of short notice demands from overseas. We had to be able to make decisions rapidly and accurately which meant that we required statistics arranged by more immediately useful breakdowns than were afforded by either the morning report or the form 127.

If a call came for fifty weather officers, twenty enlisted forecasters and ninety weather observers for China, we had to provide them from our own operating complement. We could not pull twenty of those weather officers from the Fourth Weather Region in the southeastern U. S. if the Fourth already was fifteen officers under strength, for the Fourth had to continue to provide crack service from the South Atlantic Coast to the Mississippi.

Different Classifications by World Regions

To COPE with these frequent demands the more easily the Personnel Division, using the unit morning reports for a basis, made up what it called Personnel Status Reports on a simple form of its own invention twice each month. These Personnel Status Reports were made up separately for officers (all but a handful of whom were rated forecasters), warrant officers, enlisted forecasters, weather observers, radiosonde operators and weather equipment technicians, and for miscellaneous non-technical enlisted men. The number of men authorized in each category was listed for each weather region. And then the number of men assigned was listed.

The number of men assigned frequently exceeded the number authorized, but this fact was misleading, as we frequently had occasion to point out to higher echelons. Many of our men always were away for special training or on temporary or detached duty with other commands to perform special missions. Moreover, it was necessary that we maintain an overage of both officers and enlisted men—then we could—to be in position to meet overseas demands. Included in these semi-monthly status reports were statistics for the regions in the North and South Atlantic, the Caribbean and Upper Canada which were assigned to the Asheville headquarters.

Included also were reports from weather regions in Europe, Africa, the Pacific and the Far East. Although these last might be a month or more out of date, they were required so that our Personnel Division could both evaluate and anticipate demands from overseas. Such controls as this enabled us to supply men in what might be called bulk demands—fifty forecasters, ninety observers, and so on. A demand for one officer especially equipped for a special job was a different matter.

Officers Qualification Record

To a certain extent a weather forecaster is a weather forecaster, and so is a weather observer. But obviously this cannot be one hundred per cent true. Moreover, we had many special research and staff jobs to fill which demanded special backgrounds. Suppose—to take a fairly extreme but far from impossible example—we received a call for a weather officer trained in forestry. We could fill such a call and fill it rapidly—provided we had any officers at all trained in forestry, and I'm sure we did. In Asheville we kept for every officer assigned to us an Officers Qualification Record on a form known to AAF personnel men as the 66-2. On this form was a complete history of the officer's civilian and military careers including major extra-occupational interests such as photography, wood working or small-boat handling. To provide an even readier reference, we maintained a Kardex file on every officer in the Service.

These cards contained a brief summary of the information recorded on the 66-2's. This file was to have been extended to include all enlisted specialists. Though the Army frowns upon the keeping of individual personnel records in any manner other than those laid down by Army regulations, our Kardex file and other devices were approved time and again by inspectors as necessary if we in Asheville were to fill our world-wide responsibilities.

Statistical Control Section

To fill the demand suggested above it would be possible to go through several thousand 66-2's or through the Kardex file manually until we found one or more men with forestry as part of their civilian backgrounds. However, to do it this way was, we found long ago, a laborious process. Being only human we were inclined at times to take the first man who came along. Since weathermen were of a high order, this hit-or-miss system was not as bad as it sounds, but it was bad enough to warrant improvement. In 1944 we established a statistical control section in Asheville which worked closely with our Personnel Division as well as with the other headquarters divisions. The Statistical Control Officer punched information from the 66-2's and the Kardex file on IBM cards. Thus, if we still wanted that weather officer trained in forestry we could run the IBM cards through the machine and come up with—say—five candidates. Then we could go to the individual records and check the details of each man's background.

At this point, of course, human judgment entered the picture and in that variable control tool we were especially fortunate. Although Asheville was headquarters for an organization of global extent, the service always was sufficiently small and integrated so that somebody at headquarters knew everybody. He had gone to school with him or served with him in this country or overseas. By the time we had selected one of the five we could be as close to 100 per cent confident of the wisdom of our choice as was humanly possible.

Personal Angle

THE personal angle was an invaluable tool in assessing men and in controlling assignments. And certainly it insured that we in Asheville possessed an intimate knowledge of field problems from France to the Philippines. But it did not provide an objective means of evaluating personnel nor did the record systems I have outlined. To accomplish such evaluation we contrived a number of means including tests of observing and forecasting proficiency and the aforementioned manpower yardstick. From the standpoint of the personnel officer, the yardstick was—and is— the most important. While the yardstick which was developed by our Operations Division was designed for use in the continental U. S. it actually can be used for weather stations anywhere in the world, and can be used now as profitably as when the B-29's were battering Japan's crowded cities. In fact, now when all commands must re-evaluate themselves to meet peace time requirements the yardstick is particularly valuable.

What the yardstick accomplished can best if somewhat tritely be defined as manpower streamlining. Last winter it became apparent that the end of the war in Europe would not mean any immediate diminution of our service in European and Atlantic areas. At the same time, we well knew that there would be increased demands from the Pacific and Far East as more and more power was brought to bear upon the Japanese. Accordingly we anticipated excessive drainage from our field service at home. We also wished to establish sound control methods for a post-war weather service. These factors combined to constitute a demand for re-evaluation of our operations in terms of manpower utilization. Hence the yardstick. It meant applying the principles of time and motion studies to a highly developed and exacting technical service. This was something the Army never had attempted before.

Performance Standards

THE big question was what were the reference points by which we could evaluate our personnel and set performance standards. We were not a factory producing so many motors or so many wheel assemblies a day; we were a technical service providing information and advice. "Efficiency expert" methods could not provide the answer. We wanted no Bedeaux-like speed-ups where men become only robots; we had to maintain and encourage individuality if we were to complete our mission.

One possible approach was to re-evaluate the needs of the people who used our service. We investigated the operations of various transport, training and combat organizations. We determined by analysis exactly what information was required for each type of operation and what we had to do to provide it. We found certain constant factors: so many observations to be made each day, so many maps to be drawn. And we found certain variable factors; so many formal briefings per day, so many individual aircraft clearances. From this point on we could concentrate on job analysis and determine the man-hour requirements for each step of each job.

Man-hour Requirements

THE yardstick gives us the man-hour requirements for specific jobs in any weather station. We have several different types of stations each one of which varies considerably in the field, but the sum of proper job combinations can give us man-hour requirements for any type of station or any individual station. All we have to know is what service the station is supposed to provide and what special meteorological and operational problems it must meet. The manpower requirements can be obtained from the man-hours by allowing eight hours per man per day. We have worked out normal or typical man-hours and manpower requirements for each station type to serve as controls.

Because no such scheme can cover all contingencies in detail we employ a loading factor of twenty-five per cent which is applied directly to the apparent man-hour requirements of each station type. In other words, if it takes 100 man hours to run a station for twenty-four hours, we add twenty-five more hours to compensate for several more or less imponderable elements. Among the things covered by this twenty-five per cent are leaves and furloughs, illnesses, training, meals, rotation of shifts, time off, and emergency and peak demands.

Typical Station Used as Base

FOR instance, we have found that a typical A-type weather station, one which provides 24-hour observing and forecasting service both, requires 117.5 man hours a day in the absence of special contingencies. To this we add the 25 per cent loading factor and the man hours rise to 147. When we divide this total by the eight hours per man we find that 18.4 men are required. This figure is still somewhat tentative but will serve until we find a more precise one.

However, even when the loading factor has been applied, we still have only the manpower requirements of a typical station. Weather Service operations in the field are not uniform. To say that a station is of a particular type is not to say that it is typical. Consequently, using the manpower requirements of a typical station as a norm, we have derived a rather simple arithmetical formula by which the manpower requirements of any single weather station can be determined with a precision in which we are beginning to have great confidence. Since we are just beginning to use the yardstick we can expect that the formula will be subject to many adjustments. However, we can reasonably hope that those adjustments will be minor. What may cause sizable adjustments will be new methods of weather observation and forecasting which will alter our job analyses.

Knows Manning of Each Station

A T PRESENT we are collecting quarterly time and motion statistics regarding every detail of our operations station by station. Some of these statistics probably will be collected on a monthly basis later on and many of them eventually will be punched into IBM cards to furnish data for further statistical investigations. From the periodic reports we will have not only a check on the efficiency of each station but a constant check on the yardstick itself. Certainly the yardstick will relieve our Personnel Division of many a headache.

In the future, when they are asked to provide men for twenty or a hundred stations they will know the man-power answer with a certainty they never have had before. Since the difference between war and peace is one of quantity more than anything else so far as the Weather Service is concerned we continue to find more and more uses for the yardstick despite the fact that the war is over.

By an application of the yardstick we can plan for the field, using proven reference points in relation to the work load presented by changing demands of air ferrying operations, training missions, military air transport, and ground organizations. Obviously the greatest problem faced by a service organization is that of knowing the plans of using agencies sufficiently in advance to be prepared for them. We have attempted to solve this by having a series of plans of our own encompassing all of the known factors and allowing liberally for emergencies.

Any one of these plans can be implemented immediately by direction from Asheville to the field where the service is directly assigned to us, and by suggestion where the weather service is assigned to an overseas theater. The manpower yardstick is only a guide in the adaptation of a given plan, but it is a dependable one.

Monthly Personnel Digest

N O ONE man nor ever one group of men can develop a personnel control system including necessarily elaborate records and manpower utilization analyses affecting a large number of people unless he knows what those people are doing and thinking and unless those people know what he is doing. There are problems of manpower utilization in the Weather Service which we in Asheville might never hear of, there are decisions made at headquarters which might be misunderstood and there are isolated practices in the field which might never receive merited circulation if we did not have a medium of exchange.

This is true of any large organization, especially if it is geographically widely dispersed. Accordingly, last winter Headquarters, Army Air Forces, directed that each AAF command circulate an informal monthly personnel digest to its lower echelons. Meanwhile the Assistant Chief of Air Staff for Personnel was to circulate a digest of his own to the various command headquarters.

We have been circulating such a digest to all our weather stations since last spring. In preparing this digest we have aimed at the station weather officer, bearing in mind that he is not an expert in personnel management but a busy meteorologist upon whose shoulders rests a possibly unwanted administrative burden. Therefore we have stressed the practical aspects of management rather than the theoretical. And we have done our best to stimulate interest and outright participation in the management problem.

Suggestions Welcomed

WE HAVE encouraged station weather officers to send in their solutions to knotty local problems of management and manpower utilization, and those accounts which have seemed of general interest we have published in the digest. For instance, if the weather officer at an air base where the barracks area and mess halls are remote from the weather station has so scheduled his forecasters and observers that a minimum amount of time is lost in transit, we give publicity to his scheduling method for it will be applicable to other air bases similarly dispersed. We have also used the digest to explain to the field our own studies of manpower utilization including both the yardstick and special studies ordered by Headquarters, Army Air Forces.

We exchange our monthly digest for those of other commands, and it is my opinion that we have made a more thoroughly useful application of the digest idea than they have. This opinion is supported by a letter which came to us from the Assistant Chief of Air Staff for Personnel in which a recent issue was described as "one of the most practical and effective digests received."

Manpower Yardstick Formula

ON THE following page is a summary of the operation of the manpower yardstick as it is applied to a typical A-type station of the AAF Weather Service. We begin with an analysis of the man-hour requirements necessary to operate the station for twenty-four hours. These requirements, as empirically determined, are:

REQUIREMENTS OF A TYPICAL TYPE "A" STATION
(Man hours per day)

	hours
Forecasters Activities..	42.5
Analyzing charts and current weather...	18
Analyzing standard charts	11
Familiarization with current weather.	4
Additional charts required by the using agency.	3

hours

Briefing pilots, preparing clearances and forecasts, telephone calls, and conferences   7

A dozen or more Forms ✳ 23 per day (10 minutes each), and a few Forms ✳ 23A
per day (1 hour each).   4

Briefing   1

Informal personal and inter-office calls.   2

Miscellaneous Duties:

Determining mean temperatures, spotting aircraft reports, verifying doubtful
data, canned maps, etc.   3

Training, administration, maintenance, and installation. 11.5

Station management and administration   6

Meteorological training.   5

Chart discussion (1 hour/week for 6 fcstrs)

Short Range Verification (1.5 hour/week/man)

Refresher classes, study of recent developments, seminars, etc. (1.5 hours)

Maintenance and installation. 0.5

Military duties:

Orientation, combat training, OD, guard, KP, etc.   3

Observers' Activities. 75.0

Taking regular observations   31

Making and transmitting 24 hourly observations @ 15 minutes each (sequence,
inter-office, and delays).   6

4 Pibals @ 1.5 hours.   6

Special and check observations.   1

Plotting charts   30

Standard charts   20

Additional charts.   6

Aircraft reports; deciphering canned analyses; etc.   4

Maintaining "Service Aids"

Displaying sequences; ditto work; visual aids; etc. 16.5

Administration and Maintenance. 9.5

Administrative duties of the chief observer (Check forms, type letters, superin-
tend observers, etc.).   6

Maintenance duties (Installing new equipment; maintaining teletypes; minor instrument repairs; "keeping up" manuals).   2

Training of observers (.75 hour/week/man). 1.5

Military duties:

Inspections, cleaning weather station, KP, CQ, guard, etc. 6.0

          ——

        117.5

Below Are the Conclusions Arrived at in the Latest Study of Union Security Plans. The Studies of This Subject by This University Cover both USA and Canadian Experience. They Are Excellent. Copies of Full Reports May Be Obtained from the Author.

Union Security Plan

By J. C. Cameron

Department of Industrial Relations
Queen's University
Kingston, Ont.

THE *continuance of disputes over the inclusion of union security clauses in collective agreements prompted the Department of Industrial Relations to continue its examination of the union security question. This study is a development of some of the suggestions contained in Bulletin No. 9, The Closed Shop: A Study of the Methods used by Unions to Attain Security. It presents compromise arrangements which do not appear to be open to the serious social and economic disadvantages of either the closed shop or the union shop. However, these arrangements are not above question. Their advantages and their limitations will probably continue to be the subject of debate for some time to come. This Bulletin will accomplish its purpose if it stimulates these discussions and, in some measure, clarifies the issues involved.*

The nature of the dispute over union security and the position of the protagonists has been discussed in detail in our Bulletin Number 9. It seems desirable, however, to repeat here the main reason advanced by each side for its opposition to the other's position and for its persistent refusal to give ground.

The employer who opposes union security does so because he hesitates to strengthen an organization whose aims and objectives seem to him to be diametrically opposed to his own. He cannot see how a stronger union will prove to be anything other than a more vigorous opponent, more eager and more capable of driving a harder bargain for "better" working conditions. Why, then, he asks himself, should I do anything that will strengthen this union?

Why Union Demands Security

THE union demands union security to free itself from the arduous task of preserving its existence in the face of the opposition of rival unions, of non-union employees and of the reactionary employer. It maintains that, lacking security, it is compelled to engage in tactics which are objectionable to it and to the employer. It must continuously raise contentious matters and initiate disputes in order to maintain the interest of its members.

Most of its efforts are dissipated in this way. If it were made secure in its position as bargaining agency for the employees, through a union shop agreement, it contends that it could devote all its energies to the constructive aspects of unionism. It would be able to promote better employer-employee relationships, greater efficiency of the working-force and so create larger returns for all those interested in the business. Therefore, in the union's view, a demand for a union shop is a demand for an institution which will benefit not only the union securing it but also the employer who agrees to it.

Should Not Be Imposed

IT is not proposed to examine the soundness of these arguments. It is sufficient to say that each side is convinced of the validity of its claims and the righteousness of its cause. It does seem necessary, however, to reiterate the conviction that disputes such as this can be settled to the complete satisfaction of the parties concerned only through the process of collective bargaining. No third party can intervene to lay down a settlement that would take the place of one devised by the disputants themselves. It should be clear, then, that it is not the purpose of this Bulletin to discover a solution to the union security issue that can be regarded as ideal and so properly imposed on companies and unions by some administrative board. Such settlements bid fair to destroy the voluntary nature of collective bargaining and so eliminate the very feature that holds most promise for the success of employer-employee negotiations.

Compromise Not Urged

IT was pointed out at the very beginning of this Bulletin that it is not the purpose of this study to urge disputants to compromise. The aim is rather to assist those who have decided to compromise in finding some arrangement that might prove satisfactory to both.

The provisions presented here are free from the serious social and economic objections that can be raised against the closed or the union shop. They are not undemocratic arrangements. They do not interfere with an employee's freedom of association or freedom of action. They do, however, require the employer to assist the union and so increase its strength. Furthermore, each implies an admission by the union accepting it of some lack of ability to administer its own affairs.

Questions will doubtless arise as to which of the three compromise arrangements is the most desirable. It is usually considered that the voluntary, revocable check-off is the one which appeals to employers, while maintenance of membership is favoured by unions. Circumstances will, of course, alter these views and will dictate the particular form most satisfactory to both parties.

Why Check-off?

EXPERIENCE with union security provisions in the United States and the more limited experience in this country shows that unions are not long satisfied with any arrangement which does not include the check-off. It seems that neither the union shop, the ultimate form of union security, nor maintenance of membership solves one of the most serious administrative problems with which union executives have to deal, the collection of dues. Or, to put it another way, two things have become evident: first, these union security provisions do not prevent union members from becoming delinquent and, second, the most serious cause of these delinquencies is failure to pay dues.

It may seem strange, at first sight, that union members become delinquent in spite of a union shop or a maintenance of membership provision. Each of these arrangements makes continuance in the union as a member in good standing a condition of employment for those employees who come under its terms. Apparently they give the union adequate power to deal promptly and effectively with delinquents. Why, then, do members become delinquent?

The first and perhaps the most common cause of the delinquency of union members is the unwillingness of union officials to impose penalties on some delinquents for fear of losing the good will of the union's constituents. The executives of a local union must frequently feel that there is little to be gained by imposing penalties rigorously. The union member who, for example, fails to pay his dues is lost forever if he is expelled for failing to maintain his membership. Moreover, his expulsion may arouse the sympathy of many others who will become hostile to the union. The safest course and the least difficult to follow is to wink at some delinquents and hope for their reformation.

Delinquent Members

To THIS first cause, which will be found in the most efficiently administered local unions, must be added another that will increase in importance as the efficiency of the union executive diminishes, namely, the failure of the executive to discover and keep track of delinquents, even of those amenable to mild punishment.

It is no small task, even in a small local, to administer the collection of dues, to keep careful account of those who have paid and of those who have not, to go back repeatedly to persons who for some apparently valid reason did not pay the first time or the second, to separate those who have not paid but will pay from those who have no intention of paying. It is small wonder that there are union members from whom dues are not collected regularly and others whose arrears of payments are carelessly allowed to accumulate.

There is reason to believe that neither the union shop nor maintenance of membership does much to lighten the administrative tasks of local union officials. They merely add another item to the list of penalties that may be imposed on delinquent members. They do not make it much easier or less necessary for union officials to find and take positive action against delinquents.

The fact that the penalty which they impose, loss of employment, is a severe one may make union officials somewhat hesitant to take action and less anxious to find delinquents. So it is that delinquents continue to be a problem even with the union shop or maintenance of membership. The problem is a serious one for the union, for delinquency usually comes of failure to pay dues and such failure to pay may embarrass the union financially.

Check-off Is Self-administrative

A UNION's demand for a check-off to supplement the union shop or maintenance of membership is clearly a demand for relief from the administrative difficulties which the collection of dues presents and which the other forms of union security do not remove. The check-off, unlike the "stronger" forms of union security, is, from the union's point of view, self-administrative.

A union has only to persuade its members to sign orders for dues deductions, a thing much easier to accomplish in most cases than the collection of actual money. Furthermore, a union is not obliged to canvass each member *monthly* to secure his dues. A single canvass may well secure orders for the check-off that will stand for many months.

The failure of the union shop and maintenance of membership to enforce the payment of dues and the consequent demand of the unions for the check-off leads to the conclusion that the union shop may not be the true "ultimate" in union security from the point of view of a union. Perhaps the goal of organized labour should be some form of maintenance of dues-payments rather than the union shop which emphasizes the broader thing, maintenance of membership.

Perhaps it is not true that maintenance of membership carries with it maintenance of dues-payments, while it may be true that maintenance of dues-payments does secure maintenance of membership. It may be that a person who is interested enough to contract to pay his dues to an organization is interested enough to participate in its activities. Moreover, such a person may feel that he has his money in the undertaking and has therefore some responsibility for its policy and programmes.

It follows that the most satisfactory compromise from the point of view of the union may prove to be the one which the employer usually accepts most readily, the check-off. It is the only form which ensures the stability of income which is essential to any union pursuing an active programme.

If Counseling Veterans with Reemployment
Rights Is Undertaken with Full Knowledge of
Its Implications It Will Avoid Much of the
Chronic Unemployment Tendencies Nurtured by
Adjustment Delays After the Last War.

Reemployment Counseling

By Frederick W. Novis
Division of Rehabilitation
Conn. State Department of Education
Hartford, Conn.

IF "WHAT the soldier thinks" (9) can be considered a fair criteria of their post-war plans, it is clearly evident that the majority may seek to return to their former employment. Over one-third of the white enlisted soldiers, who were working for wages before the war, expect to go back to their former employer; another one third are not so sure but say that they may return. If the plans of these soldiers materialize, it is expected that about three million men will seek out their former employer in order to exercise their reemployment rights on their old jobs, under the Selective Service regulations.

The problem of counseling these veterans is important and should warrant the attention and concern of all employers, whether they have lost one or one thousand workers to the Service. The job of reemployment counseling will be characterized by a number of factors:

There Will Be Legal Ramifications

THE legal implications of reemployment rights may force many employers, acting in good faith, to return men to their old jobs or to other speedily contrived opportunities, which may be unsuitable or even harmful. In their eagerness to help the veteran or in the fear of legal entanglement, many employers may rush an adjustment with resulting over or under placing. This danger is neatly pointed out by Drought (23) who discusses some psychological factors related to the reemployment of discharged War Veterans.

Awaiting a Reemployment Adjustment Will Be Costly

A LOSS of time in the proper adjustment of these men will be costly in money and morale. The expenditure for unemployment compensation will be far more costly than the provision of the most elaborate counseling services. The discouragement which may face many soldiers in either not finding their old job or even a better one after they "have fought for our country" will shatter morale, if employers do selected reemployment, rather than reemployment counseling of all who return to them.

Most Employers Will Not Be Prepared

WHILE many employers, particularly large industrial firms have set up or are setting up facilities to deal with this problem and are studying their responsibilities (19) (20) (21) (24) (25) (26) (27) (28) (29) (30) (37), most employers are struggling under personnel methods which have not achieved a professional level. For years, even large industry has shunned from the more modern scientific counseling tools and psychological techniques, and have clung to an age belonging to phrenology. Those who have kept pace with rapid development of counseling and occupational techniques realize that they will need to fully utilize them or depend upon community counseling and veteran centers.

Many such services are springing up. Meyer (45) depicts the community resources made available thru the Community Advisory Service at Bridgeport, Conn. Likewise, Handville and Fleming (44) describe the functions of school advisors as points of contact and counsel for veterans. Other plans, some of which have achieved nationwide attention, describe community and State action, Gray (42), Corcoran (42) Burch (41), Allen (40) Aherne (39).

Employers Cannot Completely Avoid a Counseling Problem

IN SPITE of the rapid development of counseling services under a variety of auspices, it is necessary for employers and desirable also, that they actively participate in aiding in the individual adjustment. In the first place, the employers problem of counseling for his own firm becomes easier because he has a better knowledge of his industry than a counselor working with various groups could accumulate. As one experienced personnel executive puts it: The knowledge of physical and job demands must be at the personnel man's finger tips. He cannot stop to make a job analysis each time he sees a different veteran no more so than the physician stops to make a study of pharmaceuticals before he prescribes.

The Veteran May Return a Changed Person

THE mail boy who left at 18, may return at 21 with a wife and baby; the riveter discharged an N.P. and can't stand noise; the insurance clerk who attained the rank of Captain; the man who has lost a limb, etc. These are counseling problems employers will have to face, in spite of the help of Rehabilitation Services. These and other counseling problems may need to be faced in the midst of reconversion and mass lay-off. Those who have already seen many returned servicemen, know that he can do well even though he has changed, Ward (38) ("One million men have come back!") if good counseling and reemployment procedures are used.

More Adequate Analysis of Service and Work Experience

EVEN the relatively small employer who may be discouraged by psychological and other valuable occupational analysis techniques, Gleason (4), 18, can observe such factors as *variability* of work record which may yield data as to the workers job stability. The factor of *job variability* studied in connection with *job duration* should indicate whether a person has been a job shifter or has advanced so rapidly that he held no one job over a long period of time. In addition, individual job trends can be determined.

Has the person worked within the same skill level for different employers, or has there been an upward or downward trend in skill of responsibility? Or is there no particular trend, but simply a scattered history? These criteria will be helpful, particularly in making the employer's interview more factual and realistic, rather than just another application blank. The same criteria can be adapted to the analysis of service assignments, service promotions and ratings.

Further Studies Necessary

FURTHER research along these lines seems desirable as it appears that it would be helpful in counseling and reemployment to have more accurate records of past work history. It would appear that further research may be able to seek out an "Occupational Age" for an adult individual, and that this "O.A." will be considered in the light of such variables as *job frequency* or variability, *job trend, job duration*, and *job recency*. The O.A. can be considered to be that span of time during which the individual could have worked if he so chose or if he could find work. It means that, that span of time since leaving school to the present would be more adequately expressed, and that gaps would be checked to determine whether they were due to individual factors, economic factors etc.

Analyses of work history, however, are but one phase of the counseling problems of Veterans. Suitable reemployment, particularly where a mental or physical handicap exists, cannot be worked out in isolation by industry alone, or by agencies alone, who have expert counseling to offer. An attempt to coordinate and unite the adjustment and rehabilitation services with the utilization and employing sources is described by Novis and Panciera (46) who project a counseling technique known as Experimental Training.

Three Plans

THE plan provides for a laboratory which can be used by employers and others who may pose either specific problems, or seek recommendations in the readjustment of their problem cases. For the purpose of meeting employer problems, the Experimental Training Center proposes three divisions: a medical division, a psychological division and training laboratory, and a training division. These divisions working together on each case, will suggest action, arrange tryout where indicated, conclude as to feasibility for reemployment for particular work or under certain conditions, arrange and provide skills or training found suitable. Plans now being studied for such a State-wide Experimental Training Center, include a three plan admission basis:

Plan I

consists of a one day clinical study of individuals. This involves medical and psychological diagnosis with recommendations. This plan would appear to be helpful to employers who seek to reemploy a Veteran, but desire medical and other safeguards.

Plan II

is designed for persons whose study will require over one day and less than six days. This plan includes the one day clinical study plus some occupational fact finding. This plan would appear to be helpful for persons who desire to exercise their reemployment rights, but are confused or are not sure they want to return to their own previous work; or an employer may desire to verify whether some new work which they now desire, comes within the scope of their ability.

Plan III

is designed where more extensive study is needed. It includes Plan II plus assignment to the training laboratory and training division. This plan is designed for the difficult cases who because of some physical, mental or emotional difficulty, the employer quite definitely feels that the person cannot be used in any capacity that he has available or can make available.

Arrangements for living maintenance and housing, while individuals are under study at the Center is proposed. This will enable the staff to maintain close supervision over the total individual, including his educational, social and recreational activities.

If the problem of counseling veterans with reemployment rights is undertaken with full knowledge of its vast implications, it will not only help the veteran to find his most suitable civilian place, but will avoid much of the chronic unemployment tendencies nurtured by adjustment delays in World War I. It will also act to forestall premature displacement of present valuable civilian workers, who have found their groove in a job which some day soon legally belongs to someone else.

Counseling References

(1) FLETCHER, RICHARD D. "Why Counsel Now?" Manpower Review, 12: 3-4 March 1945.
Points to need of counseling because of: 1) legal responsibility for reinstatement of many returning servicemen with consequent displacement of others; 2) assistance to veterans who need readjustment; 3) absorption of war wage earners into civilian production is essential; 4) aid is needed for young workers with no experience; 5) necessity for adjustment of older workers whose occupations may be obsolete.

(2) FOSTER, TERRY C. "Manual for Case Workers" No. 23, 1934, U. S. Printing Office, Washington, D. C. 69 pp.
A guide for rehabilitation supervisors, giving instructions, policies and procedures in guiding the handicapped to their adjustment.

(3) FOSTER, TERRY C. "Vocational Guidance in Rehabilitation Service" No. 20, Rev. 1935, U. S. Printing Office, Wash., D. C. 56 pp.
A simple and practical approach to the principles and procedures of counseling the physically handicapped.

(4) GLEASON, C. W. "The Use of Job Families for the Physically Handicapped" Psychol. Bull. 1943, 40: 714-718.
A helpful guide to suitable selection of training or jobs for the handicapped. Divides disabilities into eleven types and indicates range of activity which these types can perform.
Cross indexes occupation in reference to disability limitations and recommends as to suitability of employment for any of the eleven types.

(5) GREENBERG, VIRGINIA. "Employment Counseling of U.S.E.S." Manpower Review, 12: 5 March 1945.
Outlines the projected U.S.E.S. counseling program and explains steps of program, under the following categories: 1) Analysis of applicants problems; 2) Giving information; 3) Assistance in formulation and launching of vocational plan; 4) Locating suitable job, 5) Preparation for job referral; 6) Follow-up on placement or training.

(6) JAGER, HARRY A., AND ZERAN, FRANKLIN R., "Community Adult Counseling Centers" Occupations, 23: 261-304 Feb. 1945.
Describes the counseling problem; who is to be counseled; community services and their organization. Gives concise outline description of Community Adult Counseling Services in eleven United States communities, located in various parts of the country. Gives suggested books, pamphlets and other reference material and a suggested outline for training counselors.

(7) KITSON, H. D. "Vocational Guidance for the War-Dislocated" Teach. Coll. Rec. 1944, 45: 526-531.
The author estimates that at least 12,000 additional counselors should be trained.

(8) LINDGREN, H. C. "The Navy counsels the War-Disabled." Occupations, 1944, 23: 133-135.
Description of testing and counseling procedures in the Navy amputation center which should be helpful in Veteran counseling.

(9) Army Service Forces, War Dept. "What the Soldier Thinks" 1945, Wash., D. C. 16 pp.
Analyzes poll of soldier's post war plans, touching upon migration, career, business and educational plans.

(10) MATHEWSON, R. H. "Organizing a Community Adjustment Program" State Dept. of Education, Hartford, Conn. 1940, 28 pp.
Outlines practices and procedures for youth leaders, teachers, educational supervisors and guidance workers in field of guidance and adjustment.

(11) O'CONNOR, E. "Vocational Counseling" Crippled Child, 1944, 21: 143-144 and 165-166.
The author emphasizes the need for counseling before the student leaves high school. The employment experience of a number of handicapped individuals is described.

(12) O'Neil, W. M., and Young, J. P. "Vocational Guidance of the Disabled Soldier." Sydney L Government Printer, 1943, pp. 28. (Abstracted Review; original not seen).

Study of 556 medical dischargees, who were interviewed, tested and given further orientation and planning interviews. Large minority were unwilling to return to former occupations even when able to do so. Many tend toward novel and new occupations.

(13) Orner, A. T. "Counseling the individual who happens to be disabled." Crippled Child, 1944, 22: 35-36; 54-55.

Urges a total view of client, and to consider defect in a positive sense of limitation rather than as a defect.

(14) Shartle, C. L., Dvorak, B. J. and Others, "Occupational analysis activities in the War Manpower Commission." Psychol. Bull., 1943, 40: 701-713.

Describes the tools used and being developed for the placement of the country's manpower. Includes mention of physical demands form used in placing physically handicapped. Other tools surveyed are: Trade questions, Job descriptions, Manning tables, and job families. All of these are techniques aiming at better placement, counseling and employment adjustment.

(15) Shartle, C. L. "Occupational and Vocational Counseling of Military and Civilian Personnel during the Period of Post-War Demobilization and the Years immediately thereafter." Psychol. Bull., 1944, 41: 697-705.

Discussion of counseling, training and counseling problems. Some of the problems treated are: transfer to civilian jobs, testing, physical demands, additions and conversions between civilian occupations for Job Dictionary.

(16) U. S. Veterans Administration, "Counseling Services of the Veterans Administration." Manpower Review March 1945, 12: 10-11.

Counseling services offered veterans include: vocational advisement; placement counseling; educational guidance, and personal adjustment counseling.

(17) War Manpower Commission, "Technical Counseling Tools of W.M.C. Manpower Review," March 1945, 12: 6-7; 24.

Techniques outlined are: labor market information; monographs, manual on employment counseling; job dictionary; job families; occupations suitable for women; special aids for placing Navy and Military personnel in civilian jobs; trade and aptitude tests; job descriptions; physical demands.

(18) War Manpower Commission; "Ten Years of Occupational Research," Occupations, April 1944, Vol. 22. Historical survey of techniques developed for manpower utilization. Includes bibliography.

Reemployment References

(19) Automotive Council for War Production. "Responsibilities of the Employer in the Employment of Veterans." Detroit, Mich. 1944, 11 pp.

Discusses reemployment rights under the Selective Service Act.

(20) Dedrick, F. R. "Ready for Disabled Veterans." Factory Management and Maintenance, March 1944, 102: 100-102.

A report on the reemployment of 100 discharged servicemen at Bullard Co., Bridgeport, Conn. plant.

(21) deWeerdt, Esther H. and deWeerdt, Ole N. "You and the Returning Veteran—A guide for Foremen." Allis-Chalmers Mfg. Co.

Offers a valuable guide in the personal readjustment and reemployment of veterans. Emphasizes the importance of the foreman in this readjustment.

(22) Drought, Neal E. "Employers Plan Welcome for their Veterans." Occupations, Jan. 1945, 23: 197-201.

Suggests planning include some of the following steps: determination of reemployment rights of various service and service related groups; survey of expected after the war jobs; survey to determine which eligible employees now in Armed Forces, who plan return to former place of employment; the proportion of present employees who expect to keep working after the war. Urges use of "veteran interviewer" who knows details of Selective Service Act and suggests careful selective placement with due consideration to physical and mental defects.

(23) DROUGHT, NEAL E. "Psychological Factors Related to Re-employment of Discharged War Veterans." J. Consult. Psychol., 1944, 8: 100-106.

Factors of adequate adjustment of discharged veterans are discussed, with emphasis upon avoidance of over or under placing in view of war experience; fostering good industrial morale; insuring maximum satisfaction and performance by expansion of psychological service in industry.

(24) Liberty Mutual Insurance Co. "Employment of Physically Handicapped." Boston, Mass., Dec. 24, 1943.

A brief guide, aimed at industry, for disability examination, evaluation and classification.

(25) Manufacturers Association of Conn. Inc. "When the Veteran Returns" A Reemployment Digest. July 1944, 54 pp.

A guide to employers in rehiring the disabled and men out of uniform. Summarizes various services now available to aid in adjustment, employment, training and rehabilitation.

(26) Metropolitan Life Insurance Co. "The Employment of the Handicapped Veteran." 1 Madison Ave., N. Y. 10, N. Y. 56 pp.

Pictorial review and outline on employment of handicapped in industries throughout the country; includes 39 companies and reports on Peoria, Ill., Worcester, Mass., and Bridgeport, Conn., plans of community organization for rehabilitation of veterans.

(27) MOREY, A. A. "Rehabilitation" Safety Engineering. April 1944, P. 61-66.

Aids in solving industry's problems with World War II physically handicapped.

(28) National Association of Manufacturers, "Rehabilitation and Training for Postwar Employment." Dec. 1943, New York, 38 pp.

Panel discussion at second War Congress of American industry.

(29) National Association of Manufactures. "Reconversion and Re-Employment Problems of American Corporations." New York, December 1943, 48 pp.

Industry discusses production and human post-war problems.

(30) NORRIS, R. "Kansas City employs the handicapped." Occupations, 1944, 23: 80-85.

Study of 534 Kansas City firms which employ handicapped, with description of types of jobs which they fill.

(31) SKILTON, ROBERT H., ED. "Our Servicemen and Economic Security." Amer. Academy of Political and Social Science, 1943 (Annals of the American Academy of Pol. and Soc. Sci.) Vol. 227.

"Readjustment upon termination of service" is section devoted to articles on re-employment and government aid. Also contains article on "Re-education of the returning serviceman" by Morse A. Cartwright of Columbia University.

(32) SWEETLAND, C. "The adjustment of handicapped persons to employment in wartime. Smith Coll. Stud. Soc. Work, 1944, 15: 66-82.

A follow-up study of 73 persons who received training and later were employed. One year after employment 75% made good adjustment—others were improving their adjustment with work experience.

(33) TRUNDLE, GEORGE T. JR. "Returning to the old Job." Occupations, Oct. 1944, 23: 16-17.

Uses illustrative cases to indicate fallacy of expecting many ex-servicemen to fit into their old job. Urges need for Army records and what individual can do *now*, rather than use of person indiscriminately on his old job.

(34) U. S. Civil Service Commission, Wash., D. C. "Operations Manual for Placement of the Physically Handicapped." July 1943, 276 pp.

A coded guide which takes into consideration the functional and physical demands of jobs as regards specific parts of the body. Also considers environmental job factors.

(35) U. S. Civil Service Commission, Wash. D. C. Press Reports on Clinics for the Physically Handicapped." 1945, 19 pp.

News stories on subject of placement clinics held for physically handicapped in Tennessee, South Carolina, Georgia, Florida and Alabama.

(36) U. S. Civil Service Commission, Wash. D. C. "Untapped Manpower" 1943.

Gives facts on employment of handicapped, such as type of work, abilities, opportunities, trends, training and preparation required.

(37) War Manpower Commission "Industry Reintegrates Veterans." Manpower Review, March 1945, 12: 17-18.

Discusses problems of placing the handicapped in suitable jobs and finding better jobs for for former employees whose skills and experience warrant such advancement. Notes attention being given to this problem by R. C. A., Caterpillar Tractor Co., International Harvester Co., Curtiss-Wright Corp.

(38) WARD, M. F. "One million men have come back!" "Occupations," 1943, 22: 109-113.

Rehabilitation and re-employment procedures of handicapped veterans described. Several typical case histories are given and these augur well for the employment fate of war-injured veterans yet to return.

Special Veteran Plans and Services

(39) AHERNE, PHILIP P. JR. "Veterans Plan in Wichita." Manpower Review, Dec. 1944, 11: 5.

Brief outline of plan for veterans which emphasizes coordination of civic and community organizations.

(40) ALLEN, RICHARD, D. "Community Responsibility for Guidance—Education Plans." Adult Education Journal, July 1943, 2: 139-144.

Describes work of Providence Institute for Counseling and Personnel Service, which has served many agencies in counseling, information and advice regarding educational and occupational opportunities.

(41) BURCH, G. "Counseling the Veteran." Adult Education Journal, 1944, 3: 137-141.

Discussion of plans for community adjustment services. Describes projects in several New York and New Jersey communities.

(42) CORCORAN, THOMAS J. "Syracuse Plan for Training Veterans." Manpower Review, Dec. 1944, 11: 6-7.

The Plan defines the new roles of U.S.E.S.; Central Guidance; High School training for veterans; special college training at Syracuse Univ. In addition to special educational offerings outlined, the plan recommends arrangements for credit for work done in service and acceleration of veteran training.

(43) GRAY, CARL. "The Gray Plan for Post War Employment " Occupations, Oct. 1943, 22: 3-9.

Presents plan for adjustment of servicemen to civilian life. Proposes machinery which resembles selective service methods in reverse. Urges careful guidance; use of psychological techniques; vestibule schools; and fuller coordination among many agencies interested in the same problem.

(44) HANDVILLE, R. D., AND FLEMING, R. D. "A County aids Returning Veterans." Occupations, Oct. 1944, 23: 8-10.

Analyzes results of survey of vocational and educational desires of servicemen; describes the functions of school advisors as points of contact and counsel for the veteran.

(45) MEYER, AGNES E. "Community Service—The Model Center at Bridgeport, Conn." The Washington Post, 1945, pp. 12.

A series of articles depicting community resource utilization and coordination in providing a single center for various veteran, civilian and youth adjustment problems resulting from war, injury and employment displacement.

(46) Novis, Frederick W., and Panciera, Ernest. "The Conn. Rehabilitation Center." Conn. State Journal, April 1945, P 7, 31.

The Conn. Division of Rehabilitation launches an experimental training program to accomplish a careful medical and psychological study of war and civilian handicapped. Facilities at the Center provide for work sampling, occupational exploration as well as physical and mental capacities study.

A Distinction Is Made Between "Technical Supervision" in Which the Supervisor Knows How to Do the Job Himself, and Can Direct Methods and "Administrative Supervision" in Which the Supervisor Does Not Have Such Job Knowledge, But Knows Only the Results to Be Attained.

Memorandum *to* Supervisors

By John W. Dunham
Office of Supervising Architect
Public Buildings Administration
Washington 25, D. C.

IT is assumed that you are anxious to do your work well, and that you feel you know your job. It is further assumed that you like to be told the results required and trusted to select, originate, develop, or improve the methods of doing it, taking personal pride in its accomplishment. Aren't these the assumptions that you would like your superiors to make concerning you?

Your subordinates, if they have been properly selected, want you to make the same assumptions about them. This fact is the key to what follows.

Two Classes of Supervision

OBSERVANCE of a few fundamental principles of supervision is necessary to the efficiency of any organization. None of us is perfect and occasional lapses are inevitable, but continued neglect of these principles will ruin the morale of your group, spoil its efficiency and eventually result in your replacement.

I think you will recognize cases in your own experience, particularly as a subordinate, where trouble has been caused by neglect of these principles. I am sure that some of my own subordinates will recognize such cases.

Before discussing principles, let us distinguish two general classes of supervision.

The first class is that in which the supervisor knows not only the results required but methods of doing the work to achieve those results. He can do the work himself if necessary. An example is the supervision of a plumbing installation by a foreman plumber. Let's call this technical supervision.

In the second class the methods used in doing the work require special training which the supervisor has not had. The supervisor knows only the results required. Examples are the supervision of a stenographer's work by an engineer, or the supervision of the work of a locksmith by a building superintendent trained in electrical engineering. Let's call this administrative supervision.

Job Knowledge

A SUPERVISOR should have a clear understanding of the result to be accomplished before attempting to put a subordinate to work. If, for instance, a desk with a broken leg is received in your carpenter shop to be repaired, you must not expect the carpenter to whom you assign the work to guess whether or not that includes refinishing a scarred top as well as replacing the broken leg. If you are in doubt about the extent of the repairs required, it is up to you to find out before assigning the work. You cannot supervise work properly until you know definitely what is to be done.

Orders

THE supervisor's orders to his subordinates should be plain, accurate, and complete. Few things are more irritating to an intelligent subordinate than vague instructions. You cannot expect your subordinates to read your mind.

Remember that you have no moral right to criticize a performance which is a reasonable interpretation of your instructions. Finding fault with a performance that is reasonably in accordance with your orders can break down morale and destroy cooperation.

Orders may be of two general sorts. You can either order a subordinate to produce a certain result or you can order him to do his work in a certain manner. You should not do both.

Say Method to Be Used

IN TECHNICAL supervision you have a choice of the sort of orders you will use. In some cases, for instance in training a new man, your orders will necessarily prescribe the method to be used.

In administrative supervision it is usually necessary to limit orders to the results required.

Specify Results Required

WHERE it is possible with either class of supervision it is better to use orders of the second sort. It is almost always practicable with well-trained subordinates. Instructions specifying results only, encourage initiative on the part of the subordinates. Moreover, it is usually easier for you to describe a result clearly than to be specific regarding methods.

Suppose for instance, it is desired to fix the cause of a fire that has occurred in a certain office in a building of which you are the superintendent. If you elect to make your order of the first sort you might call a competent guard and tell him what people to see and what questions to ask. In this case you must accept responsibility for the result. If the guard does what you have told him to do and comes back without knowing the cause of the fire, it is your fault not his.

If you elect to make your order of the second sort, you might call the same guard and tell him to investigate, determine the cause of the fire, and report. This is a challenge to the man's ingenuity. It infers that he knows his position and that you have confidence in him. He has an incentive to do a good job. In this case he will fix the cause of the fire if it is at all possible for him to do so.

If in any case you elect to confine your orders to results and expect to hold your subordinates responsible for these results, you must leave the methods to the subordinates. You may make suggestions regarding method but you must not insist on their adoption.

Decisions

Decisions should be prompt and definite.
You will have to decide from time to time between ideas advanced by two subordinates or whether to modify or amplify a previous order. When such cases arise, take a reasonable time to consider matters soundly, talk things over with your subordinates, your superiors, or anyone competent to advise, then make up your mind and give a definite decision. Never leave any of your subordinates in doubt about what you have decided.

It is your responsibility to settle such matters. Reluctance to decide against one subordinate in favor of another must not stand in the way. Be courteous and as tactful as possible but be definite. Any other course not only wastes the time of all concerned but lowers your subordinates' opinions of you.

Interference

Orders to subordinates from persons of higher rank not in the subordinates' direct line of supervision should never be tolerated. Let's make this clear. Suppose the line of supervision is building superintendent, foreman of the cleaning force, charwoman. The captain of the guard is not in this line although the position is superior to that of charwoman.

If you are a foreman it is up to you to protect your subordinates from the confusion and annoyance of orders from anyone but yourself and the building superintendent. Preferably the orders should be issued only by you.

In the above situation, if the captain of the guard wishes his locker room cleaned more thoroughly, he should be required to go to the building superintendent and not to either the foreman or the charwoman. As foreman it is your responsibility to see that he does. Otherwise, either you will have lost proper control of your subordinates or they will be deviled by conflicting orders. If because of such circumstances your charwomen do not get their work done, you are the one who must answer, not the captain of the guard or whoever interfered.

Criticism

CRITICISM should always be of a performance, never of a person. It should be well considered, as specific as an order, and constructive.

Before criticizing any performance you should first be sure that you are not wholly or partly to blame. If you are partly to blame and the criticism is still necessary, you should acknowledge your part of the blame before proceeding with the criticism. Often you will find that incomplete orders or a vague decision have been largely to blame for an unsatisfactory performance.

The only excuse for criticism is the avoidance of a repetition of the same mistake. It should not be used for relief of your feelings. The criticism should indicate not only what was wrong but how the operation should have been done or what its results should have been.

Criticism should be restrained for mistakes occurring on a subordinate's first assignment and correspondingly severe for repetitions of the same mistake. Incidentally, criticism will be doubly effective if it is balanced by commendation for every performance that is better than usual.

Intelligent and desirable subordinates will not resent just and helpful criticism. Any intelligent subordinate will resent an unjust or poorly expressed criticism.

Suggestions

SUPERVISORS should encourage and consider seriously all suggestions from their subordinates.

You should realize that no matter how good you are or how good you think you are, which is something else, your subordinates will have some ideas that are better than yours. It will pay you to be big enough to realize it. You will find that sizable dividends in loyalty and efficiency result from use of good suggestions and from giving proper credit to their authors. Each of us needs to feel that he contributes something to his job.

You should answer every suggestion. This is the hard part of the job. Many suggestions will be worthless but they must be received in a manner that will not discourage further suggestions and cut off the few good ones that are bound to come.

If you disagree with a suggestion, thank the subordinate for submitting it and explain your reasons for not using it. When you agree with a suggestion put it to use and be sure that the subordinate receives credit for the idea.

Never leave a subordinate in doubt as to whether his idea will be used. Never fail to give credit for an acceptable idea.

Assignments

ASSIGNMENTS should be commensurate with the abilities of the subordinate. It is your business to know the quantity and quality of work that it is reasonable to expect from a subordinate in each of the grades that you supervise. It is also your business to know what can be expected of each of your subordinates.

It is well to give subordinates an occasional opportunity to do more or higher grade work than their positions require. It should be done in a manner to whet their appetites. In each case the subordinate should be made conscious of the fact that he is doing more or a higher grade of work than is ordinarily required of a person in his grade.

The above idea must not be confused with continual overloading. Such a course will surely lead to resentment and loss of efficiency on the part of subordinates.

Advancement

SUPERVISORS should not only seek to develop their subordinates' abilities: they should also do their part in helping the subordinates to secure the advancement which that development deserves. This is a duty that you owe to your subordinates. In common with most of the other duties you owe them, its proper performance is to your own advantage. Subordinates will work well only for supervisors who treat them fairly. They will not remain loyal long nor work efficiently for supervisors who do not care for their interests properly.

Conclusion

MOST supervisors will recognize the validity of the foregoing principles. However, you may feel that conditions peculiar to your *own* job preclude their application. . . . Think it over.

It Would Seem that a University, Particularly
One Supported by a State, Should Gear Its Ac-
tivities in with Those of the Community in
Which It Is Set. Few Do, But Here is an Ambi-
tious Program along These Lines. (For Further
Information Apply to Author.)

Personnel Research
at Ohio State

By Personnel Research Board
Ohio State University
Columbus 10, Ohio

THE Ohio State University recently established a new University-wide program
of research, service, and instruction in the field of personnel relations in business, industry, government, and education.

The program also includes technical services to education, industry, business,
and government. This is accomplished, for example, through institutes, workshops,
internships, and consultation with specialists. The results of both the research and
services are incorporated into the appropriate regular college curricula to aid the
University in the development of its courses.

Research Plans

THE Program of Personal Relations has as its foundation a continuous program of
research. Problems which call for immediate as well as long range research are
investigated. Both phases of research are useful to the University in its instructional
program and in its services to business, education, government, and industry.

The following is a summary of present research plans for the University. Some
of the projects are already under way. Others will be started later when funds are
available.

Personnel Practices for Small Business

FREQUENTLY the statement is made that small business is handicapped because a
personnel department cannot be supported. Studies should be made in cooperation with small business to determine which personnel practices are necessary and
feasible and how they may be applied. By cooperative arrangement with the University, small business would obtain information and services that might otherwise
not be available.

Worker Attitudes

WHILE some progress has been made in the methods of measuring the attitudes of workers, a good deal of research still remains to be undertaken. Both management and labor are interested in such studies and their cooperation with the University could lead to the development of research which would have wide usefulness.

Scope of Personnel Administration

THERE is need to develop standards in terms of costs, results, component parts, and optimum size of various personnel organizations. The University proposes to carry out such research in cooperation with a number of establishments of different sizes and types. Included in this research will be an attempt to develop quantitative standards for measuring the effectiveness of the performance of personnel departments. Such criteria are necessary in order to determine the feasible scope and limits of personnel administration.

Organization and Executive Leadership

THERE is a wide variety of organizational patterns and a variation in the manner in which executives carry out their work. It is proposed to study selected organization structures with the view to determining which types of executive methods are best suited to various types of organizational patterns.

Absenteeism

ABSENTEEISM is a problem which requires careful study regarding the causes and the feasible methods of reduction. The University plans to work with several plants and several unions in carrying out such a research project.

Study of Executive and Supervisory Talents

QUESTIONS are often raised regarding executive and supervisory talent. For example, how can it be measured, and how early in life can it be discovered? The University proposes to work cooperatively with business, industry, government, and education in studying such aspects as the groupings of various types of executive and supervisory positions, and the development of measures of the traits and other qualifications required for such positions.

Job Potentialities in Ohio

STUDENTS and job seekers could plan their courses of study and select job careers much more effectively if they knew the relative opportunities in various fields. The University proposes to work with governmental agencies, employers, and unions in developing and making available such information.

Job Analysis for Distributive Industries

THE University plans to cooperate with a number of establishments in the distributive industries in studying job analysis methods and in preparing a guide for job analysis and job specifications which are suitable for the retail trade, the wholesale trade, and other phases of the distributive field.

Practical Problems of Wages

PROBLEMS in connection with wages in industry, government, and education are now and will likely remain numerous and important. The University will undertake to make certain studies from which it is believed practical benefit can result. There is the problem of the yearly annual wage. How feasible is it? If feasible, how can it be put into effect? There is also the problem of incentives and their relationship to wage problems. The University plans to pursue immediately one or two phases of this problem in cooperation with industry, business, government, education, and organized labor.

Sales Engineering

ONE of the important occupations in the engineering field has been that of sales engineering. The University will undertake studies regarding the definition and scope of sales engineering, the personal requirements for success in this occupation, and how the University curriculum should be best arranged for preparing students for sales engineering jobs. It is planned to contact a number of employers of sales engineers and to work with them cooperatively in discovering important factors which both the University and employers need to know about this occupation.

Studies of Graduate and Undergraduate Engineers

THE University, employers, students, and graduates are interested in criteria for the selection of candidates for admission to study engineering. Research on the University campus as well as in establishments employing engineers is now being undertaken.

A study is also being undertaken to discover what graduate engineers do for a living, one, five, ten, twenty years after graduation from college. The evaluation of aims, content, and emphasis in engineering education will be studied in relationship to the results of this investigation.

Re-engineering Jobs for the Handicapped

IT is important that jobs be studied in an effort to employ fully, handicapped workers. The University in cooperation with a number of different establishments plans to determine the possibility of redesigning working arrangements (work place, standard tools, machine tools, etc.) in order to enable physically handicapped employees to function effectively.

Study of Tool Engineers

THE University has begun a nation-wide study of tool engineers in cooperation with the American Society of Tool Engineers. The duties of and qualifications for jobs now being held by tool engineers are being studied together with the probable resulting effects of these findings on the courses of study offered in technical schools, colleges, and universities.

Evaluation of Interviewing and Counseling

A STUDY is already in progress evaluating some of the basic techniques in personnel work, particularly those of interviewing, group counseling, and discussion groups in education and also in industry. The effect of providing recreational facilities for students, using student committees, living in cooperative houses, and other methods are being studied and appraised.

Supply and Demand of Personnel Workers

ALTHOUGH personnel workers are widely employed in business, industry, education, and government little is known regarding the current and future demand for such workers, especially in relation to the numbers being trained. This is a desirable field of research to which the University is already giving attention.

Jobs in Radio and Television

AN ANALYSIS will be made of jobs in the radio broadcasting industry and aptitude measures and other predictors of success will be developed. The study will be extended to include jobs which are developing in television and frequency modulation.

PERSONNEL
Journal

The Magazine of

LABOR RELATIONS AND PERSONNEL PRACTICES

Published by PERSONNEL RESEARCH FEDERATION

Lincoln Building, 60 East 42nd Street, New York City

Volume 24   *Number 6*

Contents for December 1945

Analyses of Labor Relations

THE recurrent waves of strikes to which American industry has been subject during the past ten years, and which show no signs of diminishing, either in intensity or frequency in the foreseeable future, leads us to wonder whether there are not more deep seated causes for them than we ordinarily think about. We present three analyses in this issue.

The first suggests the possibility that American industry has oversold the private enterprise system, or has sold it in such a way that it appears to have made promises to the workers which it has been unable to fulfill, and has raised exaggerated expectations in their minds which cannot be met.

The second analysis, which is of English socialism, purports to show how the apparent inability of capitalists there to meet the grave national and international economic problems led to their government being voted out of office.

This analysis also shows the great difficulties that a socialist government faces in introducing and developing its nationalization program; the fact that workers can expect no immediate improvement in their living standards under it: the fact that socialism is an adventurous experiment, by no means guaranteed of success; and is a grave warning to those who might think that socialism is an easy road to prosperity and internal peace.

Both these papers are based upon interpretations and applications of the ideas of Harold J. Laski, probably the world's leading socialist. While of course we do not endorse his views, we do think his criticisms, both constructive and destructive, are well worth study.

The third paper, which is excerpts from a talk by Hon. P. J. Clarey, President, Australian Council of Trade Unions, outlines Australian government policy, which has been to discourage wage raise demands, but to improve living conditions of workers through the provision of a wealth of social services, provided by the government out of general revenues.

Charles S. Slocombe,
Editor.

I. American Strike Scene

IN VIEW of our American situation we think it may be profitable to look into the analysis of capitalist democracy made by Harold J. Laski, perhaps the leading socialist in the world today.

He analyzes the situation this way. The owners of the means of production in the capitalist democracies—that is until recently, in America, England and France—have for many years told the working population that as production expanded and became more profitable the living conditions of the workers would improve. While they have not explicitly said so, they have implied that when production is not expanding, or is diminishing then a halt must be called to the improvement of living standards, or they may have to be reduced. (This has been soft-pedalled.)

Production Expansion

THE owners, particularly in America, have pretty consistently said that they were capable of expanding profitable production almost indefinitely and far into the foreseeable future. Thus the working population could be assured that, barring circumstances beyond the owners' control, such as international upsets, their standard of living would continue to improve indefinitely.

Thus over the years the working population has developed an expectation of improvement in their living standards, almost annually.

And they almost seem to have lost sight of the fact that the advances are to be proportionate to the expansion of profitable production. They want a continual advance anyway.

Thus the owners of the means of production have oversold their idea to the workers and there is a consequent disastrous kickback in the form of strikes, when improvements in living standards are not forthcoming, or when, as now, there is a tendency for the owners to ask labor to accept a reduction in living standards, as compared with the immediate past.

Too Slow Improvement of Living Standards

THERE has furthermore developed in the minds of workers a dissatisfaction with the rate of advance of their living standards, and a demand that this rate be accelerated. This again is in part due to the overselling by the owners, who have boasted overmuch about their ability to expand profitable production, and share the benefits with labor.

At present we have an anomalous situation, in terms of this analysis, in which industry has just proven in their war production achievements what they can do in rapidly expanding profitable production; labor has, according to its own view, accepted a freezing of its living standards by accepting the Little Steel formula for some time, but is now asked to accept a reduction of those standards, instead of an advance such as might be expected, considering that America is the richest country in the world.

There does appear to be soundness in the implication that labor has jumped the gun in making its wage demands before reconversion has proceeded very far. It is to be noted that some industrialists hold to the usual owner's formula, that if labor will be patient their demands for improved standards of living will be met.

Continued Use of Formula

BUT we are not so much concerned over the immediate situation, serious as it may be, but over the continued use by owners of the formula of promising, indefinitely, advances in the standard of living of workers, the continued acceptance of that formula by workers, with expectations that are increasing at a rate far beyond what the owners can meet.

It seems to us that this formula must be dropped or modified, or a new one found. We are so used to this one that it is very hard to think of another. Perhaps no change in the formula might be necessary if a way could be found to put into the hands of the millions of people in the lowest income brackets sufficient funds to purchase the products of an ever-expanding industry. But no one has worked out a formula for that yet.

Another Formula

IN ENGLAND the workers have developed or accepted a different formula—to the effect that if they themselves take over, through nationalization, the means of production they can advance their living standards to the required degree. In some ways this looks like an attempt to achieve by a third formula the objectives of both formulas mentioned above.

But this, even in the eyes of Laski, is a dubious experiment, not at all certain of successful application, and certainly not at present acceptable to any substantial proportion of American people.

The Australians over the past forty years, largely under Labor governments, have used another formula, which is described elsewhere in this issue. Instead of placing emphasis on increasing wages as a means of improving living conditions, they believe in improving living conditions by providing more and more social services for the people out of state revenues.

Thus by the provision of old age pensions, invalid pensions, maternity allowances, child endowment, widows' pensions, funeral benefits, sickness benefits, etc. by the government they do two things. They make available to workers funds, which in most countries are used to take care of the hazards of life, for the purchase of the products of primary and secondary producers. Secondly, they relieve industry and agriculture of the constant pressure of wage demands.

As long ago as 1904 Australia passed a Conciliation and Arbitration Act. This makes arbitration compulsory, provides for the regulation of wages, and the regulation of labor unions. It set up a Court of Conciliation and Arbitration for this purpose.

Child Endowment but No Wage Increase

THE policy of this Court may be understood from a case which came up in 1940, when the labor unions asked for an increase in the basic wage. The Judge of the Court stated that "the basic wage at the very best could support only a wife, a husband and one child. He stressed that unless some form of Child Endowment was introduced by the government he would feel impelled to increase the basic wage." Child endowment was provided for, but no increase in basic wage was approved.

American owners and unions are definitely against the use of this formula, but it seems to have merit as a possibility.

There is another possibility for America, and that is to retain the present formula of improving living standards of workers as profitable production expands, but placing less emphasis on promises of expansion, and more emphasis on the fact that advances in living standards must be proportionate to rate of expansion

Form Application of Formula

HIS would need a firmness on the part of owners. In the face of public opinion, and the exaggerated expectations of workers which owners in the past, and unions in the present, have encouraged, this would be exceedingly difficult to adhere to, as a policy.

It would undoubtedly lead to many long and bitter strikes, possibly accompanied by bloodshed. It would lead to intense political battles. These consequences must be avoided if possible, first because of the distress and hardship to which the general population would be subject, and second because there is no guarantee that the owners would come out on top in such conflicts.

Whether the firmness can be adopted in the collective bargaining room, and confined there, is at the present time doubtful. This is where it belongs, and where it can be most effectively used as an educative means to get workers and owners to realize more fully the relation of living standards improvement to production expansion.

Many owners have succeeded in using the formula this way, and over the years have stabilized their labor relations, and brought wage and working conditions demands within reasonable bounds. This has been possible even with such radicals as Harry Bridges, and should be possible with almost all the labor leaders, with the possible exception of John L. Lewis.

Summing up our conclusions, in terms of this analysis, it seems that the owners of American industry in general have oversold their formula that production is going to continue to expand indefinitely, and that consequently workers are going to get ever-increasing advances in their living standards; that they have promised more than they could deliver; and that they have raised undue hopes and expectations in the minds of workers.

Hence they are hoist with their own petard, and labor strife is the inevitable consequence. To get themselves out of this most awkward situation is going to be no easy matter, but it must be done somehow, lest the situation grow immeasurably worse.

The Last Capitalist Democracy

ONE final word: in the last six months two major capitalist democracies have gone socialist—England and France—in their first post-war elections. At least in England this was completely unexpected, and showed how quickly public opinion can change. America now remains as the only large capitalist democracy in the world. It has not yet had a post-war election. Depression or anticipated depression threw both England and France into the socialist camp.

It is not entirely beyond the bounds of possibility that if serious depression comes to America or is threatened, before capitalism mends its fences, there will be a runaway movement toward socialism and nationalism here. We certainly do not want that to happen.

II. English Socialism

THE growth of English labor unions has finally led to the election of a socialist government there—under a Labor party largely backed and financed by labor unions. Will the growth of American labor unions, and their inevitable stronger influence on political parties here lead us toward socialism?

This prospect looks a long way off, because neither the AFL nor the CIO show any truly socialistic leanings. Lewis shows no sign of desiring nationalization of the coal mines. The only unions talking seriously of nationalization are some of the railroad brotherhoods, and it has always been a question as to whether they are serious, or whether they hold this over the heads of the railroads as a threat in collective bargaining.

Rapid Change in Viewpoint

HOWEVER, it must be remembered that English labor unions right up till the beginning of the war showed few socialistic leanings—at least among their leaders—and were as conservative in the matter as our AFL. So that the change to socialism in England was unexpectedly rapid, and in fact happened more quickly than the socialists there·anticipated, and they were consequently caught unprepared to take over the government, when it was handed to them on a silver platter.

To try to understand the English socialism that has come, to appraise its chances of success, and the possibilities for this country, we have thought it advisable to study the textbooks written on the subject of Government by Professor Harold J. Laski over the past fifteen years.

Laski happened to be the Chairman of the Executive Committee of the Labor Party in England at the time that the socialists were elected to office. But that does not mean that he was the most influential man in winning the election, or that his ideas in running the socialistic government are the ones that will prevail.

However his ideas give us a good basis on which to evaluate what is happening there, and what may happen here.

The Government's Function

HIS first and most startling statement is that the common assumption, which is more than three hundred years old, that the function or job of the state is to look after the best interests of all its citizens, is absolutely wrong.. Or rather perhaps that no state has ever operated that way.

He says that the state fundamentally operates *only* in the interests of the owners· of the means of production. In the western capitalistic democracies such as America and England, that means that the government, whether Democrats or Republicans or Conservatives or Liberals, operates in the interests of the capitalists, and of the capitalists only.

This does not mean that there is an absence of pressure from the working class for a better life and more privileges, but that the government never grants these except when the capitalists give their approval. This they never do except at such times as when they are very prosperous and can afford to throw a few crumbs from their fat table to the underdogs below.

This does not mean either that the lot of the worker and his family has not, by and large, vastly improved particularly in the last one hundred fifty years—this made possible by the vastly improved production methods of the period, the consequent general prosperity of the capitalists, which has caused them in expansive moods to throw sizable crumbs under the table.

A Place at the Table

THIS however only serves to take the edge off their hunger, and postpone the day when the vast mass of the working population will demand, as their right, places at the table. That day comes when, as in England right now, capitalists are not prosperous, and can afford no concessions to the working class, and as during the last English election could make no satisfactory promises as to when they would be able to do so again.

Laski, in short, says that the only way the working man can really raise his standard of living, commensurate with the inherent possibilities of modern production techniques, is to obtain for himself the ownership of the means of production—that is to nationalize everything. A gradual program of this sort is under way in England now.

Bloodless Revolution

THIS amounts to revolution, and Laski holds that capitalists being what they are, there is no way for the masses of the people getting ownership of the means of production except by revolution. The English coming into power of the socialists with a program of nationalization has been accomplished by constitutional means, and is called revolution by consent. So far it has been bloodless—but there is no guarantee that it will stay that way when the nationalization really starts.

This is Laski's basic thesis. He holds however that revolutions, bloodless or not, are not guaranteed to succeed, and that they are adventurous experiments, not lightly to be undertaken. We interpret his writings as indicating that the difficulties of a bloodless revolution, such as has now taken place in England are greater than those of a bloody revolution, but that the ghastly aftermath of failure of a bloody revolution is such that it is better to try constitutional revolution.

He discusses the Russian revolution, pointing out the special circumstances that made its success—so far as it can be judged successful—as due to a special set of circumstances and the guidance of it by men of exceptional character, notably Lenin and Stalin. He sees no evidence of significant communistic leanings on the part of any substantial portion of the people of America or England.

Social Service State

L ASKI says that England under capitalistic governments has been for many years a social-service state. This means that there has been a recognition that the state must provide for the people such things as housing, workman's compensation, unemployment insurance, education and the like. England, among western democracies has no monopoly on this idea, but has probably talked more about it.

These services however can only be provided to the extent that the capitalistic government thinks they can be afforded. They have all, in their introduction, been opposed by capitalists, and their extention repeatedly postponed on the ground that they could not be afforded, at the time.

So, while at the time that an appetite for social services to the underprivileged has been whetted, at the same time a process of stalling has gone on, until finally the masses came recently to come out openly and say, by the election of a socialist government, that they did not believe that the capitalists had really any sincere intention of granting the people proper social services and wages. The arrival at this position was of course aided by the hardships of the war, and is part of the general pattern that revolutions in general follow wars

Diversion of Profits

T HIS problem of lack of provision of adequate social services is one of the basic reasons for the socialistic government. Laski said that only by the people taking over for themselves the ownership of the means of production could proper social services and living standards be provided. The diversion of the profits of private industry to investment in luxury trades, to ostentatious wasteful high living by the rich, the use of monies in unprofitable ways, all tended to draw off money that should be used for extending the education system for the masses, for giving them reasonable hospital and health facilities, for aid in times of sickness and old age, as well as raising their wages to a point where their living standards would be reasonable, and their demands for the products of industry sufficient to keep all employed.

The second basic reason is said to be that the ownership of the means of production by capitalists leads to gross inefficiency. The coal industry in England is of course the most glaring instance of this. Commissions of inquiry, most of whose members have been capitalists, have been saying this for over twenty years.

But it is not limited to coal. The same thing is said to be true of power and light, steel, cotton and other industries, as well as agriculture. This has been due to lack of coordination in use of facilities, overlapping, lack of capital for rationalization and modernization, lack of managerial ability. The diversion of capital to industries that are not essential to the national welfare, and the export of capital to other countries for the development of manufacturing facilities in them, which has been highly profitable because of the use of low paid native labor—but which has competed with English manufactures on world markets, and thus militated against the development of English industries—are also indictments of the English capital system.

The only way seen to stop this has been the idea that when the people own the capital in a socialism they will see to it that it is properly used for the benefit of the people.

Previous Dominant Position

Laski points out that when England held the dominant position she did in the years leading up to the first world war she could afford the meagre social services that were doled out, and she could afford the inefficiencies and mistakes of capitalists. But when she came out of that war with the situation entirely changed as regards her position in world markets these matters should have been changed.

During the interim between the two wars there was almost a complete halt in the extension of social services, and the capitalists showed no evidence that they were aware of the necessity for a change in their general policies. Hence the people lost faith in them.

The socialist government therefore takes over at a most difficult time, because it has to remedy the mistakes of the past twenty years, as well as deal with a world situation that is infinitely more difficult.

Basis of Economy

The basis of the English economy has been the fact that she could import raw materials, put them through her manufacturing processes and sell them on the world markets at a profit. This profit was in large part used to purchase food of which she has always been a large importer as well as to purchase more raw materials for processing. Investments abroad, shipping, and other world services have also helped to pay for the imports.

With other countries improving their manufacturing processes and setting up new ones—largely with the use of English capital—it has been increasingly difficult for England to maintain her world markets. The capitalists have not seen this as necessitating improving their policies and practices to maintain their position of leadership as efficient manufacturers—as equal or better than manufacturers in other countries—but have used it as an excuse for curtailing or blocking all extension of social services, and keeping wage rates as low as possible.

In other words, though the theory of capitalism, and free enterprise as it is called in America, is that the profit motive will lead to capitalists rising up to meet their problems, and overcome their difficulties, English capitalism has on the whole simply not risen to the occasion, but has thrust the burden occasioned by the difficulties on to the backs of the poor.

Capital Needed

Now the socialist government has the job of modernizing the English industrial plant, introducing the necessary coordinations, directing investment into the proper channels and winning back England's position as a country largely concerned with manufacturing for export. This is no easy job.

Basically a fundamental problem is to get the capital to do this with. That is why she is trying to get a long term loan from the United States. She needs this to modernize her plant, and to purchase the raw materials she will process in her industries.

The socialist government is also committed to an extension of social services, though where it can get the money from to do this in addition to all other things to be done is hard to see. Yet they are absolutely necessary, both to retain the support of the mass of people, and to improve the morale and working efficiency of the population.

Problem of Support

Laski points out the difficulties of a revolution by consent such as has happened in England, in the matter of the uncertainty of its continued support long enough to carry out its program. Many people who voted it into office had and have very little notion of the specific way in which its program would effect them and alter their modes of life.

And most people, even the poorer classes and certainly the labor unions, are very set in their ways, and while wanting the supposed benefits of socialism, will withdraw their support if they are too much disturbed. The capitalists of course will resent anything the socialist government does that takes away their property, power and privilege.

As Laski says, "Anyone who considers its position will not be inclined, I suggest, to under-estimate the magnitude of the dilemma that will confront it. If it goes too slowly, it will suffer from all the difficulties which confront any government which tries, upon the basis of capitalist postulates, to effect their piecemeal transformation. It tends to irritate its opponents by undermining confidence; and it fails to attract its supporters by inability to offer them the exhilarating spectacle of conviction turned into deed. If it proceeds rapidly—and the case for rapid action is overwhelmingly strong—it is likely to meet with sabotage and resistance."

No Following Russian Pattern

It was a basic thesis of Lenin and Stalin in the Russian revolution that all counter-revolutionaries must be got rid of by death, emigration or sentences to hard labor. The capitalists of England are counter-revolutionaries, but cannot be liquidated in the same way. The non-cooperators in Russia or those who changed their minds after the revolution, and wanted to withdraw their support from it.

or who attempted slow-down or sabotage tactics were very promptly spotted by the communist party members and punished severely. This culminated in the 1937 purge. But England cannot deal with people this way, but must endeavor to retain their support and cooperation by other means.

Compulsions, not ordinarily found in a capitalist democracy, will be absolutely necessary. And it is the manner of administering these somewhat dictatorial compulsions, and educating the people into understanding their necessity that must be relied upon to win their acceptance. The first act passed by the socialist government was a definite recognition of this Laski dictum—that was the extension of wartime powers of control for the five year duration of the first socialist government.

Pay Fair Value

THE compulsory nationalization of any industry such as coal immediately highlights the problems. In Russia this would be accomplished by the simple expedient of the government taking over ownership without any recompense to the owners—converting them overnight from wealthy aristocrats to poverty ridden fugitives. But that cannot be done in England. Not only would there be an almighty howl from the owners, and all other capitalists, but it would so shock all but a minor proportion of the supporters of the socialist government that they would refuse to vote the necessary legislation.

So the Socialist government must, and has agreed that when it takes over an industry it will, pay the owners fair value for the properties taken over. This immediately reduces or buys off opposition to the socialist regime on the part of the counter-revolutionary capitalists.

But two consequences follow, which are distinct handicaps to the socialist program. In the first instance it brings into being or continues in existence a wealthy class who live on dividends and interest, who do nothing for a living, who must be supported in idleness by the government, who therefore become a millstone round the neck of the economy, and who are continuous opponents of everything the socialist government attempts to do.

Must Borrow Money

THE second, and perhaps more serious result of this policy, is the fact that in order to buy out these owners the government must borrow the money to do so, and pay interest on the money so borrowed. True, on the deal, the government gets more or less profitable properties, and has to pay only interest and not presumably higher profit. But the difference, or net gain is not large—certainly not large enough to provide sufficient improvements in the standard of living of workers, and compete in world markets.

The main purpose of the nationalization is more efficient production, through planning, coordination, introduction of mass production methods, better machinery, closing down of marginal outlets, etc. All these things take capital in large quantities. Socialism of course needs capital, just as capitalism does. But much of the capital which could be used for this modernization program will be swallowed up in paying for the properties—thus seriously limiting the amount of additional capital that can be raised for modernization; and further seriously delaying the improvement in the standard of living of the workers and the provision of social services.

This is a most serious situation, but one which is unavoidable at this time, (foreseen by Laski ten years ago) for socialism could not survive a week unless the thing is done this way. Yet it slows up the socialist program immeasurably, and may even wreck it completely.

Apply Compulsions to Labor

SO MUCH for an instance of mild compulsion as applied to the counter-revolutionary capitalists. Labor probably does not yet realize that much more harsh compulsions are going to be applied to it, even though it is the supporter of the revolution.

The coal industry must be made more efficient. This means the introduction of modern labor-saving machinery; the opening up of new well laid out high yield mines in parts of the country where they do not now exist, with a consequent shift in residence of miners and their families; the laying out anew of old mines which are unprofitable because of their poor layout determined by the private ownership of the land; it means the closing down of marginal and unprofitable mines, and the shift of the mining population from these areas, or their engagement in other occupations; and finally it means that the miners will have to vastly increase their individual daily outputs.

This means a new outlook on the part of the miners as to their part in the prosperity of the country, and a willingness to make sacrifices of habit, convenience and traditional points of view. It was all very well for miners not to overexert themselves for private employers, to live on the dole when work was short, and to refuse to move from the so-called distressed areas. But now they have to realize they have a part to play in helping their country.

Judging by their past actions and outlook, compulsions will be necessary to force them into line. They may be brought into line by appeals to their patriotism, propaganda and other means, and doubtless many of them will—but many won't.

Fifty Per Cent Coal Output Increase

THE Minister of Fuels in England is calling for a fifty percent increase in coal output during the next year. But many miners have left the coal fields and refuse to go back, and the output of those at work in the mines is said to be very low—possibly due to insufficient food.

The government has the power to order any worker to work where it wants him to, and at such work as it determines. As soon as it nationalizes the mines it will undoubtedly have to order the miners back into the mines, from wherever they are; to get the miner's union to urge its members to drop any limitation of output policy they may have; if necessary extend hours of work; and use appeals, competitions, commendations and other such morale builders as were used by the Russians when they were faced with the similar problem of increasing output without increasing cost.

How much compulsion the miners, and later other workers, will stand remains to be seen. How much they will have to be given in immediate higher wages or more social services remains to be seen. The more money that is invested in immediately improving their lot the less will be available for the long run improvement of their industry.

Must Make Same Promises

IN SHORT, it looks as if the socialist government has and must make the same promises to the workers as were made by the capitalists over the years—namely that when business picks up they will be better treated. But the workers finally came to disbelieve that the capitalists ever could get business to pick up sufficiently, or that if it did the capitalists would come across with improved conditions. Now the workers have put their faith in the socialists, thinking that they have the ability to make business pick up, and that they will then stick to their promises.

But the workers cannot now pass the buck for a failure of business improvement to anyone. Basically its prospects are in their hands—though of course not completely—and it is up to them to hitch up their pants and pull in their belts and do the job.

The nationalization program has not proceeded very far, but there is scant evidence that the essentials of the situation have been presented to the working population of England yet, with any degree of force. The mild mannered realistic practical, though academically stated, understanding of the situation by Laski is good from a socialistic point of view, but it does not carry the conviction to the people that is necessary to put the thing over.

At the annual meeting of the major labor unions in Blackpool this summer all the leaders of the socialist government who spoke talked as if they were breathing on egg shells. Ernest Bevin, now foreign secretary, and former boss of the Transport and General Workers union, who used to be a fire-eater of the Lewis type, recently made a speech in parliament, which was reported to be the strongest speech he had made in years—its subject, the poor starving Germans.

Why not strong speeches about the poor English who will be starving in a few years unless they wake up?

Why No Cracking Down

WHY has the government not cracked down on the striking longshoremen? It has the power to do so—if necessary to draft them into the army. Admittedly the docks are not on the nationalization program, but trouble there can have serious repercussions on the progress of the socialist program. The fact that these men are selfishly disloyal to their socialist government is an augury of things to come, whenever the convenience of any group of workers is disturbed or they have some grievance.

This of course is an illustration of Laski's realization of the difficulties of the socialist government—in that it cannot afford to alienate the support of those who voted for it.

Few Consumers' Goods

As to people generally it has another problem of compulsion: That is the continued rationing of all forms of consumer goods and of food. With its vast debts abroad, the so-called blocked sterling, its limited credits abroad, even if it gets $4,000,000,000 from America, the socialist government must use as great a proportion as possible of this to purchase raw materials, machine tools, essential foods, etc. It cannot afford to use it for gasoline for pleasure car driving, or for any type of luxury goods.

It must have its manufacturing industries manufacture goods suitable for export, and sell them abroad. This means that goods manufactured in England must not, any more than can be helped, be sold to the people of England. They must continue to do without automobiles, washing machines, electric irons, sewing machines, silk stockings, and other items which they have had to do without during the war.

The compulsory refusal to the people of consumers' goods after five years of doing without during the war is not going to be easy to put across. It is going to be a serious cause of dissatisfaction with the administration, as it has been and is in this country. Furthermore, according to reports, it is having a serious affect on the morale of workers who as in the cotton industry, want more wages, and refuse to go back into the cotton mills without them, yet when they do go back are not interested in working long hours or regularly, because they say there is nothing to spend their money on if they do earn much.

Modernization of Plant and Methods

THE revolution by consent socialist government of England in fact seems to be faced with much the same problems as faced the bloody communistic revolutionary government of Russia. Though Russia was not concerned with export markets while England is, yet in both countries the vital thing is the building up and modernization of the industrial plant, and the improvement of social services.

Material comforts, higher wages and luxury living are all matters which must be sacrificed until the primary objective is realized. Then and only then can consumers' goods become freely available. As far as Russia was concerned it was not until 1937, twenty years after the revolution started before there was any appreciable loosening up of the consumers' goods market. This of course was short lived, because at that time Russia realized the threat of Hitler, cut off consumer goods manufacture, and started building armaments.

England does not start from such a low point in her economic depression as Russia did, but the socialist government starts off from a point which we suspect is much lower than most English people are aware of. The gross neglect of sound measures to put the economy on a proper basis in the years between the wars, topped off by the consequences of the war recently over, will take some heroic measures to remedy.

What if Socialists Thrown Out

LASKI brings up the point as to what will happen if the socialist government is thrown out of office at the end of five years. It is pretty obvious that some part of the nationalization program will have been accomplished by that time. If the capitalists get back into power will they reverse the nationalism, and turn the industries back to capitalists, or will they leave those nationalized still in the hands of the government, but put a halt to further nationalization? He gives no conclusive answer, but we interpret his writings as indicating a suspicion that the matter will be resolved by the seizure of the government by those with fascist views.

It is said to be more profitable to consider the matter in terms of what the socialist government can do to ensure its reelection, so that it can go on with and consolidate its program. This carries over into the consideration of social services. In the absence on store shelves of consumers' goods on which increased wages can be spent, and the competitive condition of world markets, necessitating keeping wages down, the best way in which the lot of workers can be improved is through improved social services. (No matter if it does involve expenditures that might be used for direct economic purposes, the government has to give the people something.)

Housing, Education and Health

AGAIN looking at Russian experience we see that the social services upon which they immediately started investing money were housing, education and health measures. These are the three things needed in England.

Housing needs no discussion, because of the blitz situation, except to say that it is related to the movements of population determined by new factory locations, to the question of financing or subsidizing low cost housing, and an improvement of the construction industry. There is nothing definite in the reports we have seen on this, as to the government's policy.

Economics of Education

FOR years the education system of England has been unbelievably poor. While a few of the capitalist governments during the past forty years have shown some interest in the subject nothing much has been done. Some of the governments have frankly stated that they did not believe in the education of the worker—he was troublesome enough with what little he had. Others found that the costs would be too great, and the opposition of the church groups too strong.

Consequently, in England only a very small percentage of the children go to high school, and of course very much fewer to technical schools or colleges. Most children quit at the official leaving age of fourteen, and go to work to help support their families. The economics of this situation was of course one of the reasons for not raising the compulsory school leaving age to sixteen. For not only would there be the expense of buildings and equipment, and teachers' salaries, but an inevitable demand on the part of the working class for increased wages to make up for the loss of earnings of the children.

You cannot build a modern industrial nation with a population whose education has fitted most of them for only unskilled labor. You must have an abundance of people with education sufficient to develop them into highly skilled and semi-skilled workers. The comparative shortage of such people in England is one of the reasons for its backwardness in manufacturing. Not only at the work level is there a dearth of people with the training to make the best use of the machines, and to make suggestions as to improvements in processes, and an ambition to improve themselves, but at the supervisory level there is a lack of imagination and coordinative capacity.

Higher up at the executive level again there is small-mindedness, lack of organizing ability, lack of aggressiveness and a fear of branching out into new enterprises. Most English companies are small, and they have to be, because there is such a shortage of men capable of organizing and operating large scale mass production industries.

Poor Personnel

ENGLAND cannot regain her place in world markets with such personnel, any more than Russia could develop her industries with the people the Bolsheviks found when they took over. Russia immediately started to set up schools of all grades in large quantities to educate and train the technical, operating and administrative personnel needed. At the start the schooling was unbelievably poor and make-shift, with poor teachers, little equipment and textbooks. Much of the instruction was given by factory supervisors after work to workers after work, both being fatigued in the extreme. Gradually of course the thing improved.

Again England does not start from such a low point, but she has a very long way to go, even to catch up with American standards, which are admittedly, capable of much improvement. The socialist government there must start properly educating the English people, in the elements of reading, writing and arithmetic as well as history, science, and, for a large number of them, in the technical and mechanical arts. This would be at the high school level.

In the upper levels the need for technical institutes and engineering and business colleges is equally obvious.

Will English Workers Want Education?

IN AMERICA we are used to our people making great sacrifices to obtain education and training in day and night institutions, and have difficulty in providing all the facilities to supply the demand. In Russia, when the Bolsheviks came in, and started providing educational facilities they found a demand on the part of the people for self-improvement and training that was incredible. Perhaps it was stimulated by the communist party, and the promises of promotion and privileges that would be obtained by those above the level of common labor. But whatever its origin it equalled the urge of the American people for education and training.

Perhaps because they have been starved of opportunity, or have been too poor, or have not seen that they would get much improvement in their lot if they did secure education and training, or their ambitions have been dulled by being forced to labor at too young an age, there is little evidence in England of any comparable urge toward self-improvement.

Apart from the necessity of this for the survival of England as an industrial nation, here is an opportunity for the socialist party to do a real job of social service for the English working class. No one knows whether, if free education at all levels were provided, the English people would show the same interest in self-improvement as Americans and Russians, or whether they would continue to guzzle beer in pubs, etc.

If they do not take readily to it, then they will have to be sold the idea. We are not thinking, in this regard of raising the compulsory school leaving age, for the economics of the situation at present, probably do not make that possible, apart from the labor shortage. We are thinking rather of making a start, as Russia did, with afterwork schooling. There is of course much of this in America.

Improvement of Morale

THAT such an educational program would do much to improve the morale of the working population of England seems self-evident. This is particularly true if the modernization and rationalization of her industries gave increasing opportunities for employment and promotion to those who made use of the facilities.

It would also take the edge off the demand for higher wages now, at a time when England can ill afford to pay them, and when there is nothing much to spend them on anyway. In short the socialist government should try to develop workers who if they have holes in the seats of their pants, don't go and buy a new pair, but have them patched and go and buy books on algebra or mechanical drawing. (The capitalist governments of the past missed a good bet when they discouraged education and training of the working population.)

Since the above was written the following item appeared in the New York Times:

Britain Will Compel Attendance

LONDON, Oct. 30—A compulsory part-time college education is in store for 1,500,000 boys and girls between the ages of 15 and 18 as a result of the new British Education Act. The program is to be co-educational.

The students will attend college at least one whole day or two half days a week for forty-four weeks a year. One continuous period of eight weeks or two periods of four weeks may be substituted in certain cases.

This vast new educational undertaking will mean that 20,000 specially trained teachers will be required. The plan applies only to those young people who are not already in full-time education.

If our analysis is in any way correct two other consequences would follow from such a program. Those who improved their positions and their life prospects from the socialist government provided facilities for education and training, and their parents and families, would be everlastingly grateful to the socialist government In this way the government could be sure of retaining their support when it comes to the problem of reelection.

Indoctrination with Socialism

IN ADDITION to the positive aspect of this problem, there would, in view of the history of past governments and their methods, be an awareness on the part of workers of the hazard of these educational facilities being curtailed or abolished by a capitalist government in an economy mood.

Laski points out that one of the ways by which capitalistic democratic governments have managed to perpetuate themselves is through their control of the education system. There is nothing sinful about this—it is done in America, all the time.

Here then is a well tried and approved method by which the socialist government of England can help to continue itself in office for many years. With an expanded educational program of youth and adult education, including such subjects as history, elementary economics, etc. it has an excellent opportunity of inculcating the doctrines of socialism.

It would of course be unwise to use this as a means of deriding capitalistic democracy in the interest of politics. But it could be used as a means of ensuring support of the socialistic measures which it is trying to introduce.

The indoctrination of workers with the communist viewpoint was one of the objects of the Russian educational program, of course.

Government to Pay for Health Measures

THE high incidence of sickness, premature death, and low birth rate among the low paid English workers is known. It is not as bad as in some countries, but it is nothing to be proud of. The provision of proper medical attention, hospital facilities, maternal care, dental care, recreation facilities is a social service that is obviously needed, for the general welfare and happiness of the people, for increasing their efficiency as workers, for reducing their sense of insecurity, for improving their morale, and to aid in taking the edge off wage demands.

As with education its introduction would be a means of earning the gratitude of a large number of the working population, and aiding the defeat of any party whose past history might indicate that it would, in a mood of economy, abolish or curtail these services.

It is implicit in the socialist doctrine that both health and education services should, for the most part, be provided by the government without contribution on the part of the people, except through taxes.

Books Studied

The State in Theory and Practice. By Harold J. Laski. New York. The Viking Press. *1935.* Price $3.50.

Democracy in Crisis. By Harold J. Laski. Durham, N. C. The University of North Carolina Press. *1935.* Price $1.50.

Behind the Urals. By John Scott. Boston. Houghton Mifflin & Co. *1940.* Price $3.00.

III. Australian Social Service

By Hon. P. J. Clarey, M.L.C.
Canberra, Australia.

IT is from production alone that living standards can be increased. If a community is static in production, then normally the living standards would also remain static. The only improvement which might be made would be an exceedingly slight improvement made by taking some from those in the top stratum and distributing it amongst those on the lower stratum. In a steadily expanding economy with increasing production both in volume and per head, it is possible for substantial improvements to be made in the living conditions of the people. Increased production is the only way by which living standards can be increased.

Commonwealth Conciliation and Arbitration Act

IN 1904, the Commonwealth Conciliation and Arbitration Act was passed by the Federal Parliament. This Act was modelled closely upon the lines of an Arbitration Act which had been passed by the New Zealand Government. It was passed in pursuance of the powers of the Commonwealth Government to make laws in respect of conciliation and arbitration for the prevention and settlement of industrial disputes extending beyond the limits of any one State. One of its effects was to promote the growth of Trade Unionism in Australia. It enabled Unions to be registered under the Commonwealth Conciliation and Arbitration Act, and gave them many legal rights.

(An Australian 1/- used to be worth about 25¢. It is now worth 15¢. An Australian £ used to be worth $5. It is now worth $3.25 approx.)

The Commonwealth Arbitration Court adopted the 7/- a day as its basic or minimum wage. From 1907, Australian trade unionists took up the struggle to secure this standard.

This basic or minimum wage has been increased from time to time, but the most notable thing about Australian policy has been the improvement of living conditions through extended social services, rather than through great increases in wages.

Improved Living Conditions Through Social Service

IN THE field of social services, Australia has journeyed far. This field covers a very wide range, extending from old age and invalid pensions to pharmaceutical benefits and medical care. In the early part of the century some progress had been made principally in old-age pensions by some of the States. Gradually, however, the Commonwealth has extended its sphere of influence and its legislative enactments have taken over some forms of social services previously carried on by individual States, and has resulted in giving a nation-wide standard throughout the Commonwealth.

In this field it is much easier to measure the actual advantages secured by Australian citizens as a whole and to estimate the annual cost these social services entail to the Commonwealth.

Commonwealth Old Age Pensions Scheme

THE first venture in social services by the Commonwealth was made on 1st July, 1909, when the Commonwealth Old Age Pension Scheme came into operation. Prior to that date the States of Victoria and New South Wales had instituted old age pensions as State measures. The Queensland Government had passed an Old Age Pensions Act, but before it came into operation the Commonwealth scheme superseded it. The original payment was 10/- per week. Throughout the years many changes have been made in the rate, and according to the financial position of the Commonwealth and the views held by varying Governments concerning the conditions under which pensions should be paid, varying qualifications for pensions were laid down.

At the present time the full pension payable to an old age pensioner is 27/- per week. During the year 1943 no less than 325,320 people in Australia were receiving either an old age or an invalid pension.

Invalid Pensions

THE invalid pension scheme was instituted by the Fisher Government on 15th December, 1910. The rate of pension paid to invalid pensioners who are totally incapacitated has always been the same rate of pension as would be granted to an old age pensioner.

Briefly, the basis of eligibility for an old age pension in respect of a male is that he is aged 65 years or over, and as respects females, 60 years of age or over. Invalids aged 16 years or over who are incapacitated permanently to the extent of 85 per cent. or over, are, with old age pensioners, entitled to 27/- per week. In addition, pensioners, whether old age or invalid, are entitled to supplement their incomes to an extent of 12/6 per week. Property of £400 or more (excluding the home in which the pensioner lives) debars applicants from receiving either the old age or invalid pension. In the case of husband and wife, the property limit for both pensioners is £800. Blind pensioners may earn £260 per annum, and retain their pensions. Where husband and wife are both blind, either one may earn up to £260 and both retain their full pension. The annual cost of invalid and old age pensions to the Commonwealth Government is £22,300,000 per annum

Maternity Allowances

AN ORIGINAL innovation in social services was the introduction by the Fisher Government on 10th October, 1912, of what is called "maternity allowances." The original payment on the birth of a child was the sum of £5. When maternity allowances were first introduced there was no income limit. During the depression period, however, the Financial Emergency Act imposed an income limit which the present Government (the Curtin Government) recently removed. The grant is now universal.

The system of payment of maternity allowances has now gone past the stage of making a straight-out grant on the birth of a child. The Curtin Government recently made a very important alteration, which provides that an allowance of £1/5/- per week shall be paid to the mother for the four weeks before and the four weeks after the occasion of the birth, plus an additional allowance for twins and triplets. The total allowance payable on the birth of the first child is £15, the second child £16, the third child £17/10/-. Where twins are born the allowance payable is £20, £21 and £22/10/-, and in the case of triplets £25, £26 and £27/10/-.

Since the advent of the Maternity Allowances Scheme the total number of claims paid by the Commonwealth Government from the year ended 30th June, 1913, to the year ended 30th June, 1943, was £3,387,933. The cost per annum to the Commonwealth Government of the increased maternity allowances is estimated to be £2,500,000.

It seemed with 1912 that from a Commonwealth standpoint the tendency toward social services disappeared, since the next step did not take place until 1st July, 1941. In the meantime, some of the States had introduced social service schemes of their own.

Unemployment Insurance

IN QUEENSLAND, an Unemployment Insurance Scheme, and in New South Wales, a Child Endowment Scheme, had been put into operation. The Commonwealth Government in 1921 introduced Child Endowment as part of wages for its own Public Servants.

Some States have introduced the Widows' pension, whilst in most of the States there was some scheme of Child Welfare payments by which the State made weekly payments to foster-parents on behalf of children who were entrusted to their care. These schemes varied according to the political tendency in each State. In Queensland, which from 1915 until 1929 had had an unbroken succession of Labor Government, the Government went further in social service schemes than any of the other States. In New South Wales, where Labour Governments seem to alternate with anti-Labor Governments, there was also a greater tendency towards social services than was found in Victoria, South Australia, Western Australia and Tasmania.

Developments Since 1941

However, in 1941 the Commonwealth Government again entered the field of social services, and since then there has been one long succession of Acts placed upon the Statute Books introducing new and additional forms of social services.

Child Endowment

THE first important step taken by the Commonwealth Government was the introduction on 1st July, 1941, of a Child Endowment Scheme. This followed a very forcible and clear statement by the late Chief Judge Beeby, of the Commonwealth Court of Conciliation and Arbitration, who, in his judgment on the application of the Australasian Council of Trade Unions on behalf of the Trade Union Movement of Australia in 1940 for an increase in the basic wage, stated that the Commonwealth basic wage at the very best could support only a wife, a husband and one child. He stressed that unless some form of Child Endowment was introduced by the Commonwealth Government he would feel impelled to increase the basic wage.

This Act made provision for a grant of 5/- per week for the second and all subsequent children under the age of 16 years who were maintained in a family. A similar grant of 5/- per week was made to all children maintained in institutions. There are residential and nationality qualifications, but there is no means tests before child endowment is paid.

On 30th June, 1943, 491,121 individual endowment claims, embracing 891,221 endowed children, were being paid at an annual cost of £11,585,873, whilst 16,938 children in 315 institutions cost £220,194. The annual cost is now estimated at £12,300,000.

Widows' Pensions

THE Child Endowment Scheme was rapidly followed by a Widows' Endowment Scheme, which went into operation on 30th June, 1942, and the estimated cost to Australia is £2,750,000.

Pensioners are classed into three grades. Class A are widows who, irrespective of age, have a child under the age of 16 to care for and maintain. Such a widow receives a pension of 32/- per week. A widow, however, holding property to the value of £1000 or more is debarred from the receipt of the pension. In Class B the widow must be over 50 years of age. As such, a widow would receive 27/- per week, but the possession of property to the value of £400 or more debars her from the receipt of a pension. Class C deals with widows who are in indigent circumstances and to whom a temporary grant is made for a period not exceeding six months.

On 30th June, 1943, there were 38,408 widows drawing pensions amounting to £2,620,678 per annum. There is undoubtedly abundant evidence that the Widows' Pension has been of material assistance to thousands of women and children throughout the Commonwealth.

Funeral Benefits

A VERY interesting development in regard to social services occurred on 1st July, 1943, when an Act came into operation granting funeral benefits to invalid and old age pensioners. The amount of the grant was not to exceed £10, to be applied to the cost of the funeral. The estimated cost of funeral benefits to the Commonwealth is £150,000 per annum.

Family Allowances to Invalid Pensioners

A WEEK after funeral benefits to invalid and old age pensioners came into operation an additional provision affecting old age pensioners also came into force. From 8th July, 1943, a scheme which makes allowance to the wife and unendowed child of an invalid pensioner came into operation. This allowance is a grant of 15/- per week to the wife of an invalid pensioner, and 5/- per week to the unendowed child of the invalid pensioner. The unendowed child would be the first child in the family, who under the present Act is debarred from receiving the benefits of Child Endowment. The annual cost to the Commonwealth of this allowance is £331,000 per annum.

Unemployed and Sickness Benefits

THE most far-reaching Act passed by the Commonwealth Government in respect of social services was that of Unemployment and Sickness benefits. The Act creating these benefits received the Royal assent on 5th April, 1944, but the provisions of the Act are not yet in operation. It is anticipated the Act will be proclaimed early in 1945.

It is estimated for each 1 per cent. of unemployment in the Commonwealth the cost will be £2,000,000 per annum. If 5 per cent. of the workers were unemployed it would cost £10,000,000 per annum; if 10 per cent. were unemployed it would cost £20,000,000 per annum. The estimated cost to Australia for sickness benefits is £8,500,000 per annum.

Pharmaceutical Benefits

AN ADDITIONAL social welfare scheme which was assented to in April, 1944, and which it is expected will be proclaimed early in 1945, is that known as Pharmaceutical Benefits. Under this measure, which will be universal, a doctor's prescription will be dispensed free of charge to the patient, provided the doctor uses the formulary adopted by the Commonwealth Government.

This formulary is now in use in big hospitals, and is found satisfactory for most cases. It is flexible; it will be added to from time to time. As the scheme is universal, all persons in the community, irrespective of income or of property, will be entitled to benefit. The estimated cost to the Commonwealth is £3,000,000 per annum.

It will thus be seen that during the last four years considerable progress has been made in Commonwealth social service legislation. With the exception of Child Endowment and the original Old Age Pensions Scheme, the whole of these social services have been introduced by Labor Governments. The Invalid Pensions Act and the Maternity Allowance Act were passed by the Fisher Government. Child Endowment was passed by the Menzies Government, and the remaining Social Services legislation was all passed by the Curtin Government

Contemplated Social Service Extensions

THE intentions of the Curtin Government, however, have by no means yet been exhausted. Very extensive future legislation is contemplated, including a Hospital Contribution Scheme, which aims at the payment of 6/- per day on the basis of beds occupied in public and private hospitals throughout the Commonwealth. This scheme is estimated, when brought into operation, to cost about £4,000,000 per annum.

It is proposed also to introduce a special allowance for pulmonary tubercular sufferers, which will have a maximum cost to the Commonwealth of £50,000 per annum. This allowance will be payable on the basis of a one pound payment by the Commonwealth Government to the State on the basis of each pound paid out by the State for tubercular treatment.

Plans have been drawn up for a comprehensive general medical scheme, including hospital care. This scheme, however, it is anticipated will not be implemented in full until after the conclusion of the war.

Total Cost of All Services

WHEN the Unemployment and Sickness Benefits Scheme, and the Pharmaceutical Benefits Scheme come into operation, it is probable that the annual total cost of social services to the Commonwealth will be in the neighborhood of £53,000,000. (The population of Australia is about 7¼ million.)

It is noteworthy that, with the rapid increase in the Australian national income as the result of war activities, tremendous advances have been made in the realm of social service. It is reasonable to say that were it not for the increased national income it might have been difficult to have advanced so far in such a short period.

It is important to remember, however, that so far as Australia is concerned all social service benefits are paid direct from Consolidated Revenue. Social insurance schemes, such as are in operation in New Zealand and Great Britain, have not been introduced into this country.

The Trade Union Movement of Australia from the beginning of the century had advocated social services of the class and character which have been now introduced into the Commonwealth. The Trade Union Movement has always claimed that these provisions should be paid from Consolidated Revenue. It was felt that by a universal system of taxation that all social service benefits could be met.

From an address delivered at meeting of members of the Institute of Industrial Management, Australia, at Assembly Hall, Melbourne.

The Fear Known by Disabled Ex-Servicemen
that They will No Longer Be Employable is
Being Discounted by Schemes Arranged to Ensure that They Will Be Given . . .

Another Chance
to Live

By W. H. BOLTON

London, England.

IT was just after D-Day, when the German Panzer Divisions were trying to force
their way through Normandy to cut off the American Army on the Cherbourg
peninsula, that a British soldier, Frederick J. Clarke was badly injured when his
tank was hit. Both his legs had to be amputated on the battlefield.

He Becomes a Welder

SOME months later, in an invalid propelling chair, he called upon officials of
Britain's Southern Railway Company, who had employed him previously in
one of their iron foundries.

"I shall not be of much use to you now," he said with pardonable bitterness.

"Nonsense, we have another job for you," was the answer. "One which will
not be affected by your disability. You shall be trained as a welder in our locomotive works."

Now the ex-trooper of the Tank Regiment sits in a specially made chair at his
bench and for six months has been carrying out highly satisfactory welding, even
moving his work between his bench and the floor. He is a skilled, cheery craftsman, happy and confident in his new job.

Ernest Page, waiter at one of the Railway's hotels has had a similar experience.
While serving in North Africa with the Black Watch, his arm was blown off. No
longer able to carry a tray, he was trained to be a telephone enquiry clerk at which
work he has proved most successful.

Blindness No Handicap

A MORE difficult problem was that of Roland Cloke, former locomotive engineer, who was blinded in an enemy air-raid. The National Institute for the Blind which for many years has assisted blinded civilians, took him in hand. First they restored his self confidence, pointing out that if his blindness were a handicap it need not mean total disability.

They trained him to tell by touch; first to tell the time by a special watch made without glass but strong hands, and the hours marked with dots. This watch is given to blinded persons as soon as they can use it.

That was the first step, and something was accomplished. The blind man learned that he need not be entirely dependent on others. After that advancement was steady. He was taught telephone switchboard operating and returned to his old employers in that capacity. By his switchboard, the ex-loco engineer even has a braille machine operated by touch which enables him to write down any message he wishes to record.

Broad Policy of One Company

THEY are a few of the men whom this progressive and humane railway organiza-tion have re-settled in post-war jobs. They have long had a similar scheme for dealing with injured or sick employees, planned to help them carry out duties normally undertaken by the physically fit. This scheme, with the assistance of representatives of the workers, is now being broadened in its scope. Its revision is being carried out under the following categories:

Persons disabled in War Service.
Persons disabled in the service of the Railway.
Persons broken down in health or grown old in the Railway service, and unable to perform their ordinary duties.

"We owe these men much," said Col. Gore Brown, Chairman of the Company, to his shareholders. "And we endeavour to arrange their re-habilitation so that hope may grow in their hearts and confidence in the value of their work. They must share to the full the British way of living."

Wounded Men's Fear

DOCTORS in the War hospitals declare that wounded men suffer more from intro-spective surveys as they lie on their beds of pain, than they do from their wounds. They go though nightmares of fear when they think of the days ahead.

Blinded or crippled for the rest of their lives, they feel "crocks." Once out of hospital, what is there they can do? Hopes, plans for the future, pre-war ambitions die down to a flicker. They know that after every major war there has been that endless procession of the blind and the halt dependent on the charity of their fel-low men.

The British Government has assured these wounded warriors that all will be well. They have not been over-looked in the Government's wide scheme of Vocational Training for men and women who have been in the Forces or engaged in work of national importance.

Under the Disabled Persons (Employment) Act of 1944, all important employers are compelled to find work for these disabled men and women. The Act also provides for other workers who through injury, however caused, disease or lifelong deformity, are handicapped in obtaining or keeping employment. For the time being the quota of such workers to be employed has been fixed at two per cent of the total staff.

Selection of Work

APART from the more severely disabled, for whom training is arranged at special residential centers, it has been found that most disabled workers can hold their own in a suitable trade, side by side, with able-bodied colleagues. That is provided, of course, that they have been carefully chosen for the occupation in which they were trained. Therefore disabled workers, once selected will be trained with able-bodied persons.

The effect upon these trainees is astonishing. It is proved to them that although disabled, they are not finished, nor useless, nor inferior to other workers. Real work is to be found for them, not stop-gap jobs, work in which they can take a pride and regain their confidence and dignity as workers.

They may not be entirely cured in body, that is impossible, but they will be cured in spirit.

A Serviceman, in the Lowest Pay Grade with a
Wife and Two Children, Has an Annual Income
Which Is Equivalent to a Civilian's Earnings of
About $2,800. We Are Going to Need Some
Very Good Personnel Work to Be Able to Pay
Workers that Much.

Better Personnel
Administration

By Forrest H. Kirkpatrick

Bethany College,
Bethany, W. Va.

IN BARGAINING about wage rates in these next few years, labor and management
will confront a combination of common and opposing interests that will be
more disturbing than in any other period of our history. Both labor and
management will want to expand markets, for employment will depend on sales as
truly as do profits. The sales of any product depend, in turn, on keeping its unit
price so adjusted to the prices of other goods as to attract buyers.

Prices and Wages

AS A rule the lower the selling price in relation to other prices, the larger the
sales. But prices must cover costs if prices and employment are to be assured.
In most industries, labor charges are the largest item of expense next to materials.
So if unions seek to maximize incomes of the total membership—which not all
unions do—they will have to consider what effect such wage demands will have
upon unit costs, unit selling prices, physical volume of sales and employment.

To find what wage rates, between the admittedly too low or too high, will be
most advantageous to labor will tax the shrewdest judgement. The wage rates
most advantageous to the employer are no easier to determine. An employer might
suffer from rates so high that they would force an advance of selling prices sufficient
to reduce sales drastically. Very low rates on the other hand cannot suit an employer who must get an adequate supply of competent labor in competition with

other industries. Unfortunately, sober analysis of common and conflicting interests is seldom the sole factor in collective bargaining on wages.

Present Wage Demands

Most of the large unions recently announced their demands for higher wage rates. In general, the increases demanded are designed to offset the reduction in wartime earnings attending the decline in the number of hours worked, the elimination of premium overtime pay and related factors. Thus the rubber workers ask for a wage increase of 30 cents an hour, steel workers 25 cents an hour, auto and clothing workers an increase of 30 per cent. Increases of these magnitudes would in most instances enable workers to retain their wartime take-home pay and the demands are apparently designed to accomplish that objective.

In effect, the labor unions are insisting that high wartime wages represent a legitimate immediate aspiration for their members. They are saying that the increase in workers' incomes resulting from the extra work required by our war effort must be retained in the pay envelope, even though that extra effort is no longer expended. They are also saying that productivity has increased so significantly during the war that these wage increases can be made without requiring price increases. In effect the social argument is that the wartime level of earnings must be continued to prevent workers' living standards from being impaired.

Military Pay Provisions

Undoubtedly wage adjustments are desirable in many cases and are justified on the basis of the expected post-war earning position, the rise in living costs and changes in productivity. But it is a big step from such justifiable wage increases to the 30 per cent increases now being demanded. Such an increase on top of the 36 per cent rise in average straight-time hourly earnings during the war will present industry with a sharp increase in costs which inevitably will require sharp increases in price. These price increases in turn may decrease the buying power of the wages received and in turn become the basis for new demands.

Many people overlook the possibility that present military pay provisions may have some effect upon post-war wages and collective bargaining. Government statisticians estimate that at the present time actual pay plus cash value of food, clothing, shelter, medical care, and other essentials is equivalent to an annual income of $1,700 for a private or apprentice seaman. To this amount should be added a tax saving of about $239. The dependents allowance for a married serviceman with two children increases his pay by $936 (tax exempt). This means that a serviceman in the lowest pay grade with a wife and two children has an annual income which is equivalent to a civilian's earnings of about $2,800. Non-commissioned officers in the highest grades have an income equivalent up to $3,500 of civilian's earnings.

Veterans Ideas of Justifiable Wages

THESE figures exceed the annual income received by many workers before and even during the war. I am inclined to think that many discharged soldiers will reflect upon these earnings and benefits and will count on finding even more attractive financial returns in civilian occupations. If I am correct in this, there may also be a tendency to carry their service-engendered notions about "minimum pay" over into civilian life. If such should happen, it would have a strong impact not only upon wage rates, but even more significant, upon collective bargaining for annual wages.

The matter of family allowances may not be without post-war significance either. Though confined in the United States to servicemen only, it is worth noting that in recent years family allowances have been adopted for civilian employees in at least 15 countries. The movement developed during 1914–1918 as a device to bridge the gap between wages—particularly those of workers with large families— and the rising cost of living. Provisions for these payments outlived the war in only two countries—France and Belgium. The reason lay in national concern about low birth rates and high infant mortality. Similar considerations of a "national" character revived the movement, particularly after the onset of the depression. And the British government has now indicated that it will include family allowances as part of the Beveridge social security program.

Family Allowances in Foreign Countries

OBSERVERS here are particularly intrigued by the family allowance scheme which went into effect in Canada recently. The Canadian law provides for monthly payments to range from $5 to $8 per month for each of the first four children, plus smaller amounts for additional children. At the present time, labor groups in this country are opposed to family allowances on the ground that "family wages" tend to prevent general wage increases. But that used to be the attitude of labor in Canada and Great Britain too.

It may be assumed, however, that as long as wages remain at a high level for at least a majority of United States workers, an important movement for the establishment of family allowances to benefit civilians will hardly get underway. Some forecasters, in the field of labor economics, however, think that the introduction of family allowances may well receive favorable consideration as a benefit to workers employed in some of the low-paying but essential industries.

WLB Sponsored Practices

THERE is the strong possibility that wartime developments in settling labor disputes may come to be almost folkways. We may be working under a new frame of reference that we do not yet recognize. It might be useful, therefore, to take stock of the practices which have come to be accepted in large part through War Labor Board sponsorship. Among the most important are:

(1) Equal pay for equal work regardless of sex, color, or race.
(2) Minimum wage rates to eliminate substandards of living.
(3) Maintenance of membership and its latent corollary of union responsibility.
(4) Job classification and integrated wage rate schedules.
(5) Premium pay for shift work.
(6) Arbitration as the capstone of union-management relations.

Moreover, it requires no bold prophet to suggest that three other policies, already perceptible, might take on a more definite shape in the immediate future. These are: (1) extension of collective bargaining to include group insurance, employee benefit plans, and other "fringe issues"; (2) recognition of the right to collective bargaining on the part of organizations of supervisory employees; and (3) development of guaranteed wage plans or some scheme to stabilize employment.

It is clear that the economics of war have served to wipe out pay differentials as between men and women, or white and negroes, who do the same work. Not only has this become national policy, but to an important extent, it has become national reality. It must be anticipated, therefore, that a movement to re-emphasize or re-establish differential pay will meet with considerable resistance. Plants that have been able to classify jobs in terms of "female jobs" and "male jobs" will soon have to give attention to a more realistic job classification and evaluation program.

Stronger Personnel Departments Needed

TRENDS that seem closer to day by day operations make it advisable for industry to review the organization structure of personnel departments. It is apparent that there should be a revision—or shift of emphasis—of functions and staff. There is nothing to indicate that industry dare count the responsibility of good personnel administration as being less important or less needed. On the contrary, there is an urgency in the present situation to indicate that we need stronger departments, more able men, and clearer guide-posts for this work.

As part of the job of looking ahead, it would be well to recall the factors which have largely shaped personnel department organization during the war years. These factors may be roughly grouped under two headings—despite the fact that there is a good deal of inter-relationship: (1) non-government factors, and (2) government factors. The essentially non-government factors which have affected personnel organization are: (1) recruitment, (2) employee training, (3) supervision, and (4) union relations. Government factors which have helped to shape the organization of our personnel department are: (1) wage stabilization, (2) Selective Service, (3) War Manpower Commission, and (4) National Labor Relations Board.

Shifts of Emphasis

THE organization structure of personnel departments has reflected the primary importance of these non-government and government factors. The extent to which organization structure has responded to these factors has varied, of course, with the size of the company. The present trends are not new in the sense that they represent completely new developments, but new in the sense that they represent a shift of emphasis. To some extent they will affect the organization structure of personnel departments in the immediate future, viz:

    (1) Decreasing importance of recruitment and job training. Smaller work forces in many plants, the changed labor market, lower labor turnover, will contract sharply the work involved in recruiting and training employees.

    (2) Decreasing importance of government factors to the ultimate point of elimination. The elimination point may be a year or even two years in the distance but the decline has set in.

    (3) *Increasing* importance of union relations. We are entering what will probably be a very critical period with respect to management-union relations.

    (4) *Increasing* importance of supervisory relations. This factor is increasing in importance from two angles: (a) The need for better supervision in competitive civilian production, and (b) the need for better supervisory relations as a deterrent of supervisory unionization.

    (5) *Increasing* importance of direct company-employee relations, both from the angle of company-employee contract and from the angle of company-employee communication.

Wise management will review personnel department functions, staff and budget, with an eye to the trends currently visible and will plan to devote more emphasis and more people to the increasing trends. Departments or people which have been concerned with recruitment, training, wage stabilization or Selective Service may or may not be departments or people which can be re-assigned to union relations, supervisory relations, or direct company-employee relations.

Chief executives in every industry are beginning to realize that personnel problems, like the poor, will always be with us and that successful personnel administration lies in keeping ahead of the times. These executives are viewing this work not as welfare or paternalism, but as the means for improving quality, reducing costs and increasing profits—in other words, as an integral element of management. Such executives are looking for personnel officers who know something of the technical aspects of the work, who understand the social scene in which we must live and work, and are not thinking of "union baiting" as one of their major interests or responsibilities.

Lawyers in the Business

LEGALISMS flourished and grew during the war years as a substitute for understanding and it is one of the things that must be purged in these post-war years. It is often easier and quicker to write procedures and lay down rules than to teach people how to get along with each other. Relations between employer and employee, between foreman and worker are essentially psychological and social. To surround such a relationship with legalisms stressing "rights", "prerogatives", "responsibilities", "duties", and "obligations" covers human relationships with a sheath of tar which makes the struggle for better understanding well nigh fruitless.

Of necessity, personnel departments have had to follow the ways of the National Labor Relations Board and—during the war years—the War Labor Board. Management, not knowing where else to turn for advise, has often asked lawyers to handle such matters. Many intelligent lawyers recognized, at once, the dividing line between the legal and management aspects of such problems, and have cooperated with personnel men. But some attorneys, without personnel experience, have tried to become "industrial relations experts" and have advised clients on a wide variety of personnel policies and procedures. There is no reason, of course, why a lawyer should not become a skilled personnel man, but most attorneys realize that legal training *per se* does not qualify men for this type of work.

Collective Cooperation

COLLECTIVE bargaining is one of the activities that must receive new emphasis by personnel departments. Some personnel men have been able to convince their employers that they should take a leaf from the British book of experience and rely upon the administrative rather than legislative method in labor relations. Compared with labor agreements in this country, British agreements are singularly simple. British employers depend upon good personnel management to insure union responsibility and not upon complicated regulations.

In a few companies where the management has never made union recognition an issue and where mutual confidence and respect exist, the personnel department is exploring the possibilities of increasing efficiency and improving personnel relations through collective cooperation. In some companies, labor-management committees meet regularly with the local officers of the company and of the union to discuss such matters of mutual interest as quality control, cost reduction, accident prevention, and elimination of waste.

Conference Basis

CAREFUL planning for the handling of specific personnel problems in the years of readjustment and reconversion is the major responsibility of every industry and every plant. Even with the best of plans and intentions, there will be some friction and tension during these months of readjustment. The accumulated gripes, grievances, and general unrest of the war years will let loose. There will be some strong reaction from time to time and much sounding off about "anti-union employers", "hard-hearted management", and "paternalistic capital". To many working men right now, the world seems to be filled with selfish interests, each fighting for its share of the spoils, with neither employers or government doing much for the underdog.

It is pointless to argue about the validity of such attitudes. The best we can do is to be prepared to meet each situation and each personnel problem with patience, intelligence, and honesty. Friction and tension can be diluted by the use of sound policies and procedures, by constant and firm determination to keep relationships between management and labor on a "conference basis", and by lifting personnel administration to a higher level of professional competence and management acceptance.

First Rate Methods and Men

ALL of this means that first rate methods and first rate men must be brought into the field of personnel administration. The problems we face call for something better than informal and careless methods of dealing with employment, placement, training, grievances, wage rates, and collective bargaining. We have passed the time when the personnel manager can be selected on the basis of his ability to be a slap-happy extrovert.

He must be a thoughtful student of the social scene, a man with training and experience in labor economics, social psychology, and industrial management, and he must bring to the conference table his own self-control and objectivity, tempered always by insight and appreciation for human values. I hasten to say too, that the job cannot be done by pamphlets and posters, by soft ball teams or company picnics, and it cannot be done by trying to pass the responsibility on to some government agency.

Personnel Administration Still Haphazard

PERSONNEL administration—now somewhat haphazard and confused in purpose and techniques—must be redesigned and given a new place in industrial and business management. Emphasis must be put upon better methods and procedures and upon sound and even-handed policies. But most of all personnel administration must have men who can give leadership in helping plan and set into motion the kind of labor-management relations that will offer some chance for industrial peace and prosperity, and with it, the best opportunity for workers to find satisfaction and security in their work.

Technological and manufacturing development outraces social ideas and planning. Under such conditions frictionless operation of an industrial society is well nigh impossible. It is inevitable, therefore, that the problems of human relations will come to the front. This means that in an industrial civilization there is need— and will be an increasing need—for perfecting the science and art of human relations in industry. It is our privilege to be in this work now. And, in spite of the rough roads and hard fare, that seem to be a part of the day-by-day job, most of us are sturdy enough to endure.

From an address delivered at the fall, 1945, Southern Conference on Human Relations in Industry, held at Greenville, S. C.

Book Reviews

Book Review Editor, MR. EVERETT VAN EVERY

California Council of Personnel Management, 442 Flood Building, San Francisco, 2, Cal.

MANAGEMENT OF INSPECTION & QUALITY CONTROL

By J. M. Juran. Harper & Brothers. New York. 1945. 233 pp. $3.00

The growing importance of inspection functions and methods of executive control in manufacture have been the most conspicuous developments in scientific management in recent years. Much has been written about the importance of cost control, uniform flow of work, job methods, timestudy, etc., but this is the first book we have found on the managerial aspects of inspection procedures and quality control.

Conversion to peacetime operations will hasten the necessity for careful attention to inspection tasks. Competition will force manufacturers to heed fine lines of costs and product-perfection and the responsibilities of management in this field will be greater than they were before the war.

The author is an engineer who has found the many problems of human relations in this work of checking for imperfections, maintaining high standards and assuring quality production. More than once throughout the text the author warns his readers that the human problems often transcend the technical engineering issues in complexity. The fact that specifications and much of the technical performance are administered by fallible human beings creates risks and problems that will be even more acute in our postwar competitive production race. The designer, the engineers, the checkers and operators ... all will find themselves in more discussions and disputes with factory personnel.

Juran advocates that Standards, Shop Practices, and Codes be converted through proper training into factory habits in the same manner that citizens outside the factory learn to live by laws and written statutes.

Greater precision and reduction in the inspection effort is, of course, accomplished through measuring devices. But the measurement problem requires careful delegation of authority, fixing of responsibility, division of labor and many other devices of scientific management if the resultant judgement of the product and the resultant inspection data are to really do their part in the over-all inspection function.

Errors in measurement are closely associated with the whole measurement problem and the author describes the many important sources of error, the techniques that are generally employed to judge integrity of inspectors, how the accuracy of inspectors is determined, ways of reducing temptations of inspectors, use of adequate incentives and the types of discipline found most successful in controlling errors.

In describing the responsibility of the chief inspector for the cost of exercising control, Juran concludes that the cost of finding defects is often greater than the loss incurred if the defects were not found. He goes on to say that what he calls "judicious gambling" can reduce the cost of control of quality with no appreciable reduction in the adequacy of the control. And throughout all this technical wordage the reader is not lost. He can easily follow all the complex variables, the inspection techniques based on the theory of probability and the reflected nature of the uninspected pieces produced by the sampling process.

The personnel-minded reader will find this book interesting because it explores so many simple processes and refines so many simple tasks that he has never analyzed before. Indeed the work is an exhaustive source-book on management principles and practices in what the reader is ready to admit is rapidly approaching a status of inspection and control administration.

In all manufacturing processes we can expect greater emphasis on the function of inspection and the necessity for more rigid quality control. And as these systems of operations expand we can look for the greatest obstacles to be those affecting the changing habits of people. These human problems exceed the technical problems in complexity and in difficulty and require a corresponding increase in leadership and administrative responsibility.

Personnel managers who are concerned with perfecting manufacturing processes, and the employee relations problems that accompany such improvements, will find this book as interesting and helpful as will the engineers, planning officials, designers, and those who are directly engaged in inspection and quality perfection.

PERSONNEL
Journal

The Magazine of

LABOR RELATIONS AND PERSONNEL PRACTICES

Published by PERSONNEL RESEARCH FEDERATION

Lincoln Building, 60 East 42nd Street, New York City

Volume 24   *Number 7*

Contents for January 1946

EDITORIAL BOARD

Much Has Been Written about Supervision but There Have Been Very Few Attempts at Studying the Matter Scientifically. Hence There Is Too Much About It that We Know Very Little About.

Are Management's Views *of* Supervision Faulty?

Digests and Interpretation of Study

By QUENTIN W. FILE

Purdue University, Lafayette, Ind.

How much do industrial managements know about supervision? Apparently they have many ideas and strong opinions, but most of these are faulty, in the opinion of so-called experts. Most management views are not based upon sound knowledge arrived at by any thorough studies of the problems.

No Proper Basis of Selection

HENCE management has no proper basis on which to select supervisors, to promote them, to train them, or to determine their worth or uselessness to the organization. So the most important link in the management worker contact is actually in many cases the weakest link. It may not be, but the point is that in many companies there is almost a total lack of knowledge as to what, in supervision, constitutes a strong or a weak link, and little knowledge of any supervisor, as to whether he is strong or weak, or whether he is the man who keeps labor relations on an even keel, or is the man who rocks and finally upsets the boat.

This inadequacy of management's knowledge of the facts of supervision has recently come to light as a result of a study which set out to find out if supervisory quality could be measured. In brief the study showed that the type of supervisory quality that experts think supervisors should possess can be measured, but that the vague and conflicting notions of supervisory quality that managements have are so sketchy that they cannot often even be stated, much less measured.

Management's Ideas

Management's definite ideas are of the following kinds. It believes:

(a) that technical and trade ability is of primary importance.

(b) that the primary job of a supervisor is to get out production at minimum cost.

(c) that standardized methods of dealing with supervisory problems are best—without regard to the personality differences of workers.

(d) that the supervisor's first and foremost responsibility is to management.

(e) that it is undesirable to delegate responsibility for improved working conditions to workers.

(f) that workers should not be told their chances of promotion or of getting raises, except by management.

(g) that workers should be "kept in their place".

(h) that supervisors should use negative rather than constructive methods of handling supervisor-worker relations.

These are samples of the faulty, limited and often unrealistic concepts of management regarding supervisory jobs. In general, it was found that management thinks in terms of a host of single specific items in the supervisory job, and in so far as it attempts to judge the quality of supervision does so on the basis of a supervisor's ability to handle each or all of these specific functions.

That these specific factors are often contradictory is not recognized. Nor is the fact recognized that there is a *general* factor of supervisory ability, which is common to all supervisory jobs in all companies, enabling a man if he has a high degree of this general supervisory ability to be good in any situation and in any company.

General Supervisory Ability

Without this general supervisory ability, or with only a limited quality of it, a supervisor cannot satisfactorily carry out the specific functions management might legitimately regard as important. This general supervisory ability can be measured; supervisors with not much of it can be trained in it, and when so trained can easily be trained to handle the specific items; it is better to select men with good potential supervisory ability, and then train them in the specific items of a particular job, rather than to select men on the basis of their apparent knowledge of specific items of the job, and then hope to develop in them general supervisory ability.

We may illustrate this problem of specifics by the story of a training director of a company, who in his foreman classes, thought to find out what things he should train the men to be better in handling, by asking the group of foremen to name the items on which they had been balled out by the company. Twenty supervisors came up with 272 items on which management had balled them out.

This approach to supervisory problems is, we are afraid, all too representative of management thinking, and of the thinking of most foreman training instructors.

It is obvious that such an approach is based upon faulty understanding of the supervisory job, and puts the problem in terms to which there can never be any satisfactory solution. (The management of this company fired this trainer, because he stirred up the foremen so much, and then hired another of the same way of thinking.)

A direct quotation from the published report of this study follows:

Report Quoted

Construction of the Test

IN THE construction of an instrument for measuring supervisory quality, consideration must be given to the relative importance of both the general and the specific factors involved. The seemingly predominant importance of the general factors of supervision is emphasized by the large number of books and articles now expressing the need for improved understanding of human relations and the importance of personalities in achieving industrial harmony.

Most industrial supervisors are obtained by some form of upgrading. It seems quite possible, therefore, that any individual, who is able to qualify for a supervisory position on the basis of his general abilities, will either have acquired, or can acquire, the specific knowledge necessary for handling the job. It was on the basis of the hypothesis that *factors generally common to industrial supervisory positions are the really important quantities* that this project of constructing a valid measure of supervisory quality was conceived.

When developing any test, it is necessary to make certain basic assumptions. The principal assumptions of this study were:

1. That ability to supervise workers is something general in nature rather than highly specific to a given job or company. The supervisor's effectiveness is, in the long run, dependent upon his understanding of and ability to deal with *human relations*.

2. That lack of this general ability to deal with workers is the greatest single cause of supervisory failures and of management-worker friction.

3. That knowledge of how to handle the supervisory function can be tested by obtaining responses to certain significant questions which are drawn directly from problems which frequently confront the supervisor.

4. That such questions can be obtained by direct contact with supervisors on the job, by careful study of the literature concerning supervisory fundamentals and supervisory problems, by taking into account the relevant principles of psychology, and by systematically "weeding out" those items which prove unfruitful.

In selecting the items for the supervisory ability test, *How Supervise?*, three definite objectives were kept in mind.

1. The items must be presented in problem form calling for an operational response, i.e., the items should ask "What should be done . . . ?" or "Is it desirable to . . . ?", etc.

2. The items must have "face" as well as statistical validity. They must present problems which are pertinent to industrial supervisors regardless of the department or the company from which the supervisors are selected.

3. These items must be simply worded so that *any* supervisor can see the problem involved.

Item Selection

Items for *How Supervise?* were selected from three distinct sources: publications concerning industrial supervision, suggestions from industrial supervisors and personnel men, and contacts with labor leaders. The most fruitful and readily available source of potential items was the industrial literature.

Contacts with various supervisors in a sizable manufacturing company offered a means of checking on the practicality of the problems presented and of obtaining additional items.

(*End of Direct Quote*)

After some 204 suitable questions to be included in the first test of supervisory ability had been picked, as described above, the next job was to find out the best or correct answers to the questions, and to discard the questions which seemed to be unsuitable because there was disagreement as to the correct answer. Also the best questions had to be determined.

Good Supervisors Know Best Answers

IT WAS assumed that good supervisors would know and agree upon the correct answers, and the best questions as a group. It was also assumed that men who write books on supervision, and those actually engaged in supervisory training would, as a group, know and agree upon the correct answers and best questions (so-called experts).

This was where the first snag occurred. The assumption that the best supervisors would know the correct answers was unworkable, because it was impossible to find out who the best supervisors were. It was thought that if the supervisors were rated by those working below them, and by those to whom they reported—in other words their bosses, the best supervisors could be ascertained.

Five hundred and fifty-seven sets of four ratings on each supervisor by members of management above the supervisors were obtained.

There was an almost total lack of agreement among the four raters of each supervisor, so that the same man might be rated excellent, good, average or poor by four different supervisors, all of whom were supposed to know him well enough to rate him. So that it was totally impossible to find out who the best supervisors were from management ratings.

Supervisory Ratings Unreliable

Tʜɪs, of course, is just finding out over again, that supervisory ratings by management are totally worthless. It has sometimes been assumed that rating of a supervisor by the man over him being unreliable, if three or more men rate him, the averaging of the ratings will give the correct rating. This study shows that this assumption is wrong. Four errors do not make a right. This assumption has as much sense in it as getting four children to do an arithmetic problem to which they all give wrong answers, and trying to get the right answer by averaging their four wrong answers.

So the investigators were blocked in their attempt to get a group of good supervisors to say what the correct answers to their questions on supervisory problems were.

The experts selected to say which were correct answers to the best test questions were eight writers on the subject, and thirty-seven men on the staff of the Training Within Industry division of the Government.

These forty-five men were found to have a high degree of agreement as to the correct answers, and the writers agreed well with the practical foremen trainers. So that the answers upon which they agreed were accepted as correct for the test.

Of course, the judgment of the actual supervisors which management had rated as to the correct answers to the questions were in almost total disagreement with each other, so that 557 supervisors gave almost 557 different answers to each question. And of course there was no agreement as to the correctness of answers as between the supervisors and the experts. This completely blocked the use of management's or supervisors' opinions as to the correctness of answers or the value of questions to be included in the test. Reliance had to be placed entirely upon the views of experts.

Lack of Agreement among Management People

Tʜɪs lack of agreement of management people as to the correct answers to questions was seen in one company (not included in this study) where an attempt was made in supervisory training classes to educate the men in understanding written company policy in labor relations matters. The training director had selected twenty questions dealing with problems that had been brought up by the union as grievance cases, and next to each question had put four different answers, which the union alleged had been given by top-ranking supervisors. The class was asked to mark the correct answer, and then any differences would be discussed.

Among the men in this class there was absolutely no agreement by all as to the correct answer to any question. Obviously the company had a long way to go in supervisory training, meantime the workers were irritated by different interpretations of written policy by different supervisors. The union was putting it all over the company in collective bargaining, because the company would say, when the union asked for a ruling on a grievance, that it was impossible, would ruin the company, or was an infringement on management rights, and so could not be granted, and the union would just bring to their attention that in Dept. K, or Division X, the ruling asked by the union was actually in effect.

The Human Relations Aspects

THE main point of disagreement between the experts and the management representatives was on the importance of questions relating to the human or mental hygiene aspects of supervisors relations. The experts thought these most important, but the supervisors passed them over as relatively unimportant. Modern writings on industrial relations, particularly at the supervisory level, have all stressed the great importance of the individual human relations angle. Even top flight industrialists generally give lip service to this idea.

But in so far as management-selected supervisors do reflect management's actual opinion as to what are the important items of good supervision, then actually it is obvious that management is unaware of the true importance of human relations in supervision. Another possible explanation is that top management is as well aware of the importance of this as it says it is, but that the principles of improved personnel relations have barely trickled through to operational levels.

A further direct quotation from the published report of this study follows:

Report Quoted
Summary and Conclusions

CONCLUSIONS drawn from this study can best be made in terms of the hypotheses advanced when plans for the experimental project were conceived. These hypotheses logically fall into three categories: (1) those which deal with the nature of industrial supervision, (2) those which are concerned with criteria against which supervisory quality can be measured, and (3) those which deal with methods of scoring and computing data. Both the hypotheses and findings concerning them are discussed below.

The hypotheses advanced as to the nature of industrial supervision were:

1. *Important aspects of industrial supervisory ability can be measured by test items which are equally applicable to all industrial concerns.* True. 140 discriminating items were found in this study; items which showed no significant variation with respect to the size or nature of the industrial concern. Confidence in the importance of these items was expressed by both industrial experts and management.

2. *The mental-hygiene aspects of industrial supervision are of primary importance.* In other words, *supervisor-worker relations are among the key determinants of good or poor supervision.* True. Several indications of the validity of this hypothesis were found.

a. The average discriminating power of the items of *How Supervise?* which dealt with human relations was significantly greater than the average discriminating power of factual items.

—247—

b. In response to a felt need, the last decade has witnessed innumerable publications of books and articles dealing with the human-relations aspects of industrial supervision.

c. Supervisory training courses, which place considerable emphasis on this area, are now being given.

d. The existence of labor troubles, so frequently blamed on conflicting personalities, adds further emphasis to the importance of mental hygiene in industrial relations.

3. *A general test of supervisory ability can be used to evaluate the outcomes of supervisory training programs.* True. The experimental edition of the test was used by two different companies for this purpose. Significant gains were found in both cases, especially among the poorer supervisors.

4. *Age, education, and miscellaneous other variables are highly important factors in good supervision.* Generally false. Of all the personal information examined, only education revealed a relationship above bare significance with respect to total scores on the test. It should be pointed out, however, that experience was measured in terms of two-year intervals. Differences which exist between a supervisor of one and a half years of experience and one with no experience at all may well have been overlooked.

Validating Criteria

THE hypotheses advanced concerning criteria for validating the test were:

1. *Four members of management can be found who are sufficiently well acquainted with any particular supervisor to rate his abilities accurately.* Questionable. Ratings obtained for this study were not sufficiently valid for use as a criterion for determining test item discrimination. Differences in standards set by different raters, lack of knowledge about the supervisor rated, and logical error (halo effect) concerning relations between rating traits all tended to make the obtained ratings invalid.

2. *Industrial experts as a group give reliable answers to the problems presented in the test items.* True. Two completely different groups of experts agreed closely as to the best answers to the items of the test ($r = +.91$).

3. *Top management and industrial experts agree on what constitutes good supervision.* False. Validity of this hypothesis would have eliminated the need for two criteria for the validation of test items.

Management and Experts Disagree

IN ADDITION to the hypotheses accepted or rejected, other observations were made for the analysis of the experimental data. Assuming that management-selected supervisors do reflect the attitudes of top management in their responses, the following observations can be made:

1. Management and industrial experts significantly disagree:

a. On methods of handling dissatisfied workers. Industrial experts favor transfer; management opposes.

b. On methods of handling complaints. Management favors standardized pro-cedures for each type of complaint; the experts favor the recognition of individual differences.

c. As to the desirability of delegating responsibility to workers for improving working conditions. Management opposes.

d. As to the wisdom of allowing regular rest periods. Management opposes.

e. As to whether a worker should be told what promotions he can expect provid-ing he attains a certain level of proficiency. Management maintains that these matters of salary and promotion are company business which should not be disclosed.

2. Industrial supervisors, selected by management as best, are not fully aware of the importance of human-relations problems in industrial supervision. Very few of these problems as presented in the test items approached significance with respect to the management-ratings criterion. The same items were highly significant with respect to the total score criterion.

Test Believed Useful

FROM the hypotheses investigated and observations made, we may conclude that general factors of supervision do exist and that these quantities can be measured. The human-relations aspects of supervision are vital and are, of necessity, receiving an ever-increasing amount of attention from management. Industrial experts, both theoretical and practical, have rather clear-cut ideas about these general factors. In-dustrial management tends to be less progressive and seems to favor keeping the worker "in his place," rather than encouraging him to become interested in "com-pany affairs." Management's idea of what it wants in a good supervisor seems rather inclined toward negative rather than constructive methods of handling supervisor-worker relations. Management is, however, well aware of the factual problems in industry and how they should be handled. Only on items dealing with the mental-hygiene aspects of supervision were there indications of significant weak-nesses.

From this study, a test of the general aspects of supervisory quality has been de-veloped. It is believed that this test, *How Supervise?*, will prove valuable for selecting candidates for and evaluating the outcomes of supervisory training programs, for selecting individuals for direct promotion to supervisory positions, and for checking on the quality of present supervisory personnel.

(End of Direct Quote)

Sources of Information

THE *above is a condensed interpretation, with some direct quotes, of a published report on the Measurement of Supervisory Quality in Industry. The article, published in the Journal of Applied Psychology, Vol. 29, No. 5, October, 1945, pp. 323–337, is based upon the author's thesis in partial fulfilment of the requirements for his Ph.D. degree at Purdue University.*

The work was done under the direction of Professor H. H. Remmers, in collaboration with ten industrial companies. Funds for the study were provided by the University.

The more technical description of the supervisory test and its construction may be obtained from the original article. Sample copies of the final test may be obtained from the Psychological Corporation, 522 Fifth Avenue, New York, N. Y.

HAVE YOU SPARE PERSONNEL JOURNALS?

Some issues of the Personnel Journal (as listed below) are required by reconverting industries, but are out of print.

If you have copies of these issues, which you are not now using, will you kindly return them to us, so that we may send them out to the companies requiring them. We will pay full price for them.

Vol. 23, No. 7. January, 1945.

Vol. 23, No. 9. March, 1945.

Personnel Research Federation
60 East 42nd St.,
New York, 17, New York

Appraisal of Mr. File's Study

By the Editor

MANAGEMENTS may not agree with the conclusions drawn by Mr. File from his study. But whether they do or not, the study is important because it throws some new light upon the supervisory problem.

That this problem continues to exist in an increasing manner is evidenced by foreman unionization tendency, by the increased labor tensions of the country, and by the reported reduction or lack of progress in worker output of today. More and more attention is given to the problem, but it often seems as if little progress is made in solving it because old concepts of foremanship, many of which are probably faulty, continue to dominate the thinking of management and training directors. The most serious points made in this study seem to be:

Management Does Not Know Its Good Men

THE fact that management, by its usual method of rating supervisors as to their work, completely fails to arrive at any reliable judgment as to who are its good supervisors, and who are its poor ones. It is therefore in complete ignorance as to the strength or weakness of its most important contact with workers.

We have long contended that this was true, and that all attempts to arrive, by rating, at any reliable judgment of supervisory performance having failed, the whole plan of rating should be discarded.

We hold that in every business and industry, there are objective records normally kept, which with due study can be used as the main basis of evaluating supervisory performance. We contend that the time that has been wasted in vainly trying to improve rating methods would, had it been devoted to developing and testing objective methods, have by this time really have gotten us somewhere in judging supervisors.

Reliable Records

RECORDS are available by supervisory unit, or can be developed, showing such matters as productive output, unit costs, amount of scrap, rejects by inspection department, accidents, absenteeism, labor turnover, training costs, hiring and training costs, grievances, complaints of customers, etc. A properly worked out composite of these items would, we contend, give a reliable picture of the quality of each supervisor, and give a sound basis for improvement of supervision by selection, training, transfer, etc. (These are the specific factors of supervisory quality. Their composite is probably the general factor. See below.)

There is an almost total lack of agreement among supervisors themselves as to what are the most important and crucial elements of good supervision (as revealed by their lack of agreement on best test items).

It is probable that this reflects the fact that managements have not worked out any well-defined or well-understood concepts of the supervisory function. Perhaps if they have, they have not made sure, in selecting supervisors, to pick those who reflect management's point of view.

Capricious and Differing Views

THE seriousness of this, from the point of view of efficiency and smooth worker relations, cannot be over-emphasized. Workers transferred from one department or job to another must readjust themselves to the differing emphases of different supervisors. These different viewpoints of supervisors present to workers a crazy-quilt pattern, having no basis other than the personal idiosyncracies of supervisors. In so far as workers get their impressions of management efficiency from their contacts with supervisors, the presence of this condition serves further to undermine workers' confidence in management as a well directed organization, that knows what it is about.

This affects not only workers transferred, but also the general aspect of worker thinking, because of the interchange of comment and experience among workers outside of working hours. It perpetuates an atmosphere of complaint and grievance, because of the sense of injustice arising out of differential treatment by different supervisors.

It gives ample scope for union officials to keep things stirred up, and to promise to set to right, or protect workers from the daily petty injustices of treatment by different supervisors—a protection much needed by workers, and one which, if provided by the union, strengthens the loyalty of workers to unions, meantime lessening the already weak loyalties of workers to managements.

The same comments apply to the lack of agreement among supervisors as to the correct answers to problems presented in the test. When supervisors were asked "What should be done. . .?" or "Is it desirable to. . .?", etc. their answers varied all over the map.

Does Test Measure Supervisory Ability?

WE DO not see that Mr. File has proved his point that "important aspects of industrial supervisory ability can be measured by test items". He has proved, within the limits of his study, that a set of questions relating to supervision can be developed, that a group of experts will agree that these cover important aspects of supervision, and that supervisors to whom these questions in a test form are put will show considerable variation in their ability to arrive at the same answers as the experts.

But this is a far cry from proving that this test measures actual supervisory quality or ability as shown on the factory floor. In fact, his exposure of the wide discrepancy between what management regards as important in supervision and what experts regard as important negates his conclusion.

Not until there are developed reliable objective measures of supervisory performance, enabling supervisors to be classified according to the quality of their supervision, and a test is found which classifies supervisors into the same or corresponding grades, can it be proved that the test measures supervisory quality.

Once this is done more reliance may be placed on the test, and less need arise for the maintenance of records of supervisory performance.

Is There a General Supervisory Ability?

WE DO not, for much the same reasons, think that Mr. File has proved his point that "general factors of supervision do exist". The fact that "industrial experts, both theoretical and practical, have rather clear-cut ideas about these general factors" proves nothing.

These general factors, if they exist, are nowhere defined in Mr. File's paper. There is much talk of the primary importance of mental-hygiene aspects, and that "supervisor-worker relations are among the key determinants of good or poor supervision," and a statement that "several indications of the validity of this hypothesis were found". But what are these general factors? Are they definable in exact terms? What are their limits? How do they relate to specific factors?

Mr. File has apparently taken over the concept of general and specific factors which was first investigated in theoretical psychology in regard to the measurement of intelligence—so called. In that theory, which has now been widely used, statistical methods were developed to show that there is a general factor of what may be briefly called reasoning ability.

Comparison with General Intelligence

SOME people possess more of it, others less. But you cannot expose your intelligence or reasoning ability except in specific ways. Thus the general factor of intelligence shows itself in working out arithmetic problems, in making up sentences, in judging distances, etc.

A person must have so much of this general intelligence factor before he can be successful in given ways. A person with high intelligence may use it in the specific occupation of his choice, such as an engineer, a doctor, etc. If he has but medium intelligence then he cannot succeed in these occupations, but may do well as a semi-skilled worker, a supervisor, or a clerk. With less intelligence he may be limited to unskilled work.

Mr. File has not used any such means to show a general factor or general factors of supervisory ability. We may grant the possibility of such general factors, without which a man can never be a good supervisor, or may do well as a supervisor in a limited capacity, or may be capable of becoming a first class supervisor or executive. But he has not proven this point.

Does Supervisory Test Measure only Intelligence?

As a matter of fact, in so far as intelligence is a well recognized limiting general factor, it is obvious that a dumb man cannot be a good supervisor. But Mr. File has not related the results of his test to the results of an intelligence test he might have given the supervisors. Further it would probably be found that his test is in large part merely a test of intelligence.

It is, in fact, certain that the ability of the supervisors to give correct answers to his questions was in large measure determined by their ability to understand the questions, and to reason from that understanding.

We conclude therefore that Mr. File's study is important in exposing some new considerations of considerable value in helpful industrial companies, and personnel research workers, to set seriously to work to improve supervision. We would advise caution in using the test until much further work has been done on it, to show that there are general factors of supervisory ability, and that these can be measured.

The Avoidance of Discrimination in Employment Practices Is Very Difficult. A Guide to
What May and May Not Be Considered Discrimination Is Contained in the Following
Excerpts from an FEPC Annual Report.

The Elimination
of Discrimination

By Fair Employment Practices Committee
Washington, D. C.

THE hearings held by the committee pursuant to paragraph numbered 5 of the Executive order which authorizes the committee to 'conduct hearings, make findings of fact, and take appropriate steps to obtain the elimination of dis-crimination' have resulted in the establishment of a body of interpretive principles. . . . Not all of the principles thus established have been included in the listing which follows.

For the sake of convenience the selected principles have been arranged under five classifications: discrimination by employers; discrimination by unions; defenses to charges of discrimination; directives; and enforcement. (Four classifications included here.)

DISCRIMINATION BY EMPLOYERS
Facts Which Do Not Establish Discrimination

THE fact that an employer hires no minority group workers or employs them only in small numbers may be considered by the committee in arriving at a determina-tion that such employer has discriminated against members of minority groups in their efforts to secure employment. However, the mere fact that no members of minority groups or few members of minority groups are employed in any specific plant does not, in itself, constitute sufficient evidence to justify a finding of dis-crimination. The committee has found discriminatory hiring practices to exist, however, when (a) a company hired no Negroes; (b) it contended, as justification, that 'certain skills were concentrated in certain nationalities'; and (c) the plant guard turned Negroes away at the gate pursuant to his function of determining 'what applicants [were] entitled to consideration for employment.'

2. The practice of an employer of requiring applicants for employment to state their race or religion, or both, on application forms, or otherwise, does not violate the provisions of the Executive order but is a factor which may be considered by the committee in arriving at a determination that the employer is discriminating against applicants for employment because of race, creed, color, or national origin. The committee may, however, direct the removal of such inquiries from application forms for employment where it finds, after hearing, that the employer has engaged in discriminatory hiring practices forbidden by the Executive order.

Facts Which Establish Discrimination

FACTS showing that it is the policy or practice of an employer to hire members of a minority group as laborers or in custodial work only, regardless of their particular skills, are adequate to support a finding of discriminatory employment practices forbidden by the Executive order.

2. When an employer recruits a substantial group of skilled workers from a technical school numbering Negroes and Jews among its students, but fails to employ any of the Negro students and hires a proportionately small number of Jewish students, the employer is engaged in discriminatory hiring practices forbidden by the Executive order.

3. Evidence that an employer has placed a personnel recruiting advertisement in a newspaper containing racial or religious specifications is adequate to support a finding of discriminatory employment practices forbidden by the Executive order.

4. Evidence that an employer has submitted to the United States Employment Service requests for workers containing racial or religious specifications is sufficient to support a finding that such employer has engaged in discriminatory employment practices forbidden by the Executive order.

5. The discharge of employees who refuse to salute the American flag or to stand during the playing of the National Anthem because of their religious convictions constitutes a discriminatory employment practice forbidden by the Executive order.

6. Evidence that an employer has expressed a 'preference' for employees of a particular race to subordinates entrusted with hiring responsibilities is sufficient to support a finding that such employer has engaged in discriminatory employment practices forbidden by the Executive order.

7. Evidence that an employer refused to hire a Negro craftsman on a war project unless he obtained a permit from a labor organization which barred him from membership on a parity with white craftsmen is sufficient to support a finding that such employer has engaged in discriminatory employment practices forbidden by the Executive order.

8. Evidence that an employer hires Negroes under a quota system which restricts employment to the approximate percentage of Negroes residing in the area is sufficient to justify a finding of discriminatory employment practices forbidden by the Executive order since the quota system operates to the disadvantage of individuals in both minority and majority groups by permitting considerations of race rather than those of qualifications and availability to operate. The use of the racial quota system to select employees for layoff purposes is likewise contrary to the Executive order even though it occasionally operates to the advantage of Negro employees and to the prejudice of white workers. The Executive order forbids discrimination against white as well as against colored employees.

DISCRIMINATION BY UNIONS

EVIDENCE that a labor organization subject to the jurisdiction of the committee bars Negroes from membership by practice, custom, tradition or other devices, rather than by written rule or constitutional provision is sufficient to justify a finding that such labor organization has engaged in discriminatory employment practices forbidden by the Executive order.

2. Evidence showing the existence of an agreement between an association of employers and a labor organization which prevents the employment or upgrading of qualified Negro workers on war projects, because of their race, is sufficient to justify a finding that both parties have engaged in discriminatory employment practices forbidden by the Executive order.

3. Evidence that a building trades union refuses to admit Negroes to membership and also refuses to permit Negroes to work on war construction projects so long as members of the union are unemployed is sufficient to justify a finding of discriminatory employment practices forbidden by the Executive order.

4. Evidence that a building trades union, composed entirely of white workers, opposes the employment of Negroes on war construction projects except on condition that the employer arrange to have whites and Negroes work on separate buildings is sufficient to justify a finding that the union has engaged in discriminatory employment practices forbidden by the Executive order.

5. Evidence that a union subject to the jurisdiction of the committee denies Negroes membership in its regular local but sets up an auxiliary organization for them, under which equal union rights and privileges are denied, is sufficient to justify a finding that such union has engaged in discriminatory employment practices forbidden by the Executive order if, in addition, it (a) has a closed-shop contract with the employer and (b) refuses to clear Negroes for employment or orders them discharged if they decline membership in the auxiliary while indicating a willingness to become members of the regular local.

6. Evidence that a union has construed its contract with an employer so as to bar its Negro members from employment in certain job classifications is sufficient to

justify a finding that such union has engaged in discriminatory employment practices forbidden by the Executive order. A finding of discriminatory employment practice in such a case is proper even when the contract is not discriminatory on its face.

DEFENSES TO CHARGES OF DISCRIMINATION

Agency

WHERE personnel officers or other hiring agents have clearly engaged in discriminatory employment practices, the committee will not sustain a defense by the employer that such personnel officers or other hiring agents were acting outside the scope of their authority. The committee has held that the prompt dismissal of an employment manager who refused to employ Negroes is a proper means of correcting such practices. However, where a company established that a request to the United States Employment Service specifying 'White Christian' workers was placed without the knowledge of any 'responsible' official, the committee directed that the charge and complaint be dismissed.

Partial Compliance

WHEN an employer is charged with failing to hire Negro women contrary to the Executive order, because of their race, it is no defense for him to show that he hires Negro men. Partial compliance is partial violation and any violation is forbidden by the Executive order.

2. The fact that an employer complies with the Executive order in certain of his plants is no defense to a charge of violation in his other plants although this fact may be considered by the committee in conjunction with all the other circumstances as bearing upon a determination of discriminatory employment practices.

Confession and Avoidance

THE contention by an employer that his white workers will refuse to work alongside Negroes is no defense to a showing that such employer has engaged in discriminatory employment practices forbidden by the Executive order, particularly where it appears that Negroes have been traditionally employed in the industry involved or in other war industries in the area.

2. The contention by an employer railroad that 'the community served . . . is made up of a dominant white citizenship in which Negroes are not permitted to exercise control over white people' and that consequently it cannot upgrade Negroes to positions in which they may be required to exercise authority over white workers, is entirely without merit.

3. An employer charged with discriminatory hiring practices under the Executive order cannot effectively set up as a defense the existence of a labor contract authorizing or requiring discrimination.

4. An employer charged with discriminatory hiring practices cannot set up as a defense that his contractual obligation with an employee's bargaining representative requires him to employ only union members under a closed shop contract when he is aware of the fact that the union does not accept Negroes except as members of an auxiliary which is different in union rights and privileges.

5. The contention of a labor organization that Negro building craftsmen refused to submit to an 'agreement' which would have permitted them to work only in Negro communities and then only on Negro buildings is not a valid defense to evidence showing that the union has refused to admit Negroes to membership and refused to permit Negroes to work so long as members of the union were unemployed.

6. When an employer has been duly notified that the committee will hold a hearing on charges brought against him but fails to be present or represented at the hearing, he cannot thereafter object to the findings and directives of the committee. The committee may, in such a case, issue findings and directives if the evidence adduced at the hearing establishes that the party charged has engaged in discriminatory employment practices forbidden by the Executive order.

DIRECTIVES

IN IMPLEMENTATION of its power 'to take appropriate steps to obtain the elimination of . . . discrimination' the committee may, after finding that a party has engaged in discriminatory employment practices, direct that it:

1. 'Cease and desist' from such practices;

2. Adjust its employment policies and practices so that all needed workers will be hired or upgraded without regard to race, creed, color, or national origin;

3. Extend in-plant training to all qualified employees without regard to race, creed, color, or national origin;

4. Issue formal instructions to all personnel officers and employees having authority to hire and upgrade workers, to carry on their activities in the recruiting, training, or upgrading of workers and prospective workers solely on the basis of the qualifications of workers or applicants for employment without regard to their race, creed, color, or national origin;

5. Give formal notice to all employment agencies, public or private, through which it recruits workers or trainees, that it will accept workers for all classifications of work or training, solely on the basis of their qualifications without regard to their race, creed, color, or national origin;

6. Submit monthly statistical reports revealing the classification of newly hired employees;

7. Abrogate wherever necessary provisions of existing contracts which are repugant to the policy expressed in the Executive order;

8. Submit periodic compliance reports;

9. Eliminate all questions as to race and religion from employment application forms.

We Have Some Examples in the United States of
Direct Government Operation at Federal, State
and Municipal Levels, Mostly of Utilities.   In No
Case Is There Wide Representation in Manage-
ment.   Nationalized French Industries Give a
Picture of What This Might Be Like.

Representation
in Management

As Decreed
By the Government of France

Two French Orders, of 16 January 1945 and 13 December 1944 respectively,
provided for the nationalisation of the Renault factories (automobiles) and of
the coalfields in the Departments of the Nord and Pas-de-Calais, and specified
that representatives of the staff were to be included in the agencies responsible for
administering the nationalised undertakings.   The composition and functions of
these agencies were defined in two Decrees, described below.

Administration of the National Renault Factories

A DECREE of 7 March 1945 governs the organisation and working of the National
Renault Factories and defines the respective functions of the President and
General Manager, the Governing Body, and the works committees, for whose
appointment provision had been made in the Order of 16 January.

The President and General Manager

THE President and General Manager of the undertaking is appointed by a Decree
issued on the recommendation of the Minister of Industrial Production after
consultation with the Minister of National Economy..   He is in charge of the general
direction of the undertaking and exercises, in addition to his administrative powers,
supervision over the entire staff.   He enters into individual contracts of employment
or collective agreements, and engages or dismisses members of the staff of every category, under the conditions prescribed in such contracts and agreements.   He also
acts as chairman of the Governing Body and the central works committee.

The Governing Body

THE Governing Body consists of the President and 15 other members appointed by order of the Minister of Industrial Production, as follows: two members designated by the Minister of Industrial Production, one of whom is to serve as vice-chairman; one member each designated by the Ministers of National Economy, Finance, Public Works and Transport, Labour and Social Security, and War; two members designated by agreement between the Minister of Industrial Production and the Minister of Public Works and Transport to represent users of motor vehicles; three representatives of manual workers; one representative of salaried employees and foremen; and two representatives on engineers and heads of services. The staff representatives are chosen by the Minister of Industrial Production from among the regular staff delegates to the central works committees.

Members of the Governing Body, with the exception of the President, are appointed as a rule for a term of six years, but one third of their number are renewed every two years reckoned from the date of the first appointment.

The Governing Body is convened by the chairman whenever its services are required and must meet at least ten times a year. It may also be called together under exceptional circumstances on the application of two thirds of its members. One half of its members constitute a quorum, and decisions are taken by the majority vore of those present; in case of equal voting, the chairman has the casting vore.

A record of the proceedings of each session, signed by the chairman, is first adopted by the Governing Body and then sent to the Ministers of Industrial Production, National Economy, and Finance.

Duties and Powers

THE main duties and powers of the Governing Body are as follows:

(1) Examination and approval, for each financial period, of production programmes and programmes of expansion or reconstruction;

(2) Approval of plans for the establishment of new factories or new branches of the undertaking;

(3) Preliminary examination and approval of estimates of income and expenditure;

(4) Examination and approval of the President's annual report to the Minister;

(5) Preliminary examination and approval, for each financial year, of the working account, the profit and loss account, the balance sheet for the previous year, and the proposed distribution of profits;

(6) Approval of long- and short-term loans, even if they do not imply giving security or mortgages, and previous approval of all issues of bonds;

(7) Approval of purchases and sales of real property and of the establishment of securities or mortgages;

(8) Approval of investments in other undertakings under conditions specified by the Order of 16 January 1945.

In case of disagreement between the Governing Body and the President, the latter may refer the matter to the Minister of Industrial Production, who will make a decision after consultation, if necessary, with the Minister of National Economy or the Minister of Finance.

The President will report to the Governing Body on all important developments in the general administration of the undertaking, the carrying out of production programmes, the development of capital goods, and the financial position.

Members of the Governing Body are pledged to professional secrecy.

Works Committees

THE Decree provides for the appointment of a central works committee attached to the general manager of the National Renault Factories, and a local works committee attached to the manager of the Mans factories of the undertaking.

The central works committee is composed of the President, or his representative, and a delegation of the staff, consisting of 11 titular delegates and 11 substitutes who will replace titular members when they are absent. The members of the staff delegation are appointed as follows: (1) five titular members and five substitutes from manual workers of the Boulogne-Briancourt factories; (2) one titular member and one substitute from the salaried employees of these factories; (3) two titular members and two substitutes from their supervisory staff; (4) two titular members and two substitutes from the engineering staff; and (5) one titular member and one substitute to represent the local works committee of the Mans factories.

The local works committee of the Mans factories is composed of the manager of the undertaking, or his representative, and a delegation of the staff consisting of five titular members and five substitutes, chosen as follows: two titular members and two substitutes from manual workers; one titular member and one substitute from salaried employees; one titular member and one substitute from the supervisory staff; and one titular member and one substitute from the engineering staff.

The duties and powers of the central and local works committees are substantially the same as those outlined in the Order of 22 February 1945 relating to works committees in general.

The procedure for electing, appointing, replacing, and dismissing representatives of the staff on the central and local works committees will be fixed by Decree.

ADMINISTRATION OF NATIONAL COALFIELDS

A DECREE of 4 May 1945 provides for the appointment of a President and General Manager, an Advisory Council, and works committees to administer the nationalised coal mines.

The President and General Manager

THE President is appointed by Decree of the Minister in charge of mines. He is assisted by five assistant general managers and a general secretary. He directs the working of all mines placed under the National Coalfields. In addition to his general administrative functions, he may conclude individual contracts of employment and collective agreements, appoint or dismiss any member of the staff (managerial, salaried, or wage earning), and fix their salaries, wages, remittances, bonuses and share of profits in accordance with the individual contracts and collective agreements and with the regulations in force.

The Advisory Council

THE Advisory Council attached to the President consists of 24 members: nine representing the State, eight the various categories of staff, five the coal consuming industries, and two the companies that formerly operated the mines.

The President is chairman of the Council and must keep it informed of the progress of work programmes, the results of operation, the conditions of work, and the financial position. He must also consult it concerning the issue of long-term loans, and proposals to set up new commercial or industrial establishments or new branches of the undertaking.

The President may refer to the Advisory Council, or its permanent executive, any question on which he thinks it useful to have its advice.

Works Committees

THE Decree provides for staff representation at three levels: local works committees in each pit or industrial undertaking; group works committees attached to the management of each group of mines, as defined by decision of the President; and a central social services committee attached to the general management of the National Coalfields.

Each local works committee is composed of the head of the undertaking and the engineers, on the one hand, and a delegation of the staff, on the other, consisting of: the miners' safety inspectors and the workers' delegates and their respective substitutes; representatives of underground and surface manual workers; and representatives of the supervisory staff.

Each group works committee consists, on the one hand, of the manager of the group of mines, or his representative, assisted by the heads of the principal services, and, on the other, of a delegation of the staff, which includes representatives of trade unions and of the miners' safety inspectors, the workers' delegates, the engineers, the supervisory staff, and the salaried employees, as well as representatives of the workers' members of the local works committees.

Finally, the central social services committee is composed of the President, or his representative, the director of social services, and a delegation of the staff, comprising three titular delegates and three substitutes from the manual workers; one titular delegate and one substitute from the supervisory staff; one titular delegate and one substitute from the salaried employees; one titular delegate and one substitute from the engineering staff; one titular delegate and one substitute each (from different categories of staff) appointed by each of the works committees set up in the different groups of mines.

The local and group works committees have the same rights and duties in the social and economic field as those conferred on works committees by the above-mentioned Order of 22 February 1945.

The central social services committee is required to co-operate with the President in the management of all social services established for the benefit of the staff of the National Coalfields or their families, irrespective of the method of financing the services.

(From International Labor Review, October, 1945)

References

Labour Gazette, May 1945, p. 620

Cf. *International Labour Review*, Vol. LI, No. 6, June, 1945: "Economic and Social Policy in France," by C. Bettelheim, pp. 732–733.

Cf. *International Labour Review*, Vol. LI, No. 6, June, 1945, p.770.

Journal officiel de la République française, 8 Mar. 1945, p. 1215.

Many Specialized and Technical Occupations Have Been Studied and Described by the War Manpower Commission, and Can Be Used as Guides to Those in and Seeking to Enter Different Professions.

The Profession *of* Personnel Administration

By National Roster of Scientific and Specialized Personnel

Washington, D. C.

PERSONNEL administration is that phase of management which is concerned with the effective use of human beings in an organized enterprise—business, governmental, educational, or social. It deals with the human relationships within the organization—the relationships between the worker and management, between the worker and his job, and between the worker and his fellow workers. By centering attention on the worker's well-being, morale, and capacity to produce, it increases the effectiveness of management.

Professional Workers

PROFESSIONAL workers in this field may: (a) act in an advisory capacity to management in formulation of policies with respect to employees (staff functions) and, or (b) they may have operational responsibility for carrying out personnel policies at various levels of operation (line functions). To attain these ends they must be familiar with the basic operations and purpose of their organization; they must provide for the full development of employees' interests and capacities; and they must utilize special methods and procedures that make the personnel aspect of management more precise and measurable.

Professional personnel workers are employed in business and industry, in government, and in schools and colleges. In industry and government they are generally concerned with the staffing of operating departments and agencies with competent, trained personnel and are thus responsible for the development and fulfillment of policies affecting recruitment, evaluation, selection, placement, training, transfer, discipline, job standardization and classification, rate setting, wage payment plans, counseling, grievances, health and safety, morale, labor relations, compliance with federal and state laws, separations, etc. In addition, they may be responsible for public relations by obtaining the understanding and support of the personnel program from management, employees, the legislative bodies, the press and the public.

In the government service, personnel work falls into three broad classes: civil service personnel management, military personnel work, and public employment service. In the public employment service, close contacts are made with private employers, schools, and community agencies in order to keep abreast of supply and demand in the labor market. In schools and colleges the personnel worker is generally a counselor and placement officer, serving students who are seeking either vocational guidance of a general nature, or specific help in obtaining employment.

Employer-Employee Relations

PERSONNEL workers here are concerned with procedures affecting employees during and outside of working hours; with formulation of a harmonious relationship between management and workers; with bringing problems and potential problems to the attention of management; and with the maintenance of records and reports. In industry this field is usually designated as union relations or labor relations. Elements involved are collective bargaining with employee representatives; arranging for mediation, conciliation and arbitration of disputes between management and labor; devising procedures for hearing and settling grievances; maintenance of discipline; preparation of efficiency or service ratings; counseling, such as vocational, psychiatric, or social.

Technicians also deal with the development and supervision of social and recreational programs, athletic groups, educational classes, cooperative cafeterias, credit unions, beneficial associations, group insurance plans, employee handbooks and magazines, and housing facilities. In most of these activities the personnel office may initiate action and give general guidance as well as provide facilities, but employees are encouraged to operate the projects themselves

Recruitment, Selection, and Placement

IN THIS area the technician is concerned with discovering and utilizing sources of labor; devising techniques for attracting applicants; setting up requirements for various positions; preparation of tests and testing techniques to determine intelligence levels, achievement, and aptitude. Psychological and statistical methods are employed in construction and validation of written, oral and performance tests. In the Government service (Federal, state, local), personnel workers set up eligible lists of job applicants, certify eligibles to requesting agencies, and check work performance during the probationary period. In appointment offices, in private industry, technicians analyze personnel needs, initiate recruitment, and make selections.

Placement involves finding the right job for the right man. Placement begins with the proper assignment of those newly selected and also covers all movement of personnel within a particular government agency or business establishment, whether it be promotion, transfer, detail assignment, demotion, follow-up, or reassignment. The placement of the physically handicapped is a specialized aspect of this activity.

Training

THE training technician seeks to cultivate ability, interest, and good-will among employees through an effective advisory leadership and improved on-the-job instruction. He must be acquainted with procedures and methods of induction and orientation; have a knowledge of work-methods and of the many techniques for training employees for their jobs; understand techniques for training supervisors, foremen, and apprentices; be familiar with special devices such as visual aids, the vestibule school, etc. He must be familiar with a wide variety of jobs and understand the principles of job analysis. He must be able to prepare courses of training and to apply the psychological principles of learning and incentives. He devises in-service training programs to improve the worker's ability to perform his job and to develop supplementary skills and abilities, and cooperates with schools and colleges in the development of educational programs for particular classes of occupations.

Position Classification and Pay Plans

POSITION classification involves making an analysis of individual positions as to duties, responsibilities, and qualifications requirements; the establishing of classes of related positions, and developing specifications for these classes; assigning the positions to the proper class and grade; and setting up rules for operating the classification system.

The technician sets up a pay plan upon the basis of the position-classification system. Such pay plans or schedules in private industry are generally based on a study of duties of a position, and with due regard to prevailing rates of pay for similar work in the community or industry. This frequently involves negotiations with union officials.

Separations

THE personnel worker here studies reasons why employees are separated from service and attempts necessary adjustments to retain those requesting releases. Separations may be due to voluntary resignation, lay-off, reduction in force for various reasons, dismissal for any reason, retirement for age or disability, and death. The technician develops uniform policies; utilizes the exit interview to determine individual reasons for leaving, to evaluate personnel policies and to create better understanding with employees; and studies the retirement systems of comparable agencies to develop an equitable system for his own agency.

Health and Safety

THE concern of personnel workers is with the working environment and the maintenance of adequate standards of health and safety of employees. Certain elements which are usually the province of the safety engineer may also be the concern of the personnel director. The goals here are to provide adequate medical and nursing facilities; optimal lighting and ventilating conditions; a minimum of unnecessary noise; clean, pleasant surroundings; first aid facilities; and protection of worker against accidents. The technician studies the causes of accidents on the job and conducts campaigns for the prevention of such accidents. He also analyzes absenteeism and sick leave records to discover means for eliminating unnecessary lost time.

Counseling

COUNSELING is now provided in educational institutions, in industry, and in government. In public school systems, the counselor is in an advisory capacity to the principal on vocational and disciplinary problems. In industry and government, he seeks better adjustment of the worker to his job by providing skilled advice on occupational, social and emotional problems. He usually possesses carefully prepared statistical data, validated psychological tests and personnel information.

Functional Specializations

PERSONNEL workers may specialize in any of the following:—

1. *Research:* in a phase of personnel administration, such as improvement of testing techniques or in efficiency ratings.
2. *Editing and Writing:* writing of reports, books, manuals, or articles on personnel matters, or editing journals of personnel administration, textbooks, house-organs or other employee publications.
3. *Consulting:* Personnel consultants are utilized in organization and planning, in classification and pay studies and in devising training programs.
4. *Teaching:* Personnel administration at the college level.
5. *Administration:* The management of personnel agencies or departments in government, industry, educational institutions, and other organizations.
6. *Statistical:* The use of statistical techniques in the maintenance of personal records, interpretation of surveys and studies, and in the construction of psychological tests.

Civil Service Ratings

RATINGS as personnel officer, director, technician, assistant; administrative officer, assistant; classification examiner, counselor, or training specialist are acquired as the result of examinations given by Federal, state, or municipal civil service commissions, and are indicative of the professional status of the person holding such positions.

Educational and Experience Qualifications

POSITIONS with the Federal service generally require the minimum of a bachelor's degree in personnel or public administration, or in psychology, or the equivalent of such education in experience at a professional level. Positions in the higher levels usually call for many years of experience in personnel work; a combination of such experience and a graduate degree in the field is also acceptable. Personnel workers in colleges usually have the master's degree in psychology, and frequently a Ph.D. is required. Industry varies in its requirements for professional personnel workers, but college training is becoming increasingly important. Personnel work in secondary schools is usually combined with teaching, so that on these levels, requirements for teachers must be met; i.e., a college degree with certain credits in education. In various aspects of personnel it is highly desirable that the professional workers be trained not only in personnel administration but also in the broad fields of business management, public administration, safety engineering, economics, statistics, psychology and political science. Only thus can the perspective and insight necessary in this field be gained.

Related Non-Professional Occupation

THERE are a number of occupations related to personnel work which are at a non-professional level; personnel record clerk, reviewer of personnel forms, payroll clerk, coding clerk and interviewer.

Alternate Titles and Related Fields

THE term "personnel administration" is sometimes limited to a narrow sense to recruiting, hiring, training and placement, and the term "industrial relations" or "labor management" is sometimes used in a broad sense for the entire employment relationship. Professional workers in personnel are referred to by various titles: employment manager; personnel director, supervisor, officer; training director; classification analyst; placement analyst; labor manager, personnel technician, etc.

Personnel workers draw upon the resources and tools of many fields, such as: psychology, public administration, statistics, economics, safety engineering, social welfare and management. Individuals in any of these fields may transfer into the field of personnel administration, and personnel workers themselves may transfer into the broader fields of management or public administration.

Sources of Employment

PERSONNEL workers are employed in nearly all industries and types of business enterprise, in government, and in schools and colleges.

At Various Times in Their Working Lives Many
Workers Seem to Reach Plateaus in Their Prog-
ress and Have Great Difficulty in Breaking
Through to Resume Their Upward Progress.
Seldom Do Companies Regard Aid in This
Matter One of Their Functions.

Stuck *at* Thirty-five

By Correspondent

(To The Editor, Personnel Journal:)

VOLUME 23 Number 9 of PERSONNEL JOURNAL contained an article by Mr.
Ellsworth S. Grant that interested me very much. It was titled "Let the
Foreman Manage". I read it through a number of times and then discussed
it with a number of fellow workers. For the past three years the subject matter in
this article has been on our tongues day in and day out. The article put into
plain and concise language just about all of the things we have been "hashing over".

Group of College Men

WE ARE a group of college trained men who started work at the bottom of the
pile and after going through a training program of about 6 to 10 years we have
finally been placed by management in positions varying from Foreman (12 million
dollar outlay on equipment and 100 men) of production units to engineering consultant work, and my own particular assignment of assistant industrial manager. Our
plant is a large one, better than 2000 men, and is an important part of one of the
largest industries in the country, i.e., oil.

While we were going through the mill we worked shift work, did all the assignments eagerly, and in general tried to emulate Horatio Alger at his best. Now that
we have all gotten more or less "good" positions we ask management, "Where do we
go from here?". They stare at us blankly and tell us how much we mean to the
company, and stalk off in great fear. We bring up the subject again and they get
slightly annoyed. After a bit we are on the well known list and are definitely
persona non grata from there in.

The article hits the foremen in our group right in the eye. They are fed up being told how good they are—typical quotes "You foremen are some pumpkins", "Part of Management", etc., but the whole thing is lip service and nothing more. A number of us have diplomatically brought this to the general manager's attention but each time we are rebuffed. We know that the men at the top of the organization are fair and broad minded and would be willing to listen, but in a number of instances where members of the group have gone above the general manager they have been slapped down because "they hadn't gone through channels".

Some of us have thought that we merited more money. We have asked for frank discussions of our worth to the company and have been put off with all sorts of nonsense. Salaried folk seem to be in the "hush hush" class, and as long as they have been given good titles they should feel grateful to have the job. One instance of this is that our foremen are salaried men and are on a 24 hour basis. They work all kinds of hours and get no compensation whatsoever.

The men working for them in many cases make more money than the boss. The labor rate is well over a dollar an hour and the first class mechanic rates are half again as much. Some of the shops work their men 11 hours a day 6 and 7 days a week when necessary. The foreman comes in and gets nothing for it.

How to Better Conditions

Now the problem is this. How would you advise us to go about bettering this condition without incurring the wrath of that all powerful tin god management? We are not interested in unionization but in due time we would be forced to it or to quitting and looking elsewhere for work. The first thing is distasteful to us because our abilities and sympathies lie with executive management by whom and for whose use we have been trained. We are trained and ready, but no definite path is open to us. The second alternative is also distasteful because we have 10 years or more service and the pension plan of the company is excellent and many of us believe strongly in this company.

The group I talk about consists of college men from about a dozen different technical colleges and universities from as many parts of the country. Our interests and ideas are diversified by this fact but we all feel very strongly about the above. Could you help us in any way? If so we would appreciate it very much.

(A Correspondent)

EDITORIAL REPLY

THE supervisory or junior executive problem exposed in the above letter is, we suspect, much more common in large industrial companies than they are ordinarily aware of. Hence we think it merits considerable discussion. In general there are two aspects; what the management can do; and what the employee can do.

In one sizable company the matter came up rather dramatically when it was found that three of its junior executives had committed suicide in one year—work situations at least contributing to the unbearable tensions leading to the suicides, or suspected of doing so. This was brought to the attention of the company president by an interested outsider.

This led to the setting up of a plan by which all supervisors were interviewed by their immediate bosses to try to find out the extent to which the men were dissatisfied with their jobs, their working relations, and their prospects.

Little direct result came from this, for few men would admit to their bosses that they had dissatisfactions. Of three out of 1600 men who did, two were transferred and one quit. The company was inclined to let it go at that, some executives—particularly the interviewing ones—thinking that the result proved that men were well satisfied.

Supervisory Counseling

However, the top executives were less complacent, and when last heard from had inauguated a plan of employee counseling, at the supervisory level, somewhat similar to the Western Electric plan for hourly rated employees.

This is one solution to the problem from both the management and employee angle—if properly carried out. For in one operation it appraises management of the feeling of its men; informs them of the specific problems existing, pointing to matters of general policy that require improvement; shows the specific problems of individual employees requiring transfer or other treatment; and gives an opportunity of advising individual employees with special problems as to how they may get out of the *cul de sac* in which they apparently find themselves.

Unfortunately such programs cannot be undertaken or started unless top executives are sold on the necessity of them, even for exploratory reasons. They cannot be sold by the junior executives, such as our correspondent—or had better not be. Either a wide-awake personnel officer, or some outsider must do the job.

Multiple Management Plan

The next possible way out is for management to set up or try out some plan such as the Multiple-Management idea described by Charles P. McCormick in a book by that title published by Harper & Bros. in 1938. A discussion of this plan appears under the title "Junior Executive Boards" in the November 1937 issue of the Personnel Journal.

Briefly under this plan executives at different levels are organized into advisory boards, with powers of recommendation regarding all operating and marketing problems and policies to the next higher level, and with the responsibility of each level to inform the lower board of the action taken on recommendations.

This, on paper, is an excellent idea. How it has worked out in practice during the years we do not know, but the information could be obtained through the publishers of the book, presumably. (Address Editor, Business Books, Harper & Bros., 49 E. 33, New York, 16, N. Y.)

Such a plan might be suggested to a top executive in a company such as that of our correspondent, by a group of junior executives, and might receive sympathetic consideration, if they took the trouble to examine the matter thoroughly, and work up fairly definite plans for the executive before presenting them. Even if he did not accept the plan *in toto*, it would at least form the basis of an intelligent discussion of the Junior Executives' problems with him.

Pyramid Conference Plan

A PERHAPS less formal plan, which requires no great change in relationships is the so-called pyramid conference plan, which though not called by that name, is fairly common in industry. Under this arrangement the top executive meets periodically with those reporting immediately to him. Then, as exemplified in an operating vice-president or general manager, a regular meeting is held each Monday with the divisional superintendents to discuss plans for the week, proposals for the future and progress of past approved plans, and difficulties encountered in carrying them out.

Immediately after, each divisional superintendent meets with his next lower level of executives and holds similar discussion with them regarding such points brought up in the higher executive meeting as are of direct interest to them, and in the implementation of which they must play their part.

These lower level executives, who would generally be at the higher supervisory levels, then take up matters discussed with their individual subordinates, and discuss them with them. Frequent or infrequent meetings of lower supervisory and technical groups are held as found necessary.

Keeps Organization Well Coordinated

THIS plan serves to keep an organization well coordinated, and gives all levels an opportunity of having their say in what is being done. It stimulates new ideas, and points up the men who are most capable of promotion.

Generally such a plan as this can be sold to top executives by the personnel officer, particularly if he is that rare bird, a student of organization problems. In our experience, one of the things that a top executive will always be interested in, and spend time discussing, is his organization of executives and their functions, provided it is carried out by someone who does not have some particular axe to grind.

The increasing technical knowledge required of foremen and junior executives in modern industry has created situations such as that described by our correspondent. College graduates have been hired for these positions in increasing numbers, but the technology requirements have been such that while a fairly large number of these men are needed up to a certain level, the number required above that level is sharply restricted.

Squat Bottle with Long Neck

HENCE, in a company requiring much technical skill, the normal pyramid structure of less technical companies, or departments such as sales and distribution, does not obtain. Instead there appears an organization structure which in contour resembles a squat bottle, with sharp shoulders and a long narrow neck.

In this situation, while there are fairly frequent opportunities for employment of graduates of technical institutions—more so than previously—there are very few opportunities for advancement to higher levels. The very competence of high levels of supervisory employees and junior executives reduces the number of higher level executives necessary to supervise and direct their work. Hence promotional opportunities quickly become rare, and most of the men become stuck for life at the level they reach after ten years of service.

Men Become Stuck

THIS situation is becoming more common, but only a few companies seem to be aware of its effect on the morale of their men, and few of the technical men going into these industries with fairly rosy immediate prospects realize where they are going to be stuck just when their wives, generally ambitious college girls, develop social ambitions, and have an acute problem of the expense of child education.

The problem is aggravated by the fact that the development of new or improved processes, and new products, does not come out of the operating departments, but from such special departments as engineering methods or research. New ideas from operating men are frequently not encouraged or even frowned upon, and opportunities for promotion, and a sustained interest in the job are frustrated for them.

Where companies have vaguely recognized the repercussions of this situation, they have sought to deal with it in their hiring of technical men. They have adopted a policy of hiring, as far as they were able to select correctly, only those men whose scholastic records and personalities indicated that they were little above average in ability or ambition, and would not become dissatisfied or cause difficulties for the company by wanting promotions at a rate beyond the ability of the company to grant, under the organization structure existing.

Top-notch Men Excluded

IN UTILITIES and oil companies we have seen top-notch graduates of engineering colleges turned down because they were too good. Of course, a company adopting such a policy makes some mistakes and does let through the hiring screen some few men of high competence, who are sufficient to get the few higher jobs that become available.

While such a policy is realistic from a short term point of view, it has four objectionable features. (1) It condemns to a life of mediocrity men who might do much better in other occupations or industries. Where a pension plan exists it helps to tie a man to an almost intolerable life of bondage. (2) It clutters up the operating organization with a group of conservative unprogressive supervisors and executives who will continually buck and oppose the introduction of up-to-date manufacturing processes developed by engineering and other technical specialists. (3) It keeps on the payroll men with high seniority who are not adaptable, particularly when old lines of products are discontinued, and new lines requiring new processes and methods are introduced. (4) Where problems of contact with the public are concerned it damages the public relations of the company seriously. At almost every party discussion, someone is always ready to open up the subject of their infuriation at the dumbness of some utility employee with whom they have had to deal.

Better to Hire Representative Group

A MUCH more realistic plan would be to set up a hiring policy for technical men by which a representative group from colleges would be hired containing some top-notchers and some of lesser ability, and then set up a transfer and promotion policy by which men could gain different experiences in the company, and have wider opportunities for promotion. This would involve unified hiring, in which men would be interchangeable between the operating, sales and specialized departments.

This might mean that men would be required to serve an appropriate period in operations and then, if showing promise be transferred to specialized departments. This would have an additional advantage in that the specialists would have more knowledge of manufacturing processes, so that their proposals for new methods and products would have a greater and more immediate practical value.

Elevator Riders

IN ONE company visited the operating vice-president complained of the fact that his men from the engineering design department seem to spend most of their time riding up and down the elevators from their offices on the top floor to the production lines below, to consult with the operating people as to the practicality of their designs.

The company put in a suggestion system, and was amazed at the number of practical suggestions that came from all ranks of operating people as to improvements and short cuts in manufacturing methods.

This he saw as evidence of the wonderful helpful spirit of the operating employees. He was amazed when we gently suggested that it was probably due to the fact that, in spite, or perhaps because of, the elevator riding habits of his engineering design people they did not know enough about his manufacturing processes and products to properly design the machines and methods for them.

When we left him last he was considering shifting the specialized departments down on to the manufacturing floors. A much better plan would be to set up a realistic hiring, transfer and promotion policy.

Self-help of College Men

Such a plan calls for a degree of self-help on the part of the technical men in operations, which is quite pertinent to the problem of our correspondent. Whether aided and guided by the company or not, a technical man must keep up his studies, either by attending classes or by reading or attending meetings, so that he better fits himself for his present job, as well as preparing himself for promotion either in his own department or company or elsewhere.

A man who carries out such a program of his own volition must, sooner or later, unless he has personality disqualifications, come to the attention of his or other companies and obtain merited promotion or transfer to a more satisfying occupation. Even if he is unfortunate and does not get early recognition, he will at least fill his life with something of great personal satisfaction to himself.

The post-graduate studies of a technician need not be confined to his own speciality. In one case we know of, an industrial chemist, feeling himself stuck after ten years with a company, interested himself in training, labor relations and other personnel matters. As a consequence he is now a successful general manager of a plant in another company.

Studies of Federal Men

Personnel men in the Federal service are an outstanding example of this. Even before the expansion of opportunities during the war.

Most of them were pretty inexpert and home-grown when they started, but a personnel administration society was formed in Washington, and these men flocked to it, not only to listen to speeches, but to attend serious study groups on particular problems. They thus got to so improve themselves, that, though under civil service regulations, promotion other than by the process of time passing is almost impossible to get, they opened up promotional opportunities for themselves that would ordinarily have been thought impossible.

Beefing-fest of Personnel Men

This is in distinct contrast to the way most industrial personnel men operate. At a recent annual meeting of such men at a well known university they let loose and indulged in a beefing-fest in which they blamed all the labor troubles of the country on the fact that their bosses, top executives, would not listen to their personnel and labor relations recommendations.

In discussing this phenomenon with one of the maligned $100,000 a year bosses we could see much merit in his statement that, while personnel men often come up with recommendations for change in policy, most of the time their recommendations showed lack of study and appreciation of all the factors involved, and their possible consequences. Thus while they recommended that things be done differently, they failed to convince that these would be any better than methods currently in use.

In short, the boss was disgusted, not because the personnelers put up implied criticisms of his policies, constructive and otherwise, but because their recommendations showed that they had such a poor grasp of the subject matter in which they were supposed to be and claimed to be specialists.

We cite this example from the personnel field, because we think it often applies in the technical engineering field. Our correspondent gives no evidence that he and his associates who wish to participate in the management of their company have anything worthwhile to contribute.

Participants Should Qualify

WHILE appreciating to the full, for many reasons, the desirability of lower ranking employees participating to a greater extent in company operations, we feel that those wishing to participate should show their qualifications for so doing.

In the industrial field we cite two examples, which prove nothing but illustrate the point. In one department we visited it was obvious that there was plenty of waste motion. We discussed this with the foreman in charge, who belly-ached about it. Consulting higher-ups we found that plans to redesign the whole department had been worked out by the engineering methods department, they thought the bugs had been taken out of these plans, and were going to put them in at the first appropriate opportunity.

As the policy of the conpany was, in general, not to introduce new methods, which involved the reduction of the number of employees in a department unless and until there was opportunity for their employment in some other expanding department, they were awaiting this turn of events.

Company Policies Misunderstood

IN VIEW of the unsettlement of employees, if they were informed too early of their impending transfers, and of the fact that the foreman himself would have to leave the department, management decided not to say anything about it until the appropriate time came. Thus the foreman had to be left to beef, and any suggestions he had to make, in view of his limited knowledge of the whole picture, had to be politely but firmly turned down.

In another case a young industrial engineer became very restless because the company refused to accept his recommendation that a conveyor system be installed in a department. The company was what might be called tough, and instead of telling the young enthusiast that their engineering methods department had thoroughly explored this matter years before and found it impracticable, let him carry on till he quit in disgust.

The moral of all these stories is that men who wish to participate in management problems must know their stuff thoroughly, and must realize that they often see only a segment of a problem. Management, on the other hand, is foolish if it does not give consideration to employee ambitions and motives of helpfulness and help them to a broader understanding. These are not so easy to deal with as they seem at first glance. The only methods we know which begin to approach this problem are described above.

Too Much Tied to Job

AGAIN dealing with the problem of our correspondent, we have long thought that, apart from pay matters, there is far too much tendency for hourly rated employees and supervisors to center the whole of their lives around their jobs. Hence when they are blocked back, perhaps temporarily, in their jobs they quickly lose heart, become emotional, and in some cases suffer nervous breakdowns. Their lives become so limited that they lose all sense of proportion, fail completely to properly understand the motives and problems of their employers, and stifle their own latent wishes for self-improvement through their own efforts.

Participation in external activities, such as social work, politics, church matters, avocations (gardening, carpentry, inventions, etc.), hobbies, studies of biography, art, music, etc., all help to fill out life, and make up for inevitable disappointments in the work situation. They aid in the development and rounding out of a well-balanced point of view.

Tough Spot

PERHAPS our correspondent and his associates will be disappointed in our discussion of his and their case. Admittedly they are in a tough spot, and we should hate to be similarly placed (and should hate to be the bit boss of a company that remained in ignorance of or indifferent to their situation). But they have to get out of it themselves, and unquestionably if they are able or lucky enough to find the way they will have benefited by their experience.

Book Reviews

Book Review Editor, Mr. Everett Van Every

California Personnel Management Association, San Francisco, Cal.

GROUP HEALTH INSURANCE AND SICKNESS BENEFIT PLANS IN COLLECTIVE BARGAINING

By Helen Baker and Dorothy Dahl. Princeton, N. J. Princeton University. 1945.
89 pp. $1.50

Foreword by J. Douglas Brown

Compared to the progress made in providing protection against unemployment and dependent old age during the last decade in the United States, our progress in attacking insecurity due to illness has been meagre, spotty and timid. A nation which can outproduce the world in waging two great wars at once seems strangely incapable of working out an effective social mechanism to protect and care for the few million people who become sick from week to week. The genius of American industry has created great urban centers in which millions are dependent on weekly wages. But the genius of American statesmanship and of the American medical profession have failed to assure adequate, timely and self-respecting medical care to great segments of our people.

It is not surprising, therefore, that the American labor movement has felt obligated to seek through the means of collective bargaining that protection during illness which the government seems unable to assure. In the absence of governmental action, a large number of progressive employers have developed sickness benefit and medical care programs for their employees. These have usually existed in companies fully aware of the mutual advantage of financial security and good health in industrial relationships. Many trade unions have made valiant efforts to establish and operate sick benefit schemes on a local or national basis financed by member assessments alone. Without strong financial backing and expert administration, most of these schemes have faced serious difficulties from the outset. In sharp contrast to similar developments elsewhere, neither employers nor trade unions in the United States have had any real assistance from government in these worthy endeavors. In far too many instances, the organized medical profession has fought bitterly any departure from century-old individualistic business practices.

Unwilling to depend upon employer initiative and sponsorship and increasingly discouraged by inaction in Congress, a number of national unions have more recently included demands for employer financing of sickness benefit schemes among those for improved wages and working conditions. The national war-time policy of wage stabilization has encouraged this trend, but underlying it has been the concern for security in time of illness which has pervaded all associations of wage earners since the Industrial Revolution. The arrangements proposed and established under joint company-trade union benefit plans are worthy of careful study. They have been analyzed in the following pages. Even more important for the employer, the trade union leader, and the American citizen is the earnest consideration of the question, is this the best way to assure protection in time of illness to all our people?

Nature abhors a vacuum. If the American wage earner needs self-reliant health protection, and needs it badly, sooner or later he will get it. If employers and trade unions acting alone fail to cover the vast majority of people, perhaps, acting jointly through collective bargaining, they will cover a wider group. But if schemes arising out of collective bargaining are complicated, difficult to administer, uncertain and inadequate, the only alternative remaining seems to be an effective governmental system of health insurance. Perhaps experimentation under joint voluntary programs will convince all parties to these experiments of the necessity of government action.

This report is an excellent one covering a survey of current American practice in this field, and should be on the shelves of every labor relations man concerned with collective bargaining, and health problems in industry and business. It may well be studied, for comparative purposes, along with the description of Australian policies described in the December, 1945 issue.

Contents include: union experience with sickness benefits, union aims in this matter, employer attitudes. Plans developed through collective bargaining, specific programs sought by unions, existing company benefit plans that have been liberalized. Major policies and problems in plans studied, determinations of benefits and financial arrangements, problems presented by layoffs, relationship of private group insurance, the future of group sickness insurance, and sample health insurance plans arising out of collective bargaining.

PERSONNEL

Journal

The Magazine of

LABOR RELATIONS AND PERSONNEL PRACTICES

Published by PERSONNEL RESEARCH FEDERATION

Lincoln Building, 60 East 42nd Street, New York City

Volume 24   *Number 8*

Contents for February 1946

EDITORIAL BOARD

A Personnel Department Must Be Skilled in 3
Ways. It Must Know What the Personnel
Problems of Management Are and Give an Ac-
curate Factual Picture of Them: It Must Design
and Administer Programs to Minimize Them:
It Must Continually Evaluate Their Effects.

Personnel Work
on The Grill

By D. A. Stewart and D. J. Bolanovich,
Radio Corporation of America,
Camden, N. J.

In the September, 1945 issue of *Personnel Journal*, Mr. H. G. Heneman described
the necessity for accurate appraisal of the results of personnel work if personnel
is to function as an arm of management. He touched briefly on the use of statistics for this purpose. The writers recently participated in a series of meetings under
the sponsorship of the American Statistical Association which were devoted to
statistical problems of personnel administration. All participants in these meetings
would undoubtedly have seconded Mr. Heneman in his comments. However, the
place of statistics in personnel work needs to be brought into a more proper perspective.

Personnel Work Must Be Accurate

Personnel administration is a dynamic function of management. To exist as
such it must be intelligent and objective in all phases of its operations. As a
part of management, the personnel department must be skilled in three ways: (1)
It must determine what the personnel problems of management are, and present an
accurate factual picture of these problems; (2) It must formulate and administer
programs designed to minimize these problems; and (3) It must continually evaluate
programs to show their effects on the problems. Unless the personnel department
does all these things, the personnel executive does not deserve a seat at the management table.

All these operations are accomplished with the aid of pertinent factual information
gleaned from appropriate company records. For example, the personnel department

is concerned with production records, quit and discharge rates, labor market statistics, costs of distribution and overhead, wage and salary rates, etc. It is in terms of these records that personnel problems are identified and personnel procedures evaluated.

Without understanding of the meaning and implication of these records, personnel problems may be misrepresented, personnel programs misdirected, and personnel work incorrectly evaluated. The understanding of these records is accomplished through statistical analysis. Arithmetic and even cost accounting methods can be uneconomical, and can result in erroneous and misleading conclusions; whereas statistical treatments of data save unproductive effort, point up appropriate interpretations to be made from records, and define the amount of confidence that can be placed in arithmetic and cost accounting figures.

Identification of Personnel Problems

PERSONNEL problems should not be determined by arbitrary opinion that problems exist, but by an analysis of facts indicating such problems. However it is not uncommon to find personnel departments strenuously trying to find and correct causes of turnover, quits, or absenteeism, or instituting new placement or training programs in the absence of any problem in these areas whatsoever.

As an example, one plant of a company showed what appeared to be a quit rate much in excess of its other plant. The first reaction of the company was to call this to the attention of the plant manager and institute a program to reduce quits. However, simple statistical analysis of the quit rates showed that the plant with a high quit rate also had a high proportion of female hourly workers, a group which is characteristically higher in turnover than other employees. When quit rates were adjusted for proportions of hourly and salary, male and female workers, the difference in quit rates between the plants was not significant at all.

Quality Control Charts

CONVERSELY, we might cite a case where statistical analysis led to immediate identification of sources of high turnover. A plant whose turnover rate was very high was to be analyzed for causes of turnover. The methods for discovering causes and trying to correct them could have run into elaborate analysis of termination records and surveys of the plant. Instead figures were compiled showing the percentages of turnover in each department.

Here is where statistics came in—personnel statisticians, borrowing a very handy technique from their quality control contemporaries, set these percentages up on a quality control chart. The control limits, which are based on expected chance fluctuations, immediately showed those departments which were significantly high or low in turnover rate. Personnel department representatives talked with supervisors of these departments and discovered readily that the two low departments had excellent orientation and training procedures, while those high in turnover never realized the importance of close employe-supervisor relationships. The cure was a training program to educate the latter supervisors in better relations techniques.

Incidentally, quality control charts have much to offer in the way of identifying personnel problems and evaluating programs. Their unique contribution is that they show immediately when significant changes occur. Control charts of production records, turnover rates, absenteeism, etc., can be used to indicate when changes occur which warrant investigation and corrective action. They have been applied to accident frequencies, overtime hours worked, and efficiency records to the writers' knowledge as well as to the turnover records cited above. (*Control Chart Method of Controlling Quality During Production*, Z1.3–1942. American Standards Association, 29 W. 39th Street, New York.)

Correlation and multiple correlation techniques are additional aids to uncovering and analyzing personnel problems. These are used often in placement programs. For instance, let us say that sales records show that in a similar group of salesmen some are very successful and some are failures. A placement problem exists, and is minimized by discovering the factors responsible for this difference and by making changes in placement methods. First correlation methods point out which factors are related to good performance. Then multiple correlation methods show which of these factors are interrelated and which are most important. Placement procedures then are adapted to give more attention to important factors responsible for success as a salesman.

Similarly these techniques have been applied to study the assignment of weights to job evaluation and merit rating factors and to determine the proportionate amount they contribute to the value of a job or an employee. To evaluate the importance of such factors in placement, job evaluation, and merit rating by "expert opinion" or guesswork can lead to results actually contrary to those sought.

Administration of Personnel Programs

THE need for statistical information and procedures in the administration of personnel programs is obvious to one having a knowledge of statistics and working close to personnel activities.

The area of employment is a fruitful vineyard for improving operations through the application of statistical procedures. Simple analysis of the sources of applicants may very possibly reduce recruiting costs. Figures kept on the number of applicants per month give an understanding of how high selection standards may be set in hiring applicants. In fact few companies have ever considered the application of selection standards. The Army Air Corps has shown that a simple weighting of a few personal history items was very effective in selecting pilots, navigators, and bombardiers. Industry has had similar experience in selecting salesmen, and there is reason to believe that it can be extended to other occupations.

Complex Statistical Treatment

ALTHOUGH such selection standards are extremely simple to use, their development involves fairly complex statistical treatment. Also in the employment area is the use of psychological tests. Competent psychologists are justly dismayed at the flagrant abuse of tests in industry, most of which is due to ignorance of statistical operations and inferences necessary or deliberate neglect of them. On the other hand many companies through intelligent use of statistical data have demonstrated dramatically the value of psychological tests.

The rôle of statistics in the formulation of good industrial wage and salary structures is important. Any skilled wage and salary administrator is aware of the dependence of this work on statistical know-how. Personnel circles are frequently witnesses to tales of thousands of dollars lost through unwise manipulation of wage curves by untrained wage administrators. One can probably infer that many such cases are not even recognized. Sound company wage structures are built around factual information concerning industry, area, and company practices. Statistical measures of relationship are important tools in the intelligent interpretation of this information.

Job Evaluation and Merit Rating

THE field of job evaluation is only too little understood today. Much of its technique is of the type that should require multiple correlation applications. This is not to imply that through such applications any magic formulae can be developed. Rather there is a need for practical interpretation of information gained through statistical analysis. Merit rating is a closely allied field of personnel operations which continues to confuse its users with problems that are properly in the bailiwick of statistics.

Another phase of personnel operations which requires a better understanding through statistical examinations of its data is training. Few companies today understand what is being accomplished through training. Industry could borrow from our educational procedures in clearly formulating objectives of training and means of measuring the achievement of these objectives. As a matter of fact industrial objectives should be easier to formulate and measure since they are mostly in terms of specific skills and knowledge. The needs for and accomplishments of industrial training should be determined as far as possible through examination of such records as graded quality inspections, amount of production, learning times and curves, and other objective measures of knowledge and skills.

Personnel research, which pilots personnel operations in identifying problems and developing methods is dependent in large measure upon statistics to maintain itself as a field of scientific inquiry. Experimentation is a prime tool of scientific research. The multiplicity of forces—economical, psychological and sociological—acting in personnel research problems makes statistical methods of experimental design a prerequisite to intelligent experimentation. Sampling procedures used by the statistician can affect great economies in personnel research studies, and the ability to interpret results intelligently is needed to avoid costly mistakes. Everyone, of course, is familiar with the faulty sampling procedures of the late *Literary Digest* straw vote polls and their results in the election of 1932.

Employee Attitude Surveys

O NE might also examine the use of employee attitude surveys, sometimes applied to indicate company-employee relations. To our knowledge, no method has yet been devised for interpreting the results of such attitude surveys. The extent to which the conditions under which surveys are made either prejudices answers or elicits truthful responses is not known. Psychologists would agree that they could have great influence. Technical experts in the U. S. Bureau of Census have pointed out that the manner of asking questions makes a difference in the answer received, and suggested that the Bureau correct its records for the type of bias which will result. ("Report from the Committee on Quality Control," April 1, 1944, United States Department of Commerce, Bureau of the Census, Washington.) Yet some companies will poll their employees with an elaborate questionnaire, tabulate the results arbitrarily, and smugly sit back and say, "This is a darn good company; 98% of our employes are happy and contented with their work."

The field of employe relations suffers also from the need of statistical thinking. It has already been mentioned how methods can be applied to judge the effects of employee relations policies on such significant records as turnover and absentee rates and production records. It is very possible that from such records an "employee relations index" could be composited whose fluctuations from month to month would act as a thermometer registering the effects of the company's personnel practices on its personnel. But the development of such an index, and the interpretations of its fluctuations is a difficult statistical job, since it must be composed of several variables and will be affected by both controllable (company practice) and uncontrollable (general business conditions, social-political events) factors.

Evaluation of Personnel Practices

T HE field of evaluation should be one of the most important for statistical applications. In fact evaluation implies some method of quantitative measurement. Personnel, dealing as it does with the elusive human factor, is inclined to assign the job of measurement to the realm of impossibility. It has been pointed out here, however, that personnel work receives its direction and operates in terms of certain types of quantitative records. Consequently, its appraisal can be made in terms of resulting modification of these records. For example, if personnel research reveals that workers on a job vary greatly in the amount they produce, and selection and training programs are operated to bring the production level up to that of the best workers, then appraisal of the personnel program is in terms of measurable amounts of increased production against measurable additional expenses of the selection and training programs.

Cost Accounting

ON THE surface it seems that such evaluations are largely accomplished by good cost accounting as Mr. Heneman pointed out. This is not entirely true. The cost accounting can be no more reliable than the arithmetic figures given the cost accountant. Neither the best arithmetic measures nor the best techniques of cost accounting give an adequate picture. The application of statistical analysis to these figures gives them significance. Take our production workers in the previous paragraph. Suppose that figures showed the average daily production per worker after the selection and training program has operated for a year to be 100 units higher than before. Suppose that also careful cost accounting showed the net monetary return as a result was $4,000 in excess of the cost of the program. The immediate reaction is that the personnel program instituted has been profitable and justifies continuance.

Now turn these figures over to a statistician. His first reaction would probably be to test the significance of the difference of 100 units per day per worker. That is, if the workers usually produced a large number such as 2000 units a day and varied considerably from day to day, the difference might be a chance occurrence. The statistics show that this difference could have occurred without a personnel program at all by pure chance, indicating that continued production at the higher rate is not probable. In this case, instead of a $4,000 yearly savings there was only the loss of the personnel program expense, and it does not justify continuation. Furthermore, even if the difference were significant, it is possible that other causal factors are present.

Supplemented by Statistics

STATISTICALLY the influence of other factors can be measured and the effect of the amount of increased production can be defined. Then the figures can be handed again to the cost accountant and evaluated. Perhaps the personnel program brought about a small change which did not justify its expense. Or, on the other hand, in addition to saving $4,000, the personnel program may have offset the effects of an increasingly poorer grade of supervision (for example, under war conditions) and really saved $8,000 for the year.

The cost accountant has no way of finding this out. Most records he works with have a statistical reliability which should be determined, and in the personnel field most results measured are influenced by many variables which should be considered.

In summarizing, the evaluation process is this: (1) Arithmetic figures summarize personnel records and give the basis for evaluation, (2) Statistics give meaning to the arithmetic figures, and (3) Cost accounting converts the figures and interpretation into dollars and cents.

The need for more and better factual information and increased precision of statistical inferences based upon this information is obviously important in all phases of business administration. Personnel management is not exempt from this need. Under the guidance of substantial facts accompanied by professional analysis, the personnel executive is able to establish his worth as administrator of an integrated program of personnel administration.

Most People in America Do Not Think the Country is Going to be Socialized Within Their Lifetime. Probably It Isn't, But Unless Industry Wakes Up Industry Probably Will Be. English Industry's Neglect Led To It There.

Neglect Leads
to Socialism

By Robert Watson,
The Metal Box Company,
London, England

IN ALL publications on the need for maintaining a high and stable level of employment there is little mention of the need for progressive employment policies by individual companies. By "employment policy" we mean the opportunities leading to a healthy and satisfactory career extended by a company to all its employees and the proper recognition of rights, statutory and otherwise. It is obvious that a state of full employment is a state of competition for labour, but what is not so obvious is that this calls for the maintenance of high minimum standards of employment on the part of all employers.

Lack of Consistency

EMPLOYERS pay particular attention to every move made by their competitors in the utilisation of machinery. Yet there is an amazing lack of consistency in the treatment and working conditions of human beings. The phenomenon of the backward and enlightened employer in the same trade in the same locality is easily explained in an era of labour surplus.

It is certain that in an area of labour competition those employers who have shown a marked disregard for enlightened personnel management will be at a disadvantage, and should any degree of direction of labour be maintained by the Government, there will be disgruntlement among employees accustomed to decent treatment when they are directed to firms which still employ Victorian methods.

In the United States the era of prosperity following the last war produced intense competition for labour. Companies had to give the very best possible conditions of employment, and recognition of individual merit was the keystone of the management-employee relationship. But in this country in the slump thousands of employees would have worked in a dump to be removed from the "dole."

Mr. Bevin, an ex-trade union leader, has consistently stressed the need for enlightened personnel management—

> "In spite of much good work carried out by a few firms between the two wars, I found industry as a whole quite unprepared to give this side of management its proper status, so much so that I had to say in the House of Commons, even in 1942: 'Our great weakness in British industry is the failure of employers to put personnel managers on equality with works managers in an undertaking . . . and I urge British industry that they should pay attention to these modern requirements in handling the human being'."

Enlightened Employers Few

HE HAS had trained for these posts hundreds of men and women under Government grant. Yet the enlightened employers in this country, judged by modern standards of personnel management, are few in number and often regarded by other employers with cynical contempt for their "paternalistic" outlook. But sound employment policy, which is the framework for sound personnel management, has nothing in common with the old paternalistic outlook. Its foundation is the fact, proved by experience, that the efficiency of an undertaking, and the well-being of all who work within it, are indivisible.

This survey of employment policies revealed that, even among the best employers, a published statement of Conditions of Employment is a rarity, although a number issue Handbooks of Information which usually cover only the bare rudiments of knowledge of privileges and rules.

In the following, the group have set down in general terms some of the main elements of employment policy which should be pursued in a progressive firm.

It shall be the policy of this company to regard the human problems of all grades of employees and management as of the greatest importance to the efficient conduct of its business, and:

Continuity of Employment

1. To recognise that a high level of employment is essential to the community; to co-operate wholeheartedly with the Government in the carrying out of employment policies.

2. To pay particular attention to the possible termination of certain occupations because of changes in production, with a view to the redistribution of displaced personnel or of production in other branches of the company; to make such

change-over possible by long-term production planning. If jobs become redundant, to use fairness in determining which employees have to be released and to give one month's notice in writing to each redundant employee and to the Ministry of Labour and National Service.

3. To terminate employment, except in the case of redundancy, only after two weeks' notice has been given and the employee has had the right of appeal.

4. To discuss all matters affecting continuity of employment and redundancy with the trades unions concerned and their factory representatives.

Joint Consultation

1. To give the utmost support to agreed forms of joint consultation at factory, district and national levels and to regard this as one of the major functions of management.

2. To operate joint consultation through a main joint committee and sub-committees for particular subjects.

3. To operate joint departmental committees, giving adequate representation to operatives on production matters.

4. To give to supervision, as a group, regular means of consultation with the higher management.

5. To allow employees, supervision, and works management regular means of discussion on all matters of policy with the board of directors.

6. To give every member of the organisation a copy of the constitution and rules of the joint consultative body which represents their interests.

7. To regard all joint consultative assemblies in the works or offices as democratic bodies invested with constitutional rights of consultation and advice on any matters concerned with the success of the business as a whole, and to observe the requirements of Parliamentary procedure in regard to elections and dignity of discussions.

Trade Unions

1. To recognise the free right of employees to join a trade union and to guarantee that an employee's position with the company will not be prejudiced in any way either by membership of a trade union or while acting as an officially accredited representative. To make known that the company openly invites the attention of its employees to the benefits of membership in a national trade union recognised by the Trades Union Congress.

2. To honour strictly any agreements or arrangements officially entered into between the company and trade unions, and wherever possible to display the same.

3. To co-operate with trades unions on all employment matters, but to maintain the management's final right of decision in regard to employment of any person or group of persons.

4. To allow official trade union representatives reasonable access to factories for the conduct of official business; to provide reasonable facilities for the display of official trade union literature; and to arrange for the collection of trade union membership dues by accredited representatives.

5. To ensure that no lock-out or stoppage of work shall take place without adherence to the agreed negotiating machinery and to regard such unauthorised lock-out or stoppage of work as a breach of contract.

Conditions of Employment

1. To maintain conditions of employment of a high standard which will make a contribution to the social and economic life of the communities in which we operate.

2. To recognise agreements concluded between the company and the trades unions as a condition of employment, whilst leaving the individual employee free to choose whether to join a trade union.

3. To make agreement to the staff or works regulations, either signed individually before the employee and the company, or posted on notice boards, a condition of employment.

4. To ensure that every employee is made aware of the proper channels of approach to the management or the trade union representative or both, in the event of any individual or group question arising which may be settled without reference to negotiating machinery.

5. To reward long and efficient service with the company.

6. To provide joint contributory sickness and pension schemes for employees.

Working Conditions

1. To provide the best possible working conditions, facilities for medical care and protection at work, accident prevention, canteens and other amenities.

2. To maintain the five-day, 40-hour week, or its shift equivalent, under normal peace-time conditions and to discourage systematic overtime or long hours of work.

3. To pay for all Bank Holidays and to observe annual holiday arrangements for all employees not less favourable than those established by the better employers, or under trade union agreements applicable to the trade.

Rates of Pay

1. To pay rates of salary not less than those paid by the better employers and to consider salary increases at regular intervals on a system of salary committee (representative of management and staff) recommendations and merit rating.

2. To pay the "rate-for-the-job" as determined by national or district trade union agreements and to apply payment-by-results in consultation with the trade union

representatives of the employees, no price or bonus to be changed without the prior consent of both parties.

3. To discuss at any time all general conditions of employment and rates of salary and wages with the elected representatives of the staff and workers, but to maintain the right of the individual to approach the management at any time.

Selection and Placing

1. To endeavour, as far as practicable, to place those engaged in occupations which will suit their natural abilities, or in which they have proved successful elsewhere, and to use the scientific methods which have been developed to assist selection in any occupation.

2. To require physical examination of any employee or prospective employee at the discretion of the management.

3. To obtain references from applicants for employment from employers, institutions or persons, but not before obtaining the prior agreement of the applicant.

4. To give priority in placing after the war to company employees released from H. M. Forces.

5. To give special consideration to the employment of disabled persons over and above carrying out legislative provisions; to co-operate with rehabilitation centres and to change job operations for disabled persons when practicable and necessary.

Promotions

1. To give just consideration to, and equal opportunity for, engagement and promotion of employees, on the basis of merit; length of service not to be regarded as a decisive factor in promotions unless all other considerations are equal; to promote, if possible, from within the organisation before considering outside applicants.

2. To maintain merit grading as an aid to fair and equitable judgment in making promotions

3. To maintain a promotion panel, representative of management and employees, which will sit as an advisory and consultative body.

Education and Training

1. To give every employee assistance and encouragement to develop his or her powers to the maximum.

2. To provide or arrange suitable education and training on or off the job for all grades of present employees, new employees, reinstated ex-Service personnel and disabled persons.

3. To endeavour to make the maximum use of the services of all employees who have availed themselves of the company's educational and training facilities,

but to recognise that some of them may wish to find scope for their ability and knowledge elsewhere.

4. To regard juvenile education, in its widest sense, as a preparation for citizenship.
5. To grant time off for attendance at approved courses during working hours, without loss of pay up to a maximum equivalent of one day per week.
6. To give assistance to trainees attending outside approved courses by the payment of tuition and examination fees and approved out-of-pocket expenses, provided that examination results and reports of progress are satisfactory.
7. To encourage trainees showing special ability to take a University Degree or other higher qualification by giving special leave of absence for full-time or part-time study, and financial assistance.
8. To ensure that practical courses of training within the company for craftsmen and skilled staff are devised to assist the trainee to reach a nationally or professionally recognised level of competence.
9. To provide or arrange for special job-training for employees reinstated after national service. This will include retraining, continuation of interrupted training or new training, according to the needs of the individual.
10. To provide or arrange for job-training of disabled persons in co-operation with the Disablement Rehabilitation Officers of the Ministry of Labour and National Service.
11. To encourage the development of conference groups throughout the company on a voluntary basis for managerial and supervisory staffs.
12. To encourage adult education of a general nature and community recreation outside working hours.
13. To give company awards for merit in education and training.

Co-operation with Outside Bodies

1. To co-operate with the Ministry of Labour and National Service and to grant company representation wherever possible on employment panels, committees and appeal boards; to co-operate closely with the Factory Inspectorate.
2. To co-operate with the Institute of Labour Management, the Industrial Welfare Society, the Industrial Management Research Association, the British Psychological Society and the National Institute of Industrial Psychology in regard to job selection, placement, personnel management and employee services.
3. To co-operate with educational authorities, both at national and local levels and to exchange information which will assist proper selection and placement of applicants for employment at our factories.
4. To co-operate with employers' federations and trades unions on all personnel matters.
5. To make contact with the International Labour Office and personnel management organisations in other countries.

6. To encourage employees to take part in the civic life of the community and to regard absence on such official duties during normal working hours as time worked.

Reprinted from Labor Management, the Journal of the Institute of Labor Management, London, England.

Evaluate Applicants for Jobs in Terms of What
They Can Do and Not What They Cannot Do.
Infirmities and Afflictions Can Very Easily Be
Used as a Basis for High Efficiency.

One Hand, One Ear,
One Voice

By C. C. Fracker,

Wright Aeronautical Corporation,
Cincinnati, O.

IT HAS often been said that necessity is the mother of invention. Necessity also
at times becomes the mother of innovation. The necessity of manning hundreds of new plants during the war brought about innovations in personnel
practices, and one of the most far reaching was the widespread discovery that
physically handicapped people can be efficiently used in industry. While some companies did an outstanding job in using handicapped people before the War, most
plants merely established blanket physical requirements regarding health and a
full complement of appendages.

Use Under War Conditions

LABOR conditions during the War made it necessary for industry to explore heretofore unused labor sources. The use of female labor was greatly expanded.
Special hoists and jigs were designed so that women could handle parts previously
processed or machined exclusively by men. Wage differentials were eliminated and
a policy of equal pay for equal work, regardless of sex, was established nationwide.
Such practices have enabled six and a half million women to join the labor force
since Pearl Harbor. Another potential was tapped by establishing training schools
for negroes. Many of these individuals had great capacity for machine shop work,
but never before had an opportunity to use it.

But perhaps the most impressive of all the labor sources explored was that of the
"handicapped." We took another look, not so much at the applicant, but at the
job he had to fill. Specific job analysis of physical requirements indicated that
there was a place in industry for the halt, the lame, and the blind.

Here at the Cincinnati Plant of Wright Aeronautical Corporation we examined our jobs carefully and critically, and we asked ourselves, "What do these jobs *really* require, physically?" Well, we got some rather surprising answers. For instance, we discovered that the announcer's job on our public address system *really* required only one hand to operate the switch and answer the telephone, one ear with which to hear, a voice with which to speak, and that is absolutely all. One hand, one ear, one voice, and whatever else was needed in between to maintain life.

Physical Capacities Appraisal Form

In our examination of applicants, we made use of a Physical Capacities Appraisal form. This form lists twenty-seven specific physical activities, such as, sitting, reaching, lifting, carrying, throwing, and the like, and eighteen working conditions, such as, odors, noise, moving objects, cramped quarters, sudden temperature changes, wet, dusty, etc. On this form was matched the requirements of the job and the physical capacities of the individual. By this means we were able to fill the above job with a blind boy. He had a beautiful voice with a facility for enunciating clearly and distinctly. Was he "handicapped" because he had no eyes? Not occupationally, at least.

In our dark rooms, where X-ray photographs of engine parts are developed, we used two more blind men. Here the affliction proved to be an advantage for these men were perfectly at home in the dark, their entire lives had been spent in total darkness. There was no fumbling, no awkwardness, they were among the best film developers we ever had.

In our Inspection Department we used more than a dozen blind or semi-blind people on jobs which only involved the use of plug, thread, and go-nogo gages. No handicap here. Again the lack of sight proved an advantage, for these employees weren't distracted by visual disturbances. An interesting side light concerns one blind employee who was fortunate in having a Seeing-Eye dog. This dog was photographed, had his paw prints taken, and was issued a regular employee's badge with his picture thereon. What an inspiring sight that was to see dog and master confidently walking down the long aisles of a modern machine shop, going to their place of work.

Afflictions Found Blessings

Other afflictions were found to be blessings in disguise. Have you ever been in a foundry? Ever hear the roar of the furnaces, the clatter of dollies and conveyors, the rumble and roar of the shakeout-knockout crews? How would you like to conduct delicate experiments in a laboratory adjacent to such a din? Well it doesn't bother one of our metallurgists, for he is almost stone deaf. Oh, he has a hearing aid he can turn on when it's necessary to converse with associates, but most of the time he is blissfully unaware of the racket as he conducts his delicate tests and makes his computations. Why not take a look at your noisy jobs and see if deaf people might not be your solution to high absenteeism, low morale, irritability, and the like?

Neither does lack of appendages need offer any particular hardship to employees on certain jobs. Of what occupational use are legs to an assembler who sits at a bench all day? Of what occupational use is more than one arm to messengers, tool boys or employees in a myriad other occupations? We have a one arm tool boy who is a most excellent worker. We hired a young auditor in our Controller's Department whose right arm had been removed at the shoulder. His work was so notable that he soon became the supervisor of his unit, and besides being an effective worker he contributes greatly to our company sponsored recreation programs. He drives a terrific golf ball with his left hand, shooting consistently in the low nineties. He bowls regularly in one of the plant leagues with an average of 160 to 165. He plays on the department soft ball team and is one of the best hitters. Yet I can envision many employment managers turning this man down—"Poor chap, he only has one arm."

One man with an artificial left leg offered a problem. No machine shop or allied experience was indicated on his application, and our testing showed that his mechanical ability and manual dexterity were very low. This man was definitely not suited for bench assembly or similar jobs. However, we did note that in the past he had at one time been a painter. Did we have a painter's job he could fill? Let's see. Back in Paint and Impregnate Department there is a job where the operator stands in one spot all day and sprays engine parts which go by the spray booth on a conveyor. No stooping, no lifting, or walking connected with this job. Of course he could fill it, and he did.

We found out some other things too. We found that people physically afflicted with various types of chorea were adaptable, and after the first few days when the novelty to fellow employees wore off, they made good workers. We found that careful placement enabled us to get diligent and sometimes brilliant work from known epileptics who were under Medical care, for after all, an epileptic is in complete possession of his faculties the great majority of the time.

We Should Not Be Afraid

Surely it is apparent then that we need no longer be afraid of the jobs the handicapped can perform. Let's make good use of the portions of the human body which are needed to do the job and disregard the malfunctioning or lack of other portions which have no relations whatever to the work to be done. With the return of thousands of physically disabled veterans it is up to industry to learn to accept them, and in so doing benefit by obtaining workers who will in many ways surpass their physically normal brothers.

Take a good look then, at the jobs in your plant. Itemize specifically and actually the physical requirements of a job. Base these requirements on what is absolutely necessary to perform the work, and not on the physical qualifications of the employees now holding that job. The medical division then will be required merely to indicate the handicaps of the applicant on the report to the employment interviewer who will match the man with the available job for which the handicapped person is qualified. This function will supplement their responsibility to discover contagious diseases, chronic illness, etc. Evaluate your applicants in terms of what they *can* do and not what they *can't* do.

Remember, too, that infirmities and afflictions which once might have been considered stumbling blocks can very easily be used as stepping stones.

The Male Rate of Dismissal Was Higher than the Female Being Mostly Boys Under 18 Because of Poor Attitudes Towards Their Work and Men Over 36 Because of Developing Unsuitable Personality Qualities.

Who Quits,
and Why

By Ronald Taft and Audrey Mullins,

Institute of Industrial Management,
Melbourne, Australia

I T IS by now a well-established fact that labor turnover is an expensive proposition; and, at the same time, an expense that can be reduced. Labor turnover involves an expense made up of the cost of training new employees for a job, of hiring and terminating employees and the consequent lowering in efficiency and morale. Therefore any method which may reduce its incidence should be of interest to those whose task it is to control industry.

Why Workers Quit

THERE are several spheres in which improvements may be brought about; the rate of labor turnover may be reduced by endeavoring to employ those groups that have the lowest turnover, by promoting those employees who tend to be more permanent, and by paying special attention to the elimination of the main causes of turnover amongst the employees. Therefore, in order to reduce turnover, the following prerequisites are essential; (a) there should be a definite policy on employment and supervision of employees issuing from top management, and (b) research should be conducted into the groups of employees who have the highest turnover rates, and the main causes for which they terminate.

Unfortunately, many studies on labor turnover deal purely with symptoms rather than the more basic cause in terms of the individuals revealing those symptoms. Consequently, this study has concerned itself with such personal characteristics as sex, age, marital status, intelligence and degree of responsibility as a function of labor turnover.

In *Personnel Journal*, September 1944, an article appeared under the title "Why Workers Quit", which set out the results of an analysis of causes of turnover in terms of the type of employees terminating for each cause. The present study is complementary to that one in that emphasis is placed on establishing the turnover rate for the various types of employees, as well as the reasons for their termination, so that the results may be used to modify the employment policy with regard to the type of employee that should be recruited.

In order to illustrate the application of this analytical method to the task of reducing labor turnover, this article embodies the results of an analysis of figures for an Australian factory, and demonstrates the use to which these results might be put.

The Organization Concerned in This Study

THE employees dealt with in this study are all salaried administrative employees of an organization manufacturing munitions. This organization has been engaged solely on high priority war work since its inception in 1940, and the groups of administrative employees from which the subjects were selected number over 2,000 (males and females in approximately equal proportions).

Nearly all of the employees in this organization are selected by means of aptitude tests, although the acute shortage of manpower has made it necessary for the tests to be used more in scientific placement than in the selection or rejection of the employees. The Personnel Department includes counsellors and social welfare officers, and exit interviews are used in connection with all terminating employees, irrespective of the reason for which they are being terminated.

When it is finally decided that an employee's services should be terminated, a post-mortem examination is made of circumstances leading up to the separation, the causes, the type of employee concerned, and how the termination might have been prevented; and it is largely from the information obtained in these 'post-mortems' that the material for this article was derived.

Note: For the benefit of American readers it should be stated that in Australia during the war no employee could leave a 'protected' industry without the permission of the Manpower Directorate, which was seldom given unless the separatee industry agreed to the release. This considerably lowered the rate of turnover, and particularly affected the number of employees terminating to accept other employment

So that the results could be used to modify the selection policy and the supervision where required the study is divided into two parts—the types of persons having a high turnover rate, and the main causes of turnover.

Personal Factors in Turnover
Influence of Sex

THE number of staff terminations for the various reasons, considered later in this study, totalled 237. Of these 146 were women employees, representing a turnover rate of 30%, which is nearly double the male rate of 17%. As we shall see later, this is due mostly to the effect of personal reasons, such as marriage and pregnancy. There is a greater tendency for males to leave after short periods of service, however (48% under 12 months' service).

Influence of Age

THE turnover rate of men under 26, in which group are 40% of the total male staff, is 32%; in the 14–18 years group it is 43%, which is 2½ times that of total male staff. As the rate is 13% for males over 26 years, a progressive decrease is noticed from the youngest to the oldest age groups. The average age of male employees is 31 years.

This situation is reversed with women, where there is a steady increase in the turnover rate from 23% in the group 14–18 to 50% over 36 years. However, a greater proportion of women employees are in the lower age groups; 70% are under 26 and the average age is 24.

Influence of Marital Condition

THE variation with age in both men and women appears to be directly related to marital condition, the rates being as follows: Single men, 28%, Married men, 12%; Single women, 24%, Married women, 59%.

Combining the influence of age and marital condition there is a distinct tendency for a high turnover rate for young single men, and a very high rate for married women between 18 and 35 (70%). As would be expected, the profitable application of this fact is revealed in the low proportion of married women employed, i.e. less than 35% of the total female staff; the majority of males on present staff are married.

Influence of Intelligence Level

EMPLOYEES of poor intelligence, only capable of performing routine office tasks, have the only outstandingly low rate of turnover for the various intelligence levels. However, when we analyse these figures together into sex and age, significant results are revealed.

Males—There is a low rate of turnover amongst young male employees of superior intelligence, while the rate for this group of employees increases as the intelligence level declines. This trend is reversed for male employees over 25 years, young men being an exception to the overall trend of a low turnover for those of below average intelligence.

Females—The group which is above average in intelligence has a turnover rate slightly lower than the general female rate, while the rate for the group of superior women is 50% greater than the general rate. The age of the female employees makes little difference except in the extremes where the rate for superior older women is high and that for dull older women is low. This would be expected from a combination of maturity and the extent of the possibilities of finding employment outside the organization; some of the more intelligent ones are able to obtain better positions outside, but the duller ones are content with the jobs that their experience has befitted them to do.

Influence of Responsibility

A FURTHER guide to the personal qualities of an employee is the responsibility of his position in the organization. As the salary levels are evaluated according to the degree of responsibility of each job, these should provide an indication as to the influence of responsibility on turnover. Consequently, arbitrary levels were chosen, above which the employees may be described as responsible officers. These levels would make 69% of the males and 28% of the females responsible officers.

The turnover for males in responsible positions is 10% and females 16%; but for those below the critical salary levels the rates were 34% and 36% respectively. When age is included as a function of salary levels, it is found that the ratio for male employees under 36 years and female employees under 26 years who are not in responsible positions are particularly high—52% and 37% respectively, as opposed to 11% and 16% for similar categories in responsible groups. Therefore, when employing a person for a less responsible position, it is better to employ an older person (of course, within the limits imposed by the necessity to train younger employees as a recruitment pool for responsible positions in the future), and when training selected employees to become executives it is better to train young men rather than young women, apart from any other consideration.

Analysis of Reasons for Termination

WHILE the analysis of the influence of personal factors in causing separations can be used in conjunction with the employment policy to reduce the turnover rate, a further analysis into the reasons for termination should throw further light on both the employment policy and special supervisory action needed to reduce turnover.

When it is desired that an employee be terminated, a staff request is raised by that employee's supervisor stating the reason for the separation, and the employee is interviewed so that his case may be investigated. Even where it is not possible to prevent the termination, particular pains are taken to ascertain the real reason, and it is felt that in practically all cases this method has been successful in obtaining reliable data.

When classifying the reasons for separations, it has sometimes been found difficult to isolate the one cause, as several reasons sometimes contribute to the one separation, e.g. an employee resigns ostensibly to join the fighting services, but in actual practice he may be anticipating an impending dismissal for poor attention to his work. Notwithstanding, an endeavour has been made to classify each termination under one of the following headings:

Dissatisfaction (this includes any case where the employee voluntarily leaves to accept other preferred employment), Health, Military (where employee is called up by fighting services), Personal, Dismissal and Lay-off. Termination of employees hired temporarily are not included.

Reasons for Terminations

THE percentage of separations due to these reasons were as follows:

Dissatisfied	30%
Health	11%
Personal	29%
Military	5%
Dismissed	20%
Lay-off	5%

These percentages vary from one six months' period to another; for example, the percentage of dismissals has been constantly reduced over a period of time from a maximum of 33%. This has apparently been achieved mainly as a result of an employment policy based on previous studies to the present one.

Dissatisfaction

THIS reason plays a more important part in the turnover of male employees than female, particularly males of superior intelligence in positions of responsibility, and married men over 36. Nearly all married men who terminated did so because of dissatisfaction. In most cases, the reason for leaving was to obtain a better-paid, or more suitable job. Most of the males leaving through dissatisfaction left under one year's service, while a large proportion of women left between one and two years. The female employees terminating for this reason are younger women in positions of low responsibility who were in the higher intelligence groups.

From these results it is apparent that the employment policy should be modified so as not to include more employees of superior intelligence than there are suitable positions available.

Health

MORE female employees than male resigned for health reasons, although the figure for girls under 18 was low. For those in responsible positions, the female rate is high and the male rate low, results which may throw further light on the possible nerve-wracking effect of placing women in responsible jobs.

For both sexes the rate for those with above average intelligence was higher than expectation, and for those below average it was lower.

As the rate of turnover for health reasons was high two years previously, special steps were taken to reduce the rate by investigating the previous health records of new employees and by improving working conditions. As a result of this policy this cause has been lowered from 20% to 11%.

Personal

THIS reason, which includes domestic duties, transfer to other districts and preg-nancies, concerns women in nearly all cases. Only two men resigned for personal reasons during the six months' period, but personal reasons account for a large per-centage of the entire turnover of married women, particularly those below average in intelligence. There are several possible explanations of this, but the important thing is that the employment officer should take special pains to investigate the do-mestic situation of married women before recommending them for jobs.

Military

IN THE period being considered, this reason applies almost exclusively to young males who attained the age of 18 years, and it accounts for one-third of all turn-over amongst males between 18 and 25 years. As the result of a policy of employing girls rather than boys, where possible, this cause of turnover has been reduced greatly during the war, although this policy does not solve the general community problem of finding employment for boys between the time they leave school and their induc-tion into the Services at the age of 18 years.

Dismissed

THE male rate of dismissal was higher than the female, being mostly boys under 18 years dismissed because of their poor attitude towards their work, and older men over 36 who were dismissed because of unsuitable personality qualities. Only one woman in a responsible job was dismissed.

The rate of dismissal for both sexes varied inversely with the I.Q. of the employee —that is, the less intelligent he is, the more likely the employee is to be dismissed. However, the interesting thing is that the reason for dismissal was seldom lack of ability to carry out the required duties, but more often poor attitude (absenteeism etc.) or unsuitable personality (e.g. psychopathic). This seems to confirm the suc-cess of the policy of scientific selection and placement of employees according to their abilities, but shows the necessity for further research into the detection of the more intangible qualities connected with interest and personality.

Lay-off

ALL the employees laid off (i.e. surplus in a particular section, and unsuited for transfer to another) were either young men and women not in responsible positions, or older ones in responsible jobs, who were not easily adaptable to other types of work where vacancies existed.

Applications to Personnel Policy

IN THE introduction it was pointed out that an analysis of the incidence and causes of labor turnover was a necessary prerequisite for a policy of reducing turnover. Let us now consider what recommendations ensue from the findings dealt with in this article.

Employment Policy

THE policy should be framed as far as possible to avoid the necessity of employing those groups that have a high turnover rate. (Naturally, the employment policy must also consider other factors that affect the selection of the most suitable employees, such as promotion policy, and the abilities required by the job; but let us here deal only with turnover rate, which in any case is probably a good indication of a correct regard for these other factors.) We have found that the following groups of employees have shown a very high rate of turnover (over 50%):

> Young men (under 26 years) of an intelligence group close to average; that is, not capable of filling responsible positions—at least, in most cases.
> Married women between 18 and 36 years.
> Single women over 36.

Thus, assuming all other things to be equal, for positions not involving much responsibility, and where there is no chance of rapid promotion, it is better to employ women, provided that they are under 36 years and single. In such cases those of low average intelligence are to be preferred, if this level is sufficient for the job. For routine work requiring comparatively low intelligence, married women over 36 with this level of intelligence are to be preferred.

For responsible positions, married men over 26 years and all men over 36 years are to be favored, from the point of view of turnover.

Promotion and Training Policy

THE same considerations apply to training and promotion. When selecting young persons for development to hold responsible positions, young men of superior intelligence (naturally!) are to be preferred, and when selecting employees to go into responsible positions, it should be remembered that married men over 26, and all men over 36 years have the lowest rate of turnover.

Supervision and Personnel Counselling

THE results of the analysis as set down in this article must be regarded as applicable only to the conditions prevailing at the time, and inferences from the results are dependent upon these conditions

At the time this research was made special attention could well have been paid to the health of women in responsible positions. Also special counselling of married men was indicated with regard to their satisfaction with their jobs; although these men have a low overall turnover, they appear to need more advice about their progress and prospects in their jobs than single men. (Does this show the hidden hand of the wife?)

Similarly, when it was found several years ago that the rate of dismissal for officers of superior intelligence was high, steps were taken to pay special attention to the supervision of these employees, with the result that their dismissal rate has fallen considerably.

Conclusion

THE expense incurred by labor turnover is not a fixed overhead charge. Turnover is a symptom of deep-seated social, physiological and psychological forces which vary from time to time and between one type of individual and another. Therefore, a programme to reduce its effects must start from the collection and analysis of information relevant to the conditions prevailing at the time and the individuals involved in the separations. Recommendations based on the results of such a study should then be applied to the employment and supervisory policy of the industry concerned, and should be reviewed and modified at regular intervals as required.

We Could Not Do Our Share in Winning the War by the Magnitude of Our War Production Without Paying Much Attention to the Individual Needs and Wishes of Our Workers. What Are We Going to Do Now?

Warm *or* Cold Management?

By ROBERT D. LOKEN,
Lieutenant, USNR,
San Diego, Cal.

AN INDUSTRIAL shop or a business office is much more than a well-knit organization with planned procedures operating according to a controlled schedule. It is an organization of human beings—of individuals. Most problems of supervision have their source in this sphere of human action. The success of the best organization in the world, with a perfectly planned and controlled schedule of operation depends upon how effectively the plan is translated into orders through people. The responsibility of dealing successfully with individual workers is the critical point of supervision.

Attempts to Ignore Human Aspects

THERE have been numerous attempts in the industrial history of this country to ignore the human or social aspects of industrial management. During the period of rapid expansion from 1910 to 1930 this approach drew many adherents particularly in large scale industrial enterprises. This was the period when the "efficiency experts" flourished as the industrial dictators on the American scene. At first glance, the mechanized approach to the problem of handling workers on the job appeared to have many advantages.

The basis of the system was the assumption that men could be handled in the same way as the machines that were replacing them. The system was successful only as long as machines continued to replace men. As industrial conversion began to slow down, labor and employee relations problems increased. Intelligent management groups quickly recognized that successful production required more than good organization, planning and cold, impersonal control. Since production was still being accomplished by human workers, some warmth must be injected into the system. The bone and sinew of cold management principles had to be clothed with a warm, personal, human approach if full and effective production was to result.

Supervision Impossible Without Personal Knowledge

THE principles of organization and management actually imply human, individualized leadership in application. For example, the principle of span of control limits the number of persons supervised to allow the leader to get to know each worker individually. It is based on the fact that it is impossible for the leader to supervise a worker without knowing him as a human being. The same individualized approach is implied in the principle of unity of command and in delegation of responsibility with authority.

Close examination will reveal that all of the functions of management over-lap with, and are dependent upon, humanized leadership, tailor-made to the individual workers. It is impossible to talk about "good organization" without considering the human beings that fill the positions in that organization. As soon as two or more people combine their efforts in any industrial or business enterprise, individual differences inevitably give rise to human relations problems. It is, likewise, impracticable to talk about solutions to problems of human relations in industry, without considering the basic organizational, planning and control structure within which these problems arise. The two fields, job management and man-management, are, therefore, mutually dependent. A complete understanding of either field is impossible without some understanding of both.

Group Responsibility for Individual Citizen

PRESENT day recognition of the importance of social and personal factors in the work situation did not develop by chance. Public, private, religious, educational, and industrial research agencies and organizations have made a concerted effort over the past half century to sell this idea to the American public. The fruit of these efforts is to be seen in the gradual awakening of group responsibility for the individual citizen. Everyday evidence of this recognition is to be seen in new educational facilities, new laws and wider fields of activity for the labor unions.

This public recognition of responsibility has been translated by the American people into certain rights and privileges which will operate to provide the individual worker with job security. It has also resulted in numerous major changes in industrial relations policy. For example, no more than twenty years ago such services as housing, child care, education, insurance, hospitalization, and medical care were looked upon as special privileges or premiums to be offered or withheld as management desired. Today, these same services are expected, and taken for granted, by large numbers of workers in business and industry. This has come about because management has learned that it pays off in production to recognize and consider the needs of the individual.

Farsighted employers had always realized that job satisfaction, developed through individual recognition, resulted in better relations and better production. Even during the 1920's, at the peak of mechanization, these "humanized" employers were able to compete successfully with streamlined, depersonalized industries in their own fields. The apparent simplicity of the mechanized type of personnel policy attracted a large following prior to World War II. Competition was high, prices were low and operating margins at a bare minimum. There is little wonder that this approach was eagerly seized upon by so many employers as the solution to the problem of "efficiency".

Mechanized Personnel Work Abandoned in War

IT is interesting to note, however, that mechanized personnel methods were almost completely eliminated under the demand for maximum production during World War II. When full and complete production from every available worker was needed, even the hardest shelled industrialist renounced the impersonal for the individualized approach. This was a concrete admission that cooperation will result in more efficiency production than will coercion. When the chips were down management remembered that workers are social animals, not machines, and appealed to them accordingly. It required the rigorous demands of full war production to demonstrate to the country at large a fact that had been common knowledge to successful supervisors for decades—that feelings are more important than dollars to the workers.

This belief can be supported convincingly if reasons given for discharges and quits are examined carefully. When the facts and opinions gathered by exit interviewers are analyzed, it is found that the majority of people quit or are fired, not because of skill failures, lack of job knowledge, or related reasons, but for social or personal inadequacy.

Most workers quit a job because "they don't like the foreman," "they don't like the shop," "they didn't get along with their fellow workers," or similar reasons. From the supervisors point of view, most workers are fired for almost the same reasons given by those quitting. These social or personal reasons account for more than sixty-five per cent of the separations occurring each year. Wage disputes, except where they are used to mask a more basic problem, seldom furnish the basis for termination of employment.

Annual Turnover Bill

THE annual bill covering the cost of American turnover in business and industries is a staggering sum. It amounts to several billion dollars and an even larger number of man-hours wasted each year. Since more than sixty per cent of this annual loss can be charged against social and personal failure on the part of the worker or the supervisor it would seem intelligent to examine the methods employed in dealing with problems of human relations, toward the end of salvaging some of that loss. Since these problems consume more than fifty per cent of the supervisor's time, it should be well worth his time to take every opportunity to improve his methods.

During the period of industrial expansion, and continuing through the first three decades of this century the old-time, two-fisted, hard-driving boss could, and did, achieve production. But as the worker began to receive recognition and through the growth of labor unions, he increased his prestige and power, the position of this old-time boss became more and more insecure. Today, in fact, there are relatively few fields of work where the methods of the old-time boss can be applied to advantage. His "might makes right" philosophy has been replaced by the newer, more widely accepted philosophy of the modern leader. The harsh, heavy-handed, driving methods of the old-time boss did bring results—but at the expense of the worker. The increase in education and general rise in the standard of living for the American people has changed the attitude of the average modern worker and made this approach impracticable. When exposed to these methods of supervision the production of most workers today falls off seriously.

Benefit, Not Expense to Worker

IN CONTRAST with the methods of the old-time boss, the modern supervisor *leads* his group. He does not *drive* them. He is able to get more production than the old boss but these results are achieved to the benefit, and not at the expense, of the workers. Using the techniques of modern leadership the supervisor actually builds and develops his workers instead of wearing them out. This results in an increasing reservoir of knowledge, skill and ability in the individual worker so that he becomes more valuable to industry with every year on the job.

The modern supervisor has become, in effect, an instructor. This change in emphasis could have been predicted from the social and economic condition which gave it birth. It is much more than a change in name alone. To be a good instructor, to be able to build and develop employees, requires an intimate and personal knowledge of each worker within the group supervised.

You Cannot Enforce Enthusiasm

PEOPLE can only be led in terms of their own feelings, desires, wishes, and personal ambitions. The supervisor who is honestly interested in the welfare of the people under his control will soon learn to use these hopes, ambitions, and desires to build satisfied and effective workers. He soon learns also, that it takes followers to make a leader. It is impossible to force people to become enthusiastic and productive followers. High morale, job-enthusiasm, and job-satisfaction are attitudes. As such, they cannot be achieved by rules and regulations. They must develop naturally in response to the supervisor, other workers, and factors in the work situation.

Alert supervisors discovered long ago that the problems of labor relations are inevitably problems of individual relations. Problems on the group level always have their origin in some situation involving Mary, or Harry, or John as individuals. As long as people work and produce as a group, such problems will continually arise. Their basis is the simple fact that each person is different. Failure to provide for, or recognize, these individual differences on the job results in feelings of unfairness, discrimination, or some other form of grievance.

Supervisor's Stock in Trade

KNOWLEDGE of the differences between workers, their strong and weak points, their peculiar traits and personalities, their feelings and sentiments, is the supervisor's stock in trade. Since these are the factors which vary, he spends much more of his time dealing with these habits, attitudes, feelings and emotions than he does with machines, methods, and material. Certainly they furnish the focal point around which most problems arise. From the moment the new worker reports for the job until he is promoted or separated from the department, the supervisor must be constantly alert to the individual's peculiarities and must deal with each situation in terms of these differences.

For example, most supervisors have some responsibility for the placement of employees and the assignment of jobs within the group of workers. They take this responsibility seriously, but few realize its importance or potentialities with regard to production. Research in selection and placement has demonstrated that there are important differences between workers with apparently the same education and experience in terms of actual or potential production.

Best Four Times Better Than Worst

EXAMINATION of the production records of mill hands, typists, machine operators, assemblers and a variety of other trade and office groups reveals that the production of the best worker in any type of employment will average four times that of the poorest worker. This has important implications for both the worker and the supervisor. It might mean, for example, that if the "best workers" could always be selected, the same amount of work could be turned out with only one quarter the number of workers, or that the output could be tripled if each job was filled with such employees. From the worker's point of view, this can be interpreted to mean that if properly placed he could be four times as productive as he could if improperly placed. Since the majority of workers will fall around the average, proper placement could result in doubling the production of most workers.

The responsibility for proper selection and placement is important to both management and workers. A good share of this is delegated to the supervisor. Here again close personal contact with each worker is essential if the supervisor expects to be familiar enough with their skill, knowledge, education and abilities to insure proper placement.

Social Relations Not Checked at Door

WHEN an employee walks in the factory door, he doesn't check his social relations at the entrance and become an automaton. On the contrary, he steps into a social structure which is even more complex than the social world outside of work. The rules, sanctions, and penalties which dictate employee behavior within any large company are even more binding than those laid down by the courts of law. For the most part, this social structure is created by the employees themselves, and not by the management representatives. The alert supervisor is intensely aware of this social structure and its attendant limitations and rules. It is an important consideration when giving orders, making decisions, or selecting the right employee for a particular job. If management infringes upon the social rights and privileges developed by the group, individual or group problems develop.

The Old Time Clock Problem

FOR example, a large western manufacturing concern recently completed a survey which indicated that a considerable saving could be effected by expanding their time clock system to include upper-bracket and professional level employees, as well as factory workers. The change would save thousands of man-hours in computation and accounting. The system was adopted. The order to punch time clocks was not well received by the group because it offered a definite threat to their social status in the company. Much to everyone's surprise the production and morale of the group affected dropped so low that the company lost money instead of saving by the change. Many of the group reacted almost as if they had been demoted.

Socially, at least, the order to punch the clock amounted to a "de-grading" of their positions. The privilege of not punching the time clock had carried with it large, non-financial rewards of a social nature. Previous to the installation of the time clock system this group had voluntarily worked many hours of overtime and had developed considerable enthusiasm for their work which was reflected in extra effort. This voluntary contribution of effort and overtime work stopped immediately when they were ordered to punch the clock. The total output of the group was cut by more than twenty per cent. More than thirty-thousand man-hours of voluntary overtime had been lost. Since the installation of the time clock system had saved the salaries of only five people in the payroll section, the company showed a large net loss, rather than a saving, as a result of their "economy" measure.

Each Shop Has Own Customs

THIS example is only one of thousands which occur every month in industries throughout the country. It illustrates the importance of social factors in industry. The "perfect" production system, from the point of view of efficiency experts, is often not the "best" system. The cold, impersonal logic of efficiency must always be weighed against the sentiments and feelings of the workers concerned.

Each shop or office develops its own peculiar social rules and structure. Each group has symbols which distinguish its social classes. In an office this "badge of prestige" is often the placement or size of the desks. It is not unusual to find office workers who would rather move to a larger desk at the same salary than to a smaller desk at a higher salary. This occurs when a desk or a particular work area in the office has taken on the symbol of high social position or prestige. The same conditions pertain in the shop. The distinction may be in terms of parking privileges, location of work bench, rest periods, or even in terms of which washroom the worker uses. Whatever the symbol, it is an important operating factor in the industrial situation which the supervisor can't afford to overlook. There are even examples of serious labor relations problems which had their origin in whether or not the particular group of workers used paper or fabric hand towels.

Redirect Social Thinking

THE development of social and prestige factors in any work situation can be guided and controlled to a large extent by an alert supervisor. It is often possible for such a leader to re-direct the "social thinking" of the group and build up prestige around truly important and relevant features of the job. Certainly, the supervisor cannot afford to let these patterns and factors spring up at random around completely irrational objects and interfere with production. He has, therefore, a preventative rôle to play in the social structure of his group. He must not only solve problems as they arise but strive to direct the social progress so as to prevent problems arising wherever possible.

The good supervisor must take these factors into consideration in making plans and decisions which affect his employees. The key to industrial morale lies in the leader's ability to accomplish this successfully. High morale is not a condition which, once developed, continues at the same level without fluctuation. Morale is, rather, comparable to the "public health", something to be continually inspected, tested, and attended. The supervisor, like the doctor, must keep a constant watch for new symptoms, individual illnesses, and epidemics. He, like the doctor, must learn to distinguish between the symptom and the disease—must learn not to be misled by "appearances". The balance of good morale is just as precarious as that of personal health and it rests primarily in the hands of the supervisor.

Disarmingly Simple Formulae

THERE has been a strong tendency during recent years to try to reduce the job of managing or handling people to an automatic process. Disarmingly simple formulas have been developed and sold to supervisory groups as cure-alls for any supervisory problem. Step by step methods for handling grievances, reprimands, training and other job relations problems have been taught to thousands of American supervisors. The difficulty with this formula approach is that the practical example which arises on the job seldom conforms to the illustration in the book. When one of these "unusual" situations develops the inexperienced supervisor attempts to force the situation to fit the formula. The result is, of course, further and more complicated problems. This is only one of the many dangers inherent in the formula approach based on generalizations. If any valid generalization can be made regarding the management of the people it is the reminder that to handle people requires first of all that the leader must learn to handle himself.

Where Supervisor Goes Off Track

THE promotion from worker to supervisory status brings in its wake numerous changes other than the new title and the higher wage rate. One of the most important of these is the change in social position and social relations with the group of workers. All contacts with the employees, whether of a social or technical nature, undergo critical alteration. One of the most difficult transitions for the new supervisor is the change from the former responsibility for "doing work" to the supervisory responsibility for "getting work done by others."

The temptation to continue to do the work, rather than to get others to work for them, constantly confronts the new supervisor. It is at this point that most of the problems develop, and the new supervisor gets off the track. He must learn that to get people to do work requires an individual sales approach for each employee The supervisor must know his people in order to give tailor-made directions which will result in full production. He must replace his former tools of the trade such as wrenches, lathes, and hand tools, with the newer tools for handling people. These include ability to use words, ability to see a problem from the worker's point of view, ability to plan, organize, and control work and people, and, the ability to use such factors as recognition and reward for their full incentive value.

Supervisor Molds Opinion

THOSE supervisors who are capable of taking full advantage of the position of authority and direction which they occupy are becoming determining factors in American industrial education. The potential educational and social force of the supervisory group in America is tremendous. They are in closer, more intimate, and more continuous contact with the mass of American workers than any other single group. This influence continues to be a factor in molding public opinion even though the supervisor may not be aware of its existence. In those instances where the supervisor consciously uses and directs this influence it is doubly effective.

When the supervisory job is defined in terms of building and developing people, socially and technically, it begins to take on new dignity and unlimited potentialities. While he is primarily concerned with the task of getting out production, he can do this effectively only through the people under his control. This building and developing of individual workers is primarily a task of training. From one point of view, nearly every contact with employees can be looked upon as a training situation. The supervisor's rôle as an instructor is easily recognized when he is breaking a new worker in on his job, or changing an old worker over to a new job. When handling a "bawl-out" or a grievance situation, however, supervisors rarely look upon their part as that of an instructor. Yet even in these situations training should be the primary objective.

The Bawling-out

THE purpose of the "bawl-out" is to correct mistakes or, in other words teach the worker proper methods so that the mistake will not be repeated. The same sort of analysis can be made of settling a grievance, of giving orders properly, or most of the other supervisor-employee problems that arise during the day. By word, by deed, and by example, the good supervisor is constantly imparting instructions to his subordinates.

The average supervisor spends more than fifty per cent of his time instructing his workers. Training, therefore, is a very important part of his job. For this reason, effective teaching techniques should be of primary importance to the modern supervisor. Whether handling new.or old employees, skilled or unskilled workers, office or shop personnel the supervisor must carry on this program of instruction constantly. Training never stops.

What Does He Get for All He Does

THE modern supervisor's job is diversified, responsible and exacting. With the increases in responsibility, authority and knowledge, it is actually a job on the professional level. The supervisor in modern industry stands as the governor, regulating the flow of work and the utilization of manpower. He is the fulcrum on which production efficiency is balanced against employee cooperation and satisfaction.

He must be constantly aware of the relation of individual social status to production efficiency, turnover, and other crucial operating problems. At the same time he cannot afford to let his interests in individuals overshadow his responsibility for production efficiency. He must steer his group, as individual workers, down the middle course. If they become too efficiency conscious, production suffers just as it suffers if they allow personal or social problems to interfere excessively with production. To achieve this end, he must develop the ability to see the overall picture and yet remain alert to individual problems.

HAVE YOU SPARE PERSONNEL JOURNALS?

Some issues of the Personnel Journal (as listed below) are required by reconverting industries, but are out of print.

If you have copies of these issues, which you are not now using, will you kindly return them to us, so that we may send them out to the companies requiring them. We will pay full price for them.

Vol. 23, No. 7. January, 1945.
Vol. 23, No. 9. March, 1945.

Personnel Research Federation
60 East 42nd St.,
New York, 17, New York

Book Reviews

Book Review Editor, MR. EVERETT VAN EVERY

California Personnel Management Association, San Francisco, Cal.

COUNSELING METHODS FOR PERSONNEL WORKERS

By Annette Garrett. New York. Family Welfare Association of America. 1945. 187 pp. Price $2.00

We have never been sure that employee counseling was or is a proper function o management. We know that there was much of it during the war, and that in general those plants that used it had much less difficulty with their workers than those who did not use it.

Nevertheless we doubt whether it is a proper function of management, except in emergency situations. It carries with it a basic assumption that workers are incapable of managing their own affairs, and meeting life's problems.

However there are companies with a maternal instinct who wish to carry on with this type of work. For those who do, this book offers an excellent *exposé* of conventional methods.

TOP-MANAGEMENT PLANNING

By Edward H. Hempel. New York, N. Y. Harper & Bros. 1945. 414 pp. $4.50

Organization planning and the administration of such plans as applied to American enterprise is rapidly becoming of top interest to executive managements. Critics of the American business system frequently point to the lack of planning in large scale operations and the obvious conclusions are serious and damaging to what appear to be otherwise successfully conducted businesses.

This is said to be the first book to recognize planning as a major executive responsibility. Whichever way management turns at the conclusion of the wartime activities, planning will be an inevitable need. In fact wartime conditions have so depleted organizational functions and relationships as to make them wholly unfit internally to proceed under profitable peace-time production. The swift and uncompromising demands by organized labor in some industries is but one isolated example of how a complete re-study needs to be made of numerous organizations before they can be expected to operate smoothly. Markets, costs, price controls and many changes in personnel relations present many other phases that require planning control.

The policy-making efforts of top-management are facing a real challenge today with the very core of the private enterprise system being questioned at every turn. Competition promises to be sharper than it has ever been before; labor and special interest groups are indicating a kind of economic pressure that could prove ruinous to some organizations. To successfully overcome obstacles requires more than technical knowledge and a burning desire to work hard. This book shows not only what matters of practical economics all managers must consider, but dwells on the study and thought that must be given to the size of an enterprise, product planning, process planning, plant location, arrangement of machinery and an integration of these into a coordinated top-management plan that takes shape as a working policy.

This book might be called an industrial engineer's handbook, so thorough is its treatment of organization methods needed for postwar orientation of industrial firms. The principles laid down are just as applicable to any kind of enterprise as they are to a manufacturing plant; and every business will be facing the questions and problems raised by this book. It is also shown that the task of planning correctly will affect a vital portion of the national economy . . . and the author believes it will be three times as serious as the need undertaken after 1929 and five times as important as the reconstruction necessary after 1919.

The author believes it is top-management planning that has to consider economic conditions and at the same time actually creates them. The main idea in company orientation planning is to achieve steady and continued progress for the company, which naturally means the same for its employees.

It is well brought out in the book that in past decades, all this vital and basic thinking was supposed to be performed by intuition, superior abilities, and by formulas, an expectation which was not always borne out by results; nor was this thinking always done as methodically, systematically, and thoroughly as it should have been. In the final chapter the author concludes: "This new approach is based on the belief that by the 'factual' study of the root problems of top-management and by careful decisions made at the source of industrial action there should and can be created not maximum profits for some times, but maximum employment for all times, which is considered the best and most desirable basis for individual, company, and general progress."

CONFERENCE LEADERSHIP TRAINING

By Edward S. Maclin & Paul T. McHenry. Deep River, Conn.
National Foremen's Institute. 1945. 77 pp. $2.50

Reviewed by Al. Christian

Conferences as a medium for getting things done by collective agreement have come to be generally accepted as standard practice in many organizations. And yet the procedure and technique employed in such important time-consuming meetings are often loosely drawn-up or lacking entirely. The conference as a meeting technique is not new, it is quite generally used—and yet so little is really known about its structure, purpose and possibilities. Business literature today has very little information on when conferences should be called and how they should be planned and conducted.

Those who use the conference method and prefer their reading reduced to the bare essentials will appreciate this little book. Some may feel the publishers have over-priced the simply bound 77 page publication at $2.50 per copy, but others will find so many sound ideas and suggestions crammed between these covers as to be worth many times the cost of the small volume.

The authors have presented the subject in the simplest style possible and the general text is very easy reading. It is not intended as a text for the trainee, but prepared as a guide for the conference leader and those who intend to use the conference method in their work. The advantages and disadvantages of the conference technique are clearly presented and the reader is given a complete plan for laying out the procedures. In addition to the practical form and various devices used in dealing with different situations, the authors show how current practices can be compared and appraisals made for evaluating whatever conference work the reader may now be conducting.

This little volume is a work book in the technique of the conference method and should prove valuable to anyone interested in developing conference leadership. Recommended for all personnel managers, training directors, and department heads who confer with others and desire to improve their meeting and conference results.

NEWS NOTE

A group of Hartford men are reviving an organization called the Man Marketing Clinic. Sponsored by the Sales Managers Club and the Hartford Times, its members meet weekly in an effort to "find themselves."

The plan is simple. A member's letter applying for, and describing his preference for a particular job is read before the group and criticized. The resultant pool of ideas diagnoses the applicant's qualifications objectively and suggests the proper method of selling himself to the proper market. The Clinic has met with success in helping many Hartfordites "put the round peg in the round hole".

PERSONNEL
Journal

The Magazine of

LABOR RELATIONS AND PERSONNEL PRACTICES

Published by PERSONNEL RESEARCH FEDERATION

Lincoln Building, 60 East 42nd Street, New York City

Volume 24   *Number 9*

Contents for March 1946

EDITORIAL BOARD

After Negotiating a Labor Contract You Have to
Live with It—And Live with It in Such a Manner
that the Next One Isn't Worse.   Most Companies
Do Not Realize This So Year by Year Their Negotiations Get Worse and Worse.

Labor Relations Control

By Bernard C. Ashwin

San Francisco, Cal.

W ITH *disturbed labor relations filling the air, and many companies involved in disputes, those who have so far avoided trouble have a job to do in seeing that they do not
unwittingly set in motion underlying, and often hidden currents, which may suddenly precipitate a crisis.*

*One group of companies, formed into an association covering one region, and having a
uniform labor agreement, wished to see how they stood in this matter.   They have had no
troubles so far and do not want any.*

Possible Danger Spots

B ELOW *there is a report of a preliminary survey, which attempted to show wherein the strength
of their policies and practices lay, and to find out what, if any, possible danger spots there
were.*

*The industry, through its association, negotiates annually a uniform labor agreement,
which is signed annually with two unions, a skilled craft organization, and a semi-industrial
organization covering the semi-skilled and unskilled workers.   Both unions are AFL, and have
an agreement between themselves dating back to 1908 that they will not raid each other.*

*The uniform agreement under consideration here covers some 15,000 employees in 34 plants.
The first organization of the employees and drawing up of agreement coincided with the setting
up of the New Deal.*

*The grievance machinery under the agreement provides for a joint standing committee in
each plant.*

It also provides for a Joint Relations Board for the whole industry, which is the final court of appeal. On this Board are four labor representatives and four management representatives. If the Board deadlocks, it must request a U. S. district court judge to select an extra impartial person to aid in rendering a majority decision. The Board handles about one case a year. Thus it will be seen that this Board is comparatively inactive.

A curious feature of the set up is a so-called Permanent Classification Committee, which though not mentioned at all in the agreement, is used much more than the formal Joint Board. Its function seems to be to make interpretations of the uniform agreement, when such interpretations are requested by plant standing committees. Following is the report of the preliminary survey to the Secretary of the Permanent Classification Committee.

UNIFORM LABOR AGREEMENT

ONE of the important things noted in the agreement is the provision, in certain clauses, permitting some variation to meet local conditions.

This seems important, in an industry wide agreement. That is to say it should be recognized as a principle, in writing such agreements.

The areas permitting such variations, however, must be carefully demarked, and provision made for their central control.

It is interesting that there is no mention in the agreement of the Permanent Classification Committee. (More of this committee later.)

It would be interesting and valuable to trace the modifications which have taken place in the agreement over the years—at least the major ones—and the reasons which led to these changes.

It is understood that a transcript of negotiations is available through which such a study could be made. This would reflect not only internal changes, but the effect of changing social theories in regard to labor—and the necessity or advisability of going along with those, rather than putting up strong resistance. It would help future negotiations.

It is understood that negotiations are preceded by a caucus, convention or conference by each side. The nature of these meetings should be looked into, to determine their value, and their effect on negotiations.

Irrelevant Matters

IT IS understood that at times delegates in negotiation bring up matters, which may be individual, or group grievances, and do not properly belong in negotiations for an agreement.

It is said that the negotiating conference disallows these matters as irrelevant to the proceedings. It is said that in one division, any such matters attempted to be introduced, while squashed at the time, are noted and followed up, to ensure their satisfactory settlement. This is an important matter—often disregarded in negotiations—and should be an essential part of any negotiations.

This matter should be looked into to see the nature of such complaints brought up by delegates, their origins, their effect on negotiations, and the method of follow-up used.

Steps should be taken through the Manufacturers' Assn. to encourage other companies to understand their importance, and follow them up to a satisfactory conclusion.

It is recognized that these matters do not belong in annual negotiations, yet they indicate that employees have not gained satisfaction through other machinery set up for the purpose—possibly through the Joint Relations Board, which it is understood is not used a great deal.

Streamlining Negotiations

IT is understood that in negotiating the last agreement, whether by prior arrangement or not, the union in its meeting reduced the matters to go into negotiation from 95 to 3, thus "streamlining" the negotiations, and reducing the number of amendments to the agreement.

What became of the other 92 matters brought up to the union meeting by the delegates? Is there some danger that they were not satisfactorily dealt with by the union, and may continue through the year as sore spots, in which small groups of employees or locals remain discontented.

In so far as they were not brought to the attention of employers, the latter have no means of identifying them or dealing with them. Or have they?

Maybe if this procedure is to continue, the union should be encouraged to point out, where suitable, that these matters possibly should go before the Joint Relations Board, rather than have them smothered.

It is understood that the principle has been introduced, as a means of eliminating the consideration of matters affecting limited groups, from industry wide negotiations, that a delegate to the negotiations, does not represent his local, but represents his international union.

If this be so, then it must be ensured that local matters get consideration somewhere, either through appropriate action within the union setup, or through the use of some joint machinery provided. If this joint machinery is not used sufficiently its use might be encouraged.

Union Despotism

ONE of the things involved here, and it is important in terms of the possible growth of a pattern, that if it is allowed to develop too much, it might cause an unexpected explosion.

This is what might be termed despotism of union officials. They, in not a few cases, sometimes with the encouragement of the employer, have tended to squash their more dissenting members and locals, rather than deal with their problems in an attempt to gain satisfaction and understanding.

If there is any such tendency, this should be definitely guarded against in the current development—or it may breed future trouble.

This is a definite point at which an employer can assist in moulding the nature of the union structure along sound lines.

It is understood that the two internationals this year requested separate referendums on the terms of agreement. What does this portend? Is there a reason for it? What dangers for the future are involved? Does it indicate the seeds of a cleavage?

PERMANENT CLASSIFICATION COMMITTEE

THE Permanent Classification Committee comprises two men, a vice-president and the industrial relations director of one large company. This committee, solely of employer representatives, hands down approximately one interpretation of the agreement per month, and has done so for the last 8 years.

Under present arrangements copies of interpretations are sent to union representatives, with the request that they express an opinion or disagreement with each decision. Unions are also asked to participate in defining points to be submitted to the Classification Committee.

How did this committee come to be set up? It apparently deals with matters which are regarded as strictly the prerogative of management to settle. Yet where this is often formally so, yet it is deemed advisable in some cases to consult labor in regard to some matters.

What is its relation to the Joint Relations Board? Why do standing committees refer matters to it rather than to the J. R. B.? It is readily seen that it is a much cleaner process.

It is evident from the letter of March 29, 1941, dealing with the withdrawal of Interpretation 40-85, that the union does have some influence of the committee's decisions. What is this relationship?

TABLE I

INTERPRETATIONS BY SUBJECT AND YEAR

SUBJECT	YEAR							NO DATE	TOTALS
	1935	1936	1937	1938	1939	1940	1941		
Call Time and Allowances........	1	10	10	3	8	3	3		38
Overtime......................	1	3	2	5	1			2	14
Sunday Work, etc..............			3						3
Breakdowns, etc...............			2			4			6
Membership...................		2			1				3
Work Assignments and Rates.....	1	4	1	1	1	1		1	10
Misc.........................	4	3	1			2			10
Vacation Pay.................						3	2		5
Totals......................	7	22	19	9	11	13	5	3	89

Tabulated analysis have been made of the decisions and interpretations of the committee. Table I shows these by subjects and years. It shows that questions of call time and allowances have loomed large, but that their number tends to decrease as time passes. Other questions have been overtime and work assignments and rates.

There is a natural general tendency for the number or cases per year to decrease, but this is modified by new conditions, presumably setting up new clauses in the agreement, for example vacations coming in, presumably in 1940 have occasioned interpretations, as did a series of breakdowns which occurred in the fast pick up of business in 1940.

Decisions Analysed

As the Classification Committee is an employer committee, without labor representation, I analysed its decisions as well as I could to see if there was any bias. I did this adopting the Labor Dept's form. The results are shown in Table II.

TABLE II

ANALYSIS OF INTERPRETATIONS OF CLASSIFICATION COMMITTEE

Workers gain substantially what asked for	34
Intermediate result	7
Little or no gain to workers	38
Clarifications	14
Total	93

Two points are interesting. One is an absence of bias or favor in the decisions. The second point is the clear cut nature of the interpretations, one way or the other, with a negligible number of what might be called compromises.

These two points are a distinct tribute to the work of the committee. They also indicate the possible value to industries of such committees, instead of joint boards, which more often lead to compromises in order to get fairness.

I also analysed the decisions in terms of the plants which had asked for interpretations. The results show C, 15, P, 13, F, 11, H, 6. All others less than 5.

This analysis does not reveal anything to me. I do however think that where there are sufficient cases such analyses are valuable to throw light on, or cause to be considered, whether any plant is having difficulty in coming to an understanding with the standing committee, and needs some help in its negotiations.

It is an important control, in this respect, particularly with large industries and companies more scattered than yours is.

Analysis by Sections of Agreement

I ALSO analysed the number of interpretations required by Sections in the agreement, with the following result:

This analysis was made to see whether there should be thought given to the question as to whether those clauses which need more interpreting need revision, or whether the many interpretations needed arise out of the very nature of the subject dealt with, and the many local variations that may occur.

I was interested in the number of cases in which the answer was definitely "Yes" or "No". Also in the fact that you did not do this unless appropriate. In some circumstances you found it more suitable to state or clarify the principle involved, with reference to other interpretations, and put upon local managment the responsibility of making the final decision on the point.

Here is involved the question of the responsibility of local management, and standing committees to make decisions, and refer to your committee only in appropriate cases. There is grave danger, with such committees, that local people will dodge responsibility by passing the buck to such a committee. You seem to have successfully avoided this.

Your decisions refusing local groups, even by mutual agreement, from breaking away from the terms and intent of the agreement is most interesting. In a sense you are acting as a watch dog to ensure that the ever present danger of an industry wide agreement disintegrating does not take place—even where the local parties have every good faith and intention but may accidentally stumble in the direction of disintergration of the uniform agreement.

JOINT RELATIONS BOARD

I HAVE had no opportunity to inquire into the work of this board—which I understand has been little.

I should like to look into its functions, relation to your classification committee, relation to standing committees, cases so far brought before it, etc.

•   I should also like to study the facts and implications of the case in which the question of invoking section 4b (page 21 of agreement) came up. (Deadlock case.)

I should also like to see its relationship to the points made in paragraphs (5) and (7) above (Under Uniform Labor Agreement Discussion).

STANDING COMMITTEES AND LOCAL UNION RELATIONSHIPS

OUT of these come vital pressures affecting major industry wide negotiations. I should like to study this cause and effect relation.

COMMUNITY RELATIONS AND PERSONNEL ADMINISTRATION

I HAVE the most scant knowledge of these at present. While I think the former is very important, and would like an opportunity to look into it, as affecting negotiations, I would not propose to look into the latter—also important— except as it comes incidentally into the picture, or if it may seem that certain practices might be added to help the negotiating situation.

However I do think that the subject of job classification, which you have been dealing with for six years, and which is a potential danger spot in all industry wide negotiations, should be looked into, in so far as records are available. This would be with a view to making an attempt to see what might be done at some appropriate time in the future.

Overall Considerations

NOT coming under the heading personnel administration but rather Industrial Relations Administration comes the most important question of your own relationship to the unions, your mill managers and officers of other companies.

This function seems to again involve the problems of uniformity with proper adjustment to local circumstances, the question of the responsibility of local managers, your function as advisor and possibly educator to them, so that they may not come to rely too much on you, rather than stand on their own feet—always a difficult problem.

It also involves the problem of your delineating a set of principles upon which the developments of the uniform labor agreement, and its negotiation and administration, shall depend. This is so because while the relations and agreements must now be the outcome of your architecture, in large part, the structure should be so understood, that if, in the course of time, you go on to broader administrative work, and can give less attention to it, it will continue to grow and develop along the sound lines you have laid down, and the basic continuum be established.

> When Companies Have Extra Money to Give to
> Employees They Often Give It to Them for the
> Times When They Are Not Working Instead of
> Giving it to Them for the Work They Do. (Re-
> port to Company.)

Personnel Paradoxes

By Joseph H. Frost

Stanford University, California

IT IS recommended that the company modify the features of the personnel program concerned with maintenance training and financial compensation with a view to more correctly and directly satisfying the psychological needs and desires of each individual employee. The main modifications seen necessary follow:

Plan for Rapid Promotion

IT IS suggested that the company maintain a satisfied, even enthusiastic, body of workers by the unorthodox method of setting up personnel machinery to get the best workers *out* of their jobs as quickly as possible! By this I mean to provide for as rapid a promotion system within the company as is possible; aid each individual to qualify for promotion as quickly as he can by providing both general and highly specialized training; and, if positions to absorb newly qualified workers are not available within the company, to conduct a vigorous search for advanced positions outside the company for these workers. In short, do everything possible to convince the worker that his interests and his advancement are being jealously sought by the management—even to the extent of promoting him outside the company if it is to his advantage, and he desires it.

In the case of executives, develop an even more intense program of promotion within the company, and wherever possible on out of the company to better positions in other companies. This rather unusual policy is based upon the assumption that the company will be in existence for decades to come. Therefore it is wisdom itself to establish such a reputation for rapid promotions in the company that the better men entering industry each year will be inevitably drawn to the company.

The loss of well-trained men will never offset the gain to the company of a steady influx of the best men available—all eager to make good and to advance until they, too, can be promoted to the top brackets of the company, or graduated out to better positions in other firms.　Such a body of men permeating the organization would give it such life and esprit de corps that the future of the company would be practically assured, if reasonable management were practiced in other fields.

Plan Worker Participation

THERE should be established in the collective mind of all executives and all personnel department workers the conviction that in the long run workers will willingly and staunchly support a wage scale or any similar structure only if they have had a good hand in framing it.　Further, spread the recognition that in this process of not only allowing but encouraging the workers to take a firm hand in the development work lies the greatest opportunity for educating the workers in the multitudinous aspects of the organization and its operation.

More effectively here, perhaps, than in any other method, the workers can come to understand the relation of one job to another, the vexing problems of management, the ultimate justice of the plan of financial compensation, the value of further training, the relative position of each worker in the company, and all the similar items that make up comprehension of the organization and the human beings that comprise it.

Recognize Gregarious Tendencies

EXECUTIVES at all levels should be brought to recognize the gregarious tendencies and needs of all men—recognize their universal desire for friendly fraternization with their fellows.　Assist such wholesome fraternization during normal working hours and in the actual performance of the job.　The worker wishes to feel that he is in a friendly atmosphere of good fellowship while he works.　Only a rare individual is so misanthropic as to hope his fellows will not have a smile or shout of friendship for him across his machine.　This friendliness while working need not slow the job. There are many approaches to this problem.　One of the best is organizing the workers into small functional groups where:

> pay is for the group product,
> all feel that they are members of a team,
> each may come to have a definite status in the group,
> better workers may gain prestige by teaching and assisting the less skilled, or slower of their fellows,
> slower or newer workers may have friendly guidance and assistance from someone really and sincerely interested in their improvement.

Handout Policy Criticized

I WOULD in general criticize the present personnel program severely only in that it has aimed its attractive employee good will plums only at the times when the worker does not have to be at his machine (vacations-with-pay); at the time when

330

he will no longer be able to work (pensions and retirement plans); at the time when he is injured and hence away from his machine (first aid, home nurses, hospitalization); at the time when he is away from his machine after work (enjoyment of bonuses, incentive wages, etc).

Where, I question, is the effort to make pleasant the many long hours that are so very close to each man each and every day while he works at his place? Whether or not a man likes his job; whether or not he is enthusiastic about the quality of his company depend far more on his feeling of "belonging", of doing something important and significant, and of feeling that he has a respectable status in his company than they depend upon the benefits the company showers upon him. In time these benefits can all too easily come to be accepted as his due. The pleasure he finds in his work, however, is a continuing and steady source of satisfaction.

All efforts should point to improving those psychological conditions that lead to this desirable state of satisfaction.

Reorientation of Executive Viewpoint

IN A company with as forward looking and sound a personnel policy as that found, there is little room for spectacular improvement of the details of financial compensation, or of training. Hence they would require long and careful study before wise modifications could be made, and they are not discussed in detail here. Instead it is felt far more advantageous to the company to devote initial efforts to the reorientation of the viewpoint of executives and personnel workers to one of concern for the psychological needs and desires of the worker *while he is actually on the job.*

Actual details of methods for catering to these psychological needs are less difficult, less important, and less urgent than is recognition of the nature of those needs. Moreover, the proper detailed method to apply can be more or less readily agreed upon when thorough understanding of each individual need has been achieved through careful analysis. Therefore, the following pages list only the more important psychological needs, and leave the detailed procedures to future careful study on the ground.

Individual Needs

IN ORDER to achieve satisfaction in his work each man individually needs:

1. To have belief in the value and importance of his job.

2. A very clear understanding of what is to be done, and just what is expected of him, and the rewards for both normal and superior performance.

3. To have faith in the continuity of his job—or a clear initial understanding of the seasonality effects, etc., and the probability and extent of layoffs.

4. Assurance of minimum guarantees of compensation to give a feeling of security day by day.

5. To feel that compensation is adequate and just for the amount of work and the relative rank of the job.

6. To be assured that promotion is based entirely on merit and service and not on favoritism.

7. A clear understanding of the possibilities for promotion in rank, and in pay within a grade.

8. To have a feeling of partnership with management and his fellow workers through a complete knowledge of the general operation of the organization, and in particular of the part his job plays in the production of the finished article.

Social Needs

THE average worker feels a definite need to "belong". He finds greatest satisfaction in a work atmosphere where the men about him are his friends, are interested in what he is doing, believe that he is doing his part. He needs to be convinced that they approve of him and are convinced that he is carrying his part of the load. He needs to believe that they are all doing their share—in short he needs to have a *recognized status* in a group of surrounding workers whose opinion he values.

He needs to belong to some little group or "informal organization" of his fellow workmen. That is, he needs buddies. He needs to be one of a little clique that lunches together, or that pauses from their work as a group for a cigarette.

Although detailed attacks upon these problems are properly the subject only of investigation on the ground where the job is in progress, a general attack is worthy of mention since it applies throughout the company.. This is the incorporation of large size name plates into the company identification discs, and requiring that such plates be worn while at work. The greatest single barrier to friendly intercourse between two men is crossed when each can call the other by name readily. A man's sense of belonging is greatly enhanced by the acquisition of the ability to call a considerable number of his surrounding workmen by name. Just the mere exchange of "goodmorning" greetings can give a feeling of intense satisfaction—and those greetings are seldom forthcoming from a large group unless there is an easy means of becoming acquainted with each man's name.

Moreover, if the name letters are sufficiently large outsiders, particularly and importantly management personnel, can pick up a man's name at a glance without embarassing squinting at the name plate. Then it is easy to speak to him in a more cordial and friendly manner by calling his name in greeting. Such a greasing of the skids allows intercourse to slide along smoothly, and hence is an invaluable adjunct to better relations between each man and his mates.

Need for Faith in Leaders

IF EACH worker is to throw himself enthusiastically into his work, he must:

1. Be thoroughly convinced that his leaders are sincerely interested in his problems, his success and his advancement.

2. Be convinced of the fairness of his leaders.

3. Be able to believe that his company is well-organized, and efficient. He must be able to be proud of his outfit and the article it produces.

4. Believe that his interests will be considered in all actions taken by management.

5. Believe that he is being led by his immediate supervisors toward the accepted objectives of his job, and toward his own personal gain.

Need for Sense of Achievement

THE worker needs to believe that management is really interested in the quality of his work. In some fields of high skill, the need for recognition of quality is greater than the need for bonuses for increases in quantity of production. Where work is on other than a piece basis, and quality is measurable, it becomes of greater importance in giving the worker satisfaction than the quantity of output. This is particularly true of all but the highest executive positions.

Public recognition of the quality of a man's work is quite important to him no matter how much he may publicly scoff at the idea. It is the published recognition that he can take home to his wife to obtain her praise, and it is published recognition that improves his status in the eyes of his fellows. Recognition need not be in monetary form. Ribbons, cups, postings on bulletin boards, and mentions in the columns of the company paper probably furnish more lasting pleasure than a small reward in money.

Every man has a need for the hope and possibility of achievement. If large achievements, such as promotions, are not immediately possible, it is essential that small achievements be within range, such as the company paper, and bulletin board mentions indicated above.

The Army and Navy Spent Much Time and Money Training Our Armed Forces. These Men, so Trained, Should Be Much More Valuable to Industry Than a Group of Untrained Men.

Veterans
in Industry

By George E. Tucker

Tubize Rayon Corporation,
Rome, Ga.

THE returning veterans of World War II offer a source of labor to Industry that is superior to any other now existing. It is estimated that 21% of these men will choose some type of industrial work as a means for earning a living and another 25% are undecided what type of work they will take up. It is reasonable to believe that a large part of this 25% who are undecided will turn to industrial jobs. It might be profitable if Industry would make an effort to employ all of this 25%.

To fully appreciate the value to Industry of men who have been trained in the Army and have served in the field, requires some knowledge of how a soldier is trained in the Army and what he does in the field. With this knowledge, a review of the qualities desired by an employer of an employee will indicate that the veteran more than fits the bill.

False Impressions

BEFORE discussing this subject any further, the false impression that men who have been trained in the Army and have fought in combat have gone through some change which makes them problems for society, must be dispelled. It is quite true that the hazards and hardships of training and combat are a tremendous strain on the nervous system and that some few men become permanent nervous casualties. It is reasonable and logical to believe, however, that those who go through this without becoming nervous casualties have demonstrated the ability to stand up under trying conditions.

Once removed from hazards of combat and hardships of training and given a short period of rest, the veteran will be the same man fundamentally, improved as a result of his experiences and travels. These men have had vigorous physical and mental requirements to meet over a long period which has, no doubt, left its mark and the inclination will be to carry on. This may be construed to be a general improvement in the average veteran over the average man of the same age who has had no Army experience. There are, no doubt, some veterans who feel that the world owes them a living and they will use any ruse to collect their wages. These men, most likely, will play the sympathy game to the fullest. It is felt that this class is a small percentage of the whole.

Qualities Developed

TRAINING in the U. S. Army develops in each individual the following qualities: morale, discipline, health and endurance, technical proficiency, initiative, adaptability, leadership, teamwork and tactical proficiency. Successful operation in combat requires the application of all these qualities. The veteran returned to civilian life after a successful period in the Army will be possessed of these qualities. The qualities desired by any personnel manager in an employee include most of those named above. Where else can he find men who have been so trained and proven?

Industrial organizations are set up in a very similar manner to organizations in the Army. The administrative and sphere of responsibility system used in Industry in most aspects is the same, as is called in the Army, channels of command. This is the part of the organization responsible to get things done. Each commander in the Army has his staff, who are specialists and work out the details, which is comparable with the managers, superintendents, and general foremen's staffs in Industry. Every man trained in the Army thoroughly understands the system and also understands that he is required to do what he is instructed or ordered to do from the man having the proper authority. He also understands that he will some day have the next higher job if his performance and proficiency warrants the promotion.

Do Not Molly-coddle

THE success of handling the veteran in Industry will depend upon the application of two fundamental principles: (1) *forget the war* and (2) *do not molly-coddle*.

Many of the returning men have had' very violent emotional experiences, and would prefer to forget about it. In another light, no man can live on his laurels nor can he remain in the Army mentally and make progress on his new job. "Forget the War" might be considered the number one basic principle for handling veterans.

There are, no doubt, some good samaritans who insist on giving the veteran special privileges, setting him upon a pinnacle, handling him with kid gloves and giving him, always, the easiest job. No man wants to be molly-coddled. The soldier is habitually treated firmly and required to accomplish the mission regardless of self-discomfort or the risk involved. In other words, the soldier has character. Probably the surest and quickest way to make a soldier lose his self respect, character and the will to constantly improve himself is to treat him as a tin god. *"Do not molly-coddle"* might be considered the number two basic principle for handling veterans.

What Is Meant?

Existing in the minds of all is the thought that the men who fought the war should be given every consideration possible. This is as it should be. The question immediately arises: what is meant by giving a man every consideration possible? Certainly reminding a man of grim experiences and undermining his self respect and character cannot be said to be giving a man consideration. Some men recently returned from combat and oversea duty may give the outward appearance of being shaky and licked.

This is merely a superficial thing and any thought that it is a weakness is a false idea and to disregard the two basic principles mentioned above as a remedy is an injustice and not a consideration. A good example of human endurance was shown in Germany just after the cessation of hostilities. The people, although apparently shaky and licked, seriously and earnestly started the job of recovery and rehabilitation. This is not to be construed to mean that the Germans are, by any stretch of the imagination, supermen but cited as an indication of endurance since the people to the last woman and child were on the battlefield for several years.

The idea should prevail that the veteran has been through an arduous and hazardous period during which he accomplished a hard job in a superior manner and is a better man as the result.

Number of Medals Should Not Count

With the two fundamental principles for handling the veteran in mind, other thoughts must be considered in employing these men to give maximum satisfaction to both the employee and employer. As many veterans should be employed as is possible by industry. It would be unsatisfactory to lay off employees in order to employ veterans; however, the veteran should be given priority in replacing losses by normal attrition. This plan, no doubt, will show enough preference to satisfy the average veteran's feeling that he deserves some preference. Once employed, he should be processed and placed as any other new employee. In the case of a veteran who is a former employee of the company, the man should be given the opportunity to have his former job back but not automatically placed in it.

The veteran wearing the greatest number of decorations should not be given the best job because of his decorations. Certainly the decorations indicate that he has done a good job in the Army and he is to be commended for that. There are many men released from the Army, all having had the same training, who are not wearing several ribbons. These men have not had the opportunity to win decorations in many cases. Most decorations are won in unusual situations. Even in combat the situation is normal most of the time and all Infantrymen do not have equal opportunity to win medals. The average Artilleryman does not have as many chances to win a medal as the average Infantryman. It is not intended that any credit or glory be taken away from the decorated man, but it must be realized that he is not the best man for Industry because of his decorations.

Treat Like Any Other

ONCE the veteran is placed on his job it is essential that he be treated as any other employee both on the job and off the job. Management must be just and firm in handling the veteran as in handling anyone else and if necessary more so because he is trained to respond to this type of treatment. He is trained to do the job in keeping with prescribed rules and he has shown that he can and will do it under trying conditions.

Many veterans have never had a civilian job and many desire to do something new. Industry will not be gambling to hire every available one but will be making a sound investment. The employing of veterans will not present a labor handling problem but on the other hand it will ease the labor handling problem by having men who have had uniform training and experiences over a long period of time.

Trained in Teamwork

THE soldier is trained in teamwork and a great many are still living because teamwork was practiced in combat. Throughout Industry it is necessary for men to work closely with others and depend on each other's work to accomplish a given job. Even though it seems rather simple for a man to work in a group, it has been seen many times that the spirit of cooperation and teamwork is lacking and the job suffering as a result. To successfully work a veteran as a part of a team requires only the application of the principles.

The men being discharged from the Army offer Industry a large pool of men suitable in every respect for employment. Management can, with some thought on the subject and application of a few simple principles, take advantage of this supply of labor and at the same time give the veteran a deserved opportunity.

A Suggestion System Is a Peculiar Psychological Arrangement. The Suggestor Most Often Offends his Know-All Boss But Feels that He Cannot Stand Superior Dumbness All His Working Life—So Sticks His Neck Out and Makes a Suggestion.

$1000 *for* the Boss
$50 *for* Me

By Robert B. Shapiro

Formerly Picatinny Arsenal
Dover, N. J.

MORE money to workers—increased profits—higher production—lower unit costs—Utopia or impossible? It can be done—because it *has* been done.

A great deal is written and heard of the technical, atomic improvements of the War and about new and better products. Far in the background, a discriminating listener occasionally hears a timid voice whispering of less spectacular war-inspired developments. At least one of these—within the easy grasp of any business with 25 to 25,000 workers—is the method of encouraging workers to sell management their ideas as to how production can be improved—often labeled by the limiting term of Suggestions System.

Results Summarized

MUCH has been written on the subject in the past. A few outstanding examples of profitable use of such techniques are generally known to specialists in the field of Industrial Management.

Just how were 5,697,748 dollars in savings realized within four years in four plants geographically adjacent and all under one administration—along with the corresponding increases in production, reduction in unit costs and thousands of dollars of additional income to workers?

Why from 18,000 workers in 1941 were only 113 suggestions received and only three adopted; in 1942 only 1,490 ideas submitted with 128 adopted, but in 1944 a total of 4,789 suggestions were made with 962 adopted resulting in savings of $2,724,574 for that year alone?

Fortunately, objective, scientific facts are available for progressive management to answer such questions and thus make available war-developed or improved techniques which might otherwise be forgotten, discarded or lost in the shuffle.

Three Broad Phases

THE experiment divided itself into three broad phases.

Phase one was the initial period when there was a suggestion system in name only, lip service to the method, no financial awards—no publicity—no worker recognition through certificates or other written forms of commendation and no definite procedures for handling suggestions.

Second phase during 1942 and part of 1943 when everything possible was done at one time or other including use of the height of patriotic urges—*except* using financial awards.

Third phase—the addition of financial payments and recognition of the oft "forgotten man", the supervisor.

The end results of the three phases in 1941–1942 and 1944 have already been pointed out. By analyzing the three phases we find the factual answers to questions often raised but seldom answered other than by opinions. Should supervisors be paid for ideas; who should be on the evaluating committee; what to do about rejected ideas; how about improvements on improvements; must the idea be new or novel; why pay for adoption of commercially available improvements; what are the relative merits of semi-annual drives against constant "pressure"; should names of suggestors be anonymous during investigation; who whould have the responsibility of investigating submitted ideas—and the follow through; should the suggestion unit be a funnel or a sieve; best frequency of (a) picking up suggestions from boxes, (b) acknowledgements to suggestors, (c) interim reports to suggestor; what to do with suggestions that are really complaints?

This Was an Experiment

DURING the course of four years of this controlled and measured experiment, elements were added or taken away—results measured in terms of volume, caliber, extent and dollar value of suggestions. From this, definite conclusions—do's and don'ts—methods and techniques evolved.

For brevity, rather than give details of all the comparable measured results when different elements or time intervals were tried in the various phases, the ultimate major conclusions are recorded here.

Convenient, attractive suggestion boxes containing simple forms for writing suggestions and having a place for a small poster—changed every three to four weeks—not on the same corresponding day, increase volume of suggestions. Use of bi-monthly slogan or other contests with entries sent through suggestion boxes only, advertises places of suggestion depositories and increases their use.

Pick-up of suggestions from boxes every five to seven days with a written acknowledgement to suggestor within 24 hours after receipt proved to be the most efficient "frequency". Explanation by a short phrase in the letter of acknowledgement giving the expected time for investigation of the suggestion avoids worker's "anxiety". An interim report every forty days to suggestor, if no final action takes place within such time, materially enchances worker's interest and faith in the system—as well as unconsciously acting as a reminder or impulse to submit additional ideas. An outstanding example occurred while one suggestor had seven ideas pending, his eighth hit the "jack pot" with an annual saving of $155,000 resulting from a single change capable of being adopted within 5 days after receipt of suggestion.

Full Time Job for One Unit

CONFIDENCE by all concerned in the integrity, objectivity and competency of the unit handling suggestions is imperative. If such unit is also charged with other duties, the whole system will suffer in direct ratio to the amount of such additional responsibilities. Accordingly, while production engineering, planning, research and development or methods units must constantly be "keyed in", experience proved that when any one of such units were charged with the program's responsibility, results suffered. While many setups were tried, most successful operation resulted from having the suggestion unit administratively attached to the personnel department, especially for clerical assistance, procedure and routine, as well as an objective approach.

Measured control during all three phases verified that not only is the suggestion system an integral part of a healthy progressive personnel policy but for best results—a necessary adjunct to time and motion study, work simplification, training, and wage incentive plans based on unit output or group incentives—especially in avoiding worker or supervisor resistance to changes or new work habits. Like other matters, follow-up of installed suggestions proved vital and necessary not only for the actual suggested installation, but in similar situations in other work units. In one instance when tote boxes were placed on wheels in the metal shops, due to lack of follow through, wheels were not used on tote boxes in the sewing unit a mile away.

Anonymity Not Necessary

THE use of numbered suggestion blanks to guard anonymity did not prove necessary —but rather a lame apology to participants of the integrity of the suggestion unit and an obstacle to full investigation. However, during investigation, except where necessary, the source of the suggestion was not disclosed in order to minimize the possibility of jealousy or prejudice.

Best results were obtained when the suggestion unit acted as a funnel—not a sieve, and used its own investigators to personally follow through a suggestion both before and after adoption—always allowing the operating unit concerned final approval or disapproval. Thus are avoided pitfalls of jealousy, jamming new things down throats and retention of objectivity by the suggestion unit with continued confidence in it by suggestors and continued emphasis upon the necessity of diplomacy and salesmanship by the investigator. For these reasons, it was found that tact, diplomacy, inquisitiveness, salesmanship and common sense were more important attributes of an investigator than an engineering education or background. This was added value when, for various reasons, some suggestions could not be used, it was found just as important to explain the reasons in simple language to the suggestor, as any other single technique.

Dealing with Rejections

To COMPLETELY insure maximum possible suggestor satisfaction, results proved the advisability of always including and inviting exercise of the right of appeal in all letters of rejection. Psychologically, the use of the words "rejected" or "impractical" invited argument and hence were carefully avoided. The result was that contrary to prevailing opinion, there was a relatively small percentage of frivolous appeals. Instead, in several instances, reinvestigations based on additional facts or idea variations submitted with the appeals, permitted adoption of formerly rejected suggestions whose value far outweighed the time and trouble consumed by all reinvestigations and appeals.

Experience showed that unless rejections were based on good reasons, fully and tactfully explained, the next idea was *not* submitted. Furthermore, the working companions of the suggestor became exposed to an "againster", thus directly and adversely affecting their participation like a rolling snow ball ever increasing in size.

Experience also proved that few workers express their ideas as lucidly as they have thought them out. In one instance a very crude sketch with a few words of explanation in a foreign language resulted in an improvement saving $23,000. Because of this and the proven value of not overlooking a worker's ego—measured results showed the advantage of personal contact by the investigator with every suggestor and his supervisor. Thus, the suggestor would know by additional means, his work—and it is work to think and write—was receiving attention and the investigator was also able to get verbal amplification of the idea and have supervision keyed in.

Prompt Payment of Maximum Cash

IN THE second phase of the experiment, greater results were obtained through publicity in the plant newspaper; posters; rallies; awards of certificates; letters of commendation; labor-management committees; and care in acknowledging and investigating suggestions. Such methods brought good results. But even to the individual most susceptible to recognition and personal pride, the novelty soon diminishes and the gremlin of "what money is in it for me" begins to wreak havoc unless recognized by more direct financial payment than just giving the suggestor promotions in terms of a better job or increased wage rates.

The third phase proved conclusively the necessity for prompt payment of the greatest possible cash based on a percentage of net *estimated* savings for the first year. In this instance, only 5 per cent was the maximum allowed due to factors beyond local control—still the amazing results followed, and undoubtedly would have increased, in a sizable ratio if larger percentage payments could have been used. The greater the payment, the better is the antidote to the ever present thought—"I saved the boss $1,000 and all I got was a measly 50 bucks."

Delays in making awards diminished interest. Holding award ceremonies at least once a month helped to stimulate worker participation.

Until the Awards Committee was made up of a wide representation of top management, union and supervision it did not have the prestige or respect for fairness essential to obtain maximum results.

"But For" Rule

THE simplest rule of thumb adopted in cases of doubt concerning credit for a suggestion, or even improvements upon it by others than those directly employed for such purposes, was the "But For" rule. Namely, if "But For" the suggestion, an improvement would not have been made at the time nor have had attention directed to it, the suggestor was paid the highest possible amount, resolving all doubts in the suggestor's favor.

The most workable philosophy—avoiding a great deal of wrangling and valuable committee time—included recognition of the fact that human error was always possible. But the error must be in favor of the suggestor—especially since in considering yearly averages, management and the stockholder received its fair share of "pay" due to the relatively low percentage of 5 per cent paid to the suggestor.

A cross index of past suggestions, rejected or adopted, proved invaluable. Occasions arise where, due to changed conditions, ideas not usable a year or two before, become of present value. Again the "But For" rule was used—especially in cases when a different suggestor at the later date called attention to the presently adoptable suggestion. In such instances an equitable distribution of payment available was made to both suggestors.

Cash Awards Absolutely Necessary

A WORD in passing should be noted of the school of thought—sometimes called old-fashioned or hard-headed, that the submission of new ideas is always part of the job for which all workers, and especially supervisors get their regular wages, so why pay for the same thing twice. The ultimate conclusion resulting from trial and measurement of several plans again resulted in use of the "But For" rule. Facts and practical considerations, rather than opinion, definitely proved that even if such was the case (only one supervisor was ever found who refused a cash payment), as a practical matter the vast majority of worker ideas just were *not* forthcoming without the added financial incentive.

When cash payments were withdrawn, the well would dry up, including contributions from those in high supervisory positions. Not many doubt the simple truth that human beings are by nature lazy, especially im their mental processes. We just don't like the labor of "thinking", so that every method and technique known, especially financial incentive, paid dividends by overcoming such inertia.

Here—just as in many other instances—supervision can make or break the best of things. Accordingly facts proved the necessity and good business of not only allowing direct participation of supervisors, but recognition to them through their employees' suggestions by contests, and by additional financial awards. The existence of an occasional "mooching" supervisor did not disprove the greater good obtained for the greater number. Rather it proved to be one more probing searchlight into the fog of evaluating supervision.

Supervisor training had a direct bearing in getting across to them the policy of management that no supervisor was expected to have *all* the new ideas and credit. No criticism reflected upon him when his workers submitted improvements. On the contrary, the more ideas his operators turned in, the better the supervisor was doing his job. The best means of demonstrating good faith to both worker and supervisor were financial payment and foreman recognition.

Grievances in Suggestion Form

SUGGESTIONS which in reality were complaints or grievances, while at first diste garded, later proved their worth and received the same careful attention as a machine improvement including a financial payment in instances indicated that "But For" the complaint, labor turnover causes, poor supervision, safety or waste might not have been as readily known to management. Such instances, as well as many others, did not always lend themselves to exact calculation of savings. Nonetheless, somewhat arbitrary financial payments were made—leaning toward the liberal side.

Mention should be made of the "ostrich neck in the sand" position decrying any use of a suggestions system because of a fear that workers would be encouraged thereby to complain, or would be dissatisfied sellers of ideas. Controlled experiments definitely showed no appreciable difference in this in operating plants with or without the suggestions system; and that where the system was properly, fairly, and democratically operated the number of dissatisfied sellers was negligible in comparison to the greater group of satisfied workers, management and stockholders. The futility of this negative position was as discredited by the measured facts as would be the refusal of a restaurant to stop buying eggs because, on rare occasions, a bad one might be found or served.

No Panacea for All Ills

A SUGGESTION system is no panacea for all ills. The most progressive management in all phases of personnel will not entirely avoid trouble—but the incidence and intensity can greatly be reduced.

It's part of the answer to the questions—always present on, or just below, the surface: "Does it Pay—Me?" "What will I get out of it?" "Why should I line the bosses' pocket?"

Experiments showed that, just as in sales promotion, best results and stimulus are obtained by constantly keeping the system before the workers with an "all out" campaign not more frequently than once or twice a year.

Incidental Advantages

IMPORTANT as financial gain to worker and management may be, measured results proved the suggestions system paid additional dividends such as: a concrete method of recognition of the individual worker as a member of the team, rather than a number on it; a type of two-way communication between worker, supervisor and management, including a valuable adjunct to a "preventive medicine" program in the form of a safety valve and means of uncovering and eliminating friction points.

The basic question in the minds of worker, supervisor, top management, union and stockholder or owner—yes, even the customer: Does it pay? or What will I get out of it?—seems generally overlooked. Yet by constantly using such a question as the theme—successful lower unit costs; improved labor-management relationships; worker income incentives; competitive advantage—are all within easy "paying" grasp.

In a slightly different setting—democracy in action has again proven its worth with the corollary that no system is very much better than the caliber of the people who administer it and the effort expended.

If the Supreme Court Decides that Management
Must Bargain with Foremen, Management is in
For a Rough Time. If It Decides the Other Way,
then Foremen Are in For a Very Rough Time.

Is *a* Foreman
a Worker?

BY T. H. FAIRCHILD

San Francisco, Cal.

I REMEMBER in the 1930s during the renaissance of union organization in our country, the foreman was by far and large the favorite whipping boy for the unions
at the negotiation table. I began to think in those days that the bosses were very
dumb to pick men like that, or the job itself distorted and warped men's minds. I
remember that the foreman was accused of favoritism, a sometimes human trait, had
no decency with female employees, did not know how to pick a man for promotion,
and in effect would ruin the entire industrial structure of our industry unless radical
changes were made, and particularly unless you signed a contract with the union.

Unions Blame Foremen

IN SOME cases the charges were no doubt valid but the great majority of them I suspect were simply aimed at the nearest element of management convenient to the
union darts. Although I might add that the boys from the unions were not adverse
to going all the way up the ladder with their invectives.

Those were days, to use a military term, of rear guard action in defense for the
management side. I remember all too well the half-hearted acquiescence by management that they would undertake a sweeping reform movement in the supervisory level
of foreman. The professional tub-thumpers on both sides seized this issue with great
glee and after many forums finally declared that the disease could properly be labeled
"foremanititis". Much was written and declaimed on the illness, and to be sure all
sorts of panaceas were offered.

Came the war with the resultant cry to forget all else in the production of war goods for the arsenal of democracy. The dread malady seemed to be forgotten for the moment. To be sure, hastily erected governmental agencies rushed into the fray with training courses for everyone including the foremen. Except for sporadic outbursts on the part of certain members of unions more refined in the art of industrial mayhem, the foreman was buried as a subject of public concern under the stress of war production. Everybody apparently thought he was doing a pretty good job.

Foremen Became "Good Guys"

B ut lo and behold, a sudden rumble on the industrial horizon gave flashes of lightning which spelled an end to the slumbering problem of the foreman. These embattled souls were fed up with status quo and were flocking to a union known as The Foremen's Association of America. They promised that they were organizing for the purposes of gaining their own benefits and would have no truck with the A.F.L. or C.I.O. However, the shoe seemed to be on the other foot and a very nice fit withal. The two large national labor organizations gazed on this new baby o organization with benign and interested eyes.

Suddenly the foreman became to them not the ogre of the 1930s, but simply a foundling of importance that surely would need their tender care and guidance. So the merry-go-round reversed itself and became a three ring circus between the foremen's union, management and the National Labor Relations Board. The latter did several inverted loops and finally came up with something that salved its conscience but proved nothing. At this writing it appears certain that the final tune will be played by the Supreme Court of the United States when it gets around to hearing the case of Packard Motor Company versus The Foremen's Association of America. Meanwhile the end of the war may very well change the complexion of the various segments of management.

Difference Between Operating and Administrative

R ecently while reading a most purposeful and useful book penned by Mr. Richard Weil, Jr. (The Art of Practical Thinking), I happened on this:

"An operating executive is a person who is supposed to supervise, at first hand, and in some sense practically to do himself, the task which is to be accomplished. [Foremen in factories] are examples of operating executives. They are the men in whom a certain amount of authority is vested and who are, at the same time, held responsible at first hand for the accomplishment of jobs. No intervening level of authority is interposed between them and the direct supervision of the work to be done. While they cannot, with their own two hands, do all the work, they can continuously and on the spot, with their own two eyes, oversee the doing of all the work, and therefore take complete and detailed responsibility for the manner of the execution."

"An administrative executive, instead of being able either to do the work in question or at firsthand to oversee with his own eyes practically every detail of the work, is forced to work almost entirely through other people. In large organizations, having several levels of executives, the administrative executive may have to work through people, who work through people, who work through still other people."

"It is important to understand the difference between these operating executives and an administrative executive is a difference not in degree, but in kind. The work of the administrative executive is a different kind of work."

At What Level Will Line Be Drawn?

THE foregoing seems to me to be a logical and clear breakdown of executive levels. The question that proposes itself is just where in the executive ladder the courts will draw a line beyond which executives are not entitled to the protection of the National Labor Relations Act. As far as my experience and training goes, I have always been under the impression that all executives who are not owners, are employees.

Henry Ford has an explicit and written agreement for his organized foremen with the F.A.A. No one seems to have sought his opinion, but it may be that he can give the answer as to where on the executive scale industry must draw the line.

The question as to whether the foreman will survive as a part of management is still waiting for the answer. In all it may be just a passing phase of American industry that was spurred by the war and nurtured on abnormal circumstances. But we don't think so.

HAVE YOU SPARE PERSONNEL JOURNALS?

Some issues of the Personnel Journal (as listed below) are required by reconverting industries, but are out of print.

If you have copies of these issues, which you are not now using, will you kindly return them to us, so that we may send them out to the companies requiring them. We will pay full price for them.

Vol. 23, No. 7. January, 1945.

Vol. 23, No. 9. March, 1945.

Personnel Research Federation
60 East 42nd St.,
New York, 17, New York

In Response to Numerous Requests This Story of What Happened in the Good Old Employee Representation Plan Era is Reproduced. Do Such Things Still Go On? Of Course, Only Now the Battle Is a Little More Fierce.

Tragic Mistakes
in Conferences

By Charles S. Slocombe
Personnel Research Federation

THIS is the era of the negotiating conference. With collective bargaining recognized as the established practice in more and more industries, the need for skill in conducting round table negotiations is growing.

Payment of millions of dollars in wages, avoidance of strikes, the fates of unions or of individual business enterprises, sometimes depend on how well practiced in conference technique are the participants on both sides.

No Adequate Preparation

AND yet there is really no conference technique as yet. Representatives of both management and men habitually come to these sessions without sufficient preparation. Chances to smooth things out to the satisfaction of both are not made the most of, and as a result many conferences leave a sour taste in the mouths of all participants, and lead on to costly strikes or cause bad feeling lasting for years.

A case in point is a conference in a certain company, which is one among the many conferences of management and men which the Personnel Research Federation is studying and analysing. This conference ended badly. The men were left dissatisfied with the outcome and their good will which had been built up over a period of years was seriously damaged. Yet the dispute which led to the conference was over what was in itself a comparatively unimportant issue. The facts were known and had they and the issues been clearly stated, trouble could have been avoided.

The dispute arose over a moderately costly mistake which led to spoiling of materials and equipment. A worker was discharged as being responsible. The men made an issue of it. It became the chief subject of discussion for months.

Finally the President of the Company visited the plant where it occurred, and in conference attempted to settle the difficulty.

Provisions of Plan

A<small>N EMPLOYEE</small> representation plan was in operation in the Company. It provided as usual for separate meetings of the employee representatives, and a Joint Conference with equal representation by men and management to consider grievances and disputes not settled lower down in the organization. There was a provision in the Plan that in the event of failure to agree in the Joint Conference, an umpire could be appointed or appeal made to the State Labor Department.

The Joint Conference could not agree on this case, and the management refused to agree to the appointment of an umpire on the grounds that the men did not have a case. According to the plan the next step was for the men to ask the State Labor Department to mediate. But the men preferred to try to persuade management to agree to the appointment of an arbitrator whose decision would be binding on both parties.

The verbatim report of the conference between the president, general manager, and works superintendent and the employee representatives is a human document of psychological interactions of unusual interest. (An analysis of the conference is given in conclusion.)

Employee Caucus

J<small>UST</small> before arrival of the management representatives, the men held a short preliminary meeting.

Employee Chairman: What are we going to ask the president? The toughest part in asking him is that he made a statement the last time he was here that we really knew more about the plan than he did. But we want to see if he can't help us with this interpretation. I still haven't got the interpretation that the general manager and superintendent gave us. They still got us in a deadlock and can't go any further with the conciliation committee.

The Chairman was clearly guilty here of hazy thinking. If he had thought out in advance what the men wanted, he would have made a better start. There were three issues; (1) the case of the discharged worker, (2) matters that the men could bring up to the conciliation committee, and (3) procedure in case of failure to agree in this Committee.

An employee representative, then asked the Chairman, "Are we going into the details of Joe's case or just an interpretation of the plan?"

"Go as far as you can, I would say," replied the Chairman.

Here again the Chairman is muddy in his thinking. He does not answer the question, does not define definite objectives.

The preliminary conference proceeded, the workers adopting the fatalistic attitude that management would interpret the plan in management's favor, instead of themselves setting up their own idea of a fair interpretation of the plan, and then seeking agreement on it.

Meeting with Company President

THE president arrived, and the Employee Chairman opened:
Employee Chairman: Gentlemen, I will call the meeting to order. At your request the President is here. I also extended an invitation to the General Manager and Superintendent. I don't suppose, Mr. President, you have gone through the minutes in this case. I don't know whether you are familiar with it or not.

President: I don't know either. What is it?

Chairman: It concerns the discharge of a man. We had the case in the conciliation. We got in a deadlock. . . .

He then carried on thus for several minutes, mixing up the case of the man, the Joint Committee deadlock, his 20 years experience with the Company, history repeating itself and wound up with a threat. Instead of this chaos of ill defined thoughts, systematic thinking through of the three real issues would have led to three possible openings, such as:

(1) Mr. ——, you have come here specially for this conference, and I assume you know all the details. Therefore it is not necessary for me to restate them. We should like your opinion of (a) the dismissal of this man, (b) what subjects can properly be considered by the Joint Conference and (c) the best way out of the present difficulties.

or (2) An orderly brief statement of the facts and the three issues, with a request for the President's opinion.

or (3) A statement that there were three issues, briefly mention them and a request that Number 1 be settled first.

The Discharge Case

FURTHER brief discussion of the discharged employee followed:
President: Everything I have seen indicates that the man was lax or was not qualified.

Employee Chairman: That is what management attempted to prove. From the evidence we didn't see it that way. As far as the plan is concerned, if management attempts to interpret to their advantage certain paragraphs, they are not fair.

President: What advantage was it to management to discharge this man?

The Employee Chairman does not follow through the first issue, the case of the discharged employee, but brings in the Plan again. The President in his question tried to bring the discussion back to the man's case by misunderstanding the last sentence.

Employee Chairman: The management will have to answer that.

President: There can't be any possible advantage. (He then continued with a long statement in the course of which he admitted that the equipment was "not in perfect condition." He further said "I didn't agree with the complete discharge of this man. It wasn't his fault and he should be given work in some other capacity.")

Employee Chairman: I heard the other day that the man had been terribly burned before. One of the men said he thought the fellow was "heat shy," but that in time he might work out of it. When a baseball player gets up to bat and gets hit in the head, he is "bat shy" for a season or two. (The Chairman further said he thought the foreman was "just as equally as guilty as the man." He wound up as usual with a statement about the Plan.)

President Makes Admissions

THIS is a curious interchange of statements. The President made an admission regarding the equipment which the men might have used as an alibi for the man. He then said, "It wasn't his fault." Antagonistic employee representatives might have selected these admissions and used them as arguments why the man should be reinstated. Instead, they gave a reason why the man was not qualified and then inferentially admitted the fault of the man in the statement, "the foreman was equally guilty." The President could have followed up these admissions, in seeking to have the men realize that the Company had not discharged the man without due cause.

But it is unnecessary to consider what might have happened if the parties to the dispute had been unfriendly. Surely here was the basis for an amicable settlement of issue No. 1 by which the man would be rehired and given work in some other capacity at least until he recovered from his heat shyness.

Neither the employee representatives nor the President made use of this opportunity, but allowed the argument to shift back to the Plan.

President: Answering the second point you made in my opinion, and my interpretation of the plan, is that this isn't a matter for conciliation, arbitration or scarcely for the body of the representatives. It is a matter of the supervisory departments supervising the working forces, which is their duty in the Plan, as well as under any other situation. The only grounds that this committee would have for objecting to a decision would be that they could show fraud. In other words, if the Superintendent had shown personal malice against this man and carried out an unfair act and because of that, then it is a matter for this body, or conciliation, or state industrial commission, or as far as you want to go. In my opinion this is not a question for the body at all unless you can show fraud.

Agreement Clause Quoted

HE TOOK it on himself to explain the plan, and although the men asked him to do so, might well have done it in another way both to avoid unpopularity and to clarify discussion. After insisting on settling the issue of the discharged employee he might have said: "I do not need to give you management's view of this. It is quite clear in what it says. Read this paragraph:—'

> (a) The right to hire and discharge shall be vested in the Company, and only the fairness of any action under this paragraph shall be a proper subject for review by the Joint Conference.

He might have had the representatives read this and other relevant clauses, word by word if necessary. Then if it were found that there were places where the meaning was not clear, or was conflicting, he could have tried to lead the meeting to agree on meanings. In this way he would have been sitting down with the men in a true joint conference, having as its basic purpose, agreement.

Delegate Wanders from Point to Point

FURTHER mixed discussion about the discharged man and the Plan followed, in which another employee representative took up the cudgels on behalf of the man, but wandered from point to point having no thought out plan of action.

Employee Repr. No. 2: I don't see why some disputes are permitted to go into the Committee and others are not. (This should have been issue No. 2 in a planned conference.)

President: Of course the direction of the working forces must be in skilled hands. That isn't a matter for motions. That is a matter for experienced practice. The company couldn't continue to exist on any other basis. It isn't existing very heartily right now as a matter of fact.

Employee Repr. No. 2: Does that mean that it couldn't exist if the management was turned over to the men in the plant?

President: That means the appointment of people for jobs, I would say that is right, because they don't know. Take yourself for example. If you had knowledge you would be a member of the management. Automatically you would be sought out.

Employee Repr. No. 2: I wouldn't say he was unfairly discharged—that there was malice shown. In my opinion there was some mistake along the line somewhere. He might have shown a weakness, but there are no statements or any other thing that he had done that might prove him incompetent or negligent.

President: I don't think he should be discharged. I think he should be reinstated in some capacity where his services would not result in losses that affect us all. Just like Babe Ruth. He pitches sometimes and he plays center-field sometimes.

Opportunity for Agreement Not Followed Up

NOTE issue No. 1 coming up again and an opportunity for settlement present in the interchange if it had been followed up either by the President or the Employee Representative. But a new point is brought in.

Employee Repr. No. 2: Also in regard to our Committee. I don't believe we should have the Committee instructed. Don't you believe the Committee should be allowed to vote according to their own individual judgment?

President: Were you forced to vote as you didn't think?

Employee Repr. No. 2: I was not, but five members of the Committee were.

General Manager: He is referring to a statement I made in the Committee and which I will repeat. That on matters of that kind, management, as represented by me, would not agree that an umpire should be appointed.

President: Well, I don't agree either.

Employee Repr. No. 2: That would be all right if each man voted according to their individual opinion, but they didn't.

General Manager: Well, if someone guides me to a better opinion, I hope I have sense enough to take it. I don't stick to an opinion when it has been proven to me that that opinion is wrong. I never instructed them how to vote at any time.

Employee Repr. No. 2: You did instruct them.

Justice and Malice

G ENERAL *Manager:* No, I stated management's position, as I do now.

Employee Repr. No. 3: In that case what is the use in having a Conciliation Committee? Is it necessary that there must be malice or that a foreman must be crooked always to fire a man unjustly?

President: In my opinion it is.

Employee Repr. No. 3: It is not to my mind. Those foremen are not any more perfect than I am or any other man. I have never yet stated that this man was maliciously handed something. My point of view of the Plan is that we have a chance to bring out (of course, in our humble way. We can't bring it out like you fellows) that a man has been unjustly treated. The general belief of the men is that he was unjustly fired because this could have happened to the best man and he wouldn't have seen it.

General Manager: And the best man will be discharged if he doesn't see. That's his responsibility. That's something you are always missing. Of course, there might be extenuating circumstances, which we have all the time. We don't discharge men if there is not a good reason for discharging them. That's the point you are missing.

Employee Repr. No. 3: I am not missing anything. I know there isn't a bit of truth in what you say. What do you suppose I have been doing over in that department?

General Manager: I don't know.

The Big "I"

E MPLOYEE *Repr. No. 3:* Here you come out with the big "I" and you can stop something from going through the conciliation. That is why we had the President come down here to find out how something can be stopped in the Conciliation where it should go on agreeably to its completion. It always has been done. This fighting and crucifying the man. That's not what I want to hear. I argued down along the line for something, and I still argue and still stand just where I did. It hasn't been proved to me that he was justly fired and that it wouldn't have happened to anybody. I would like to ask the President for his interpretation of the paragraph in the Plan that tied up the case in the middle of the Conciliation Committee, and kept the case going from place to place skipping two procedures that have always been followed. I don't see anything to fear in a referee, and the argument you put up and brought up there is no good. It looks to me like you are just stopping the case in the Conciliation Committee.

Some bitterness at the General Manager showed in the above. It looks as if the men regarded his action in this matter as too arbitrary. The discussion proceeded, and finally Empl. Repr. No. 2, in the following question, wisely turned from passion to logic:

Employee Repr. No. 2: What is the objection of the management to have an umpire decide this case? Lawyers and judges decide situations, a lot of them being more important than this case, and their decision is binding. I don't know why a fair minded man couldn't decide a question of this type. If he decides in favor of the management, it suits me.

President: There is no objection. There is no case here unless you can show some irregularity, an action which apparently doesn't exist here.

President Gives Opening

AT THIS point the men lost an opportunity. They might have seized on the President's statement, "There is no objection," and sought an agreement that the umpire's duty should be to decide if there was a case. But the Employee Chairman interjected with a complaint against the General Manager.

Employee Chairman: It is rather startling, Mr. President. I think the General Manager will bear me out in this, that ever since he came here, all cases that came into the Conciliation have been voted in favor of management, with the exception of one case, and the management voted in favor of the man one time. Ever since Mr. —— came here, we don't ever attempt to take the advantage.

Employee Repr. No. 2, apparently the most intelligent of the employee negotiators, made some good points but does not follow them through partly because of irrelevant interjections by other employee representatives. The dialogue shows clearly that the employees spoiled their own case by not working out their plans before the conference started.

President: I think you have a feeling that the conciliation committee supersedes the management, but it doesn't in matters of that kind, such as additional equipment and questions of that nature. Matters of that kind must be run by the supervisory departments. That is specified in the Plan. For example, suppose some of the men would like to have a new building, and you go and carry it up to the Conciliation Committee, and that Committee ends in a deadlock, but they do agree to appoint an arbitrator, and he decides that a new building should be built. In that case we wouldn't do that anyway.

Employee Repr. No. 2: Why use that as an illustration? If you brought that into the Conciliation Committee, we would simply say no.

President: That is only one step removed from the assumption that the Conciliation Committee has any jurisdiction over the operation of this plant and the direction of the working forces.

President Brings Up Old Bug-a-boo

E MPLOYEE *Repr. No. 2:* That is aside from the duties of the Conciliation. It doesn't say that that should be the duty of the Conciliation Committee in the Plan, but it does say that their duties shall have to do with the settlement of disputes.

This was a very good point, "their duties (i.e. the duties of the Joint Committee) shall have to do with the settlement of disputes." The representative might have emphasized and clarified this further by saying, "This is a dispute, and therefore obviously a proper subject for the Committee's consideration."

President: It doesn't mean to pass judgment on a man's ability. That doesn't belong to the Conciliation Committee or the representatives, or anyone, except management.

Employee Repr. No. 2: Why didn't management keep it out of the committee in the first place if it was management's prerogative to say that it had no business in the Committee?

President: The Plan is perfectly clear on that. If this man has been fraudulently discharged, then immediately it becomes the business of the body of representatives, to be taken up first with the foreman, then with the superintendent, and then through the courses laid down in the Plan.

Employee Repr. No. 3: Here is a report, which shows that the man was discharged for negligence and when it came to Committee it was said he was discharged for incompetence.

Employee Repr. No. 4: Mr. President, aside from the man's case, I didn't know we were going to review the question. I thought it was a matter of interpreting the Plan. If we are going to eliminate this last provision of the Plan that calls for a hearing of all cases before the Conciliation Committee: and in case of disagreement and of an umpire or referee; if you are going to eliminate that clause and dictate that you can settle everything or any case that comes to the Conciliation Committee, then the way I see it you have discarded the whole Plan. You are no longer trying to get along with the Plan. The Plan provides that things should go through certain channels to the Conciliation Committee, and from the Conciliation Committee to an umpire, and from there to arbitration, and if you eliminate that, you are eliminating the whole Plan. We are just wasting our time here, if you are going to eliminate that part of it. I don't see anything in the Plan about fraud.

Ability vs. Negligence

H ERE was issue No. 3 (what to do in case of deadlock) being mixed in with issue No. 2 (which cases are properly subjects for consideration of the Conciliation Committee). Again the individual employee representatives bring up different aspects and arguments, instead of logically dealing with one point at a time.

President: You represent the man as an individual, not as to his ability. This is a negligence case and you representatives should have come in and demanded his discharge.

Employee Repr. No. 4: Who is the judge of this ability?

President: The management entirely. That is what they are hired for.

Employee Repr. No. 5: We are not satisfied that the man has been justly discharged and we have the right to bring this out before management. Have we got the right man? We say NO.

President: I think he has been properly dismissed. I believe he should be given work in some other capacity for his sake.

Employee Repr. No. 6: It appears to me that the President has a one sided picture of this whole thing. I wonder if he is familiar with the facts.

Little Prior Attempt to Get Facts

P RESIDENT: I have read the minutes. I haven't talked to the General Manager.
Employee Repr. No. 6: That equipment gave trouble on the batch before this one. I just wondered if this was taken into consideration.

President: I am sure it was by the management here.

Employee Representative No. 3 then made a long statement about previous troubles in the plant and that was discussed for a time. As is often the case in these conferences, when the leaders seem to be failing to develop their points properly, the followers, with no concerted action and usually with less ability, bring in other points which add to the confusion.

Employee Chairman: I can't understand why you won't let this Conciliation Committee go. We are divided in the Committee. It is up to us to take it to the State Industrial Commission if we want to take it there.

General Manager: Why don't you do it? It definitely states what you can do.

Employee Chairman: Well if that's what you want, Mr. President, when the Committee meets Friday then she goes to the State Industrial Commission.

Employee Repr. No. 4: Mr. Chairman, I make a motion we do not make any such statement and that we table it and adjourn.

President: I don't recommend you take it to the Commission. I don't think this is a case. I think it falls outside the Conciliation Committee.

Employee Chairman: You said why don't you take it there.

President: You have a perfect right to take it there. I don't recommend it because I believe that wherever you take it you will lose.

Start All Over Again

THE men then started all over again as to the duties of the Committee, the fact that the man had not yet been given other work, whether the man was unjustly discharged, whether management can make mistakes, etc.

Employee Repr. No. 4: Wouldn't it be fair to leave it up to some disinterested party?

General Manager: It isn't always true that a disinterested party is qualified to make the decision.

Employee Repr. No. 4: Why not, if he has all the evidence?

President: He would have to have the technical knowledge as well.

After a few more interchanges, the meeting adjourned in an atmosphere of bitterness. Due to bad planning, no one was satisfied, no one happy. Today, four months later, tension still rules. Management and men are still engaging in bitter arguments over the case.

Conclusions

WE HAVE said that the fruitlessness of this conference was due primarily to lack of preparation. The written records of previous meetings should have been studied carefully by both sides.

The men, in making their preparations, might have reviewed in their minds the following facts:

They were sold on the employee representation plan. For them it was a Bill of Rights which guaranteed them a hearing on all matters they might bring up. And up till this case it had always been satisfactory.

Now suddenly they came up against a case in which the machinery of the plan failed. True enough, they could appeal to the State Labor Department. But if this appeal to an outsider was necessary, did it not mean that their rights were no longer protected by the employee representation plan they so strongly believed in?

And did not the question of adequacy of the plan far outweigh the case of the discharged man, as far as the employees were concerned?

Having concluded that an adequate plan was the matter of greatest importance, the men in preparing for the conference should have asked themselves specifically what it was about the plan that made it unsatisfactory. Was there some inconsistency or ambiguity, or was management being grossly unfair?

If they had thought it over they would have concluded that the following clause was not as clear cut as it might be:

"The right to hire and discharge shall be vested in the company, but the fairness of any action under this paragraph shall be a proper subject for review, by the Joint Conference."

What Is Fairness?

THE word "fairness" in this clause was a stumbling block from the point of view of the men. What did it mean? Management, in previous conferences, had held that only deliberate intent to discriminate, or maliciousness, constituted lack of fairness, and that the case was therefore not subject to review. The men, on the other hand, held that unfairness could result from an unwitting mistake, that this was so in the case in question, and that the case was therefore one for review.

Here was a radical difference in interpretation. Through a reading of previous minutes, the men should have concluded that this should be made a separate issue to be divorced entirely from the case of the discharged employee.

The dictionary gives the following definition of the word "unfair":

"Marked by dishonesty or fraud; showing partiality or prejudice; dishonest."

The definition would appear to back up the stand of the management that the case should not be reviewed, since the men did not claim dishonesty, fraud, partiality, or prejudice on the part of the boss who fired the man. The case was really one involving not fraud but simply a mistake in judgment on the part of the management.

Preparations by Men

THE men might therefore have concluded they should strive to secure an amendment to the clause which would definitely state that *injustices* to them resulting from "mistakes" should be subject to review as were those due to fraud, partiality, dishonesty or prejudice. To negotiate such an amendment obviously did not require the presence of an arbitrator.

Finally, there is the case of the discharged man. The assistant superintendent had previously indicated his opinion that the man should be rehired in some other capacity. The representatives should have decided beforehand whether to seek to have this translated into an offer, then accept it pending the settlement of all issues, or whether keeping the case open would strengthen their position on the other issues.

In order not to hazard failure in their major aim the securing of an amendment to the plan to provide machinery for dealing with cases of alleged injustice, the men should have decided to get the discharge case out of the way first. So they should have sought and accepted the reasonable compromise the management was prepared to make, retaining, if they wished, the right to reopen the case under the amendment, if they succeeded in negotiating it.

Proper preparation for the conference would have shown the employee representatives that there were three simple objectives:

1. Reinstatement of the man,—if necessary in some other position in the plant.

2. Securing of an amendment to the plan, giving them the right to bring up cases of alleged injustice and providing machinery for dealing with such cases.

3. Possibly also the obtaining of permission to consider the man's case again through the amended plan.

Preparations by Management

WHAT preparations should the management representatives have made? In addition to thinking the dispute through to the above three simple issues, they should have reached decisions on the following points:

1. What to do about reinstatement of the man.

2. How to meet a request from the men for an amendment giving them increased rights.

3. Whether, if made, to grant a request of the men that any new amendment be made retroactive and therefore applicable to the case of the discharged man.

4. What to do in case the men, lacking education and lacking clear understanding of meanings, would not have thought the issues through clearly, and would therefore dispute the meaning of the clause in question, insist on an arbitrator, and ask for complete reinstatement of the man to his old job.

After arriving at decisions on these points, management might have considered which of the following two general attitudes to adopt:

1. An attitude of complete independence of interest, leaving the man to present their case as best they could, and letting them take the consequences of defeat if they did poorly at it.

2. An attitude of assuming responsibility for the success of the conference, and aiding the men in clarifying the issues so that an amicable basis of agreement could be reached.

(Reprinted from the May, 1935, issue of the Personnel Journal, Vol. 14, No. 1.)

Book Review

Book Review Editor, Mr. Everett Van Every
California Personnel Management Association, Berkeley, Cal.

THE INDUSTRIAL SUPERVISOR

By John M. Amiss and Traver C. Sutton. New York. The Ronald Press Co. 1944.
243 pp. $3.00

Reviewed by Al Christian

Although there are many good books on supervisory training, this one deserves special mention for several reasons. It is written in a style suitable for either conference or personal study and thoroughly treats all the essential practices of good foremanship and supervision. Those who do not have access to training facilities will find this book especially helpful, while the experienced training director will find the text material a refreshing check on current methods.

The authors approached the subject of supervisory training through a wide selection of topics which they consider to be the most essential, and formulating under those headings a comprehensive outline of training possibilities. The first chapter is devoted to general supervisory responsibilities and a practical analysis of these duties and responsibilities adds up to the real job of getting things done and what must be done about it. The second chapter is devoted to the general qualifications of a supervisor and the leadership qualities without which no foreman or supervisor can be considered prepared or qualified for his work. The self-scoring test of supervisory ability is an interesting part of this section.

The remaining chapters treat the usual headings found in such studies on foremanship, with the addition of many topical suggestions for further study. One of the faults of the book is that a little more supplementary information of a technical nature would have done much.

PERSONNEL
Journal

The Magazine of

LABOR RELATIONS AND PERSONNEL PRACTICES
Published by PERSONNEL RESEARCH FEDERATION
Lincoln Building, 60 East 42nd Street, New York City

Volume 24   *Number 10*

Contents for April 1946

If We Are to Avoid Upset Labor Relations Such
as Have Plagued Us in the Last Ten Years We
Need Much Better Trained Management and
Personnel Administrators.   Here is a Well
Thought Out and Well Balanced Program for
Doing Just That.

Management
Training Program

Radcliffe College,
Cambridge, Mass.

THE Management Training Program is a graduate course. It gives a basic
training for administration, including the administration of personnel departments.

The program occupies about ten months; it is open to a limited number of young
women of outstanding ability and character. After leaving us our students obtain
administrative positions in business and industry, government offices, social service
institutions and educational establishments. (This program is concerned with the
administration of organizations. It does not qualify a student to be a social service
worker or a teacher.)

About seven months of academic work are dove-tailed with three months of
full-time apprentice field work. The calendar is arranged to provide the greatest
possible connection between the study and the experience of actual working situations.

Close Integration

FOR each of the three academic sessions the curriculum lists a number of instructors' courses. These are not so many unrelated courses which, taken together,
might be supposed to cover the field. The method of teaching and the material
used provide close integration between the parts.

The teaching is designed to give an understanding of people in their working
situations and in their community setting. This includes a training in the observation and interpretation of human behavior and motive, and also in methods of
handling people.

The student is given some knowledge of the economic, financial, technical and other systems within which any organization must function. Practical problems which confront administrators commonly involve most of these things, including the human factor, and sound administrative action depends on a balanced judgment of the various elements which enter into a particular situation.

Certain techniques, including those of use in personnel departments, are taught to the extent necessary for a real understanding of administrative functions, and to a point where the student can continue to study these techniques for herself if her subsequent work requires it.

Continuous practice is given in administrative judgment by the method of teaching, much of which consists in the class discussion of written accounts of actual situations and problems. For instance, the student is not confronted with a financial problem in a vacuum, but with a description of a concrete situation in which one of the important factors may be the financial status of the organization in question In all, the class studies and discusses between one and two hundred such cases during the course of their training.

Previous Work Experience

SOME of our students come to us straight from college. These have almost always worked in one or more organizations during their summer vacations. Others have earned their living for varying periods of time after taking their degrees. Cases are prepared by the students in informal study groups arranged by themselves; in this way the experience of each is shared with the other members of the class in a quite remarkable degree.

Besides the regular courses listed in the curriculum, guest speakers give informal talks to the class about once a week throughout the program. These administrators, men and women, are chosen for their proven ability in their fields. These meetings, which usually take place in the evening, are confidential. One of the students is in the chair and the talk is followed by questions and discussion.

Each student is required to spend about three months of her training as an apprentice in some two or three organizations. These apprentice assignments are chosen with regard to the particular needs of each student. This is rendered possible through the public-spirited coöperation of a large and growing number of business and industrial firms, government offices, educational establishments and social service organizations.

Easier Adjustment

APART from previous experience, our students start their careers at the bottom of the professional ladder. But, as a result of their training, they are equipped to adjust themselves with a minimum of friction and delay; they have a broader understanding of their work and they can look forward to more rapid promotion and to greater professional achievement.

The Management Training Program has been developed for young women intending to enter the profession of administration; but it is to be expected, and hoped, that in the course of time most of our graduates will become involved in family responsibility to the exclusion of full-time careers. The Program teaches essential techniques of administration and it gives practice in the skills of human adjustment and leadership. These are permanent assets for any married woman who takes a practical interest in public and community affairs.

Curriculum

In general the curriculum is designed as follows:

(1) Summer Orientation Session; Human Behavior; Uses and Limitations of a Testing Program; Some Problems and Objectives of Administration.

(2) First Field Work Period.

(3) Fall Session; Human Problems of Administration; Functions of a Personnel Department; Public Administration; The Accounting Process; The Use of Graphs and Statistics; Production Management; Seminars.

(4) Spring Session; Production Management; Problems of Distribution; Psychological Testing; Labor Problems; Human Problems of Administration; The Community.

(5) Second Field Work Period.

(6) Final discussions of field work experiences. Final conference with guest speakers.

FROM DIRECTOR'S REPORT

THE students differed greatly in family circumstance, age, intellectual interests, work experience, place of residence, and even in nationality. Nevertheless, the group worked well together and their instructors did not find the heterogeneity too great for effective teaching. It is probably true that in the early weeks of the Course those students showed to advantage who had professional experience and training in the social sciences, but as time went on this initial advantage largely disappeared. For instance, in the top third of the class, as judged by academic grades and by field-work performance, were students from both the older and the younger groups and those whose field of concentration at college had been both relevant to, and far removed from, the work of the Course.

Judging from the year under review, as well as from previous years, the two characteristics which appear important for success in our training are a superior intellectual ability and a character suited to the conduct of affairs. Granted adequate ability, to which should be added an enlightening educational experience in college, the unlimited requirement seems to be for suitability of temperament and attitude; there is no such thing as a law of diminishing returns in this respect.

Older and Younger Students

IT MAY seem from the above that there is little to be gained in our Course from previous professional experience. This is a complete mistake. The work of the class gains immensely from the working experience of many of its members. The point is that, as the year goes on, the experience of each is shared with the other members of the class in a quite remarkable degree.

The younger students, straight from college, also make a positive contribution. They help to maintain a standard in the techniques of learning and their academic knowledge still retains some semblance of its original systematic form. By their very inexperience these younger students compel the older group to re-think problems which tend to get overlaid in the daily round of professional work.

I think those who have been responsible for the Training Course over a number of years would agree that a student should have performed some paid work in an organization, if only during summer vacations; though it must be admitted that one or two excellent students in past years have not had this advantage.

Appraisal of Potentialities

THIS year has been largely occupied in appraising the potentialities of the Training Course and in laying the groundwork for its future progress. During the course of the past winter the President and Council of Radcliffe College authorized an expansion of the student body up to a limit of forty students, with a corresponding adjustment in the Department's budget.

Our records of the ninety-one graduates who received their certificates on or before 1944 throw some light on the task before us. The following facts refer to March, 1945; changes since that date do not significantly alter the picture.

1. Sixty per cent of our graduates were in full-time paid work of an administrative character. These graduates were scattered through thirty-three cities in fifteen states, the District of Columbia, the Panama Canal Zone, Canada, and overseas.
2. Of those in full-time paid work, 40% were employed in commercial firms, two-thirds of these, in industry; 20% were in private noncommercial institutions, mostly in colleges and hospitals; 30% were working in federal government offices, about one-quarter of whom were stationed in Washington; nearly 10% were serving as commissioned officers in the military forces.
3. With few exceptions, the positions held by our graduates were in personnel departments or in work of similar character.
4. With one or two exceptions, every graduate in paid work was employed by one of the largest and best known institutions of its kind.
5. Forty per cent of our graduates were not seeking paid work and most of these had family responsibilities.

In some respects the Training Course is evidently fulfilling its purpose. We draw outstanding students from all over the country and their subsequent positions are equally well distributed. So far as we know, no graduate who has desired it has failed to obtain reasonable offers of employment. It is particularly significant that practically all of these young women are employed as administrators and are thus exercising the very skills for which we have prepared them. Finally, we can take satisfaction in the fact that the quality of our graduates is recognized by first-rate organizations of such very different types.

Course Broadened

ON THE negative side must be placed our failure to impress both the students and prospective employers with the value of our training for administrative positions outside of personnel or similar departments. A second limitation lies in the absence of graduates who have found opportunities in small and growing enterprises.

To meet the first-mentioned difficulty the name of the course has been changed from "Training Course in Personnel Administration" to "Management Training Program." The present catalogue for the year 1945-46 bears the new name and the scope of the training has been particularly emphasized in the explanatory text. The curriculum for the coming year is also arranged with the same thought in mind.

It will prove a more complicated matter to find suitable openings for our graduates in small and more recently established enterprises, although some of the best opportunities for young women (and men) lie in this direction. The problem has two aspects. For readily understandable reasons, most of the available teaching material is based upon practices and illustrations drawn from large and well-established concerns. Again, it is far more easy for a college and its students to make contact with the larger and better known organizations and to appraise the opportunities they offer. Nevertheless, a vigorous national economy and a healthy spirit of adventure cannot be fostered on a basis of "safety first." We are exploring means for overcoming this limitation.

Many Do Not Seek Work

THE last fact to which I wish to draw attention is that in March, 1945, forty per cent of our graduates were not in full-time work, by their own desire. Most, if not all, of these young women were occupied with family responsibilities of one kind or another. At that date a quarter of our graduates had only completed our training one year previously; nearly half had obtained their certificates within the previous two years, while three-quarters of our graduates had only left us within the previous four years. As our alumnae become more mature it is to be expected, and hoped, that an increasing proportion will become involved in family responsibilities to the exclusion of full-time careers. On the basis of college records generally, we must assume that less than half of our students will spend many years as full-time administrators. We are under an obligation to consider what we can offer to those of our students who do not continue in professional careers.

The Management Training Program gives the student an elementary knowledge of the tools and techniques of Management; it also gives her a way of thinking about the organization and control of people in working situations. As a part of this, the student practices the diagnosis of actual situations involving both people and technical considerations, and her judgment is exercised in the taking of action decisions. This is accomplished by the continual study and discussion of realistic case material, as well as by first-hand experience during the field-work periods.

Social Intelligence

An executive in a large department store recently characterized our course as a training in "social intelligence", and that describes it very well. Although our teaching is specifically pointed to responsible leadership in working situations, the basic skills of social adjustment and of leadership are of universal application. I think it is not too much to hope that, as a result of their training, our graduates acquire a greater capacity to play their part in whatever lies before them, and to enter more fully into the life and activities of their communities, whether as professional women or as responsible citizens.

Thus, our Management Training Program has a dual purpose; it trains for a professional career; it also provides a much-needed link between the rarefied atmosphere of a typical liberal education and the subsequent experience of real life. Ever since its inception in 1937 considerable attention has been paid to this second aspect of our teaching, and we are seeking to develop it still farther in the future.

As the war draws to a close, prospective students are naturally showing increasing concern with their future opportunities. It is not possible to be dogmatic on this subject for the whole situation is unprecedented; nevertheless, there are solid grounds for optimism.

The main ground for optimism must lie in our expectation that the country will achieve a sound level of economic activity in the years ahead. The reputation of the Management Training Program is growing rapidly throughout the country and our graduates have an excellent record. Added to this is the undoubted fact that resistance to the employment of women in administrative positions is steadily diminishing.

Openings for Women

In one respect at least, the near future will alter the incidence of openings for women and, to some extent, for men. At present two-thirds of our graduates in commercial enterprises are working in industrial plants. As war production declines the distributive trades will make a better showing. During the war our teaching has placed almost exclusive emphasis on production. This has already been rectified to some extent in the curriculum for 1945-46, and it is likely that a further readjustment may be desirable in the following year.

Two reasons are commonly adduced by employers who hesitate to engage women as administrators. The first is that men object to serving under women; this prejudice undoubtedly exists, but it appears to be slowly diminishing as experience is gained. The second reason for not employing women as administrators is that many of them will marry and leave the organization. This objection seems to be at least partly based on muddled thinking. Every organization which has passed through its initial period of rapid expansion finds itself unable to provide for sufficiently rapid promotion among its junior executive ranks. The result is that the age level of the juniors becomes too high and their morale is apt to decline. This difficulty would be largely met if a substantial proportion of junior executives were women, many of whom would wish to retire after a few years of service. In this way the junior ranks of an organization could be staffed by young executives of superior calibre, while promotion for the men and women who remained would not be blocked.

Comment

Mr. Dexter M. Keezer, former President of Reed College, and Public Member of the War Labor Board, writing in the Journal of Higher Education, February, 1946, on the increasing number of schools and colleges offering courses in industrial relations is very much afraid that these will constitute what he calls "a flimsy educational performance." He fears that the result will be to project into the field of industrial relations "a sizeable crop of pseudo-experts, and thus add further complications to what (he) finds an already sufficiently complicated range of activity."

We are inclined to agree with Mr. Keezer, and that is why we think the Radcliffe program well worth looking into because of the care that has been taken to ensure a well-rounded intensive training, such as he fears many other institutions do not and will not provide.

We think that companies hiring college graduates as junior executives with alleged training in personnel work would do well to make sure that the training they have received has been of the proper sort.

We further think that the larger companies might well consider setting up management training programs of the Radcliffe type themselves, instead of relying entirely upon those they hire from colleges.

(For further particulars on the Radcliffe program write Mr. T. North Whitehead, Radcliffe College, Cambridge 38, Mass.)

There is a Theory that the Traditional Wage System is Obsolete and Must Be Supplanted by One that Will Make the Operation of the Economy More Stable—Although Annual Wages May Not Be a Perfect System It Deserves a Trial.

The Challenge *of* Annual Wages

By Solomon Barkin

Textile Workers Union of America,
New York, N. Y.

THE demand for the annual wage is a challenge to American industry. The objective, to secure employment and an annual continuous flow of income is widely endorsed. It is a common yearning of all men. Those who disapprove of this proposal by referring to it as impractical, unsound, or economically audacious, are evading their responsibilities. These men have not stopped to define their functions. They are merely resisting change.

Social Purpose of Business

THE regular pursuit of personal and business profit has blinded many to the social purpose of business. This system of private enterprise, insofar as it still exists, stands on its ability to provide a safe reconciliation between individual liberty and security. Where it has failed, it has been in time supplanted. The United States is the most important country in the world which still maintains a system based largely on private enterprise. Its survival in the midst of a universe of other systems is dependent upon its success in meeting the varied social expectations placed upon every economic system. It must provide a large measure of security and an assurance of an evolutionary advance in the standard of living for all people at a minimum of social and personal cost, accompanied by a guarantee of status for all.

The gains made to assure workers' security has assumed many forms. Financial security and income stability are increasing. We have recognized such practices as the guaranteed hourly rate; the guaranteed daily rate; guaranteed reporting time pay; guaranteed pay for lost time and bad work. In some industrial and occupational groups agreements provide a weekly pay guarantee, and in still others, an annual pay guarantee. Another approach to this same problem has been that of preventing seepages in income through payments for vacations, holidays not worked, and for periods of illness. These practices are now widespread. Unemployment compensation provides partial income during periods of forced unemployment.

Extension of Previous Developments

THE demand for the annual wage is an extension of the previously listed developments. Its objective is more far reaching. It seeks to prevent the most significant source of income insecurity in our society: irregular employment and irregular income.

Conceived as a demand on employers, the proposal for annual wages is not an extension of unemployment insurance. Rather, it is a demand that management provide regular annual employment. The annual wage proposal looks toward continuous regular and normal employment throughout the year, so that the employee will not suffer lapses in actual income.

A guarantee of either part of the annual earnings, or a limited number of weeks of employment do not comprehend the full purpose. Similarly, a guarantee to limited groups does not square completely with the objectives of the annual wage. It is not conceived as a technique for concentrating employment or income further or for isolating the risks of insecurity to a select group. Nevertheless, most exponents do not present an all or nothing position. Rather, most of them favor even the partial acceptance of a program for annual wages, recognizing it as an initial step and as an exploratory venture in the direction of fully achieving the goal. The partial adoption of the program will contribute substantially to a more stable economy and will promote full employment.

Annual Employment

THE annual wage concept is basically founded on a desire for annual employment. They are complementary. An economy of full employment provides a most satisfactory climate for the successful solution of the problem of the annual wage and continued annual employment. But both present many distinct issues which need separate analysis. Neither automatically provide the answers for the second. The most fortunate economic society enjoys both.

The sound basis for the annual wage is annual employment. The annual wage is an immediate minimum charge upon an employer or group of employers which must be shouldered while they evolve full plans for continuous annual employment. Such employment may be with one employer or with a group of employers. The purpose of the charge is to press management singly or in groups to dovetail operations so as to assure full continuity of employment.

While management and the community are developing programs and shaping techniques, labor is asking that both shall share the cost of their failures. Workers have shouldered risks which are not properly theirs. The risk-takers are the property owners. They should, in our society, bear these particular costs. They cannot justly escape these costs as they have done. The social cost of business must become a substantial part of the accounting of enterprise.

Primary Responsibility of Management

THE responsibility for this technical development rests primarily with management. Organized labor will gladly share to the extent that management allows it to participate and thereby increase management's effectiveness. In some instances it is of course known that unions have taken the initiative and contributed substantially to the stabilization of employment in industry.

Management's own efforts and responsibilities can be greatly lightened by transferring part of the task to government, but management cannot divest itself of the obligation nor deny its opportunity. The limitations of the single firm must be merely a reason for coöperation with others. The need for continuous coördination and economic independence must be the *raison d'etre* for governmental intervention. Industry must deal with the issues and not take leave of them. Otherwise, labor's demands will be translated into governmental leadership, guidance and regulation.

Already management has made scattered individual attempts at regularizing plant operation and employment. These programs are not guarantees of annual employment. They are techniques for evolving a sound base for wider voluntary use of the guaranteed annual wage. They will reduce the actual cost and make the annual wage a by-product of the normal operations of a company. Every effort in the direction of greater regularization of plant operations and employment must therefore be counted as a contribution toward making the annual wage a reality.

Problems Complicated

THE problems of employment regularization are numerous and complicated. Some industries and plants lend themselves easily to this effort; others will stubbornly resist solution. Some industries are so essentially seasonal in character that the only approach may be the establishment of complementary activities. The solution in other cases may well be an integrated program of regularization for an entire community.

Every company can do much toward regularizing employment. The advance of the opening date of automobiles was significant though it did not meet the full problem. A similar step for the radio industries would minimize the sharp seasonality in that industry and thereby reduce serious sources of labor discontent.

Much work has still to be done within each organization to overcome irregular production and unemployment. Major efforts are still required to meet these challenges. Unfortunately, the study by the President's subcommittee has been stymied by lack of funds and opposition from many quarters. No more important effort could be made toward the solution of this problem than an extensive study of the problems and techniques on an industry and community basis.

Regularization of operations leads to better use of facilities and reductions in cost. Regularized production means a better work force and lower cost.

Annual Wage Practice Not Unknown

SOME efforts have been made for some select groups to remove the risk of irregular earnings for workers. The annual wage practice is not unknown but it is limited. It has not yet become a normal business practice.

Governmental employment is normally established on the basis of an annual salary. Executive and many salaried personnel in industry have annual contracts. There are millions of workers whose pay is calculated on an annual rate but who have no annual guarantees. The number of actual annual guaranteed pay programs is unknown. The Bureau of Labor Statistics reports some 42,500 workers in unionized industries as being covered by annual guaranteed wage programs. These are located primarily in service and distributive industries. A further survey indicated the presence of annual guaranteed wage programs in some 700 additional concerns. The Bureau of Labor Statistics is investigating them. This small number is an index of the failure of management to deal with this very vital problem.

In summary, the present techniques are generally classified into the following two major categories:

Guaranteed Employment Plans

THIS group, as the name implies, guarantees a minimum number of weeks of employment. Examples are the Procter and Gamble Co., which guarantees 48 weeks of 40 hrs. each to employees of 2 yrs. service or more; the Namm Stores, which guarantees 40 weeks to employees with one year's service and 52 weeks to employees with 5 yrs. service or more; the Downtown Dry Goods Jobbers Assn. which guarantees a full year's employment to a basic crew of employees.

Annual Wage Plans

THESE plans guarantee a minimum weekly pay to employees throughout the year. Examples may be found in the Nunn-Bush Shoe Co. which guarantees 52 checks equal to the total wage fund; the G.A. Hormel Plant which guarantees 52 weeks based on a projected production quota to which is added bonuses for production in excess of quota.

The wage advance or constant wage plans guarantee a minimum weekly income and provide that deficits shall be offset by increased earnings in other periods. They are not truly annual wage guarantees since they maintain only part of the standard pay. The employee receives the same pay but has his deficits offset by his credits. An example of this may be found in the General Motors program which allowed employees to receive advances up to 40 or 60% of weekly earnings depending on length of service with advances to be paid in later weeks by deducting half the earnings above 40 or 60% of standard weekly earnings.

Harbingers of a Mighty Movement

THESE programs are harbingers of a mighty movement for annual wage guarantees. These programs are a practical and an economic necessity. Industry must find means of assuring workers the continuity of employment and income which will give them the security necessary for balanced, healthy living. Some preliminary efforts may be found in the movement for employment regularization. They can make it easier and less costly to inaugurate the annual wage program. But neither society or workers can await the realization of this goal at the pace which is now being pursued.

Management is doing too little to advance regularized employment. The resistance to the current governmental study of the problems does not speak well of the interest in this problem. Labor will not continue indifferent to the current practice of making workers shoulder the costs and risks of irregular employment. It will call for governmental action unless significant progress is made. It is management's immediate responsibility to plan on a company basis and to coöperate on a community basis for regular, continuous employment for workers so that we can minimize the total cost of the annual wage guarantee. Its failure to proceed must be considered an open invitation for labor to ask government to enforce programs for employment regularization and annual income guarantees.

(Note) There is a very strong appeal in the idea of annual wages, to company presidents as well as to hourly rated employees. Much more will be heard of them. Perhaps the most readable book on the subject is "Guaranteed Annual Wages" by Jack Chernick and George C. Hellickson. Published by University of Minnesota Press, Minneapolis, Minn. $2.50.

The Author Believes that There Should Be a
Clear Cut Distinction Between Labor Relations
and Personnel Administration Because One Deals
with Employees as a Group and the Other with
Them as Individuals.

90 Years *of* Personnel Experience

BY C. C. FRACKER

Hamilton Foundry and Machine Co.,
Hamilton, O.

THE Management Almanac for 1945 indicates that 99.8% of all businesses have less than 1,000 employees. One year of personnel dealings with 30,000 employees, then, might be considered as equivalent to thirty years' experience for the majority of personnel men. At the War's end the author was Assistant Personnel Manager of a huge mid-western warplant engaged in the manufacture of aircraft engines. Employment averaged 30,000 for the three years of association with that company, and despite the anticipated criticism of the statistical gymnastics involved (especially from the old-timers), there might seem to be some justification for basing this report on "ninety years' experience" in personnel administration—at least for the purpose of arriving at a catchy title for this article.

Six Fundamentals

NEEDLESS to say, we did have the opportunity of observing a great number of individuals in an industrial situation. We tested, hired, counseled and separated many, many thousands of employees. We encountered and solved more personnel problems than we ever imagined could exist. We encountered and failed to solve some other personnel problems—some of the same problems that continue to plague personnel men across the nation.

As this mass of data continued to grow from month to month, there seemed to be certain fundamentals that stood out—and certain conclusions were inevitable. Some of these conclusions are obviously sound because we saw successful action result from an application of the principle. Others are only inferred from unsuccessful action resulting from opposite or contradictory policy. These experiences have been analyzed, studied, and summarized into the following statements which are proposed as "Six Principles of Effective Personnel Practice." Let's take a look at them.

The Importance of an Employee Lies in His Individuality

THERE has been a trend in the near past toward the combining of labor relations and personnel relations. Very often both functions are the responsibility of an industrial relations manager who is asked to consider the employees as a group on the one hand, while at the same time present day concepts indicate that personnel problems must be met on an individual basis. Plants organized in this manner should give serious consideration to reorganization so that one individual is not required to do two types of thinking at the same time.

Labor relations and personnel relations are not the same. Labor thinking treats all employees as a group—all identical, with no differentiation except possibly length of service with the company. Labor thinking necessitates that Joe receive as much money as Dick for Joe has been with the company as long as Dick; that Pete shan't be promoted ahead of Bill because Bill has seniority; that John, who is a fair worker, can't be laid off instead of Jim, who is a much better worker, because John's service exceeds that of Jim.

All employees doing the same work should receive the same pay, get their raises automatically at the same time, and receive the same consideration. But are these employees all the same? Is the productivity of their work the same? Are their reactions to their fellow workers and to their supervision the same? Is their morale and attitude the same? Are their problems and their peculiarities the same? Of course not. When one hundred men are treated as a group we find that we have geared our production to the lowest level of productivity of any one man in the group. The same one hundred men working as individuals will turn out more work and better work.

Group Dealing

THERE is no question that the consideration of employees as a group and proper dealing with their officially elected representatives in terms of their union is a desirable thing. The part that is undesirable, however, is the attempt to administer personnel practices based on the group thinking necessary for labor relations. The author is not claiming that there should be no coördination between the two. What the author is saying is that there should be no connection between the two.

Treating all employees as individuals, then, necessitates an understanding of the two basic needs of any human being. There have been many outlines compiled listing all the various things that employees require to maintain efficiency and good morale. No item has been perused yet, however, that cannot be classified either as the need for security or the need for recognition. The growing consideration of guaranteed annual wage plans is one indication of the importance of this need for security. A lack of security in the job, a lack of security in the home, which is very often dependent on the job, or a lack of security in the future of the job may readily become a source of irritation which may focalize in unjustified demands for increased wages, better working conditions, or some other unrelated thing.

Lack of individual recognition may bring about the same situation. The writer has never seen a grievance presented which stated that the employee was aggrieved because his foreman did not occasionally say "Joe, you did a good job." The author has seen hundreds of grievances *based on any number of other supposed causes*, yet those same grievances could have been prevented if the foreman had only occasionally said, "Joe, you did a good job." One small way in which individual recognition can be given is to include on the employee's badge, not only his picture and payroll number, but also his name. People usually like their names and like to see them used. Yet many organizations overlook this very obvious opportunity to provide recognition. Does yours?

Even though all employees have these needs in common as a group, the satisfaction of these needs must be on an individual basis.

The Selection and Placement of Employees Can Only Be Made by the Proper Combination of Three Factors: Personal Interview, Application Analysis, and Psychological Testing, for No One Alone nor Any Two in Combination Is Sufficient

A MAN will admit that he does not know much about statistics. He will readily agree that he has trouble with spelling, can't remember names, or procrastinates. But intimate to a man that he can't judge people by talking with them, and you've made an enemy for life. Too many employment managers rely entirely on an interview as the criterion for hiring. The interview of an applicant should be primarily for the purpose of seeing the man in action. It is a chance to evaluate his appearance and his manner, and determine whether it is consistent with that required of the job. The interview may also be a means of obtaining supplemental information which is not or cannot be shown on the application blank. In addition, it is an opportunity of presenting the company to the applicant, explaining the job, and pointing out what will be expected of him.

Perhaps we often fail to make the most of this opportunity of telling the potential employee about his future job. We ask a number of questions about him, he certainly has a right to know something about us. For the purposes outlined above, then, the interview becomes an important *part* of the hiring procedure, and not an end in itself.

Application Blanks

THE next factor in hiring, and possibly the one most neglected of all, is application analysis. By application analysis I mean a very thorough perusal of the application and the information which it supplies.

There is a very important sidelight in this connection, and that is the lack of properly designed application blanks. Many that have been seen have requested a tremendous amount of information that had absolutely no connection whatsoever with the job, and had I been an applicant filling out some of these applications there would have been a great temptation to write in many of the spaces, "It's none of your damned business!" There are a lot of things that we do not ask on applications that might well be included. Very often we ask of the previous jobs the man has had, but how often do we ask for any of the conditions under which the man worked. Or if we ask for explanations do we allow only a little space two inches by one-half inch in which to answer? Request only that information which will determine whether or not you will hire the individual. Additional personal history for record purposes may be obtained only if and after he is hired.

The third factor in the hiring procedure, no more important and no less important, is psychological testing. Arguments for the use of psychological testing have been put forward much better than I could hope to put them, and rather than repeat well worn theory, let me outline the result of "90 years' experience."

Our test battery consisted primarily of an intelligence measurement and a temperment measurement, and included other tests which might be applicable, such as arm-hand-finger dexterity, typing, clerical, and the like. Due to the tightness of the labor market we did not do a great deal of selection on the basis of these tests, for the urgency of production was so great that even a poor employee was better than no employee. However, this did give us a wonderful opportunity to evaluate the use of tests for hiring, for we not only had performance records of those who were selected, but also the performance records of those *who would not have been selected*. With data such as these, very positive comparisons can be made. Preliminary studies conclusively indicated that selection based on a consideration of psychological tests scores will result in a higher percentage of "good" employees than is possible without this consideration.

All of the test data acquired has subsequently been given to Purdue University where detailed studies are to be made and probably published.

Compensation Should Be Adequate and in the Proper Relation, for Only in Comparison with Others Do Wages Become a Matter of Contention

EUGENE BENGE has often said that an unhappy employee cannot be made happy by money. It is unfortunate that these words cannot be shouted from the house tops. The proper system of job evaluation with a fair and comparative assignment of wage rates will lessen the possibility of wages becoming the focal point for a lot of other minor infections of poor employee relations. Many of the recent surveys attempting to measure employee morale have indicated that money, as such, is not after all very important. So long as the individual doesn't feel that another employee in the plant is making more money for doing less work, and so long as his income is sufficient to provide him and his family with the accepted standard of living in his community, then there is little likelihood that he will become upset or disturbed concerning wages.

Promotions Should Be Considered First on the Ability to Do the Job, Second on Merit, and Third on Seniority

THE above statement should not imply that a promotion should be based on a combination of the three factors mentioned, for such is not the case. No matter how deserving the employee, no matter how long he has worked for the company, we do him a grave injustice to promote him to a job for which he does not have the ability. The three factors are considered this way: that if two or more employees have the same ability then the next factor, merit, should be considered. And if two or more employees have the same ability and are each as deserving as the next, then certainly seniority. If all three are equal then by all means let's add the fourth factor of personal prejudice. Why not? After all, we like to do things for people we like. A note of caution should be injected, however, that the desire to get to the fourth factor does not bring about an unfair evaluation of the previous three.

There have been a great many situations of individuals' being given jobs with additional responsibility and additional authority, only to result in miserable failures due to a lack of ability which should have been perfectly apparent at the time of promotion. But because Joe is a good old boy, and Joe works hard and has been with us a long time, we'll give him a chance. Poor Joe. You do him no favor.

No Discrimination Should Exist Because of Race, Creed, Color or Country of Origin, Except Where Local Precedent Makes Such Practice Untenable from a Production Standpoint, for at No Time Should a Company's Position Be Such That the Company Is, in Effect, Promoting Any Minority Group

IT ISN'T the writer's desire at this time to open a heated debate on racial problems or religious problems. From a purely matter of fact and practical standpoint it would appear necessary to go along with the tide regarding discrimination. A plant in the deep south is obviously in for trouble by subscribing to a policy of no discrimination towards negroes. On the other hand, a plant in Detroit which discriminates would find that they would be subject to considerable criticism, boycotting, and what not. Actually, there may be some basis for argument that a plant in the south which dictates economic equality of the races is discriminating against the whites by forcing them into situations to which they are unaccustomed. What about it?

Everyone admires an individual strong in his beliefs, no matter what they may be, but a man interested in promoting social or economic or religious equality is foolhardy to use his business as a springboard for carrying on such a program.

There Should Be Provided Only Those Employee Services Which Will Promote More Efficient Workmanship, Carefully Avoiding Any Appearance of Patronage

HUMAN nature is such that little value or appreciation is given to things which are acquired without cost or effort. Many companies, especially during the War, went all out to provide employees with every imaginable type of service. Mind the baby, take the laundry, fix the water heater, pay the gas bill, do the Christmas shopping, and a host of other measures intended to build morale and reduce turnover. It is questionable if the results justified the means. On the other hand, recreation programs sponsored by the company, *but run by the employees*, have definite value in building group spirit and good fellowship. Men who play well together usually work well together.

Indiscriminate supplies of uniforms, safety equipment, or things of that nature without cost to the employee have a definite effect of lowering their value. Free safety goggles provided without restriction will seldom be worn. Safety goggles for which the employee pays at least part are taken care of and used without urging. Lockers need only be adequate and clean. Frills in the locker room are totally unnecessary. Avoid a paternalistic attitude in whatever you do for the employee. A great amount of actual resentment is created by playing the part of "the great benefactor."

This, then, is the result of my "90 years' experience." Six principles which may or may not agree with your conception of "how it should be done."

The Writing and Evaluation of Job Descriptions,
and Dealing with Grievances Arising Out of
Them Should Not Be in the Hands of Line
Supervision.

Wage Administration

By Edward J. Redmon
Hollywood, Cal.

BIG business adjusted itself to the war economy with extensive growing pains, and created a number of agencies to foster industrial relations programs despite the overlapping functions of various Plant Personnel, Wage Administrations, Labor Relations and similar service departments.

These various hierarchies were formed and nurtured carefully in large organizations over a period of years and their continued existence depended upon the continuance of government subsidies to industry. However, the inception of a competitive economy undoubtedly marks a new era in union-management relations and industrial relations organizations.

Inception of Wage Administration Departments

THE administering of wages remains a relatively new field and Wage Administration departments have evolved ostensibly in large corporations, in some cases, as a token gesture to evidence a corporation's adherence to the maze of federal regulatory statutes, War Labor Board decisions, National War Labor Board rulings, etc.

After war corporations combined and submitted Wage Administration plans for War Labor Board approval, the inevitable controversy revolving around the proper classification of employees as contrasted against the improper classification of employees to meet the exigencies of war-time production schedules, gradually became a major struggle between company wage analysts and labor relations bargaining agents.

Authority Behind the Wage Program

THE efficient functioning of a skilled job analyst depends almost entirely upon the organization level to which the chief Wage Administrator reports. The administering of wages bears more directive authority if that function reports to the corporate level. A wage program that survives only as an advisory or staff function will not insure adherence to federal statutes and company job descriptions, inasmuch as line supervision will inevitably misclassify, create duplicate operations, and gradually evolve a chaotic disproportion of higher rated employees in all occupations if left to their own devices.

It is apparent that job descriptions should occasionally be interpreted flexibly to upgrade employees temporarily to meet accelerated production trends accompanied by labor shortages and higher living standards. However, it must be recognized that manipulation of wage structures inevitably leads to rate-wise inequities in comparable classifications within the wage structure of related jobs.

Prerequisites of the Job Analyst

THE job analyst must preferably have pursued graduate work in the fields of education, research, or public administration, and have undergone extensive training in administration prior to participating in a functional Wage Administration program. This field demands a combination of professional training, practical experience, and proven ability to deal effectively with higher management in the evolution and enforcement of wage structures. In short, he must synthesize overall manufacturing functions into valid job descriptions in view of current and future organizational changes. In this connection the writing of job descriptions must be coördinated very closely with management control functions.

The job analyst, to function successfully, must be autonomous from the coercive authority of pressure groups and prejudiced line supervision. In order to perform in an unbiased capacity, he must be attached to higher organizational levels.

As analyst must not suppose, imply, or employ conjectures, but must present facts in an objective, scholarly manner and draw conclusions on grievances, misclassifications, etc., in conformance with federal rules and regulations and company job descriptions. He must have a working knowledge of shop manufacturing methods, office and technical operations, as applied to the writing of specific jobs.

Directive versus Staff Authority

THE wage analyst, if attached to a Wage Administration set-up bearing directive authority, will act as a consultant to higher management in interpreting classification problems and the fine lines of distinction between the maze of office, technical and factory jobs.

The time-consuming and costly policy of mediating on classification issues by high-priced line supervision can be settled more economically if company discussions, prior to arbitration, are restricted to boards composed of Job Analysts and Labor Relations representatives. In this instance, facts are presented by those charged with the responsibility of compiling and interpreting grievance data, and is passed on by Labor Relations personnel, who are empowered to make concessions to Union business agents

The fields of grievance investigation, job descriptions, and the subtle lines of distinction between technical engineering jobs, intangible manufacturing engineering occupations, obviously should be restricted to specialists, and not referred to operating line supervision.

Are Job Evaluation Techniques Wholly Scientific?

JOB evaluation, as such, cannot yet be regarded as a science. Evaluation techniques thus far place primary emphasis upon actual duties performed and attempt to categorize employees into constricted mechanical fields, with the resultant reaction that industry has been accused of transforming human beings into mechanized robots. However, a scientific method of evaluating jobs, especially office and technical occupations, would, of necessity, properly emphasize the experience and technical knowledge necessary to perform technical jobs at their accepted level.

Industry today buys experience and knowledge in hiring tool planners, tool designers, and similar occupations. The sustained mental application required of technical employees cannot be fully measured and isolated in routine job descriptions. It is in this misconception that some job descriptions covering technical occupations demonstrate lack of validity.

Job Analysts versus Supervision

THE administering of wages comprises functions that are directive in nature in more progressive companies. The writing and evaluation of job descriptions and the settlement of employee grievances should be accomplished by skilled wage and job analysts and not by remotely interested line supervisors who are far removed from the actual facts.

Job evaluation remains closely related with organizational control operations and cannot accomplish desired results without close coördination with continuous organization changes. Job descriptions are tools that can be utilized to individual advantage by companies and labor bargaining units. It follows that functional wage administration programs are an objective approach to the insurance of normal manufacturing cost.

How to Improve Job Descriptions

ALL job descriptions are predicated upon the reader's ability to distinguish the meaning of words contained therein, but the latter presents fallacious reasoning that frequently falls down in actual practice. The English language remains very tyrannical and presents the same difficulty as did stone age hieroglyphics. There is no uniformity of opinion regarding the significance and scope of terms used in Company-Union job descriptions.

Valid, reliable job descriptions cannot be achieved by resorting to the naïve telegram method of presenting facts, inasmuch as the latter is much less desirable than the complete grouping of homogeneous functions into specific jobs and the establishing of definite skill levels.

Most job descriptions are vulnerable simply because, in their simplicity, levels of difficulty between grades and occupations are not clearly defined. Theoretically the total evaluation points of comparable technical jobs place the latter jobs within specific labor grades. The initial cost of originating and installing job evaluating programs is incidental compared to the cost of rigidly enforcing the application of job descriptions. For instance, in large organizations, controls must be set up to eliminate duplications of activities between divisions and departments.

As a corallary, job descriptions must be written around homogeneous job duties and not around split functions of similar occupations. For example, closely related jobs such as Tool Planner, Tool Designer, Tool Liaison Man, Production Processor, etc., revolve around the planning and designing of tools. The subtleties that distinguish these jobs from each other must be noted in job descriptions, not for layman consumption, but in the terminology of the specific occupation. Most descriptions become costly instruments not because of what is stated, but because of omissions and lack of clearly defined terms.

Evolution of Jobs in a Typical Job Family

THE evolution of jobs in a typical job family, in order, include such jobs as Planning Clerk, Parts Lister, Planning Estimator, Tool Planner, and Tool Designer. The latter shows the gradual evolution of skill levels in a typical family in manufacturing engineering departments from jobs that are relatively easily evaluated to jobs that largely involve the use of previously gained knowledge and experience, and as a result are less tangibly evaluated. Obviously, as point evaluation systems become less reliable in the rating on intangible hourly jobs, actual job descriptions must become more definite and descriptive of actual duties performed. Hence jobs involving creative, technical, or original thinking are less easily measured and cannot be standardized completely under point evaluation systems.

In Some Companies Hit by Strikes Early This Year Unquestionably Not Only Have Gross Wage Increases Been Responsible But Also Wage Differentials.

Wage Curves

By Leonard Cohen

National Steel Commission
New York, N. Y.

BEYOND a doubt, in the not too distant future, arbitrators will be faced with the problem of establishing wage curves in dispute cases. This will be most difficult as the wage curve is properly a matter individual within each and every company. In addition, there are no well established customs fixing the general shape nor anchor points of wage curves; nor are there any undebatable rules—economic engineering, psychologic, or mathematic—which state that the curve should be anchored here and there, with the shape thus and so. Indeed, the opinions of "authorities" in the field are many and divergent.

Jobs About Which There Is Agreement

IN ANTICIPATION of disputes about wage curves, these arbitrators must develop a policy, or a formula, which will be applied to the resolving of such disputes and the construction of the curves. Insofar as possible, this policy should place a great reliance on collective bargaining and derive a mutually satisfactory wage curve within the area of agreement already existing between the parties. The soundest procedure is to select 15 to 20 jobs in the organization in which there is no disagreement. Plot them; then chart the line of best fit as the pay curve. (See reference #9 in the bibliography attached.)

Developing a wage curve through such a method has the advantage of permitting the parties to establish their own monetary value per point. That is, if there is agreement on certain jobs in the scale, then the value of other jobs can be obtained by interpolation. Actually, the parties have selected their own anchor points and curve shape.

King (#18) says, "the shape that this curve would or should assume, is problematical. . . . A straight line, with a unit value per point, perhaps would be the ideal to be looked toward. . . ." But Burk (#9) states that "the correct slope of the line . . . is to . . . pay . . . the same number of cents per hour . . . per point . . . along the entire scale." Of course, this would be a straight line. Bradbury (#8) however, maintains that the curve "will be a rising parabola, for rates should rise progressively faster with greater job values."

Straight Line Best

Reasoning from a statistical and psychological point of view, the straight line function is perhaps best. It is easier to understand, the money value per point is a constant. The suggestion that the curve should rise progressively faster with greater job values is obviously in error. The more valuable the job, the more points it will have, and consequently the more pay. Intentionally making the curve a rising parabola merely will reweight disproportionately the point values of the higher rated jobs.

As a general rule, the arbitrators might permit the line of best fit, derived from the job rates in agreement, take whatever shape it may; but when a curve approaches a linear function it should be made a straight line curve.

System May Be Too Complex

After the wage curve is structured, the problem of single rates or rate-ranges and job classifications still remains. These issues can be referred back to the parties for negotiation. Viteles (#23) says, "there is psychological justification for using a range (of rates) for each group of jobs, and also for providing overlapping between grades which are adjacent to one another. . . ." This allows reward for seniority, efficiency, etc.

However, an imposition of rate ranges upon the already complex tonnage pay system in vogue in the steel industry would tend to make the entire pay system too complex for efficient administration. Once the anchor points and shape of the curve has been established, the question of job classifications can assuredly be settled through direct negotiation between the parties. The boundaries of the different classes need only be marked along the base line of the wage curve chart. The rate of pay established for each class might then become the midpoint of that class.

The arbitrators will face a more serious problem, however, if there is no agreement by the parties on any job rates in question. Here, both the anchor points and curve shape will have to be arbitrarily fixed. Hammond (#13) suggests that the lowest point on the wage curve should be determined by "considering costs of living, local labor rates, and company policy. The maximum point should be established to represent roughly a 30% spread between the minimum and the maximum." After these two points are established a straight line will be plotted between them with intermediate pay rates read from the curve.

Hammond's suggestion for obtaining the low-side anchor point is a logically sound one, but his insistence upon a 30% spread is open to grave criticism. The 30% is a figure plucked from the air which, so far, has not been empirically nor theoretically justified. And establishing such a maximum unnecessarily and arbitrarily tends to rigidify the wage structure.

The second anchor point could better be established with coördinate points at the average wage rate paid in the plant (man average, not job average) and the average number of evaluation points assigned to the jobs in the plant, considering of course, the number of employees on each job. Determining the second anchor point in this way will not increase the eventual costs of the company's pay roll, and thus not hinder its competitive position.

Bibliography

1. American Gas Association. Report of the A. G. A. Office Personnel Committee. *Am. Gas. Assoc. Proc.*, 1929, pp. 380–403.
2. BALDERSTON, C. C. Wage Setting Research. *Personnel Journal*, 15: 220–224.
3. ——— Job Evaluation Under Wage Stabilization. *Personnel Journal*, 22: 194–200, December, 1943.
4. ——— Wartime Lessons in Wage Administration. *Advanced Management Quarterly*, 10; 1: 1936, 58–60, October 8, 1936.
6. BENGE, E. J. Job Evaluation in a Paper Plant. *Personnel Journal*, 19: 42–8, June, 1940.
7. BENGE, E. J., BURKE, S. L. H., AND HAY, E. N. *Manual of Job Evaluation.* N. Y. Harpers, 1941, 198 pp.
8. BRADBURY, K. F. Job Evaluation Analyzed. *Advanced Management*, 5: 16–20, March, 1940.
9. BURK, S. L. H. Pricing the Wage or Salary Scale. *Advanced Management*, 6: 86–90, April–June, 1941.
10. ——— Salary and Wage Administration. *National Assoc. of Cost Accountants Bul.* 23: 1347–54, June, 1942.
11. COOK, W. D. Determination of Prevailing Wage Rates. *Personnel*, 14: 24–6, August, 1937.
12. ELLIS, R. W. Controlling Wages and Salaries. *American Business*, 14: 18–22, October; 18–19, Nov.; 23–4, Dec., 1944.
13. HAMMOND, A. M. Job Analysis and Merit Rating. *Society for Advancement of Management Journal*, 4: 100–4, July, 1939.
14. ——— Salary Administration Plan for Your Business. *American Business*, 9: 11–13, Nov.; 24–5, Dec., 1939, 10: 30–2, Jan., 1940.
15. HAY, E. M. Planning for Fair Salaries and Wages. *Personnel Journal*, ¹⁸: 141–50, Oct., 1939.
16. KARABASZ, V. S. Certain Difficulties in Determining the "Market Rate" of Wages. *Personnel*, 13: 147–9, May, 1925.
17. KINDALL, A. F. Job Description and Rating. *Personnel*, 14: 122–130, Feb. 1938.
18. KING, S. J. Job Evaluation. *Advanced Management*, 3: 93–8, May, 1938.
19. MINER, D. F. Standardization, Harmonizer of Human Effort. *Advanced Management*, 7: 15–22, January–March, 1942.
20. MOORE, H. Problems and Methods in Job Evaluation. *J. Consulting Psychology*, 8: 90–99, 1944.
21. PAGUETTE, N. C. AND FRASER, C. Labor-Management Joint Development and Application of Job Evaluation in a Single Unit Motor Bodies Plant. *Advanced Management*, 8: 92–6, July, 1943.
22. ROSITZKE, R. H. Job Evaluation. *Paper Trade Journal* 112: 31–8, Mar. 13; 45–50, Mar. 20, 1941.
23. VITELES, M. S. A Psychologist Looks at Job Evaluation. *Personnel*, 17; 3: 165–76, Feb., 1941.
24. YOUNG, A. H. Occupational Rating Plan of the International Harvester Co. *Management Engineering*, 4: 301–6, May, 1923.

While Illustrating Some of the Goings on in a
Closed Shop This Story Also Shows the Difficulties of Adjustment in Shifting from One Working
Environment Such as the Office to Another Such
as the Factory Floor.

Adventure *in* A Closed Shop

By Mildred L. Young
New York, N. Y.

THE advertisement in our small-town paper was unique. There is seldom any demand for workers except in the glove and leather industry, and this was an appeal to Patriotic Women to come and sew on soldier's jackets,—"Help us make the coats our fighting men need!" spread across half a page in inch high type. I can sew on an electric machine, and what could I do less than answer that ad?

My male relatives were all risking their lives in the service of our country, in the air over Germany, in the waters under the Atlantic Ocean, and at Oak Ridge doing secret work,—could I, who had nothing to do but wait for a house to be sold, refuse to spend that waiting time helping to clothe these fighters?

Not An Attractive Place

IT was not an attractive place,—the coat factory,—on a dirty out of the way street, in an old skinmill, upstairs over a rocket factory which might blow up any day. Clatter and whirr of many machines, clack of voices, piles of scraps and partly finished garments, other piles of parts ready to sew,—women, men, noise, confusion. I had always worked in a law office where the Stone Brothers, my new employers, had come for counsel.

They regarded me with something like awe as I took my place at a terrific looking machine, lunchbox in hand, comfortable shoes and apron,—like all the other women about me. I had been hired with enthusiasm by a member of the United States Employment Service, newly put in charge of the shop's personnel department.

—387—

Mr. Joyce obviously thought his advertisement a great success because I had come to work. He hoped some of my friends would follow, but nobody else from "nob hill" came to do patriotic service in the coat factory. They each had someone in their families who told them about closed shops and that they had better not invade that particular territory even as an emergency measure. I was alone.

Be Careful

THEY put me to work making bellows pockets for field jackets. I quite liked that task. It is fussy and particular, rather like making a blouse,—one of my hobbies. They did not hurry me. The girl supervisor and even one of the bosses came around to show me shortcuts and small ways of increasing my output. They told me that none of my first efforts had to be thrown out, but could be used because I had been careful,—the thing to do was to keep on in the same way, gradually increasing my speed.

But I knew that I must make a certain quota in order to earn my pay, and I wanted to earn that pay, for it is one of my firm beliefs that the worker should receive an adequate living wage and in return should do enough work to earn his keep. The wages seemed very good to me, accustomed to the wages of a stenographer. In our town a stenographer gets about eighteen dollars a week, sometimes less, seldom more. In New York, at one time, I had been paid over sixty dollars a week, and considered myself near the top of my profession. My first full week's pay in the coat factory was $19.67 after tax deductions. Not bad at all, I said to myself. But I was to learn.

Suspicions

HE women around me regarded me with suspicion. They could not understand my coming there to work. Although they had, many of them, sons or husbands in the services, they felt no obligation to clothe them, no interest in getting out the orders promised to the government by their employers. They would walk out at three in the afternoon saying "I've earned enough for today. I made my ten dollars."

Even though they knew production was lagging behind schedule, they would say "I don't feel like making another bundle" and walk out. At first I could not understand. Ten dollars a day on those machines? Impossible! "Oh, yes," the supervisor told me, "After you get up speed you can make better than that on these pockets. These pay well. You can make twelve dollars or more if you put in the whole eight hours. Some of our best operators make more than eighty dollars a week."

Objectives

I ASKED myself,—how could it be? These ignorant women, most of them speaking broken English, living in a dirty old mill and equally dirty and unattractive parts of our city and others nearby,—how did it happen that they earned such money, and what did they do with it? That was the interesting question to me. What did they do with it? I never did learn exactly, except that they were buying all the second hand gadgets they could find in every place selling out old equipment of any kind, and paying exhorbitant prices for those castoffs.

This I learned because so many took a long lunch hour in order to attend some advertised sale of household goods. Of course, they came to work in a taxi or a car belonging to their family. Some were buying homes, two family houses so they could live in one flat and rent the other. Not better houses in better neighborhoods than they had known,—but any house they could get at a "bargain," usually in their old neighborhood and with repairs needed galore.

They all had to buy bonds, but objected to that, and often cashed them as soon as possible. A few were educating a child to be a teacher, secretary or businessman, with the idea mainly that the girl would marry her boss, or the boy go away to a better city where he could make more money. The younger girls had elaborate weddings when some serviceman came home,—with gowns, gifts and parties from their fellow workers, in the shop or some restaurant. They seemed to have no life or interests outside of the mill and spending their earnings.

What the Union Would Do

EACH morning at eight o'clock, after a bout with the alarm clock, I was on the bus going to work. A friend of my father's sometimes rode the same bus and we were talking of my adventure. He undertook to tell me a little of what might lie in store for me later on. He asked if I did not know that I had entered a "closed shop" and I asked him exactly what that meant.

He explained that after it seemed certain that I would make my quota, the Union would make me join or leave, and if I exercised my prerogatives of remaining in spite of the Union so long as they were doing 100% government work, then they would begin to tinker with my machine and do me dirty tricks so that I would get fired, and if I was not fired they would make me miserable. I was rather resentful at this man at first, then I began to look around and listen more carefully and in time became very thankful to him for his interest. For matters worked out much as he had predicted,—with variations.

Jimmie

IT was the very next day after my talk with this friend that I ran head-on into the UNION. There was a small, dark complexioned man bossing the production on the floor of the shop,—passing out the work to be done, instructing, moving sewing machines about, talking with this one and that one—seemingly running things. The Stone Brothers were around too, but the women looked to this "Jimmie" as their "boss." At times the Stones were very nearly snubbed by their help.

Jimmie spoke broken English, used very bad grammar, did not hesitate to curse at anytime or anyone, and was most uncomfortable when he had to speak to me or encountered my gaze. Yet he seemed to take a swaggering sort of satisfaction in giving me his few orders. He would stand across the room with his small snaky eyes fixed on me in an odd way while talking with persons who came in from time to time.

One of these persons—a malignant, slippery sort of male dressed all in black with a briefcase, was, I learned, the district Union organizer. Jimmie would sometimes walk slowly past behind me and peer over my shoulder from a little distance, then pounce down with a loud criticism. Quite suddenly he asked me, "Do you have any objection to joining the Union?" I said at once,—"Indeed, I would not join any Union. It is not necessary on Government work when I am here only as a temporary employee doing a patriotic service." (I had already learned this from my lawyer, just in case.)

Bucking the Quota

A FEW days later the woman who collected the Union dues came to speak to me, and I fear we had rather a scrap on the subject. I began to look about to find some friendly person,—someone who had known me or a member of my family formerly. I began to take more interest in talking with the girls near me and trying to win their friendship. The machinist proved to be a former client in our law office. One of the women had gone to school with me, another had worked in the home of one of my relatives,—and it finally appeared that the woman Union representative with whom I had quarreled had known me best of all when we were both youngsters.

After she recognized me, they were all suddenly very friendly and Jimmie seemed to have forgotten me. But as I worked and watched, listened and learned, I saw that beyond a doubt, Jimmie while pretending to try and meet production quotas, was actually by many small tricks, preventing the work from going out on schedule.

The Old Wreck

THEN one day, just a month from the time I had started work, I made my quota. It was such a surprise, and I became quite excited because at last I could earn my wages. That night Jimmie changed my machine to another table, gave me an old wreck to sew on, and every night from then on, it was tampered with and had to be repaired in the morning before I could sew. The machinist worked at it daily, neglecting others, and the idle time I had while he fixed the machine, I used circulating about from pocket-maker to pocket-maker, on the pretext of watching some of the fastest makers and learning more about how to speed up my work. I did learn more.

The highly skilled operators at the completely Unionized table showed off for me on their machines. They talked continuously of how much money I could make if I "joined the Union." Their machines flew along, their work practically did itself. If I would join the union it would be the same with me. It was like an oft repeated refrain, with the not unmusical accompaniment of humming sewing machines, but it did not lull me to sleep.

I told those women from one end of the mill to the other, that their Union is their enemy. I told them that this union boss, Jimmie, was keeping production down, keeping their sons and husbands from getting the clothing they needed across the waters on the battlefields. It seemed that, one and all, they objected to "working for the company." If the Union had the money, they said, it could buy up the factories and then the workers would be their own bosses and work for themselves. The company made so much off of them that it could afford to be idle all the rest of its life. It happened that I knew the Stone Brothers scale of living pretty well. I knew that a machine operator making sixty dollars a week in the factory was getting just about as much as each member of the company used weekly to support his family. I told that to the women and proved it.

The Owning Family

THEY should have known it for themselves with five members of the family working there in the factory among them. They had to believe me. They began to think a little. They began to suspect Jimmie. Then the machinist, tired of keeping my machine working besides doing all his other work, and angry too, I suspect,—resigned. He said that since the fishing season had opened, he meant to take a long rest in the woods. Even with all the fuss going on, I could still very nearly make my quota. My employers said they were satisfied. Again and again I was urged to join the union, and again and again I refused.

Finally came the day. My nerves must have been feeling the strain for some time. And that day Jimmie insulted me, deliberately, insolently, sneeringly. He demanded to know why I was standing watching an expert worker make pockets instead of sitting at my machine. I told him that he knew well enough that somebody, possibly himself, had tampered with my machine every night for some time now. He replied, "Oh, you're just too lazy to adjust the machine yourself!"

The Final Blowup

MY HAND reached for a sharp pair of scissors—my mind told me to jab them into him hard—but instead, I dropped the shears and rushed into the Employment Office. Mr. Joyce had to soothe a fine case of hysteria before he could get the whole story from me. He begged me to take a few days rest and come back, but I never went back into that room again, even to get my shoes and apron. A man friend called for those and asked to see Jimmie. Just what happened, I do not know, but I am told that my friend offered to roll Jimmie, who is much smaller, on the floor as a means of teaching him how to address a lady and that Mr. Stone and Mr. Joyce held the two of them.

The next information I got was that Jimmie had gone back to Boston, from whence he had been sent to our county for the express purpose of making trouble,—and that the FBI were close behind him. It seems the Garment Workers Union had been attempting to affiliate the makers in the glove shops with their Union and had sent a corps of organizers into the county, placing them in various shops to manage the coup.

Elections were held and the affiliation was voted down. Apparently the girls in the coat factory had ganged up on the Union boss. When it came to a showdown they sided with an old schoolmate rather than a stranger. They told the Stone Brothers that if I were fired they would all walk out. Jimmie had planned it otherwise. He meant them to walk out if I did not join the Union. But Jimmie walked—or ran—good riddance to him!

Now a very charming local young woman is the "boss" at the coat factory, and I am told that the output is improved and that the girls still ask about me and wonder if I will ever come back to the shop.

Book Reviews

Book Review Editor, Mr. Everett Van Every

California Personnel Management Association, Berkeley, Cal.

INDUSTRIAL TRAINING AND TESTING

By Howard K. Morgan. New York. McGraw-Hill Book Company. 1945. 225 pp. $2.50

Training in industry has undergone some strange transformations during the war. Training programs were streamlined and speeded up. Permanent and lasting training techniques were cast aside in favor of getting quick results. Quality of results was not nearly so important as volume in mass production. And now with attention on quick reconversion, almost with the same suddenness with which we met the war impact, it would seem that too little attention is being paid to training.

The fast wartime training was better than no training at all, but it was a long way from the carefully designed job instruction which we need today in reverting to fulltime production.

In studying current training needs the author has not prescribed a review of all known methods; instead he has suggested a plan of industrial training which he believes will meet the need for the period ahead.

The first chapter considers turnover and training costs—one of the most baffling aspects of training and a subject that few authors attempt to handle. Morgan, however, gets right into figures and freely assumes what the various cost factors are in any normal operation. He concludes, for instance, that in a company of 1,000 workers, the saving in good testing and training should amount to $55,000 per year.

The next two chapters on Testing Programs and Selected Tests describe the most common means used to measure interests, abilities, intelligence, etc. The balance of the book is devoted to training topics with a definite recommendation for a program that can be adapted to any company.

The author believes that supervisors make the best instructors and he prescribes a carefully worked out plan in which multiple plant training and coordination between the units can make this possible. Throughout he stresses the importance of keeping management continually informed as to costs and savings in the training department.

The chapter on Training Department Organization is especially well done and shows the three essential divisions that any worthwhile department must have and be prepared to fully develop.

The instruction technique is thoroughly discussed with adequate treatment given to introductory training, shop instruction and supervisory training as three important subjects. The final chapter is a feature of the book that shows how to follow-up effectively on training and testing programs.

War-weary programs and the equally tired and weary training directors will welcome this fresh viewpoint and rather new approach to job instruction problems.

PRACTICAL MANAGEMENT RESEARCH

By Alexis R. Wiren and Carl Heyel. New York, N. Y.

McGraw-Hill Book Co. 1945. 222 pp.

Little has been written on the subject of research as applied to management. Certainly no aspect of business warrants more careful study and scrutiny than that of managing the enterprise and all its problems of human relations. The authors make it clear that this kind of research is much different in its multiple complexities. No one engaged in this work at the management level, no matter how thorough, can gather and interpret data as though he were in a physics or chemistry laboratory, where the subjects of his researches would confuse him by their capricious action.

Written by two management authorities, the work clearly shows them to be engineers with unusual experiences and viewpoints on the importance of human relations.

Business books are coming out by the hundreds of titles, but this is the first study of the scientific research techniques applied to operating a business and controlling a complicated organization through creative thinking and pre-determined designs of action and follow-through. It is the only book of its kind, simply written and yet encompassing all that is known at the top-level of gathering data, making valid interpretations and arriving at sound conclusions.

The first section of the book is devoted to the principles and practice of management research. The second section considers case examples of the systematic solution of management problems. From these case studies the reader recognizes an attempt to develop what the authors call a pattern of thinking about such problems and with the assumption that it is more important to discuss how to think about a whole class of problems than merely to show how a particular set of situations were solved.

But the book is too brief. The subject treatment is so well done, what there is of it, that the authors leave their readers more eager than ever for material of this nature. We should like to have seen far more extensive work devoted to research in personnel and industrial relations—and preferably by these authors. The book is highly important as an indication of the direction that business managements are very likely to take and we recommend it especially to executive managements, organization planners and consultants.

MANAGEMENT AT THE BARGAINING TABLE

By Lee N. Hill and Charles R. Hook, Jr. New York, N. Y.

McGraw-Hill Book Co. 1945. 300 pp. $3.00

No more important book has been written for management. In fact here is a book devoted to matters that are generally discussed in conference and corridors, but seldom reach the printed page. I earnestly believe this kind of work is long overdue and should have been available long ago.

In some respects the book is unconventional in its subject treatment and this is probably best explained by the authors who tell us that the negotiation of collective bargaining agreements is too dynamic a process and has developed too rapidly to permit the establishment of sound and trustworthy principles of universal application. So the authors merely bring out the most important issues for open discussion —and they really bring them out. There is no effort to disguise questions or reveal private information. The book is intended to stimulate discussion and afford consideration of highly pertinent topics rather than to provide solutions to problems.

In an early chapter the authors contend that the bargaining agreement in each case must be custom-built to fit the particular situation. They show how the preservation of management rights is only the first essential in the establishment of sound employer-employee relations. Having preserved its rights, management has the obligation of exercising its rights in such a manner as to build a solid foundation for stable and satisfactory relationships with its employees.

As a premise the authors point out what they call a tragic commentary on modern collective bargaining: in the heat of negotiations between unions and management representatives, the employees, in whose behalf the contract is presumably being negotiated, are frequently not aware of the demands being made, are sometimes not consulted as to which demands they consider important, may actually be forgotten by the contending parties sparring for strategic position during negotiations, and may, in the end, obtain an agreement that is victory for their representatives but a defeat for the employees themselves. Much is made of the fact that the collective bargaining agreement is signed by two parties, but the silent party—the employees themselves—is a real party in interest.

The book is divided into detailed discussion sections elaborating on the functional categories of collective bargaining agreement clauses. This is not a catalogue of clauses but an analysis of the different classifications of clauses and the various management positions reflected from them.

Although written principally from the point of view of protecting the functional rights of management, the work is also a very good review of employee interests that need auditing in any well-managed operation, and should prove a valuable guide in developing good industrial relations.

The chapter on Union Protective Clauses makes a good case for tolerant understanding on the part of management but warns that management should be alert to provide adequate control to prevent abuse of what rights are granted to the unions.

The chapter on Management Protective Clauses is the best treatment we have seen on this subject. The authors definitely recommend a strong management clause, and that careful consideration be given to the pro's and con's as well as the various devices used by unions to invade the field of management functions. These devices are carefully studied and readily recognized as mutual-consent clauses, delegation of management functions to joint-committees of labor and management, restrictions of management discretion by seniority limitations and unlimited compulsory arbitration. The chapter closes with a stern warning that the minimum consideration must be given to the problem of protecting the rights to manage. Any management which does otherwise will not long retain its right to manage and cannot long remain in the role of management.

The first part of the book dwells on the content of the collective-bargaining agreement, analyzing and classifying the various clauses, and suggesting sound positions for management negotiations together with underlying reasons for such positions. Part two deals with the actual mechanics of negotiations and techniques that have brought results. The chapters on Preparation for Negotiations and Actual Negotiations are studded with sound experience not usually found in business books.

If management is going to be free to manage, and keep itself that way, it had better make its first order of business to know what needs to be known to protect its rights and its employee's rights. This should be the business book of the month—and read by every executive who is responsible for his company's presence at the bargaining table.

CPSIA information can be obtained
at www.ICGtesting.com
Printed in the USA
BVHW07*1059180918
527831BV00010B/159/P

9 780484 168267